Learning About Politics

LEARNING

ABOUT POLITICS

A READER IN POLITICAL SOCIALIZATION

Roberta S. Sigel

State University of New York at Buffalo

 RANDOM HOUSE • NEW YORK

FIRST PRINTING

Copyright © 1970 by Random House, Inc.
All rights reserved under International and Pan-American Copyright Conventions.
Published in the United States by Random House, Inc., New York, and simultaneously
in Canada by Random House of Canada Limited, Toronto.

Library of Congress Catalog Card Number: 70-89482

Manufactured in the United States of America.

Printed and bound by Kingsport Press, Kingsport, Tenn.

Typography by Jack Ribik
98765432

Acknowledgment

This reader was first assembled several years ago in order to bring together widely scattered materials on political socialization for a new course at Wayne State University. If the book should prove of use to its readers, the thanks go largely to my students, whose interest in the topic and whose questions and criticisms often served as guidelines. If some of the comments no longer seem as applicable as they were when first written, it merely tends to confirm the book's leitmotif, that change is an essential ingredient of political socialization.

No set of acknowledgments, however, would be complete without a very special mention of Gary A. Krieger, then an undergraduate student at Wayne State University and now a graduate student at Yale University, who handled the technical aspects of editing the book. More than that, his enthusiasm, good scholarly judgment, and unfailing energy greatly added to the fun of putting this book together.

ROBERTA S. SIGEL

State University of New York at Buffalo
1970

Contents

Chapter II • The Family 103

Chapter III • Personality and Politics 231

Chapter IV • The School 311

Chapter V • College and University   375

Chapter VI • Relevant Others: The Peer Group   411

Chapter VII • Socialization in Adulthood—The Importance   427
of Role

Chapter VIII • The Political Environment—Source of Conformity and Deviancy   **491**

Chapter IX • Change, Conflict, and Socialization   **589**

Introduction

Why this sudden interest among political scientists in the topic of political socialization? Many reasons could be offered; but one in particular should not be overlooked, namely the nature of the political world in which we live today. For one thing, the world today contains literally dozens of new states whose names alone were totally unknown thirty or forty years ago. Many are emerging from long-lasting colonial status; others are the result of a hodgepodge conjoining of formerly separate territories, tribal or otherwise. The first order of business for such new nations often is the creation of a sense of we-ness, national loyalty, and consensus; in short, they need to become political socializers. Another reason for the popularity of the topic of political socialization is that the twentieth century is the century of democracy. Countries of all types describe themselves as democracies and lay claim not only to the loyalty but to the approval of their people; for democracy after all is said to rest on the consent of the governed. And finally, this is also the century of unprecedented technological, social, and ideological change. In the course of this change political systems can find their hold on people's loyalty weakening as these people find themselves dislocated by new machinery, threatened by new claimants to power, or lured by new political ideologies. The greater people's insecurity and/or dissatisfaction, the more they give the system cause to worry unless their loyalty to it overrides all momentary discomforts. It is here then that political socialization enters.*

* Parts of the subsequent two paragraphs are from Roberta S. Sigel, "Assumptions About the Learning of Political Values," *The Annals*, Vol. 361 (September 1965), with permission of the publisher.

Political socialization refers to the process by which people learn to adopt the norms, values, attitudes, and behaviors accepted and practiced by the ongoing system. Such learning, however, involves much more that the acquisition of the appropriate knowledge of a society's political norms and more than the blind performance of appropriate political acts; it also assumes that the individual so makes these norms and behaviors his own—internalizes them—that to him they appear to be right, just, and moral. The socialized human being, in other words, develops an affective commitment for the system. Successful socialization thus has both cognitive and affective dimensions. Having once internalized the society's norms, it will presumably not be difficult for the individual to act in congruence with them. For example, members of a stable democratic system are expected to learn to effect change through elections, through the application of group practice, rather than through revolutions. The goal of political socialization then is to train or develop individuals to become well-functioning members of the political society. Although the definition of a well-functioning member will vary with the political system—from obedient passive subject in one system to active participating citizen in another—a well-functioning citizen is one who internalizes society's political norms and who will then transmit them to future generations. For without a body politic so in harmony with the ongoing political values, the political system would have trouble functioning smoothly and perpetuating itself safely. And survival, after all, is a prime goal of the political organism just as it is of the individual organism.*

The term socialization conveys perhaps a much too deliberate and coercive tone to the discussion—as though there were a powerful commissar present who force-feeds political values into the resistant young organism. Nothing in the socialization process is, of course, quite that deliberate, nor is the organism very resistant. A more accurate way of describing it would be to say that man is born into a given political culture but that he partakes of it not as a culture but via people and institutions (agents) who practice the norms of the culture and who teach them to him both by example and by demands. Never having known other cultures, he has little cause to resist his own. In this respect political socialization is quite different from childhood socialization in general. The young child who is toilet trained or trained (socialized) to give up the breast or to inhibit his aggression is told to *give up* something he found pleasurable. Hence this type of socialization often entails struggles between socializer and socialized. But the young American who is told at home and in school that it is good that all people be allowed to vote is not giving up any previously acquired contrary beliefs in order to internalize this systems-appropriate one.

The path of political socialization consequently is a relatively smooth one. Norm internalization goes on casually and imperceptibly, often without either teacher or student being aware that it is taking place. Much of it is not even political in nature but is incidental to other experiences; and precisely because it is incidental, it has a more lasting effect on the acquisition of political values and behavior than does

---

* A harmonious body politic need not be unchanging and tension free. This point will be documented time and again in this volume; see especially Chapters VIII and IX.

deliberate indoctrination. It comes about as the result of observation (observing a teacher treating a well-off parent more respectfully than a poor one), overheard conversations (hearing a father talking of having a traffic ticket "fixed"), religious or moral training (many nonpolitical moral precepts are closely related to political philosophies), and—last but not least—life itself and the experience it brings to bear on people. (No poverty-stricken Latin-American peasant on a large estate needs a civics class to show him that the government caters less to his needs than to those of the well-off large landowners. Civics classes and other forms of deliberate indoctrination (national ceremonies and holidays, political mythology, propaganda, and so on) all no doubt play a part in the socialization process; but it is doubtful that they contribute as much as—let alone more than—incidental learning does to a person's political socialization.

The first chapter of this volume concentrates on the mechanics of the learning process—just exactly how this learning takes place, what principles are involved, and so on. Finding selections from political science literature for this chapter was particularly difficult because political scientists, for the most part, have not been very much concerned with the learning process and have instead concentrated on the output (what is learned). Learning psychologists, on the other hand, seldom study the learning of political roles or opinions. And neither political scientists nor psychologists have engaged in many extended on-the-spot observations of complex political responses. None, for example, have deemed it necessary actually to observe what goes on in the home or the school during the political socialization process.

The next chapters will then turn to the questions Who is it that socializes the young and the not-so-young? Who are the agents and institutions engaged in this practice? The individual, after all, is not socialized by the political system or the political culture directly; rather political culture is transmitted to him via intermediaries (agents or institutions) who themselves are part of this common culture just as he is. Chapters II, IV, V, and VI particularly deal with the agents of socialization.

The impression we might have created so far is that the path of political socialization is a very smooth and fixed one and that generation after generation agents transmit the same values to each new generation. There is some truth in that picture —at least for the older, stabler systems—but it is also a gross oversimplification. For one thing, since political culture is transmitted by many different agents, it is well to bear in mind that at times these agents transmit mutually contradictory values and norms. The culture of poverty, according to Oscar Lewis, prevents poor Mexicans from becoming integrated into the general Mexican political culture and leads them to develop "a provincial and locally oriented culture."* In the United States the Amish, a religious subgroup, socialize their youth in order to eschew many of the political and social acts highly valued by most Americans, thus occasionally provoking open conflict with society at large.

Rapid social or technological change is another source of possible socialization conflict. Such conflict—no matter how slight—is perhaps more the rule than the

* Oscar Lewis, *The Children of Sanchez* (New York: Vintage Books, 1961), p. XXVI.

exception. For if we assume that change is a fact of life as well as that modern complex societies must always be beset by at least some degree of intergroup tension, then we also have to assume that people growing up in such societies will from time to time be subject to conflict over prevailing norms. Chapters VII, VIII, and IX will focus particularly on conditions of change and conflict, although this theme actually runs like a *leitmotif* through all the chapters.

Another *leitmotif* is the interdependence of people, groups, and institutions and the difficulty of extricating one from the other for research purposes. To be sure, we have assigned some selections to the chapter on the family and others to the chapter on the political environment or the chapter on social class and other reference groups; but who is to say where the influence of one begins and of the other ends? For example, the family is a primary group, and it is also part of the class structure; and both are affected by the political environment and in turn influence it. Hence we shall, especially in the introductions to each chapter, make frequent references to selections in many different parts of the book.

The reader will also notice that in spite of the customary emphasis on childhood socialization much space is devoted to socialization through the life cycle in the conviction that man's political socialization is not completed upon reaching adulthood. Many experiences and demands a person meets in discharging his role as an adult member of society continue to shape and reshape, to socialize, resocialize, and even desocialize him (see especially Chapters VII and VIII).

Any book of readings by definition is, of course, highly selective. This one is no exception. The reader may well ask why several well known political science articles have not been included, whereas many less directly political selections from the fields of psychology and sociology have been included. The reason often was that some psychological or sociological pieces were selected in order to introduce the political science student to a mode of analysis or a way of conceptualizing that he is not apt to encounter in his own field, while he might have come across the "classics" of political socialization literature in another context.* Some such "classics" were included nonetheless, since no substitutes could be found for them.

Because literature in some areas is nonexistent, we have not been able to include some selections that we felt were necessary. Previously we alluded to the absence of observational studies of the socialization process and to the dearth of selections with a learning orientation. Another serious void concerns cross-national studies. Several articles on non-American countries have been included, but even they are sparse as yet; even more difficult to discover are cross-national studies. No far-ranging generalization about political socialization can be made until such data are available. Material on the mass media also is missing.

Another glaring omission lies in the fact that no selection addresses itself to an empirical test of the basic assumption behind political socialization thinking, namely that political socialization is essential to political stability. Is this in fact so? Conceptually a good case could be made to answer the question in the affirmative;

---

* This refers particularly to the pioneer work of Fred Greenstein and the joint work of David Easton and Robert Hess, selections from which we encounter in almost every recent American government reader.

but what seems plausible conceptually need not and often does not hold true empirically. Maybe the question instead ought to read How many citizens (located where) must have internalized the system's political norms for the system to operate smoothly and harmoniously? It is conceivable that many systems can function quite satisfactorily with a large apathetic citizen body, provided enough strategically located individuals are willing to support the existing norms, to be the "carriers of the creed." Nor have we as yet asked the question Can political systems induce a sense of legitimacy among their members without first socializing them? In other words, can a government gain the support of the governed because, for example, they thrive under it economically without the governed necessarily embracing its philosophy? It would be well if in the future political scientists conducted empirical research into these questions before blithely asserting that government stability depends on the successful socialization of the governed.

Finally, no well-developed theory of political socialization will emerge from the volume, although theorizing about political socialization exists in many articles. Here and there, especially in the later chapters, we point to variables—such as rate of change—which must be built into any future theory of political socialization;* but that is far from saying a systematic theory (or theories) of political socialization exists already. Political socialization research is perhaps no longer in its infancy but it certainly has not yet reached adolescence, let alone adulthood. If the current volume reflects the tentativeness of the current state of the discipline, we can only say: so be it!

---

* Notions as to the kind of theory that is needed are spelled out in some detail in Roberta S. Sigel, "Political Socialization—Some Reactions to Current Approaches and Conceptualizations," paper read at the 1966 Annual Meeting of the American Political Science Association, New York City. As this volume is going to press, the first major attempt at developing a theory of political socialization has appeared: David Easton and Jack Dennis, *Children in the Political System—Origins of Political Legitimacy* New York: McGraw-Hill, 1969.

Learning About Politics

Learning and Development

INTRODUCTION

In the introduction to this book we have frequently referred to political socialization as a learning process without attempting to explain the nature of the process. It is the purpose of this chapter to offer such an explanation. On the outset let it be said that as yet students of political socialization, although convinced that political behavior like all social behavior is learned behavior, have very seldom made an effort to observe *how* the behavior is learned. There are virtually no experimental and very few field studies that have recorded exactly how man proceeds step by step to acquire his political meanings, values, and behaviors. The failure to make such observations is understandable because the political scientist is not (and should not attempt to be) a learning psychologist; his main focus is not how men learn but what the consequences of

learning (or the failure to learn) are for the political system. Yet our total neglect of the learning process is unwise because it keeps us from fully understanding certain aspects of the political socialization process. It incapacitates us particularly in understanding how political concepts are acquired or discarded and how certain political deviances (socialization failures) occur. Because political socialization constitutes but one special form of social learning, we shall in this introduction attempt a very brief and simplified overview of the psychology of learning in the hope that it will facilitate the reading of the selections which follow and will link them to one another conceptually.

Learning is the result of our ability to profit from past experience. "Stated most simply, learning [in the words of a well known child psychology text] is the establishment of a connection or association between a stimulus and a response where, prior to learning no such association existed."[1] Secondly, "all learning depends on maturation, which fits the organism for learning."[2] But before learning takes place there must be motivation to learn. An organism that has no desire or need to learn usually will not learn. Let us now proceed to explain the terminology and meaning of these assertions in more detail.

Learning Principles

Motivation

Motivation (some psychologists term it "drive," and there is yet other terminology) serves as a stimulus to action as it presupposes a state of tension or felt need to gain something (or to avoid something). This tension mobilizes the organism to engage in behavior designed to bring about tension reduction. Hunger pangs may motivate a tense viewer of a TV thriller to get up and go to the refrigerator for food, something he might not do if he merely had a mild appetite. To take an example from the world of politics, Congressmen are said to have observed that they seldom receive mail complimenting them on looking out well for their constituents' interests, whereas they tend to be deluged with mail when they are contemplating legislation that some constituents might perceive as being injurious to them. The satisfied constituent whose Congressman contemplates no changes in the political setup experiences no tension and therefore no motivation to exert pressure on his Congressman, whereas the constituent who is experiencing fear that his interests might be adversely affected by contemplated legislation experiences tensions and hence is motivated to make a response, namely, to write a letter urging his Congressman to vote against the bill.

Stimulus-Response

When we talk of such terms as "association," "stimulus" (some call it "cue"), and "response" we are employing terminology familiar to learning theorists. A "cue" is defined as a distinctive stimulus that may be followed by a response. A "response" in turn is a behavior that occurs subsequent to a cue. A behavior or response can but need not be overt and visible to the naked eye. Physiological changes and even thoughts and images can be a response although the layman usually thinks of verbal or motor behavior and other overt actions when he speaks of response. Responses to cues may at first be made randomly by trial and error; but when the response meets with a reward (the technical term is reinforcement), it will be repeated when the same or a similar cue appears. Reinforcements can be verbal, such as praise, or material, such as election to a political office. The recompense for a response constitutes a reward only when it is so interpreted by the person making the response. Colonial conquerors who first tried to offer natives goods valued highly in the conqueror's homeland often found that the natives were uninterested—and therefore refused to make the response the conqueror desired to elicit—simply because the goods (reward) had no intrinsic value to the natives. When the conquerors then switched to what seemed to them rather valueless and trivial goods, such as trinkets and colored beads, they often managed to elicit the desired response because to the natives these offerings constituted a reward. Reward enhances the probability that the same response will tend to follow the same or similar cue. Thus, those voters in a sharply divided community who are anxious to avoid higher taxes will soon learn that they must turn out at every school fund election if they want to assure themselves that additional school taxes will not be levied. If they discover that indeed as a result of organizing "no" voters and making sure that they turn out to vote, the school tax will be defeated at each election, they will soon learn to make the response of registering to vote, voting, and encouraging others to vote every time the same cue, that is, increased school taxes, appears on the ballot. If, however, after a given time they find themselves consistently and overwhelmingly outvoted, in other words, if reward is no longer following the response, they may soon give up. Learning psychologists speak of extinction when a response ceases to be made after a while because of the absence of rewards. This is not to say that a reward always has to follow each individual response. A response that has been successfully rewarded over and over again becomes a habit and can sustain itself even when it is rewarded only now and then—which presumably is what takes place in elections since few people are always on the winning side of an election. But if the response is never again rewarded, the chances are the responses will become extinct. Extinction then is another factor in learning. Although rewards are essential for learning a habit and for maintaining

it, punishment, on the other hand, will teach a person not to repeat a given response. A Southern Negro may attend a civil rights rally in a church and be told about the importance of voting if he wishes to improve his lot. If, on the other hand, he attempts to register the next day but encounters delay and threats and then subsequently finds his credit at the local store cut off, he is not apt to return the very next day and attempt once more to register. In this instance, punishment has led him to avoidance behavior: in other words, to avoid the response of attempting to register. Yet we know that in spite of such punishment and even direr ones, some Negroes have attempted to register and have not been deterred by punishment. To this, the learning theorists would probably answer that a human being has, of course, a hierarchy of needs; and if his need for improvement through social action is higher and more important to him than his need for credit or illusory security, the specific punishment may well not have constituted a sufficient deterrent to unlearn the response.

Generalization

Seldom are two social situations so identical that the cues will seem identical to the observer. How can he then make a response if the cue is not identical to the cue to which he was used to responding? Human beings can make the same or very similar responses to cues or situations that are not identical, although similar, because they have learned the ability to make generalizations. This ability permits them to transfer learning from one situation to another; the more similar the situation the easier it is, of course, to make the transfer. An example of stimulus generalization can be offered when observing the behavior of young white Southern children. Observations in Southern states show that at an early age children were often snatched by their mothers from the company of young Negro children with whom they were found playing.[3] Very often this parental behavior was not followed by any explanation as to the inappropriateness of playing with Negroes. Quite quickly, though, the young child learned to avoid Negro children not just for play but for all social intercourse and to seek out white children exclusively. In short, he had learned to generalize from the undesirability of one Negro child to the undesirability of Negro children in general and from play specifically to social contact in general.

Discrimination

To make the appropriate responses the organism has to learn not only to make generalizations but also to make discriminations. Two or several cues may look quite similar (as for instance in the study of children's preferences of a nation's flag, see Edwin Lawson, pp. 321–327). To the very young child all flags that have stripes and stars look the same; and it is only the somewhat older child who can distinguish the Star Spangled Banner from a variety of seemingly similar looking flags. Discrimination is very important in social learning because it sensitizes us to variations in cues that require from us variations in response. Pity, for example the poor private who would not be able to distinguish between an enlisted man and an officer because they both

wear khaki uniforms. Chances are he would fail to salute the officer, and he would be punished for such failure. It is therefore important to him to learn to discriminate in order to avoid punishment. "The process of discrimination tends to correct maladaptive generalizations. It increases specificity of the cue-response connection."[4]

Imitation and Identification

Imitation and identification are two conditions of learning that seem of particular relevance to political socialization. Imitation is generally defined as copying or modelling the behavior of others. Imitation and identification are determined by a variety of motives, such as admiration and the desire to obtain approval or status. No doubt many political acts can be attributed to this type of learning. Studies have shown, for example, that although low-efficacious people tend to be nonvoters, this is not true in the middle class. Since voting is wide-spread in the middle class, low-efficacious people in that group apparently copy the behavior of their more efficacious peers. This type of learning is of great relevance, especially for role-learning. As Chapter VII indicates, much adult political behavior involves the learning of systems-appropriate political roles, such as Senator, bureaucrat, citizen, and so forth. Newcomers to the role, such as junior Senators, very often have to learn new response patterns congruent with the role expectancies of their colleagues. An interesting study of the United States Senate showed that many a newcomer, in order to get along well, watched closely the behavior of his colleagues and tried to imitate it in order to ease his acceptance by them.[5] Persons who did not make the imitative response soon found themselves designated as outsiders and often were kept from rewards such as desirable committee assignments.

Identification involves more than mere modeling or imitation because it implies that the respondent begins to *feel* like another person or group of persons which he values; as such the process often is quite unconscious. A good example of it can be seen in a study of concentration camp inmates. Bettelheim relates how prisoners who had been in camp the longest tended to identify with their oppressors in values and in behaviors. Having given up hope of being liberated, some prisoners learned to copy the behavior of the Gestapo guards and to treat new prisoners with the same cruelty as the guards did. "A prisoner had reached the final stage of adjustment to the camp situation when he changed his personality so as to accept as his own the values of the Gestapo."[6] Studies in this reader (see for example Theodore Newcomb, pp. 380–391 and Thomas Pettigrew, pp. 498–513) also illustrate how identification with a significant other person or group operates as a powerful political socialization force.

Observational Learning

What, however, about novel situations? Must all learning proceed by trial and error? Some psychologists would argue that it need not, that men can learn from observation. A newly-sworn-in judge who instructs a jury is making what for him is a novel response; but he has had ample opportunity as a lawyer to observe other judges and learn from them how it should be done, that is, to make the correct responses. Social learning theorists like Albert Bandura and Richard Walters[7] term this type of learning "observational learning" or "vicarious learning"; and they argue that the response which is made to a novel situation, although perhaps novel in the repertoire of the response giver, is not the result of trial and error but rather of learning acquired previously, albeit vicariously. Children learn many political behaviors in just such a way; they observe adult responses and the rewards or punishments that follow them. Later on they find themselves in similar situations, and they can then produce the correct response without ever having practiced it before. For example, they may see a customarily bossy, loud father talk softly and subserviently to a traffic policeman in order to avoid a ticket and observe that no ticket is issued. If they study the situation closely, they learn that the correct response to the stimulus "policeman" is politeness. All other things being equal, they will be able to give that response some time later when they themselves are stopped by a policeman. Eventually they may even generalize from this particular instance of citizenship vis-à-vis a specific authority to citizenship obligation to all authority.

The above exposition of learning theory was introduced to highlight some of the mechanisms by which people acquire the political knowledge, values, and behaviors characteristic of them. The question which now arises is: *What* does the individual have to learn to equip himself for citizenship? Here we are dealing with *the content, not the process, of learning*. People have to acquire skills, concepts and their application, and political values (moral judgments). Skills require the acquisition of mechanical and/or cognitive know-how; concepts require the acquisition of certain cognitive abilities; values or moral judgments in addition require certain affective commitments.

What Needs to Be Learned?

Skill Learning and Concept Learning

Different societies demand different skills of their members. To be a proficient hunter and warrior may be the most important skill in one society, whereas in a political system such as ours, the necessary, although not sufficient, minimal political participation skills for effective citizenship include reading, writing, knowing how to register for voting, how to mark a ballot, and so forth. More is demanded of some citizens: legislators, for example are expected to be able to talk before a public, follow parliamentary procedures, answer roll calls, and so forth.

The mere acquisition of more or fewer mechanical skills is, of course, but part of the story. In addition, people must acquire some rudimentary knowledge of their political system, its institutions, processes, and principles. To understand them people have to be able to think conceptually. Most people can *learn by rote* that Canada is a democracy of the parliamentary variety. To understand what this *means*, a person must be able to handle concepts such as democracy, representation, and party responsibility, to name but three. A concept refers to a collection of instances (persons, things, events) that in their aggregate distinguish one class of in-

stances from another. Government, representation, and democracy are political science concepts. They help us organize many diverse environmental acts (stimuli) that otherwise would make no sense. A new tax extracted from us without asking for our personal permission would make no sense to us if we did not have in our repertoire the concept "representation."

Concepts serve as crucial links between the environment and the individual. They are intellectual tools that man uses in organizing his environment and attacking his problems. When man employs concepts, he thinks in terms of symbols and classes. When he orders diversity into classes or categories, he begins to reduce ambiguity and imprecision.

Associated with most concepts or categories, moreover, is a set of appropriate behaviors, be they thoughts, motoric acts, or fantasies. Man thereby has a repertoire of behaviors with which to deal effectively with the environment. In fact, his responses may become virtually instantaneous, since he quickly identifies and classifies environmental cues within the context of a particular concept. Thus concepts perform a vital function in enabling us to cope with the complexities of the physical and social world.[8]

Concepts then play a crucial role in the political socialization process because concepts are the important building blocks for acquiring meaningful knowledge about one's political system and its processes. The whole process by which concepts are attained is highly complex and would be impossible to summarize within the confines of a few pages. Although it is imperative that the practitioner, such as the civics teacher, understand the process in order to teach concepts more effectively, for our purpose here it is sufficient that we are aware that the organism's ability to learn highly complex or abstract ideas and concepts must first be preceded by its mastery of simpler ones. Very young children generally cannot handle concepts such as "nation" or "sovereignty," but they can associate a given flag with their homeland. Understanding must, of course, include not only cognitive awareness of a concept or principle but the ability to apply it to a variety of situations or problems. Joseph Adelson and Robert O'Neil (pp. 50–64) notice that young children very often lack the ability to utilize a general concept, such as community and community welfare, by which to judge an individual case but that the ability is well developed by adolescence. Sigel's study of children's reactions to President Kennedy's death (pp. 152–172) also shows how difficult it is for very young children to grasp highly abstract concepts (in this case the concept of due process of law) and to think of political situations not merely in terms of the unique situation (the assassination) but in terms of general principles (due process of law). David Easton and Jack Dennis (pp. 31–49) demonstrate clearly how the child's notions of government increase in complexity and abstraction as he matures. Whereas at first he can think of the government only in terms of people, he gradually learns to think of government in terms of relations, principles, and institutions. Jean Piaget and Anne-Marie Weil (pp. 18–30) show how hard it is for young children to comprehend that they can be simultaneously citizens of Geneva and of Switzerland because to them the concept citizen is an exclusive and not a mutually inclusive one. The implication

of their study is, of course, that the understanding a child has of social events is dependent on the stage of his cognitive development at a given chronological age. All of the studies in this chapter point to the notion of progress through time, although there is considerable disagreement as to the age range for the attainment of certain developmental stages. In spite of these discrepancies, it is rather clear that by adolescence the organism has learned to handle highly complex and abstract thought processes.

Internalization of Social Values

So far we have restricted ourselves very largely to the acquisition of cognitive skills. For political socialization to be effective more is required, of course, than merely cognitive awareness of prevailing societal values—the individual must accept these values as his own because he judges them to be good and proper. Whereas all societies probably teach their young some notions of responsibility and justice, the definitions of responsibility and of justice vary with society and also within groups of the society. A person cannot be said to have been socialized effectively until he makes the societally accepted definitions his own and uses them as a guide for opinion and behavior because they seem to him the only correct, just, and good ones. In other words, he must acquire an *affective* preference for the values and behaviors preferred by the political system. We refer to this stage of learning as internalization. "Internalization can be said to occur when an individual accepts influence because the content of the induced behavior—the ideas and actions of which it is composed—is intrinsically rewarding."[9] Thus in the United States an intense partisan, upon losing an election, still would not consider contesting the verdict by force because he has internalized the notion that the majority must rule or that elections must be decided by ballots, not bullets. "When the norms, values, beliefs, and attitudes of a social system are internalized by the individual, then the efficacy of the socialization process is demonstrated."[10]

Effective socialization, on the other hand, seems to be closely related to political stability. Although there is no clear-cut evidence of just how many people (located where in the system) must be effectively socialized to insure stability, it is nonetheless logical to assume that the wider the distribution of internalized system-induced values, the greater the likelihood that citizens will eschew deviant political behaviors. To be sure, people can be *forced* by government to behave in certain ways without having internalized values from which such behavior should stem; but coerced behavior is often fragile and cannot be counted on to endure. Thus many a white Southern youngster now peacefully goes to school with Negroes because the law forces him to do so; but it would certainly be premature to predict from this behavior that we can anticipate more harmonious race relations for the South of the future. Similarly, in a now classic study of a lynch mob in a small Southern town, Neal Miller and John Dollard[11] observed that many citizens participated in the lynching once it became clear that their behavior would escape punishment. The participants knew perfectly well that lynching was illegal;

but affectively they had apparently not internalized the notion that Negroes were people entitled to the same legal protections as the participants. When behavior does not rest on internalized values, it often crumbles in periods of adversity or change. Miller and Dollard, for example, noted that the lynching they analyzed occurred during a period of economic reverses. The advent of the Third Reich in Germany took place in another period of economic distress. Heresy trials and inquisitions tended to occur in eras of great intellectual or social change and ferment. To insure against the fragility of such behavior, it seems vital that systems-appropriate values and norms be internalized.

Development

Throughout the previous pages there has been the inference that what is learned is dependent on the state of development which the organism has reached. Second graders have no understanding of the concept democracy whereas tenth graders do because they have reached a greater stage of intellectual development.[12] The organism's state of development also affects the extent to which his feelings can be socialized. The emotionally immature organism is essentially an egocentric one and hence is not yet capable of relating to others with empathy or reciprocity. Piaget and Weil, in their article on the child's understanding of the homeland, suggest that egocentrism* is one of the

* Piaget's work in this volume treats egocentrism as part of the cognitive process. Other psychologists use the term when discussing personality development, as illustrated in the following pages.

reasons the very young child cannot understand that a Frenchman who is a foreigner in Switzerland would not be considered a foreigner in France. Sociocentrism comes only at a somewhat later stage when the child is able to think in reciprocal terms. Piaget's work on the moral development of the child seems to note similar stages where the child also develops from great egocentrism to increased sociocentrism.[13]

Explanations as to why the young child finds it so difficult to think in sociocentric terms vary somewhat from personality theorist to personality theorist. But there is a considerable amount of agreement that psychologically the young organism at first is undifferentiated, that is, he cannot distinguish between self and the outside world.

The dominant principle that regulates the orientation of this initial "undifferentiated absolute" is a satisfaction of the momentary needs or wishes as they arrive. . . . In other words, child mentality and behavior are governed by the "pleasure principle," to use a term borrowed by Piaget from psychoanalysis. . . .

On account of the resistances that he meets in the external world, the individual has to make adaptation to reality. With this dawns logical consistency, which develops gradually through the stages of "egocentrism" and logical thinking. In the egocentric stage the child acts and talks as if he were the center of reference in the whole world, hence there is not much logical consistency, which is achieved only through sticking step by step to some well-established premise. In this process the undifferentiated absolute breaks down, the realization of reciprocal relations among other people and ourselves evolves.[14]

With increased maturation the organism should develop this ability, and a socio-centric orientation should follow. Such orientation in turn facilitates cooperative social living. The selections below (Adelson and O'Neil, Goodman, Piaget, and Sigel) all demonstrate how gradually such sociocentric thinking evolves. Great changes occur in children during latency and adolescence. Adelson and O'Neil notice that the biggest changes occur between the ages of 11 and 13, an observation also made by Sigel; and they attribute the observed cognitive changes to the emotional changes that occur between childhood and adolescence. The Adelson and O'Neil selection also points out that not until about the age of thirteen are children likely to meaningfully integrate the general political consensus, thus giving further proof that the growth of sociocentrism as well as sensitivity to community norms comes with increased maturity. By adolescence this process has been all but completed: and it is for that reason that voting and attitude studies often find remarkably few differences between the political outlook of high-school seniors and adults of voting age.

Adolescence in fact is the period that so far has received the most attention of political sociologists and political scientists, not only because it is a stage at which many people begin to assume some of the obligations of citizenship, such as serving in the military, voting, and so forth, but also because it is the period during which people allegedly are most likely to develop new political ideas that often may bring them in conflict with traditional and family norms. It is the period when youth searches for new answers, it is the period during which they might join extremist or radical political movements, and it is the period during which many a political leader gained his first interest and enthusiasm for politics. Psychoanalytically oriented investigators have traced this tendency towards rebellion, radicalism, and idealism to an "identity crisis." Erik H. Erikson, the originator of this term, defines the major crisis of adolescence as follows:

[At] that period of the life cycle when each youth must forge for himself some central perspective and direction, some working unity, out of the effective remnants of his childhood and the hopes of his anticipated adulthood; he must detect some meaningful resemblance between what he has come to see in himself and what his sharpened awareness tells him others judge and expect him to be.[15]

This is not the place to discuss the validity of concepts such as "identity crisis" or any other concept that tries to explain the development through which the organism passes in its path toward adulthood. It is, however, important to sensitize the reader to this type of thinking, for it seems only logical to assume that the development stages of man should also have a very profound influence on the political attitudes, cognitions, and behaviors with which he can cope. Unless we know what an organism is like at a given stage in his development, we really do not know what demands we can make on him politically, nor will we understand how he orients himself to the body politic around him. Unfortunately, so far political scentists have all but ignored this important aspect of political socialization. It is profoundly to be hoped that future studies will incorporate knowledge about man's cognitive and psychological stages into their thinking on political socialization.

Conditions of Learning

The article by Edgar Schein on the American prisoners of war illustrates yet another important aspect of learning, namely, the conditions of learning. Human beings learn in a social setting, and Schein's study points to the importance of other people in the learning process. He shows how some Americans became unsure of previously held beliefs and engaged in behaviors they would never have condoned under ordinary circumstances—all because they found themselves bereft of the validating and encouraging support of other people. Once they could no longer rely on newspapers, letters from home, and companions to reinforce their previously held beliefs, they became easy victims of a process commonly—although incorrectly—labeled "brainwashing."

Learning does not take place in a vacuum. The severity of some settings can be such as to extinguish previous learning, to facilitate or inhibit new learning, and generally to desocialize or resocialize the organism in a manner unlikely to occur if the social setting were more benevolent. The selection by Seymour Lipset shows further how much environment can influence learning. It is the author's contention that the very condition of the university environment greatly accelerates the growth of idealism and with it radicalism among students. By cultural tradition and psychological development young adults are more prone than older ones, and certainly more so than the egocentric younger child, to think of the world around them in idealistic terms. The nature of the university setting with its demands on the development of intellectualism and service and with its deemphasis of materialism and adult responsibility tends further to encourage the full development of this tendency. The selection by Urie Bronfenbrenner on character education in the Russian school is yet another example that documents how the setting itself can contribute to specific learning. The emphasis on group rather than individual achievement in the Russian primary school tends at a very early age to discourage pupils to think in terms of individual success and encourages them to subordinate self-gratification to the achievement goals of the total group. All of which tell us that the speed and direction of social learning can be manipulated by the conditions under which it takes place.

In summary then, political socialization is a learning process; as such it follows definite laws and principles of

learning. Political learning must be considered in a developmental sequence* and is dependent on the cognitive as well as the personality development of the organism. For learning to take place, the organism has to be ready to learn; and this readiness in turn is dependent on a variety of factors of which intelligence, training, biological and personal characteristics are but some of the more important. Finally, learning does not take place in a vacuum but can be greatly affected by the social setting in which it happens. The political environment is but one of such settings: and in the chapters which follow we shall constantly have reference to the political setting as one of the important variables that affect the course of political socialization.

* Not all authors would agree with each other as to the exact sequence or the exact ages at which certain types of learning take place; some might feel that some kinds of learning take place earlier, whereas others may feel that some types of cognition can be learned simultaneously, and there need not always be a lockstep, invariant sequence of learning.

NOTES

1. Paul Henry Mussen, *et al.*, *Child Development and Personality*, 2nd ed. (New York: Harper & Row, 1963).

2. Carl I. Hovland, "Learning," in Edwin G. Boring, *et al.*, *Foundations of Psychology* (New York: Wiley, 1948), p. 138.

3. E. L. Horowitz and R. E. Horowitz, "Development of Social Attitudes in Children," *Sociometry*, 1 (1938), 301–338.

4. Neal E. Miller and John Dollard, *Social Learning and Imitation* (New Haven: Yale University Press, 1951).

5. Donald R. Matthews, *U.S. Senators and Their World* (Chapel Hill: University of North Carolina Press, 1960).

6. Bruno Bettelheim, "Individual and Mass Behavior in Extreme Situations," in E. E. Maccoby, T. M. Newcomb, and E. L. Hartley, *Readings in Social Psychology*, 3rd ed. (New York: Holt, Rinehart and Winston, 1958).

7. Albert Bandura and Richard H. Walters, *Social Learning and Development* (New York: Holt, Rinehart and Winston, 1963).

8. Irving E. Sigel, "The Attainment of Concepts," Martin L. Hoffman and Lois W. Hoffman (eds.), in *Review of Child Development Research* (New York: Russell Sarge Foundation, 1964), pp. 209–210.

9. Harold Proshansky and Bernard Seidenberg, *Basic Studies in Social Psychology* (New York: Holt, Rinehart and Winston, 1965), p. 239.

10. Herbert C. Kelman, "Compliance, Identification and Internalization: Three Processes of Attitude Change," in *ibid.*, p. 142.

11. Miller and Dollard, *op. cit.*, pp. 235–252.

12. Robert Hess and Judith Torney, *The Development of Political Attitudes in Children* (Chicago: Aldine, 1967), **chap. 2.**

13. Jean Piaget, *The Moral Judgment of the Child* (London: Routledge and Kegan Paul, 1932).

14. Muzafer Sherif, *The Psychology of Social Norms* (New York: Harper Torchbook, 1966).

15. Erik H. Erikson, *Childhood and Society*, 2nd ed. (New York: Norton, 1963).

SELECTED BIBLIOGRAPHY*

BALDWIN, ALFRED, *Theories of Child Development*, New York: Wiley, 1967.

BUGELSKI, B. RICHARD, *The Psychology of Learning*, New York: Holt, Rinehart and Winston, 1956.

HILGARD, ERNEST R., *Theories of Learning*, New York: Appleton-Century-Crofts, 1956.

HILL, WINFRED F., "Learning Theory and the Acquisition of Values," *Psychological Review*, 67 (1960), 317–331.

WHITE, SHELDON H., "Learning," in Harold J. Stevenson (ed.), *Child Psychology*, 62nd Yearbook National Society for the Study of Education, Chicago: University of Chicago Press, 1963.

* Standard references cited in the Notes to this chapter are not included.

EMERGENT CITIZENSHIP: A STUDY OF RELEVANT VALUES IN FOUR-YEAR-OLDS*

• Mary Ellen Goodman

In view of the long-standing American concern for educating the young to be "good citizens"—constructive members —of a democratic society, Americans have paid remarkably little attention to "emergent citizenship." The study reported here represents a step in exploration of this essentially unknown territory.

This study was made with ninety-two four-year-olds, both boys and girls, in attendance at nursery schools in a northeastern United States metropolitan area. The children were observed and interviewed in their schools; their teachers and mothers were also interviewed.

Above selection is reprinted from: *Childhood Education*, Vol. 35, 1958–59, pp. 248–251, reprinted by permission of Mary Ellen Goodman and the Association for Childhood Education International, 3615 Wisconsin Avenue, N. W. Washington, D.C. Copyright © 1958–1959 by the Association. Deletions have been made by the editor in the interest of brevity.

* The author wishes to express sincere appreciation for the contribution made to this study by Dura-Louise Cockrell of the Department of Child Study and Education, Smith College, Northampton, Massachusetts. The investigation owes its inception and much more to Miss Cockrell. The author is grateful for sponsorship and facilities provided by Tufts University, Medford, Massachusetts, through the Department of Sociology and the Eliot-Pearson School. Thanks are due also to the directors and teachers of the eighteen different nursery schools, to the children and to their parents.

The study, a pilot project, was carried out under grant from the Ella Lyman Cabot Trust of Boston. The author is appreciative of this assistance.

The report given here is too brief to allow more than a sampling of the findings. It will serve, however, to illustrate that young children are often remarkably mature in their grasp of some values which are basic in our culture and basic to citizenship.

Premises of This Study

Children, although not yet citizens in the political sense, can be thought of as citizens in a broader sense. In this broader sense citizenship is a matter of behavior with respect to other members of society—of playing a citizenship role. The way in which this role is played reflects—and is importantly determined by—the value system which has been learned in the course of socialization.

Prominent among the child's values relevant to citizenship are those having to do with authority and authority figures, standards and limits (rules) concerning behavior, interpersonal rights and obligations, what is "good" and what is "bad" (with respect to people and their behavior).

Findings on Authority and Authority Figures

We assumed, as was reasonable, that the authority figures most likely to figure prominently in the four-year-old's scheme of things are Mother, Father, teacher and policeman (in that

15

order). Such appears to be the case, with the policeman a shadowy figure on no more than the periphery of perception for some forty-five per cent of the children.

It is significant that the majority of the children appear to value most or all of their present authority figures in a positive way (i.e., to be affectionate, friendly and accepting toward them). It should be noted, for example, that in connection with their authorities a greater proportion of children think of things they are told "to do" than of things they are told "not to do"; that "conforming and compliance responses" predominate in their projections of own behavior into imaginary situations involving authority figures; that the large majority of children are said (by both teachers and mothers) to relate to their authority figures preeminently in positive ways (fond, happy, responsive).

This prevailing positive tenor of child authority relations becomes more apparent in nature and content when juxtaposed against the most striking exceptions. In children whose stance toward authority and authority figures is generally negative, we find marked aggressiveness and hostility; erratic, unpredictable behavior; defiance and resentment of attempts at control; fantasies involving the violent and morbid; and a sophisticated and cynical command of dissimulation techniques.

Findings on Standards and Limits

As the children view the content of standards there is no vast difference between home and school. They see the authorities in both places as especially given to telling them to get on with personal routines—sleep or resting and so on—and with picking up, putting away or other chores. Parents, however, issue prohibitions about personal safety: on the street, about the car, near the stove, with respect to inclement weather —while teachers' "don'ts" have to do especially with social safety: "don't hit" and the like.

On the whole these four-year-olds are quite aware of the things they are being told to do and not to do, and the majority readily admit that there are certain things they *have* to do. A sizable minority reject this notion, and even more numerous are those who reject the notion that there are any things they must not do.

The children's values become most apparent when they tell us what they "love to do" and what they "hate to do." Most of them "love" to play and do other things which give pleasure and "hate" to do chores or other things which interfere with personal pleasure and gratification. We find that a few children declare they "love" to extend courtesies or to do things for other people. Observation of actual behavior confirms their declarations.

Clearly not all children, even at four, consistently value the self and its gratifications above other people and their gratifications.

Whatever their ideas and feelings about the self versus others and about the standards held up before them, not many of our subjects frequently behave in a fashion which in the adult world might be called "lawless." Observations show fifty per cent of them quite "civilized" in their behavior and not (in the nursery school setting) failing either in meeting standards or staying within reasonable limits for behavior. In a fair proportion of the remaining cases failures are probably infrequent.

It appears that, in this sample of four-year-old society at least, the young citizens are for the most part reasonably well habituated to accept and abide by the "laws." We infer that doing what they have learned they ought to do is, for most of the children, a positively valued mode of behavior.

Findings on Interpersonal Rights and Obligations

It is noteworthy that adults queried seldom indicated doubts whether four-year-olds do in fact think and act with respect to interpersonal obligations as well as rights. Discussion with the children sustains the view that more than half of them, at least, are enough aware of obligations to understand what we were talking about and to answer affirmatively when we asked, "Are there things you should do for other people?" They conceive these obligations as having to do especially with giving, sharing, helping and being sociable (playing with other children).

That the four-year-olds also conceive of obligations as a reciprocal matter is attested by both adults and the children themselves. More than half of the children declare that there are things other people should do for them, and the specifics they list are much like the ones they accept as their own obligations.

o   o   o

In Summary

This study supports the view that children learn very early some of the basic values essential to orderly social living and characteristic of American culture.

If this small sample is representative, we may conclude that the majority of children learn, in their first four years of life, some values fundamental to "good citizenship." It appears too that, even among children who have in common an urban middle-class background, there can be a very wide range of variation. A few will be generally and highly negative. At the opposite end of the range, a few will be generally and highly positive with respect to citizenship behavior and values.

o   o   o

THE DEVELOPMENT IN CHILDREN OF THE IDEA OF THE HOMELAND AND OF RELATIONS WITH OTHER COUNTRIES

- ## J. Piaget assisted by Anne-Marie Weil

Any psychological and sociological study of tensions presupposes some acquaintance with certain findings of child psychology. We may begin by enquiring whether in view of their particular method of development, the cognitive and affective attitudes associated with loyalty to the homeland and initial contacts with other countries may not be at the root of subsequent international maladjustments. Even if this theory does not at first glance appear to be borne out by facts, we should next proceed to investigate why the child, as he grows, does not acquire enough objectiveness and understanding of others, or readiness to give and take, to withstand those influences for tension or maladjustment that are brought to bear upon him in adolescence or adult life.

These were the two points of view on which the survey described below was based. From the very outset, we were struck by the fact that, whilst children, in the initial stages of their development, did not appear to display any marked inclination towards nationalism, a slow and laborious process in developing a faculty for cognitive and affective integration was necessary before children attained an awareness of their own homeland and that of others; this

Above selection reprinted from: *International Social Science Bulletin*, 3 (1951), 561–578. Deletions have been made by the editor in the interest of brevity.

faculty, being far more complex than would appear on first consideration, is accordingly precarious and liable to be upset by later impacts. For the purpose of studying social and international tensions in general, it is therefore worth giving close consideration to the development and nature of this faculty for integration, since subsequent disturbances will, in the last resort, depend on its strength—or its weakness.

Admittedly, our survey covered only Swiss or foreign children living in Geneva, and, in interpreting the data assembled, some allowance should be made for the influence of the children's adult environment. But, even if we make this allowance, and pending confirmation of our findings by surveys in other areas, we are faced with a paradox which, though it may be peculiar to a particular part of Europe, is none the less indicative.

This paradox may be summed up as follows: the feeling and the very idea of the homeland are by no means the first or even early elements in the child's make-up, but are a relatively late development in the normal child, who does not appear to be drawn inevitably towards patriotic sociocentricity. On the contrary, before he attains to a cognitive and effective awareness of his own country, the child must make a considerable effort towards "decentration" or broadening of his centres of interest (town, canton, etc.) and towards integration of his impressions (with surroundings other than his own), in the course of which he acquires an understanding of countries and points of view different from his own. The readiness with which the various forms of nationalist sociocentricity later emerge can only be accounted for by supposing, either that at some stage there emerge influences extraneous to the trends noticeable during the child's development (but then why are these influences accepted?), or else that the same obstacles that impede the process of "decentration" and integration (once the idea of homeland takes shape) crop up again at all levels and constitute the commonest cause of disturbances and tensions.

Our interpretation is based on the second hypothesis. The child begins with the assumption that the immediate attitudes arising out of his own special surroundings and activities are the only ones possible: this state of mind, which we shall term the unconscious egocentricity (both cognitive and affective) of the child is at first a stumbling-block both to the understanding of his own country and to the development of objective relationships with other countries. Furthermore, to overcome this egocentric attitude, it is necessary to train the faculty for cognitive and affective integration; this is a slow and laborious process, consisting mainly in efforts at "reciprocity," and at each new stage of the process, egocentricity re-emerges in new guises farther and farther removed from the child's initial centre of interest. These are the various forms of sociocentricity—a survival of the original egocentricity—and they are the cause of subsequent disturbances or tensions, any understanding of which

must be based on an accurate analysis of the initial stages and of the elementary conflicts between egocentricity and understanding of others ("reciprocity").

We shall set forth under three separate headings the facts we have been able to assemble; in the first section we shall study the cognitive and affective development of the idea of homeland (between four and five and 12 years of age); in the second section we shall analyse the reactions of children towards countries other than their own, while the third section will deal with the problem of cognitive and affective understanding of others ("reciprocity").

Over 200 children between four and five and 14 and 15 years of age were questioned.

I

The Development of the Idea of the Homeland

The child's gradual realization that he belongs to a particular country presupposes a parallel process of cognitive and affective development. This is not surprising, since any mental attitude is always a blend of cognitive and affective components (the cognitive functions determine the pattern of behaviour, whilst the affective functions provide its "dynamism," or driving force, which is responsible for the net result by which behaviour is judged). But there is more than interdependence between the two: the cognitive and affective aspects may be said to be parallel or isomorphous, since the very young find the intellectual concept of "reciprocity" as difficult to grasp as affective "reciprocity" when this passes beyond the range of their immediate practical experience.

Cognitive Aspect

We came across normal children who, until they were seven or eight years old, had none of the basic knowledge essential to understanding the idea of their country. One boy of seven was positive that Paris was in Switzerland because the people there spoke French, and that Berne was not in Switzerland. As a rule, very young children, up to five or six years of age, are apparently unaware that Geneva is in Switzerland. At the outset, then, children have only a simple notion of the territory in which they live (e.g., their home town), a notion comprising a more or less direct knowledge of certain characteristics (approximate size, main language spoken, etc.), but these ideas are mixed up with verbal notions such as "canton," "Switzerland," etc., which they can neither understand nor fit into a coherent picture. Among these verbal notions picked up from other children or adults, one finally becomes rooted in their minds at about five or six years of age: this is that "Geneva is in Switzerland." But the interesting point is whether this piece of acquired knowledge immediately affects their attitude.

Until they are about seven or eight, though children may assert that Geneva is part of Switzerland, they none the less think of the two as situated side by side. When asked to draw the relationship between Geneva and Switzerland by means of circles or closed figures, they are not able to show how the part is related to the whole, but merely give a drawing of juxtaposed units:

ARLETTE C. 7;6.[1] Have you heard of Switzerland? *Yes, it's a country.* Where is this country? *I don't know, but it's very big.* It it near or a long way from here? *It's near, I think.* What is Geneva? *It's a town.* Where is Geneva? *In Switzerland* (The child draws Geneva and Switzerland as two circles side by side).

MATHILDE B. 6;8. Have you heard of Switzerland? *Yes.* What is it? *A canton.* And what is Geneva? *A town.* Where is Geneva? *In Switzerland* (The child draws the two circles side by side). Are you Swiss? *No, I'm Genevese.*

o   o   o

We see that these children think of Switzerland as comparable to Geneva itself but situated somewhere outside. Switzerland is of course "near" Geneva and "bigger." But they do not understand, either geographically or logically, that Geneva is in Switzerland. Geographically, it is alongside. Logically, they are Genevese, and not Swiss, . . . which in both cases shows inability to understand how the part is included in the whole.

At a second stage (7–8 to 10–11 years of age), children grasp the idea that Geneva is enclosed spatially in Switzerland and draw their relationship not as two juxtaposed circles but as one circle enveloping the other. But the idea of this spatial enclosure is not yet matched by any idea that logical categories can be included one in another.[2]

Whilst the category of Genevese is relatively concrete, that of Swiss is more remote and abstract: children, then, still cannot be Swiss and Genevese "at the same time."

FLORENCE N. 7;3, What is Switzerland? *It's a country.* And Geneva? *It's a town.* Where is Geneva? *In Switzerland* (Drawing correct). What nationality are you? *I'm from Vaud.* Where is the canton of Vaud? *In Switzerland, not far away* (The child is made to do another drawing showing Switzerland and the canton of Vaud. Result correct). Are you Swiss as well? *No.* How is that, since you've said that the canton of Vaud is in Switzerland? *You can't be two things at once, you have to choose; you can be a Vaudois like me, but not two things together.*

o   o   o

These children hesitate: some, like Florence, deny the possibility of being "two things together," although they have just asserted and illustrated with their drawings that Geneva and Vaud are in Switzerland.

o   o   o

It may be said that their real loyalty is to the canton and not to their country. But we find the same response in children who are not living in or do not even know their canton, as well as in Genevese who know they belong there. We have met children who hardly know their home canton, yet stoutly declare they belong to it, out of attachment to their family. The fact is, that at this stage the homeland is still only an abstract notion: what counts is the town, or the family, etc., and the statements heard there; but the children do not yet synthesize these statements into any coherent system.

However, at 10–11 years of age, children enter upon a third stage, in the course of which their ideas are finally synthesized correctly.

MICHELINE P. 10;3. (The child replies correctly to the first questions and makes an accurate drawing.) What is your nationality? *I'm Swiss.* How is that? *Because my parents are Swiss.* Are you Genevese as well? *Naturally, because Geneva is in Switzerland.* And if I ask someone from Vaud if he is Swiss too? *Of course, the canton of Vaud is in Switzerland. People from Vaud are Swiss, just like us. Everyone living in Switzerland is Swiss and belongs to a canton too.*

JEAN-LUC L. 11;1. (The child replies correctly to our first questions and makes no mistakes with the drawing.) What nationality are you? *I'm from St. Gallen.* How is that? *My father is from St. Gallen.* Are you Swiss too? *Yes, St. Gallen is in Switzerland, even though the people there talk German.* Then you are two things at once? *Yes, it's the same thing, since St. Gallen is in Switzerland. All people from Swiss cantons are Swiss. I'm from St. Gallen and still Swiss, and there are others who are Genevese or Bernese and still Swiss.*

It is only at this stage that the notion of country becomes a reality and takes on the idea of homeland in the child's mind. The problem is then to determine whether this development is merely the outcome of a cognitive correlation (inclusion of the part in the whole); whether the age at which these correlations are understood depends on affective factors; or whether both sets of factors evolve side by side.

Affective aspect

Obviously, the child's emotions cannot be analysed in the course of a simple conversation of the kind used for ascertaining his logical make-up. Nevertheless, though no absolute significance can be ascribed to the actual content of his value judgments, and although, in particular, the importance of affective reactions he cannot put into words must not be overlooked, it is still possible, through comparison of replies made at different ages to quite common-place questions (what country do you prefer, etc.) to draw some conclusions as to both the type of motivation and the real but unexpressed motives. It is a striking fact that the three stages briefly described above correspond, as regards affective evaluations, to three stages in a clearly marked process of "decentration," starting from motives essentially bound up with subjective or personal impressions (of the most fleet-ing or even accidental kind) and progressing towards acceptance of the values common to the group, first to the family group and then society as a whole.

During the first stage, the child who is asked for a value judgment does not even think of voicing any preference for Switzerland. He likes any country that appeals to his fancy at the moment and, if Switzerland is chosen, it is for some such reason. The following are the preferences actually expressed by three Swiss youngsters.

EVELYNE M. 5;9. *I like Italy. It's a nicer place than Switzerland.* Why? *I was there these holidays. They have the loveliest cakes, not like in Switzerland, where there are things inside that make you cry. . . .*

DENISE S. 6;0. *I like Switzerland because it has such pretty houses. I was in the mountains and they were all full of chalets. It's so pretty, and you can get milk there.*

JACQUES G. 6;3. *I like Germany best because my mummy just got back from there to-night. It's ever so big and far away an' my mummy lives there.*

These childish affective reactions are analogous to the difficulty, usually experienced by children during this first stage, of integrating their country, canton or town in one logical concept. The question then arises whether it is because it does not yet represent an affective reality that the country is merely juxtaposed to the canton or town, instead of being included in it as part of a whole, or whether it is because the idea of inclusion cannot be logically grasped that the country does not yet arouse any real affective response. A third solution is obviously possible: as reality is centred around their own particular doings and immediate inter-ests, children at stage I lack the requisite logical "decentration" to conceive of their town or canton as enclosed in a larger whole; nor have they a sufficient degree of affective "decentration" to grasp collective realities outside their narrow individual or inter-individual circle: at this level, their failure to grasp the idea of their country or home-land, either on the cognitive or on the affective plane, thus represents two interdependent and parallel aspects of the same spontaneous, unconscious ego-centricity—the original obstacle to any integration of logical relationships and affective values.

Next we give the typical reactions at stage II to the same questions of preference or choice.

DENIS K. 8;3. *I like Switzerland because I was born there.*

PIERRETTE F. 8;9. *I like Switzerland be-cause it's my own country. My mummy and daddy are Swiss, so I think Switzerland's a nice place.*

JACQUELINE M. 9;3. *I like Switzerland. It's the loveliest country for me. It's my own country.*

The reader senses immediately that, despite the persistence of the same egocentric statements as at stage I, the motivation is quite different: family loyalties and traditions now begin to predominate over purely personal motives. The country becomes the *terra patria*, and, though there is still difficulty in ranging the town, canton and nation in an exact order, this is unimportant: their common and therefore undifferentiated affective appeal is based on family feeling. Thus we have here a close parallel between the inability to make logical distinctions (e.g., the idea of spatial or spatio-temporal inclusion is accepted, but not that of the inclusion of one class of ideas in another) and the inability to make affective distinctions, so that the different conceptions are reduced to a single emotional factor— that of family tradition. To be more precise, considerable progress has been made in both directions at once; we find the beginnings of logical "decentration," enabling the child to subordinate his territory (town or canton) to a larger unit in which it is enclosed; and, at the same time, the beginnings of affective "decentration," enabling him to subordinate his egocentric motives to collective values beyond his personal interests. But, in both cases, this process of "decentration" has only just begun and is restricted by the above-mentioned inability to differentiate (due to the remnants of egocentricity surviving in more extensive form in the new field of consciousness recently mastered).

At the third stage, finally, the motivations once again change and are more or less adjusted to certain collective ideals of the national community:

JULIETTE N. 10;3. *I like Switzerland because we never have any war here.*

LUCIEN O. 11;2. *I like Switzerland because it's a free country.*

MICHELLE G. 11;5. *I like Switzerland because it's the Red Cross country. In Switzerland, our neutrality makes us charitable.*

Neutrality, freedom, a country spared by war, the Red Cross, official charity, and so on: it sounds like a naïve summary of patriotic village speeches! But the very banality of these motivations is revealing: the most general collective ideals are those which make the strongest appeal to the child. Merely to state that he repeats what he has been told at school is not enough to explain why he repeats it and, more especially, why he understands it; he gives these reasons because, beyond his personal feelings and the motives of family loyalty, he is finally realizing that there exists a wider community with its own values distinct from those of the ego, the family, the town and visible or concrete realities. In brief, he is attaining to a scale of values culminating in relatively abstract virtues, and at the same time he is succeeding in integrating spatio-temporal and logical relationships into the invisible whole formed by the nation or the country: here, once more, we have parallelism between the processes of logical "decentration" or integration, on the one hand, and affective or ethical "decentration" or integration on the other.

II

Other Countries

We shall now give a brief account of this second part of our investigation, considered from the following two standpoints. First of all, we wished to determine whether ideas or feelings about other countries, or peoples of other nationalities (as far as the child was acquainted with any such) develop along the same lines as those referred to in the first section, or whether there is an appreciable difference between the two types of concepts. Our second, and more important aim, was to lead up to the analysis of "reciprocity" which is presented in the third section. For whether the child's ideas and affective reactions regarding his own and other countries develop along similar or different lines, it will be instructive to discover how, in the light of those attitudes, he arrives at that intellectual and ethical "reciprocity" which is, essentially, the faculty for social awareness and international understanding. . . .

The children at stage I are found to have the same intellectual difficulty about including the part in the whole in regard to other countries as in regard to their own, and the same judgments, based on subjective and fugitive considerations.[3]

o   o   o

PIERRE G. 9;0. (cf. Chapter I, stage II). Do you know any foreign countries? *Yes, France, Africa and America.* Do you know what is the capital of France? *Lyons, I think, I was there with daddy, it's in France* (Juxtaposed circles, Lyons touching France *"because the city of Lyons is on the edge of France"*). And what are the people who live in Lyons? *Frenchmen.* Are they Lyonese too? *Yes. . . . no, they can't be. They can't have two nationalities at once.*

o   o   o

BERNARD D. 6;3. Have you heard of any people who are not Swiss? *Yes, there are the people of the Valais* (Valais, as everyone knows, is one of the 22 Swiss cantons,

and the child himself is a native of Valais). And have you heard of other countries too? Are there any differences between the countries? *Oh yes, there isn't a lake everywhere.* And are the people the same? *No, people don't all have the same voice and then they don't all wear the same pullovers. At Nax I saw some lovely pullovers, all embroidered in front.*

HERBERT S. 7;2. Are there any differences between the different countries you know and the different people living there? *Oh yes.* Can you give me an instance? *Well, the Americans are stupid. If I ask them where the rue du Mont Blanc is, they can't tell me.*

It is superfluous to stress the analogies between the reactions of this stage as recorded above and those described in the first section: their concurrence is the less surprising since most of these children are unaware of belonging to their own particular country (cf. Bernard once again).

The reactions of children at stage II, on the other hand, reveal that their ideas of other countries have developed in exactly the same way as those concerning their own, but frequently with an antagonism between the two types of affective ideas or reactions. Identical development in the first place: in both cases, there has been a "decentration" of the original egocentric attitude, which has now given way to an acceptance of the ideas or traditions of the child's immediate environment, especially those of his family. But thereafter—and the possible antagonism originates here—the child's reactions towards other nationalities may be guided into the most varied channels, according to whether his social environment is understanding, critical, or even censorious of foreigners. Here are some instances of these acquired attitudes, the last of them shedding light on the degree of logic to which the child has attained:

MURIELLE D. 8;2. Have you heard of foreigners? *Yes, there are Germans and French.* Are there any differences between these foreigners? *Yes, the Germans are bad, they're always making war. The French are poor and everything's dirty there. Then I've heard of Russians too, they're not at all nice.* Do you have any personal knowledge of the French, Germans or Russians or have you read something about them? *No.* Then how do you know? *Everyone says so.*

o   o   o

MICHEL M. 9;6. Have you heard of such people as foreigners? *Yes, the French, the Americans, the Russians, the English. . . .* Quite right. Are there differences between all these people? *Oh yes, they don't speak the same language.* And what else? *I don't know.* What do you think of the French, for instance? Do you like them or not? Try and tell me as much as possible. *The French are not very serious, they don't worry about anything, an' it's dirty there.* And what do you think of the Americans? *They're ever so rich and clever. They've discovered the atom bomb.* And what do you think of the Russians? *They're bad, they're always wanting to make war.* And what's your opinion of the English? *I don't know . . . they're nice. . . .* Now look, how did you come to know all you've told me? *I don't know . . . I've heard it . . . that's what people say.*

o   o   o

It is easy to perceive the mechanism of such reactions. Whilst the "decentration" of attitudes towards adoption of family traditions may lead to the beginnings of a healthy patriotism, it may also give rise to a kind of tribal outlook, with values based on the dis-

paragement of other social groups. In discarding his fugitive subjective judgments, and replacing them by the judgments of his environment, the child is, in a sense, taking a step forward, since he is projecting his mind into a system of relationships which broaden it and give it increased flexibility. But two courses then lie open to him: acquiescence (with its positive and negative aspects) and reciprocity, which requires independence of judgment in those concerned. Now none of the remarks just quoted give any impression of dawning independence or "reciprocity:" everything suggests that, on discovering the values accepted in his immediate circle, the child felt bound to accept that circle's opinions of all other national groups.

It is evident, of course, that harsh judgments are not the unbroken rule, and that favourable estimates are accepted like the others. But even in the latter case, we are faced with the psychological problem that results from any action by the social group and, for that matter, from any form of education: is the spirit of understanding engendered by the content of the ideas inculcated, or simply by the process of exchange? In other words, if a child receives his opinions—even the soundest opinions—ready-made, does he thereby learn to judge for himself, and does he acquire the faculty for integration which will enable him, if need be, to rectify deviations and to overcome tensions?

o   o   o

The general conclusion of this chapter . . . is, therefore, as follows: the mastery of the concept of the homeland may be interpreted as the culmination of a gradual "decentration," correlative with a process of integration which is applied to a succession of ever larger units. But study of children's reactions towards other countries shows us that this "decentration" may take either of two possible forms: egocentricity, defeated on one plane, may reappear on another plane in the form of a sociocentricity ranging from the naive to extremely subtle; or, on the contrary, the conquest of egocentricity may mean an advance towards "reciprocity." At this point, we should try to find out whether it is possible to assess the strength of this latter factor.

III

Reciprocity

For the purpose of analysing the understanding of reciprocity as such, while still keeping to the subject of relations between the homeland and other countries, we put two types of question to the same children, 4–5 and 11–12 years of age. To investigate the formation of logical connexions, which, as we have seen, go far to reveal the stage of development of the nationalist concept, we asked each child what a foreigner was, and whether he himself could become a foreigner in certain circumstances (travel, etc.). From the point of view of affective motivations and attitudes, we put the following questions, which lent themselves to illuminating comparisons: "If you had been born without any nationality, what country would you choose, and why?" and "If I asked a little French boy the same question, what country would he choose, and why?"

On this crucial point of reciprocity, as in previous respects, we found an exact parallel between intellectual development and affective understanding. As for the formation of logical concepts, the replies at stage I reflected the notion of the foreigner as something absolute, and an inability to grasp the meaning of reciprocity, that is to say, of the essential relativity of this relationship: foreigners are people belonging to other countries (   ), whereas the Swiss (or Genevese, etc.) cannot be regarded as foreigners, even outside their own country. In the matter of affective motivations, children at this same stage thought that, if they had no homeland, they would choose their present one, but could not understand that French or English children would also choose their respective countries. At stage II, the two types of question call forth intermediate replies, showing the beginnings of reciprocity, together with obvious remnants of egocentricity; and, at stage III, reciprocity gains the upper hand in regard to both types of question.

Intellectual Aspect: The Idea of the Foreigner

As we found in section I, in connexion with the idea of the homeland at this same stage, a certain fund of knowledge is essential if the child is to understand the actual question put to him. Until the child knows the exact meaning of the word "foreigner," it is pointless to present him with the problem of "reciprocity," as the responses would only be something like the following:

GEORGES G. 6;10. What is a foreigner? *I don't know.* Have you ever seen any? *Oh yes.* How did you know they were foreigners? *By their clothes mostly. They wear old clothes. They're always going off to the country.*

CORINNE M. 6;11. Do you know what foreigners are? *I don't know, but I've seen
some. They're soldiers.*

However, once the word is understood,
the question of reciprocity may be
raised, but at stage I, the response is
usually negative.

GEORGES B. 7;5. What nationality have
you? *I'm Swiss.* Are you a foreigner?
No. Do you know any foreigners? *Yes.*
Who, for instance? *People living a long
way off.* Now imagine you were travelling
in France, could you also become a foreigner in certain ways? *No, I'm Swiss.*
Could a Frenchman be a foreigner? *Of
course a Frenchman is a foreigner.* And is a
Frenchman a foreigner in France? *Naturally.*

o   o   o

Before we conclude that these reactions
reflect a failure to grasp the essence of
"reciprocity," two possible objections
should be discussed. Firstly, it might
be argued that it is a mere verbal
misunderstanding: it is the word "foreigner" and not the idea which, in
this case, gives rise to confusion. To
put it differently, the word "foreigner"
could be wrongly interpreted as "not
Swiss" or not "Genevese," etc., thus
giving the impression of non-reciprocity,
even though the child might actually
be capable of true reciprocity. But this
objection may be readily countered by
the facts. The replies quoted above are,
in fact, typical of a category of very
general reactions up to seven or eight
years of age and persisting even longer
in relation to certain classes of ideas.
Thus it is quite common for a boy at
this level to assert that he has a brother,
but that his brother has none;[4] or
children may correctly put out their

right or left hand, but cannot tell which
is which in the case of a person sitting
opposite;[5] or they may have neighbours
but do not regard themselves as these
people's neighbours,[6] and so on. It is
no mere chance, then, if relative concepts become absolute in their minds:
this is due to the lack of any power to
construct logical relationships or to
attain to reciprocity in practice.

A second objection may then be
made: could it not be a mere deficiency
in reasoning power—affecting the sense
of relativity itself—and not a lack of
reciprocity as an attitude of mind?
There are two answers to this objection.
Firstly, relativity (in this particular case
the "symmetrical" character of the
relationships under consideration) is the
result of an operation: the deduction
that $A = B$ means the same as $B = A$,
is a conversion operation and, from
the psychologist's point of view, the
operation is the cause and the relationships deduced are the effect. Any failure
to grasp the relativity of a concept is
therefore due to a lack of adequate
operational equipment. Now the operations producing a sense of relativity are
tantamount to a system of reciprocity.
Secondly, the surest proof that we have
to do with a deep-rooted mental attitude and not merely with logical results
is, as we shall see later, that this failure
to grasp the meaning of reciprocity is
matched by an egocentric motivation
in the values themselves.

During stage II, we find a series of
reactions midway between those described above and reciprocity, as in-
stanced by the following:

JACQUES D. 8;3. Do you know what foreigners are? *Yes, they're the people who come
from Valais. I have an aunt from Valais and
when she comes to Geneva, she's a foreigner.*

ELAINE K. 8;9. What nationality have you? *I'm Swiss.* And what are you in Switzerland? *Swiss.* Are you a foreigner? *No.* And if you go to France? *I'm still Swiss.* Are you a foreigner? *No.* Is a Frenchman a foreigner? *Yes.* And what is a Frenchman in Switzerland? *French, but a little bit Swiss, too, if he's here.* And a Frenchman in France? *He's French.*

○   ○   ○

It is interesting to compare these reactions with our observations on children at the same stage II, recorded in sections I and II. It will be recalled that in their judgments on their homeland and other countries, these children reflected an attitude that might be described as bipolar, if not equivocal: there is a certain degree of logical activity, testifying to progress beyond the egocentricity of the first stage towards "decentration" and integration; but there is also a certain lack of independence, reflected in an acceptance of family opinions, thus transforming the initial egocentricity into sociocentricity, as opposed to "decentration." Here we come across the same bipolarity, but in terms of reciprocity—the new attitude to which we should no doubt look for an explanation of the above reactions. On the one hand, the child has progressed sufficiently far beyond his immediate standpoint not to claim that a Swiss living in another country can never be a foreigner, etc.; this is certainly a development towards reciprocity. But this reciprocity may be said always to stop midway, since there nevertheless remains an undercurrent of sociocentricity tantamount to the assertion that a Swiss (or Genevese, etc.) is not exactly comparable with other people. It is

surely the precarious nature of this incipient faculty for integration that accounts for this type of inconsistency.

However, at stage III, the problem appears to be entirely mastered:

MURIELLE F. 10;6. Do you know what a foreigner is? *It's someone in a country other than his own.* Could you become a foreigner? *Not for the Swiss, but I could for others if I don't stay in my country.*

ROBERT N. 11;0. You know what a foreigner is? *Yes, they're all the people who are not from the same country as ourselves.* And could you become a foreigner? *Yes, for all the other people who are not Swiss, as I was born in a different country from them, so I'd be a foreigner.*

○   ○   ○

Thus, as regards the formation of logical concepts and relationships no further obstacle to reciprocity is discernible at this level. Is the same true from the affective standpoint?

Affective Motivation

Although there appears to be no direct relationship between the question which country children would choose were they to lose their nationality, and whether they themselves are always foreigners to other people because others are foreigners for them, we found a striking concurrence between the corresponding reactions at the three stages considered.

At stage I, not only does the child choose his own country, but he also imagines that a national of another country would likewise choose Switzerland, as though no one could fail to recognize this objective pre-eminence. Here are a few sample remarks made towards the end of stage I (before then, the question is meaningless, as the children are at first quite unaware of their own nationality):

CHRISTIAN K. 6;5. If you were born without belonging to any country, which would you choose? *I'd like to become Swiss.* (The child is Swiss.) Why? *Because. . . .* Say you could choose between France and Switzerland, would you choose Switzerland? *Yes.* Why? *Because the French are nasty. The Swiss are nicer.* Why? *Because the Swiss didn't go to war.* If I asked a little French boy the same question as I asked you just now and said to him: now look, imagine you were born without any nationality and that now you can choose what you like, what do you think this child would choose? *He'd want to be Swiss.* Why? *Because he just would.* And if I were to ask him who is nicer, the Swiss or the French, or whether they're both as good as each other, what would he say? *He would say that the Swiss are nicer than the French.* Why would he? *Because . . . they know the Swiss are nicer.*

o   o   o

It is surprising to find that, as soon as the question is understood, children at this stage voice nationalist feelings that were apparently absent in the children at stage I, described in section I. But apart from the fact that, towards the end of stage I, children begin to be influenced by remarks they pick up (as they will be to an increasing extent during stage II), a factor associated with the actual interrogation should be borne in mind: the first question asked refers to the nationality of the child questioned, and thus has the force of a deliberate suggestion, whereas in section I, his attention was not drawn to this point at the outset.

During stage II, reciprocity appears as a "symmetrical" choice attributed by the child to others of different nationality:

MARINA T. 7;9 (Italian). If you were born without any nationality and you were now given a free choice, what nationality would you choose? *Italian.* Why? *Because it's my country. I like it better than Argentina where my father works, because Argentina isn't my country.* Are Italians just the same, or more, or less intelligent than the Argentinians? What do you think? *The Italians are more intelligent.* Why? *I can see the people I live with, they're Italians.* If I were to give a child from Argentina a free choice of nationality, what do you think he would choose? *He'd want to stay an Argentinian.* Why? *Because that's his country.* And if I were to ask him who is more intelligent, the Argentinians or the Italians, what do you think he would answer? *He'd say the Argentinians.* Why? *Because there wasn't any war.* Good. Now who was really right in the choice he made and what he said, the Argentinian child, you or both? *I was right.* Why? *Because I chose Italy.*

o   o   o

We see that while the child is induced to choose his own country (as at stage I) he is then easily made to place himself in the position of children from other countries. We thus have a relative parallelism with our observations concerning the intellectual "structuration" typical of stage II. But—and this further strengthens the parallel—at the end of the conversation, we only have to add "but who is really right?" to break down this incipient reciprocity and to bring the child questioned round to an attitude resembling that adopted during stage I. Lastly, at stage III, children show a genuine understanding of the "reciprocity" of points of view, and some resistance to the final suggestion.

ARLETTE R. 12;6 (Swiss). If you had no nationality and you were given a free choice of whatever nationality you liked, which would you choose? *Swiss nationality.* Why? *Because I was born in Switzerland and this is my home.* Right. Who do you think is nicer, the French or the Swiss, or do you think they are just the same? *Oh, on the whole, they're much the same. There are some very nice Swiss and some very nice French people, that doesn't depend on the country.* Who is more intelligent, a Swiss or a French person? *All people have their good points. The Swiss don't sing too badly and the French have some great composers.* If I were to give a Frenchman a free choice of nationality, what do you think he would choose? *French.* Why? *Because he was born in France and that's his country.* And who would seem nicer to a French girl, a French or a Swiss boy? *I don't know, perhaps the French for her but you can't be sure.* Which of you would be right? *You can't tell. Everyone is right in his own eyes. All people have their opinions.*

o   o   o

We see how, despite the inevitable superficiality of the questions to which we were forced to confine ourselves, the broad outline of this development may be clearly traced. We may thus draw two main conclusions. One is that the child's discovery of his homeland and understanding of other countries is a process of transition from egocentricity to reciprocity. The other is that this gradual development is liable to constant setbacks, usually through the re-emergence of egocentricity on a broader or sociocentric plane, at each new stage in this development, or as each new conflict arises. Accordingly, the main problem is not to determine what must or must not be inculcated in the child; it is to discover how to develop that reciprocity in thought and action which is vital to the attainment of impartiality and affective understanding.

NOTES

1. Editors note. 7;6 abbreviation for 7 years 6 months.

2. Geneva is drawn as a small circle within the large circle which represents Switzerland. However, Switzerland is often thought of as a large circle separate from the small circle.

3. We have come across normally intelligent school children living in Geneva who had reached age of seven without having ever heard of France ("No! I don't know what that is"), but only of Savoy, etc.

4. Piaget: *Le jugement et le raisonnement chez l'enfant.*

5. *Ibid.*

6. Nicolescu: *Les idées des enfants sur la famille et le village* (Étude sur les enfants roumains. Geneva thesis, 1936.)

THE CHILD'S IMAGE OF GOVERNMENT

• David Easton and Jack Dennis*

Political socialization refers to the way in which a society transmits political orientations—knowledge, attitudes or norms, and values—from generation to generation. Without such socialization across the generations, each new member of the system, whether a child newly born into it or an immigrant newly arrived, would have to seek an entirely fresh adjustment in the political sphere. But for the fact that each new generation is able to learn a body of political orientations from its predecessors, no given political system would be able to persist. Fundamentally, the theoretical significance of the study of socializing processes in political life resides in its contribution to our understanding of the way in which political systems are able to persist,[1] even as they change, for more than one generation.

The Theoretical Setting

A society transmits many political orientations across the generations, from the most trivial to the most profound. One of the major tasks of research is to formulate criteria by which we may distinguish the significant from the less important. Once we posit the relationship between socialization and system persistence, this compels us to recognize that among many theoretical issues thereby raised, a critical one pertains to the way in which a society manages or fails to arouse support for any political system, generation after generation. In part, it may, of course, rely on force or perception of self-interest. But no political system has been able to persist on these bases alone. In all cases, as children in society mature, they learn through a series of complicated processes to address themselves more or less favorably to the existence of some kind of political life.

But socialization of support for a political system is far too undifferentiated a concept for fruitful analysis. As has been shown elsewhere,[2] it is helpful to view the major objects towards which support might be directed, as the political community, the regime, and the authorities (or loosely, the government). The general assumption is that failure to arouse sufficient support for any one of these objects in a political system must lead to its complete extinction.

This paper seeks to illuminate one of the numerous ways in which the processes of socialization in a single political system, that of the United States, manages to generate support for limited aspects of two political objects: the regime and the government (authorities). Ultimately, comparable studies in other systems should enable us to

Above selection reprinted from: *The Annals of the American Academy of Political and Social Science*, 361 (September 1965), 40–57.

* Research from which this paper was drawn has been supported by a grant from the Office of Education. The research design and collection of data were executed jointly by the principal co-investigators, David Easton and Robert D. Hess. The analysis of the political aspects of the data is the primary responsibility of David Easton and Jack Dennis.

generalize about the processes through which members learn to become attached to or disillusioned with all the basic objects of a system.

Within this broad theoretical context our specific problems for this paper can be simply stated: How does each generation born into the American political system come to accept (or reject) the authorities and regime? As the child matures from infancy, at what stage does he begin to acquire the political knowledge and attitudes related to this question? Do important changes take place even during childhood, a time when folklore has it that a person is innocent of things political? If so, can these changes be described in a systematic way?

Government as a Linkage Point

In turning to the political socialization of the child, we are confronted with a fortunate situation. The area that the theoretical considerations of a systems analysis dictate as central and prior—that of the bond between each generation of children and such political objects as the authorities and regime— happens to coincide with what research reveals as part of the very earliest experiences of the child. As it turns out empirically, children just do not develop an attachment to their political system, in the United States, in some random and unpatterned way. Rather, there is evidence to suggest that the persistence of this system hinges in some degree on the presence of some readily identifiable points of contact between the child and the system. From this we have been led to generalize that in one way or another every system will have to offer its maturing members objects that they can initially identify as symbolic or representative of the system and toward which they feel able to develop sentiments and attitudes deemed appropriate in the system. If a system is to persist, it will probably have to provide each new age cohort with some readily identifiable points of contact with the system. But for this, it would scarcely be likely that children could relate in any meaningful way to the various basic objects in a system.

In this respect our point of departure diverges markedly from the few past studies in the area of political socialization. In these it has been customary to take for granted the object towards which the child does, in fact, become socialized. Thus, following the pattern of adult studies, efforts have been made to discover how the child acquires his party identification, his attitudes towards specific issues, or his general political orientations on a liberal-conservative or left-right axis. But such research has adopted as an assumption what we choose to consider problematic. How, in fact, does a child establish contact with the broad and amorphous political world in which he must later take his place as an adult? What kind of political objects do, in fact, first cross his political horizon? Which of these does he first cathect?

For the American democratic system, preliminary interviewing led us to conclude that there are two kinds of initial points of contact between the child and the political system in its broadest sense. One of these is quite specific. The child shows a capacity, with increasing age, to identify and hold opinions about such well-defined and concrete units among the political authorities as the President, policeman, Congress, and Supreme Court. But we also found that simultaneously another and much more general and amorphous point of contact is available. This consists of the conglomeration of institutions, practices, and outcomes that adults generically symbolize in the concept "government." Through the idea of government itself the child seems able to reach out and at a very early age to establish contact both with the authorities and with certain aspects of the regime. In a mass society where the personnel among the authorities changes and often remains obscure for the average person, the utility of so generalized and ill-defined a term as "the government" can be readily appreciated. The very richness and variability of its meaning converts it into a useful point of contact between the child and the system.

But the discovery of the idea of "government" as an empirically interesting point of reference for the child brings with it numerous complications for purposes of research. In the first place, any awareness of government as a whole is complicated by the necessary diffuseness of the idea; it applies to a broad and relatively undifferentiated spectrum of disparate events, people, structures, and processes. Government speaks with a cacophony of voices. It takes innumerable actions both large and small, visible and virtually invisible; and these locate themselves at the national as well as the local level, with many strata in between. Furthermore, the usual child is not likely to place *res publica* very high among his daily concerns.

Thus, the child's marginal interest in things political combined with the complexities of the object itself discourages a clear perception of the overall nature of government. This enormously complicates the task of isolating the specific image and attitudes that children do acquire. However, the points of contact between maturing members of the system and its basic parts are not so numerous that we could allow these obvious difficulties to discourage a serious effort to explore the nature of this connection and the part it may play in the growth of supportive or negative attitudes towards the authorities and regime.

Our Data

The children whom we have surveyed concerning what they think and feel about government, as well as about a number of other political orientations (which we will report elsewhere), are for the most part children in large metropolitan areas of the United States. They are, with few exceptions, white, public school children, in grades two through eight, and were selected from both middle-class and working-class neighborhoods. We have conducted many individual interviews and administered a series of pencil-and-paper questionnaires. The latter we read out to the children in their regular classrooms while they individually marked their answers.

The data to be reported below are some fairly uncomplicated examples of these responses; we use them to illustrate the kinds of developments of greatest interest about orientations towards "the government." In some we are attempting to discern the pattern of cognitive development about government as a whole; in others there is some mixture of cognitive and affective elements; and in a third type, the affective or supportive aspects dominate.

Preview of Findings

The findings which grew out of this analysis will, perhaps, surprise those readers who are accustomed to think of children as innocent of political thought. For not only does the child quite early begin to orient himself to the rather remote and mystical world of politics, but he even forms notions about its most abstract parts—such as government in general. Our data at least suggest this. The political marks on the *tabula rasa* are entered early and are continually refurbished thereafter.

We will, perhaps, disappoint as well those readers who are accustomed to think of the American as one who is brought up on the raw meat of rugged individualism, which supposedly nourishes our national frame. We find that the small child sees a vision of holiness when he chances to glance in the direction of government—a sanctity and rightness of the demigoddess who dispenses the milk of human kindness. The government protects us, helps us, is good, and cares for us when we are in need, answers the child.

When the child emerges from his state of nature, therefore, he finds himself a part of a going political concern which he ordinarily adopts immediately as a source of nurturance and protection. His early experience of government is, therefore, analogous to his early experience of the family in that it involves an initial context of highly acceptable dependency. Against this strongly positive affective background the child devises and revises his cogni-

tive image of government. Let us first turn to some empirical evidence bearing upon this cognition.

The Child's Early Recognition of Government

In earlier studies of the child's growing awareness of political objects and relationships, it was found that the President of the United States and the policeman were among the first figures of political authority that the child recognized.[3] In part, at least, we would expect that attitudes towards political authority would begin to take shape in relationship to these objects. They are clearly the first contact points in the child's perception of wider external authority. In general, data collected since the earlier exploratory studies have supported these findings, as will be reported in later publications.

We can, however, now raise a question which takes us beyond these findings. Does the child also establish some early perceptual contact with the more amorphous, intangible abstraction of government itself, that is, with the more general category of political authority among whose instances are counted presidents and policemen? Is the child's cognitive development such that he is likely to work immediately from a few instances to the general class of objects? This would then put him in a position to apply his concept to new instances, as well as to refurbish it as the experiences of its instances grow. If this is so, we can anticipate that, in addition to such points of contact as the policeman and the President, in the American political system the child will also be able to orient himself to political life through perceptions of and attitudes towards the more generalized and diffuse object that we call "the government."

The Crystallization of the Concept

When do our respondents first begin to recognize the general category of things labeled "government?" One simple way of exploring this is to see whether the child himself thinks he knows what the word "government" means, even if no verbalization of his understanding is called for. On this simple test we would contend that even the seven- or eight-year-old child is likely to feel that he has attained some rudimentary grasp of this general concept. This test is met in a question we asked on our final questionnaire which read as follows: "Some of you may

Table 1

Development of a Sense of Confidence in Understanding the Concept of Government (Responses of Children by Grade Level) [a]

Grade	%	N
2	27.29	1,655
3	19.01	1,678
4	17.61	1,749
5	11.15	1,803
6	12.41	1,749
7	8.36	1,723
8	9.79	1,695

[a]The questionnaire which contained this item was administered to a purposively selected group of 12,052 white, public school children in regular classrooms in eight large metropolitan areas (100,000 and over) in four major geographic regions (South, Northeast, Midwest, and Far West) in late 1961 and early 1962. The children were in grades two through eight and from both middle- and working-class areas. We will refer to this questionnaire hereinafter as simply "CA-9," which is our code name for Citizenship Attitude Questionnaire #9. This question is item #55, page 12. [Page number refers to original article.]

not be sure what □ means. If you are □ ernment means, put □ below." The changin □ sponse to this question is shown in Table 1.

What we find from thes□ □ple data is that 27 per cent of the second-grade children feel some uncertainty about the concept. This proportion declines rather regularly over the grades, however, so that for the eighth-grade children, less than 10 per cent express this uncertainty. In general, these suggest that a considerable portion of the youngest children had already crystallized some concept of government prior to our testing, and with each higher grade level the likelihood that they had not formed some concept decreases. With these data—and similar data from other protocols—as a background, it is plausible for us to proceed to a more detailed consideration of the content of the child's understanding of government.

Symbolic Associations of the Concept "Government"

Since it appears that the child is rather likely to develop some working conception of government in these early years, we can move on to ask: Is there any specific content to this concept, especially of a kind that is political in character? We might well expect that because of the inherent ambiguity and generality of the term, even for adults, considerable differences and disjunctiveness would characterize this concept for aggregates of children. Our findings do, in part, support this expectation. Yet there are clear patterns of "dominance" in these collective conceptions, these patterns vary to a large degree with the age and grade level of the children.

One way we have devised for getting fairly directly at which patterns are dominant in this period and at how these patterns change involves a pictorial presentation of ten symbols of government. These are symbols which appeared strongly in our extensive pretest data when children were asked either to define *government* or to "free associate" with a list of words, one of which was government.

What we asked in our final instrument was the following: "Here are some pictures that show what our government is. Pick the *two* pictures that show best what our government is." This instruction was then followed for the balance of the page by ten pictures plus a blank box for "I don't know." Each of the ten pictures represented a salient symbol of the United States government and was accompanied by its printed title underneath the picture. The options in order were: (1) Policeman; (2) George Washington; (3) Uncle Sam; (4) Voting; (5) Supreme Court; (6) Capitol; (7) Congress; (8) Flag; (9) Statue of Liberty; (10) President (Kennedy); (11) I don't know. The pattern of response to these ten symbols of government is shown in Table 2.

Several interesting facts emerge from this table. If we take 20 per cent as a rough guide to what we might expect purely by chance as a maximum level of response to each of the ten symbol options (for two-answer format), we see that only four of these pictures were chosen with a frequency greater than chance. These four are George Washington, Voting, Congress, and

Table 2 Development of a Cognitive Image of Government: Symbolic Associations (Per Cent of Children and Teachers Responding)[a]

GRADE	Police- man	George Wash- ington	Uncle Sam	Voting	Supreme Court	Capitol	Congress	Flag	Statue of Liberty	President Kennedy	I Don't Know	N Respond- ing	N Not Respond- ing
2	8.15	39.47	15.63	4.32	4.51	13.65	5.93	15.75	12.11	46.26	15.69	1,619	36
3	4.09	26.77	19.01	8.36	6.38	16.13	12.94	16.49	14.26	46.81	12.94	1,662	16
4	5.74	14.19	18.02	10.83	10.25	16.57	28.97	13.33	12.92	37.25	13.15	1,726	23
5	2.74	6.93	19.40	19.23	16.77	11.57	49.08	11.57	11.18	38.51	4.86	1,789	14
6	2.36	4.94	16.78	27.99	16.84	9.94	49.66	11.38	17.07	30.52	4.66	1,740	9
7	3.03	3.44	18.26	39.44	13.54	9.39	44.22	12.84	18.61	27.89	2.98	1,714	9
8	1.66	1.72	16.40	46.77	15.87	6.93	49.14	11.78	19.60	22.91	1.54	1,689	6
TEACHERS	1.00	1.00	5.00	72.00	13.00	5.00	71.00	6.00	8.00	15.00	1.00	390	1

[a] (1) Percentages should add to 200 due to the two-answer format, but do not, because of the failure of some children to make two choices. This is especially the case for those answering "I don't know." (2) 113 children failed to respond to this question. Thus the N at each grade are those responding and the percentages are of that number. (3) We have added, at the bottom, the responses of the teachers of these children, for the sake of comparison. The teachers were given a similar questionnaire at the time of administration of the children's questionnaire.

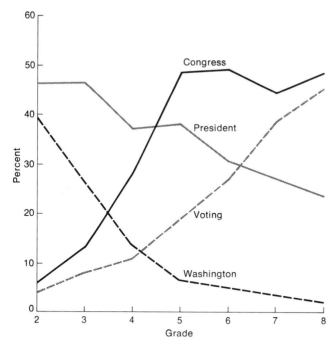

Figure 1: Development of a Cognitive Image of Government: The Four Dominant Symbolic Associations (the Number of Children Responding at Each Grade Level Varies from 1,619 to 1,789).

President Kennedy. These four are considerably more dominant than any of the others, but this dominance varies by grade level. For the youngest children, the two most popular options are the two Presidents, Washington and Kennedy. But these choices drop in the later grades. In Figure 1, the developmental curves for the four dominant options are plotted over the grade span in order to interpret more easily the major changes that are taking place.

It would appear that, in terms of these symbols, the youngest child's perception of government is quite likely to be framed by the few personal figures of high governmental authority that cross his cognitive horizon, probably both in the school (where the portraits of presidents are often prominently displayed) and outside. The young child focuses most directly upon per-

sonal or perhaps "charismatic" aspects of political authority for his interpretation of what government is. But as he moves into the middle years, there is a greater likelihood that his attention will be turned to rather different, prominent aspects of the authorities.

First, he revises his notions to include the Congress and drops George Washington—who suffers a precipitous decline after his initial showing. Undoubtedly, the growing adoption of Congress reflects an awareness of several things, and these are supported by various other data. First, the older children become more aware of the group character of government rather than simply identifying it with single persons. Second, the more frequent choice of Congress probably also reflects a greater awareness of governmental institutions—particularly the ongoing organizations engaged in *law-making* (as suggested undoubtedly in the beginning social studies, history, or civics texts). Children move, in a sense, from a very personalized conception of governmental authority to one better characterized as "legal-rational," institutionalized, or impersonal political authority, to continue the Weberian parallel.

Third, children appear to reflect a greater awareness of the representative character of these institutions. Impersonalization of authority is coincident with some growth in the recognition of regime norms, in this case of the rules of behavior that contribute to representation. This conclusion is borne out to some degree by the third marked shift which occurs—that concerning the older child's greater tendency to pick "voting" as the best picture of our government. Thus, by grade eight nearly half the children choose voting. This suggests some beginning awareness of the regime rules associated with popular democracy and the role of ordinary people in it.

The child's conception of government is, therefore, brought in stages from far to near, from one small set of persons to many people, from a personalistic to an impersonalized form of authority, and toward an awareness of the institutionalization in our system of such regime norms as are embodied in the idea of a representative, popular democracy. There are obviously a number of further tests we would wish to make on these hypotheses. We would also wish to keep in mind that by no means all of these children appear to be going through these stages of cognitive development. But the patterns which emerge seem to us at least very striking,

and they are supported in various ways from our other data.[4]

Generally, therefore, in these data about the cognitive development of this rather abstract category of the individual's political thought, we detect more than a mere glimmering of a concept. Furthermore, the emergent conception in this instance seemingly reflects some fairly wide and regularly changing comprehension for aggregates of children.

This suggests that considerable societal efforts are probably being made to transmit a concept deemed appropriate in the American political system. If we compare children with their teachers, for example, we find that the latter most roundly endorse the two options dominant for the eighth-grade children. The proportions are even higher for the teachers, however, so that in terms of the statistical norms, they stand perhaps closer to the end-state suggested by the direction of movement of the children. Thus the teachers—who are highly salient agents of the child's political and general conceptual development—have a concept that is quite in line with the child's apparent maturational tendencies. One could hypothesize, therefore, that a part of society's efforts to inform the child is reflected in the teacher's responses.

The Concept of Government and the Law-Making Function

A supporting piece of evidence which is connected to the above, but supplements it from the standpoint of governmental functions (rather than from the structural aspects of the concept alone), has to do with the child's changing

Table 3

Development of an Awareness of the Chief Law-Maker (Per Cent of Children and Teachers Responding)[a]

GRADE	Congress	President	Supreme Court	I Don't Know	N Responding	N Not Responding
2	4.79	75.55	11.49	8.17	1,627	28
3	11.41	66.14	16.93	5.52	1,648	30
4	27.51	44.11	21.07	7.31	1,723	26
5	57.39	19.35	19.85	3.40	1,793	10
6	65.06	13.25	18.30	3.38	1,743	6
7	72.14	8.88	16.41	2.57	1,712	11
8	85.33	5.44	7.87	1.36	1,690	5
TEACHERS	96.00	1.00	3.00	0.00	339	5

[a] CA-9, item 33.

awareness of the chief law-makers in our system of government. One thing we find is the fact that, of the various kinds of political or other functions that the child most readily associates with government, the making of laws is very prominent. That is, when the child is asked, "What does the government do?" he is quite likely to answer that he, it, or they make the laws.

A questionnaire item that we presented in this connection reads as follows: "Who makes the laws? Put an X next to the *one* who does the most to make the laws." The options were: (1) Congress, (2) President, (3) Supreme Court, (4) I don't know. The same pictures as before were used. In Table 3, we see the patterns of change over the grade span for this aspect of the child's understanding.

Here the President's early dominance is apparent, but Congress gradually supplants him by grade five. Thus, by the middle grades the child is both increasingly prone to identify Congress as the chief source of law-making as well as a more representative symbol of our government than the President.

If this trend should continue into adulthood, we would expect great support for Congress as the primary institution of government vis-à-vis the President. We would expect that, of the opposing observations of Max Lerner and Robert Lane, for example, those of Lane would be given support. Lerner observed (as cited by Lane) that "when the American thinks of his government, he thinks first of the President as its symbol."[5] If "first" means while he is a second or third grader, then Lerner is correct. But this does not appear to be the sense in which he is using the word.

In light of the developmental trends we see in our data, our respondents seem to resemble more closely the "common men" in Lane's Eastport study. Lane found that his respondents were more likely to perceive government in terms of its legislative functions than its administrative or judicial ones.[6] As far as the common men in Eastport were concerned, Congress was the most important focus of their concept of government. Lane also found that government (and Congress) are thought of in terms of their products, namely, the laws they make.[7] His subjects consider government and Congress as benign, helpful, and responsive—an organization "working for the people, not merely restraining them."[8]

All of these findings converge with our data as far as the developmental trends are concerned. The oldest children in our test group are those who most resemble the common men of Eastport. One can therefore interpret what we find as an indication that this image of government is one not confined to the period of Lane's study but seems to have more general application. Our respondents tend over the grades toward the adoption of a vision of government which puts great emphasis upon Congress as the center of government, upon law as its most visible product, and upon benign, helpful, protective, and responsive qualities as those most appropriately describing its manner of operation. The latter, more affective image will be discussed shortly after we present some further findings concerning cognitive development.

Differentiation of the Public Sector

Even though the children tested assert a growing awareness of government as an idea and object, are they, in fact, able to distinguish it as a sphere separate from other areas of social life? If attitudes towards the authorities as an object are to have relevance for later ties to the system, we need some evidence indicating that even in their earliest years children are, in fact, able to recognize some minimal difference between that which is governmental

and that which is not. Only under such conditions could we infer that attitudes towards government—to which we shall turn in a moment—refer to distinctively political bonds.

To discover whether the child's declared knowledge of what government means includes a capacity to discriminate governmental from non-governmental objects, we chose to test his awareness of the difference between what we normally view as the public and private sectors of life. A variety of contexts could be used to test for this differentiation—activities of various kinds, organizations, symbols, or personnel. We have chosen for our test the last because we found that the formulation, "people who do various jobs to help the community," is a rather familiar context for the child who has been exposed to the beginning social studies texts. The child learns that a variety of "community helpers" exist, ranging from doctors and nurses to firemen and street sweepers.

What we asked was very simple. Taking various occupations—milkman, policeman, soldier, judge, postman, and teacher—we said: "Here are some people. Which ones work for the government?" Then followed six questions with an appropriate picture for each such as: "Does the MILKMAN work for the government?" The options were: (1) Yes, (2) No. What we found is shown in Table 4.

Only the first of these people was considered by us to be clearly outside the governmental system as determined by his occupation.[9] Of the rest, two were more directly local government workers—the policeman and the teacher; two were clearly national government workers—the soldier and

Table 4

Development of an Awareness of the Public and Private Sectors (Per Cent of Children and Teachers Responding)[a]

GRADE	Milkman	Policeman	Soldier	Judge	Postman	Teacher	N Responding (varies by item)
2	29.12	86.04	68.33	86.42	56.87	48.01	1,601–1,626
3	30.77	89.11	79.16	88.35	62.74	54.95	1,627–1,656
4	28.03	90.98	83.17	88.70	71.35	58.29	1,702–1,730
5	20.54	88.99	90.18	90.45	80.02	62.65	1,778–1,792
6	16.24	87.84	93.28	91.70	85.53	64.48	1,730–1,747
7	12.85	82.47	95.52	94.16	89.02	64.03	1,697–1,718
8	8.38	80.95	98.11	93.72	93.20	59.31	1,681–1,692
TEACHERS	1.00	77.00	100.00	91.00	99.00	45.00	330–341

[a]CA-9, items 49-54.

the postman; and one was indeterminate as among levels—the judge.

Several things are apparent from the table. Of these workers, the milkman is the one (as we would expect) who is least often identified as a member of the public sector. Around 70 per cent of the youngest children were able to make an accurate assessment of his nongovernmental status. From grade four on, this proportion steadily increased so that by grade eight, less than 10 per cent were in error.

For the rest, the policeman and the judge are most easily recognized as belonging in the governmental system by the youngest children. Then come the soldier, postman, and teacher in that order. Both the soldier and postman—the more nearly exclusively national government workers—increase in the proportions of children endorsing them at successively higher grade levels until, by grade eight, they are the ones who, with the judge, get the greatest governmental identification.

The teacher, on the other hand, does not really make any major gains over the grades, but remains somewhat ambiguous with respect to her governmental status. And this effect holds for the teacher respondents as well. Somehow the status of the teacher is a more complex one.

That something else is probably at work is seen when we compare with the others the perception over the grades of the teacher and the policeman—both local-governmental in status. Both, over the grades, suffer some net decline in the proportions of children endorsing their governmental status while the other government workers show gains. Possibly the older child is more likely to direct his attention to the national level for his image of government, and, therefore, his differentiation is conflicted for local government workers. This would fit, at least, other somewhat similar findings about the child's greater awareness of the national than of the lower levels of government.[10] It also explains the markedly lower percentage of teachers who identify policemen and teachers as working for the government.

In general, the child in his elementary years attains the capacity to differentiate the governmental system of behavior from nongovernmental systems. This does not mean that he is able to do so in every conceivable way. Our data suggest only that he is increasingly able to do this for the personnel of government. His concept of government, therefore, does become a differential one, at least in these terms. Again, this suggests a development beyond that of only a rudimentary grasp of this complex object in these early years of political awareness.

There is thus sufficient content in the child's perception of government for us to have some confidence that when we now come to talk about his attitudes toward this object, it will reflect affect towards a genuinely political (that is, public) authority. It will also prove significant for our interpretation that there is even a tendency to think of government at the national rather than at the local level.

Summary of Findings on the Child's Developing Cognitive Image of Government

As a possible object toward which affect might be directed, the idea of government undergoes far-reaching changes in the cognitive development of the child as represented in our test group. As he passes through grades two to eight, he begins with a rudimentary notion in which government is personal in character, represented by a few high-ranking and visible leaders. But as he grows older, the child see government in less personal terms. He becomes increasingly aware of its group character and its major institutions; he learns something about the norms (voting) of a representative and popular democracy. In addition, it is crucial that the child proves increasingly able to identify government as something that is different from the private sector of life, however the latter may be defined in different epochs of society. All of these things suggest that, aside from any feelings that may be associated with government, the efforts by society to convey an adequate representation of this abstract object are by no means in vain.

The Child's Affective Response to Government

Although analytically we are able to separate the cognitive aspects of the image of government from accompanying feelings towards it, empirically they go hand in hand. For an understanding of the way in which the American political system stimulates diffuse support for the political authorities, it is critical to appreciate the fact that from the very beginning of his awareness—at its conceptually most rudimentary stage—the child interprets government as something provided to further his welfare and that of the people around him. The benevolent, protective, helpful, and otherwise good qualities of government constitute the first and continuing overall context of evaluation. Even at the end of this period—when the child is thirteen or fourteen years of age, and government and individual authorities, such as the President and the policeman, are beginning to be seen more realistically and less ideally—the child still regards them as great blessings, if slightly mixed ones.

Table 5

Attitudes Toward the Role of Government

	1. "The government is getting too big for America."		2. "The government meddles too much in our private lives."		3. "The government has too much power."		4. "The government usually knows what is best for the people."		5. "The government ought to give money and food to people out of work."		6. "The government should have more power over the people."	
GRADE	% Agree	N	% Agree	N	% Agree	N	% Agree	N	% Agree	N	% Agree	N
3	16	113	28	108	36	116	80	69	70	69	22	69
4	14	125	21	118	19	122	77	119	84	119	33	120
5	10	118	17	116	22	118	87	117	80	117	24	117
6	7	146	19	145	10	146	84	145	78	143	13	145
7	13	143	19	139	12	139	91	139	71	139	20	138
8	11	149	14	148	15	147	84	147	77	145	19	145

The child thus continues to endorse government even though what he understands it to be is changing. Having started off his evaluation in highly positive terms, he seems reluctant to give it up. In this we see, perhaps, the early formation of a bond that it is hard to loosen. It is a bond that entails future diffuse support for the governmental system.[11]

The Child's Approval of Government's Role

In our pilot data, we found such a uniformly favorable affective image of government, from the earliest grades onward, that we felt no special large-scale effort was necessary to deal with this in our final instrument. Yet we do have some data from our eight cities which bear upon the question. First, however, we shall present a few examples of our considerable body of pilot data in order to show how highly consensual our young children's ap-

proval of government is over the whole grade range.

In an instrument administered to children in the Chicago area, we proposed that the children either agree or disagree with statements such as these:

1. The government is getting too big for America.
2. The government meddles too much in our private lives.
3. The government has too much power.
4. The United States government usually knows what is best for the people.
5. The government ought to give money and food to people out of work.
6. The government should have more power over the people.[12]

We attempted as far as possible to retain the original wording of statements of children in our pretest interviews—but reversing the items in several cases. The patterns of response to these statements are shown in Table 5.

What we see is that children at all of these grade levels roundly approve of government. They reject, at a fairly high level of agreement (75 per cent or more), the first three statements about the scope of government becoming too large. Statements 4 and 5, on the other hand, reflect approval of the role of government in guiding and caring for the people, and these statements elicit a high level of agreement. Only for the last statement do we see any impetus toward restricting the role of government; that is, the children like it the way it is.

The over-all response is one which is better characterized as collectivist endorsement than individualistic disapproval of government. In spite of the great myth of rugged individualism which is supposed to pervade the American consciousness, these children, at least, seem to be inclined toward the opposite kind of feeling about government. Thus the child begins as something of a natural collectivist, and whatever individualistic tendencies he may exhibit are developed later on.

The sixth item suggests, moreover, that the child is likely to be a "conservative collectivist" in that he is not much in favor of extending the scope of government beyond its present limits. He is rather happy with government as it stands and would not give it "more power over the people." Thus, the child's early contentment with government is fairly complete, and it is one which exhibits the characteristics of a high acceptance of government as a given, necessary part of the natural environment. If the child is to develop discontent and a desire for change, it is undoubtedly yet to be learned. It thus

Think of the *Government* as it really is . . . (Circle the number of your choice)

1	2	3	4	5	6
Almost never makes mistakes	Rarely makes mistakes	Sometimes makes mistakes	Often makes mistakes	Usually makes mistakes	Almost always makes mistakes

1	2	3	4	5	6
Would always want to help me if I needed it	Would almost always want to help me if I needed it	Would usually want to help me if I needed it	Would sometimes want to help me if I needed it	Would seldom want to help me if I needed it	Would not usually want to help me if I needed it

1	2	3	4	5	6
Makes important decisions all the time	Makes important decisions a lot of the time	Makes important decisions sometimes	Makes important decisions seldom	Almost never makes important decisions	Never makes important decisions

1	2	3	4	5	6
Can punish anyone	Can punish almost anyone	Can punish many people	Can punish some people	Can punish a few people	Can punish no one

1	2	3	4	5	6
Knows more than anyone	Knows more than most people	Knows more than many people	Knows less than many people	Knows less than most people	Knows less than anyone

will be overlaid upon an early base of high regard for the government.

The Child's Rating of Government's Qualities

The early positive regard for the government is shown, as well, over a larger group of respondents in some ratings of the government in our final "eight cities" questionnaire. Using five role attributes and qualities of government as descriptions, we asked the child to "think of the Government as it really is." The items (CA-9, items 32–36) read as on page 44.

We asked for these ratings at grades four to eight. The results are shown in Table 6.

Over-all, on these five ratings[13] approval of government is high across the grades. There is some decline for two of these ratings, however, and an increase on three. The most apparently affectively loaded item, "would want to help me if I needed it," for example, shows a greater tendency of the older child to rate the government's willingness to help him "almost always" or "usually" rather than "always." And the same is true for the somewhat affectively loaded item "makes mistakes." The more cognitively directed, role-relevant items show steady increases in the more positive categories although the perception of government's capacity to punish is seemingly never as high as the other two—"makes important decisions" and "knows more than other people."

Perhaps the most interesting observation is that the most directly affective item, "would want to help me if I needed it," elicits a high regard for

government over the whole span of grades, with a small drop of this support for the older children.

Summary of the Child's Affective Response to Government

The child's affect in this context begins high but diminishes somewhat as he learns more about the political world. He begins with deep sympathy for government, and this early aura of approval is likely to remain at the base of this acceptance of the government, whatever later modifications and limitations he puts on his trust and approval. These limited data, at least, suggest that he certainly begins with highly supportive feelings.

Conclusion

To maintain a social construct as varied, extensive, and demanding of social resources as government, a broad panoply of forces need to be set in motion to provide the requisite support. The political socialization of new members is one of the most far-reaching and most consequential of these forces. The political system must somehow provide a flow of information about and continuously create deep feelings of loyalty and obedience for its basic forms. One of these is its government or authorities. Government is a primary focus for the generation of politically supportive or disaffective orientations. Our data suggest that in the United States a supportive image of government is being widely and regularly reproduced for young new members. The average grade school child of our test group appears to experience some

Table 6

Ratings of the Qualities of Government (Per Cent of Children Responding)

1. "Makes mistakes"

GRADE	1. Almost Never	2. Rarely	3. Some-times	4. Often	5. Usually	6. Almost Always	Mean Rating	N Responding	N Not Responding
4	29.75	42.70	25.02	1.13	.87	.53	2.02	1,499	250
5	23.95	45.72	27.87	1.90	.39	.17	2.10	1,787	16
6	22.18	47.93	27.18	1.67	.40	.63	2.12	1,740	9
7	16.78	48.89	31.59	2.21	.12	.41	2.21	1,716	7
8	13.44	45.51	38.25	2.26	.18	.36	2.31	1,681	14

2. "Would want to help me if I needed it"

GRADE	1. Always	2. Almost Always	3. Usually	4. Some-times	5. Seldom	6. Not Usually	Mean Rating	N Responding	N Not Responding
4	25.27	31.72	23.92	11.63	5.17	2.28	2.47	1,488	261
5	16.60	31.01	27.80	16.26	5.29	2.98	2.72	1,777	26
6	16.60	31.12	28.36	16.43	4.50	3.00	2.70	1,735	14
7	15.64	29.00	30.92	15.99	5.72	2.74	2.75	1,714	9
8	13.66	28.82	32.34	15.93	6.26	2.98	2.81	1,676	19

3. "Makes important decisions"

GRADE	1. All the Time	2. A Lot of the Time	3. Some-times	4. Seldom	5. Almost Never	6. Never	Mean Rating	N Responding	N Not Responding
4	35.01	47.93	13.92	2.21	.54	.40	1.87	1,494	255
5	38.75	46.89	12.00	1.63	.45	.28	1.79	1,783	20
6	47.70	40.39	9.78	1.32	.35	.46	1.68	1,738	11
7	54.32	35.06	8.75	1.46	.06	.35	1.59	1,714	9
8	57.81	35.16	5.72	.83	.18	.30	1.51	1,678	17

4. "Can punish"

GRADE	1. Anyone	2. Almost Anyone	3. Many People	4. Some People	5. A Few People	6. No One	Mean Rating	N Responding	N Not Responding
4	13.90	29.28	24.11	19.01	9.13	4.57	2.94	1,489	260
5	13.68	33.67	25.45	16.61	6.53	4.05	2.81	1,776	27
6	19.83	31.82	23.29	14.47	6.22	4.38	2.69	1,735	14
7	22.46	31.79	23.75	13.43	5.34	3.23	2.57	1,705	18
8	26.44	30.58	21.28	12.83	5.52	3.36	2.50	1,668	27

5. "Knows"

GRADE	1. More Than Anyone	2. More Than Most People	3. More Than Many People	4. Less Than Many People	5. Less Than Most	6. Less Than Anyone	Mean Rating	N Responding	N Not Responding
4	13.68	44.67	36.35	2.88	1.41	1.01	2.37	1,491	258
5	11.35	52.11	33.56	1.46	.79	.73	2.30	1,779	24
6	14.02	52.05	29.95	2.25	.75	.98	2.27	1,733	16
7	16.05	54.09	27.34	1.65	.53	.35	2.18	1,701	22
8	15.34	58.24	23.83	1.56	.60	.42	2.15	1,662	33

rather basic changes in his conception of government—changes which move him toward a cognitive image that conforms to the requirements of a democratic political system.

He begins, as a "political primitive," with a vision of government as the embodiment of a man or a small set of men who constitute a yet dimly recognized form of external authority. This authority applies to the immediate environment of the child in a rather abstract way as well as to the wider world beyond. Probably the first recognizable shadow that flickers across the wall of the cave of the child's unformed political mind is that of the President. He forms the initial visible object of the political world, and, from him, the child builds down, gradually incorporating more and more objects below him until the image becomes rounded and complex.

The child, moving down toward a plural, complex, and functional conception of government (as our unpublished data show) runs upon representative and popular institutions. He raises Congress and voting in his mind's eye to positions of dominance as symbolic associations and thus elicits democracy in his interpretation of what our government is. At the same time, he is beginning to sharpen his knowledge about the boundaries of government by sorting what is outside the realm of government from what is within it.

This finally adds up to a picture supportive of a democratic interpretation and evaluation, a picture that becomes rapidly and forcefully exhibited in these years, as other data, not reported as yet, confirm. The child is initiated into a supportive stance by what is probably high exposure to cues and messages about government, even while he is essentially unconcerned with such matters and too young to do much about them even if he wished. He learns to like the government before he really knows what it is. And as he learns what it is, he finds that it involves popular participation (voting) and that this is a valuable part of its countenance. It is further reason for liking it; and liking it is what the child continues to do. The child has somehow formed a deep sympathy for government even before he knows that he is in some way potentially part of it.

We know of course that such a process of changing understanding and feeling must go beyond these early years. And later experiences may upset these earlier formed images. Yet we know as well, from what little evidence there is directly about support for government *per se*, that adult Americans are also highly supportive of their government, whatever exaggerations may exist about their belief in limited government.[14] In these exploratory data that we have presented, we think we see growing the deep roots of this supportive sentiment.

Furthermore, our data enable us to link up our discussion of the cognitive and affective aspects of the child's image of government, at least in a speculative way. Two things stand out in our data. First, the child begins with a view of government as composed of palpable, visible persons—such as the President or a past President, Washington. Second, as he makes his initial contact with government, it becomes a symbol of orientation to political life that is charged with positive feelings. If we now make the plausible assumption that a child of seven or eight is not likely to develop such feelings about *impersonal* organizations or institutions, we can appreciate the significance of the fact that his first glimpse of government is in the form of the President. It permits the child to express toward a figure of political authority sentiments that he is already accustomed to displaying to other human beings in his environment.

From this we would draw the hypothesis that the personalizing of the initial orientation to political authority has important implications for the input of support to a political system as the child continues through his early years into adolescence. As he fills in his picture of government, adding, to leading figures, such institutions as Congress and such regime rules as voting, we would suggest that the affect originally stimulated by his personalized view of government subtly spills over to embrace other aspects of government and the regime itself.

But for this process it is difficult to see how impersonal, remote, and complex organizations such as Congress or practices such as voting could possibly catch the imagination of a child and win his affection. Yet our data do show that positive sentiment towards government, even after the child has begun to see it it in impersonal terms, is so high as to approach a consensual level. When we add to this the fact that children tend to view government as national rather than local in its scope, we can appreciate the unifying force that this image must have in a system such as the United States.

This interpretation carries us far beyond its immediate significance for socialization into the American political system. In effect, we may have encountered here a central mechanism available to many political systems in building up diffuse support in each wave of children as they enter a political system through birth into it. In many ways a child born into a system is like an immigrant into it. But where he differs is in the fact that he has never been socialized to any other kind of system. That is to say, he is being socialized politically for the first time rather than resocialized as for an immigrant. The fact that the new member is a child rather than an adult with a pre-existing set of attitudes towards political life, creates a need for special devices to build support for the regime and authorities. Each system will, of course, have its own specific mode of personalization. It may take the form of a monarch, a paramount chief, a renowned elder or ancestor, a charismatic leader, or a forceful dictator. But the pattern of making government a warm and palpable object through its initial symbolization as a person, the high affect that this permits for a child and the possible subsequent overflow of this feeling to cold and impersonal institutions and norms may form a complex but widespread mechanism for attaching to the system those members who are new to it by virtue of their birth in it.

NOTES

1. For the idea that persistence includes change, see D. Easton, *A Framework for Political Analysis* (Englewood Cliffs, N.J.: Prentice-Hall, 1965) and *A Systems Analysis of Political Life* (New York: John Wiley & Sons, 1965).

2. *Ibid.*

3. David Easton, with R. D. Hess, "The Child's Changing Image of the President," 24 *Public Opinion Quarterly*, pp. 632–644; "Youth and the Political Systems," *Culture and Social Character*, ed. S. M. Lipset and L. Lowenthal (New York: Free Press of Glencoe, 1961); and "The Child's Political World," 6 *Midwest Journal of Political Science* (1962), pp. 229–246.

4. Some of these supporting data will be presented below; other kinds of data will be shown in other publications.

5. Max Lerner, *America as a Civilization* (New York: Simon and Schuster, 1957), p. 377.

6. Robert Lane, *Political Ideology* (New York: Free Press of Glencoe, 1962), p. 146.

7. *Ibid.*, pp. 147–148.

8. *Ibid.*, pp. 145, 149.

9. Pretesting had indicated that "the milkman" was as good an indicator as numerous other private roles.

10. See Fred Greenstein, *Children and Politics* (New Haven: Yale University Press, 1965), pp. 60–61.

11. For the concept "diffuse support," see D. Easton, *A Systems Analysis of Political Life, op. cit.*

12. These questions are from our pilot questionnaire "In My Opinion —# III," items 50, 125, 169, 170, and 151, respectively.

13. We have the same five ratings, as well as others, for the President, the child's father, the policeman, the average United States senator, and the Supreme Court. We will present comparisons of these ratings in a later report.

14. See V. O. Key, Jr., *Public Opinion and American Democracy* (New York: Alfred A. Knopf, 1961), pp. 28–32; M. Janowitz, D. Wright and W. Delaney, *Public Administration and the Public: Perspectives toward Government in a Metropolitan Community* (Ann Arbor: Bureau of Government, University of Michigan, 1958), pp. 31–35; and Donald E. Stokes, "Popular Evaluations of Government: An Empirical Assessment," *Ethics and Bigness*, ed. Harlan Cleveland and Harold D. Lasswell (New York: Harper, 1962), pp. 61–72.

...ITICAL IDEAS IN ADOLESCENCE:
...OMMUNITY[1]

...ı and Robert P. O'Neil

During adoı... ..ce the youngster gropes, stumbles, and leaps towards political understanding. Prior to these years the child's sense of the political order is erratic and incomplete—a curious array of sentiments and dogmas, personalized ideas, randomly remembered names and party labels, half-understood platitudes. By the time adolescence has come to an end, the child's mind, much of the time, moves easily within and among the categories of political discourse. The aim of our research was to achieve some grasp of how this transition is made.

We were interested in political ideas or concepts—in political philosophy—rather than political loyalties per se. Only during the last few years has research begun to appear on this topic. Earlier research on political socialization, so ably summarized by Hyman (1959), concentrated on the acquisition of affiliations and attitudes. More recently, political scientists and some psychologists have explored developmental trends in political knowledge and concepts, especially during child-

Above selection reprinted from: *Journal of Personality and Social Psychology*, 4, 3 (July-December 1966), 295–306.

[1] The research was supported by grants to the first author from the H. H. Rackham Faculty Research Fund of the University of Michigan and from the Social Science Council. It constituted a portion of the second author's doctoral dissertation submitted to the University of Michigan.

hood and the early years of adolescence; the studies of Greenstein (1965) and of Easton and Hess (1961, 1962) are particularly apposite.

Our early, informal conversations with adolescents suggested the importance of keeping our inquiry at some distance from current political issues; otherwise the underlying structure of the political is obscured by the clichés and catchphrases of partisan politics. To this end, we devised an interview schedule springing from the following premise: Imagine that a thousand men and women, dissatisfied with the way things are going in their country, decide to purchase and move to an island in the Pacific; once there, they must devise laws and modes of government.

Having established this premise, the interview schedule continued by offering questions on a number of hypothetical issues. For example, the subject was asked to choose among several forms of government and to argue the merits and difficulties of each. Proposed laws were suggested to him; he was asked to weigh their advantages and liabilities and answer arguments from opposing positions. The interview leaned heavily on dilemma items, wherein traditional issues in political theory are actualized in specific instances of political conflict, with the subject asked to choose and justify a solution. The content of our inquiry ranged widely to include, among others, the following topics: the scope and limits of political authority, the reciprocal obligations of citizens and state, utopian views of man and society, conceptions of law and justice, the nature of the political process.

This paper reports our findings on the development, in adolescence, of *the sense of community*. The term is deliberately comprehensive, for we mean to encompass not only government in its organized forms, but also the social and political collectivity more generally, as in "society" or "the people." This concept is of course central to the structure of political thought; few if any issues in political theory do not advert, however tacitly, to some conception of the community. Hence the quality of that conception, whether dim, incomplete, and primitive, or clear, complex, and articulated, cannot fail to dominate or temper the child's formulation of all things political.

The very ubiquity of the concept determined our strategy in exploring it. We felt that the dimensions of community would emerge indirectly, in the course of inquiry focused elsewhere. Our pretesting had taught us that direct questions on such large and solemn issues, though at times very useful, tended to evoke simple incoherence from the cognitively unready, and schoolboy stock responses from the facile. We also learned that (whatever the ostensible topic) most of our questions informed us of the child's view of the social order, not only through what he is prepared to tell us, but also through what he does not know, knows falsely, cannot state, fumbles in stating, or takes for granted. Consequently we approached this topic through a survey of questions from several different areas of the schedule,

Table 1

Distribution of Sample by Grade, Sex, and Intelligence

	Boys		Girls	
	Average IQ	Superior IQ	Average IQ	Superior IQ
5th grade: *N*	10	5	10	5
Mean IQ	106.1	127.8	105.1	128.4
7th grade: *N*	10	5	10	5
Mean IQ	104.1	140.0	104.5	134.4
9th grade: *N*	10	5	10	5
Mean IQ	106.6	133.2	105.1	134.0
12th grade: *N*	10	5	10	5
Mean IQ	106.1	140.8	103.8	134.8

chosen to illuminate different sides of the sense of community.

Method

Sample

The sample was comprised of 120 youngsters, equally divided by sex, with 30 subjects at each of 4 age-grade levels—fifth grade (average age, 10.9), seventh (12.6), ninth (14.7), and twelfth (17.7). The sample was further divided by intelligence: At each grade level, two thirds of the subjects were of average intelligence (95–110) and one third of superior intelligence (125 and over), as measured by the California Test of Mental Maturity. Table 1 shows the distribution by grade, intelligence, and sex. For each grade, school records were used to establish a pool of subjects meeting our criteria for age, sex, and IQ; within each of the subgroups so selected, names were chosen randomly until the desired sample size was achieved. Children more than 6 months older or younger than the average for their grade were excluded, as were two otherwise eligible subjects reported by their counselor to have a history of severe psychological disturbance.

This paper will report findings by age alone (to the next nearest age) and without regard to sex or intelligence. We were unable to discover sex differences nor—to our continuing surprise—differences associated with intelligence. The brighter children were certainly more fluent, and there is some reason to feel that they use a drier, more impersonal, more intellectualized approach in dealing with certain questions, but up to this time we have not found that they attain political concepts earlier than subjects of average intelligence.

The interviews were taken in Ann Arbor, Michigan. We were able to use schools representative of the community, in the sense that they do not draw students from socio-economically extreme neighborhoods. The children of average IQ were preponderantly lower-middle and working class in background; those of high intelligence were largely from professional and managerial families. Academic families made up 13% of the sample, concentrated in the high IQ group; 5% of the "average" children and somewhat over one quarter of the "brights" had fathers with a professional connection to the University of Michigan. In these respects—socioeconomic status and parental education—the sample, which combined both IQ groups, was by no means representative of the American adolescent population at large. Yet our inability to find differences between the IQ groups, who derive from sharply different social milieux, makes us hesitate to assume that social status is closely associated with the growth of political ideas as we have measured them, or that the findings deviate markedly from what we would find in other middle-class suburbs.

Interview

The aims, scope, and form of the interview schedule have already been described. In developing the schedule we were most concerned to find a tone and level of discourse sufficiently simple to allow our young-est subjects to understand and respond to the problems posed, yet sufficiently advanced to keep our older interviewees challenged and engaged. Another aim was to strike a balance between the focused interview—to ease scoring—and a looser, more discursive approach —to allow a greater depth of inquiry and spontaneity of response. Our interviewers were permitted, once they had covered the basic questions of a topic, to explore it more thoroughly.

The interviews were conducted at the school. There were six interviewers, all with at least some graduate training in clinical psychology. The interviews were tape-recorded and transcribed verbatim. Those conducted with younger subjects were completed in about 1 hour, with older subjects in about 1½ hours.

Reliability

In order to appraise the lower limits of reliability, only the more difficult items were examined, those in which responses were complex or ambiguous. For five items of this type, intercoder reliabilities ranged from .79 to .84.

Results

When we examine the interviews of 11-year-olds, we are immediately struck by the common, pervasive incapacity to speak from a coherent view of the political order. Looking more closely, we find that this failure has two clear sources: First, these children are, in Piaget's sense, egocentric, in that they cannot transcend a purely personal approach to matters which require a sociocentric perspective. Second, they treat political issues in a concrete fashion and cannot manage the requisite abstractness of attitude. These tendencies, singly and together, dominate the discourse of the interview, so much so that a few sample sentences can often distinguish 11-year-old protocols from those given by only slightly older children.

The following are some interview excerpts to illustrate the differences: These are chosen randomly from the interviews of 11- and 13-year-old boys of average intelligence. They have been asked: "What is the purpose of government?"

11A. To handle the state or whatever it is so it won't get out of hand, because if it gets out of hand you might have to . . . people might get mad or something.

11B. Well . . . buildings, they have to look over buildings that would be . . . um, that wouldn't be any use of the land if they had crops on it or something like that. And when they have highways the government would have to inspect it, certain details. I guess that's about all.

11C. So everything won't go wrong in the country. They want to have a government because they respect him and they think he's a good man.

Now the 13-year-olds:

13A. So the people have rights and freedom of speech. Also so the civilization will balance.

13B. To keep law and order and talk to the people to make new ideas.

13C. Well, I think it is to keep the country happy or keep it going properly. If you didn't have it, then it would just be chaos with stealing and things like this. It runs the country better and more efficiently.

These extracts are sufficiently representative to direct us to some of the major developmental patterns in adolescent thinking on politics.

Personalism

Under *personalism* we include two related tendencies: first, the child's disposition to treat institutions and social processes upon the model of persons and personal relationships; second, his inability to achieve a sociocentric orientation, that is, his failure to understand that political decisions have social as well as personal consequences, and that the political realm encompasses not merely the individual citizen, but the community as a whole.

1. "Government," "community," "society" are abstract ideas; they connote those invisible networks of obligation and purpose which link people to each other in organized social interaction. These concepts are beyond the effective reach of 11-year-olds; in failing to grasp them they fall back to persons and actions of persons, which are the nearest equivalent of the intangible agencies and ephemeral processes they are trying to imagine. Hence, Subject 11A seems to glimpse that an abstract answer is needed, tries to find it, then despairs and retreats to the personalized "people might get mad or something." A more extreme example is found in 11C's statement, which refers to government as a "he," apparently confusing it with "governor." Gross personalizations of "government" and similar terms are not uncommon at 11 and diminish markedly after that. We counted the number of times the personal pronouns "he" and "she" were used in three questions dealing with government. There were instances involving six subjects among the 11-year-olds (or 20% of the sample) and none among 13-year-olds. (The most striking example is the following

sentence by an 11: "Well, I don't think she should forbid it, but if they, if he did, well most people would want to put up an argument about it.")

Although personalizations as bald as these diminish sharply after 11, more subtle or tacit ones continue well into adolescence (and in all likelihood, into adulthood)—the use of "they," for example, when "it" is appropriate. It is our impression that we see a revival of personalization among older subjects under two conditions: when the topic being discussed is too advanced or difficult for the youngster to follow or when it exposes an area of ignorance or uncertainty, and when the subject's beliefs and resentments are engaged to the point of passion or bitterness. In both these cases the emergence of affects (anxiety, anger) seems to produce a momentary cognitive regression, expressing itself in a loss of abstractness and a reversion to personalized modes of discourse.

2. The second side of personalism is the failure to attain a sociocentric perspective. The preadolescent subject does not usually appraise political events in the light of their collective consequences. Since he finds it hard to conceive the social order as a whole, he is frequently unable to understand those actions which aim to serve communal ends and so tends to interpret them parochially, as serving only the needs of individuals. We have an illustration of this in the data given in Table 2. Table 2 reports the answers to the following item: "Another law was suggested which required all children to be vaccinated against smallpox and polio. What would be the purpose of that law?"

A substantial majority—about three

Table 2

Purpose of Vaccination

	Age			
	11	13	15	18
Social consequences (prevention of epidemics, etc.)	.23	.67	1.00	.90
Individual consequences (prevention of individual illness)	.70	.33	.00	.10

Note.—X^2 (3) = 46.53, $p > .001$. In this table and all that follow $N = 30$ for each age group. When proportions in a column do not total 1.00, certain responses are not included in the response categories shown. When proportions total more than 1.00, responses have been included in more than one category of the table. The p level refers to the total table except when asterisks indicate significance levels for a designated row.

quarters—of the 11-year olds see the law serving an individual end—personal protection from disease. By 13 there has been a decisive shift in emphasis, these children stressing the protection of the community. At 15 and after, an understanding of the wider purposes of vaccination has become nearly universal.

Parts and Wholes

Another reflection of the concreteness of younger adolescents can be found in their tendency to treat the total functioning of institutions in terms of specific, discrete activities. If we return to the interview excerpts, we find a good example in the answer given by Subject 11B on the purpose of government. He can do no more than mention some specific governmental functions, in this case, the inspecting of buildings and highways. This answer exemplifies a pattern we find frequently among our younger subjects, one which appears in many content areas. Adolescents only gradually perceive institutions (and their processes) as wholes; until they can imagine the institution abstractly, as a total idea, they are limited to the concrete and the visible.

Table 3 is one of several which demonstrates this. The subjects were asked the purpose of the income tax. The responses were coded to distinguish those who answered in terms of general government support from those who mentioned only specific government services. (In most cases the services referred to are both local and visible—police, firefighting, etc.) We observe that the percentage of those referring to the government in a general sense rises slowly and steadily; all of the high school seniors do so.

Negatives and Positives

Before we leave this set of interview excerpts, we want to note one more important difference between the 11- and 13-year-olds. Two of the former emphasize the negative or coercive functions of government ("To handle the state . . . so it won't get out of hand;" "So everything won't go wrong . . ."). The 13-year-olds, on the other hand, stress the positive functions of the

Table 3

Purpose of Income Tax

	Age			
	11	*13*	*15*	*18*
General support of government	.23	.33	.47	1.00*
Specific services only	.23	.17	.23	.00
Do not know	.53	.50	.30	.00

Note.—*p* level refers to row designated by asterisk.
*χ^2 (3) = 9.54, $p < .05$.

government—keeping the country happy or working properly. This difference is so important and extensive that we will treat it in depth in a later publication, but it should be discussed at least briefly here. Younger subjects adhere to a Hobbesian view of political man: The citizenry is seen as willful and potentially dangerous, and society, therefore, as rightfully, needfully coercive and authoritarian. Although this view of the political never quite loses its appeal for a certain proportion of individuals at all ages, it nevertheless diminishes both in frequency and centrality, to be replaced, in time, by more complex views of political arrangements, views which stress the administrative sides of government (keeping the machinery oiled and in repair) or which emphasize melioristic ends (enhancing the human condition).

The Future

The adolescent years see a considerable extension of time perspective. On the one hand, a sense of history emerges as the youngster is able to link past and present and to understand the present as having been influenced or determined by the past. On the other, the child begins to imagine the future and, what may be more important, to ponder alternative futures. Thus the present is connected to the future not merely because the future unfolds from the present, but also because the future is *tractable;* its shape depends upon choices made in the present.

This idea of the future asserts itself with increasing effect as the child advances through adolescence. In making political judgments, the youngster can anticipate the consequences of a choice taken here and now for the long-range future of the community and can weigh the probable effects of alternative choices on the future. The community is now seen to be temporal, that is, as an organism which persists beyond the life of its current members; thus judgments in the present must take into account the needs of the young and of the unborn. Further, the adolescent becomes able to envision not only the communal future, but himself (and others) in possible statuses in that future as well.

The items which most clearly expose the changing meaning of the future are those dealing with education. When we reflect on it, this is not surprising: Education is the public enterprise which most directly links the generations to each other; it is the communal activity through which one generation orients another toward the future. Several questions of public policy toward education were asked; in the answers to each the needs of the communal future weigh more heavily with increasing age. One item runs: "Some people suggested a law which would require children to go to school until they were sixteen years old. What would be the purpose of such a law?" One type of answer to this question was coded "Continuity of community;" these responses stress the com-

Table 4

Purpose of Minimum Education Law

	Age			
	11	*13*	*15*	*18*
Continuity of community	.00	.27	.33	.43

Note.—χ^2 (3) = 11.95, $p < .01$.

Table 5

Should People Without Children Pay School Taxes?

	Age			
	11	*13*	*15*	*18*
Continuity of community		.10	.10	.47	.60

Note.—$\chi^2(3)$ = 18.61, $p < .001$.

munity's need to sustain and perpetuate itself by educating a new generation of citizens and leaders. Typical answers were: "So children will grow up to be leaders," and "To educate people so they can carry on the government." Looking at this answer alone (analysis of the entire table would carry us beyond this topic), we find the following distribution by age (see Table 4).

Another item later in the interview poses this problem: "The people who did not have children thought it was unfair they would have to pay taxes to support the school system. What do you think of that argument?" Again the same category, which stresses the community's continuity and its future needs, rises sharply with age as shown in Table 5.

Finally, we want to examine another education item in some detail, since it offers a more complex view of the sense of the future in adolescent political thought, allowing us to observe changes in the child's view of the personal future. The question was the last of a series on the minimum education law. After the subject was asked to discuss its purpose (see above), he was asked whether he supports it. Almost all of our subjects did. He was then asked: "Suppose you have a parent who says 'My son is going to go into my business anyway and he doesn't need much schooling for that.' Do you think his son should be required to go to school anyway? Why?"

Table 6 shows that as children advance into adolescence, they stress increasingly the communal function of education. Younger subjects respond more to the father's arbitrariness or to the economic consequences of the father's position. They are less likely to grasp the more remote, more general effects of a curtailed education—that it hinders the attainment of citizenship. Representative answers by 11-year-olds were: "Well, maybe he wants some other desire and if he does maybe his father is forcing him;" and ". . . let's say he doesn't like the business and maybe he'd want to start something new." These children stress the practical and familial aspects of the issue.

Older subjects, those 15 and 18, all but ignored both the struggle with the father and the purely pragmatic advantages of remaining in school. They discoursed, sometimes eloquently, on

Table 6

Should Son Be Required to Attend School Though Father Wants Him to Enter Business?

	Age			
	11	13	15	18
Yes, education needed to function in community	.00	.23	.43	.77***
Yes, education good in itself	.03	.23	.20	.27
Yes, education needed in business	.40	.47	.23	.13
Yes, prevents parental coercion	.57	.47	.43	.23

Note.—p level refers to row designated by asterisk.
***χ^2 (3) = 25.54, $p < .001$.

the child's need to know about society as a whole, to function as a citizen, and to understand the perspectives of others. Here is how one 18-year-old put it:

. . . a person should have a perspective and know a little bit about as much as he can rather than just one thing throughout his whole life and anything of others, because he'd have to know different things about different aspects of life and education and just how things are in order to get along with them, because if not then they'd be prejudiced toward their own feelings and what *they* wanted and they wouldn't be able to understand any people's needs.

Older subjects see education as the opportunity to become *cosmopolitan*, to transcend the insularities of job and kinship. For the older adolescent, leaving school early endangers the future in two ways. On the personal side, it threatens one's capacity to assume the perspective of the other and to attain an adequate breadth of outlook; thus, it imperils one's future place in the community. On the societal side, it endangers the integrity of the social order itself, by depriving the community of a cosmopolitan citizenry.

Claims of the Community

We have already seen that as adolescence advances the youngster is increasingly sensitive to the fact of community and its claims upon the citizen. What are the limits of these claims, the limits of political authority? To what point, and under what conditions can the state, acting in the common good, trespass upon the autonomy of the citizen? When do the community's demands violate the privacy and liberty of the individual? The clash of these principles—individual freedom versus the public welfare and safety—is one of the enduring themes of Western political theory. Many, perhaps most, discussions in political life in one way or another turn on this issue; indeed, the fact that these principles are so often used purely rhetorically (as when the cant of liberty or of the public good is employed to mask pecuniary and other motives) testifies to their salience in our political thinking.

A number of questions in the interview touched upon this topic tangentially, and some were designed to approach it directly. In these latter we asked the subject to adjudicate and comment upon a conflict between public and private interests, each of these supported by a general political principle—usually the individual's right to be free of compulsion on the one hand, and the common good, on the other. We tried to find issues which would be tangled enough to engage the most complex modes of political reasoning. A major effort in this direction was made through a series of three connected questions on eminent domain. The series began with this question:

Here is another problem the Council faced. They decided to build a road to connect one side of the island to the other. For the most part they had no trouble buying the land on which to build the road, but one man refused to sell his land to the government. He was offered a fair price for his land but he refused, saying that he didn't want to move, that he was attached to his land, and that the Council could buy another piece of land and change the direction of the road. Many people thought he was selfish, but others thought he was in the right. What do you think?

Table 7

Which Party Is Right in Eminent-Domain Conflict?

	Age			
	11	13	15	18
Individual should sell; community needs come first	.30	.20	.30	.40
Detour should be made; individual rights come first	.60	.47	.27	.37
Emphasis on social responsibility; individual should be appealed to, but not forced	.10	.17	.17	.07
Ambivalence; individual is right in some ways, wrong in others	.00	.13	.27	.17

Somewhat to our surprise, there are no strong developmental patterns visible, though we do see a moderate tendency (not significant statistically, however) for the younger subjects to side with the landowner (see Table 7). The next question in the series sharpened the issue somewhat between the Council and the reluctant landowner:

The Council met and after long discussion voted that if the landowner would not agree to give up his land for the road, he should be forced to, because the rights of all the people on the island were more important than his. Do you think this was a fair decision?

The phrasing of the second question does not alter the objective facts of the conflict; yet Table 8 shows decisive shifts in position. It is hard to be sure why: perhaps because the second question states that the Council has considered the matter at length, perhaps because the Council's decision is justified by advancing the idea of "the people's rights." Whatever the reason, we now see a marked polarization of attitude. The younger subjects—those 11 and 13—continue to side with the landowner; those 15 and 18 almost completely abandon him, although about one quarter of the latter want to avoid coercion and suggest an appeal to his sense of social responsibility.

The final question in the series tightened the screws:

The landowner was very sure that he was right. He said that the law was unjust and he would not obey it. He had a shotgun and would shoot anyone who tried to make him get off his land. He seemed to mean business. What should the government do?

The landowner's threat startled some of the subjects, though in very different ways depending on age, as Table 9 shows: The younger subjects in these cases did not quite know what to do about it and suggested that he be mollified at all costs; the older subjects, if they were taken aback, were amused or disdainful, saw him as a lunatic or a hothead, and rather matter-of-factly suggested force or guile to deal with him. Nevertheless, this question did not

Table 8

Should Landowner Be Forced to Sell His Land?

	Age			
	11	13	15	18
Yes, rights of others come first	.40	.37	.63	.70
No, individual rights come first	.57	.50	.33	.07**
No, social responsibility should suffice	.03	.10	.00	.23

Note.—p level refers to row designated by asterisk.
**χ^2 (3) = 12.17, $p < .01$.

Table 9

What Should Government Do If Landowner Threatens Violence?

	Age			
	11	13	15	18
Detour	.60	.63	.37	.10
Government coercion justified	.23	.27	.57	.83

Note.—χ^2 (3) = 29.21, $p < .001$.

produce any essential change in position for the sample as a whole. Those older subjects who had hoped to appeal to the landowner's social conscience despaired of this and sided with the Council. Otherwise, the earlier pattern persisted, the two younger groups continuing to support the citizen, the older ones favoring the government, and overwhelmingly so among the oldest subjects.

These findings seem to confirm the idea that older adolescents are more responsive to communal than to individual needs. Yet it would be incorrect to infer that these subjects favor the community willy-nilly. A close look at the interview protocols suggests that older adolescents choose differently because they reason differently.

Most younger children—those 13 and below—can offer no justification for their choices. Either they are content with a simple statement of preference, for example: "I think he was in the right;" or they do no more than paraphrase the question: "Well, there is really two sides to it. One is that he is attached and he shouldn't give it up, but again he should give it up for the country." These youngsters do not or cannot rationalize their decisions, neither through appeal to a determining principle, nor through a comparative analysis of each side's position. If there is an internal argument going on within the mind of the 11- or 13-year-old, he is unable to make it public; instead, he seems to choose by an intuitive ethical leap, averring that one or the other position is "fair," "in the right," or "selfish." He usually favors the land-owner, because his side of the matter is concrete, personal, psychologically im-mediate, while the Council's position hinges on an idea of the public welfare which is too remote and abstract for these youngsters to absorb. Even those few children who try to reason from knowledge or experience more often than not flounder and end in confusion. A 13-year-old:

Like this girl in my class. Her uncle had a huge house in ———, and they tore it down and they put the new city hall there. I think they should have moved it to another place. I think they should have torn it down like they did, because they had a law that if there was something paid for, then they should give that man a different price. But then I would force him out, but I don't know how I'd do it.

What we miss in these interviews are two styles of reasoning which begin to make their appearance in 15-year-olds: first, the capacity to reason consequen-tially, to trace out the long-range implications of various courses of action; second, a readiness to deduce specific choices from general principles. The following excerpt from a 15-year-old's interview illustrates both of these ap-proaches:

Well, maybe he owned only a little land if he was a farmer and even if they did give him a fair price maybe all the land was already bought on the island that was good for farm-ing or something and he couldn't get another start in life if he did buy it. Then maybe in a sense he was selfish because if they had to buy land and change the direction of the road why of course then maybe they'd raise taxes on things so they could get more money cause it would cost more to change directions from what they already have planned. [Fair to force him off?] Yes, really, just because one person doesn't want to sell his land that don't mean that, well the other 999 or the rest of the people on the island should go without this road because of one.

In the first part of the statement, the subject utilizes a cost-effectiveness ap-proach; he estimates the costs (economic, social, moral) of one decision against another. He begins by examining the effects on the landowner. Can he obtain equivalent land elsewhere? He then considers the long-range economic con-sequences for the community. Will the purchase of other land be more ex-pensive and thus entail a tax increase? Though he does not go on to solve these implicit equations—he could hardly do so, since he does not have sufficient information—he does state the variables he deems necessary to solve them.

The second common strategy at this age, seen in the last part of the state-ment, is to imply or formulate a general principle, usually ethico-political in nature, which subsumes the instance. Most adolescents using this approach will for this item advert to the com-munity's total welfare, but some of our older adolescents suggest some other governing principle—the sanctity of property rights or the individual's right to privacy and autonomy. In either instance, the style of reasoning is the same; a general principle is sought which contains the specific issue.

Once a principle is accepted, the youngster attempts to apply it consistently. If the principle is valid, it should fall with equal weight on all; consequently, exceptions are resisted:

I think that the man should be forced to move with a good sum of money because I imagine it would be the people, it said the rights of the whole, the whole government and the whole community, why should one man change the whole idea?

And to the question of the landowner's threatening violence: "They shouldn't let him have his own way, because he would be an example. Other people would think that if they used his way, they could do what they wanted to." Even a child who bitterly opposes the Council's position on this issue agrees that once a policy has been established, exceptions should be resisted:

Well, if the government is going to back down when he offers armed resistance, it will offer ideas to people who don't like, say, the medical idea [see below]. They'll just haul out a shotgun if you come to study them. The government should go through with the action.

The Force of Principle

Once principles and ideals are firmly established, the child's approach to political discourse is decisively altered. When he ponders a political choice, he takes into account not only *personal* consequences (What will this mean, practically speaking, for the individuals involved?) and pragmatic *social* consequences (What effect will this have on the community at large?), but also its consequences in the realm of *value* (Does

this law or decision enhance or endanger such ideals as liberty, justice, and so on?). There is of course no sharp distinction among these types of consequences; values are contained, however tacitly, in the most "practical" of decisions. Nevertheless, these ideals, once they develop, have a life, an autonomy of their own. We reasoned that as the adolescent grew older, political principles and ideals would be increasingly significant, and indeed would loom large enough to overcome the appeal of personal and social utility in the narrow sense.

To test this belief we wanted an item which would pit a "good" against a "value." We devised a question proposing a law which, while achieving a personal and communal good, would at the same time violate a political ideal—in this case, the value of personal autonomy. The item ran: "One [proposed law] was a suggestion that men over 45 be required to have a yearly medical checkup. What do you think of that suggestion?" The answer was to be probed if necessary: "Would you be in favor of that? Why (or why not)?"

Table 10

Should Men over 45 Be Required to Have a Yearly Medical Checkup?

	Age			
	11	*13*	*15*	*18*
Yes, otherwise they would not do it	.50	.07	.00	.03***
Yes, good for person and/or community	.50	.80	.70	.60
No, infringement on liberties	.00	.13	.27	.37**

Note.—*p* level refers to rows designated by asterisk.
**$\chi^2(3) = 11.95$, $p < .01$.
***$\chi^2(3) = 33.10$, $p < .001$.

Table 10 shows the distribution of responses.

The findings are interesting on several counts, aside from offering testimony on the degree to which good health is viewed as a summum bonum. The 11-year-olds, here as elsewhere, interpret the issue along familial and authoritarian lines. The government is seen in loco parentis; its function is to make its citizens do the sensible things they would otherwise neglect to do. But our primary interest is in the steady growth of opposition to the proposal. The basis for opposition, though it is phrased variously, is that the government has no business exercising compulsion in this domain. These youngsters look past the utilitarian appeal of the law and sense its conflict with a value that the question itself does not state. These data, then, offer some support to our suggestion that older adolescents can more easily bring abstract principles to bear in the appraisal of political issues. Strictly speaking, the findings are not definitive, for we cannot infer that all of those supporting the law do so without respect to principle. Some of the older adolescents do, in fact, recognize the conflict implicit in the question, but argue that the public and personal benefits are so clear as to override the issue of personal liberties. But there are very few signs of this among the younger subjects. Even when pressed, as they were in a following question, they cannot grasp the meaning and significance of the conflict; they see only the tangible good.

Discussion

These findings suggest that the adolescent's sense of community is determined not by a single factor, but by the interaction of several related developmental parameters. We should now be in a position to consider what some of these are.

1. *The decline of authoritarianism.* Younger subjects are more likely to approve of coercion in public affairs. Themselves subject to the authority of adults, they more readily accept the fact of hierarchy. They find it hard to imagine that authority may be irrational, presumptuous, or whimsical; thus they bend easily to the collective will.

2. With advancing age there is an increasing grasp of the *nature and needs of the community.* As the youngster begins to understand the structure and functioning of the social order as a whole, he begins to understand too the specific social institutions within it and their relations to the whole. He comes to comprehend the autonomy of institutions, their need to remain viable, to sustain and enhance themselves. Thus the demands of the social order and its constituent institutions, as well as the needs of the public, become matters to be appraised in formulating political choices.

3. *The absorption of knowledge and consensus.* This paper has taken for granted, and hence neglected, the adolescent's increasing knowingness. The adolescent years see a vast growth in the acquisition of political information, in which we include not only knowledge in the ordinary substantive sense, but also the apprehension of consensus, a feeling for the common and prevailing ways of looking at political issues. The child acquires these from formal teaching, as well as through a heightened cathexis of the political, which in turn reflects

the generally amplified interest in the adult world. Thus, quite apart from the growth of cognitive capacity, the older adolescent's views are more "mature" in that they reflect internalization of adult perspectives.

4. We must remember that it is not enough to be exposed to mature knowledge and opinion; their absorption in turn depends on the growth of *cognitive capacities*. Some of the younger subjects knew the fact of eminent domain, knew it to be an accepted practice, yet, unable to grasp the principles involved, could not apply their knowledge effectively to the question. This paper has stressed the growth of those cognitive capacities which underlie the particular intellectual achievements of the period: the adolescent's increasing ability to weigh the relative consequences of actions, the attainment of deductive reasoning. The achievement of these capacities—the leap to "formal operations," in Piaget's term—allows him to escape that compulsion toward the immediate, the tangible, the narrowly pragmatic which so limits the political discourse of younger adolescents.

5. In turn the growth of cognitive capacity allows *the birth of ideology*. Ideology may not be quite the right word here, for it suggests a degree of coherence and articulation that few of our subjects, even the oldest and brightest, come close to achieving. Nevertheless there is an impressive difference between the younger and older adolescents in the orderliness and internal consistency of their political perspectives. What passes for ideology in the younger respondents is a raggle-taggle array of sentiments: "People ought to be nice to each other;" "There are a

lot of wise guys around, so you have to have strict laws." In time these sentiments may mature (or harden) into ideologies or ideological dispositions, but they are still too erratic, too inconsistent. They are not yet principled or generalized and so tend to be self-contradictory, or loosely held and hence easily abandoned. When younger subjects are cross-questioned, however gently, they are ready to reverse themselves even on issues they seem to feel strongly about. When older subjects are challenged, however sharply, they refute, debate, and counterchallenge. In some part their resistance to easy change reflects a greater degree of poise and their greater experience in colloquy and argument, but it also bespeaks the fact that their views are more firmly founded. The older adolescents, most conspicuously those at 18, aim for an inner concordance of political belief.

These then are the variables our study has suggested as directing the growth of political concepts. We must not lean too heavily on any one of them: The development of political thought is not simply or even largely a function of cognitive maturation or of increased knowledge or of the growth of ideology when these are taken alone. This paper has stressed the cognitive parameters because they seem to be so influential at the younger ages. The early adolescent's political thought is constrained by personalized, concrete, present-oriented modes of approach. Once these limits are transcended, the adolescent is open to influence by knowledge, by the absorption of consensus, and by the principles he adopts from others or develops on his own.

A Developmental Synopsis

We are now in a position to summarize the developmental patterns which have emerged in this study. It is our impression that the most substantial advance is to be found in the period between 11 and 13 years, where we discern a marked shift in the cognitive basis of political discourse. Our observations support the Inhelder and Piaget (1958) findings on a change from concrete to formal operations at this stage. To overstate the case somewhat, we might say that the *11-year-old* has not achieved the capacity for formal operations. His thinking is concrete, egocentric, tied to the present; he is unable to envision long-range social consequences; he cannot comfortably reason from premises; he has not attained hypothetico-deductive modes of analysis. The 13-year-old has achieved these capacities some (much?) of the time, but is unable to display them with any consistent effectiveness. The *13-year-olds* seem to be the most labile of our subjects. Depending on the item, they may respond like those older or younger than themselves. In a sense they are on the threshold of mature modes of reasoning, just holding on,

and capable of slipping back easily. Their answers are the most difficult to code, since they often involve an uneasy mixture of the concrete and the formal.

The *15-year-old* has an assured grasp of formal thought. He neither hesitates nor falters in dealing with the abstract; when he seems to falter, it is more likely due to a lack of information or from a weakness in knowing and using general principles. His failures are likely to be in content and in fluency, rather than in abstract quality per se. Taking our data as a whole we usually find only moderate differences between 15 and 18. We do find concepts that appear suddenly between 11 and 13, and between 13 and 15, but only rarely do we find an idea substantially represented at 18 which is not also available to a fair number of 15-year-olds.

The *18-year-old* is, in other words, the 15-year-old, only more so. He knows more; he speaks from a more extended apperceptive mass; he is more facile; he can elaborate his ideas more fluently. Above all, he is more philosophical, more ideological in his perspective on the political order. At times he is consciously, deliberately an ideologue. He holds forth.

REFERENCES

Easton, D., and Hess, R. D. Youth and the political system. In S. M. Lipset and L. Lowenthal (Eds.), *Culture and social character*. New York: Free Press of Glencoe, 1961. Pp. 226–251.

Easton, D., and Hess, R. D. The child's political world. *Midwest Journal of Political Science*, 1962, 6, 229–246.

Greenstein, F. *Children and politics*. New Haven: Yale University Press, 1965.

Hyman, H. H. *Political socialization*. Glencoe, Ill.: Free Press, 1959.

Inhelder, B., and Piaget, J. *The growth of logical thinking from childhood to adolescence*. New York: Basic Books, 1958.

SOVIET METHODS OF CHARACTER EDUCATION: SOME IMPLICATIONS FOR RESEARCH

- ## Urie Bronfenbrenner

Every society faces the problem of the moral training of its youth. This is no less true of Communist society than of our own. Indeed, Communist authorities view as the primary objective of education not the learning of subject matter but the development of what they call "socialist morality." It is instructive for us in the West to examine the nature of this "socialist morality" and the manner in which it is inculcated, for to do so brings to light important differences in the ends and means of character education in the two cultures. For research workers in the field of personality development, such an examination is especially valuable, since it lays bare unrecognized assumptions and variations in approach. Accordingly, it is the purpose of this paper to provide a much-condensed account of Soviet methods of character education and to examine some of the provocative research questions that emerge from the contrast between the Soviet approach and our own.

The Work and Ideas of A. S. Makarenko

To examine Soviet methods of character training is to become acquainted with the thinking and technology developed

Above selection reprinted from the Research Supplement to the July–August 1962 issue of *Religious Education* by permission of the publisher, The Religious Education Association, New York, New York.

primarily by one man—Anton Semyonovich Makarenko. Makarenko's name is virtually a household word in the Soviet Union. His popularity and influence are roughly comparable to those of Dr. Spock in the United States, but his primary concern is not with the child's physical health but with his moral upbringing. Makarenko's influence extends far beyond his own voluminous writings since there is scarcely a manual for the guidance of Communist parents, teachers, or youth workers that does not draw heavily on his methods and ideas. His works have been translated into many languages and are apparently widely read not only in the Soviet Union but throughout the Communist bloc countries, notably East Germany and Communist China. Excellent English translations of a number of his works have been published in Moscow (1949, 1953, 1959) but they are not readily available in this country.

Makarenko developed his ideas and methods over the course of a lifetime of practical work with young people. In the early 1920's, as a young school teacher and devout Communist, Makarenko was handed the assignment of setting up a rehabilitation program for some of the hundreds of homeless children who were roaming the Soviet Union after the civil wars. The first group of such children assigned to Makarenko's school, a ramshackle building far out of town, turned out to be a group of boys about 18 years of age with extensive court records of house-breaking, armed robbery, and man-slaughter. For the first few months, Makarenko's school served simply as the headquarters for the band of highwaymen who were his legal wards. But gradually, through the development of his group-oriented discipline techniques, and through what can only be called the compelling power of his own moral convictions, Makarenko was able to develop a sense of group responsibility and commitment to the work program and code of conduct that he had laid out for the collective. In the end, the Gorky Commune became known throughout the Soviet Union for its high morale, discipline, and for the productivity of its fields, farms and shops. Indeed, Makarenko's methods proved so successful that he was selected to head a new commune set up by the Ministry of Internal Affairs (then the Cheka, later to become the GPU and NKVD). In the years which followed, Makarenko's theories and techniques became widely adopted throughout the USSR and now constitute the central core of Soviet educational practice.

To turn to the ideas themselves, we may begin with an excerpt from what is possibly the most widely read of Makarenko's works, *A Book for Parents* (1959).

But our [Soviet] family is not an accidental combination of members of society. The family is a natural collective body and, like everything natural, healthy, and normal, it can only blossom forth in socialist society, freed of those very curses from which both mankind as a whole and the individual are freeing themselves.

The family becomes the natural primary cell of society, the place where the delight of human life is realized, where the triumphant forces of man are refreshed, where children— the chief joy of life—live and grow.

Our parents are not without authority either, but this authority is only the reflection of societal authority. The duty of a father in our country towards his children is a particular form of his duty towards society. It is as if our society says to parents:

You have joined together in good will and love, rejoice in your children and expect to go on rejoicing in them. That is your personal affair and concerns your own personal happiness. Within the course of this happy process you have given birth to new human beings. A time will come when these beings will cease to be solely the instruments of your happiness, and will step forth as independent members of society. For society, it is by no means a matter of indifference what kind of people they will become. In delegating to you a certain measure of societal authority the Soviet State demands from you the correct upbringing of its future citizens. Particularly it relies on you to provide certain conditions arising naturally out of your union; namely, your parental love.

If you wish to give birth to a citizen while dispensing with parental love, then be so kind as to warn society that you intend to do such a rotten thing. Human beings who are brought up without parental love are often deformed human beings (Makarenko, 1959, p. 29).

Characteristic of Makarenko's thought is the view that the parent's authority over the child is delegated to him by the state and that duty to one's children is merely a particular instance of one's broader duty towards society. A little later in his book for parents, the author makes this point even more emphatically. After telling the story of a boy who ran away from home after some differences with his mother, he concludes by affirming: "I am a great admirer of optimism and I like very much young lads who have so much faith in Soviet State that they are carried away and will not trust even their own mothers" (Makarenko, 1959, p. 37–38). In other words, when the needs and values of the family conflict with those of society, there is no question about who gets priority. And society receives its concrete manifestation and embodiment in the *collective*, which is an organized group engaged in some socially useful enterprise.

This brings us to Makarenko's basic thesis that optimal personality development can occur only through productive activity in a social collective. The first collective is the family, but this must be supplemented early in life by other collectives specially organized in schools, neighborhoods, and other community settings. The primary function of the collective is to develop socialist morality. This aim is accomplished through an explicit regimen of activity mediated by group-oriented punishments and rewards.

Makarenko's ideas are elaborated at length in his semibiographical, semifictional accounts of life in the collective (1949, 1953). It is in these works that he describes the principles and procedures to be employed for building the collective and using it as an instrument of character education. More relevant to our purposes, however, is the manner in which these methods are applied in school settings, for it is in this form that they have become most systematized and widely used.

Socialization in the School Collective

The account which follows is taken from a manual (Novika, 1959) for the training and guidance of "school directors, supervisors, teachers, and Young Pioneer leaders." The manual was written by staff members of the Institute on the Theory and History of Pedagogy at the Academy of Pedagogical Sciences and is typical of several others prepared under the same auspices and widely distributed throughout the USSR.

This particular volume carries the instructive title: *Socialist Competition in the Schools*. The same theme is echoed in the titles of individual chapters: "Competition in the Classroom," "Competition between Classrooms," "Competition between Schools," and so on. It is not difficult to see how Russians arrive at the notion, with which they have made us so familiar, of competition between nations and between social systems. Moreover, in the chapter titles we see already reflected the influence of dialectical materialism: Conflict at one level is resolved through synthesis at the next higher level, always in the service of the Communist collective.

Let us examine the process of collective socialization as it is initiated in the very first grade. Conveniently enough, the manual starts us off on the first day of school with the teacher standing before the newly assembled class. What should her first words be? Our text tells us:

It is not difficult to see that a direct approach to the class with the command "All sit straight" often doesn't bring the desired effect since a demand in this form does not reach the sensibilities of the pupils and does not activate them.

How does one "reach the sensibilities of the pupils" and "activate them?"

According to the manual, here is what the teacher should say: "Let's see which row can sit the straightest." This approach, we are told, has certain important psychological advantages. In response,

The children not only try to do everything as well as possible themselves, but also take an evaluative attitude toward those who are undermining the achievement of the row. If similar measures arousing the spirit of competition in the children are systematically applied by experienced teachers in the primary classes, then gradually the children themselves begin to monitor the behavior of their comrades and remind those of them who forget what needs to be done and what should not be done. The teacher soon has helpers.

The manual then goes on to describe how records are kept for each row from day to day for different types of tasks so that the young children can develop a concept of group excellence over time and over a variety of activities, including personal cleanliness, condition of notebooks, conduct in passing from one room to the other, quality of recitations in each subject matter, and so on. In these activities considerable emphasis is placed on the externals of behavior in dress, manner, and speech. There must be no spots on shirt or collar, shoes must be shined, pupils must never pass by a teacher without stopping to give greeting, there must be no talking without permission, and the like. Great charts are kept in all the schools showing the performance of each row unit in every type of activity together with their total overall standing. "Who is best?" the charts ask, but the entries are not individuals but social units—rows, and later the "cells" of the Communist youth organization which reaches down to the primary grades.

At first it is the teacher who sets the standards. But soon, still in the first grade, a new wrinkle is introduced: Responsible monitors are designated in each row for each activity. In the beginning their job is only to keep track of the merits and demerits assigned each row by the teacher. Different children act as monitors for different activities and, if one is to believe what the manual says, the monitors become very involved in the progress of their row. Then, too, group achievement is not without its rewards. From time to time the winning row gets to be photographed "in parade uniforms" (all Soviet children must wear uniforms in school), and this photograph is published in that pervasive Soviet institution, the wall newspaper. The significance of the achievements is still further enhanced, however, by the introduction of competition between *classes* so that the winning class and the winning row are visited by delegates from other classrooms in order to learn how to attain the same standard of excellence.

Now let us look more closely at this teacher-mediated monitoring process. In the beginning, we are told, the teacher attempts to focus the attention of children on the achievement of the group; that is, in our familiar phrase, she accentuates the positive. But gradually, "it becomes necessary to take account of negative facts which interfere with the activity of the class." As an example we are given the instance of a child who despite warnings continues to enter the classroom a few minutes after the bell has rung. The teacher decides that the time has come to evoke the group process in correcting such behavior. Accordingly, the next time that Serezha is late, the teacher stops him at the door and turns to the class with this question: "Children, is it helpful or not helpful to us to have Serezha come in late?" The answers are quick in coming. "It interferes, one shouldn't be late, he ought to come on time." "Well," says the teacher, "How can we help Serezha with this problem?" There are many suggestions: get together to buy him a watch, exile him from the classroom, send him to the director's office, or even to exile him from the school. But apparently these suggestions are either not appropriate or too extreme. The teacher, our text tells us, "helps the children find the right answer." She asks for a volunteer to stop by and pick Serezha up on the way to school. Many children offer to help in this mission.

But tragedy stalks. The next day it turns out that not only Serezha is late, but also the boy who promised to pick him up. Since they are both from the same group, their unit receives two sets of demerits and falls to lowest place. Group members are keenly disappointed. "Serezha especially suffered much and felt himself responsible, but equal blame was felt by his companion who had forgotten to stop in for him."

In this way, both through concrete action and explanation, the teacher seeks to forge a spirit of group unity and responsibility. From time to time, she explains to the children the significance of what they are doing, the fact "that they have to learn to live together as one friendly family, since they will have to be learning together for all of the next ten years, and that for this reason one must learn how to help

one's companions and to treat them decently."

By the time the children are in the second grade, the responsibilities expected of them are increased in complexity. For example, instead of simply recording the evaluations made by the teacher, the monitors are taught how to make the evaluations themselves. Since this is rather difficult, especially in judging homework assignments, in the beginning two monitors are assigned to every task. In this way, our text tells us, they can help each other in doing a good job of evaluation.

Here is a third grade classroom:

Class 3-B is just an ordinary class; it's not especially well disciplined nor is it outstandingly industrious. It has its lazy members and its responsible ones, quiet ones and active ones, daring, shy, and immodest ones.

The teacher has led this class now for three years, and she has earned the affection, respect, and acceptance as an authority from her pupils. Her word is law for them.

The bell has rung, but the teacher has not yet arrived. She has delayed deliberately in order to check how the class will conduct itself.

In the class all is quiet. After the noisy class break, it isn't so easy to mobilize yourself and to quell the restlessness within you! Two monitors at the desk silently observe the class. On their faces is reflected the full importance and seriousness of the job they are performing. But there is no need for them to make any reprimands: the youngsters with pleasure and pride maintain scrupulous discipline; they are proud of the fact that their class conducts itself in a manner that merits the confidence of the teacher. And when the teacher enters and quietly says be seated, all understand that she deliberately refrains from praising them for the quiet and order, since in their class it could not be otherwise.

During the lesson, the teacher gives an exceptional amount of attention to collective competition between "links." (The links are the smallest unit of the Communist youth organization at this age level.) Throughout the entire lesson the youngsters are constantly hearing which link has best prepared its lesson, which link has done the best at numbers, which is the most disciplined, which has turned in the best work.

The best link not only gets a verbal positive evaluation but receives the right to leave the classroom first during the break and to have its notebooks checked before the others. As a result the links receive the benefit of collective education, common responsibility, and mutal aid.

"What are you fooling around for? You're holding up the whole link," whispers Kolya to his neighbor during the preparation period for the lesson. And during the break he teaches her how better to organize her books and pads in her knapsack.

"Count more carefully," says Olya to her girl friend. "See, on account of you our link got behind today. You come to me and we'll count together at home."

In the third grade still another innovation is introduced. The monitors are taught not only to evaluate but to state their criticisms publicly.

Here is a typical picture. It is the beginning of the lesson. In the first row the link leader reports basing his comments on information submitted by the sanitarian and other responsible monitors: "Today Valadya did the wrong problem. Masha didn't write neatly and forgot to underline the right words in her lesson, Alyoshi had a dirty shirt collar."

The other link leaders make similar reports (the Pioneers are sitting by rows).

The youngers are not offended by this procedure: they understand that the link leaders are not just tattle-telling but simply fulfilling their duty. It doesn't even occur to the monitors and sanitarians to conceal the shortcomings of their comrades. They feel that they are doing their job well precisely when they notice one or another defect.

Also in the third grade, the teacher introduces still another procedure. She now proposes that the children enter into competition with the monitors, and see if they can beat the monitor at his own game by criticizing themselves. "The results were spectacular: if the monitor was able to talk only about four or five members of the row, there would be supplementary reports about their own shortcomings from as many as eight or ten pupils."

To what extent is this picture overdrawn? Although I have no direct evidence, the accounts I heard from participants in the process lend credence to the descriptions in the manual. For example, I recall a conversation with three elementary school teachers, all men, whom I had met by chance in a restaurant. They were curious about discipline techniques used in American schools. After I had given several examples, I was interrupted: "But how do you use the collective?" When I replied that we really did not use the classroom group in any systematic way, my three companions were puzzled. "But how do you keep discipline?"

Now it was my turn to ask for examples. "All right," came the answer. "Let us suppose that 10-year-old Vanya is pulling Anya's curls. If he doesn't stop the first time I speak to him, all I need do is mention it again in the group's presence; then I can be reasonably sure that before the class meets again the boy will be talked to by the officers of his Pioneer link. They will remind him that his behavior reflects on the reputation of the link."

"And what if he persists?"

"Then he may have to appear before his link—or even the entire collective— who will explain his misbehavior to him and determine his punishment."

"What punishment?"

"Various measures. He may just be censured, or if his conduct is regarded as serious, he may be expelled from membership. Very often he himself will acknowledge his faults before the group."

Nor does the process of social criticism and control stop with the school. Our manual tells us, for example, that parents submit periodic reports to the school collective on the behavior of the child at home. One may wonder how parents can be depended on to turn in truthful accounts. Part of the answer was supplied to me in a conversation with a Soviet agricultural expert. In response to my questions, he explained that, no matter what a person's job, the collective at his place of work always took an active interest in his family life. Thus a representative would come to the worker's home to observe and talk with his wife and children. And if any undesirable features were noted, these would be reported back to the collective.

I asked for an example.

"Well, suppose the representative were to notice that my wife and I quarreled in front of the children [my companion shook his head]. That would be bad. They would speak to me about it and remind me of my responsibilities for training my children to be good citizens."

I pointed out how different the situation was in America where a man's home was considered a private sanctuary so that, for example, psychologists like myself often had a great deal of difficulty in getting into homes to talk with parents or to observe children.

"Yes," my companion responded. "That's one of the strange things about your system in the West. The family is separated from the rest of society.

That's not good. It's bad for the family and bad for society." He paused for a moment, lost in thought. "I suppose," he went on, "if my wife didn't want to let the representative in, she could ask him to leave. But then at work, I should feel ashamed." (He hung his head to emphasize the point.) "Ivanov," they would say, "has an uncultured wife."

But it would be a mistake to conclude that Soviet methods of character education and social control are based primarily on negative criticism. On the contrary, in their approach there is as much of the carrot as the stick. But the carrot is given not merely as a reward for individual performance but explicitly for the child's contribution to group achievement. The great charts emblazoned "Who IS Best?" which bedeck the halls and walls of every classroom have as entries the names not of individual pupils but of rows and links (the link is the smallest unit of Communist youth organization, which of course reaches into every classroom, from the first grade on). It is the winning unit that gets rewarded by a pennant, a special privilege, or by having their picture taken in "parade uniforms." And when praise is given, as it frequently is, to an individual child, the group referent is always there: "Today Peter helped Kate and as a result his unit did not get behind the rest."

Helping other members of one's collective and appreciating their contributions—themes that are much stressed in Soviet character training—become matters of enlightened self-interest, since the grade that each person receives depends on the overall performance of his unit. Thus the good student finds it to his advantage to help the poor one. The same principle is carried over to the group level with champion rows and classes being made responsible for the performance of poorer ones.

Here, then, are the procedures employed in Soviet character education. As a result of Khrushchev's educational reforms, they may be expected to receive even wider application in the years to come, for, in connection with these reforms, several new types of educational institutions are to be developed on a massive scale. The most important of these is the "internat," or boarding school, in which youngsters are to be entered as early as three months of age with parents visiting only on weekends. The internat is described in the theses announcing the reforms as the kind of school which "creates the most favorable conditions for the education and communist upbringing of the rising generation" (Communist Party of Soviet Russia, 1958). The number of boarding schools in the USSR is to be increased during the current seven-year plan from a 1958 level of 180,000 to 2,500,000 in 1965 (figures cited in *Pravda*, November 18, 1958), and according to I. A. Kairov, head of the Academy of Pedagogical Sciences, "No one can doubt that, as material conditions are created, the usual general educational school will be supplanted by the boarding school" (Kairov, 1960).

If this prophecy is fulfilled, we may expect that in the years to come the great majority of Soviet children (and children in some other countries of the Communist bloc as well) will from the first year of life onward be spending their formative period in collective settings and will be exposed daily to the techniques of collective socialization we have been describing. It is therefore a matter of considerable practical and scientific interest to identify the salient features of these techniques and subject them to research study, in so far as this becomes possible within the framework of our own society.

Guiding Principles of the Soviet Approach to Character Training

As a first approximation, we may list the following as distinguishing characteristics or guiding principles of communist methods of character education.

1. The peer collective (under adult leadership) rivals and early surpasses the family as the principal agent of socialization.

2. Competition between groups is utilized as the principal mechanism for motivating achievement of behavior norms.

3. The behavior of the individual is evaluated primarily in terms of its relevance to the goals and achievements of the collective.

4. Rewards and punishments are frequently given on a group basis; that is to say, the entire group benefits or suffers as a consequence of the conduct of individual members.

5. As soon as possible, the tasks of evaluating the behavior of individuals and of dispensing rewards and sanctions is delegated to the members of the collective.

6. The principal methods of social control are public recognition and public criticism, with explicit training and practice being given in these activities. Specifically, each member of the collective is encouraged to observe deviant behavior by his fellows and is

given opportunity to report his observations to the group. Reporting on one's peers is esteemed and rewarded as a civic duty.

7. Group criticism becomes the vehicle for training in self-criticism in the presence of one's peers. Such public self-criticism is regarded as a powerful mechanism for maintaining and enhancing commitment to approved standards of behavior, as well as the method of choice for bringing deviants back into line.

There are of course many other important features of the Soviet approach to socialization, but the seven listed above are those which present the greatest contrast to the patterns we employ in the West.

o   o   o

UNIVERSITY STUDENT POLITICS

• Seymour Martin Lipset

Interest in the character, intensity, and extent of university student involvement in politics has increased sharply in recent years. In the United States, much of the civil-rights revolution has been manned by students, in both the North and the South. The recent disturbances at the Berkeley campus of the University of California, which appear to resemble events observed in recent years only on the campuses of underdeveloped nations, were in large measure an outgrowth of controversies that stemmed from the demands of students involved in civil-rights activities to use the university as a base for their off-campus demonstrations and sit-ins. During 1964, student demonstrations played a major role in unseating governments in Bolivia, South Vietnam, and the Sudan. The Syngman Rhee regime in Korea was finally overthrown in 1960 as a result of student demonstrations, and similar actions have been directed against the military regime during the past year. Mass demonstrations in Japan, manned almost entirely by students and directed against the passage of the Japanese-American Security treaty, prevented President Eisenhower from visiting that country in 1960. The list of countries in

Above selection reprinted from: "University Student Politics" by Seymour Martin Lipset. From *The Berkeley Student Revolt* by Seymour Martin Lipset and Sheldon S. Wolin. Copyright © 1965 by Seymour Martin Lipset and Sheldon S. Wolin. Reprinted by permission of Doubleday & Company, Inc.

Asia, Africa, and Latin America in which student political activity has formed a major threat to the stability of the polity could be extended almost indefinitely.

In the Communist countries, also, students have played a major role in efforts to change the status quo. This was especially true in Poland and Hungary in 1956. In Poland, the chief organ of criticism was a student journal, *Po Prustu (Plain Talk)*, which served as the main rallying point for the liberal elements as long as it was permitted to exist. In Hungary, too, university students were a major force among the groups taking part in the uprising. In the Soviet Union, students have played an important role in demands for reform, insisting on more freedom and more intellectual integrity. A former student of Moscow University reports that while "it is difficult to give exact figures . . . my estimate of the proportion of Soviet students whose political discontent was revealed during the thaw of 1956 would be from one-fourth to one-third of the total. With the exception of the professional activists, the remaining played the familiar role of 'the masses:' their attitude toward the political avant-garde was sometimes sympathetic, sometimes uncomprehending, but rarely hostile." In Communist China, the year 1957 witnessed the "Hundred Flowers" campaign in which open criticism was encouraged by the Party. The results startled the regime, since for five weeks it was exposed to a barrage of sharp attacks by older intellectuals and students. As René Goldman, a French journalist present in China at the time reported: "What really shook the party was a feeling that it faced the loss of its control over the youth. Young people brought up under Communist rule had become the loudest in denouncing the party which had vested its hopes in them." Yugoslavia also faced student protest in the late fifties.

The efforts by the rulers of Communist countries to repress student political activities may be explained in part by their awareness of the importance of student movements in undermining the pre-Communist regimes of these countries. In nineteenth-century Russia, university students were almost the only group to engage in demonstrations demanding freedom and economic reform, from the middle of the century onward. Student disorders occurred almost annually at the University of Moscow from the late eighties to the Revolution of 1905. Historians report that the Russian workers learned the value of street demonstrations from students. In China students helped greatly in bringing about the downfall of the Manchu Dynasty at the turn of the century. Student politics reached a second climax in May 1919, when the huge student demonstration that began in Peking inaugurated the second Chinese revolution. In the 1930s student movements, demonstrations, and strikes played a major role in undermining Chiang Kai-shek, and following World War II, student riots contributed greatly to the final downfall of the Nationalist regime.

It is interesting to note that shortly before he died, C. Wright Mills, in seeking to specify the conditions favoring social revolution, challenged the Marxist beliefs in the political potential of the working class as an agency of "historic change," and suggested that the record of revolutionary movements indicated students and intellectuals are more likely than the proletariat to be the "immediate radical agency of change."

The special political behavior of students, their greater propensity to participate in radical or other protest movements, is an outgrowth of elements specific to the situation and environment of university life, disposing students toward deviant behavior. University students are generally at an age defined as biologically adult; many non-students of the same age have already entered upon adult activities, marrying, earning money, and spending it as they wish. Students are often at the age where they may vote and marry, and many do both. Yet few university students earn all their livelihood; many remain financially dependent on their parents, and the society at large still treats them in many ways as adolescents without responsibilities, permitting and even approving their "sowing of wild oats." They may even violate the law in various ways without being punished. (At Santa Barbara, not too long ago, a student was killed during a fraternity initiation; at Berkeley this past fall, a police car was surrounded and held captive by student demonstrators who used its roof as a speaker's podium for thirty-six hours. In neither case was anyone punished.) In many countries, particularly in Latin America, police are restricted by law from entering university precincts; campuses are privileged sanctuaries to which students may flee after carrying out attacks against institutions of the surrounding society.

If students are defined as socially irresponsible, they are also encouraged to be idealistic. Value-transmitting agencies such as the family, church, and school, tend to present morality in absolute, right or wrong terms. The famed German sociologist Max Weber observed that youth has a tendency to follow "a pure ethic of absolute ends," while mature men tend to espouse an "ethic of responsibility." The advocate of the first fears that any compromise on matters of principle will endanger the "salvation of the soul;" the proponent of the second fears that an unwillingness to confront the complex "realities of life" may result in the "goals . . . [being] damaged and discredited for generations, because responsibility for *consequences* is lacking." University students, though well educated, have generally not established a sense of close involvement with adult institutions; experience has not hardened them to imperfection. Their libidos are unanchored; their capacity for identification with categories of universal scope, with mankind, the oppressed, the poor and miserable, is greater than it was earlier or than it will be later in life. Their contact with the articulated moral and political standards of their society is abstract; they encounter them as principles promulgated by older persons, as imposed by authority, rather than as maxims incorporated into and blurred by their own experience. Increasingly in the modern world, which includes the highly educated sector of the emerging nations, equality, efficiency, justice, and

economic well-being are represented as the values of the good society. Poverty, racial discrimination, caste systems, social inequality, administrative and political corruption, and cultural backwardness are all violations of such principles. In all countries, of course, reality is usually at variance with principles, and young persons feel this strongly. Educated young people everywhere thus tend to support idealistic movements which take the ideologies and values of the adult world more seriously than does the adult world itself. Youthful idealism, even when it leads to sharp rejection of adult practices and the use of extremist methods is often expected and respected by older people.

An opinion survey based on a random sample of University of Warsaw students reports that those students who were most committed to socialism and its egalitarian ideals were much more likely to have actively participated in the demonstrations against the regime in 1956, than were those who had less faith in, or were opposed to, socialism as a goal. In Berkeley during this past fall, the study of the University of California student body by Robert Somers printed here indicates that the factor most highly associated with support for the student demonstrations and sit-ins, the demands of which were the elimination of all campus controls on any form of political activity, is commitment to political liberalism.

Another factor that affects the likelihood of young people to deviate from accepted adult norms rests on the need of new generations to differentiate themselves from older ones, in effect, from their parents. Such needs are most prevalent in societies that stress individualism, the need for separate identity, characteristic of most Western countries. However, even in the more traditional societies of the under-developed world, the university system itself represents an incursion of modern individualistic values stressing creativity and innovation.

The relations of youth with the parental generation is also complicated by the fact that the institutions within which they have been socialized before entering the university, the family church, and school are more likely to be concerned with transmitting the values of older generations, with shielding youth from the effects of changes that erode older beliefs, than with preparing youth to cope with change. But since youth become aware of major changes in values, even if teachers, parents, and preachers do not discuss or frown on such changes, the relative "conservatism" of adult educators will serve to undermine their authority and to lead young people to think they know more and better than their elders. This attitude may predispose them to support innovating concepts and organizations as soon as they reach the freedom from familial restraint provided by the university.

The particular attraction of extremist movements to young people, the willingness among those most disposed to question ancient verities in the name of freedom to accept uncritically new doctrinaire solutions, may be related to the very uncertainty about what is right and wrong inherent in the situation of many university students. At a university, youth learn that there are attractive values and ways of life that differ sharply from those urged on them by their parents. This contact with a variety of possibilities not taught within the family is confusing, and rather than remain in a state of doubt, many youth seek a new certainty in beliefs opposed to those taught at home. Radical movements give young people an idealistic rationale for breaking with their families, especially when parents are perceived as supporters of the reactionary system.

A major source of tensions which fosters the availability of young people for organized "deviance" is their situation as socially "marginal" individuals, as people whose status and future are not yet established. The student has left the security of the family, and does not yet have the security and emotional involvement he will attain on entering his own occupational career and marriage. The longer and more intensive this insecurity concerning career and marriage, the less likely is the recognition that it flows from anxiety about an inherently ambiguous personal situation, and the greater the tendency to blame it on society and the adult world. Many will seek a socially acceptable explanation for their fear of possible personal failure, and this is often readily available in the ideologies of radical social movements.

The extent to which students will seek and accept such ideological outlets is related to their degree of uncertainty about the future. Those studying for courses that do not readily lead to a secure career should be more available for rebelliousness than those in fields of study that resemble apprenticeships to a definite position, e.g., engineering, preparation for school-teaching, and the like. The most insecure of all are those who hope to be creative intellectuals, and consequently those in the liberal arts (more the humanistic than the scientific disciplines), especially graduate students, should be expected to play a leading role in student protest, a hypothesis that research on the subject bears out.

Studies of support for extremist movements in many countries indicate that social dislocation, changing from one significant environment to another, predisposes individuals to accept new values, ideologies, and affiliations in the religious and political spheres. University-student communities probably contain a larger proportion of socially displaced individuals than any other type. Many students, sometimes almost all, on most campuses, have left home, have changed communities, have given up old friends, and must adapt to a totally new environment. One would expect, therefore, to find a disproportionate number of extremists among them. And, in line with these assumptions, research on student behavior indicates that student political activists and supporters of more radical politics are more likely to be found among those students who are living away from home than among those who live with their families and commute to school.

In addition to the various sources of motivation for student radicalism, there are factors inherent in the ecological structure of universities that facilitate collective action. Like a vast factory, a large campus brings together great numbers of people in similar life situations, in close proximity to each other, who can acquire a sense of solidarity and wield real power. At Berkeley, there are close to 30,000 students, at Mexico City over 65,000, at Buenos Aires over 70,000, at Calcutta more than 100,000, at Rome about 50,000, at the University of Paris over 75,000, and at Moscow over 30,000. It is relatively easy to reach students; leaflets handed out at the campus gates will usually do the job. These conditions facilitate quick communication, foster solidarity, and help to arouse melodramatic action.

The need of a younger generation to establish its independence corresponds to the tactic of radical activist movements to seek recruits among those who are not well integrated in the institutional system. The fact that students constitute the group that is most available for radical social movements because of its social situation, discontents, and accessibility, is not lost on movements seeking support. Communist parties, particularly, have concentrated considerable resources on university campuses in the United States and other countries for precisely these reasons. In many of the underdeveloped countries, most parties seriously concern themselves with student politics, though the more extreme ones are almost always much stronger on the campuses than in the nation as a whole. Thus the concentrated effort to reach students with political messages should be added to the list of factors predisposing and exposing students to political activism.

On a comparative level, it is clear that the extent of political concern among students in different countries is in part a function of the degree of tension in the larger polity. In societies that have a stable democratic order with legimate government and opposition, as in the United States and much of western Europe, students may be disproportionately to the left of nonstudents of similar social strata, but on the whole they exhibit much less interest in politics and give less support to extremist groups than do students in those nations that have unstable polities. It has been argued that the greater significance of radical student politics in Latin America reflects characteristics of the national political structures. In conditions of political tension, where the existing adult elites and counter-elites are badly organized and ineffectual, student political organizations are likely to be important. Thus countries in which governments may be easily toppled by the political action of the military are often the same nations as those in which student political activity is of major importance. South Korea, Bolivia, the Sudan, and South Vietnam are the most recent cases in point.

National university systems vary in academic standards and in the extent to which they require students to toe the mark. The greater the pressures placed on students to work hard in order to retain their position in the university, the less they will participate in politics of any kind. In much of Latin America, India and Japan, students are not faced with the need of taking rigorous, severely competitive, regular examinations. Among faculties and departments within the universities, similar variations also hold. Fields like the natural sciences, which require more concentrated study and work than the humanities or social sciences, will inhibit the inclination of students toward active politics.

The greater the number of years the student spends at the university, the greater the likelihood of significant student activity. Where the university system permits students to "hang around" for years, to finish at their own discretion, one finds the phenomenon

of the professional student, from whose ranks political leaders and activists are likely to be recruited. Observers of student politics in much of Latin America and southern Asia have pointed to the presence there of such "professional students," many of whom are not enrolled, as being "often the catalysts who agitate lambs into lions." Currently in large centers of graduate training in the United States, one also finds "students" who remain in the university community for many years, nominally preparing for doctoral examinations or supposedly writing theses. Many commentaries on the upheaval at Berkeley have pointed to the significant role played by the large number of semipermanent "graduate students" in creating the Bohemian and politicized atmosphere there.

The quality of the relationships between students and their teachers, which depends in part on the traditions of the various university systems and on the student-faculty ratio, affects the extent to which students feel committed to, or alienated from, the academic culture. Where there is a drastic separation between students and teachers, where faculty must depend on extra-university employment because of low salaries, or where there is a very great number of students per faculty member, students are more likely to engage in radical political activities to express their discontent.

Participation in politics may be viewed as an alternative to other forms of student extracurricular activities. Universities in many parts of the underdeveloped world, in Latin America, the Near East, and parts of Asia, have almost no organized extracurricular activity other than political. In the

United States, organized sports were expressly introduced into colleges and universities to divert the adolescent energy that in many college communities had gone into brawls and "town and gown" riots. Determined but unsuccessful efforts to provide alternative activities in order to reduce the energies available for political activity, have been attempted in universities in the Arab world and in Japan.

It should be noted in conclusion that even though radical and extremist attitudes and actions occur frequently among highly politicized students, most students in most countries are not so politicized, and insofar as they have political beliefs, these are conservative, moderate, or liberal. Surveys of student attitudes in many universities of Latin America and Asia indicate that the large majority in most of them do not support radical politics. The discrepancy between the image of students in these nations as predominantly leftist and the data reported in the opinion surveys is a consequence of the fact that the less radical the politics of students, the less likely they are to be interested in or take part in any form of politics. Hence one finds the majority of the politically interested and active students located toward the far left of the political spectrum, creating the public impression that most students agree with this position, when in fact this is not the case.

Basic to any understanding of the critical political stance which characterizes the politics of the university community, whether faculty or student, as compared to the predominant politics of other privileged high-status sections of the population, is the fact that those engaged in intellectually creative activities, whether inside or outside of the academy, are involved in an enterprise requiring them to criticize, revise, and supplant tradition. They value new discoveries and innovation, not the reproduction, copying, and transmission of old discoveries and ideas. Originality, departure from what is established and officially accepted, is a central value in the outlook of the modern intellectual. Universities by their stress on scientific discipline and detachment from the idols of the market place, have nurtured a critical attitude. Especially in the social sciences has there been a tension between the affirmation of the dominant systems of practice and belief and a critical attitude toward these systems. And it is the anti-tradition and anti-Establishment attitudes of modern intellectual life that provide a point of departure for and help legitimate student politics which are generally to the left of national politics on many campuses of the world.

In general, however, it may be said that where the society, the university, and the student are committed to the fullest development of research and teaching in an atmosphere of complete academic freedom, and where adequate resources are available in the form of faculty, libraries, laboratories, and financial support, students are less likely to engage in extreme forms of political activity and are more likely to allow themselves to be assimilated into the corporate life of the university as an institution devoted to the interpretation of what is inherited, the discovery of new truths, and the training of students to do both of these and to prepare themselves for careers based on these activities. Universities to be successful must form a community that embraces students as well as faculty and research workers. Universities must develop a culture of their own, whose concerns are in many ways sharply distinct from those of groups political or others outside the campus. This culture must transcend the bodies of specific knowledge which are taught and cultivated, and foster a scholarly ethos of attitudes and sensibilities, of standards and canons of judgment which must be assimilated and cannot be explicitly taught. These tasks of the university cannot be performed without the assimilation of the student body into the university community, which is a graded community, inevitably hierarchical by virtue of differences in age and competence. This task is not an easy one, but on its effective performance depends the success of the university in fulfilling its essential tasks.

A high incidence of intense student political activity is in some sense an indication of the failure of a university as an academic community, particularly since in most cases such activity involves a rejection of the intellectual leadership of the faculty, a denigration of scholarship to a more lowly status than that of politics within the university itself. And where a campus becomes highly politicized as many have in some parts of the underdeveloped world, academic freedom, the principal condition for a meaningful university life, is threatened, if not destroyed. Where professors must worry about the political reactions of students and colleagues, there is no freedom to teach, study, or do research. Few student movements may be in a position to overturn governments, but they may sharply weaken or even destroy the independence of the university. Thus the problem of student politics is more than academic for both the academy and for society.

THE CHINESE INDOCTRINATION PROGRAM FOR PRISONERS OF WAR: A STUDY OF ATTEMPTED "BRAINWASHING"

- Edgar H. Schein

In this paper I shall try to present an account of the "typical" experiences of United Nations prisoners of war in Chinese Communist hands and to interpret these experiences in a social-psychological framework.

o   o   o

The data were collected during August 1953 at Inchon, Korea, where the repatriates were being processed, and on board the U.S.N.S. *General Black* in transit to the United States from September 1 to September 16.

o   o   o

Of approximately 20 repatriates selected at random at different stages of the repatriation, each was asked to tell in chronological order and in as great detail as possible what had happened to him during his captivity. Emphasis was placed on what the Chinese or North Koreans *did* in their handling of the prisoners and how the men reacted. The men were particularly encouraged to relate the reactions of *others*, in order to avoid arousing anxiety or guilt over their own behavior and thereby blocking the flow of memories. The interviews varied in length from two to four hours.

The picture presented is not to be viewed as the experience of any single

Above selection reprinted from: *Psychiatry*, 19 (1956), 149–172. Deletions have been made by the editor in the interest of brevity.

person nor as the experience of all the men. Rather, it represents a composite or typical account which, in all its details, may or may not have been true for any one prisoner.

o   o   o

[Before proceeding with the discussion of the American prisoners' "retraining," Schein discusses the primitive physical conditions under which prisoners lived (hard work, low rations, and poor housing but no physical torture). Although many Chinese and Koreans perhaps did not live a great deal more lavishly themselves, the Chinese captors always suggested to their captives that "those stresses could be brought to an end by the adoption of a 'cooperative attitude'" (ed.).]

The Indoctrination Program

All of these conditions in the permanent camp were, in actual practice, interlocked with the indoctrination program. This program should not be viewed as a collection of specific techniques routinely applied, but rather as the creation of a whole set of social conditions within which certain techniques operated. Whether the Chinese manipulation of the social setting to create certain effects was intentional can only be conjectured; intentional or not, it was an important factor in such success as the indoctrination program achieved.

Removal of Belief, Attitude, and Value Supports

On matters of opinion, people tend to rely primarily on the opinions of others for determination of whether they themselves are "right" or "wrong" —whether these opinions of others are obtained through mass media of communication or through personal interaction. All of the prisoners' accustomed sources of information concerning daily events on a local, national, or international level were cut off by the Chinese, who substituted their own, usually heavily biased, newspapers, radio broadcasts, and magazines. *The Daily Worker* from various cities was available in the camp libraries, as were numerous magazines and journals from China, Poland, Russia, and Czechoslovakia. Radio news broadcasts usually originated in China. The camp headquarters had no scruples concerning accuracy in the news announcements made over the camp public-address system.

The delivery of mail from home was systematically manipulated; the evidence indicates that all mail which contained information about the war or the truce talks, or which contained favorable personal news, was withheld, while letters containing no general information, or bad personal news, were usually delivered.

Personal contact with visitors from outside the camps was very limited, mainly restricted to Communist news correspondents. For most prisoners, there was simply no way to find out accurately what was going on in the world.

The Chinese also attempted to weaken the means of consensual validation by undermining personal contacts among the men. First of all, the men were segregated by race, apparently in order to put special indoctrination pressure on members of certain minorities, especially Negroes. The men were also segregated by rank, in what appeared to be a systematic attempt to undermine the internal structure of the group by removing its leaders. Thus, the noncommissioned officers, who were at first in the enlisted camps, were put into a special camp when the Chinese found out that they were quite effective in keeping the other men from various kinds of collaboration. It was reported that this segregation was often followed by a considerable increase in collaboration, particularly among the younger enlisted men.

o   o   o

There was also persistent emphasis on undermining all friendships, emotional bonds, and group activities. For instance, the Chinese prohibited all forms of religious expression and ruthlessly persecuted the few chaplains or others who tried to organize or conduct religious services. Bonds to loved ones at home were weakened by the withholding of mail, as the Chinese frequently pointed out to the men that the lack of mail meant that their friends and relatives no longer cared for them.

The systematic use of Chinese spies and also informers from prisoner ranks made it possible for the Chinese to obtain detailed information about almost all activities going on in camp. The men reported that the Chinese were forever sneaking around their quarters and listening to conversations or observing activities from hidden posts, and they also knew that some of their number were acting as informers. These circumstances helped to create a feeling of general distrust, and the only fully safe course was to withdraw from all intimate interaction with other prisoners.

o   o   o

From the point of view of this analysis, the most important effect of the social isolation which existed was the consequent emotional isolation which prevented a man from validating any of his beliefs, attitudes, and values through meaningful interaction with other men at a time when these were under heavy attack from many sources and when no accurate information was available.

Direct Attacks on Beliefs, Attitudes, and Values

The chief method of direct indoctrination was a series of lectures that all prisoners had to attend at some time during their imprisonment. These lectures were given daily and lasted from two to three hours. Each camp had one or more political instructors who read the lectures from a prepared text. Often one _ instructor read while another seemed to follow a second copy of the text, as if to make sure that the right material was being presented. The lectures were direct, simple, black-and-white propaganda. They attacked the United Nations and particularly the United States on various political, social, and economic issues, at the same time glorifying the achievements of the Communist countries, and making strong appeals for "peace."

Most men reported that the anti-American material was naïve and seldom based on adequate or correct information about the United States. Even the pro-Communist arguments were sometimes weak and susceptible to attack. Occasionally a well educated prisoner debated points on communism successfully with instructors who had little knowledge of the classical works of communism. Usually the instructors presented the neo-Communist views of writers such as Mao Tse-tung and were unable to counter the arguments of prisoners who knew Marx and Lenin. The number of prisoners with sufficient education to engage in such arguments was, however, extremely small.

The constant hammering at certain points, combined with all the other techniques used—and in a situation where the prisoners had no access to other information—made it likely that many of the Chinese arguments did filter through enough to make many of the men question some of their former points of view. It is also likely that any appeal for "peace," no matter how false, found a receptive audience among combat-weary troops, especially when it was pointed out that they were fighting on foreign soil and were intervening in a civil war which was "none of their business." Both lectures and didactic "interrogations" emphasized detailed predictions of what would happen to the prisoners upon repatriation, some of which turned out to be accurate.[1] The Chinese implied that certain problems which would arise would be the result of the "weakness" or "unfairness" of the democratic ideology.

Another direct technique was the distribution of propaganda leaflets and the showing of Communist films glorifying the accomplishments of the Communist regime in Russia and China, and pointing out how much more had been done by communism for the peasant and laborer than by the capitalist system. While such films might have been highly ineffectual under ordinary circumstances, they assumed considerable importance because of the sheer lack of any other audio-visual material.

Perhaps the most effective attack on existing values, beliefs, and attitudes was the use of testimonials from prisoners who were ostensibly supporting Communist enterprises. These included peace petitions, radio appeals, speeches, and confessions. The use of such testimonials had a double effect in that it further weakened group ties while presenting pro-Communist arguments. As long as the men unanimously rejected the propaganda, each of them could firmly hold to the position that his beliefs must be right, even if he could not defend them logically. However, *if even one other man became convinced, it was no longer possible to hold this position.* Each man was then required to begin examining his beliefs and was vulnerable to the highly one-sided arguments that were repeatedly presented.

Of particular importance were the germ-warfare confessions which were extracted from a number of Air Force officers and enlisted men. The Chinese made a movie of one or two of the officers giving their testimony to the "international" commission which they had set up to investigate the problem and showed this movie in all the camps. Furthermore, one or two of the officers personally went from camp to camp and explained how United Nations forces had used these bombs; this made a powerful impression on many men who had, until then, dismissed the whole matter as a Chinese propaganda project. The great detail of the accounts, the sincerity of the officers, the fact that they were freely going from camp to camp and did not look as if they were then or had previously been under any duress made it difficult for some men to believe that the accounts could be anything but true.

The Chinese also used Koreans to give testimonials concerning the barbarity of the United Nations; in one instance women and children told one of the peace committees how United Nations planes had dropped toys which exploded when children tried to pick them up. It is difficult to evaluate the effects of such propaganda, but it is not likely that many prisoners believed stories of such extremity.

Indirect Attacks on Beliefs, Attitudes, and Values

In the direct attacks which I have been discussing, the source of propaganda was external. In the indirect attacks, a set of conditions was created in which each prisoner of war was encouraged to participate in a way that would make it more possible for him to accept some of the new points of view. One attempt to accomplish this was by means of group discussions following lectures.

Most lectures ended with a series of conclusions—for example, "The South Koreans started the war by invading North Korea," or "The aim of the capitalist nations is world domination." The men were then required to break up into squads, go to their quarters, and discuss the material for periods of two hours or more. At the end of the discussion each squad had to provide written answers to questions handed out during the lecture—the answers, obviously, which had already been provided in the lecture. To "discuss" the lecture thus meant, in effect, to rationalize the predetermined conclusions.[2]

A monitor was assigned to each squad to "aid" the men in the discussion, to make sure that they stayed on the proper topic, and to collect the answers and make sure that they were the "right" ones. Initially, the monitor for most squads was an English-speaking Chinese but whenever possible the Chinese turned the job over to one of the squad members, usually the one who was most cooperative or sympathetic to the Communist point of view. If one or more members of the squad turned in "wrong" answers— for example, saying that the North Koreans had invaded South Korea— the entire squad had to listen to the lecture again and repeat the group discussion. This procedure might go on for days. The Chinese never tired of repeating the procedure over and over again, apparently believing that group discussion had a better chance of success in converting men to their point of view than individual indoctrination.

The success of such discussions often depended on the degree of supervision. If the monitor was lax, the groups would talk about anything but the required material. But a prisoner-of-war monitor who was actively pro-Communist or a Chinese who had a good understanding of English idiom might obtain considerable discussion. Supervised discussion did not necessarily lead a man to question his own beliefs; in many cases it permitted POW's to strengthen their former beliefs by giving them an opportunity for consensual validation.

A second means of indirect attack was interrogation. Interrogations were carried on during all stages of internment, but their apparent function and the techniques utilized varied from time to time. Almost all men went through lengthy and repetitive military interrogations. Failure to answer questions seldom led to severe physical punishment. Instead, various psychological pressures were applied. For instance, all information was cross-checked against earlier interrogations and against the information from other men. If an answer did not tally with other information, the respondent had to explain the discrepancy. Continuous pressure to resolve contrary answers often forced a man to tell the truth.

The Chinese tried to create the impression that they could obtain *any* information from *anyone* by the following interrogation technique: If a man continued to refuse to answer a question, despite great fatigue and continued repetition of the question, the interrogator would suddenly pull out a notebook and point out to the man the complete answer to the question, sometimes in astonishingly accurate detail. The interrogation would then move on to a new topic and the same procedure would be repeated, until the man could not assess whether there was indeed *anything* that the Chinese did *not* know. In most cases the man was told that others had already given information or "confessed," so why should he hold back and suffer?[3]

A further technique was to have the man write out the question and then the answer. If he refused to write it voluntarily, he was asked to copy it from the notebooks, which must have seemed like a harmless enough concession. But the information which he had copied could then be shown to another man as evidence that he had given information of his own volition. Furthermore, it could be used to blackmail him, because he would have a hard time proving that he had merely copied the material.

o   o   o

The Eliciting of Collaboration by Rewards and Punishments

For a number of propaganda purposes the Chinese seemed to want certain men to cooperate in specific ways, without caring whether they accepted communism or not. These men did not seem to enjoy as much status as other pro's[4] and were cast off by the Chinese as soon as they had ceased to be useful. Such collaboration was elicited directly by a system of rewards and incentives on the one hand, and threats and punishments on the other. It was made clear to all prisoners, from the time of their capture on, that cooperation with the Chinese would produce a more comfortable state of affairs, while noncooperation or open resistance would produce a continuing marginal existence. Which rewards were of primary importance to the men varied with their current condition. On the marches and in the temporary camps physical conditions were so bad that more food, any medication, any

clothing or fuel, better and less crowded living conditions, and the like constituted a powerful reward. Promises of early repatriation, or at least of marked improvement of conditions in the permanent camps, were powerful incentives which were chronically exploited.

In the permanent camps there was some improvement in the physical conditions, so that the basic necessities became less effective incentives. The promise of early repatriation continued to be a great incentive, however, despite the fact that it had been promised many times before without result. Communicating with the outside world now became a major concern. To let those at home know they were alive, some prisoners began to collaborate by making slanted radio broadcasts or filling their letters with propaganda or peace appeals in order to make sure that they were sent.

As conditions continued to improve, some of the luxury items and smaller accessories to living assumed greater significance. Cigarettes, combs, soap, candy, small items of clothing, a cup of hot tea, a drink of liquor, fresh fruit, and other items of this kind were sought avidly by some men.[5] Obtaining such items from the Chinese was inextricably linked with the degree to which the prisoner was willing to "cooperate." Any tendency toward "cooperation" was quickly followed by an increase in material rewards and promises for the future.

In some cases rewards were cleverly linked with participation in the indoctrination. For example, highly valued prizes such as cigarettes or fresh fruit were offered for essays dealing with certain aspects of world politics. The winning entries were published in the camp newspaper or magazine. Usually the winning entry was selected on the basis of its agreement with a Communist point of view, and the winner was usually someone well on the road to collaboration anyway, but the whole competition succeeded in getting the men to participate—to consider the various sides of an issue and to examine their previous views critically.

The Chinese also used rewards and punishments to undermine group organization. For example, shortly after capture, a number of men were led to believe that if they made radio broadcasts to the United Nations lines they would be repatriated early. The content of the broadcasts was not specified, but the men agreed to make them in the hope of letting their relatives know that they were alive. These men were then conspicuously assembled in front of other prisoners and were taken to a special location some distance away, where the broadcasts were to be made. In the meantime, other prisoners were encouraged to believe that these men were obtaining special privileges because they were "cooperating" in bringing "peace" to Korea.

The actual content of the radio messages turned out to be a peace appeal which tacitly condemned the United Nations, and a statement that the prisoners were being well treated by the Chinese. When the men saw the messages that they were to read, some of them refused to make the broadcast, despite threats of severe punishment. Other men agreed to make the broadcast but tried to code a message into the prescribed text, and still others hoped that the recipients of the broadcasts would somehow know that they were under duress. At least their families would know that they were alive if they broadcasted something.

When these men rejoined the other prisoners, they found that they had aroused the suspicion and hostility of many, especially since the Chinese showed their "appreciation" by ostentatiously bestowing favors on them. In order to retain these special privileges—and having in any case incurred the hostility or even ostracism of their own group—some of these men continued to collaborate, rationalizing that they were not really harming the United Nations cause. They became self-appointed secret agents and attempted to infiltrate the Chinese hierarchy to gather "intelligence information," in which capacity they felt that they could actually aid the United Nations cause.

Among the most effective rewards used by the Chinese were special privileges and certain symbolic rewards, such as rank and status in the prison hierarchy. Perhaps the most important of the privileges was freedom of movement; the pro's had free access to the Chinese headquarters and could go into town or wherever they wished at any time of the day or night. They were given certain preferred jobs, such as writing for the camp newspaper, and were excused from the more unpleasant chores around the camp. They were often consulted by the Chinese in various policy matters. They received as a status symbol a little peace dove to be worn in the lapel or a Mao Tse-tung button which served as an identification badge. And many rewards were promised them for the future; they were told that they were playing a vital role in the world-wide movement for "peace," and that they could enjoy positions of high rank in this movement if they stayed and continued to work for it.

If one asks why men "fell" for this kind of line—why they were able to believe this kind of promise—one must look to the circumstances described earlier. These men had no sources of contrary information to rely on, and once they had collaborated even a little they were ostracized by their buddies, thus losing the support of the group which might have kept them from collaborating further.

Just as the probability of collaborative behavior could be increased through the use of rewards, the probability of resistance could be decreased through negative or painful stimulation. Usually threats of punishment were used when prisoners refused to "cooperate," and actual punishment was meted out for more aggressive resistance. Threats of death, nonrepatriation, torture, reprisals against families, reduction in food and medication, and imprisonment were all used. While the only one of these threats which was carried out with any degree of consistency was imprisonment, which sometimes involved long periods of solitary confinement, the other threats were nevertheless very effective and the possibility that they might be carried out seemed very real. Especially frightening was the prospect of nonrepatriation, which seemed a likely possibility before the prisoner lists were exchanged at Panmunjom. The threat of death was also effective, for the men knew that they could be killed and listed officially as having died of heart failure or the like.[6] With regard to food and medication, the men could not determine whether they were actually being punished by having these withheld, or whether the

meager supply was merely being reserved for "deserving" prisoners.

An effective threat with officers was that of punishing the whole group for which the officer was responsible if he personally did not "cooperate." The incidence of such group punishment was not revealed in the accounts, but it is clear that if an officer did "cooperate" with the Chinese, he was able both to relieve his own fears and to rationalize his cooperation as being the only means of saving the men for whom he was responsible.

Reinforcing all these threats was the vague but powerful fear of the unknown; the men did not know what they were up against in dealing with the Chinese and could not predict the reactions of their captors with any degree of reliability. The only course that led to a consistent reduction in such tension was participation in Chinese enterprises.

Overt punishment varied with the offense, with the political situation, and with the person administering it. Shortly after capture there were numerous incidents of brutality, most of them committed by North Koreans. During early interrogations the Chinese frequently resorted to minor physical punishment such as face-slapping or kicking when answers were not forthcoming, but a prisoner who continued to be silent was usually dismissed without further physical punishment.

Physical punishments in permanent camps had the effect of weakening rather than injuring the men. They varied from severe work details to such ordeals as standing at attention for long periods; being exposed to bright lights or excessive cold; standing on tiptoe with a noose around the neck; being confined in the "cage," a room too small to allow standing, sitting, or lying down; being thrown in the "hole," a particularly uncomfortable form of solitary confinement; or being kept in filthy surroundings and denied certain essentials for keeping clean. Those who were *chronically* uncooperative were permanently segregated from the rest of the group and put into special camps where more severe forms of discipline backed by harsher punishments were in effect. Basically, the "lenient policy" applied only to those men whom the Chinese hoped they could use.

More common forms of punishment for minor infractions were social in character, intended to degrade or embarrass the prisoner in front of his fellows. Public confessions and self-criticisms were the outstanding forms of such punishment, with blackmail being frequently used if a prisoner had once collaborated to any extent. There is *no* evidence that the Chinese used any drugs or hypnotic methods, or offered sexual objects to elicit information, confessions, or collaborative behavior. Some cases of severe physical torture were reported, but their incidence is difficult to estimate.

General Principles in All Techniques

Several general principles underlay the various phases of the Chinese indoctrination, which may be worth summing up at this point. The first of these was *repetition*. One of the chief characteristics of the Chinese was their immense patience in whatever they were doing; whether they were conducting an interrogation, giving a lecture, chiding a prisoner, or trying to obtain a confession, they were always

willing to make their demand or assertion over and over again. Many men pointed out that most of the techniques used gained their effectiveness by being used in this repetitive way until the prisoner could no longer sustain his resistance. A second characteristic was the *pacing of demands*. In the various kinds of responses that were demanded of the prisoners, the Chinese always started with trivial, innocuous ones and, as the habit of responding became established, gradually worked up to more important ones. Thus after a prisoner had once been "trained" to speak or write out trivia, statements on more important issues were demanded of him. This was particularly effective in eliciting confessions, self-criticism, and information during interrogation.

Closely connected with the principle of pacing was the principle of constant *participation* from the prisoner. It was never enough for the prisoner to listen and absorb; some kind of verbal or written response was always demanded. Thus, if a man would not give original material in question-and-answer sessions, he was asked to copy something. Likewise, group discussions, autobiographical statements, self-criticisms, and public confessions all demanded as active participation by the prisoner.[7]

In their propaganda campaign the Chinese made a considerable effort *to insert their new ideas into old and meaningful contexts*. In general this was not very successful, but it did work for certain prisoners who were in some way not content with their lot in the United States. The obtaining of autobiographies enabled each interrogator to determine what would be a significant context for the particular person he was dealing with, and any misfortune or setback that the person had suffered served as an ideal starting place for undermining democratic attitudes and instilling communistic ones.

No matter which technique the Chinese were using, they always structured the situation in such a way that the correct response was followed by some form of *reward*, while an incorrect response was immediately followed by *threats* or *punishment*. The fact that the Chinese had complete control over material resources and had a monopoly of power made it possible for them to manipulate hunger and some other motives at will, thereby giving rewards and punishments their meaning.

Among the various propaganda techniques employed by the Chinese, their use of *prestige suggestion* was outstanding. The average prisoner had no way of disputing the germ-warfare confessions and testimonials of Air Force officers, or the conclusions of an investigation of the germ-warfare charges by ostensibly impartial scientists from many nations.

Among the positive propaganda appeals made, the most effective was probably the *plea for peace*. The Chinese presented an antiwar and laissez-faire ideology which strongly appealed to the war-weary combat soldier.

In addition the Chinese used a number of *manipulative tricks*, which were usually successful only if the prisoner was not alert because of fatigue or hunger. One such trick was to require signatures, photographs, or personal information for a purpose which sounded legitimate, then using them for another purpose. Some prisoners reported that they were asked to sign "camp rosters" when they first arrived in camp and

later found that they had actually signed a peace petition.

In essence, the prisoner-of-war experience in camp can be viewed as a series of problems which each man had to solve in order to remain alive and well integrated. Foremost was the problem of physical privation, which powerfully motivated each man to improve his living conditions. A second problem was to overcome the fears of nonrepatriation, death, torture, or reprisals. A third problem was to maintain some kind of cognitive integration, a consistent outlook on life, under a set of conditions where basic values and beliefs were strongly undermined and where systematic confusion about each man's role in life was created. A fourth problem was to maintain a valid position in a group, to maintain friendship ties and concern for others under conditions of mutual distrust, lack of leadership, and systematically created social disorganization. The Chinese had created a set of conditions in which collaboration and the acceptance of communism led to a resolution of conflicts in all these areas.

Reactions to the Indoctrination

In discussing the reactions of the POW's to these pressures it is necessary to distinguish between collaboration and ideological change, for neither of these necessarily implies the other. *Collaboration* may be considered as any kind of behavior which helped the enemy: signing peace petitions, soliciting signatures for peace petitions, making radio appeals, writing radio scripts, writing false information home concerning conditions in the camps (or recording statements to this effect), writing essays on communism or working for the

Communist-controlled newspaper, allowing oneself to be photographed in "rigged" situations, participating in peace rallies or on peace committees, being friendly with the enemy, asking others to cooperate with the enemy, running errands for the enemy, accepting special privileges or favors, making false confessions or proenemy speeches, informing on fellow prisoners, divulging military information, and so on.

Nothing about ideological conversion is implied in this definition. A man who engaged in any of these collaborative behaviors because he wanted an extra cigarette was just as much a collaborator as one who did so because he wanted to further the Communist cause. Moreover, the definition does not take into account the temporal pattern of such behavior. Many men collaborated at one time during their imprisonment when one set of conditions existed but did not collaborate at other times under other conditions. The man who moved from collaboration to resistance was obviously different from the man who moved from resistance to collaboration. Perhaps most important of all, this definition says nothing about the particular pattern of motivations or circumstances that drove a man to the first collaborative act and subsequently into a situation in which it was difficult to stop collaborating.

Ideological change may be defined as a reorganization of political beliefs, which could vary from acquiring mild doubts concerning some aspects of the democratic ideology to the complete abandonment of this ideology and a total embracing of communism. The latter I shall label *conversion*. The problem of measuring the *degree* of ideological change is complicated by the lack of good behavioral criteria. One might be tempted to say that anyone could be termed a convert who actively attempted to convince others of the worth of communism, who took all the advanced courses in camp, and who was able to demonstrate in his overt behavior a disregard for democratic values. But such behavior might also characterize a relatively intelligent man who had begun to read Communist literature out of boredom, only to find that both his friends and the Chinese took this as evidence of his genuine interest in communism. He might then be ostracized by his friends and pressed into collaboration by the Chinese, who, it was rumored, severely punished anyone who deceived them.

Of all the prisoners, 21 refused repatriation; one might assume that these represent the total number of converts, but such a criterion is inadequate on at least two grounds. On the one hand, some converts would undoubtedly have been sent back to the United States to spread communism and form a potential fifth column. On the other hand, some collaborators who had not changed ideologically might have been afraid to return, knowing that court-martial proceedings and personal degradation probably awaited them.

Thus, it is more difficult to determine how the prisoners responded to indoctrination techniques ideologically than it is to determine what overt collaboration occurred. What the prisoners *did* is, relatively speaking, a matter of fact; why they did it is a matter of conjecture. In presenting a classification of types of reactions and the motivation patterns or situations that elicited them, one must rely primarily on the *consensus* of the accounts of the repatriates and must recognize the possible biases that can arise in such an analysis after the fact. I am not implying that each prisoner could be placed into one of the categories to be presented below; it is more likely that each man fell into several categories at any given time, and, moreover, that his motivation-situation complex shifted as different sets of circumstances presented themselves.

The "Get-alongers"

The predominant reaction of prisoners was to establish a complex compromise between the demands of the Chinese and the demands of their own ideology. This kind of behavior was labeled "playing it cool" by the men and consisted primarily in a physical and emotional withdrawal from all situations which might arouse basic conflict. Men who reacted in this way were unwilling to do anything that did not have to be done and learned after some months to "suspend" their feelings about most events, no matter how provoking they might be. This was not an easy adjustment to maintain, since the prisoner had to make some concessions to the Chinese to avoid the more severe physical or psychological pressures, at the same time avoiding cooperating to such an extent as to arouse the suspicion and hostility of his fellow prisoners. The safest course was to withdraw emotionally both from the Chinese and from the rest of the prisoner group; this withdrawal was made easier by the apathy and physical weakness induced by life under marginal conditions.[8]

Most of the men who achieved this kind of compromise successfully without too great a toll on their personality were well integrated and retained secure and stable group identifications from before their prisoner-of-war experience. Their judgment concerning the extent to which they could collaborate safely had to be relatively unimpaired, and they had to be able to evaluate objectively and dispassionately threats made by the Chinese.

The Resisters

A number of men developed chronic resistance as their main mode of behavior in camp, refusing to go along with even the most trivial of Chinese requests. This lack of cooperation varied from passive resistance to active, organized obstructionism. Such men were a great trial to the Chinese, who labeled them "reactionaries" and either imprisoned them, if they felt they had some justification, or segregated them in special camps. According to the dynamics involved, these men seem to have fallen into four somewhat separate classes.

The obstructionist. These men were characterized by a life-long pattern of indiscriminate resistance to all forms of authority,[9] and had histories of inability to get along in the United Nations Army just as they were unable to get along with the Chinese. They openly defied any attempt to get them to conform, and performed deeds which other prisoners considered heroic, such as withstanding severe torture. Usually these men spent a major part of their internment in the camp prison, in solitary confinement, or in the "hole."

The Idealist or martyr. These men had unusually powerful identifications with groups whose ideology demanded that they actively resist all forms of pressure from the Chinese. The best example would be the man who was deeply religious and whose faith demanded absolute noncooperation with a "Godless enterprise" of the type the Chinese represented.

The anxious guilt-ridden person. This was the man who was afraid of his own inclination to be tempted by the positive rewards that the Chinese offered for collaboration and who could handle these impulses only by denying them and overreacting in the other direction. He was chronically guilt-ridden over his unpatriotic and antisocial impulses and absolved himself by indulging in exaggerated forms of resistance.

The well-integrated resistance leader. Probably the majority of resisters fell into this class, although there is no way to estimate their number. Because of extensive experience in difficult situations and a thorough understanding of the military, they were able systematically to organize other men and to set important precedents for resistance. The chief characteristic of these men seemed to be their ability to make valid judgments concerning possible courses of action in a situation in which there was little information on which to base such judgments. They had to be able to guess what Chinese reactions would be, what United Nations reactions would be, and most important, how to handle the other prisoners.

The Cooperators

This group is the most difficult to delineate, since I am attempting to include not only those whom the Chinese considered progressives but all those who collaborated to any significant extent. The accounts of prisoners concerning men who collaborated make possible the discrimination of six somewhat separate

patterns of motivation for such behaviors.

The weakling. This was the man who was chronically unable to resist any form of authority and who was unable to withstand any degree of physical or psychological discomfort. Such men probably became collaborators very soon after their internment, with a minimum of ideological involvement, because it was the easiest way. They often found that the more they collaborated, the more collaboration was demanded of them. They were highly susceptible to threats of blackmail by the Chinese, who could exhibit the evidence of their collaboration to the other prisoners or the United Nations authorities. From the point of view of these men, collaboration was an acceptable adjustment under the physical strains of internment, and they developed elaborate rationalizations to justify their behavior and to convince themselves that they would not suffer for it in the future.

The opportunist. These men exploited the role of pro for all its material benefits, again without any ideological involvement, and with little consideration for the future welfare of themselves or others. They were characterized chiefly by their lack of stable group identifications either inside or outside the Army. They met all situations as they arose and tried to make the most out of them for themselves.

The misguided leader. A minority of commissioned and noncommissioned officers engaged in various types of collaborative activities under the firm impression that they were furthering the United Nations cause and resisting the enemy. Their primary error was one of judgment. They reasoned that the best way to resist indoctrination was to go along with it, to find out what the Chinese were up to, to get into the inner circle so as to better plan resistance. In most cases, they managed merely to set a bad precedent for other prisoners, who felt that if their superiors were getting special privileges they should be getting them as well. These officers, like others, found that once they had begun to collaborate it was difficult to stop. Some of these men were probably weakling types who personally preferred the path of least resistance, but who, because of their responsible positions, had to develop adequate rationalizations. They could not see that their course of action was highly inappropriate; they saw only a justification which met their own needs.

The bored or curious intellectual. Of the very small number of men who had superior education, some turned to Communist literature out of boredom or curiosity, and they found that they had aroused both the hostility of their own group and the expectations of the Chinese that they would collaborate. Only a few managed to interest themselves in the Communist literature without falling into this dilemma. More often, material rewards for the intellectual's interest resulted in his ostracism from his own group and drove him in the direction of collaboration. Some of these men were fooled by the promise of early repatriation in return for collaboration, and they felt that their collaboration would be sufficiently minor not to damage their own futures. These men, like those previously described, seldom became ideologically confused or converted. Essentially they used bad judgment in an ambiguous situation.

The "low-status" person. The man who was most vulnerable *ideologically* was one who had never enjoyed any kind of secure or rewarding status position either in his home community or in the Army. This type included the younger and less intelligent, the malcontent, and the man whose social reference groups made the attainment of status difficult— that is, the member of various racial, religious, national, or economic minority groups. These men had little realization of the benefits of democracy because they had never experienced them in a meaningful way. They felt that the society was more to blame for their failures than they were. Such men were ready to give serious consideration to an ideology that offered remedies for their misfortunes. As pro's within the Communist hierarchy they could, for the first time, enjoy some measure of status and privilege, and the Chinese wisely promised them important roles in the future of the "peace movement." Some of these men were probably among those who declined repatriation—perhaps out of fear, when they realized how seriously they had jeopardized their position in the Army and at home, perhaps in order to stay with the cause which had for the first time allowed them to be important. It is difficult to determine whether such men underwent a complete ideological conversion, but there is no doubt that they gave serious consideration to the Communist cause, at least to the limit of their intellectual capacity.[10]

The accounts of the repatriates were unclear regarding the reactions of members of the various minority groups, especially the Negroes. The Communist technique of segregating the Negroes and giving them special indoctrination was probably a tactical error. Many Negroes felt that if they were going to be segregated, they might as well be segregated in the United States—that there was nothing new or better about communism in this respect. Moreover, the propaganda given them was too extreme; even the very low-status Negro knew that his circumstances in the United States were not as bad as the Communists painted them.

However, because of the low-status category of most of the Negroes, the positive appeals made to them must have struck responsive chords in some. They had an opportunity to be leaders and to enjoy fully equal status if they became pro's, and they could rationalize that they would be able to improve the position of their race by participating in Communist peace movements which advocated equality. It is not possible to determine to what extent these positive appeals outweighed the deterrents, and thus to estimate the degree to which ideological change occurred among the Negroes. In any case, the Chinese probably could have persuaded more Negroes to collaborate and to embrace communism had they not made the fundamental errors of segregation and poor propaganda.

The Communist sympathizer. This was the man who, even before he had joined the Army, was sympathetic to the Communist cause and who, therefore, felt no conflict about his course of action in the prisoner-of-war camp. However, if there were loyal Communists in the camps, it is unlikely that the Chinese divulged their identity by calling them pro's, since they would be of far more use as undercover agents.

Attitudes toward Progressives

The reaction of most men toward the pro's was one of perplexity, fear, and hostility. They could not understand how anyone could "swallow the junk" the Chinese were presenting, yet they were afraid that they, too, might be swayed, for among the pro's were many men like themselves. If the pro was a "weak-minded guy" or a man who did not have the stamina to resist the physical pressures, other men felt some sympathy for him, but at the same time they resented the extra privileges that his weakness gained for him. If the pro was perceived to be an opportunist, he was hated and threatened with retaliation during internment or following repatriation. If the pro was a person who had status or rank, the men felt perplexed and afraid; they could not decide what they themselves should do especially if such a pro tried to convince them that it was acceptable to collaborate.

The pro's were made conspicuous in camp by their identification symbols, by their special privileges—which they did not hesitate to flaunt—and by the fact that they usually congregated around camp headquarters. This made them ideal scapegoats and targets for hostility.

They were ostracized by the other prisoners who often refused even to carry on conversations with each other when a pro was present, forcing the pro's into interaction with each other. Thus they tended to form tightly knit groups, which continued even after the end of their internment. The men accused the pro's of informing, imputed to them many motives about which they themselves felt guilty, and attributed any punishment they suffered to some report by a pro. They threatened the pro's with physical violence, but were usually prevented by the Chinese from carrying out such threats. Later, on board ship, the men frequently said that they would now "get even," but the low rate of incidents suggests that no realistic plans underlay the threats. Perhaps most men felt too guilty about their own actual or fantasied collaboration to be comfortable about retaliating against those who had succumbed to the temptations.

The attitudes of the pro's varied with their motivations. Those who had been tricked or "seduced" into collaborating before they could fully realize the consequences remained aloof from other prisoners because they felt guilty and afraid. The opportunists or low-status prisoners felt their collaboration to be entirely justified by the prison-camp situation and viewed noncollaborators as "fools who don't know a good thing when they see it." They tried to persuade others to collaborate—in some cases because they sincerely believed part of the Chinese propaganda and in other cases because they knew that the Chinese would reward them still further if they succeeded. Many pro's tried hard to remain liked both by the Chinese and by the other prisoners, but few succeeded. Since the Chinese presented themselves as benevolent captors, the pro's were the only group in camp who could consistently be used as an outlet for all the hostility engendered by the prison-camp situation.

The Effectiveness of the Indoctrination Techniques

By disrupting social organization and by the systematic use of reward and punishment, the Chinese were able to elicit a considerable amount of collaboration. This is not surprising when one considers the tremendous effort the Chinese made to discover the weak points in individual prisoners and the unscrupulousness with which they manipulated the environment. Only a few men were able to avoid collaboration altogether—those who adopted a completely negativistic position from the moment of capture without considering the consequences for themselves or their fellow prisoners. At the same time the number of men who collaborated to a sufficient extent to be detrimental to the United Nations cause was also very small. The majority collaborated at one time or another by doing things which seemed to them trivial, but which the Chinese were able to turn to their own advantage. Such behavior did not necessarily reflect any defection from democratic values or ideology nor did it necessarily imply that these men were opportunists or neurotics. Often it merely represented poor judgment in evaluating a situation about which they had little information and poor foresight regarding the reactions of the Chinese, other prisoners, and people back home.

The extent to which the Chinese succeeded in converting prisoners of war to the Communist ideology is difficult to evaluate because of the previously mentioned hazards in measuring ideological change and because of the impossibility of determining the *latent* effects of the indoctrination. In terms of *overt* criteria of conversion or ideological change, one can only conclude that, considering the effort devoted to it, the Chinese program was a failure. Only a small number of men decided to refuse repatriation— possibly for reasons other than ideological change[11]—and it was the almost unanimous opinion of the prisoners that most of the pro's were opportunists or weaklings. One can only conjecture, of course, the extent to which prisoners who began to believe in communism managed to conceal their sympathies from their fellows and the degree to which repatriates are now, as a result of their experience, predisposed to find fault with a democratic society if they cannot make a go of it.

It is difficult to determine whether to attribute this relative failure of the Chinese program to the inadequacy of their principles of indoctrination, to their technical inefficiency in running the program, or to both these factors. In actual practice the direct techniques used were usually ineffective because many of the Chinese instructors were deficient in their knowledge of Western culture and the English language. Many of their facts about America were false, making it impossible for them to obtain a sympathetic audience, and many of their attempts to teach by means of group discussion failed because they were not sensitive to the subtle ways in which prisoners managed to ridicule them by sarcasm or other language devices. The various intensive pressures brought to bear on single prisoners and the fostering of close personal relationships between prisoner and instructor were far more effective in producing ideological change, but the Chinese did not have nearly enough trained personnel to indoctrinate more than a handful of men in this intensive manner.

The technique of breaking up both formal and spontaneous organization was effective in creating feelings of social and emotional isolation, but it was never sufficiently extended to make the prisoners completely dependent on the Chinese. As long as the men lived and "studied" together, there remained opportunities for consensual validation and thus for resisting indoctrination. However, as a means of social control

this technique was highly effective, in that it was virtually impossible for the prisoners to develop any program of organized resistance or to engineer successful communication with the outside by means of escapes or clandestine sending out of information.

The most powerful argument against the intellectual appeal of communism was the low standard of living which the men observed in the Korean villages in which they lived. The repatriates reported that they were unable to believe in a system of values which sounded attractive on paper but which was not practiced, and they were not impressed by the excuse that such conditions were only temporary.

Most men returned from prison camp expressing strong anti-Communist feelings.

In summary, it can be said that the Chinese were successful in eliciting and controlling certain kinds of behavior in the prisoner population. They were less successful in changing the beliefs of the prisoners. Yet this lack of success might have been due to the inefficiency of a program of indoctrination which could have been highly effective had it been better supported by adequate information and adequately trained personnel.

Collaboration with the enemy occurs to a greater or lesser extent in any captive population. It occurred in the Japanese and German prisoner-of-war camps during World War II. But never before have captured American soldiers faced a *systematic effort* to make them collaborate and to convert them to an alien political ideology. The only precedent in recent history was the handling of political prisoners by the Nazis, described by Bettelheim.[12] By means of extreme and degrading physical and psychological torture the Nazis attempted to reduce the prison population to an "infantile" state in which the jailer would be viewed with the same awe as the child views his father. Under these conditions, the prisoners tended, in time, to identify with the punitive authority figures and to incorporate many of the values they held, especially with respect to proper behavior in camp. They would curry the favor of the guards, would imitate their style of dress and speech, and would attempt to make other prisoners follow camp rules strictly.

It is possible that such a mechanism also operated in the Chinese prison camps. However, the Nazis attempted, by brutal measures, to reduce their prisoners to docile slave laborers, while the Chinese attempted, by using a "lenient policy" and by treating the prisoners as men in need of "education," to obtain converts who would actively support the Communist point of view. Only those prisoners who showed themselves to be "backward" or "reactionary" by their inability to see the fundamental "truths" of communism were treated punitively.

The essence of this novel approach is to gain complete control over those parts of the physical and social environment which sustain attitudes, beliefs, and values, breaking down interactions and emotional bonds which support the old beliefs and values, and building up new interactions which will increase the probability of the adoption of new beliefs and values. If the only contacts a person is permitted are with persons who *unanimously* have beliefs different from his own, it is very likely that he will find at least some among them with whom, because of growing emotional bonds, he will identify and whose beliefs he will subsequently adopt.

Is the eliciting of collaborative behavior in itself sufficient to initiate the process of ideological change? One might assume that a person who had committed acts consonant with a new ideology might be forced to adopt this ideology in order to rationalize his behavior. This might happen especially if the number of possible rationalizations were limited. The situation in the prison camps, however, allowed the men to develop rationalizations which did not necessarily involve Communist premises. Furthermore, it is likely that whatever rationalizations are adopted, they will not acquire the permanence of beliefs unless supported by social reinforcements. When the prisoners re-entered the democratic setting, most of them gave up whatever Communist premises they might have been using to rationalize their collaboration and found new rationalizations that attempted to explain, from the standpoint of democratic premises, why they had collaborated. Apart from the technical difficulties the Chinese experienced in running their indoctrination program, they were never able to control social interactions to a sufficient extent to reinforce in meaningful social relationships the Communist rationalizations for collaboration.

Taken singly, there is nothing new or terrifying about the specific techniques used by the Chinese; they invented no mysterious devices for dealing with people. Their method of controlling information by controlling the mass media of communication has been a well-known technique of totalitarian governments throughout history. Their system of propagandizing by means of lectures, movies, reading materials, and testimonials has its counterparts in education and in advertising. Group discussions and other methods requiring participation have their counterparts in education and in psychiatry. The possibility that group discussion may be fundamentally superior to lectures in obtaining stable decisions by participants has been the subject of extensive research in American social psychology. The Chinese methods of interrogation have been widely used in other armies, by the police, by newspaper reporters, and by others interested in aggressively eliciting information. Forced confessions and self-criticism have been widely used techniques in religious movements as a basis for conversion or as a device to perpetuate a given faith. The control of behavior by the manipulation of reward and punishment is obviously the least novel of all the techniques, for men have controlled each other in this way since the beginning of history.

Thus, the only novelty in the Chinese methods was the attempt *to use a combination of all of these techniques and to apply them simultaneously* in order to gain complete control over significant portions of the physical and social environment of a group of people.

NOTES

1. The various problems that faced repatriates have been discussed by Segal, *op. cit.* [Henry A. Segal, "Initial Psychiatric Findings of Recently Repatriated Prisoners of War," *Am. J. Psychiatry*, 1954, CXI, pp. 358–363, aptly describes such prisoner groups as "groups of isolates"], and by Robert J. Lifton in "Home by Ship: Reaction Patterns of American Prisoners of War Repatriated from North Korea," *Am. J. Psychiat.*, 1954, CX, 732–739.

2. During the last year or so of imprisonment, many of the features of indoctrination which earlier had been compulsory were put on a voluntary basis. Any prisoners who were interested in learning more about communism could attend special lectures and group discussions. The men who participated in such voluntary programs were known as "self-study pro's" and were given many privileges not accorded to other prisoners.

3. Many men reported that they felt the Chinese were boasting when they told what they knew—that they were very proud of their ability as interrogators and felt a need to show off to their captors.

4. [The collaborators, called "Progressives" by the Chinese, were commonly called "pro's" by their fellow prisoners (ed.).]

5. A number of men reported that black-market activities flourished among the prisoners. Those items of value which men did not wish to use themselves were bartered or sold to other men. Even valuable medicines could sometimes be obtained only by bartering with pro's who had obtained them from the Chinese.

6. There is evidence that the Chinese sometimes staged "executions" in order to elicit cooperation. A prisoner might be marched out into a field, an empty gun placed to his head, and the trigger actually pulled. This procedure first created a state of high anxiety and then a state of grateful relief when it was discovered by the prisoner that he would not be executed after all.

7. The Chinese apparently believed that if they could once get a man to partici- pate, he was likely to continue and that eventually he would accept the attitudes which the participation expressed. However, it may have also been true that the interrogators, for instance, were in danger of losing face with their own group if they could not produce concrete evidence that they had obtained some in- formation; at times they seemed to want any kind of answers, so long as they had something to show in headquarters as proof that they had done their job. Simi- larly, the material obtained at the end of the group discussions was perhaps used as evidence that the instructors were doing their jobs properly. Thus, it is possible that part of the aim was a check by the Chinese on each other.

8. For Puerto Ricans and other foreign nationals whose knowledge of English was very shaky, the problem was easily solved. These men conveniently forgot what little English they knew, and because the Chinese did not have instructors who could speak their languages, they were permitted to withdraw to a relatively comfortable existence of doing details or routine chores. A few others success- fully convinced the Chinese that they were illiterate or in some other way in- capacitated for study. Some men resolved the conflict by volunteering for all the heavy or unpleasant details, but obviously such a solution was available only to the physically strong and healthy.

9. This pattern has been well described by Lifton, *op. cit.*

10. The men who were most vulnerable to ideological appeals were not necessarily the ones the Chinese encouraged to become pro's. There is considerable evidence that the Chinese were quite selective in giving important jobs to prisoners and that they favored more mature and stable ones. Thus, the younger, less intelli- gent, and less stable person was exploited by the Chinese in the same manner as he had probably been exploited before. The Chinese made what use they could of such men and then rejected them when they ceased to be useful.

11. A discussion of some background factors in the lives of these men is presented by Virginia Pasley in *21 Stayed* (New York: Farrar, Strauss & Cudahy, Inc., 1955). Unfortunately her study is inconclusive because she did not investigate the background factors in a control group of men who decided to be repatriated.

12. Bruno Bettelheim, see preceding article. [*Journal of Abnormal and Social Psychology*, XXXVIII (1943), pp 417–452.]

2

The Family

INTRODUCTION

"The family provides the major means for transforming the mentally naked infant organism into the adult, fully clothed in its own personality" (Davies, page 108–118). Among the items of clothing the family bestows upon the individual are his political beliefs, opinions, behaviors, and even his partisan identification. In the United States, for example, fully three-fourths of the offsprings' generation share the same partisan preferences as their parents, notwithstanding the fact that the two generations may find themselves in vastly different socioeconomic environments. Why should the family exert such a pull over its offspring? The family is so influential because (A) of the role it plays in the life of a young child; (B) a family represents a system of social (or asocial), moral, and personal values that the child observes; and (C) families utilize specific techniques or child-rearing practices that often have permanent effects on the young and that will determine his political behavior in adult life.

(A). *Crucial Position of the Family.* The family's importance lies in the fact that for many years it is the sole provider (or denier) of the child's physical and emotional needs. The family's love and approval is crucial to him, and so are the material benefits as well as the status it has to confer upon him. Being so dependent on the family and having few means for nonfamilial validation, the child readily identifies with its politics as well as with the rest of its value system. Just as he accepts his parents' explanation of death or of who made the world, so he accepts their views when they tell him that Republicans are better than Democrats or that union men are more trustworthy than management.

And even the youth who does not mold easily often finds it comfortable or prudent to accede to the family's political values; for, after all, who else has so many opportunities to reward him for conformity and punish him for deviance? Identification, desire for reward, and fear of punishment thus all operate to make the child develop in the political image of his family. The similarity of views between parents and children on such issues as foreign affairs, civil rights, economics and many other vital topics of the day is truly phenomenal. In the 1940s, Richard Centers[1] discovered much agreement between parents and youth on such questions as civil liberties, labor-management relations, and so forth; and the selections by Lawrence Wrightsman and Roberta Sigel below show similar agreement between parents' and children's reactions to the threat of nuclear war and the Kennedy assassination respectively. An unpublished study by Joan Laurence and Harry Scoble[2] observed that liberal parents raise liberal children, whereas another study by M. Kent Jennings and Richard Niemi[3] found fair, although not perfect, resemblance between parents' and high-school youth's political ideas.

Individual rebellion against the family seldom seems to be expressed in political revolt from parents—at least not in the United States (see article below by Russell Middleton and Snell Putney), or at least not until recently. One may argue that this is so because politics does not occupy a very central role in the lives of most American families and, therefore, rebellion in this sector simply would not upset the family enough for the youth to bother with it.

(B). *Family Value System, Philosophy, and Status.* Why, however, should youth not shed some of these familial beliefs once they get older and can test parental opinions against the reality of their own experiences? The answer is that, of course, they do shed some of them (see, for example, the article by Richard Dodge and Eugene Uyeki); but a great proportion of the parental politics do get transmitted to the next generation. At times the answer to this phenomenon can be found in the similarity of social position occupied by later generations: black parents of one generation and of the next may see themselves subject to very similar frustrations, so may two generations of coal miners in Appalachia (see article by Dean Jaros). Similarly, children born to great wealth are as a rule not apt to be paupers during adulthood. Consequently there is little wonder that they will see their political and economic interests much as their fathers saw theirs. Another answer may be that politics is an outgrowth of a general value system or *Weltanschauung*. As the child absorbs the familial *Weltanschauung*, it absorbs the political values that go along with it. A young man who grew up in a family that emphasized the virtue of hard work and looked upon poverty as just punishment for indolence or stupidity will in adulthood see little commendable in the war on poverty. Childhood socialization has provided him with a value screen that highlights some aspects of the social scene and filters out others.

The reference to a value screen, which in itself implies a high degree of congruence between the values of the young and those of their parents, should not blind us to environmental forces that make for intergenerational conflict.

Changes in the social or political environment lead parent and offspring to consider different political solutions. Richard Flacks argues that the conflict between liberal youth and their parents results not from different value systems —both are humanitarian—but from generational differences in ideas of how best to implement these values.

(C). *Child-Rearing Practices*. Political socialization occurs in many other ways too. Many political values that the child acquires are the result not of political or social teachings but of the family's interaction style, especially its child-rearing practices. The family is the first type of authority with which the child has to learn to cope. The way in which this authority is exercised (and the way in which the exercise is perceived by the child) often profoundly affects the young person's general adjustment to authority. Some never learn to adjust to it; others overlearn it. Some, therefore, become rebels or withdrawers from society, whereas others become submissive and unthinking robots for the state. As yet our knowledge about the precise extent to which experience with familial authority is later on projected upon political authority is meager. But the selections below (Part C) give rather eloquent proof that the family contributes to political socialization not only by *what* it tells the child about politics but also by the *manner* in which it transmits its sense of values. Child-rearing methods vary from nation to nation generation to generation, and often from family to family. Karen Orren and Paul Peterson seem to feel that social class, for instance, affects the very way in which parents "teach" children about politics. Middle-class parents tended to draw historical lessons

from President Kennedy's assassination, whereas blue-collar families preferred to moralize but generally communicated less verbally and more emotionally with their offspring. The inclination to train and manipulate children verbally is quite characteristic of American middle-class families and tends to produce highly verbal youngsters who then —as we shall see in Chapter IV—use verbal skills effectively in school. This skill, in turn, facilitates later political participation, effectiveness, and even rise to leadership. We may no longer believe—as some were inclined to during World War II[4]—that child-rearing methods explain why nations espouse dictatorships or go to war; but the articles that follow do demonstrate that different child-rearing strategies can have different personality and behavior payoffs and that some of these payoffs, in turn, tend to affect politics. For example, Robert LeVine in a later section demonstrates how different child-rearing practices in two otherwise similar African societies differentially affect their ability to maintain an impersonal judicial system (pp. 535–549). Frank Pinner demonstrates that parental overprotection leads to political distrust in Belgian youth. The landmark research resulting in the book *The Authoritarian Personality*[5] reveals that prejudiced, racist, and jingoist adults were likely to have been raised with little respect and affection but instead with much harshness and ridicule. An earlier study of Nazis and anti-Nazis[6] also found systematic differences in the child-rearing experiences of the two populations. The articles by Elena Calas, Lucien Pye, and Richard Flacks show that youth in Soviet Russia, Burma, and a certain segment of the United States behave differently from one another—politically speaking—because their parents handle them differently. In Soviet Russia youths are treated strictly but consistently, in Burma inconsistently, and in the United States permissively. The political results speak for themselves.

Families, however, do more than help shape personalities; they also aim to shape behaviors and habits. Families who solicit their children's opinions—or at least listen to them with patience—tend to raise children who develop the habit of self-expression. Results from a comparative study of five nations[7] have demonstrated that this habit, when learned in childhood, is likely to lead to active political participation in adult life. Without the skill for self-expression adults often find political participation difficult, if not impossible—a phenomenon which can be seen clearly in four of the men described by Robert E. Lane.

In fact, families train children in a great variety of interpersonal behaviors, all of which can have vital bearing on politics. For example, families may teach children to play games fairly and by the rule, win or lose; or they may teach them to put winning ahead of all other considerations. They may teach children never to give in to playmates, or they may teach them to compromise graciously in a childhood feud. Again, some parents train children "to go it alone" ("don't share your books—don't do a *joint* science project," etc.), whereas others parents encourage their young to cooperate with one another. Shared books and gracious yielding in a game may seem far removed from politics; but on second thought it should be obvious that the ability to cooperate and to compromise is essential to the capacity for nation-building and to peaceful political activity.

One of the most politically relevant lessons taught in the family is trust or distrust of other people; ability to trust in one's fellow-man may well lie at the bottom of a nation's capacity for effective self-government. Later selections (by Edward Banfield, Lucien Pye, and Adamantia Pollis) demonstrate vividly how lack of such trust is keeping some nations from developing as fully as they might. But lack of trust is not inborn in the child. Children have to be taught to mistrust other people. Adults often tell them from early childhood on to beware of strangers and to expect the worst from most human beings except members of the family. Since life is often harsh and bitter for the parents as well as the children, frequently children see little around them to disconfirm their parents' view. Consequently, by the time they are adults, mistrust has become part of their personality structures. Misanthropes, however, are not likely to organize with others for mutual benefit! Hence the perpetual factionalism, intrigue, and self-isolation that are so characteristic of politics in some sections of the world. In frontier America, in contrast, Alexis DeTocqueville observed great propensity for friendship—toward neighbor and stranger alike—based on trust in one's fellow-man and on the conviction that united we are strong, singly we are weak.

The literature on the political consequences of trust-inducing or trust-discouraging child-rearing practices is all but nonexistent. All one can do, therefore, is to speculate that trust may well be the great unexplored variable in socialization literature and to hope that it will soon be explored.

Although the selections in Part C of this chapter have attempted to demonstrate the linkage between child-rearing methods and subsequent political behaviors in the offspring, we must bear in mind, however, that families do not bring up their children in a vacuum. Articles in subsequent sections will show that familial authoritarianism in Greece yields different political results than it does in China or Germany. In short, the effectiveness of familial methods depends in no small measure on the sociopolitical milieu in which they are practiced. Thus, no family is an island unto itself; and the political consequences of its child-rearing techniques are embedded in a cultural context that profoundly affects their efficacy.

NOTES

1. Richard C. Centers, "Children of the New Deal: Social Stratification and Adolescent Attitudes," *International Journal of Opinion Attitude Research*, 4 (1950), 315–335.

2. Joan Laurence and Harry Scoble, "Ideology and Consensus Among Children of the Metropolitan Socio-Economic Elite," Unpublished, mimeographed manuscript (University of California, 1967).

3. M. Kent Jennings and Richard Niemi, "Family Structure and the Transmission of Political Values," *American Political Science Review* (forthcoming).

4. Ruth Benedict, *The Chrysanthemum and the Sword* (Boston: Houghton Mifflin, 1946), Geoffrey Gorer, *Exploring the English Character* (London: Cresset Press, 1955); Gorer and John Richmond, *The People of Great Russia* (London: Cresset Press, 1949); and Bertram Henry Shaffner, *Fatherland: A Study of Authorianism in the German Family* (New York: Columbia University Press, 1948).

5. Theodore Adorno, *et al.*, *The Authoritarian Personality* (New York: Harper & Row, 1950).

6. David M. Levy, "Anti-Nazis: Criteria of Differentiation," in Alfred H. Stanton and Stewart E. Perry (eds.), *Personality and Political Crisis* (New York: Free Press, 1951).

7. Gabriel Almond and Sidney Verba, *The Civic Culture: Political Attitudes and Democracy in Five Nations* (Princeton, N.J.: Princeton University Press, 1963).

THE FAMILY'S ROLE IN POLITICAL SOCIALIZATION

- James C. Davies

The family provides the major means for transforming the mentally naked infant organism into the adult, fully clothed in its own personality. And most of the individual's political personality —his tendencies to think and act politically in particular ways—have been determined at home, several years before he can take part in politics as an ordinary adult citizen or as a political prominent.

The politicizing process starts early. Easton and Hess have indicated that in America it begins at about the age of three and is basically completed by the age of thirteen. And it usually remains stable, at least in terms of party loyalty, for life. These statements suggest the strength of family influences on political behavior. In what follows I will try to indicate why and how the family influence is so strong, among both ordinary citizens and political prominents and in polities that are either relatively stable and constitutional or unstable and unconstitutional.

The Mother, the Father and the Child's Basic Needs

There are at least four basic needs that appear to be innate and therefore common to all human beings—the physical needs for food, clothing, shelter, health, and safety from bodily harm; the need

for love and affection, which antiseptically may be called the social need; the need for establishing the identity or selfhood that Maslow calls self-esteem; and the need for self-actualization.[1] The ways in which these needs are met— during the longest maturation process required by any species—expose the human organism to a range and intensity of conditioning that are unique. The family provides the individual initially with all his environment for need satisfactions and throughout his entire life is the locus for most of them.

As the initial provider for the newborn child, the mother constitutes the biggest portion of his environment. She is—as Freud indicated—indistinguishable in the infant's primitive mental processes from himself. He and his mother are the same. As he grows, the infant begins gradually to distinguish himself from her and other aspects of the environment. As this distinction emerges, the child nurtured with food, warmth, and affection begins the process of establishing his own identity and at the same time begins the process of deciding with whom he wants to identify. This internal dialogue, beginning before the child can talk, continues through his later life, so that he must forever not only establish his distinct self but relate that self to others whom he would like to be, to be like, or, minimally, to be with. Even the aged citizen who freely and secretly casts his last ballot in an election that presents

Above selection reprinted from: *The Annals of the American Academy of Political and Social Science*, 361, September, 1965, 11–19.

free alternatives to him is never quite free of those people who have influenced him—most particularly his childhood family. And the political leader, like all others, likewise remains under the influence of his family background—if not in the content, then at least in the style, of his rule. Throughout his presidency, Woodrow Wilson remained a preacher and remained in unconscious rebellion against his Presbyterian preacher father.

The basic, innate, organic needs appear to emerge generally in the order stated above: first, the physical; then the social; then the self-esteem; and lastly the self-actualization needs. The family is the most prominent environmental source not only of what may be deemed its inherent function of providing affection but also of satisfying other needs. This is probably the central reason that the individual comes to think and act like his family more than he thinks and acts like those who are less regularly relevant to his need satisfactions. In the process of fulfilling his needs, the individual establishes who he is and whom he is like. In short, he thus establishes his identity.[2] This definition emphasizes the continuing purposes, the continuing functions, which his lifelong interaction with others serves.

There is a dearth of research on the relationship between the family as a source of physical deprivation, and no great amount of research on the political consequences of physical deprivation itself. The research on brainwashing clearly establishes the (usually transitory) political pliancy that occurs when the victim realizes that his very existence depends on his conformity to his captors' (his pseudo parents') ideology.[3]

Dependency is a very common reaction to physical deprivation, but we may thus far only hypothesize that such dependency associated with the family will heighten the tendency to conform to the familial political outlook. This hypothesis helps explain the greater tendency of wives in America to conform to their husbands' politics than vice versa, because the husband is usually the breadwinner.[4]

Social deprivation arising from maternal deprivation has been examined empirically and throws light by inference on the political consequences of the individual's failure to receive normal affection during his early years. The profundity of the consequences of affection deprivation is indicated by research both with primates and with human beings.

Harlow has compared monkeys raised with mechanical mothers—devices to which a nursing bottle is attached—to ones raised under the normal care of their natural mothers. Some of the monkeys raised with mother-surrogates would rage at passers-by or, internalizing their tension, would rage at themselves by biting or picking at their own bodies. Others displayed deep apathy. At the age of six months, they could not play normally with normally raised monkeys or with one another. When they became adults and were placed together with other monkeys that were breeding, they were incapable of normal sexual activity. These "childhood" deprivations had permanently abnormalized the behavior of the mature monkeys.[5]

Comparable systematic but non-experimental research by Spitz has indicated the consequences of maternal deprivation among infants. He was able to compare infants raised by their own mothers in a nursery home with infants raised in a foundling home without mothers. All the former category were still alive at the age of two years. Among the ninety-one raised without mothers, over a third had died. All but a couple of cases in the foundling home became "human wrecks who behaved either in the manner of agitated or of apathetic idiots."[6] The same polarization between hyperexcitability and apathy occurred in the behavior of the Harlow monkeys and the Spitz children.

One of the major discontinuities in the research in political socialization lies between the degree and kind of physical and social nurturance or deprivation of the child within the family and the degree and kind of politicization of the adult. We can not yet report systematically any such research that might establish ties between these phenomena and political socialization.[6] It is again only possible to hypothesize that the general political apathy (and transient hyperexcitability)—the lack of politicization—that still prevails in most of the world is traceable to the apathy (and transient hyperexcitability) resulting from childhood deprivation of these basic needs within the family.

Achieving Political Identity Through the Family

The minimal normal family unit consists of mother, father, and child, but this unit is by no means the universal one. There are both larger and smaller ones. At one extreme are the extended families in which various combinations of nuclear family units are (usually) intergenerationally combined. Research on the politicization consequences of extended family experience for the growing child is again lacking, despite some analysis of the quasi-extended family units in the Israeli kibbutzim. But these novel social units have not been in existence long enough to predict what are the political consequences for kibbutz-raised adults.

But there is the opposite extreme of the minimal and subnormal family unit, typically consisting of the mother and child. On this phenomenon there is some evidence, including some that relates to politicization. One study compared children raised in normal nuclear families with children of families in which the fathers were sailors absent from home for long and irregular periods. Among the findings were these: the father-absent boys, compared with those raised with both parents, strove more to identify with their fathers and at the same time were uncertain of their own masculine identification and tried to act more masculine. Both the boys and girls in father-absent families remained more dependent on their mothers.[7]

In an intensive study of Japanese youth experiencing the profound emotional crisis of their country after its first resounding national defeat in the Second World War, Lifton made comparable observations. Although the fathers were physically present, Japanese youth were very dependent on their mothers. Fathers often were incapable of managing the tensions of young Japanese in cultural transition from a still semifeudal and authoritarian family structure to a still unstabilized new set of interpersonal relationships. They consequently have withdrawn into ineffectual noninvolvement. The mother has remained as the source for satisfying a basic need for stable affection quite without ideological or other cultural content. The great intergenerational gap has been bridgeable emotionally only with the mother. The political consequence has been a high anxiety level among the youth and a tendency to oscillate between quiescence and extreme activity that has involved engaging in massive demonstrations in which the individual finds strong extrafamilial social identification and release from his own private tensions.[8]

Langton, in comparing maternal with two-parent families in Jamaica, has found that authoritarianism in maternal families is higher and both political interest and a sense of political efficacy are lower. The effect is more pronounced among male then female children, and the relationship, with some exceptions, holds regardless of the social class of the children studied.[9]

Even in the relatively more equalitarian father-mother authority relationships that prevail in American families, the father is generally more dominant. On the more specific question of the father's political influence, Langton has found that in Jamaican father-present families it is the father, by a ratio of better than two to one over the mother, who is looked to for political advice and influence.[10]

The reasons for this preponderant influence of fathers in family decision-making, including political decisions, remain imperfectly explored. It is not adequate to explain the phenomenon in such altogether environmental terms as authoritarianism or father-centered cultures. There is the possibility that, in addition to environmental forces, organic ones may be operating. A study of 27 males and 27 females for whom

data were gathered from childhood (ages 3–10) and adulthood found a change that was strikingly different as between the men and women. The boys and girls had been rather alike in their emotional dependence on parents and their tendency to withdraw passively from problem situations. As adults, the males showed a pronounced reduction in these tendencies; females were much less likely to change.[11] This finding may be one link in a still unformed and long chain of explanation for the fact that fathers and husbands are more politically influential in the family than mothers and wives.

The causes for family influence on political socialization do remain very largely unexplored. Even the detailed knowledge of the early life of Lee Harvey Oswald, Kennedy's probable assassin, does not adequately explain his unique political behavior. But there is enough provocative description of just what happens politically in childhood to promise that more analytical, causally oriented work may be done in the future.

Easton and Hess have indicated that one decade is the critical period for basic politicization, starting at the age of three. Just how the first filaments of political identification are formed is not quite clear, but these first ties, well established by the age of seven, are to the broad political community, on an emotional basis that starts with a warm and positive attachment to schools, the "beauty of their country," and "the goodness and cleanliness of its people."

These relatively concrete attachments to community are followed by similar ties to the wielders and visible symbols of public authority, represented by the President of the United States, the local policeman, and the flag. The attachment to the flag becomes almost religious and the flag salute almost a prayer to God. As the child grows, his attitudes toward political authority become increasingly impersonal.

To his quasi-religious set of political attachments, which reach some sort of plateau by the age of nine or ten, is added a more abstract set of identifications with such concepts as democracy, voting, and various aspects of civic liberty. An awareness develops of people as citizens and of one's obligations as a future citizen.[12]

How much of this politicization derives from the family is uncertain, but the likeness between the child's positive, warm appraisal of his own father and the President is clear and may relate to the relatively generous, benign, and nonauthoritarian behavior that is deemed fairly common in American fatherhood. Greenstein emphasizes another characteristic of children's appraisal of the President, namely, that they are remarkably lacking in cynicism about him and other political leaders. Part of this is attributed to the tendency of parents to protect their children from harsh realities of the adult political world and part to the tendency of children to establish a univalent picture free of unpleasant coloration.[13]

The reasons for the warm and trusting attitude toward political authority remain speculative but are seen by Easton and others as relating to the child's anxiety about his dependency on his parents. We can add an explanatory link by again suggesting that the child identifies with both parents because they are the early and the continuing primary source for his need satisfactions. And he identifies more with the father than the mother as an authority figure

because—for surely cultural and also perhaps organic reasons—the father is typically the prime exerciser of authority in the family.

The research of Sigel in analyzing both child and adult responses to the assassination of President Kennedy in November 1963 extends earlier research. She found that the younger the child, the greater the emotional shock and the worry about what would happen after the sudden removal of the central power figure. The President's death produced a reaction that he was not quite so powerful after all, because the presidency and the government continued without interruption after he died. But the younger children more often were unconcerned with the rule of law, more often approving the murder of the assassin. And in a response that may reflect what Greenstein described, the younger children were more inclined to regard the assassination as the act of a single specific individual and not of a conspiracy.[14]

Changes from Political Identification with Parents

The high degree of conformity in America to the political system has been attributed by Lane and others to the lack of deep political controversy, because the system and its parts generally work well.[15] But quite aside from the system's effectiveness, most of the forces *internal* to the family tend strongly to produce a likeness in political attitudes and action from generation to generation. Correlatively, when the child becomes alienated from its parents, it tends also to become politically alienated.[16] One cause for this alienation (which is in any case a common phenomenon of adolescence) is strict parental control, which has been found to make some children more conforming and others more deviant politically.[17] And in families that are highly politicized, politics is "available as an object of protest."[18]

Intrafamilial sources of change from political identification with parents inevitably ramify into extrafamilial influences. Perhaps the most important of these operate in schools, where it is the peer group of students and the tall authority figure of teachers that interpose and superimpose their influence on the strong family forces. And a young man's change in political orientation may reflect a change in socioeconomic or ethnic status from that of his parents. The Irishman, the Jew, the Negro, the Ainu, or the Untouchable who is becoming integrated into the great society is likely to abandon the views of his parents, as these derive from any political ties that were established on an ethnic and social-class basis.

Such changes reflect a measure of tension resulting from mental conflict within the individual child as he grows and his needs emerge. Changes that are extrafamilial in origin involve the family as the arena where outside forces operate. Long-lasting stability in the social and political system reinforces the custom-conserving familial forces. During times of rapid social and political change the conflicting intra- and extrafamilial influences interact most vigorously on the growing individual. And these relate not only to the forces exogenous to the individual (within and without the family) but also to those generated by his own organism as his own needs and other mental processes emerge, change, and grow.

The Impact of External Crisis

External threats to members of a family produce a variety of responses in the individual member. Severe economic crisis poses a threat to the physical well-being of the growing child. As Bakke and others have indicated, when the father becomes unemployed, his role as provider of food, clothing, and shelter is so diminished as to affect his role as the chief authority figure in the family.[19]

Natural disaster, like explosion or tornado, does not have necessarily the same effect as economic crisis in altering the power structure within the family, but it does have the remarkable consequence of breaking down ties to the larger community. People hit by such catastrophe have the initial impulse to protect and be protected by their immediate family and to quite forget the broader community welfare.[20]

In a nuclear or extended family in a preindustrial and predemocratic society, the process may be different. We may suppose that there is little of the politicization process that has been described as taking place in industrialized and democratic societies. The large community in the former case is not characteristically national, perhaps not even regional, but is more likely to be bounded by the local village or large rural estate.

When such premodern societies are in transition, the forces for economic, social, and political change probably operate qualitatively the same as in industrialized but still-changing societies. But they are far more widespread and intense, traumatizing the family more severely than natural or economic disaster in a modern society. They both draw the family together and pull it apart.

Within the family arena two contradictory politicizing functions develop, as the growing child begins the move from the traditional to the modern. One family function is to serve as the shield protecting its members from external forces that threaten not only its traditional roles but also its high degree of autonomy and integrity.[21] When the family acts thus as a shield against external threats, one consequence is likely to be concerted hostility to the regime itself or—more likely, if the threat is severe—of withdrawal from any kind of political activity whatever.

When the external forces are seen by the young not as a threat but as an opportunity, there is likely to be conflict between parents and children and therefore a long-lasting reduction in the role the family plays in the politicization process and a correlative increase in the role of school, of the young person's age-mates, and of youth organizations which directly demand the loyalty of the young to the government rather than to the family. Many of the needs, including the dependency needs, that hitherto had been largely met within the family are now met outside it.

This crisis to the family in a society in transition may diminish with time, as exemplified in the growing emphasis in the Soviet Union—more than a generation after the 1917 revolution—on loyalty and obedience to family. But the "concluding" stable familial state is unlikely to be like the one before the transition began. It is likely to include an acceptance by the family that its politicization role, while still perhaps the strongest, is not exclusive and that other social groups, notably schools, have relatively free access to the growing children. And renewed crisis, whether it be economic, as in the Great Depression of the 1930's, or social, as in the American civil rights crisis of the 1950's and 1960's or the profound postwar crisis in Japan, or more directly political, as in the foreign policy crisis in America of the 1960's, is likely to reactivate intrafamilial tensions as the youth diverge from familial political loyalties and outlook.

The Family and the Production of Political Prominents

For lack of systematic research, it is here possible only to outline the role of the family in producing that small portion of the citizenry who emerge from the great genetic and social pool of infancy and obscurity to mature prominence as national leaders. There are some psychologically insightful biographies, like Huizinga's of Erasmus, Erikson's of Luther, the Herndon and Charnwood biographies of Lincoln, and, perhaps, Bullock's of Hitler. But this field of study is so undertilled that any outlines of general principles governing the development of national leaders remain fragmentary.[22]

About the only generalization that may have universal validity is that political leaders are, psychologically speaking, marginal men. That is to say, whatever their particular genetic make-up, circumstances have pushed them to various boundaries—between old eras and new, traditional and static social status and modern fluid social status, and, more deeply, between the mental insecurity of alienation from parents and identification with new social and political movements affecting the great society whose profound change they experience and interact with.[23]

Whatever their idiosyncratic characteristics, leaders all seem to experience profound conflict as to their own identifications with others and as to their own identity. They do not quite know to whom and what they belong and who and what they are, and they spend their political lives in a never-quite-ending search for resolution of this manifest conflict and its deeply hidden tensions. In this they probably do not differ in kind from their fellow citizens but do differ in the intensity of their response. Their intensity may be a consequence of greater ego strength—of ability to resolve the conflict rather than to withdraw from it into passivity or insanity—and of an extraordinarily high energy level. But these remain only hypothetical suggestions helping to explain the acute marginality of political prominents.

The Family, Political Childhood and Maturity

The child is nurtured in all ways primarily within the family. Until he reaches maturity, he remains in a condition of dependency on the family. However, his achievement of political maturity depends not only on the family but also on other social influences. And, in the contemporary world, which for the most part remains politically apathetic, dependent, and immature, neither the political system nor the family is sufficiently prepared to insure that the transition to maturity will be made with less than enormous turmoil in the minds of both the child and the parents. Tribal and feudal societies generally contain family power relationships in which the child is regarded less as a potential equal than as a person who must learn to conform and to rise only slowly in the hierarchy and who must never expect to live in other than superior and subordinate relationships with others.

The retarding influence of autocratic and authoritarian social relationships, within and without the family, is usually accompanied by circumstances of endemic physical deprivation during which the growing child must quickly learn to provide physically for himself, then his parents, and then his children. Without the potentially leveling, anti-hierarchizing influences of modern integrated and industrialized society, the child is likely to move from authoritarian dependency to authoritarian support of those dependent on him. He is unable to learn adequately anything other than authoritarian ways of acting and reacting and therefore unable to achieve with any facility the transition from dependency to autonomy. So he uneasily remains authoritarian within the family and in his political relationships.

As he starts the transition from tribal or feudal to modern society, he shifts his dependency on parents to a dependency on a new national movement and new political father figure. There is, perhaps, more often than not, some net gain, because the authority influence of the political father cannot, over a prolonged period, be so strong as the proximal familial influence. In consequence, when the transition has progressed somewhat, he is less likely to be as dependent as he was previously on either familial or political father and, in that case, has achieved the beginning of his own autonomy. In turn, he is likely to be less authoritarian toward his own dependent children than his father was and so to facilitate both the broad social transition and the internal transition of the single growing individual.

The transition period is heavy with anxiety, chronic in the individual and endemic in the society, but as the dialogue of change develops and stabilizes, the loyalties to family become re-established on a new basis and new ties to other groups develop—including ones to party, leadership, nation, and the social institutions of an increasingly pluralistic society. As the universal, residual social unit, the family can thus serve not only authoritarian social and political functions, in which the in-

dividual's value derives from his status as a subordinate or a superior, but equalitarian functions in which the individual's value becomes equal to that of others as he acquires the sense of security, responsibility, and autonomy of a mature member of the family and the democratic polity.

Families as the major matrix for individual political maturation have endured intact a centuries-long transition from feudalism to pluralism and individualism in the Western world. And individuals in transition have similarly remained intact. There is no reason to assume that the experience thus accumulated will not both facilitate and accelerate the process in the rest of the world.

NOTES

1. This listing of needs is borrowed directly from Abraham H. Maslow, "A Theory of Human Motivation," *Psychological Review*, 50 (July 1943), pp. 370–396, who lists a fifth need (for security) that I regard as a need for being secure in the satisfaction of the physical, social, self-esteem, and self-actualization needs. See J. C. Davies, *Human Nature in Politics* (New York: John Wiley & Sons, 1963), chap. 1.

2. A closely reasoned and comprehensive analysis of the family's role in the identification process defines it as "the more or less lasting influence of one person on another," in Robert F. Winch, *Identification and Its Familial Determinants* (Indianapolis, Ind.: Bobbs-Merrill, 1962), p. 3. Identification may be more causally defined as the process by which an individual is influenced in his behavior in the course of satisfying each of his basic needs.

3. Among the many reports, a most penetrating analysis is Robert Jay Lifton, *Thought Reform and the Psychology of Totalism* (New York: W. W. Norton, 1961). [See also the selection by Edgar H. Schein in this volume, pp. 82–101 (ed.).]

4. See Angus Campbell *et al.*, *The Voter Decides* (Evanston, Ill.: Row, Peterson, 1954), Table C.3, p. 205.

5. Harry F. Harlow, "The Nature of Love," *The American Psychologist*, 13 (December 1958), pp. 673–685 and H. F. and M. K. Harlow, "Social Deprivation in Monkeys," *Scientific American*, 207 (November 1962), pp. 136–146.

6. R. A. Spitz, "The Role of Ecological Factors in Emotional Development in Infancy," *Child Development*, 20 (September 1949), pp. 145–155. [But note the article by Robert Lane, "Fathers and Sons," pp. 119–131, in this volume (ed.).]

7. David B. Lynn and William L. Sawrey, "The Effects of Father-Absence on Norwegian Boys and Girls," *Journal of Abnormal and Social Psychology*, 59 (September 1959), pp. 258–262.

8. Robert Jay Lifton, "Youth and History: Individual Change in Postwar Japan," *Daedalus*, 91 (Winter 1962), pp. 172–197.

9. Kenneth P. Langton, *The Political Socialization Process: The Case of Secondary School Students in Jamaica* (Unpublished Ph.D. dissertation, University of Oregon, 1965), pp. 113, 115–117.

10. *Ibid.*, p. 118.

11. Jerome Kagan and Howard A. Moss, "The Stability of Passive and Dependent Behavior from Childhood through Adulthood," *Child Development*, 31 (September 1960), pp. 577–591. The authors' speculative explanation is environmental, but it does not seem to preclude an organic inference that is no more speculative.

12. David Easton and Robert D. Hess, "The Child's Political World," *Midwest Journal of Political Science*, 6 (August 1962), pp. 229–246, notably at pp. 236–239. For a very preliminary cross-national research report, see R. D. Hess, "The Socialization of Attitudes toward Political Authority: Some Cross-National Comparisions," *International Social Science Journal*, 15 (4: 1963), pp. 542–559.

13. Fred I. Greenstein, "The Benevolent Leader: Children's Images of Political Authority," *American Political Science Review*, 54 (December 1960), pp. 934–943.

14. Roberta S. Sigel, "Some Explorations into Political Socialization: School Children's Reaction to the Death of a President" [In this volume, pp. 152–172 (ed.).]

15. Robert E. Lane, "Fathers and Sons: Foundations of Political Belief" [In this volume, pp. 119–131 (ed.).] or Lane, *Political Idealogy* (New York: Free Press of Glencoe, 1962), chap. 17.

16. Herbert McClosky and Harold E. Dahlgren, "Primary Group Influence on Party Loyalty," *American Political Science Review*, 53 (September 1959), pp. 757–776, at 766.

17. Eleanor E. Maccoby *et al.*, "Youth and Political Change," *Public Opinion Quarterly*, 18 (Spring 1954), pp. 23–39.

18. Langton, *op. cit.*, Table 27, p. 140 and p. 223.

19. E. Wight Bakke, *Citizens without Work* (New Haven: Yale University Press, 1940), chap. 6. See also P. Eisenberg and P. F. Lazarsfeld, "The Psychological Effects of Unemployment," *Psychological Bulletin*, 35 (June 1938), pp. 358–390; Ross Stagner, *The Psychology of Personality* (New York: McGraw-Hill, 1937), p. 399.

20. L. M. Killian, "The Significance of Multiple-Group Memberships in Disaster," *American Journal of Sociology*, 57 (January 1952), pp. 309–314.

21. In a study of expatriates from the Soviet Union, one finding was that 47 per cent of the expatriates who had experienced the arrest of a family member expressed hostility to the regime, in contrast to 27 per cent who had experienced

neither their own arrest nor that of a family member. See Raymond A. Bauer, "Some Trends in Sources of Alienation from the Soviet System," *Public Opinion Quarterly*, 19 (Fall 1955), pp. 279–291 and Bauer *et al.*, *How the Soviet System Works* (Cambridge, Mass.: Harvard University Press, 1956), chaps. 12 and 13. [See also, in this volume the selections by Urie Bronfenbrenner, pp. 65–73 and Elena Calas, pp. 201–203 (ed.).]

22. The work of Donald R. Matthews—*The Social Background of Political Decision-Makers* (Garden City, N.Y.: Doubleday, 1954) and *U.S. Senators and Their World* (Chapel Hill: University of North Carolina Press, 1960)—is more sociological than psychological, giving socioeconomic family background data on leaders in mainly Western politics. The two studies of Lucian W. Pye—*Guerrilla Communism in Malaya* (Princeton, N.J.: Princeton University Press, 1956) and *Politics, Personality, and Nation-Building* (New Haven: Yale University Press, 1962)—do apply psychological concepts to an analysis of the emergence of prominents in non-Western contexts. [A selection from Pye appears in this volume, pp. 192–200 (ed.).]

23. For marginality as a criterion for distinguishing prominents from nonprominents in a politically portentous riot situation, see G. Wada and J. C. Davies, "Riots and Rioters," *Western Political Quarterly*, 10 (December 1957), pp. 864–874.

FATHERS AND SONS: FOUNDATIONS OF POLITICAL BELIEF*

• Robert E. Lane

Loosely speaking, there are three ways in which a father lays the foundations for his son's political beliefs. He may do this, first, through indoctrination, both overt and covert as a model for imitation, so that the son picks up the loyalties, beliefs, and values of the old man. Second, he places the child in a social context, giving him an ethnicity, class position, and community or regional environment. And, he helps to shape political belief by his personal relations with his son and by the way he molds the personality which must sustain and develop a social orientation. The combination of these three processes produces the "Mendelian law" of politics: the inheritance of political loyalties and beliefs. But while imitation and common social stakes tend to enforce this law, the socialization process may work to repeal it. It is the socialization process, the way in which fathers and sons get along with each other, that we examine in this paper.

Some perspective is gained by noting a number of possible models of the way

Above selection reprinted from: *American Sociological Review*, 24 (August 1959), 502–511.

* I wish to acknowledge financial assistance in the form of a Faculty Research Fellowship from the Social Science Research Council, a Fellowship at the Center for Advanced Study in the Behavioral Sciences, and a modest but indispensable grant from the former Behavioral Sciences Division of the Ford Foundation. This article is a revised version of a paper presented at the annual meeting of the American Political Science Association, September, 1958.

fathers through their rearing practices may affect their sons' social outlook. The German model of the stern father who emphasizes masculine "hardness" and "fitness" in the son, and who monopolizes the opportunity for conversation at the dinner table, is one that has been explored at length.[1] The Japanese father, partially deified like his ancestors, strictly attentive to protocol and detail in the home, is another.[2] The Russian father image—the gruff, indulgent, somewhat undisciplined but spontaneous and warm individual—is a third.[3] And the American father is said to be more of a brother than a father, joined with his son under the same female yoke, uninspired but certainly not frightening.[4] Here is an image to compare with others and, as with the other models, its caricaturistic exaggeration nevertheless represents an identifiable likeness.

The father-son relationship may be explored with the help of data on the lives and politics of fifteen men interviewed recently at considerable length. These men represent a random sample drawn from the voting list of 220 citizens living in a moderate income housing development in an Eastern industrial city. Out of fifteen asked, fifteen (prompted by a modest stipend) agreed to be interviewed, even though these interviews ranged from ten to fifteen hours, administered in from four to seven installments. The characteristics of the sample are as follows:

They were all white, married, fathers, urban, and Eastern.

Their incomes ranged from 2,400 to 6,300 dollars (with one exception: his income was about 10,000 dollars in 1957).

Ten had working class occupations such as painter, plumber, policeman, railroad fireman, and machine operator. Five had white collar occupations such as salesman, bookkeeper, and supply clerk.

Their ages ranged from 25 to 54 years—most of them were in their thirties.

Twelve were Catholic, two Protestant, and one was Jewish.

All are native-born; their nationality backgrounds include: six Italian, five Irish, one Polish, one Swedish, one Russian (Jewish), and one Yankee.

All were employed at the time of the interviews.

Three concluded their schooling after grammar school and eight after some high school; two finished high school, one had some college training, and one went to graduate school.

The interviews were taped, with the permission of the interviewees, and transcribed for analysis. There was an agenda of topics and questions but the interviews were not closely structured, being conducted with probes and follow-up questions in a conversational style. The topics included: (1) current social questions, such as foreign policy, unions, taxes, and desegregation; (2) political parties; (3) political leaders and leadership; (4) social groups and group memberships; (5) ideological orientation toward "democracy," "freedom," "equality," and "government;" (6) personal values and philosophies of life; (7) personality dimensions—partially explored through standard tests; (8) life histories, including attitudes towards parents, brothers and sisters, school, and so forth.

In addition to the interviews, a group of tests were administered on anxiety, authoritarianism, anomie, information, and certain social attitudes.

The characteristics of the sample, as in any study, affect the relationships discovered. It should be stressed that this is a sample of men who, by and large, are well adjusted to society: they are married and have children, hold steady jobs, they are voters. This probably implies that any warping of personality which may have taken place in childhood was marginal. We are, then dealing with the relationships of childhood experiences and political expression in a moderately "normal" group. We are not involved with the extremes of personality damage, or the bottom rung of the social ladder, or a highly socially alienated group. Unlike the studies of American Communists[5] or of nativist agitators,[6] this paper is concerned with middle and normal America, with more or less adjusted people. This is an important point because our findings differ in certain respects from those of other studies, but they do not necessarily conflict with them.

The Unfought War of Independence

The influence of the son's rebellious attitudes towards his father has often been said to be important in explaining radical movements, particularly "youth movements." The son's basic position is one of growing from complete dependence to independence. During the later stages of this growth he and his father each must make a rather drastic adjustment to the changing relationship called forth by the son's maturation. Under certain circumstances the son may rebel against the family and particularly against the father. Is this the typical American pattern—as Erikson denies? Unlike German youth, he argues, American youngsters do not rebel, although willing and able to do so, because the paternal discipline is not something to rebel against.[7]

We explored the question of rebellion, particularly in its political aspects, with our fifteen men and found that there was indeed very little evidence of the kind of relationship that Erikson describes in the German situation. Apparently, only rarely did a family-shattering clash of wills occur when the son thought himself old enough to behave as a man. The father-son opposition took relatively minor forms: the question of what hour to come in at night, the use of the family car, the son's conduct in school. Concerning the political expression of such rebellious feelings, there were strong indications that this subject remained on the periphery of the men's world of experience.

Although the major evidence comes from the biographical material, answers to a question on youthful rebellion or radicalism are revealing. Rapuano, an auto parts supply man with a rather undisciplined tendency to vent his aggression on social targets (communists and doctors), responds in bewilderment and finally denies any such tendency. O'Hara, an oiler in a large factory and one of the more class-conscious interviewees, is confused and takes the question to mean rebellion against his brothers and sisters. Woodside, a policeman who rejected his father with venom, responds to an inquiry about his own youthful rebellion or radicalism:

I do remember through the depression that my folks mentioned that it seems as though more could have been done—that the parties should have made more means of work so that the poverty wouldn't be existing so much around you—and, not only around you—but with you yourself.

He turns the question of his own rebellion and radicalism into a family matter: the family was more or less disgruntled. Only one man, better educated than others, speaks of his own moderate radicalism in a way which could be interpreted as a search for independence from or opposition to his parents.

There are several reasons why political expression of youthful defiance failed to come off. One is the low salience of politics for the parents. Few of the men could remember many political discussions in the home and some were uncertain whether their parents were Democrats or Republicans. If the old man cared so little about politics, there was little reason to challenge him in this area. Another reason is that when there is a need to assert independence there are ways of doing it which come closer to the paternal (and generally American) value scheme. One of these is to quit school. Four or five men sought independence and the economic foundations for a life no longer dependent on paternal pleasure by leaving school shortly before they were ready to graduate—thus striking directly at the interests of parents determined to see their children "get ahead in the world." Of course this act had compensations for parents in need of money, but there seems to have been more of a genuine conflict of wills in this area than in any other. Quitting school, in some ways, is the American youth's equivalent of his European opposite of conservative parentage joining a socialist or fascist party.

Two reasons then for the apolitical quality of youthful revolt are the low salience of politics in the American home and the opportunity for rebellion in other ways. A third reason may be—to use a hyperbole—the relatively low salience of the father in the American scheme. We asked our men, "Who made the important decisions in your parents' household?" One replied that they were jointly made, two that their fathers made the important decisions, and twelve testified that mother was boss. The statement of Ruggiero, a maintenance engineer and supply man from a remarkably happy home, typifies the most frequent point of view:

'Which of your parents would you say was the boss in your family?'—I'd say my mother. My father was easy-going in the house. . . . We found that mother ran the house exactly the way she wanted to. She took care of the money, too. Paid all the bills. She still does.

Now it may be that from a child's perspective that Mother is usually boss. But the near unanimity on this point is convincing, all the more so because the accompanying comments generally show no overlord in the background. Even in this immigrant and second generation population Mom had taken over.[8] Why, then, rebel against Father?

There is a fourth reason for the generally low rate of political rebellion. In the American home a child is given considerable latitude. "Permissiveness" is the term used currently to express this idea and although the term and idea are in bad odor among some critics, it is clear that the prevailing standards of child care even twenty years ago allowed a degree of freedom in school, neighborhood, and home not generally prevalent in Europe or Asia.[9] To a large extent, the boy is on his own. This is Erikson's

point, but we can illustrate it in detail. Thus Farrel, a man from a working class background whose schooling included graduate study, reports on his tendency to political radicalism in his youth: "I think there must also be the adolescent revolt aspect, which was never acute with me. . . . There was, as far as I was concerned, no necessity for it to be acute. I didn't feel hemmed in by my parents." Rapuano talks of his "reckless" youth in which he ran free with other boys, and some of the men speak of their parents' preoccupations that gave them opportunity to live a "free life." Many of the boys had earned money for their own as well as their families' use by selling papers, working in grocery stores, or cleaning up the school. Nor was this freedom attributable to parental indifference. When Rapuano was struck by a school teacher, his mother (*not* his father) visited the school to beat the teacher with a stick. A free child assured of supportive parental assistance when in need does not need to rebel.

A minority of four or five of these children, however, had suffered under controls which seem strict by most American standards.

Four Men Whose Fathers Failed Them

Although it is true that the symptoms of *rebellion* are rather slight and that its political expression is minuscule, it does not follow that the American son, particularly the son of immigrants, identifies with his father—introjects the paternal ideal, as the psychoanalysts might say—and accepts the male role as it has been played on the home stage. At least four of our fifteen men probably had experienced seriously damaged relations with their fathers and even in the roseate glow of remembered childhood do not like the old man. Interpretation of this situation must be circumspect, since people are supposed to love their parents and are even commanded to honor them. During the interviews, however, interstitial comments, reportorial selection of incidents, and graphic silences, as well as the explicit expressions of like and dislike, present a clear picture of father-son relations.

There are, of course, many varieties of both bad and good father-son relations. In these four cases of damaged relations we note two patterns. One is *identification without affection*, represented by only one case. The other, the *rejection pattern*, is illustrated by three cases. This section briefly pictures the father-son relationships of these four men. In the following sections their political expression is explored.

Identification without affection. The American youth, as we have noted, typically does not invest much emotional energy in a father rebellion on the European scale. But of course the latter does occur. And sometimes the process resembles the German pattern where the youth identifies with his father, struggles for his approval, gradually asserts himself against him as though assaulting a fortress, departs, and returns to be like him—another paternal fortress against his own son.

Sullivan, a railroad fireman and former semi-professional boxer follows this tradition. Now, at the age of 25, he stresses his respect for his father, but his report shows little affection. Of discipline he says:

He was pretty strict—very strict. He'd been brought up strict, and in an old Irish family

there, and of course, all the way through school it was very strict [the father went to a Catholic seminary]. So he was pretty strict with me, more so than with the two girls.

When asked about his father's good points he responds in the same terms as though everything else were blotted out: "Well ... (long pause) ... his good points were that he knew when to be strict and when to be lenient." Except on the question of sports (where the father gave instruction, but nothing is said of a good time), there is little joy in this relationship.

Yet there is identification. The son has adopted his father's strict manner. Sullivan had left his family because his wife would not follow his orders about the management of the home; he now sees that the children should, properly, give instant obedience. His rebellion— and he did rebel—is over:

Oh, I knew everything when I was 19. Nobody could tell me nothing. Boy oh boy I found out, though. That's one thing my father would always try and ... teach me things, and offer advice and so on. But no, I wouldn't listen. He told me especially about discipline and orders and so on. I never used to like to take orders. I don't think I was in the service a month when I wrote and told him, "Boy, you were right. You said some day I'm going to say that—and boy, you are." The service was a good thing for me.

Sullivan is a "hard" man to deal with, not mean, but there is a steely quality about him which reflects his experience in and exaltation of the Marine Corps, as well as his father's values.

Reflection of the father. Unlike Sullivan, three others, Woodside, Dempsey, and DeAngelo, reject their fathers outright. There is no effort to cover over their feelings, to take back the criticism, undo the damage, unsay the words. Something within them is quite clear and solid on this matter and they are not shaken by fear or guilt at the thought of such rejection.

DeAngelo is a factory machine operative, whose father and mother separated when he was an infant; he subsequently acquired a step-father. Of his father, who lives in the same town, laconically he says: "I don't bother with him." Of his step-father:

He was a good guy when he was sober, but he was bad when he was drunk. I never had too much respect for him. . . . When he was drunk he wanted to argue, you know. But my mother was bigger than him—didn't have too much trouble taking care of him. After a while my mother left him, you know, and we were on our own.

DeAngelo narrowly missed reform school when in high school—from which the principal ordered him to leave, possibly through a misunderstanding. But some maternally inspired internal gyroscope kept him on an even keel through a series of such adversities. Today he is the father of six boys, a steady breadwinner, and union shop steward in the plant.

Woodside, a policeman with a conscience, remembers his childhood with horror because of the irresponsible drunken behavior of his father and particularly his father's "outside interests," women. He says, quite simply: "At one time I felt I'd hate my father— that if anything ever happened to him it would be a wonderful thing." But today he plays checkers with the pathetic old man and helps him when he's in trouble. He hated his father in the past for the beatings he gave his mother, the humiliation he brought on the household, and

the physical suffering to the children: "It's a pretty gruesome thing to tell anybody that a father could neglect his kids so much. Believe me, a good many days I've seen where I had just water, and I was lucky to have water—for a meal for the whole day."

Dempsey is an older man who married a widow when he himself was 40, having previously lived with his mother and, until they were married, with his brothers. In comparison with DeAngelo and Woodside, his reactions to his father are more veiled and he identifies somewhat more with him. He thinks of him as "a hard working man, the same as I am now, and couldn't get much further than I probably will . . . although my hopes are probably a little bit higher." But through the veil we see more granite than flesh and blood:

'Did your father have a sense of humor?'— Well, that I couldn't say. As I say, we were never too chummy with him. He never was a fellow to be chummy with us children. . . . He was one of them guys—it had to be it, or there was no way out of it.

There apparently were few family outings, little fun, and strict curfews. What things did Dempsey admire about his father? "Only that he was a hard worker, and gave us a chance to do—to choose what he wanted to—at the time [reference to choice of religion in which they chose the mother's religion.] Outside of that he was a very hard man." And a few minutes later he repeats, "he was a hard—a very hard and stern man."

The Politics of Filial Alienation

Having examined a model American pattern of father-son relationships and isolated four deviant cases, we turn to an inquiry into the politics of these latter four men.

Low information and social interest. The question of political information is considered first, partly because it indicates the degree of interest in the social world outside oneself. Our measure of political information is made up of questions on local, national, and international institutions and events. The local events, in particular, are not usually learned in school, since they include such items as "Who is the local boss of New Haven?" and "How would you go about getting a traffic light put on your corner?" It is therefore especially significant that these four men, concerning political information, rank as the four lowest of the fifteen cases.

There are several reasons for this. The loss or lack of a secure parental model encouraged each of these four to frame his own life style and to engage in the life-long business of self-discovery. Each man is his own Pygmalion. More importantly, the development of a personal sense of security, of being a loved and wanted and respected person, which is a bulwark against psychic conflict, is lacking. This lack seems to be borne out by the evidence of severe anxiety in all four cases. Dempsey and DeAngelo rank among the four highest scorers on the "neurotic anxiety" scale. Sullivan ranks third on a social anxiety scale and shows evidence of severe sex-tension, as indicated by his top score in this area (and his marriage is breaking up). DeAngelo ranks fourth on this sex-tension scale. Woodside, while less troubled by sexual problems and not "neurotically" anxious, ties for first place on the scale of social anxiety; he is, by his own account and other evidence, a worrier, a searcher for

all around "security" and has somatic difficulties.

Anxiety can lead into politics as well as away from politics. People can defend themselves against anxiety by knowing more than others—or people may succumb to the demands of anxiety by knowing less. Generally in the American apolitical culture the anxious man does not employ politics as a defense against his conflicts. One of the little appreciated benefits of such a culture is the low premium on politics for the anxious and neurotic.

Authoritarianism. Three of the four men score strongly on authoritarianism: DeAngelo has the highest score in the group, and Sullivan and Woodside tie for fourth; only Dempsey's ranking is moderate. The genesis of authoritarianism and its close connection with father-son relations are well known. Here it is sufficient to note that in order to believe that people can live and work as cooperative equals or at least as trusting partners, a person must have experienced such a relationship. In their relations with their fathers, these men had no such experience.

Speak no evil of the political leader. There is a third area of political outlook which seems to be shared by these four men with damaged father relations, a quality which in some measure sets them apart from the others. Although political lore would have it otherwise, people generally prefer to speak well of political leaders than to speak ill of them.[10] But the average citizen can criticize such leaders, designate those he dislikes, and weigh the good and bad points of each on occasion. Our four deviant cases found such criticism or even objectivity more difficult than the others.

Sullivan admires Monroe, Lincoln,

Truman, and Eisenhower. He defends Truman against those who believe that his attack on the music critic was out of order. He defends Ike for the vacations he takes. When asked about political leaders he dislikes: "Well, from what I learned in history, Grant seemed to be pretty useless . . . [pause]. He didn't seem to do too much [mentions that he was a drunkard]. And [pause] I mean I don't dislike him, either, but—I don't dislike any of them." Question: "How about living leaders, or recent leaders, which of these would you say you had the least respect for?" Answer, after a pause: "Well [long pause], none that I could think of."

Dempsey likes Washington and Lincoln, and, when probed, Wilson and Truman, for whom he voted. Asked about "any particular feelings about Dewey" he says, "No, I wouldn't say that." Roosevelt was "a very good man." Eisenhower is also a "very good man, doing everything he possibly can." He can think of no mistakes he has made.

DeAngelo says he doesn't particularly admire any political leaders. But: "I like them. I mean I didn't think anything bad about them, y'know." Questioned about an earlier reference to Robert Taft, he replies:

Well, I mean, I thought for being President, I thought he'd be a little better in know-how and savvy than Eisenhower, y'know. I ain't got nothing against Eisenhower—he's good, he seems to be honest enough, but I don't . . . I don't . . . I don't think he should have run again because I think his health is—his health was good enough.

DeAngelo has trouble expressing his reservations about Eisenhower even on the question of health. When asked specifically about people he dislikes, distrusts, or thinks to be weak or wrong for the job: "Well, I don't know, not offhand."

Woodside's views are a little different. He likes Eisenhower but is more willing to discuss his weaknesses (particularly his signing of an order to execute a deserter). He likes MacArthur as a "big man" and mentions Lincoln favorably. Asked about his dislikes and those he thinks did a poor job, he mentions others' criticisms of Roosevelt but then rushes to his defense, except to say that he thinks Eisenhower is "a little bit more mannish" than Roosevelt. The only political leader he mentions unfavorably is Adlai Stevenson, who strikes him as a man who could say "yes" when he means "no."

With the possible exception of this last comment, these remarks convey three themes: (1) Conventional leaders like Washington, Lincoln, and Monroe are admired. (2) The independent leader who doesn't let outsiders tell him what to do is admired—Truman would stand for no nonsense (Sullivan), Stevenson is too much influenced by his advisors (Woodside). (3) Authority figures are not to be criticized—an especially important point.

These four men are not notably deficient in their general ability to criticize or to express hostility. Why, then, do these four, whose relations with their fathers are strained, find it so hard to criticize political leaders in a wholehearted way?

In answering this question, Sullivan's case should be distinguished from the others. Sullivan feels guilty about his negative feelings toward the original political authority in the family. He cannot bring himself to express his hostility without quickly withdrawing his remarks and saying something of a positive nature. The expression of hostility to authority figures is painful and Sullivan simply avoids this pain.

The other three men express outright hostility toward or unrelieved criticism of their fathers. Why not also of political authority? In the first place, there is a carryover of fear from the childhood situation which has not been obliterated by the adult emancipation. Men do not easily forget those childhood moments of terror when the old man comes home drunk, abuses the mother, or gets out the strap to deal with the child in anger unalloyed with love. Secondly a combined worship and envy of strength exists, which father-hatred fosters in a child, for it is the father's strength in the family that penetrates the childish consciousness. Finally, there is the persistent belief in the futility and danger of countering and rebelling against authority. Although DeAngelo was a rebel in high school and was expelled and Woodside stood up to his father threatening him with a log behind the wood shed, both are successful now partly because they have curtailed these anti-authority impulses that threatened to bring disaster once before. Their consciences are composed of anti-rebellion controls; this is why, in part, they can be good citizens.[11]

Utopia and conservatism. The basis for a hopeful view of the world lies in the self; the world is ambiguous on this point. In the self, the notion that we can move toward a more perfect society is supported by the belief that people are kindly by nature and considerate of one another. Moreover, when the idea of a better social order is developed even a little, the mind quickly turns to the nature of authority in such a society. Is there a kind of authority which is strong and directive, yet at the same time solicitous and supportive of the weak in their infirmities—in short, paternal?

We asked our subjects about the nature of their vision of a more perfect society (with results which must await detailed analysis). At the end of the discussion we inquired whether or not there is evidence that we are moving closer to such a society. Although the men were not asked if the world was possibly moving in the opposite direction, some volunteered this answer. Our fifteen men answered the questions on an ideal society as follows:

	Damaged Father-Son Relations	Others
We are moving closer to ideal society	0	8
We are not moving closer to ideal society	3	2
(volunteered) We are moving away from ideal society	1	1

The pattern is clear. Woodside first touches on the drift from a peacetime to a wartime society. Then speaking of only the peacetime society, "like we're in peace now, the society is about the same as it has been back along. . . . I would say that throughout history it has been about the same." Asked if people are happier now than they were a hundred years ago, he is reminded ironically of the phrase, "There's nothing like the good old days," and he digresses to say that people adjust so quickly to mechanical progress that their degree of satisfaction and dissatisfaction remains about constant.

Dempsey, as always, is more laconic.

Asked the same question about possible progress toward a better society, he says: "No. I don't think so. I think we're going to stay on the same lines we are on right now."

And Sullivan: "Never. We'll never get any place close to it, I think." He first modifies his answer by noting that "prejudice" may decline but is skeptical because "you can't change human nature."

DeAngelo takes the dimmest view of all: "I don't think we'll ever get any closer [to a more perfect society]. We're getting farther and farther away from it, I guess. All indications are we're moving away from it. There's not enough people trying to make the world perfect." Asked why we are retrogressing, he cites what he regards as the drift away from religion and the rise of communism. These are perhaps the two most convenient pegs today on which to hang a deeply rooted pessimism regarding the social order.

Contrast these views with those of five cases selected because of their close identification and warm relations with their fathers. One says flatly that "I don't think we're far from it." Another points out that the population increase will bring about troubles but he is hopeful because of the parallel increase of the proportion of good people. A third declares that every mistake we make teaches us something, hence the world is getting better. A fourth believes that a socialist society is developing, which he thinks is probably a "good thing" although socialism is not an "ideal" society. Only one of these five holds that such progress is unlikely, attributing this to the increase of governmental controls; but he adds, characteristically, "Maybe concurrently with such controls you're getting more of the things that most people seem to want made available to them."

Fathers and Sons—and History

The state is "man writ large;" the family is a microcosm of society. The history of a nation may, in considerable measure, reflect the changes in the ways children and parents, sons and fathers, struggle to get along with one another. Some of the characteristics of a nation's politics may rest on the resolution of these struggles.[12] With this point in mind, we turn to certain aspects of American and foreign politics.

To recapitulate in American society: (1) "good" father-son relations are the norm; (2) of those youth with rebellious feelings against their fathers there are few for whom the rebellion takes political form; and (3) there is a tendency for moderately damaged father-son relations to be associated with relatively low levels of hope, interest, and capacity to criticize political leaders. These tendencies are revealed in what may be called the American political "style" in the following ways:

1. American politics is often said to embody a kind of consensualism in which both sides tend to come together, rather than a bipolarization or radicalism. At the same time, campaigns become quite heated with highly critical comments passed between the partisans of one candidate and those of another. This situation parallels the qualities we find associated with sons of strong but nurturant fathers: lack of alienation but a capacity for outspoken criticism.

2. Compared with the citizens of other nations, the American citizen is reported to be relatively well informed about current events and civic matters. On the

other hand, his intensity of concern is relatively low. He can exchange blows during campaigns and then accept the victory of the opposition without much trouble. This pattern (a considerable cultural achievement) is difficult, as we have seen, for the poorly socialized and again suggests an important family component in American democracy.

3. It is often noted that a strain of idealism exists in American international politics which distinguishes it from the hard-boiled realism of the Continent. Wilson's Fourteen Points, Roosevelt's Four Freedoms, and Truman's Point Four illustrate the character of this idealism, an idealism nourished by the hope that we can do away with war and establish a peaceful world order. Behind these beliefs and supporting them in their many expressions lies that quality of hope and trust which are forged in boyhood, when the son is apprenticed to a protective and loving father.

Summary: Some Hypotheses

With a humility based on an appreciation of the great variety of experience that goes into the making of political man, we suggest the following hypotheses.

1. Compared with other Western cultures, American culture discourages youthful rebellion against the father. It further discourages political expression of whatever rebellious impulses are generated. This is because: (a) There is less need to rebel in a permissive culture. (b) Rebellious impulses are less likely to be expressed against the father because of his relatively less dominant position in the family. (c) The low salience of politics for the father means that rebellion against him is less likely to be channeled into politics or political

ideology. (d) The high salience of the father's ambition for the son (and the resulting independence) means that rebellion against the father is more likely to be expressed by quitting school and going to work, or by delinquent conduct.

2. Damaged father-son relations tend to produce low political information and political cathexis. This is because, *inter alia*: (a) Without an adult model the youth must give relatively greater attention to the process of self-discovery and expend greater energy in managing his own life problems. (b) Failure of father-son relationships creates anxiety which is often (not always) so preoccupying that more distant social problems become excluded from attention.

3. Damaged father-son relations tend to develop an authoritarian orientation.

4. Damaged father-son relations tend to inhibit critical attitudes toward political leaders because: (a) The damaged relations encourage an enduring fear of expressing hostility toward authority figures. (b) They stimulate a reverence for power over other values. (c) In children they provoke the belief that it may be useless to rebel or petition authority.

5. Damaged father-son relations discourage a hopeful view of the future of the social order because: (a) The damaged relations often give rise to a less favorable view of human nature. (b) They help to create skepticism about the possibility of kindly and supportive political authority. (c) They encourage a cynical view of the political process: it is seen in terms of corrupt men seeking their own ends.

6. The history, political style, and future development of a political community reflect the quality of the relationship between fathers and sons. The

permissive yet supportive character of modal father-son relationships in the United States contributes to the following features of the American political style: (a) a relatively high consensualism combined with a capacity for direct and uninhibited criticism; (b) a relatively large amount of interest and political information combined with relatively low emotional commitment; and (c) a relatively strong idealism in foreign affairs (and in general social outlook).

NOTES

1. See Bertram H. Shaffner, *Father Land, a Study of Authoritarianism in the German Family*, New York: Columbia University Press, 1948; David M. Levy, "Anti-Nazis: Criteria of Differentiation," in Alfred H. Stanton and Stewart E. Perry, editors, *Personality and Political Crisis*, Glencoe, Ill.: Free Press, 1951.

2. See Ruth Benedict, *The Chrysanthemum and the Sword*, Boston: Houghton Mifflin, 1946.

3. See Henry V. Dicks, "Observations on Contemporary Russian Behavior," *Human Relations*, 5 (May, 1952), pp. 111–176.

4. See Erik Erikson, *Childhood and Society*, New York: Norton, 1950.

5. Gabriel Almond, *The Appeals of Communism*, Princeton: Princeton University Press, 1954; Morris L. Ernst and David Loth, *Report on the American Communist*, New York: Holt, 1952.

6. Leo Lowenthal and N. Guterman, *Prophets of Deceit*, New York: Harper, 1949. For an interesting case analysis of father-son relationships and virulent fascism, see Robert Lindner, "Destiny's Tot" in his *The Fifty Minute Hour*, New York: Rinehart, 1955.

7. Erikson, *op. cit.*, pp. 280–283.

8. Compare Margaret Mead, *And Keep Your Powder Dry*, New York: Morrow, 1942.

9. On this point, see Robert R. Sears, Eleanor E. Maccóby, and Harry Levin, *Patterns of Child Rearing*, Evanston, Ill.: Row, Peterson, 1957; and Robert J. Havighurst and Allison Davis, "A Comparison of the Chicago and Harvard Studies of Social Class Differences in Child Rearing," *American Sociological Review*, 20 (August, 1955), pp. 438–442.

10. In 1948 between a quarter and a third of a national sample could find nothing unfavorable to say about Truman or Dewey, but almost everyone could mention something favorable about both candidates. See Angus Campbell and Robert Kahn, *The People Elect a President*, Ann Arbor, Mich.: Survey Research Center, 1952; and Angus Campbell, Gerald Gurin, and Warren E. Miller, *The Voter Decides*, Evanston, Ill.: Row Peterson, 1954.

11. The view that men with damaged father-son relationships do not like to criticize authority figures may seem to fly in the face of a popular interpretation of radicalism. This contradiction is more apparent than real. The effect of failure of socialization on normal populations is more likely to be apathy than radicalism. (See, e.g., P. H. Mussen and A.B. Warren, "Personality and Political

Participation" [in this volume, pp. 277–292 (ed.)]. There are exceptions, of course, since relationships are always expressed as probabilities. In radical groups, moreover, the tendency to criticize authority figures is focused on those who are seen as illegitimate, usurpers, or leaders who are considered to be weak. This was Woodside's approach to Stevenson, and it was precisely the latter's "weakness," his lack of decisiveness, which Woodside critized. Our findings are complementary, not contradictory, to other similar studies in these respects.

12. Melancholy experience suggests that it is prudent to note that I am not denying the importance of a nation's history or of its geography and economics, or of its current leadership, in shaping its destiny. I do not imply, for example, that German Nazism arose because of an authoritarian family pattern rather than the Versailles treaty, or Article 48 of the Weimar Constitution, or the weakness of von Hindenberg, or what not. Within Germany, however, those whose fathers forbade them from speaking at the dinner table were more likely to be Nazis than those whose fathers were more indulgent. (See Levy, *op. cit.*) German fathers were more likely to be repressive in this and other ways than fathers in certain other nations. The *combination* of defeat in World War I, the nature of Germany family life, and other factors, no doubt, helped to create a public responsive to Hitler's appeals.

POLITICAL EXPRESSION OF ADOLESCENT REBELLION

- Russell Middleton and Snell Putney

In his pioneer psychoanalytic study of political attitudes Lasswell pointed out that, although political beliefs may be expressed in a highly rational form, they are often developed in highly irrational ways. "When they are seen against the developmental history of the person, they take on meanings which are quite different than the phrases in which they are put."[1] Using a series of case studies, he attempted to demonstrate that family relationships were one of the nonrational determinants of whether or not an individual became an anarchist, a socialist, a highly conservative Republican, or a political assassin.

Political beliefs can be influenced by family relationships through rebellion; a youth may, for example, express rebellion against his parents by rejecting their political beliefs and adopting a divergent set. The probability of such political rebellion is enhanced by the fact that adolescence, which most authors regard as a period of generalized rebellion in American society,[2] is also the age at which most individuals seem to crystallize their political viewpoints.[3]

Clearly adolescent rebellion cannot be attributed solely to the biological maturation process, for adolescence is not a period of storm and stress in every society.[4] Rather, there appear to be

Above selection reprinted from: *American Journal of Sociology*, LXVIII, 5 (March 1963), 527–35 by permission of The University of Chicago Press. Copyright © 1963 by the University of Chicago Press.

structural features in American society conducive to youthful rebellion. Parsons, for example, argues that, since there is a sharp limitation of "objects of cathexis" in the isolated conjugal family typical of American society, children tend to be highly dependent emotionally on their parents, especially on the mother.[5] As the individual nears adulthood, however, he is expected to break this dependency and choose his occupation and sexual partner with little adult support. In adolescence, therefore, a reaction formation may be generated against the dependency needs and may find expression in a rebellious youth culture, compulsively independent and defiant of parental norms and authority, and, at the same time, compulsively conformist to the peer group that satisfies individual dependency needs. Parsons maintains that the rebellion is especially strong among adolescent boys because of an additional reaction formation of compulsive masculinity against an original identification with the mother.

The question remains, however, whether the adolescent is likely to use political beliefs as an instrument of rebellion. Hyman believes that he is not: "The almost complete absence of negative correlations [between the political attitudes of parents and children] provides considerable evidence *against* the theory that political attitudes are formed *generally* in terms of rebellion and opposition to parents."[6] The absence of negative correlations between the political beliefs of adolescents and their parents, however, does not demonstrate that rebellion tends to be non-political. It might simply indicate a relative lack of rebellion, even though such rebellion as occurred might often be political.

A recent study by Lane based on depth interviews with fifteen working-class and lower-middle-class men selected at random from an eastern housing development focused on how often rebellion against the parent was expressed politically.[7] Concentrating on rebellion against the father, he found that only four of his subjects had impaired relationships with their fathers. In none of these cases did the rebellion take a political form, and the subjects' general level of interest in politics was low. On the basis of these scant but suggestive data Lane argues that, compared with other Western cultures, American culture (because it is more permissive and the father is less dominant) tends to discourage youthful rebellion against the father. Moreover, when such rebellion does occur, it tends to discourage its expression in political terms because politics is relatively unimportant to the father, making other forms of rebellion more appealing.[8]

Maccoby, Matthews, and Morton conducted a study of the circumstances under which political rebellion against the parent was most likely to occur in American society.[9] Seeking to test the hypothesis that the young tend to become radical in their political views because of adolescent rebellion against strict parental authority and discipline, they interviewed 339 first-time voters between the ages of twenty-one and twenty-four in Cambridge, Massachusetts, immediately after the 1952 presidential election. Each respondent was

asked: "In your case, when you were in your teens, did your family want to have quite a lot to say about your friends and the places you went and so on, or were you pretty much on your own?" They found that there was maximum political conformity to parents among those subjects who said that their parents had "about an average amount to say." Those who reported that their parents "had a lot to say" and those who said their parents left them "on their own" were both more likely to deviate politically from their parents. The researchers thus concluded that political rebellion was correlated with the type of discipline prevalent in the adolescent's family.

On the other hand, Nogee and Levin, in a study of 314 Boston University students eligible to vote for the first time in the 1956 presidential election, found no evidence of any relationship between strict parental control in early adolescence and political rebellion: "Although a small number do 'revolt' against their parents' political views, there is no evidence that the likelihood of such revolt is related to the strictness of parental control."[10] This study, like the previous study by Maccoby, Matthews, and Morton, did not investigate whether strictness of discipline was correlated with estrangement between the youth and his parents; rather they implicitly assumed such a relationship and concentrated on measuring the degree to which it might be expressed politically.

Previous research thus presents an incomplete and contradictory picture of adolescent political rebellion. It is generally agreed that adolescence is a period of general rebellion in American society. Hyman and Lane, however, are doubtful that this rebellion is likely to take a political form in the context of

American culture. And when political rebellion occurs, Maccoby, Matthews, and Morton disagree with Nogee and Levin as to whether it is associated with the perceived degree of strictness of parental control.

In the present study we have attempted to investigate further some of the problems raised by the earlier studies. Are youths who are estranged from their parents no more likely to deviate from parental political views, as Lane suggests, than youths who are close to their parents? Does parental indifference to politics, as Lane further suggests, inhibit the political expression of rebellion by those who are estranged from their parents?

Our basic hypothesis is that estrangement from parents is associated with political rebellion if the parents are interested in politics, and perceived extremes of parental discipline (strict or permissive) are associated with lack of closeness between parent and child and thus with political rebellion.

Methods

Anonymous questionnaires were administered late in 1961 to classes of students in sixteen colleges and universities in the United States. A state university, a state college, a private university, and a private liberal arts college were included in each of four regions—Far West, Middle West, Northeast, and South. Four of the institutions were church affiliated. Thus, although the individual subjects were not selected in a strictly random fashion, the sample does include a broad range of types of institutions and regions. Caution should be used in generalizing the findings on this sample to American college students in general, but analysis of the sample has not revealed any marked biases correlated with political rebellion or adolescent rebellion.

A total of 1,440 completed questionnaires was obtained from students attending the sixteen colleges and universities included in the survey. Almost all the subjects were between the ages of seventeen and twenty-two, a group in transition to young adulthood. At their age, the storms of adolescence are recent enought to be recalled, but distant enough to be viewed with a certain objectivity. Fully three-fourths of these students reported that they had fairly clear political views while still in high school, and it can be assumed that the effects of adolescent rebellion on their political beliefs are now largely complete.

There were 824 males and 616 females in the sample. Since the relations of males and females to their mothers and fathers are somewhat different—especially in psychoanalytic theory, but also in terms of culturally defined relations between the sexes—we have considered the sexes separately throughout the analysis.

Each student was asked how close he was to each of his parents (response categories: "Very close," "Fairly close," "Not very close," and "Hostile"). If a parent died early in a child's life, lack of closeness is hardly indicative of rebellion, nor is the parent likely to have had a significant influence on the child's political views. When examining the personal nexus between parent and child in relation to political rebellion, therefore, we have excluded those cases in which the parent died before the child entered high school.

In order to measure political views, each respondent was presented with a set of five political categories and asked:

"Which of these political positions is closest to your own views?"

1. Socialist
2. Highly liberal
3. Moderately liberal
4. Moderately conservative
5. Highly conservative
6. I have no political views

Extensive pretesting indicated that this set of categories was meaningful to American college students, involving as it does an extremely simple left-to-right continuum, and few students experienced any difficulty in characterizing their views in terms of the categories. At the same time, this approach avoided some of the knotty methodological problems involved in the use of political party affiliation or attitudes on substantive political issues as indexes of political position.[11]

To determine whether or not the student was deviating from his parents' political views, he was also asked to use the same categories to characterize the views of his mother and his father. In many cases the students' perceptions of their parents' views may have been incorrect. Yet it is precisely the perceived rather than the actual views of the parent that are of crucial importance in the present study. As the Thomas theorem states, "If men define situations as real, they are real in their consequences."

For purposes of this study a student was defined as a political rebel if he placed himself to the left or right of his parent. If the student agreed with his parent, had no political views, or simply remained unaware of the views of his parent, he was considered a non-rebel.

Each student was asked, "How close are (were) you to your father?" and "How close are (were) you to your mother?" Further, in a question patterned after that used by Maccoby, Matthews, and Morton, we asked each student to report on the strictness of his parents' discipline: "When you were in high school, did your parents want to have quite a lot to say about your friends and the places you went and so on, or were you pretty much on your own?" (Response categories: "Parents had a lot to say," "Parents had an average amount to say," and "Parents left me pretty much on my own.")

As a rough index of generalized rebellion against the parent, each student was asked: "When you were in high school, how often did you defy your parents and do things contrary to their instructions or wishes?"

Finally, each student was asked how much interest he thought each of his parents took in political matters. Parents were classified as interested in politics if the student reported that they were very much interested or moderately interested most of the time. If the student believed that they were only slightly interested or not at all interested, they were classified as not interested in politics. Once again, it is the student's perception of his parent that might influence the pattern of his rebellion, not necessarily the actual views or interests of the parents.

The X^2 test of significance was applied throughout the analysis, and the rejection level for the null hypothesis was set at .05.

Findings

As shown in Table 1, approximately half the students hold political views different from those they attribute to their fathers, and nearly half hold political views different from those they attribute to their mothers. Male students are more likely than female students to deviate from the political views of their fathers and also from those of their mothers, and these tendencies are statistically significant beyond the .05 level ($P < .001$).

Thus our findings indicate that divergence from parental political views, as measured by our categories, is fairly common, especially among male students. The question remains as to how much of this difference between viewpoints can be attributed to the nature of parent-child relationships. If deviation from parental political viewpoints is motivated by rebellion against the parents, it might be expected that those students who have a history of conflict with the parents would deviate more often than those who do not. In Table 2, the students who report that they defied their parents often or very often while in high school are compared to those who report that they did so only occasionally or rarely. Except in the case of male students in relation to their mothers (where there is no difference), those who report frequent defiance deviate from the parental political viewpoints more often than those who do not. However, the differences observed in the sample

Table 1

Per Cent Rebelling from Political Views of Parents, by Sex of Student and Parent

	From Position of Father		From Position of Mother	
	Per Cent	*N*	Per Cent	*N*
Male students	54	781	49	812
Female students	42	584	38	605
Total	49	1,365	45	1,417

Table 2

Relation of Defiance of Parental Wishes While in High School to Political Rebellion, by Sex

	Per Cent	*N*
	Rebelling from Political Views of Father	
Male students:		
Defied parents often or very often	56	130
Defied parents occasionally or rarely	53	650
Female students:		
Defied parents often or very often	48	71
Defied parents occasionally or rarely	41	515
	Rebelling from Political Views of Mother	
Male students:		
Defied parents often or very often	49	135
Defied parents occasionally or rarely	49	678
Female students:		
Defied parents often or very often	44	73
Defied parents occasionally or rarely	37	533

are small, and none are significant at the .05 level. It might, nevertheless, be expected that when the parents of defiant students were interested in politics, there would be markedly more political rebellion than when the parents were indifferent to political issues. However, when the data are broken down according to the degree of perceived parental interest in politics, no consistent pattern emerges, and no statistically significant relationships are found. Our data thus lend little support to the contention that political rebellion is related to a generalized rebellion against the parents, and are consistent with Lane's contention that generalized rebellion in America is likely to be expressed primarily in non-political terms.

Nevertheless, political rebellion might occur under particular circumstances. Following Maccoby, Matthews, and Morton, we therefore examined the relation of parental discipline to political deviation (Table 3). In every case, there is a maximum of political rebellion in students who perceive their parents as having imposed strict discipline. Moreover, we find (as did Maccoby, Matthews, and Morton) that those who perceive their parents' discipline as average are least likely to rebel politically (except in the case of males in relation to their mothers). However, the association between political rebellion and parental discipline is significant at the .05 level only for females ($P < .01$ for rebellion against the father's political views and $P < .02$ for rebellion against the mother's political views). Moreover, the percentages do not differ sufficiently to suggest that parental discipline is generally a decisive factor in determining whether or not the student deviates from the political views of the parents.

Discipline, however, is likely to influence the degree of closeness between parent and child. Accordingly, we examined the relation between the student's perceptions of his parents' discipline and his degree of closeness with his parents (Table 4). The relationship revealed is non-linear, with those students who regard their parents' discipline as average having stronger emotional ties than those who regard it as either strict or permissive. All of the

relationships are significant at the .05 level ($P < .001$ for male students in relation to their fathers, and $P < .01$ for the other three). This finding may explain why Maccoby, Matthews, and Morton found a maximum of political conformity among those young people who perceived their parents' discipline as average. These are the young people who are likely to be closest to their parents, and if nexus to parents is related to political conformity, there would thus be an indirect relationship between discipline and political rebellion. It must first be established, however, that closeness between parent and child is related to political conformity.

In general, there is a linear relationship between parent-child nexus and conformity to parental political views (Table 5). The associations are significant at the .05 level, except in the case of male students in relation to their mothers where it is non-linear and not significant. The factor of parental interest in politics needs to be explored, however, inasmuch as politics is a relatively pointless instrument of rebellion unless it is of some importance to the parents.

Accordingly, the factor of perceived parental interest in politics is introduced into the examination of the relationship between parent-child closeness and political rebellion (Table 6). When the student perceives his parent as not interested in politics, no consistent relationship emerges between closeness to the parent and political rebellion, and none of the comparisons are statistically significant at the .05 level. When the student perceives his parent as interested in politics, however, a linear relationship is observed in all cases between political rebellion and estrangement of the

Table 3

Relation of Perceived Strictness of Parental Discipline to Political Rebellion, by Sex

	Strict Discipline		Average Discipline		Permissive Discipline	
	Per Cent	*N*	*Per Cent*	*N*	*Per Cent*	*N*
Rebelling from political views of father:						
Male students	56	97	53	379	54	304
Female students	55	104	36	315	46	166
Rebelling from political views of mother:						
Male students	53	102	50	393	47	318
Female students	49	106	34	331	40	168

Table 4

Relation of Perceived Strictness of Parental Discipline to Closeness of Relation with Parent, by Sex

	Strict Discipline		Average Discipline		Permissive Discipline	
	Per Cent	*N*	*Per Cent*	*N*	*Per Cent*	*N*
Feel close to father:						
Male students	73	97	86	379	70	304
Female students	73	104	83	315	70	166
Feel close to mother:						
Male students	87	102	94	392	88	317
Female students	85	106	94	331	86	167

Table 5

Relation of Closeness to Parent to Political Rebellion, by Sex

	PER CENT OF STUDENTS REBELLING FROM POLITICAL POSITION OF PARENTS			
	Father		Mother	
	Per Cent	*N*	*Per Cent*	*N*
Male student:				
Very close to parent	46	210	46	311
Fairly close to parent	56	399	53	424
Not very close or hostile to parent	57	172	47	77
Female students:				
Very close to parent	37	205	34	333
Fairly close to parent	43	249	41	211
Not very close or hostile to parent	50	130	49	61

Table 6

Relation of Closeness to Parent to Political Rebellion by Interest of Parent in Politics, and by Sex

	PER CENT OF STUDENTS REBELLING FROM POLITICAL POSITION OF PARENT							
	Father				Mother			
	Interested in Politics		Not Interested in Politics		Interested in Politics		Not Interested in Politics	
	Per Cent	N	Per Cent	N	Per Cent	N	Per Cent	N
Male students:								
Very close to parent	44	165	53	45	50	165	40	146
Fairly close to parent	57	263	54	136	63	165	56	259
Not very close or hostile to parent	63	80	53	92	74	19	38	58
Female students:								
Very close to parent	35	188	53	17	36	214	32	119
Fairly close to parent	44	193	38	56	40	108	42	103
Not very close or hostile to parent	58	76	39	54	50	22	49	39

student and his parent. Three of these four relationships are significant beyond the .05 level ($P < .01$ for male students and fathers, $P < .01$ for female students and fathers, and $P < .05$ for male students and mothers).

Conclusions

The data thus support our basic hypothesis that deviation from parental political viewpoints is associated with estrangement between parent and child —if the parent is interested in politics. This finding is consistent with Lane's contention that parental indifference to politics inhibits adolescent political rebellion. In general, the association between estrangement and rebellion is more marked in relation to fathers than in relation to mothers, perhaps because enough of the traditional male predominance in politics remains to render the

father's political views a more obvious basis for rebellion than those of the mother.

Our data, moreover, generally support the conclusions of Maccoby, Matthews, and Morton (as against those of Nogee and Levin) that deviation from parental political views is related to the kind of discipline experienced in the home. However, the associations observed are not extremely high, a point consistent with Hyman's contention that political attitudes in America are not in general generated by adolescent rebellion.

Some caution should be observed in imputing a causal relationship to the associations observed between impairment of parent-child relationships and deviations from parental political views. Rebellion against the parent, arising from strained parent-child relationships, may provoke political deviation. But it may also be the case that political deviation arising from factors unrelated to the parent may be the source of alienation between parent and child. For example, one of our subjects reports that he and his father have drifted apart in large measure because he acquired different political views while attending college. When he visits home he and his father now become involved in bitter arguments over political questions, although once they were fairly close. Here the causal sequence seems clearly reversed.

One unexpected finding adds another dimension to the picture of political attitudes and parent-child relationships. Our data disclose a positive relationship between parental interest in politics and closeness of the student to the parent. In fact this tendency of students to feel closer to parents who are interested in politics is significant well beyond the .001 level in all four relationships: father and son, father and daughter, mother and son, and mother and daughter. Any interpretation of this finding is necessarily ex post facto, but a plausible explanation would be that there is a relation between frequent and rewarding parent-child communication and the student's perception of the parent as interested in politics. In many cases of alienation between parent and child there may be too little communication for the student to perceive clearly his parents' political interests, whereas when the parent and child are close, communication of political viewpoints may be facilitated.

In any case, our data suggest that, while some students express rebellion against their parents in political terms, many, if not most, do not. Family relationships are an influence on political attitudes, as Lasswell suggested, but many other factors, including education, reference groups outside the home, mass media, and perhaps even rational evaluation of issues, may influence political beliefs.

NOTES

1. Harold D. Lasswell, *Psychopathology and Politics* (Chicago: University of Chicago Press, 1930), p. 153.

2. Kingsley Davis, "The Sociology of Parent-Youth Conflict," *American Sociological Review*, V (August, 1940), 523–35; Kingsley Davis, "Adolescence and Social Structure," *Annals of the American Academy of Political and Social Science*, CCXXXVI (November, 1944), 8–15; Ernest A. Smith, *American Youth Culture* (Glencoe, Ill.: Free Press, 1962); Florence Kluckhohn and John P. Spiegel, *Integration and Conflict in Family Behavior* (Group for the Advancement of Psychiatry, Report No. 27 [Topeka, August, 1954]); P. Blos, *The Adolescent Personality* (New York: Appleton-Century-Crofts, Inc., 1941); Ruth Benedict, "Continuities and Discontinuities in Cultural Conditioning," in Clyde Kluckhohn and H. A. Murray (eds.), *Personality in Nature, Society and Culture* (New York: Alfred A. Knopf, Inc., 1955), pp. 522–31. For a variant view, however, see Frederick Elkin and W. A. Westley, "Myth of Adolescent Culture," *American Sociological Review*, XX (December, 1955), 580–84, and William A. Westley and Frederick Elkin, "The Protective Environment and Adolescent Socialization," *Social Forces*, XXXV (March, 1957), 243–49.

3. See Herbert H. Hyman, *Political Socialization* (Glencoe, Ill.: Free Press, 1959), pp. 51–68, and Robert E. Lane, *Political Life: Why People Get Involved in Politics* (Glencoe, Ill.: Free Press, 1959), p. 217.

4. Margaret Mead, *Coming of Age in Samoa* (New York: William Morrow & Co., 1928); Margaret Mead, "Adolescence in Primitive and in Modern Society," in Eleanor E. Maccoby, T. M. Newcomb, and E. L. Hartley (eds.), *Readings in Social Psychology*, (3rd ed.; New York: Henry Holt & Co., 1958), pp. 341–49; and Yehudi A. Cohen, "'Adolescent Conflict' in a Jamaican Community," in *Social Structure and Personality* (New York: Holt, Rinehart & Winston, 1961), pp. 167–82.

5. Talcott Parsons, "Psychoanalysis and the Social Structure," in *Essays in Sociological Theory* (rev. ed.; Glencoe, Ill.: Free Press, 1954), pp. 336–47.

6. Hyman, *op. cit.*, p. 72.

7. Robert E. Lane, "Fathers and Sons: Foundations of Political Belief;" [in this volume, pp. 119–131 (ed.)].

8. *Ibid.*, p. 510.

9. Eleanor E. Maccoby, Richard E. Matthews and Anton S. Morton, "Youth and Political Change," *Public Opinion Quarterly*, XVIII (Spring, 1954), 23–39.

10. Philip Nogee and M. B. Levin, "Some Determinants of Political Attitudes among College Voters," *Public Opinion Quarterly*, XXII (Winter, 1958–1959), 463.

11. For a detailed discussion of the problems of measuring variations in political views and the rationale for the particular categories we have selected, see Russell Middleton and Snell Putney, "Student Rebellion against Parental Political Beliefs" (paper presented at the annual meeting of the Southern Sociological Society, Louisville, Kentucky, April 3, 1962, to be published in *Social Forces*).

PARENTAL ATTITUDES AND BEHAVIORS AS DETERMINANTS OF CHILDREN'S RESPONSES TO THE THREAT OF NUCLEAR WAR*

- Lawrence S. Wrightsman

Why are some American children more fearful about the possibilities of nuclear war than other children? What are some of the causes of their fears? Can these fears be related to family influences and to the children's personalities?

This research is an attempt to determine if certain family influences and children's personality characteristics are related to children's fears about nuclear war. Common-sense speculation, as well as a large quantity of research evidence (*Campbell*, 1958; *Newcomb and Svehla*, 1937) would imply that one of the major contributors to a child's attitudes is the family in which he lives; parents are necessarily imitated and used as sources of information and orientation by the child. Although the child's attitude is often not a direct and recognizable facsimile of the parents' attitude, it should show some relationship to that of the parents. Such relationship should exist for attitudes toward war and fears about war, just as they have been shown to exist for prejudices, voting preferences,

and religious attitudes. Therefore it is hypothesized that the extent of a child's fears about nuclear war will be related to how much his parents worry about war and to how much they discuss at home the possibilities of war.

A second source of a child's fears about war should be his own personality dynamics. *Collins and Wrightsman* (1962), whose subjects were some of the junior-high school boys used in the present study, have shown that general personality maladjustment is related to such diverse attributes as dissatisfaction with one's self-concept, aggressiveness, and unfavorable views of human nature. It may be reasoned that maladjustment may be related to fears about war because the maladjusted boy, according to the previous study, admits to his own hostile feelings and projects unfavorable characteristics onto others. Given this Weltanschauung, he sees in his expectations about a war a justification and proof of his views. It is therefore hypothesized that children's fears about nuclear war will be related to the extent of their personality maladjustment.

Method

Subjects (*Ss*) of this study were the 72 boys in the seventh and eighth grades of an elementary school in a town of 30,000 in Tennessee together with their parents. All the boys were white, and the majority came from middle-class homes.

Above selection reprinted from: *Vita Humana* 7 (1964), 178–185. Deletions have been made by the editor in the interest of brevity.

* Presented as a part of a symposium on Reactions of Children to Nuclear War and Related Threats, given at the annual meeting of the American Psychological Association, Philadelphia, August 1963.

The author wishes to thank the following persons for assistance in collection of the data: *Walter Collins, Susan W. Gray, Baxter Hobgood, Rupert Klaus,* and *Donna McMullen.*

Attitudes toward war were collected through the use of questionnaires which were constructed specifically for use in this study. The children's questionnaire consisted of questions dealing with the possibility of war (in the next year, the next five years, the next 10 years, and the next 20 years), the number of people who would be killed, who would start and who would win the war, how one would feel about being a soldier in the war, and how much one worried about the possibilities of war. The parents' questionnaire contained some of the same questions—those dealing with the possibilities of war at varying times and the extent one worries about the possibilities of war. Additional questions on the parents' questionnaire dealt with the desirability of fallout shelters and the extent to which the family talked about war. All the questions on both forms of the questionnaire could be answered by circling a response; there were no open-ended questions.

The boys filled out their questionnaires during class in May 1963. The parents were mailed their questionnaires over a month later, and were asked to return them in the enclosed stamped envelope. Because of the time interval between administration of the children's and parents' questionnaires, it is felt that the chance of direct influence in filling them out was minimized. A total of 49 sets of parents (or 68%) returned the questionnaires.

A year previously, as part of another study (*Collins and Wrightsman*, 1962), 60 of the boys in this study had been administered a variety of paper-and-pencil measures of personality and attitudes. Among these were the following:

1. The Buss Hostility Scale (*Buss*, 1961), an inventory measuring aggressiveness in various areas.

2. Bi-polar ratings of 20 personality characteristics. *S*s rated themselves as they were and as they would like to be. A self-ideal discrepancy score (S-ID), as a measure of dissatisfaction with present self-concept, was derived from the self ratings.

3. A modified form of the Philosophy of Human Nature Scale (*Wrightsman*, 1963), a Likert-type scale dealing with positive and negative aspects of human nature, as revealed by such characteristics as trustworthiness, altruism, etc.

These instruments were administered to small groups of students by a person not connected with the school system. Care was taken that each student understood the meaning of each item.

Results

First, consideration will be given to some of the findings from the children's questionnaire. The children were almost unanimous in their answers to some of the questions. For example, of the 72 children, only 5 felt that America, rather than Russia, would start a war; only 4 felt that Russia would win, and only 2 reported that they would be happy if we got into a war with Russia.

Expectations about the possibility of war in the future were more varied. No one expected a war in the next year, but 22 (31%) expected a war within 5 years, 34 (47%) expected war within 10 years, and 50 (70%) expected war within 20 years.

The extent of worry about the possibility of war also revealed individual differences. Table 1 indicates the number and percentage of children responding to each alternative. The most frequent responses were to say one worries "some" or "very little" (73%); but almost 20% admitted that they worried about war "a lot" or "all the time." About 7% stated that they "never" worried about war.

To test the first hypothesis, parents' responses were compared with those of their children. (Since few children selected the extreme categories regarding worry over war, in the analysis answers falling in the 2 extreme categories were combined with answers in the next categories.)

Table 2 presents information about the extent that parents talk about war and the extent to which children say they worry about war. There is a definite relationship ($X^2 = 15.49$, $p < 0.01$), with families who discuss war more frequently being more likely to have children who fear war.

Table 3 relates parents' expectations regarding war to the extent of their child's worry about war. Parents, like children, were asked whether they expected a war one year from now, 5 years, 10 years, and 20 years from now. The question ". . . 10 years from now"

was chosen for analysis because approximately 50% of the parents answered yes and 50% answered no. As can be seen in Table 3, there is a decided relationship between parents' expectations and and extent of their son's worries ($X^2 = 13.61$, $p < 0.01$). Of the children who worried "never" or "very little," 13 out of 15 had parents who did not expect war in 10 years. On the other hand, 11 of the 12 children who worried "a lot" or "all the time" had parents who expected war in 10 years.

Table 4 presents information about the relationship between extent of parents' worry and extent of their child's worry. Again there is a clearcut relationship in the predicted direction ($X^2 = 16.05$, $p < 0.01$). Parents who

Table 1

Children's Responses to the Question: " Do you worry much about the possibilities of war?"

Response	N	% $(N = 72)$
I worry about war all the time	2	2.8%
I worry about it a lot	12	16.7%
I worry about it some	27	37.5%
I worry about it very little	26	36.1%
I never worry about it	5	6.9%
Total	72	100.0%

Table 2

Relationship between Family's Talking about War and Extent of Child's Worry about War

Family talks about war:	Child's response: I worry			Total
	Never or very little	*Some*	*A lot or all the time*	
Almost every day	0	0	4	4
Once a week or so	0	4	2	6
Once a month or so	7	11	6	24
Almost never	8	7	0	15
Total	15	22	12	49

$X^2 = 15.49$, p. < 0.01 (using Yates' correction).

Table 3

Relationship between Parents' Expectation of War within 10 years and Extent of Child's
Worry about War

	Child's response: I worry			
Parents' expectation	Never or very little	Some	A lot or all the time	Total
War within 10 years	2	12	11	25
No war within 10 years	13	10	1	24
Total	15	22	12	49

$X^2 = 13.61$, p. < 0.01 (using Yates' correction).

Table 4

Relationship between Extent of Parents' and Children's Worry about War

	Child's response: I worry			
Parents' response: We worry	Never or very little	Some	A lot or all the time	Total
A lot or all the time	0	2	4	6
Some	1	10	5	16
Never or very little	14	10	3	27
Total	15	22	12	49

$X^2 = 15.05$, p. < 0.01 (using Yates' correction).

reported worrying a lot about war tended to have children who reported worrying a lot, whereas parents who reported being unconcerned tended to have unconcerned children. Thus the first hypothesis—that children's fears about the possibilities of war are related to how much their parents worry about it and how much their parents discuss it —was confirmed.

The second hypothesis predicted a relationship between the extent of children's fears and personality maladjustment. To test this hypothesis, children were again categorized according to their response to the question dealing with the extent of their worry about the possibility of war.

Table 5 indicates that extent of worry about war was unrelated to any of the measures assessing personality maladjustment. None of the differences between groups for each variable were significantly different; and in the case of aggressiveness, the means did not follow the expected order. Hypothesis 2 was therefore not confirmed.

Discussion

These results appear to mean that parental attitudes and behavior are greater determinants of children's fears about nuclear war than are the children's personalities.

The findings about parental attitudes

Table 5

Mean Scores on Personality Measures for Children who Differ in Extent of Worry over War

Children who:	N	Aggressiveness	Mean score on: Self-ideal discrepancy	Unfavorable view of human nature
"Worry all the time or a lot"	11	38.4	24.2	19.1
"Worry some"	25	40.4	23.9	18.3
"Worry a little or never"	24	37.5	22.2	17.9

Significance of mean differences for each column were tested by Analysis of Variance. For each variable, mean differences were not significantly different.

and behavior are an extension of previous findings in this area; and a simple finding that children learn their attitudes from their parents is not earth-shaking. Perhaps what is surprising is the extent of this relationship. There were several reasons to have expected that any such hypothesized relationship would be attenuated: the questions were direct, easily-faked, and limited in the variety of available responses; and there was also a certain amount of subjectivity in the terms used, such as "worry some" and "possibilities of war in 10 years." Nevertheless, a very strong relationship emerged. This relationship, it should be emphasized, is between the verbal report of parents and the verbal report of their child. To be precise in our conclusions, we must always state that parents who *report* much worry about war tend to have children who *report* much worry. If one wished to be a devil's advocate, one might argue that what is common among family members is a response set, rather than a behavior. However, if any response set is present, it appears to be a response to worry or not to worry. Lack of relationship with the personality variables tends also to preclude the possibility of the operation of a response set.

The commonality between parents' and children's attitudes is due not only to the direct inculcation of the child by his parents—but also, probably, due to indirect influences, such as the newspapers allowed in the home, the television news commentators the parents choose to have the family watch, and the adult-age friends who visit the family. Thus, in effect, the parents "manage the news" unconsciously by exposing the child to a selected type of attitude.

There are several interpretations for the findings of the second hypothesis. The reasons why maladjustment was not found to be related to extent of worry over war may center around the methods used to assess maladjustment. Although these measures had been found in an earlier study to be related to each other and to teacher's ratings of maladjustment, they may not be as direct as measures of anxiety, external locus of control, or lack of ego strength. It is also possible that in the year's interim since the indicators of maladjustment were administered, the children changed radically. These measures of maladjustment appear to be relatively stable, however, and the time interval does not seem to be an acceptable explanation for the negative finding, although it may have reduced the possible relationship.

The next step in relating personality measures to fears about war would seem to be one which concentrates on variables conceptually similar to fear of war. Such measures as manifest anxiety, test anxiety, and guilt would be examples. Until then, it would appear that specific fears of war are unrelated to maladjustment.

o   o   o

REFERENCES

Buss, A. H.: *The psychology of aggression* (Wiley, New York, 1961).

Campbell, E. Q.: "Some psychological correlates of character in attitude change." *Soc. Forces* 36: 335–340 (1958).

Collins, W. E. and Wrightsman, L. S.: "*Indicators of maladjustment in adolescent and preadolescent boys.*" Paper delivered at American Psychological Association Convention, St. Louis, August 1962.

Newcomb, T. M. and Svelha, G.: "Intra family relationships in attitude." *Sociometry* 1: 180–205 (1937).

Wrightsman, L. S.: "*The measurement of philosophies of human nature.*" Paper delivered at Midwestern Psychological Association Convention, Chicago, May 1963.

PEYRANE AND THE OUTSIDE WORLD

- Laurence Wylie

When Madame Arène says, "They (*ils*) have raised the price of coffee on us again," she is not referring to the *ils* of the village, but to a more dangerous set of *ils*. She means the *ils* that threaten from beyond the limits of the commune. Of course, the *ils* within Peyrane are a nuisance, but since they are specific individuals whom one knows and sees every day, one can guard against them. The *ils* outside Peyrane are dangerous because they are anonymous, intangible and overpowering. Against the outside *ils* an individual has little defense, and yet from them come the greatest evils that beset the people of Peyrane: inflation, taxation, war, legal restrictions, administrative red tape. It is the outside *ils* who are blamed for raising the price of fertilizer, for forcing young men to spend eighteen months in the army, for preventing a farmer from planting as many wine grapes as he wishes, for taking a substantial portion of the family income in the form of taxes, for complicating existence with waiting-room queues and forms to be filled out.

The identity of the outside *ils* varies. The term may refer to Big Corporations or to Newspapers or to the *Syndicat d'Initiative d'Avignon*. It may refer to the French People or to the Americans or to the Russians or to People in general. Usually, however, it refers to the French Government in all its manifestations, for it is the Government which collects taxes, makes war, controls the wine production, and employs impersonal civil servants.

This attitude is in direct conflict with what the children are taught in school. In their civics books they read that the Government is simply the concrete manifestation of the State, which is the political personality of *la patrie*. They learn by heart such sentences as:

The French nation has a body formed by the soil and the men who live on it; a soul formed by the history, language, tradition, and symbols.

When men feel love for their nation it becomes a *patrie*.

The State is the nation organized and administered.

The Government is the directing organism of the State.

A good citizen always seeks to become educated. He respects the law, pays his taxes loyally, accepts the military obligation, and defends his *patrie* when it is threatened.

A good citizen possesses the spirit of coöperation and mutual aid.

Politics too often arouses distrust, disdain, and even disgust.

Politics should not be an excuse for furthering private interests and above all it should not unleash our passions.

Politics should be a great public service, the art of bringing about more justice and happiness among men."*

* These sentences are taken from the section entitled "Retenons par coeur" of chapters 26, 36, and 37 of Ballot and Aveille, *Education morale et civique. Classe de fin d'études* (Paris: Charles-Lavauzelle, 1952).

The children have no difficulty in accepting the concept of *la patrie*, for at home and throughout the village they hear *la patrie* spoken of only with love and respect. One of the most hallowed spots in the village is the *Monument to Those of Peyrane who Died in Defense of the Patrie*. Several times a year they see the men of the village temporarily forget their personal differences and march together to lay a wreath at the foot of the monument. The children know that France is a country favored above all others—"Sweet France" of the marvelous hexagonal shape. They know that the French language is the language of Civilization and that Civilized People everywhere consider France as their second *patrie*. Culturally, emotionally, geographically, aesthetically, the people of Peyrane feel they are an integral part of *la patrie*. They recognize also that officially, legally, statistically, they are a part of the State, which they respect but do not love.

Unfortunately, *la patrie* and the State must be translated into human terms, and it is at this point that the people of Peyrane refuse to accept the "beautiful sentences" of the civics textbook. Theoretically, Government may be an alter ego of *la patrie*, but in point of fact it is made up of men—weak, stupid, selfish, ambitious men. It is the duty of the citizen *not* to cooperate with these men, as the civics books would have people do, but rather to hinder them, to prevent them in every possible way from increasing their power over individuals and over families.

This is a point on which everyone in Peyrane would agree: a man with power over you is essentially evil. They readily admit that a man may be virtuous when he goes into politics, but they would deny that he can remain virtuous if he attains power. Except for a few supporters of the MRP, the voters of Peyrane say that the heads of their parties, and of all other political parties, are "a pile of bandits." Even people who are not in politics but in government administration are tainted by the corrupting force of power. They become insensitive to the feelings of others.

In preaching civic virtue to the school children, the authors of the civics book recognize that their precepts describe an ideal rather than an actual state of things. They warn:

Many honest and intelligent people, who could be the best guides in public life, avoid politics, and condemn it harshly.

1. Indeed, politics arouses much *distrust*. People avoid talking about it in family gatherings, in friendly professional or social groups. It is excluded from the army, which must remain impartial (*la grande muette*), and from the judiciary branch of the government. It must be kept out of school. This phrase is almost always found in the constitutions of clubs and societies: "All political and religious discussions are formally forbidden." Thus, distrust seems general.

2. The *disdain* in which politics is held is no less great. "Politics is a specialty which I am willing to leave to the specialists," says the writer Georges Duhamel. Thus he expresses the *disdain* which many intellectuals feel for what one of them calls "the housework of the nation."

3. Hence the *distaste* for politics and for politicians who are often portrayed as men of little morality, of slight merit, incapable of making their way honestly and serving usefully.

The authors of the civics text then go on to preach a different and democratic ideal to the students, but in these paragraphs they have described the reality that the children have witnessed. They constantly hear adults referring to

Government as a source of evil and to the men who run it as instruments of evil. There is nothing personal in this belief. It does not concern one particular Government composed of one particular group of men. It concerns Government everywhere and at all times—French Governments, American Governments, Russian Governments, all Governments. Some are less bad than others, but all are essentially bad.

Of course much of the talk against Government and politicians must not be taken too seriously. People do not mean all they say. They recognize the necessity of government, and on a rational level they recognize the necessity of a certain amount of civic spirit. However, when they are confronted by the frustrations caused by these outside *ils*, they fulminate against them. The outside *ils* are like the weather: they are necessities which one must accept, because "that's the way it is." It makes a person feel better to curse the weather and to curse the outside *ils*. We should be naïve to take much of the cursing seriously, but still we should be equally naïve to ignore the cursing. The hostility toward government is real and it is deep.

o   o   o

In 1945, when Peyrane was liberated along with the rest of France, the chief of the local *maquis*, Raoul Chanon, took over the government of the commune. A few hours afterward he received a telegram from the departmental *Comité d'épuration* saying: "Arrest the following collaborators—Barbier (Notaire and Vichy Mayor), Viquier (Town Clerk and Légionnaire), Allibert (owner of ochre mines), Reynard (the principal grocer), Baume (owner of the bus and taxi), Bonerandi (the baker), Marnas,

Anselme, Sanape, Laplace, Massot, and Arnoux (the last six among the wealthiest farmers).

When Chanon read the telegram he did not hesitate. He tore it into pieces and said, "Nous réglons nos affaires en famille!"

No act and no phrase could have more completely captivated the people of Peyrane. I heard this story from many sources, from Communists on the Left and from the intended victims, Barbier and Reynard, on the Right. Regardless of what people thought of Chanon's role in the resistance, and regardless of what people thought of him as a farmer, as a businessman, as a husband, he became the village hero. By his action he had defied what then seemed to be the Government, and he had gotten away with it. He had thumbed his nose at the worst of the *ils*. He had asserted the right of the people of Peyrane to manage their own affairs. He had given expression to their feeling that in spite of all the squabbles (or because of them?) Peyrane is one big family, composed of individuals who disagree among themselves, but who unite when faced by a common enemy threatening from outside.

This feeling of unanimity is in reality only a vague emotion which disappears if an attempt is made to translate it into action. People agree that war, inflation, taxation, restrictions, and red tape are evil, and they agree that Governments are largely responsible for them. They agree that Government and the men who run Government are essentially evil because they have power over individuals and over families. They agree that individuals and families should be protected against Government, but at this point action rather than feeling is required, and when action is required, unanimity disappears. Just how to make Government, the necessary evil, function so as not to crush the individual and his family, so as to help them if possible, is a question on which disagreement within the community is extreme and bitter.

Thus political bitterness is more than an effect of people's disagreement. It is also a cause for their not getting along together. The existence of party labels gives them the opportunity of blaming on each other not just the evils that arise from living together but also the evils that threaten from without.

When the price of coffee goes up, Pouget can blame it on "Reynard and people like him who vote for men who help Big Business rob us little men." Reynard, on the other hand, blames the high taxes on "people like the Pougets who live like animals, have lots of children, then vote for politicians who pay them to have still more children—paying them out of the pockets of 'decent' people (like Reynard, that is) who have only two children."

o   o   o

AN EXPLORATION INTO SOME ASPECTS OF POLITICAL SOCIALIZATION: SCHOOL CHILDREN'S REACTIONS TO THE DEATH OF A PRESIDENT[1]

- Roberta S. Sigel

o   o   o

When, . . . an event is of crisis or pseudo-crisis dimensions, it is a particularly propitious setting in which to study political socialization. A political crisis is by definition a situation in which existing norms or values are under attack. It thus affords an opportunity to test how firmly children share in the adult political consensus and how much they have internalized the norms of the existing political order, i.e., how politically socialized they have become.

The study we are about to report is an attempt to look at a political and national crisis—the events of the November 22, 1963, weekend—as it looked from the point of view of school children.[2] The tragic events of that weekend tested first a child's understanding of and feeling for the Presidency in general and the murdered President in particular and hence pertained to children's relation to a crucial part of American political authority. The murder of Oswald, on the other hand, tested their understanding of American norms of justice, the rights of other people, due

process, etc. The complexity of the events provided clues to both children's attitudes toward authority and their comprehension of American norms and principles of political conduct, thereby testing their socialization in two different spheres (which are really two different levels): understanding of the more personalized aspects of political institutions (as symbolized in the Presidency) and understanding of the more de-personalized, conceptual aspects. Responses to these two aspects of socialization can be used to test: 1.) the nature and stability of the child's faith in political authority, and 2.) the child's attachment to and understanding of abstract principles. Taken together the responses constitute a partial index of socialization into American political norms.

o   o   o

[To the American child the most visible political authority figure is the President, who is usually seen as benevolent, competent, and powerful. The tendency of children to idealize the President was interpreted by some researchers as a sign that the child saw him either as a father or as an ideal father. This was the reasoning originally adopted by Hess and Easton (ed.).]

image of the President [is] an extension or transfer of the image of the father to other authority figures in the child's perceptual world. If this is a valid hypothesis, we would expect that the image of the father and of the President would be highly congruent.[3]

The data, however, do not show any such clear-cut congruence. In a later paper Hess . . . offers

an alternative explanation [which] is that the child is not projecting onto the President the image he has of his own father but that of the ideal father of his culture.[4]

He continues:

In the United States the highly benign, even nurturant image of the President is congruent with the image of the paternal role which, in the United States, greatly overlaps that of the mother in expressive and nurturant components.[5]

Even the alternative explanation, however, seems to us most tenuous because it assumes that political figures are a source of personal identification for individuals. Observation of the American scene does not permit such assumption. The explanation also seems untenable because it does not sufficiently consider the role of social class. If familial experience, especially with the father, determined the child's view of authority, we would expect to find great variance in the political imagery of children of different social backgrounds. One of the marked class differences in the United States is in patterns of child rearing and the degrees of authoritarianism of the father.[6] If the nature of the child-father relationship predetermined the child's image of the Presidency, the image should show variability from class to class. Yet in the studies cited no very pronounced differences were discovered. This suggests that something other than

family and father must contribute heavily to the child's image of the Presidency.

An examination of the Chicago and the Greenstein data, as well as our own, indicates that the school is probably one of the important contributors to the child's image of political authority (witness the high number of children who know the President's name, can identify Presidents of history, etc.). And most school texts and children's books do not contain much about Presidents that is critical; on the contrary, they are designed to increase pride in our Presidents and our history.[7]

The wider American political culture also tends to bolster faith in our officials. Americans in general seem neither overawed by public officials nor concerned about whether chosen officials are competent to discharge the job entrusted to them. Presidents and presidential candidates especially are usually judged to be competent to handle the job even by those who do not intend to or did not vote for them.[8]

Whatever people may think of minor politicians, they apparently prefer to believe that the nominees for the highest office in the land are worthy men.[9]

All this plus the fact that in the United States politics has low tension and adults view government as worthy of trust,[10] may well explain why neither home nor school is apt to undermine a child's faith in his President.

The President, being far away, enjoys an added advantage over local authority figures: the child has no opportunity to check against reality the idealized image taught him by the adult world. Whereas the child may soon learn from personal experience that the policeman at the corner or the librarian in the public library are at times less friendly and helpful than their portraits on the illustrated pages of such children's books as *Our Friend the Policeman* and *Community Helpers*, few children have an opportunity to compare the real President with the one discussed in school and books. Under these circumstances we suggest that the idealized image the child has of the President is a function of: 1.) school learning and indoctrination; 2.) the absence of traumatic experiences with political authority, especially on the national level; 3.) the political culture which is generally optimistic and trusts government; and 4.) the absence of any personal observation which might indicate that the President would *not* be benign. These four alternate explanations do not deny that political orientaiton may also be rooted in psychological needs and/or experiences but they take the discussion out of the realm of the exclusively psychological and place it in a cultural, political, and experiential context.

A composite image of the President, as seen by school children, would probably be of a man occupying the most prestigious profession known to a child, a man who is judged to be very competent, hard-working, well informed, with a tremendous amount of power; a man who cares a great deal about people, wants to help them and to protect them. Although seen as powerful, he is not seen as punitive, particularly not by older children of upper social status.[11]

Scope of Our Study

Given the fact that a child has such an idealized image of the President and sees in him the benevolent leader who protects child and country, how would we expect the child to react to the news of his assassination? No firm hypothesis seems warranted because little systematic data exists as yet on the ways adults or children cope with death and bereavement in general.[12] Even less is known of

the generalized massive bereavement which occurs at the death of certain public figures, such as kings, presidents or entertainment idols like Valentino. One can perhaps assume that the bereavement in these situations is qualitatively different from that experienced by close relatives, yet it is nevertheless genuine.[13]

In view of the general lack of knowledge, we shall not attempt to formulate rigorous hypotheses but rather restrict ourselves to a few assumptions, some of which we will be able to test.

Assumptions

Since the President is such an important figure to the child, and since the young child relates to government through the person of the President rather than the Congress, the court, or the law, we would expect that:

1. The child would conceive of the President's death as a threat to his own security. Because he tends to think of adult authority as steady, firm, nurturant, and nearly unassailable, the President's death would lead the child, and especially the very young child, to worry greatly about either the future of the country or his personal safety or that of the group to which he belongs. Great worry that the country's safety depends on the "leader," we would therefore interpret as a sign of incomplete political socialization because it

indicates that the child has not yet learned to separate the institutions of government (in this case the Presidency) from the persons who occupy the governmental positions.

2. The more the child identifies the President as a person who meets his needs, the more he identifies with him, the more upset and worried we would expect him to be. Thus we would expect children who identify themselves as Democrats to have been more upset than Republicans, and Negroes (irrespective of party) to have been more upset than whites.

3. Since the death was brought on by such a wanton act as assassination, the child's image of the omnipotence of personal political authority (such as the President's) would be altered—he would think of the President as somewhat less powerful.

4. Because an assassination is an assault on political authority, because it is a departure from the political norms on which they had begun to rely, we would expect children to react to it with shock, horror, and sadness, and the overt behavioral manifestations associated with such emotions, as, for example, weeping, loss of appetite and sleep, occasional headaches, etc.

5. Because of the grief, shock, and fears resulting from the experience, and because of the love and admiration that children have for the Presidency, we would expect them to portray anger, hostility, and aggressive feelings toward the person who caused the loss to the child. We would expect children at times to give vent to these feelings in wishes for revenge and punitive treatment of the perpetrator of the misdeed. This we would expect particularly among younger children, and we would

predict that these feelings of anger and hostility would become most visible in their reaction to the murder of Oswald. We would predict that they would be far less concerned over the wrong done to Oswald. We base this assumption on the knowledge that notions such as due process of law, "every man is entitled to a fair trial," etc. are rather abstract notions acquired only with increasing maturity. Another reason why they would show less concern is that children recoil less than adults from the use of violence and aggression. Mastery of aggressive impulses is one of the primary tasks the developing organism has to learn.

Within the confines of this chapter it will not be possible to test all of the above assumptions, or to undertake the detailed developmental comparisons such an analysis requires. We shall have to restrict ourselves here to a preliminary investigation into the nature of political socialization by performing three types of analyses:

1. A comparison of adult and children's reactions to the assassination, on the assumption that the greater the similarity between adults' and children's responses, the more children have partaken of the general political consensus. Since we operate from the premise that political socialization is a developmental process, we will compare children's reactions at different age levels to see if they do indeed change with age.

2. A partial investigation of children's attitudes toward the Presidency. Here we are particularly interested in discovering whether or not children's views of the omnipotence and/or benevolence of the President suffered as a result of the events of November 22. We entertain the possibility that children will report

slightly less idealized images of the Presidency, especially in its power aspects, than they had previously. If a President can be killed that easily, children might argue, he is not all that powerful. Self-defense might then dictate that it would be wise for the child to minimize the President's importance. This analysis will also permit us to inquire once again into children's views of the Presidency. If children should turn out to have been noticeably more indifferent to the President's death than were adults, then, obviously, the President plays a less crucial role in the political world of children than had generally been assumed. His death therefore constituted no threat.

3. An exposition of children's understanding of some fundamental aspects of the American system of justice. The way children reacted to the murder of Oswald would offer us insights into the extent to which they understand such concepts as due process, justice, etc. The idea that so heinous an act as the murder of a President could be avenged by the murder of the assassin should not be uncongenial to young children, especially since they see justice of this type meted out almost daily on their favorite TV shows. The more a child rejects the idea of Ruby's deed and the more he can conceptualize the need for due process and justice, the more he presumably has become politically socialized.

Methodology

To perform the above analysis a written questionnaire was administered to 1349 primary and secondary school children in Metropolitan Detroit within a twenty-one day period after the assassination.

The urgency to move in immediately was modified only by the time required to make the necessary arrangements with school officials. While some pretesting was undertaken, ample pretesting was foregone in the interest of administering the questionnaire while the impact of the event was close to its maximum in the minds of children. A cross section of the Metropolitan Detroit school population is represented in the sample. Care was taken to have adequate representation of lower-class, working-class, middle-class, and also upper-class children and to have a sizable sample of Negro as well as white children. Three private schools were included along with ten public schools in order to get a genuinely upper-class sample. (For an exact breakdown of the sample, see Chart I, page 157.) All the 1349 children were within the normal school population; we did not use any classes with disturbed, gifted, handicapped, or otherwise exceptional children. There were approximately the same number of children for each grade, and a good representation of social class and race in each grade as well.

For grades six and up the questionnaire administrator introduced the questionnaire briefly, stating that its aim was to explore children's reactions to certain public events and that it was in no way related to their school standing. They were assured of the complete anonymity of their answers, and their teachers were not in the room while the questionnaire was given. Children were urged to answer the questions without concern about how parents or teachers might want them to answer them but rather to write down or check off how they really felt at that particular moment. The children then went ahead to

Chart I

Composition of Sample

	Number	Per Cent
Boys	629	47
Girls	720	53
White	1006	74
Negro	342	26
Oriental	1	—
Grade 4	264	20
6	281	21
8	339	25
10	249	19
12	216	16
Children in lower-class schools	373	28
middle-class schools	644	48
private, upper-class schools	332	25
Children with working-class fathers	580	43
Children with white collar fathers (service trades, clerical and sales help)	225	17
Children with fathers owning businesses or in managerial positions	249	19
Children with fathers in the professions	182	13
Children who don't know father's occupation	113	8

answer the questions. They were helped with the reading of questions and spelling of answers if they requested such assistance.

For children in the fourth grade the introduction was the same, but the questionnaire was then read aloud to them item by item, and the children followed along answering each item as it was read. Care was taken to make sure that each child answered each question. Several graduate and advanced undergraduate student assistants were available in the room to help the children with reading and spelling.

The questionnaire consisted of 71 items, some open-ended, some check-off items, and a few matching items. Nine items came from a Hess-Easton study; 17 items from a national survey conducted by NORC (National Opinion Research Center) one week after the assassination; and an additional 45 items were constructed by us.

The items repeated from the Hess-Easton instrument dealt with the President's role relevance and his place in the American system of representative government.[14] For the most part they were concerned with the President's competence to do his job, his responsiveness to people, and his general powerfulness. In repeating the items we used the phrasing of their pilot studies[15] rather than the scalelike format of their as yet unpublished national studies which offers six multiple choices to the child on each item. Most of the six scalelike choices portrayed the President in a favorable light when compared to others. We preferred the three-item choice not merely for simplicity's sake but because the existence of so many positive choices over negative ones on the Hess-Easton instrument might pressure the child toward choosing the highly positive items and thus have the effect of exaggerating the extent to which children actually place the President above other people in their esteem. Further, the absence of any neutral items precludes any casual reaction. Yet some children may well feel casual or neutral toward the President. But when forced to decide whether a President knows more or less than most people, without being able to put him on the same level as other people, what could we expect but that the average child would place him *above* other people? To guard against this forced idealization, we preferred the format containing the more neutral item. Proof that children did not indiscriminately flock to the neutral choice can be seen in the section on results, which shows that the moderate alternative was chosen for some items but clearly not for others.

The Hess and Easton items were utilized to see: 1.) how competent the President seemed in the child's eyes (knows more, etc.); 2.) how much children thought he cared about them ("If you write the President, he cares a lot what you think," etc.); and 3.) how powerful he seemed ("Who does the most to run the country?" etc.). It is with this last item that we will most concern ourselves here. A thoughtful analysis of children's image is well beyond the scope of this paper and will be attempted at a later time. For purposes of our analysis here we interpret a marked decrease in the power image of the Presidency as a sign that the assassination weakened children's faith in the President's powerfulness.

From the NORC check lists we repeated those items that probed into: 1.) people's intellectual and emotional reactions to the news of the assassination, and 2.) people's physical sensations or psychosomatic complaints following the news. In instances where the NORC language seemed quite adult to us we simplified it slightly, but the items remained essentially unchanged.

The 45 items we constructed were designed not only to get at children's immediate reactions to the death of the President, but to gain some insight into their conception of the Presidency, their image of the relation of the President to the general governmental structure, their understanding of American concepts of justice. We also inquired into the depth or shallowness of their political knowledge of a specific President (in this case Kennedy) and into their reactions to the TV coverage. Only three of these topics will be analyzed in this paper: children's views of the Presidency; their view of his relation to government in general; and their views of the Oswald/Ruby affair.

Wherever relevant the data were analyzed on the basis of grade in school, sex, race, and social status. Children's social status was determined by the father's occupation, not the school. We divided the sample into four groups:

1. blue collar trades (U.S. Census classification 4–9)
2. white collar trades, such as service trades, clerical, and sales (U.S. Census categories 1 and 2)
3. managerial and business (U.S. Census classification 0)
4. professional (for which the U.S. Census classification also is 0)

Where no refined social class breakdowns seemed warranted, we limited ourselves to the conventional breakdown into blue collar and white collar occupations.

Table 1

Comparison of Children's and Adults'* Reactions

Item	Adults (n = 1384)			Children (n = 1349)	
	Felt it deeply or very deeply	*Crossed mind*	*Never occurred to me*	*Felt that way*	*Did not feel that way*
Felt the loss of someone very close and dear	79%	9%	12%	71.417%	25.390%
Worried what would happen to our country	47	32	21	65.35	30.85
Worried what would happen to our relations with other countries	44	33	23	62.31	34.26
Felt so sorry for his wife and children	92	6	2	93.32	4.47
Felt worried how the U.S. would carry on without its leader	41	29	30	58.90	36.84
Felt angry that anyone should do such a terrible thing	73	14	13	81.95	14.85
Hoped the man who killed him would be shot or beat up	11	13	76	40.48	55.19
Felt ashamed that this could happen in our country	83	10	7	82.71	14.70
Was so confused and upset I didn't know what to feel	38	14	48	43.06	52.00
Felt in many ways it was the President's own fault	4	11	85	16.07	79.61
Hoped the next President would be better	—	—	—	35.55	58.76
I did not feel bad	—	—	—	13.26	80.97

* NORC Study SRS 350

Results and Discussion

I. Comparison of Children and Adult Reactions

The most interesting phenomenon is the similarity of adults and children in their emotional reactions, while at the same time they show pronounced differences in some of their political and quasi-political reactions and interpretations. Mourning and sadness encapsulated children and adults, testifying to the crucial role such a political figure plays in the lives of our children and indicating how far back into childhood the roots of political socialization reach. Table 1 clearly shows that grief, sympathy (for Mrs. Kennedy and the children), shame, and anger were the reactions most frequently given on the NORC items— given by well over two out of every three adults and children. The children's behavior was also strikingly similar to adults'. They report about the same incidence of headaches, loss of appetite, trouble going to sleep, etc. (See Table 1.) Interestingly enough, parents tended to underestimate the extent to which their children were upset. According to NORC 32 per cent thought children were "not upset at all," and only 23 per cent thought they were "very upset."

The index we developed for measuring children's emotional upset showed children to be considerably more upset, as we shall demonstrate later on. This is just one example of the difficulty one encounters when trying to measure feeling. It may also be an illustration of adults' tendency to minimize the extent to which children are capable of experiencing rather adult reactions.

Only in respect to crying do children distinguish themselves from adults. Children of all ages professed to have cried less than adults (39 per cent and 53 per cent respectively). (See Table 2.) Roughly four out of ten fourth-graders and twelfth-graders denied having cried. Boys of all ages denied it almost categorically. If we were to believe the children, 81 per cent of all the crying was done by girls. We refuse to believe our children and base this refusal on teachers' and parents' reports to the contrary.

The items developed by us, especially the open-ended ones, offer further insight into children's reactions. When asked to tell in their own words how they felt when they heard the news, over half (52 per cent) said they could not believe it. Shock and disbelief usually are the first reactions of a grief-stricken person. Sheatsley and Feldman regret not having asked this question because they think "it is probable that the response of disbelief was as prevalent as those of loss, sorrow, pity, shame, and anger."[16] We tend to agree with them. Sadness was the other frequently reported emotion (30 per cent said they felt sad or bad), while anger, shame, and disgust are mentioned by only a few children. Obviously, then, disbelief (shock) was the most salient emotion. Sixty per cent of the children and 53 per cent of the adults could not recall ever having felt that way before. Most of those children who did had experienced the death of a relative or friend or possibly of an animal. Unlike adults, they never mentioned a public event or the death of a public figure (a third of adults did). Death was thus related to in a very personalized fashion.

A word or two are in order here about the developmental pattern we observed in this context. Generally, we take it for granted that children behave more like adults as they increase in age. For example, Sheatsley and Feldman "presumed

Table 2

Behavior of Adults and Children During the Weekend

Symptom	Adults (n = 1384)*	Children (n = 1349) All children	By Grade				
			4	6	8	10	12
Didn't feel like eating	43%	37%	50%	38%	33%	35%	28%
Had headaches	25	22	33	26	17	19	16
Had an upset stomach	22	18	31	23	11	12	12
Cried	53	39	39	35	39	45	41
Had trouble getting to sleep	48	45	69	48	36	39	31

* NORC Study SRS 350

Table 3

Adults' and Children's Worry for the Nation

Item	Adults*	All Children	By Grade				
			4	6	8	10	12
Worried how the U.S. would get along without its leader. (NORC wording: "Worried how U.S. would carry on.")	41%	59%	76%	69%	59%	45%	41%
Worried what would happen to our country. (NORC wording: "Worried about future U.S. political situation.")	47	66	76	69	68	59	60
Worried what would happen to our relations with other countries. (NORC wording: "Worried about international situation.")	44	63	59	63	63	64	65

* This includes adults with the following response intensities:
1. Very deepest feelings; 2. Felt it quite deeply.
(NORC Study SRS 350)

that teenagers would react in much the same manner as adults . . . but [they] were curious about the emotions of the four-to-twelve age groups. . . ."[17] Working from this assumption, they failed to ask parents about teen-agers' reactions. If our data are any guide, their assumption was unwarranted in this instance. Teen-agers did not prove very similar to adults in their overt emotional reactions; instead we found that it was the younger children who behaved more like the adults. The frequency with which somaticized emotional reactions were reported decreased with age (see Table 2); in fact, for several items each increase in age brought a decrease in emotional reaction. How are we to explain this? To us it seems in keeping with the adolescent's desire to appear "tough,"[18] "cool," unemotional, uninvolved, and his horror of making a sentimental display of himself. An overt disclaimer of strong feelings may or may not be indicative of emotion experienced.

In their assessment of the political consequences and in their interpretations of the events, children were not the carbon copy of adults that they were in their emotional reactions. Both adults and children worried about the country, but children seem to have worried more than adults. Whereas on all three "worry" questions majorities of adults responded that such worry never occurred to them or at best just "crossed [their] mind but not deeply," majorities of children seem to have worried (See Table 3.) The adult and youth figures are not quite comparable since we gave the child only two check-off choices (either he felt that way or he did not) while NORC offered four, representing different degrees of worrying. Nevertheless we doubt that the higher worry scores for children are a result of our dichotomized question wording. Worrying does not remain stable in children. It decreases sharply with increase in age (except in the realm of foreign affairs). Younger children were heavy worriers.

Over three quarters worried about the country's future and how it would get along without its leaders (fourth grade 76 per cent; twelfth grade 41 per cent). Such accentuated worrying in the lower grades is in line with our prediction that young children, because of their greater dependency needs, are more upset when adult authority is shaken. In the political sphere, the most salient authority figure seems to be the President. Presumably he meets their dependency needs. It is through him that they relate to governmental authority, rather than through political institutions or principles. No wonder that the younger the child, the higher his worry score—testifying to the trauma a Presidential assassination represented.

How did children interpret the events compared to adults? Children and adults both were quite sure Oswald had killed the President (see Table 4), although 49 per cent of the children thought he might have been found innocent at a later trial. There was no consensus in either group as to why Oswald had wished to kill the President. Twice as many adults (33 per cent) as children (15 per cent) attributed it to mental illness. Also far more adults than children attributed it to Oswald's Communist leanings (16 and 6 per cent respectively). Several other items on the table indicate that more adults than children took a conspiratorial view of the assassination. When asked who was to blame for the President's death, children (in an open-ended question) tended to think exclusively of Oswald. Russia and Communism were mentioned by only four children. No child mentioned Castro, Cuba, or extremists of the right and left. Adults did to a fair extent (Russia and Communism 15 per cent, Castro and Cuba 37 per cent). Thus it would seem that children viewed the event with a refreshing absence of cabalism. Nor did children express much of the generalized guilt feeling to which some adults seem to have been prone. Not one child answered "we are all to blame" (8 per cent of adults did) and only 7 per cent blamed the American public (adults 25 per cent). Children seem to have seen the event in a simple and concrete way: blame must be put on the man who pulled the trigger, although many children (38 per cent) were at a total loss to explain why anyone would want to do such a thing. Such straightforwardness is perhaps an encouraging sign; children do not see any conspiratorial plots endangering the United States, and they are not yet given to the now fashionable stance of *mea culpa*, which assumes personal guilt for acts not of one's own doing. On the other hand, the straightforwardness may have come from their lack of sophistication. Such concepts as mental illness and collective guilt[19] are rather abstract and perhaps hard for young children or children from relatively simple backgrounds to comprehend. The children who did offer explanations in these terms not only tended to be older but consistently came from professional or upper middle-class homes.

Where children showed themselves most distinctly different from adults was in their reactions to the Oswald-Ruby aftermath. Oswald put attachment to American values of justice and due process of law to a severe test—a test many children could not pass. Few adults hoped the man who shot the President would be shot down, but 41 per cent of the children did, expecially the younger children. Similarly, only 16 per cent of the children expressed regret that the murder of Oswald deprived him of a trial (for adults NORC reports 33 per cent), which is, of course,

Table 4 *Comparison of Adults' and Children's Interpretation of the Events*

Item	Adults*	Children
Felt certain Oswald killed the President	72%	75.3%
Undecided about it	28	19.1
Reasons why Oswald did it:†		
Insanity	15	14.9
Paid to do so		4.9
Communists behind it	16	5.8
Dislike for Kennedy	12	13.9
Disliked government		3.9
Bad man		.5
Too much for Negroes		1.1
Hatred	12	5.1
Publicity		2.2
Misc.	8	10.0
Don't know	15	37.9
Who is to blame for the President's death?		
Oswald	†	72.6
Security measures	22	2.0
Russia or the Communists	15	.3
God's will		.8
No one person		4.5
Hatred, bigotry, fanaticism	10	3.1
Misc.	‡	3.5
No answer	‡	4.5
The public in general	25	7.4
We are all to blame	8	
Tension and decline of morality	6	
Castro or Cuba	37	not offered
People of Dallas	15	by children
Birchers	15	
Negroes in this country	6	
Did the assassin plan it?		
Alone	24	35.4
With others	62	46.4
Don't know	14	17.7
Who do you think planned it with him?†§		
Ruby		18.5
Russia		2.7
Communists		4.1
Misc.		15.1
How do you feel about what happened to Oswald?†		
Glad	20	19.0
Now we will never know	33	24.4
Should have had trial	33	15.5
Sorry for his family		.7
Didn't care		6.1
Thought it unfair		3.6
Killing always bad	not offered	1.4
Felt a bit bad	by adults	7.1
Felt bad or unhappy		12.7
Misc.		4.2
No answer		5.3

* NORC Study SRS 350
† Answers not quite comparable because children's question open-ended
‡ Figures not broken down this way
§ Percentages less than 100 because only those listed who said he planned with others

in keeping with the previously cited feelings of aggression children demonstrated toward the President's assassin. When asked how they felt about Oswald's death (open-ended question) 19 per cent (the percentage was the same for adults) spontaneously said they were "glad"; 6 per cent said they did not care; and 24 per cent expressed regret that "now we will never know" (33 per cent for adults). And yet, 85 per cent knew it was wrong of Ruby to kill Oswald even if he was the assassin. Children's reactions thus show a certain amount of ambivalence. They seem to have felt extreme hostility toward Oswald along with the awareness that what Ruby did to him was wrong.

Here again clear-cut developmental patterns can be observed. Expressions of revenge declined steadily with age. Two thirds of the fourth-graders and 53 per cent of the sixth-graders "hoped the man who killed the President would be shot or beat up." By the eighth grade this constituted minority sentiment (37 per cent). In the tenth grade, 24 per cent felt this way, and by the twelfth grade it had dropped to a mere 17 per cent. We interpreted a pro-revenge answer as indicating two things: that the child did not yet understand the inappropriateness of such a response in the setting of the American system of government, and, more importantly, that the child was coping with a frustrating or threatening event by resorting to hostility and aggression—at least in his wishes. We take this to mean that younger children have not yet been completely socialized into one important aspect of politics, namely the rejection of violence as a method of retribution. This should come as no surprise to students of child development. Yet in a political system like ours the internalization of politically

nonhostile and nonaggressive norms even toward the offender is one of the crucial goals of political socialization.

Adolescents not only disapproved of what had happened to Oswald but gave adultlike responses on this item and on a variety of other questions dealing with due process and similar principles of American political life. Adolescents may show emotional reactions to a political event that differ from adults', but their political orientations apparently are similar. This is, of course, in keeping with most political socialization studies, which indicate that by adolescence a person has acquired the major political orientations that he will espouse throughout most of his adult years.

Rejection of aggression and acceptance of American concepts of justice is also related to a child's social class. Children from lower socioeconomic backgrounds at all age levels condoned aggression more readily than did upper-class children, especially those from professional families. True, the younger the child, irrespective of class, the easier he finds it to condone aggression, but even at a young age it is slightly harder for children of higher socioeconomic background, and the discrepancy between the classes increases rather than decreases with age, so that by the twelfth grade there was hardly a child of professional parents who wished to see Oswald get killed, while over a third of the working class and white collar children did (see Chart II). The impact of upper-class standing seems to be first, that it accelerates rejection of violence, and, second, that it all but obliterates acceptance of violence by adolescence. Consequently the gulf between the classes has widened by adolescence, not narrowed, or—to put it another way—while all children become more

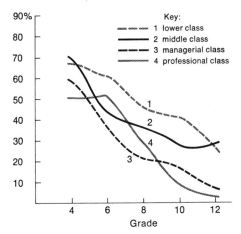

Key:
- — — 1 lower class
- —— 2 middle class
- – – – 3 managerial class
- ～～ 4 professional class

Chart II Children Who "Hoped the Man Who Killed President Kennedy Would be Shot or Beat Up"

socialized with age into the rejection of violence, upper-class children are the most politically socialized to this norm. Findings such as these demonstrate the political consequences of the different child-rearing practices of the various social classes, which some scholars have observed.[20]

II. Differential Involvement and Reactions to the Event

We had predicted that even though all children love and admire the President, children who identified more with the President, for partisan or other reasons, might feel his loss most severely. This assumption was tested with respect to Negro/white children and to Republican/Democratic children.

The comparison of Negro and white reactions was undertaken on the assumption that Negroes would have particularly strong reasons for mourning the President's death. Sheatsley and Feldman comment on the fact that adult Negroes seem to have shown more

pronounced grief over the President's death than did any other population group. This seems to hold even among school children. Almost without fail the Negro children were considerably more upset and worried. (See Table 5.) Many of these children wrote that they worried "how my folks will now get along." One Negro girl attending a high school in the worst part of the city poignantly wrote, "It was as though my father had died all over again."

The reactions of Negro children are interesting in many ways, but a thorough analysis would take us beyond the scope of this chapter. Here we can point out merely that they showed much more hostility toward the assassin and much more worry about how the United States would get along without its *leader*. They had far greater worries than white children about what would happen to the country domestically. Obviously in the minds of Negro children Kennedy was intimately associated with the fate of the Negro. No wonder that more of them reported trouble sleeping and loss of appetite!

It is also noteworthy that of all the groups Negro girls showed themselves the most deeply affected. While girls generally were more emotionally affected than boys, Negro girls' reactions were far more severe than white girls' and than Negro boys'. The least affected, apparently, were the white boys. These differences maintained themselves even when partisanship and socioeconomic status were taken into account.

We further predicted that children who identified with the President's party (those children who said they would vote Democratic if they were old enough to vote) would show more signs of grief and fear over the future of the country

Table 5

Reactions of White and Negro Children

A) NORC checklist	White (n = 1006) %		Negro (n = 342) %	
When I Heard the President Was Dead I:	*This is how I felt*	*I did not feel that way*	*This is how I felt*	*I did not feel that way*
Felt the loss of someone very close and dear	68.6*	29.0*	80.7*	13.5*
Was so upset and mixed up, I did not know what to feel	43.5	53.1	40.1	51.2
Was mad that anyone should do such a terrible thing	81.6	16.0	83.6	10.8
I cried	39.6	56.7	39.5	51.8
Worried about what would happen to our country	63.1	34.3	74.3	19.0
Felt sorry for his wife and children	93.9	4.7	91.2	4.7
Hoped the man who killed him would be shot or beat up	35.9	60.3	53.9	39.2
I did not feel bad	10.0	85.7	22.8	67.5
I did not feel like eating	26.5	60.4	38.9	51.8
Worried what would happen to our relations with other countries	61.9	35.2	64.0	30.7
Felt in some ways it was the President's own fault	14.7	80.4	18.4	73.7
I had trouble getting to sleep	42.2	55.1	51.8	42.8
Hoped the next President would be better	29.7	66.0	54.7	35.9
Felt ashamed that this could happen in our country	85.6	12.8	75.1	19.6
I had a headache	21.0	74.9	22.9	65.5
I had an upset stomach	16.6	78.6	21.6	66.9
Worried how the U.S. would get along without its leader	55.4	41.5	69.6	23.7

B) Answers to the open-ended question: "Tell us, in a few words, just how you felt when you first heard that President Kennedy was dead."	White Children %	Negro Children %
I could not believe it	55.9	40.9
I felt sad	15.6	21.1
I felt very bad	10.3	18.1
I felt frightened	2.2	1.5
I felt sick	1.3	5.5
I felt ashamed	1.2	1.5
I felt mad	.9	2.6
Combination of the above answers	6.6	1.8
Misc.	5.1	4.9
No answer	.8	2.1

"Did you ever feel that way before?"		
Never	61.1	53.8
At the death of a relative	22.1	30.1
At the death of a friend	5.7	3.8
At sickness of a friend	2.8	4.1
At loss of animal	1.9	.9
At divorce of parents	.6	—
Misc.	4.3	4.1
No answer	1.2	2.9

* Percentages do not add up to 100% because some children failed to check each item.

than those not so identified. Table 6 indicates that this was indeed the case, although it showed up mainly in the area of emotional responses. Democratically inclined children reported more trouble sleeping, more loss of appetite, crying, etc. More of them identified with the President—"worried how the U.S. would get along without its leader" (Democrats 66 per cent, Republicans 58 per cent). And, not unexpectedly, more of them showed feelings of aggression toward Oswald (Democrats 50 per cent, Republicans 38 per cent). The President may have a firm niche in American children's affections and admiration, but partisanship is apparently an intervening variable, which either strengthens or loosens this bond. Even in death and tragedy children are aware of their partisanship—although not to a very marked degree.[21]

III. Comparison of Presidential Image Before and After November 22

The image our children[22] had of the Presidency was essentially positive and idealized just as Easton and Hess had reported it to be. But in one aspect of the image, the power aspect, children who were interviewed after the assassination differed from those Easton and Hess had interviewed before. As we had predicted, after the assassination the President seemed slightly less powerful. Whereas in the Easton-Hess study most children thought the President did most to run the country,[23] in our sample barely half did. His role image ("He knows more," etc.), however, remained unchanged.

Personal idealization of the President increased. In our sample somewhat more children than in the Easton-Hess group liked him very much, and hardly any disliked him. Although we were careful to tell children not to think of the late President when answering the question, but to think instead of Presidents in general, personal liking shot up.

The image of the Presidency thus remained positive and idealized among children, but their belief in his powerfulness noticeably decreased. This indicates to us that the impact of the assassination made children less sure of the President's omnipotence, perhaps brought the image closer to reality.

Another example of realism is seen in children's evaluations of American Presidents. Invited to make a guess whether

America has had Presidents who did their job well and Presidents who did not do a good job

or

American Presidents have almost all done their job very well

slightly over half (51 per cent) chose the more critical answer. Only five children refused to pass judgment. As was expected, the tendency to idealize *all* Presidents decreases with age, and decreases sharply (76 per cent of the fourth-graders said almost all Presidents have been good, as opposed to 16 per cent of the twelfth-graders). Most significant, however, is the fact that children were willing to admit at all that we have had Presidents who did not do a good job.

Children apparently were also able to make a distinction between the person of the President and the institution. In answer to our question

When a President dies . . .
There is no government for a while

or

Table 6

Reactions of Children Who Identify as Democrats and Republicans

NORC checklist	Democrats (n = 459) %		Republicans (n = 231) %	
When I Heard the President Was Dead I:	*This is how I felt*	*I did not feel that way*	*This is how I felt*	*I did not feel that way*
Felt the loss of someone very close and dear	79.3*	16.1*	63.3*	34.6*
Was so upset and mixed up, I did not know what to feel	38.3	54.7	47.2	48.9
Was mad that anyone should do such a terrible thing	85.6	10.5	80.5	16.0
I cried	44.4	49.9	34.2	62.3
Worried about what would happen to our country	66.7	28.1	69.3	28.6
Felt sorry for his wife and children	91.7	4.6	93.9	5.2
Hoped the man who killed him would be shot or beat up	49.9	45.5	37.7	59.7
I did not feel bad	9.6	82.8	16.9	80.1
I did not feel like eating	41.2	53.4	32.4	64.9
Worried what would happen to our relations with other countries	63.8	31.4	61.1	37.2
Felt in some ways it was the President's own fault	14.4	79.3	17.8	79.7
I had trouble getting to sleep	48.2	47.1	39.8	58.4
Hoped the next President would be better	37.7	55.1	38.5	58.0
Felt ashamed that this could happen in our country	78.4	18.1	82.3	15.2
I had a headache	21.1	72.1	22.5	74.0
I had an upset stomach	16.6	75.4	19.5	76.6
Worried how the U.S. would get along without its leader	65.8	29.8	58.4	37.7

* Percentages do not add up to 100% because some children failed to check each item.

Government goes on just the same

an overwhelming majority (84 per cent) expressed faith that government goes on just the same. It is possible, of course, that faith in the continuity of the institution of government was in part attributable to the emphasis TV coverage put on precisely this point. Thanks to television, children, shortly after learning of Kennedy's death, watched President Johnson take the oath of office aboard the Presidential plane—in the presence of the widow of the just deceased President. One may well wonder if children's faith in the stability of government would have been equally emphatic if television had not enabled them to follow with their own eyes and ears the swift and orderly succession. On this point it is interesting to note that, even so, 33 per cent of all fourth-graders thought that there is *no* government for a while. Nonetheless the answers indicate that though the assassination caused many children to worry about the future of the country, they had faith in the stability of their government.

The responses to the last two items, especially when analyzed in conjunction with the Easton-Hess items, suggest that children's highly positive image of the Presidency is not untinged by realism, and that children can apparently—in a rudimentary way—distinguish between the person of the president and the institution of the government. Their sense of political security seems to be a function of their faith in the institution of government as well as of their faith in individual Presidents.[24]

Summary

Children appear to have been greatly moved by the President's death. Their reactions were similar in many ways to those of adults. Their socialization, however, does not yet seem complete (at least in grades four through six), for many showed feelings of revenge and slight regard for due process of law. High school students, however, seem to be nearly as politically socialized as most adults.

Negro children and children who intend to vote Democratic were noticeably more upset than white children or those who identified themselves as Republicans.

The image of the Presidency remains highly positive although a slight decrease in the power image has occurred.

All of which would lead us to believe that, probably due to the influence of home, school, peers, and mass media (especially television), even young school children quickly learned to join the adults in national mourning and in the appropriate civilized responses to the event. The optimists among us should be permitted to believe that this reaction of the young was spontaneous and a function of successful political socialization.

The fact that even young children's reaction patterns were so similar to adults' should further alert us to the fact that political socialization begins at an early stage—a fact all too often ignored.

NOTES

1. Initial assistance for the project came from Wayne State University and the Merrill-Palmer Institute but the major financial support for this investigation came from grants from the National Institute of Health (MH10112-01) and from the Society for the Psychological Study of Social Issues.

Special thanks here are due to the administrations and administrators who permitted us access to their schools within the span of a few days. These are the Boards of Education of the cities of Detroit and Dearborn, Michigan, and the headmasters of Grosse Pointe University School, Grosse Pointe, Michigan, Brookside School and Kingswood School for Girls, both of Bloomfield Hills, Michigan.

Most particularly, however, the author wishes to acknowledge the help of the following people: Judith Brent and Elinor B. Waters of the Merrill-Palmer Institute; Drs. Sandor Brent of the Department of Psychology, Wayne State University and William Kooistra, Pine Rest Christian Hospital, Grand Rapids, Michigan; and last—but certainly not least—the co-investigator, Dr. Irving E. Sigel, Chairman of Research, Merrill-Palmer Institute.

The above people need assume no responsibility for the report (since they have not seen it), but without them the study could never have taken place, as they helped in the questionnaire design, administered it, and generally saw to it that we could get to the schools before the children dispersed for Christmas vacation.

2. One may, of course, argue that the event never was, strictly speaking, a crisis since no real threat to the continuity of government was ever present. If one, however, accepts the looser dictionary definition (Webster) of a crisis as a "turning point . . . a state of things in which decisive change is impending" one might well call the event a crisis.

3. Hess and Easton, 1960, p. 640.

4. Hess, 1963, p. 14.

5. *Ibid.*, p. 24.

6. Davis and Havighurst, 1946; Miller and Swanson, 1958; Whiting, 1963; Sewell, 1961.

7. Two old, but still valid, volumes on the subject are Charles E. Merriam, *Civic Education in the United States* (New York: Scribner's, 1934) and Bessie Louise Pierce, *Citizens' Organizations and the Civic Training of Youth* (New York: Scribner's, 1933).

8. Sigel, 1964.

9. Lazarsfeld, Berelson, and Gaudet, 1948, p. 38.

10. Lane, 1962.

11. Greenstein, 1965, 104.

12. Volkart, 1957, writes, "No summary analysis of the social psychiatry of bereavement and separation can be made, since none as yet exists." P. 285.

13. Wilson, in Leighton, Clausen, and Wilson, 1957, p. 306.

14. The above terminology is not Hess and Easton's but our own. They break them down as: a.) perception of responsiveness; b.) personalized as opposed to institutionalized conceptualization of the government; c.) role competence; d.) power index. (From a personal communication to the writer by Judith V. Torney, March 20, 1964.)

15. Hess and Easton, 1960.

16. Sheatsley and Feldman, 1964, p. 195.

17. *Ibid.*, 200–201.

18. In keeping with this toughness stance, fewer teen-agers than elementary school children reported having felt "sad," "sick," or "bad."

19. Political science literature has as yet not furnished us with any data on young children's concepts of political justice and morality. However, the work of Piaget, 1948, with respect to children's morality is of great relevance here.

20. Davis and Havighurst (1946). For a contrary view, cf. Maccoby and Gibbs (1954) as well as the Havighurst-Davis rejoinder to Maccoby and Gibbs (1955).

21. Sheatsley and Feldman also noted that supporters of the late President seemed more upset than his former opponents.

22. In part of the analysis we have eliminated the tenth and twelfth grade children

in order to make our sample more comparable to the Hess and Easton one which included no children beyond the eighth grade.

23. Personal communication to the author. We are withholding exact percentage citations on this and several other items until the official publication of the Hess-Easton report.

24. We are sorry that we failed to inquire in more detail just how children perceived of this latter relationship. Such an inquiry would undoubtedly have yielded valuable insight into the role of the leader vis-à-vis the institution.

LIST OF REFERENCES

Davis, Allison and Robert J. Havighurst. 1946. "Social Class and Color Differences in Child-rearing," *American Sociological Review*, XI, 698–710.

Greenstein, Fred I. 1965. *Childrer. and Politics*. New Haven, Conn.: Yale University Press.

Hartley, Eugene L. and Ruth E. Hartley. 1952. *Fundamentals of Social Psychology*. 1st edition. New York: Knopf.

Havighurst, Robert J. and Allison Davis. 1955. "A Comparision of the Chicago and Harvard Studies of Social Class Differences in Child Rearing," *American Sociological Review*, XX, 438–42.

Hess, Robert D. 1963. "The Socialization of Attitudes Toward Political Authority: Some Cross National Comparisons," *International Social Science Journal*, XV, 542–59.

Hess, Robert D. and David Easton. 1960. "The Child's Changing Image of the President," *Public Opinion Quarterly*, XXIV, 632–44.

Hyman, Herbert. 1959. *Political Socialization*. Glencoe, Ill.: Free Press.

Lane, Robert E. 1962. *Political Ideology: Why the American Common Man Believes What He Does*. New York: The Free Press of Glencoe.

Lazarsfeld, Paul F., Bernard Berelson, and Hazel Gaudet. 1948. *The People's Choice*. New York: Columbia University Press.

Leighton, Alexander H., John A. Clausen, and Robert N. Wilson. 1957. *Explorations in Social Psychiatry*. New York: Basic Books.

Maccoby, Eleanor E. and P. K. Gibbs. 1954. "Methods of Child Rearing in Two Social Classes." In William E. Martin, and C. B. Stendler (eds.) *Readings in Child Development*. New York: Harcourt, Brace, pp. 380–96.

Miller, Daniel R. and Guy E. Swanson. 1958. *The Changing American Parent*. New York: John Wiley & Sons.

Piaget, Jean. 1948. *The Moral Judgment of the Child*. Glencoe, Ill.: Free Press.

Prothro, James W. and Charles M. Grigg. 1960. "Fundamental Principles of Democracy: Bases of Agreement and Disagreement," *Journal of Politics*, XXII, 276–94.

Sewell, William H. 1961. "Social Class and Childhood Personality," *Sociometry*, XXIV, 340–56.

Sigel, Roberta S. 1964. "The Effect of Partisanship on the Perception of Political Candidates," *Public Opinion Quarterly*, XXVIII.

Sheatsley, Paul B. and Jacob B. Feldman. 1964. "The Assassination of President Kennedy—A Preliminary Report of Public Reactions and Behavior," *Public Opinion Quarterly*, XXVIII, 189–215.

Torney, Judith V. and Robert D. Hess. 1962. "The Child's Idealization of Authority." Paper presented at the American Psychological Association annual meeting, St. Louis, August 30, 1962.

Volkart, Edmund H. 1957. "Bereavement and Mental Health." In Alexander H. Leighton, John A. Clausen and Robert N. Wilson, *Explorations in Social Psychiatry*. New York: Basic Books.

Whiting, Beatrice R. 1963. *Six Cultures: Studies of Child Rearing*. New York: John Wiley & Sons.

POLITICAL AFFILIATION AND IMAGERY ACROSS TWO RELATED GENERATIONS*

- ## Richard W. Dodge and Eugene S. Uyeki

Introduction

In recent years students of politics have become increasingly concerned with the problem of the acquisition and formation of political attitudes. In the past much useful information of a descriptive nature has been accumulated from a wide range of election studies in which the relation between demographic variables and voting behavior has been studied in great detail. A further development in increasing our understanding of the political process has been an emphasis on the "intervening variables," exemplified in the work of the Survey Research Center of the University of Michigan.[1] These are the psychological factors which reveal the basic set of the individual with respect to politics. More knowledge of this basic attitudinal pattern—how it is formed, how modified, and under what conditions—should contribute to an understanding of specific acts of political behavior.

Research along these lines has studied the development of voting decisions in the course of a political campaign.[2]

Above selection reprinted from: *Midwest Journal of Political Science*, 6, 1962, 266–276 by Richard Dodge and Eugene Uyeki by permission of the Wayne State University Press. Copyright © 1962 by the Wayne State University Press.

* We are grateful to the Case Reasearch Fund for a grant which made this study possible. We appreciate the generous help which Kurt and Gladys E. Lang gave us during the preliminary stages of the research.

Among the influences that have an important bearing on political choice are those of family, friends, and co-workers. The family's influence is, of course, of great importance as the primary school for the inculcation of approved values and modes of behavior. This instruction includes both a general orientation toward politics as a type of activity and toward a particular political preference. This is not to suggest that the family is *the* key to understanding how the political outlook of the younger generation is shaped, but its influence can be inferred from the fact that approximately 70% of young voters follow the political predilections of their parents.[3] In these cases, other influences, such as schools, churches, friends, etc., may serve to reinforce this initial outlook. On the other hand, not all the influences to which one is subjected in the process of acquiring a set of political attitudes and predispositions are likely to converge so neatly. If the preponderance of influence is in one direction, any contrary views can by explained away by the individual without too much difficulty. In other cases there may be disagreement either between the parents themselves, or between the parents and the general environment.[4] The effect of these situations has not been too extensively studied, but it is probable that young voters, finding themselves in such a conflict situation, may withdraw from political action until such time as the conflict has been resolved. This is suggested as a partial explanation for the low voting turnout among the young.[5] There may also be situations where attitudes acquired from parents are brought into question by a new environment in which the family member finds himself. Newcomb documented one such situation a generation ago in his study of a college community.[6]

In addition to these factors, the larger political context cannot be ignored. Political attitudes and preferences are substantially influenced by the particular historical era in which a person comes of age.[7] The common experience of adolescence may impart a similar outlook to a generation which sets it off from that of its parents. The issues which excited partisan division in an earlier time have been resolved and the resulting compromise has become part of the given situation, no longer controversial and accepted by everyone. In the meantime, new issues have arisen to provide the basis for contemporary controversy —but, depending on the era involved, the partisan division may be sharp or muted. This process has been aptly designated as "dualism in a moving consensus" by V. O. Key.[8] Even though the "stuff" of partisan debate changes, there is evidence to suggest that the shifts of individual allegiance within the body politic are of lesser amplitude. The influence of the family in inculcating a fundamental outlook on society, including a set of attitudes toward politics, is frequently sufficient to persist despite fluctuations in the substance of political combat. Wholesale political realignments have been the exception rather than the rule in American politics. The usual pattern has been that of periods of national dominance by one or the other of the major parties. Lubell has shown that in the case of the transition from Republican to Democratic dominance at the time of the New Deal, it was the coincidence of economic grievances and the desire for improved status on the part of underprivileged groups that provided the stimulus for a coalition inside the Democratic Party.[9] In this massive party shift, family ties were undoubtedly less persuasive than ordinarily seems to be the case. Since then, despite the unique nature of the Eisenhower appeal, the Democrats seem to have maintained their position as the majority party—if not as prominently as in the middle 1930s. A study of the political differences between generations today would presumably continue to reveal a substantial agreement within families with respect to political preference. The major purpose of this article is to examine two related generations with regard to stability and change in political affiliation and in their general outlook on political issues and events.

Method and Description of the Sample

This study is based on a sample of 175 students and one or the other of their parents. The respondents were all full-time undergraduates at Case Institute of Technology, Cleveland, Ohio, in the fall semester of 1956–57. Since the student body at Case is already preselected—above average in intelligence, family income, and status of parent's occupations—it was felt that no particular gain would result from taking a representative sample.[10] The respondents were mainly freshmen (76%), plus seniors and juniors taking electives offered by the Department of Humanities and Social Studies. The vast majority were intended majors in engineering, with some in science and management.[11] A ten-page questionnaire was administered to 264 students a week prior to the election of November, 1956. A similar questionnaire was mailed to the parents of each student. To achieve the highest return possible, a stamped addressed envelope was included with each questionnaire, together with a covering letter from the Dean of the undergraduate school, explaining the nature of the study and allaying possible parental fears about the confidential nature of the data and the probity of the researchers. Questionnaires returned completed and in usable form numbered 175, or nearly two thirds of those sent out, a high return for this kind of survey. Fathers filled out the questionnaires in about 64% of the cases.[12] The remainder were filled out by the mothers. The important factor was that the respondent should be a generation removed from the students. To this parent sample, the 175 comparable student questionnaires were added for purposes of the following analysis.

A comparison of the Republican and Democratic parents on a series of demographic variables, which earlier studies have shown to be related to political affiliation, demonstrates substantial diversity between the two groups. Democratic families are about equally divided in their ancestry between Britain and Northwest Europe (the "old" immigration) and Italy and Southeast Europe (the "new" immigration), whereas the Republicans are overwhelmingly from the former areas. This contrast is also reflected in the figures for religious preference where the two major religions divide Democratic parents equally, but the Republican parents are predominantly Protestant. Nearly half of the Republican parents have had some college education, but only 21.7% of the Democratic parents have advanced beyond high school. (Perhaps even more significant than this difference is the fact that in *all* these families at least one son is now obtaining a college education, indicating the great expansion in higher education since the Second World War.) Occupationally, the two sets of parents are not as far apart, but Republicans do have greater percentages in the professional and managerial categories, while the Democrats have more persons who are craftsmen, operatives, and service workers. Finally, the respondent's own ratings on social class demonstrate the American preference for the middle class which has long been noted by sociologists. However, again we can observe a distinction between Republican and Democratic parents, with the former placing themselves considerably more in the upper middle class than the latter. In summary, then, even though the sample of parents is not a cross section of the U.S. population, being more highly educated and holding "higher" occupations than the average, it nevertheless exhibits substantial differences in certain demographic characteristics when it is divided according to political preference. These differences are in the direction one would expect based on previous studies of political behavior.

Political Affiliation

A person's subjective party preference or identification is of great importance in conditioning his attitudes toward political issues, campaigns, and candidates. It is obviously a significant item

Table 1

Political Identification, by Generation

POLITICAL IDENTIFICATION	Parents	Students
Republican	42.4%	40.6%
Ind. Republican	20.0	29.8
Independent	2.3	5.1
Ind. Democrat	13.1	9.7
Democrat	21.1	14.8
Not Ascertained	1.1	—
	100.0%	100.0%
	N = 175	N = 175

in a study of two political generations. The question on political identification occurred well along in the questionnaire, after all the other questions of a political nature had been answered. The wording of the question was: "Do you consider yourself basically a Democrat? a Republican? an Independent?" For those who picked Independent, a further question was asked: "Do you consider yourself closer to the Democratic Party? Republican Party?" The breakdown for the parent and student groups is given in Table 1.

Two conclusions emerge from this overall comparison. First, there is substantial stability of political preference from one generation to the next. But, second, there is a slight shift toward the

Republicans, possibly reflecting a combination of the effects of the era in which the students have been reared as well as their general striving for upward mobility.[13]

In order to probe more deeply into the nature of this continuity of political identification, the preferences of the parents have been compared with those of their own sons. The results are shown in Table 2.[14]

The Republicans (combining the two sub-groups for the purposes of this discussion) experience scarcely any "loss" in the transmission of political identification between the generations. Only four students (out of 109) move over to the Democratic Party. The Democrats, although a majority of sons stay in the fold, suffer a defection of one-third to the Republicans (20 out of 60). Why there should be a greater degree of "apostasy" among the sons of Regular Democrats than among the Independent Democrats is not clear. In general, the sons of Democratic parents in our sample are probably in more of a cross pressure situation than would be the case in most Democratic families— or than exists for the sons of Republican parents. It is known on the basis of comparative data that engineering students

Table 2

Intergenerational Transmission of Party Affiliation

Affiliation of Sons	Parent's Affiliation			
	Democrat	Ind. Democrat	Ind. Republican	Republican
Democrat	32.4%	47.8%	5.7 %	0.0%
Ind. Democrat	18.9	21.7	2.9	1.4
Independent	8.1	8.7	2.9	2.7
Ind. Republican	29.7	17.4	45.7	28.4
Republican	10.8	4.3	42.9	67.6
	99.9%	99.9%	100.1%	100.1%
	N = 37	N = 23	N = 35	N = 74

Table 3

Class Placement of Sons, by Party Affiliation of Parents and Sons

CLASS SHIFT	Republican Parents Republican Sons	Democratic Parents Democratic Sons	Republican Sons
Upward	20.6%	25.7%	50.0%
Same	63.7	62.9	35.0
Downward	15.7	11.4	15.0
	100.0% N = 102	100.0% N = 35	100.0% N = 20

are upwardly mobile in greater proportions from lower parts of the social structure than most of the other professions.[15] Where the career goal of engineer seems to reinforce the political orientation in Republican families, it serves to compete with political traditions and values in Democratic families.

A clue as to why the Democratic parents were less successful in transmitting their political affiliation to their sons is suggested by a closer examination of the data on social class. In Table 3, the student responses to the class question have been compared with those of their parents. Using the class of the parent as the base line, the responses of the students are presented in terms of agreement, shift upward, or shift downward. (Democratic sons of Republican parents have been eliminated as there were too few to give meaningful results.)

Where political identification remains the same from one generation to the next (varying only within the two categories of partisanship), the sons exhibit similar behavior, regardless of political affiliations. In both Republican and Democratic families a majority of the sons choose the same social class as their parents with a very slight net upward shift overall. The divergence of those sons of Democratic parents who

prefer the Republican Party is clear and in the direction of substantially greater upward mobility. The pull of their career goal seems stronger than the influence of family political orientation. This change very likely may have been induced by the parents themselves as they taught their children to aspire to higher educational and career opportunities than they themselves have had. Comparing the two groups of sons of Democratic parents—those who remain Democratic and those who switch to the Republicans—on demographic variables as religion, father's occupation, ancestry, and education does not reveal any significant differences. Thus, we are probably justified in believing that the dichotomy can better be explained on psychological rather than sociological grounds.

Perceptions of Political Issues

In order to investigate the nature of political perception within and between the generations, two fairly complex questions were devised. The first was concerned with exploring the image which the respondents held of the two parties with respect to their ability to handle current issues, while the second sought to uncover attitudes toward events of the present day and recent past, introducing an element of historical perspective.

On current images of the two parties, fourteen issues were selected as being representative of major domestic and foreign problems.[16] The respondents were asked to indicate which of the major parties was better qualified to handle each of the problems. Our expectations were confirmed that there would be a great amount of agreement on the allocation of these issues to the Republican and Democratic parties by both the parent and student generation, irrespective of party bias. With the issues placed in rank order for each of the two generations according to the greatest percentage credited to the Republicans and Democrats, respectively, the rank order correlations between the generations are .91 for the former and .93 for the latter. The principal exceptions are "Looking after the interests of the working man" and "Holding prices down," where a greater percentage of students chose the Democratic party as being better qualified to handle these than their parents did. Even when the sample is controlled for party affiliation, the rank order remains pretty much the same for most of the generational comparisons as evidenced by coefficients which range from .82 to .91.

We noted the suggestion of a moderating aspect to the student responses. On most of the issues, the students chose the party of their avowed affiliation as better qualified by a lower percentage than the parent generation of the same affiliation (comparing Democratic students and Democratic parents, Independent Democratic students and Independent Democratic parents, etc.)

and the other party as better qualified by a higher percentage than the parent generation of the same affiliation. The conspicuous exception is the small group (26) of Democratic students who are more partisan than their parents.

Another dimension of political behavior was obtained by having respondents indicate their views on a series of 15 statements dealing with political events of the present day and recent past.[17] These statements were deliberately "loaded" to force the respondent to take a position either pro or con in line with his general party orientation. Respondents were given four choices, strong or moderate agreement and strong or moderate disagreement, on each of the 15 statements.

Our expectation of similarity on the part of the student and parent generation is upheld. The rank order correlation coefficient between the parents and students when the statements are ranked according to percentage agreement (sum of agree strongly and agree somewhat) on each of the 15 issues is .78. When we introduce political affiliation as a control, the intergenerational correlations are .67 for Republican parents and Republican students and .91 for Democratic parents and Democratic students. In only three cases is there substantial disagreement—two of these involve statements critical of Roosevelt and the New Deal in which the students, despite a slightly more Republican orientation, are much less inclined to agree with the extreme Republican position than are their parents. The greater divergence is found to lie within the Republican group on these questions. The other case where a divergence emerges concerns Eisenhower's stature as a war hero. Again, the students agree less than their parents that he was the greatest general, but the greater discrepancy is within the Democratic ranks.

On these perceptions of the political past, we also noted a greater tendency on the part of the student generation—except for the Democratic students—to take a moderate position (greater percentage of students chose agree or disagree *somewhat*) as compared with the parent generation (greater percentage of parents chose agree or disagree *strongly*). The conspicuous exception is the statement regarding the halting of aggression in Korea, where the students support Truman's intervention more strongly than their parents do.

Conclusion

We have a highly selected parental sample with somewhat diverse backgrounds, but heavily overrepresenting the more highly educated, higher status occupations. Most of the student sample were freshmen who can be presumed to rely primarily on parental guidance in reacting to politics. In the process of preparing for careers in engineering and science they can be expected to converge in their value orientations. And the environment of Case Institute probably supports a conservative orientation. Within this context, the nature of our sample produces a cross pressure situation for students from Democratic families: a professional career goal which conflicts with the family orientation. We noted earlier that the Democratic families in our sample are less typical of all Democratic families than is true of the Republicans. They are certainly less partisan in their party outlook, which can be further documented by noting that while 95.4% of

Republican parents signified an intention of voting for Eisenhower, only 53.3% of the Democratic parents expected to vote for Stevenson. Allowing for this, there still remains the fact of a substantial shift of the sons toward the Republican party, and not merely its candidate. This is undoubtedly strongly rooted, as the class question suggests, in the drive for higher status.

There is a close correspondence between the generations, excepting the Democratic students, in political affiliation, in images of the parties, and in attitudes on issues. This over all generational "transfer" is qualified by the fact that the students as a group are both more Republican and more moderate than their parents. Their Republicanism, however, derives from a more recent historical era than that of their parents and thus leads them to accept as part of the existing order of things, matters which their parents remember as controversial. For instance, FDR and the New Deal are viewed from a less partisan perspective than that of their parents. However, on a contemporary issue such as the influence of big business in the Eisenhower administration, the students react in more partisan ways than they did to similar questions about the Hoover and Roosevelt eras. Thus, despite a greater preference for the Republican party than their parents, these students tend to be more moderate, to see more merit in some Democratic positions, and to respond slightly more to the non-party appeal of the Eisenhower administration.

Finally, then, while the evidence in this study suggests a great stability in political affiliation and great influence in political attitudes from one generation to the next, there are hints that a more volatile attitude complex is veiled. Specifically, the effects of the general context of the times and of the personal goals of the students are visible. Granting that engineering and science students may be an atypical group, we feel that a deeper probing into attitudinal patterns with other samples of related generations will provide additional insights into the components of political change.

NOTES

1. This line of investigation started with and is reported in A. Campbell, G. Gurin, and W. E. Miller, *The Voter Decides* (Evanston, Ill.: Row, Peterson, 1954).

2. See, for instance, the following: P. F. Lazarsfeld, B. Berelson, and H. Gaudet, *The People's Choice* (New York: Duell Sloan and Pearce, 1944); B. Berelson, P. F. Lazarfeld, and W. McPhee, *Voting* (Chicago: University of Chicago Press, 1959).

3. A. Campbell, P. E. Converse, W. E. Miller, D. E. Stokes, *The American Voter* (New York: Wiley, 1960), pp. 147–149. Even where neither parent was "politically active," if both were Democrats, 76% of the offspring identified with the same party, and if both parents were Republicans, 66% of the offspring identified with the Republican party. When one or both parents were "politically active," the percentages of party transmission to their offspring were 79% for Democratic parents and 71% for Republican parents.

4. However, the Michigan study of the 1952 campaign showed that there was very little disagreement between husband and wife pairs in their political preference (Campbell et al., *The Voter Decides*, pp. 200–201).

5. S. M. Lipset, *Political Man* (Garden City, New York: Doubleday, 1960), p. 210.

6. T. M. Newcomb, *Personality and Social Change* (New York: Dryden, 1943).

7. D. Riesman, with R. Denney and N. Glazer, *The Lonely Crowd* (New Haven: Yale University Press, 1950).

8. V. O. Key, Jr., *Politics, Parties, and Pressure Groups* (4th ed. New York: Crowell, 1958), p. 243.

9. S. Lubell, *The Future of American Politics* (New York: Harper, 1951), especially Chapter 3, "Revolt of the Cities," pp. 28–57.

10. Our purpose was to examine the relationship between two consecutive generations in a tentative and exploratory way, primarily to suggest another approach to the problem of the formation of political attitudes among young people. For another study of the political behavior of youth by means of a specific and not entirely representative sample, see E. E. Maccoby, R. E. Matthews, and A. S. Morton, "Youth and Political Change," *Public Opinion Quarterly*, XVIII (Spring 1954), 23–39.

11. Some indication of the proportionate distribution of these students between the various majors may be gotten by looking at the data for the most recent graduating class at Case (1961). Of the total graduating class of 278, 70.2% were in

engineering, 16.9% in the sciences (physics, chemistry, and mathematics), and 12.9% in management.

12. The assumption was that fathers were the more politically aware of the parents and also more influential in shaping the student's views about politics.

13. There is also a tendency for a greater proportion of the parents (63.5%) to indicate straight party affiliation unqualified by protestations of independence. The comparable figure for the students is 55.4%.

14. The four Independents among the parents have been eliminated from Table 2.

15. For instance, to quote from a very recent study, among the "careers preferred by students who come from families with income under $7,500 a year and in which the father has completed less than 4 years of high school are electrical and civil engineering. . . ." See J. A. Davis and N. Bradburn, *Great Aspirations: Career Plans of America's June 1961 College Graduates* (Chicago: National Opinion Research Center, September 1961), p. 57.

16. Of the fourteen issues, six were clearly perceived by the respondents as being "Republican:" keeping us out of war, keeping the economy at a high level, holding prices down, looking after the interests of businessmen, keeping Communists out of government, and running an efficient government. Five issues were clearly perceived as "Democratic:" looking after the interests of the working man, looking after the interests of older people, extending social security, giving the farmer his fair share, and conserving our natural resources. Three were perceived as more neutral in tone: guaranteeing civil rights, promoting world disarmament, and looking after the interests of young people.

17. The 15 statements were as follows: (a) During the Hoover administration, Big Business ran the government. (b) Hoover did nothing to get us out of the depression, except make promises. (c) It took World War II to bring us prosperity and pull us out of the depression. (d) The New Deal did far too much to interfere with private enterprise. (e) Unions got too big under Roosevelt and Truman. (f) Roosevelt was far too friendly with the Russians. (g) Roosevelt was a power-hungry individual who wanted to perpetuate his administration. (h) Because of his great contributions in getting us out of the depression and winning World War II, Roosevelt will go down in history as one of our greatest Presidents. (i) Without the Truman doctrine of aid to Greece, the Marshall Plan, and NATO, the Communists would have engulfed Western Europe. (j) Truman's decision to drop the atomic bomb stopped the war with Japan and saved the lives of thousands of Americans. (k) Trueman's decision to send troops to defend South Korea was a major step in halting Communist aggression. (l) As a war hero, Eisenhower stands unequalled among all generals both in Europe and the Pacific. (m) The economic policies of the Eisenhower administration have favored big business at the expense of the little man. (n) Eisenhower followed through on his campaign promise and brought the war in Korea to an end. (o) Eisenhower is a great President because he stands above party and represents all of the people.

THE REVOLT OF THE ADVANTAGED: AN EXPLORATION OF THE ROOTS OF STUDENT PROTEST*

- ## Richard Flacks

As all of us are by now aware, there has emerged, during the past five years, an increasingly self-conscious student movement in the United States. This movement began primarily as a response to the efforts by Southern Negro students to break the barriers of legal segregation in public accommodations —scores of Northern white students engaged in sympathy demonstrations and related activities as early as 1960. But as we all know, the scope of the student concern expanded rapidly to include such issues as nuclear testing and the arms race, attacks on civil liberties, the problems of the poor in urban slum ghettoes, democracy and educational quality in universities, the war in Vietnam, conscription.

Above selection excerpted from: *The Journal of Social Issues*, XXIII, 3 (1967).

* The research reported here stemmed from a coalescence of interests of the author and of Professor Bernice Neugarten of the Committee on Human Development of the University of Chicago. The author's interests were primarily in the student movement and the families and social backgrounds of student activists. Professor Neugarten's interests have been primarily in the relations between age-groups in American society. The plan to gather parallel data from students and their parents accordingly provided a welcome opportunity for collaboration. The Research has been supported in part by grant # MH 08062 National Institute of Mental Health; in part by grants from the Carnegie Fund for the Advancement of Teaching and the Survey Research Center of the University of Michigan. I wish to thank Professor Neugarten, Charles Derber and Patricia Schedler for their help in preparing the manuscript; its flaws are entirely my own responsibility.

This movement represents a social phenomenon of considerable significance. In the first place, it is having an important direct and indirect impact on the larger society. But secondly it is significant because it is a phenomenon which was unexpected—unexpected, in particular, by those social scientists who are professionally responsible for locating and understanding such phenomena. Because it is an unanticipated event, the attempt to understand and explain the sources of the student movement may lead to fresh interpretations of some important trends in our society.

Social-Psychological Roots of Student Protest: Some Hypotheses

How, then, can we account for the emergence of an obviously dynamic and attractive radical movement among Americans students in this period? Why should this movement be particularly appealing to youth from upper-status, highly educated families? Why should such youth be particularly concerned with problems of authority, of vocation, of equality, of moral consistency? Why should students in the most advantaged section of the youth population be disaffected with their own privilege?

It should be stressed that the privileged status of the student protesters and the themes they express in their protest are not *in themselves* unique or surprising. Student movements in developing nations—e.g., Russia, Japan and Latin America—typically recruit people of elite background; moreover, many of the themes of the "new left" are reminiscent of similar expressions in other student movements (Lipset, 1966). What is unexpected is that these should emerge *in the American context* at this time.

Earlier theoretical formulations about the social and psychological sources of strain for youth, for example the work of Parsons (1965), Eisenstadt (1956), and Erikson (1959), are important for understanding the emergence of self-conscious oppositional youth cultures and movements. At first glance, these theorists, who tend to see American youth as relatively well-integrated into the larger society, would seem to be unhelpful in providing a framework for explaining the emergence of a radical student movement at the present moment. Nevertheless, in developing our own hypotheses we have drawn freely on their work. What I want to do here is to sketch the notions which have guided our research; a more systematic and detailed exposition will be developed in future publications.

What we have done is to accept the main lines of the argument made by Parsons and Eisenstadt about the social functions of youth cultures and movements. The kernel of their arguments is that self-conscious subcultures and movements among adolescents tend to develop when there is a sharp disjunction between the values and expectations prevailing in the occupational sphere and those embodied in the family. The greater the disjunction, the more self-conscious and oppositional will be the youth culture (as for example in the situation of rapid transition from a traditional-ascriptive to a bureaucratic-achievement social system).

In modern industrial society, such a disjunction exists as a matter of course, since families are, by definition, particularistic, ascriptive, diffuse, and the occupational sphere is universalistic impersonal, achievement-oriented, functionally specific. But Parsons, and many others, have suggested that over time the American middle class family has developed a structure and style which tends to articulate with the occupational sphere; thus, whatever youth culture does emerge in American society is likely to be fairly well-integrated with conventional values, not particularly self-conscious, not rebellious (Parsons, 1965).

The emergence of the student movement, and other expressions of estrangement among youth, leads us to ask whether, in fact, there may be families in the middle class which embody values and expectations which do *not* articulate with those prevailing in the occupational sphere, to look for previously unremarked incompatibilities between trends in the larger social system and trends in family life and early socialization.

The argument we have developed may be sketched as follows: First, on the macro-structural level we assume that two related trends are of importance: one, the increasing rationalization of student life in high schools and universities, symbolized by the "multiversity," which entails a high degree of "self-rationalization," impersonality, competitiveness, and an increasingly explicit and direct relationship between the university and corporate and governmental bureaucracies; two, the increasing unavailability of coherent careers independent of bureaucratic organizations.

Second, these trends converge, in time, with a particular trend in the development of the family; namely, the emergence of a pattern of familial relations, located most typically in upper middle class, professional homes, having the following elements:

—a strong emphasis on democratic, egalitarian interpersonal relations
—a high degree of permissiveness with respect to self-regulation
—an emphasis on values *other than achievement*; in particular, a stress on the intrinsic worth of living up to intellectual, aesthetic, political, or religious ideals.

Third, young people raised in this kind of family setting, contrary to the expectations of some observers, find it difficult to accommodate to institutional expectations requiring submissiveness to adult authority, respect for established status distinctions, a high degree of self-rationalization, a high degree of competition, and firm regulation of sexual and expressive impulses. They are likely to be particularly sensitized to acts of arbitrary authority, to unexamined expressions of allegiance to conventional values, to instances of institutional practices which conflict with professed deals. Further, the values embodied in their families are likely to be reinforced by other socializing experiences—for example, summer vacations at progressive children's camps, attendance at experimental private schools, growing up in a community with a high proportion of friends from similar backgrounds. Paralleling these experiences of positive reinforcement, there are likely to be experiences which reinforce a sense of

estrangement from peers or conventional society. For instance, many of these young people experience a strong sense of being "different" or "isolated" in school; this sense of distance is often based on the relative uniqueness of their interests and values, their inability to accept conventional norms about appropriate sex-role behavior, and the like. An additional source of strain is generated when these young people perceive a fundamental discrepancy between the values espoused by their parents and the style of life actually practiced by them. This discrepancy is experienced as a feeling of "guilt" over "being middle class" and a perception of "hypocrisy" on the part of parents who express liberal or intellectual values while appearing to their children as acquisitive or self-interested. Fourth, the incentives operative in the occupational sphere are of limited efficacy for these young people—achievement of status or material advantage is relatively ineffective for an individual who already has high status and affluence by virtue of his family origins. This means, on the one hand, that these students are less oriented toward occupational achievement; on the other hand, the operative sanctions within the school and the larger society are less effective in enforcing conformity.

It seems plausible that this is the first generation in which a substantial number of youth have both the impulse to free themselves from conventional status concerns *and can afford to do so*. In this sense they are a "liberated" generation; affluence has freed them, at least for a period of time, from some of the anxieties and preoccupations which have been the defining features of American middle class social character.

Fifth, the emergence of the student movement is to be understood in large part as a consequence of opportunities for prolonged interaction available in the university environment. The kinds of personality structures produced by the socializing experiences outlined above need not necessarily have generated a collective response. In fact, Kenneth Keniston's recently published work on alienated students at Harvard suggests that students with similar characteristics to those described here were identifiable on college campuses in the Fifties. But Keniston makes clear that his highly alienated subjects were rarely involved in extensive peer-relationships, and that few opportunities for collective expressions of alienation were then available. The result was that each of his subjects attempted to work out a value system and a mode of operation on his own (Keniston, 1965).

What seems to have happened was that during the Fifties, there began to emerge an "alienated" student culture, as students with alienated predispositions became visible to each other and began to interact. There was some tendency for these students to identify with the "Beat" style and related forms of bohemianism. Since this involved a high degree of disaffiliation, "cool" non-commitment and social withdrawal, observers tended to interpret this subculture as but a variant of the prevailing privatism of the Fifties. However, a series of precipitating events, most particularly the Southern student sit-ins, the revolutionary successes of students in Cuba, Korea, and Turkey, and the suppression of student demonstrations against the House Un-American Activities Committee in San Francisco, suggested to groups of students that direct action was a plausible means for expressing their grievances. These first stirrings out of apathy were soon enmeshed in a variety of organizations and publicized in several student-organized underground journals—thus enabling the movement to grow and become increasingly institutionalized. The story of the emergence and growth of the movement cannot be understood solely as consequences of the structural and personality variables outlined earlier—in addition, a full understanding of the dynamics of the movement requires a "collective behavior" perspective.

Sixth, organized expressions of youth disaffection are likely to be an increasingly visible and established feature of our society. In important ways, the "new radicalism" is *not* new, but rather a more widespread version of certain subcultural phenomena with a considerable history. During the late 19th and early 20th century a considerable number of young people began to move out of their provincial environments as a consequence of university education; many of these people gathered in such locales as Greenwich Village and created the first visible bohemian subculture in the United States. The Village bohemians and associated young intellectuals shared a common concern with radical politics and, influenced by Freud, Dewey, etc., with the reform of the process of socialization in America—i.e., a restructuring of family and educational institutions (Lasch, 1965; Coser, 1965). Although many of the reforms advocated by this group were only partially realized in a formal sense, it seems to be the case that the values and style of life which they advocated have become strongly rooted in American life. This has occurred in at least two ways: first, the subcultures created by the early intellectuals took root, have grown and been emulated in various parts of the country. Second, many of the *ideas* of the early twentieth century intellectuals, particularly their critique of the bourgeois family and Victorian sensibility, spread rapidly. It now seems that an important defining characteristic of the college-educated mother is her willingness to adopt child-centered techniques of rearing, and of the college educated couple that they create a family which is democratic and egalitarian in style. In this way, the values that an earlier generation espoused in an abstract way have become embodied as *personality traits* in the new generation. The rootedness of the bohemian and quasi-bohemian subcultures, and the spread of their ideas with the rapid increase in the number of college graduates, suggests that there will be a steadily increasing number of families raising their children with considerable ambivalence about dominant values, incentives and expectations in the society. In this sense, the students who engage in protest or who participate in "alienated" styles of life are often not "converts" to a "deviant" adaptation, but people who have been socialized into a developing cultural tradition. Rising levels of affluence and education are drying up the traditional sources of alienation and radical politics; what we are now becoming aware of, however, is that this same situation is creating new sources of alienation and idealism, and new constituencies for radicalism.

These hypotheses have been the basis for two studies we have undertaken.

Study One, begun in the Summer of 1965, involved extensive interviews with samples of student activists and non-activists and their parents. Study Two, conducted in the Spring of 1966, involved interviews with samples of participants, non-participants and opponents of the tumultuous "anti-ranking" sit-in at the University of Chicago.

1. Activists Tend to Come from Upper-Status Families

Our study of the Chicago sit-in suggests that such actions attract students predominantly from upper-status backgrounds. When compared with students who did not sit-in, and with students who signed the anti-sit-in petition, the sit-in participants reported higher family incomes, higher levels of education for both fathers and mothers, and overwhelmingly perceived themselves to be "upper-middle class." One illustrative finding: in our dormitory sample of 24 students reporting family incomes of above $15,000, half participated in the sit-in. Of 23 students reporting family incomes below $15,000, only 2 sat in.

Certain kinds of occupations are particularly characteristic of the parents of sit-in participants. In particular, their fathers tend to be professionals (college faculty, lawyers, doctors) rather than businessmen, white collar employees or blue-collar workers. Moreover, somewhat unexpectedly, activists' mothers are likely to be employed, and are more likely to have "career" types of employment, than are the mothers of non-activists.

Also of significance, although not particularly surprising, is the fact that activists are more likely to be Jewish than are non-activists. Furthermore, a very high proportion of both Jewish and non-Jewish activists report no religious preference for themselves and their parents. Associated with the Jewish ethnicity of a large proportion of our activist samples is the fact that the great majority of activists' grandparents were foreign born. Yet, despite this, our data show that the grandparents of activists tended to be relatively highly educated as compared to the grandparents of non-activists. Most of the grandparents of non-activists had not completed high school; nearly half of the grandparents of activists had at least a high school education and fully one-fourth of their maternal grandmothers had attended college. These data suggest that relatively high status characterized the families of activists over several generations; this conclusion is supported by data showing that, unlike non-activist grandfathers, the grandfathers of activists tended to have white collar, professional and entrepreneurial occupations rather than blue collar jobs.

In sum, our data suggest that, at least at major Northern colleges, students involved in protest activity are characteristically from families which are urban, highly educated, Jewish or irreligious, professional and affluent. It is perhaps particularly interesting that many of their mothers are uniquely well-educated and involved in careers, and that high status and education has characterized these families over at least two generations.

2. Activists' Parents Are More "Permissive" Than Parents of Non-activists

We have just begun to get some findings bearing on our hypothesis that parents of Activists will tend to have been more "permissive" in their child-rearing practices than parents of equivalent status whose children are not oriented toward activism.

One measure of parental permissiveness we have been using is a series of rating scales completed by each member of the family. A series of seven-point bipolar scales was presented in a format similar to that of the "Semantic Differential." Students were asked to indicate "how my mother (father) treated me as a child" on such scales as "warm-cold;" "stern-mild;" "hard-soft"—10 scales in all. Each parent, using the same scales, rated "how my child thinks I treated him."

Table 1 presents data on how sons and daughters rated each of their

Table 1

Sons and Daughters Ratings of Parents by Activism (Percentages)

TRAIT OF PARENT	Males		Females	
	Hi Act	Lo Act	Hi Act	Lo Act
Mild-stern				
% rating mother "mild"	63	44	59	47
% rating father "mild"	48	33	48	32
Soft-hard				
% rating mother "soft"	69	61	60	57
% rating father "soft"	50	50	62	51
Lenient-severe				
% rating mother "lenient"	94	61	66	63
% rating father "lenient"	60	44	47	42
Easy-strict				
% rating mother "easy"	75	50	77	52
% rating father "easy"	69	44	47	37

parents on each of four scales: "mild-stern;" "soft-hard;" "lenient-severe;" and "easy-strict." In general, this table shows that Activist sons and daughters tend to rate their parents as "milder," "more lenient," and "less severe" than do non-Activists. Similar data were obtained using the parents' ratings of themselves.

A different measure of permissiveness is based on the parents' response to a series of "hypothetical situations." Parents were asked, for example, what they would do if their son (daughter) "decided to drop out of school and doesn't know what he really wants to do." Responses to this open-ended question were coded as indicating "high intervention" or "low intervention." Data for fathers on this item are reported in Table 2.

Another hypothetical situation presented to the parents was that their child was living with a member of the opposite sex. Responses to this item were coded as "strongly intervene, mildly intervene, not intervene." Data for this item for fathers appears in Table 3. Both tables show that fathers of Activists report themselves to be much less interventionist than fathers of non-Activists. Similar results were obtained with

Table 2

Father's Intervention—"If child dropped out of school" (Percentages)

| Degree of Intervention | Activism of Child | |
	High	*Low*
Low	56	37
High	44	63
N	30	30

Table 3

Father's Intervention—"If child were living with member of opposite sex" (Percentages)

| Degree of Intervention | Activism of Child | |
	High	*Low*
None	20	14
Mild	50	28
Strong	30	58
N	30	30

mothers, and for other hypothetical situations.

Clearly both types of measures just reported provide support for our hypothesis about the relationship between parental permissiveness and activism. We expect these relationships to be strengthened if "activism" is combined with certain of the value-patterns to be described next.

3. Activism Is Related to a Complex of Values, Not Ostensibly Political, Shared by Both the Students and Their Parents

Data which we have just begun to analyze suggest that the political perspectives which differentiate the families of activists from other families at the same socioeconomic level are part of a more general clustering of values and orientations. Our findings and impressions on this point may be briefly summarized by saying that, whereas non-activists and their parents tend to express conventional orientations toward achievement, material success, sexual morality and religion, the activists and their parents tend to place greater stress on involvement in intellectual and aesthetic pursuits, humanitarian concerns, opportunity for self-expression, and tend to de-emphasize or positively disvalue personal achievement, conventional morality and conventional religiosity.

When asked to rank order a list of "areas of life," nonactivist students and their parents typically indicate that marriage, career and religion are most important. Activists, on the other hand, typically rank these lower than the "world of ideas, art and music" and "work for national and international betterment"—and so, on the whole, do their parents.

When asked to indicate their vocational aspirations, nonactivist students are typically firmly decided on a career and typically mention orientations toward the professions, science and business. Activists, on the other hand, are very frequently undecided on a career; and most typically those who have decided mention college teaching, the arts or social work as aspirations.

These kinds of responses suggest, somewhat crudely, that student activists identify with life goals which are intellectual and "humanitarian" and that they reject conventional and "privatized" goals more frequently than do nonactivist students. More detailed analyses which we are just beginning to undertake support the view that the value-patterns expressed by activists are highly correlated with those of their parents.

4. *Activists Are More "Radical" Than Their Parents; but Activists' Parents Are Decidedly More Liberal Than Others of Their Status*

The demographic data reported above suggests that activists come from high status families, but the occupational, religious and educational characteristics of these families are unique in several important ways. The distinctiveness of these families is especially clear when we examine data from another study on the political attitudes of students and their parents. In that study, activist and non-activist families were roughly equivalent in status, income and education. Our data quite clearly demonstrate that the fathers of activists are disproportionately liberal. For example, whereas 40% of the non-activists' fathers said that they were Republican, only 13% of the activists' fathers were willing to describe themselves as "highly liberal" or "socialist," whereas 67% of the activists' fathers accepted such designations. Forty percent of the non-activist fathers described themselves as conservative; none of the activists' fathers endorsed that position.[1]

In general, differences in the political preferences of the students paralleled these parental differences. The non-activist sample is only slightly less conservative and Republican than their fathers; all of the activist students with Republican fathers report their own party preferences as either Democrat or independent. Thirty-two percent of the activists regard themselves as "socialist" as compared with 16% of their fathers. In general, both non-activists and their fathers are typically "moderate" in their politics; activists and their fathers tend to be at least "liberal," but a substantial proportion of the activists prefer a more "radical" designation.

A somewhat more detailed picture of comparative political positions emerges when we examine responses of students and their fathers to a series of 6-point scales on which respondents rated their attitudes on such issues as: U.S. bombing of North Vietnam, U.S. troops in the Dominican Republic, student participation in protest demonstrations, civil rights protests involving civil disobedience, Lyndon Johnson, Barry Goldwater, congressional investigations of "unAmerican activities," full socialization of all industries, socialization of the medical profession.

Table 4 presents data on activists and non-activists and their fathers with respect to these items. This table suggests, first, wide divergence between the two groups of fathers on most issues, with activist fathers typically critical of current policies. Although activists' fathers are overwhelmingly "liberal" in their responses, for the most part, activist students tend to endorse "left-wing" positions more strongly and consistently than do their fathers. The items showing strongest divergence between activists and their fathers are more interesting. Whereas activists over-

whelmingly endorse civil disobedience, nearly half of their fathers do not. Whereas fathers of both activists and non-activists tend to approve of Lyndon Johnson, activist students tend to disapprove of him. Whereas activists' fathers tend to disapprove of "full socialization of industry," this item is endorsed by the majority of activists (although fewer gave an extremely radical response on this item than any other); whereas the vast majority of activists approve of socialized medicine, the majority of their fathers do not. This table provides further support for the view that activists, though more "radical" than their fathers, come predominantly from very liberal homes. The attitudes of non-activists and their fathers are conventional and supportive of current policies; there is a slight tendency on some items for non-activist students to endorse more conservative positions than their fathers.

It seems fair to conclude, then, that most students who are involved in the movement (at least those one finds in a

Table 4

Students' and Fathers' Attitudes on Current Issues (Percentages)

ISSUE	Activists		Non-Activists	
	Students	*Fathers*	*Students*	*Fathers*
Bombing of North Vietnam	9	27	73	80
American troops in Dominican Republic	6	33	65	50
Student participation in protest demonstrations	100	80	61	37
Civil disobedience in civil rights protests	97	57	28	23
Congressional investigations of "un-American activities"	3	7	73	57
Lyndon Johnson	35	77	81	83
Barry Goldwater	0	7	35	20
Full socialization of industry	62	23	5	10
Socialization of the medical profession	94	43	30	27
N	34	30	37	30

city like Chicago) are involved in neither "conversion" from nor "rebellion" against the political perspectives of their fathers. A more supportable view suggests that the great majority of these students are attempting to fulfill and renew the political traditions of their families.*

* Data from our research which have not yet been analyzed as of this writing, will permit a more systematic analysis of the political orientations of the two generations.

NOTES

1. For the purposes of this report, "activists" are those students who were in the top third on our Activism index; "non-activists" are those students who were in the bottom third—this latter group reported virtually no participation in any activity associated with the student movement. The "activists" on the other hand had taken part in at least one activity indicating high commitment to the movement (e.g. going to jail, working full-time, serving in a leadership capacity).

REFERENCES

Coser, L. *Men of Ideas*, New York: The Free Press, 1965

Erikson, E. "Identity and the Life-Cycle", *Psychological Issues*, 1959, *1*, 1–171

Eisenstadt, S. *From Generation to Generation*, Glencoe: The Free Press, 1956

Keniston, K. *The Uncommitted*, New York: Harper, 1957

Lasch, C. *The New Radicalism in America*, New York: Knopf, 1965

Lipsit, S. "University Students and Politics in Underdeveloped Countries," *Comparative Education Review*, 1966, *10*, 320–349

Parsons, T. "Youth in the Context of American Society." in E. Erikson (ed.), *The Challenge of Youth*, Garden City: Doubleday Anchor, 1965

A NOTE ON THE BURMESE FAMILY

• Lucian Pye

Burmese politics are in part a distillation of certain fundamental qualities of Burmese culture and personality.

o   o   o

Two themes emerge in nearly all the early Western attempts to describe Burmese character. The first relates to the quality we have placed at the center of contemporary Burmese political culture, the contradiction between gentleness and violence. Whether the point of view was friendly or critical or objectively neutral toward the Burmese, all observers agreed that there were many paradoxes in the Burmese character.

One side to the Burmese character was usually described with such words as: happy, carefree, tension-free, outgoing, easygoing, cheerful, spontaneous, laughing, without a thought for the morrow, loyal, noncompulsive, and childlike. To this day the Burmese themselves tend to use these same words in describing what they consider to be their better national characteristics. The other side of Burmese character was usually referred to by such words as: touchy, overly sensitive, cocky, agressive, sullen, quick tempered, cruel, quick to take offense, shy, selfish, opportunistic, and other terms suggesting a potentiality toward anger and violence. Not surprisingly, in present-day Burma

Above selection reprinted from: Chapter 13, *Politics, Personality, and Nation Building*, Yale University Press, 1962. Deletions have been made by the editor in the interest of brevity.

these same words are used to describe what are still considered to be national weaknesses and faults.

The second theme which emerges from a survey of the literature on Burma is that Burmese character has consistently been corrupted by government and politics no matter who the rulers have been. The persistent assumption has been that all the generalities of the Burmese are attributable to governmental policies, and that, therefore, if the government could only be changed —or better still, if all government could be completely eliminated—the positive and profoundly good qualities of the Burmese would readily emerge triumphant and uncompromised. Significantly, the Burmese of today have also taken over this theme and customarily attribute the negative qualities of their character to the evils of governments, either past or present.

o   o   o

Contemporary anthropologists see many of the same qualities in Burmese culture, but they tend, as should be expected in this post-Freudian epoch, to link Burmese character more closely with the pattern of early childhood experiences. In seeking enlightenment on the Burmese family, we are primarily dependent upon the work of four social scientists. Hazel Hitson has produced a data-rich and penetrating report on the basis of a year of field work in a Burmese village.[1] A second recent study of Burmese national character was done by Lucien M. Hanks on the basis of field observations in Arakan at the end of World War II.[2] The third suggestive study of Burmese personality, an outstanding example of studying a culture from afar, was done by Geoffrey Gorer during World War II when field observations were impossible.[3] The fourth analyst of Burmese character, U Sein Tu, is possibly the most sensitive and certainly the most explicitly Freudian.[4]

On the basis of these four interpretive analyses and other sources,[5] it is possible to outline the most significant features of the early socialization process within the family setting. Broadly speaking, the Burmese family resembles the type of family common to most of tropical Asia. The Burmese, however, have tended to make less of a formal ideological issue over the importance of family associations than many other Asians, such as the Chinese, Japanese, and even the Filipinos. They are less prone to employ explicitly such concepts as family honor and loyalty, and they have not surrounded the principles of filial piety with quasi-religious sanctions. In spite of these qualifications, it remains true that no other institution in Burmese society places a greater demand on the individual. The family provides the unmistakable focus for all Burmese social life.

The atmosphere of the Burmese family conveys the impression of an intimate, active, crowded, and noisy way of life. Whether the home is that of the rural peasant or the wealthier resident of Rangoon, it provides almost no possibility for developing a sense of privacy. As the physical size of dwellings expands, the number of people who are expected to live together increases in almost direct proportion; so the amount

of space for the individual does not change greatly with income levels. Consequently the Burmese is brought up to feel that nearly all activities should normally occur in a group setting. This characteristic of the family situation may help explain why throughout life any urge toward privacy is more than counteracted by the comforts of being in the center of activities. Certainly a striking quality of the Burmese political class is that its members are never alone throughout their waking hours; they tend to surround themselves with at best an entourage and with at least a few cronies who never leave their sight. Just as in the family setting, well-being is associated with a constant need to interact with others and not to experience any of the sensations of physical isolation.

Within the family context, children are generally treated with a very high degree of indulgence; in Western eyes Burmese children are constantly in danger of being "spoiled." They are warmly accepted as a source of happiness and amusement, and almost no demands are placed on them until they are ready for schooling. The Burmese mother displays a high degree of genuine happiness and affection toward her child. The nursing relationship is apparently a physically and psychologically satisfying one for the child; he is nursed whenever he cries so that feeding occurs frequently and under quite matter-of-fact circumstances. The child is the object of attention by all members of the family, who casually pass him around among themselves while freely fondling, cuddling, and playing with him. Nobody, however, except the mother has any sense of responsibility for the child; others, when bored with him or attracted to something else, will unexpectedly break off the affectionate relationship.

There is also substantial anthropological evidence that the mother herself tends to vacillate between extremes of warmth and affection and of disinterest and exasperation. She too can become unexpectedly cold, distant, and uninterested. Frequently she may tease the child, excite him, arouse him, and then, if her mood changes, suddenly stop and seem to put him out of her mind. The child is thus brought up to feel that he has no control over the ways in which he is treated by others. Whether he is the object of kindly affection or completely ignored has little relationship to his own behavior; it is not a question of reward and punishment but of the mood of his mother. Thus from the time of his earliest experiences the child exists in a world in which there is no rational relationship, no recognizable cause-and-effect connection between his powers of action and choice and the things he most desperately wants. From this beginning the Burmese child comes to feel unconsciously that the world is fickle, and that those who seem warmest and closest can become the primary source of one's isolation. The Burmese child thus learns the most profound lesson of his life: there is impermanence in life, a far more profound form of impermanence than that implied by Buddhist preaching about the transitory nature of physical things, for this is the impermanence of human relationships.

As the child grows older, the spirit of permissiveness continues but in an erratic fashion. He is expected to cause his parents less trouble and absolutely no anxieties. He is not, however, given a clear set of standards of performance,

the achievement of which might yield predictable rewards. The parents make few demands for achievement; indeed, there appears to be very little in the Burmese socialization process which would produce what David McClelland has called a high sense of the need for achievement.[6] The world becomes increasingly demanding and dangerous, but the child is not taught in any firm fashion how to behave in order to reduce the element of danger and unpredictability in social relationships. He learns only that he should avoid as best he can becoming in any sense a nuisance. He thus tends to expect security from being subservient and yielding to all who are his superiors.

In addition, there is considerable evidence that the Burmese tend to rely heavily upon shame and ridicule in the socialization process, with the result that the child becomes extremely sensitive to the opinions of others. His sense of self-esteem is socially conditioned so that his sense of identity is determined to an unusual degree by the way in which others regard him. Fear of shame and need for praise and reassurance become all-important guides to behavior. Basically, however, the Burmese becomes dependent upon the opinions of others because the socialization process has left him with few internalized standards of behavior that are self-exacting and self-demanding.

Another feature of the early socialization process is the explicit use of fear. The child is apparently frequently controlled by being told that unless he submits to the will of his parents, he will be carried off by ogresses, bogies, or *nats* of the spirit world. The parents frighten him, but they themselves display no sense of fear. Thus in time fear becomes associated with loneliness, and conversely, loneliness and isolation become in themselves fearful; thus a Burmese can experience the sensations of fear when socially isolated, and it is possible and understandable for him to lose his head to fear when others about him are keeping theirs and appear relaxed.

The Burmese child is explicitly taught to think of his family as the center of his existence and as a shelter against all the dangers of the outside world. Loyalty and subservience to parents is the ultimate test of the character of the individual. From earliest childhood, the Burman is taught that he should always be infinitely careful not to bring any distress or unhappiness to his parents. Since the child is not trained to highly explicit standards of behavior, "good" conduct tends to become subservient and docile conduct. To yield to the wishes of the parents is to please them and to act in an exemplary fashion. Hence at a very early stage in life the Burmese child is taught to be completely submissive before any form of authority and to expect that a passive and yielding attitude is most likely to please those with power.

It is significant that in the relatively loosely structured Burmese society almost the only cumulative and reinforcing patterns of social pressures are those prohibiting any explicit revolts against the family. Once the child has entered the age of reason he is not expected to demonstrate even the slightest sign of opposition to family control. We may speculate that in Burma, as in much of the rest of Asia, the continued denial to youth of any possibility to express legitimately any sense of revolt against parental authority has led young people to direct their spirit of rebellion to an inordinate degree against other and less sacredly protected forms of authority. Thus in these societies many modern forms of authority become the ready objects of attack of a youth who paradoxically wishes to rebel against the old authorities and to accept the new ones. The sentiments of family are still far too powerful to be directly challenged, and yet the necessity of yielding to an authority that is unable to give psychic satisfaction, especially in a changing world, produces an increasingly rebellious spirit.

From the anthropological evidence about the Burmese family we can draw some very tentative conclusions about the early stages of the Burmese socialization process which may throw light on some of the problems of nation building. Specifically, it is possible to identify within the family relationships practices that may contribute to the paradoxical sentiments so central to the Burmese political culture. In terms of the early years of life, the contradictions take the form of an odd combination of optimism and distrust, a combination which in varying degrees seems to be present in many transitional societies having difficulties in modernizing.[7]

Personality theory might suggest that the qualities of cheerfulness and optimism so frequently noted in descriptions of Burmese character may be related to the relaxed, generous, and even blissful pattern of infant nursing. The family setting and the sympathetic spirit of the Burmese mother are conducive to a powerful sense of omnipotence, for in the beginning the world belongs to the child, responding to his every demand and eliminating his every frustration. Every time he signals displeasure or tension his world reacts to bring him food and oral gratification. This may possibly provide the dynamic basis for the irrational and almost compulsive sense of optimism which is never lost in spite of all the tests of reality.

Yet right after this phase of infant bliss comes the "betrayal" by the mother, who turns out to be controlled more by her own unpredictable moods than by the wishes of her child. The relationship that has shown the potentiality of being the warmest and closest has turned out to be unreliable—a traumatic experience. Thereafter it may always be hard for the Burmese to push aside a basic distrust of any relationship that pretends to be constant, loving, and generously helpful. For him, there is true danger and uncertainty in all human relationships.

A comparable and hence reinforcing sequence of experiences occurs when the boy is suddenly confronted at about school age with the shock of responsibility. The early and highly permissive years are devoted to instilling in the child a diffuse but powerful sense of dependency upon his family. The open, cheerful, noisy, and active qualities of young Burmese children, and for that matter most young Asian children, may be closely associated with this permissive and undemanding period. The sharp increase in demands for conformity at school age may contribute to the more withdrawn, cautious, and even sullen and suspicious airs of the older children when confronted with the outside world.

The sum effect of these early experiences appears to be a peculiar blending of a perennial capacity for optimism with a diffuse, all-pervasive distrust and suspicion of others in any particular relationship. The need to suppress all protestations against the very one who

has done the most to damage faith in human associations may be the origin of the violence and cruelty, the touchiness, the explosive tempers, and the readiness to take offense that many have observed to be one side of the Burmese character. These aggressive tendencies may spring from the child's denial of any legitimate way of expressing his aggressive and hurt feelings over his mother's having forsaken him. As in most traditional Asian cultures, he is forced to display unqualifiedly submissive respect to both his parents irrespective of how they may tease, ignore, love, or punish him. Any suggestion of hostility toward the parents is likely to be met on the manifest level with severe punishment, and on the latent level it is likely to appear as an attack on the mother, the one person with whom the child is seeking intimacy. Thus, deep down, the danger of offending the mother is that of courting isolation and loneliness. The child cannot strike back either directly or symbolically, but instead must show only greater respect and submissiveness. Aggressive feelings are thus dammed up, to explode later in other contexts where it is safer to drop the front of courtesy and deference.

These conflicting experiences within the family may possibly stand behind and give strength to the extraordinary resilience of the Burmese people, making it possible for them to believe constantly that the present is "the best of all possible Burmas," even while always acting on the basis of a profound distrust of those with power. Unable to resist the temptation of enjoying the pleasures of a superficial optimism, the Burmese at the same time seem equally unable to take a trusting view of the motives of others. On the one hand, the sense of optimism makes it possible for the Burmese people to go through crisis after crisis with remarkably little psychic damage; on the other hand, their fundamental feeling of distrust in human relationships, and particularly of the possibility for stable relationships, makes it extremely difficult for them to perform effectively in any organizational context. In terms of the requirements of nation building, it would seem that this peculiar combination of faith in the diffuse and suspicion of the particular is precisely the opposite of what is needed. A greater distrust of institutions and of forms of power and a greater faith in people would provide a far stronger basis for nation building. At least this would seem to be the case if we contrast these Burmese attitudes with those of people in more industrially developed societies. For example, the very basis of the American governmental system and its division of powers is a diffuse suspicion of institutions and of man's motives in general which, however, is coupled with an open and trusting approach toward particular relationships among individuals.

[In the section that follows, Pye goes on to give specific examples illustrating how the Burmese socialization process leaves adults ill prepared to handle what we have come to conceive of as the essence of politics, namely the management of conflict (ed.).]

o   o   o

Since so much of politics involves management of conflict and tests of loyalty, a crucial dimension of the socialization process relates to how people are trained to perceive and differentiate between a friend and foe. What are the obligations of friendship and how should a person react to enemies? Are people taught to think in terms of a continuum extending from the poles of amity and enmity, or in terms of two categories? In classifying people, how important are such differences as those between neighbors and strangers, between those in high places and those with no status to lose? Are most people like "us" and can they therefore be trusted to act as we do; or are most people "theys" who are different and dangerous?

There is possibly no aspect of the socialization process to which Burmese parents give more attention than teaching their children about the differences between friends and potential enemies. Nothing is more important than instructing the child to have absolute faith and loyalty in his family and unrestrained suspicion of strangers. Hitson has observed that the Burmese child is taught in countless ways to feel that he is safe only among his family while all outsiders and especially strangers are sources of danger to be treated with caution and suspicion.[8] Thus, for example, when the young child cries he is fed, but if he cries as he grows older, he is frightened into silence by threats that ogresses, or strangers, or Indians will carry him off. The child begins to learn that his society has a vertical dimension, consisting of authority figures that extend on into the supernatural realm, and also a horizontal one consisting of the in-group of which the family is the center and all the out-groups which are to be feared. The child learns to look upward toward a social hierarchy in which all above are to be treated with complete deference; and he also learns to look outward from his immediate family to his relatives, his neighborhood, his village, on to distant strangers, and to feel that each concentric circle is increasingly an area of danger.

In teaching the child to think of the family as a relatively safe island in a dangerous world, the parents give him a picture that is realistic in many respects. Loyalty to family is strong, and one never consciously harms another member of one's immediate family. However, in a deeper psychological sense there seems to be a basic conflict between family and self in Burmese culture. The test of a good child is whether he is *lein-mah-deh*. A *lein-mah-deh* child is one who is always ready to deny and sacrifice himself for his parents. The concept is a somewhat secularized version of the Chinese concept of filial piety. Not only is the child supposed to show respect for his parents, he is expected to be cunning and crafty in helping them against all outsiders. Even the daughter is expected to continue after her marriage to make sacrifices for her own parents. (Thus the insecure Burmese male must accept the fact that his wife, just as his mother before, has a prior obligation and commitment to someone else.) A deep sense of conflict arises because the *lein-mah-deh* child is expected to forget himself for his family, but his parents may act in an unpredictable manner toward him. He is told that the family is the safest of all places, and yet it is precisely within the family that he has received his deepest psychological damage, which has left him insecure. All the sentiments that might make him want to turn his back on his family come into conflict with the demand of continual sacrifice for them. His desires to forget the family in his quest for security conflict with the ideological belief that the family is the only safe place.

This sharp distinction between the in-group and all outsiders teaches the Burmese to believe that very few relationships can be affectively neutral. Casual relationships are almost impossible, for others may turn out to be more dangerous than they appear. Ideally the commitment of loyalty within the circle of friends is a powerful and demonstrative emotion, while actually the absence of conspicuously warm feeings suggests that there is a need to be wary. Since there is little middle ground, most relationships call for strong emotional reactions of one kind or another.

The intensity of Burmese feelings of friendship is revealed in the extraordinarily tight cliques common to student life. The groups of friends that form at Rangoon University tend to become the central forces of nearly all the activities of the individual student. The group may determine not only his extracurricular interests but also the subjects he studies. Moreover, the bonds of association are expected to last throughout his life, and particularly among the political class they can become the most basic ties of the individual's life. The loyalty is not to the idea of fraternity but to a particular set of individuals. Within the AFPFL many of the most basic relationships could be traced back to these university associations.

In many respects the Burmese seem to ask too much of friendship, especially in the light of their feeling of inner unsureness about others. The basic pattern of much of Burmese social life, whether in the village, the university, or national politics, is one of an anxious search for friends leading to the formation of a small but demanding clique, which becomes increasingly more intimate and all-encompassing until the strain becomes unendurable, there is an explosive falling out, and the search for friends begins again.

The problem of enmity is peculiarly great because to Burmese the socialization process does not provide the individual with explicit rules for handling conflicts. The individual is only taught that violence and disagreement are bad and dangerous, and cooperation and unanimity are good. There is little recognition that honest differences can arise and that conflicts can be conducted in orderly and lawlike ways. Within the society or within its politics there is little room for the concept of the opponent who is still the friend, and of a loyal opposition.

NOTES

1. Hazel Hitson, "Family Pattern and Paranoidal Personality Structure in Boston and Burma," dissertation, Radcliffe College, 1959. Hitson's thesis is that there is a relationship between the type of family culture, the socializing process, the way in which anger is handled, and the most likely form of mental illness in the culture. In particular, she advances the hypothesis that if the family culture deals with anger by turning it outward toward the environment there is likely to be a high incidence of violence and homicide, and if mental illness develops it is likely to take the paranoidal form. Conversely, if the home environment results in turning anger inward there will be a greater incidence of suicide, and mental illness will take a depressive form. On the basis of her data, Hitson concludes that the high incidence of violence in Burmese culture is related to the pattern of directing hostility against others.

2. Lucien M. Hanks, "The Quest for Individual Autonomy in the Burmese Personality," *Psychiatry*, *12*, no. 3, 285–300.

   Hanks concludes that at the basis of the Burmese character is a compulsive quest for autonomy, a need to be freed from all restraints, particularly those of superiors, and to escape from the dangers and uncertainties of human relationships. Hanks relates their urge to be rid of all superiors to the childhood experience of, first, extremely permissive early years, and then, the sudden introduction into the highly disciplined monastery schools.

3. Geoffrey Gorer, "Burmese Personality" (mimeographed; New York, Institute of Inter-Cultural Studies, 1943).

   After perusing carefully all available literature on Burma and interviewing people with firsthand experiences in the country, Gorer hypothesized that the Burmese socialization process produces a high proportion of insecure males, who as children were indulged but whose treatment by parents was subject to extremes of mood, and more competent women who early in life were forced to assume responsibilities. Thus for Gorer the final Burmese paradox is that "the dominant women act as though they were subservient . . . and the hen–pecked passive men talk and strut and pose as though they were really in control, consulting their wives surreptitiously, but announcing the decisions as if they were their own. The Burmese character is doubly distorted; the broken male struts like a master; and the dominant woman smiles and gives way to him."

4. Sein Tu, "Ideology and Personality in Burmese Society" (mimeographed; Harvard University, 1955).

The heart of Sein Tu's analysis is the hypothesis that the Burmese family provides an intense oedipal situation which is homosexually resolved. The child is extremely close to the mother and feels small and helpless before the domineering and frightening father who offers no basis for the son to identify with him. The son resolves this situation by identifying even more closely with his mother and emulates her in psychologically submitting passively to the father. By linking himself in this way to his mother the boy is able to feel closer to her, reduce his fear of being forsaken by her, and at the same time by "identifying himself with the aggressor" he is able to view his father as a seductive rather than destructive threat.

To the extent that this pattern is psychologically valid in Burmese life, one is inclined to speculate that it may leave the Burmese peculiarly sensitive to any appeals to changing his identity—a sensitivity which certainly exists, as we shall be observing in our discussion of the acculturation process. This is to say that the complex of feelings that the child may have toward his father may later be re-enacted in a psychological sense in his reactions to the modern world which he can perceive as threatening, demanding, but also attractive and seductive.

Thus while the child may long to be possessed by the father (feeling deep down a sense of competition with the mother), he also fears and repudiates his desires; hence he has the need to deny what he truly feels, and he may experience the transition from "I love him," through "I hate him," to "he hates me," which is the basis of a paranoid reaction. (O. Fenichel, *The Psychoanalytic Theory of Neuroses*, New York, Norton, 1945, pp. 427 ff.) As we shall be observing, the same pattern of transition seems to be basic to the reactions of many Burmese to the initially attractive but fundamentally threatening, appeals of modern culture and of the West.

5. The most useful general description of upper-class Burmese family life which conveys some nostalgic sentiments for the prewar Burmese life, is Mi Mi Khaing, *Burmese Family* (Calcutta, Longmans, Green, 1946).

6. David McClelland et al., *The Achievement Motive* (New York, Appleton-Century-Crofts, 1953).

7. The tendency to vacillate between unfettered optimism and profound suspicion emerged as a dominant characteristic of Indian personality as analyzed by A. Morris Carstairs, *The Twice Born: A Study of a Community of High-Caste Hindus* (London, Hogarth Press, 1957).

8. Hitson, "Family Pattern and Paranoidal Personality Structure in Boston and Burma," pp. 73–76.

SUMMARY OF CONCLUSIONS OF RESEARCH ON SOVIET CHILD TRAINING IDEALS AND THEIR POLITICAL SIGNIFICANCE

(Conducted as Part of Studies in Soviet Culture)

- ## Elena Calas

From the earlier official attitude, which reflected the belief that socialist society would take upon itself in full the up-bringing of children, the Soviet Government has shifted to an emphasis on the significant role of the family and family upbringing of children. Recent laws, decrees, and public announcements of leaders encourage the growth of a closely knit family and of parental authority. From the strengthened and united family the state expects full cooperation in the matter of molding "the moral countenance" of future Soviet citizens. Parents are held totally responsible for mental attitudes which they wittingly or unwittingly transfer to their children; they are called on to examine their own attitudes and behavior and to struggle against possible carry-overs (*perezhitki*) from the capitalist past. Parents must serve as models of political and social activity, industriousness, unselfishness, and optimism. This will guarantee them the love and respect of their children. Children become emotionally alienated from parents who do not act in accordance with the precepts and ideals which the children learn in school and in the Pioneer or Komsomol organization.

In relation to children, parents must be unremittingly vigilant, exacting, and consistent in disciplinary demands and in the imposition of duties; no relaxation of effort on the parents' part is permissible for fear that the child may fall under bad influence and be controlled by anti-social elements. While parents should show warmth, affection, and understanding, they should not permit excessive intimacy, which might undermine their authority. Parents must not be all-forgiving, for conduct deviations in children cannot be tolerated. Parental indulgence interferes with proper upbringing and turns a child into a despot at home and into a difficult child in the school collective. The ideal parents are little differentiated as to their function in relation to the child, the father being encouraged to assume equal responsibility with the mother in the matter of upbringing.

Upbringing must develop in children the qualities of personality which, combined, form the moral countenar.ce of a future fighter for communism: ideological purposefulness, strong convictions, patriotism, sense of duty, courage, endurance, tenacity, self-control, humanism, vigor, industriousness, optimism, generosity combined with the care of property, modesty, neatness, politeness, and sensitivity to the needs of others. Obedience is seen as the first step toward developing a disciplined will. Anxiety related to performance of duty is viewed as a virtue. Qualities are regarded as

Above selection reprinted from: Margaret Mead, *Soviet Attitudes Toward Authority: An Interdisciplinary Approach to Problems of Soviet Character*, McGraw-Hill, 1951.

virtues if they are socially oriented; they are undeserving of approval when used to further purely personal interests. Training from early infancy is recommended; constancy of effort on a child's part and the carrying through of any undertaking to the end receive heavy stress. The will to overcome obstacles must replace the intolerable tendency to follow the line of least resistance. Most related "noncompulsive" behavior is ascribed to the influence of the past through the medium of faulty family relations and attitudes. The planned transformation of man is rationalized by the concept of the moral betterment of man: "The process of remaking man which is taking place under the influence of socialistic conditions, as well as the creation of a new man, must attract the exclusive attention of Soviet pedagogy." It is admitted that the process of forming the new morality involves a difficult and tense struggle.

In all circumstances, personal interests must be subordinated to collective ones. The desirability of a large family is stressed because it affords the child his first experience of collective life, accustoming him to respect older siblings and to give succor to the younger. From an early age a child should be trained in a feeling of responsibility to the collective and in upholding the honor of the group (his class, or Pioneer brigade). The child should be trained to value highly the approval of the collective and to fear its disapproval. "The rules of conduct adopted by the collective become binding on the member, and finally one's sense of responsibility to the collective becomes the basis of self-evaluation." While it is one's duty to confess errors and misdeeds, to accept criticism with respect and without offense, and to

subordinate oneself to the demands of the collective, the moral gain for the culprit is placed in the foreground: "Courage is developed by the need always to say the truth, not to commit dishonorable, amoral deeds, and, if such are committed, courageously to recognize one's guilt before the collective and its leader, to submit to the condemnation of the misdeed and to become imbued with the determination to mend it." The emphasis is not on the cathartic release of guilt feelings but on moral growth. Adults may enlist the disapproval of a child's peers or may delegate authority so that corrective action comes from the child's collective. Organized collective (such as the Pioneer organization) may instigate corrective action independently by resorting to group accusation. While the role of comradeship and friendship is extolled, solidarity with the collective is placed above personal feelings of friendship. While interpersonal relations are generally approved, there is always the conditional factor: personal relations must fit into the required pattern, that is, they must serve the ultimate strengthening of the state.

Correct discipline should lead gradually to self-discipline. Every influence of the adult on the child, be it of encouragement or punishment, has as its aim the molding of the child's behavior, interests, views, and impulses, and the development of the convictions which will determine his future conduct. There is consistent emphasis on punishment as correction rather than as retribution. The nature of a misdeed dictates the handling of it, and when punishment is indicated it must fit the concrete circumstances of each case. Parents and teachers must be aware of the "point of application" of their educational influence (*vozdeistvie*), which requires an understanding of a child's motivations in committing a deed. There are frequent warnings against an abuse of punishment and scolding as well as of praise and reward, because through repetition they lose their effectiveness. An "eye to eye" talk is a recommended corrective measure which must be carried out when both the adult and the child are calm, because an adult's raised, irritated voice throws the child into either a state of sharp excitation or of inhibition. All forms of verbal reaction must be controlled, and in no event may they be used as catharses for adult feelings. Corporal punishment is outlawed, and other forms are warned against. Irony and humbling of arrogance are resorted to in cases of inadequate performance or bragging. A recommended punishment is the withholding of a treat, but this may not involve food. Repeated misdeeds which reveal bad traits of character and distorted concepts call for starting anew all the work with the child, and it is recommended that in the first place the parent place himself "under the microscope" to see in what way he himself has been inadequate to his task.

PARENTAL OVERPROTECTION AND POLITICAL DISTRUST

- Frank A. Pinner

The long-term objective of any student of political socialization is to specify how experiences account for personality orientations, and in what way the latter explain specifically political dispositions and actions. We are still a long way from this goal. Many of the available studies describe either relationships between individual experience and broad social orientations or else connections between social orientations and specifically political attitudes.[1] In the first case, the probable political effects of general social orientations can only be guessed; whereas in the second, the social experiences underlying general social orientations remain obscure.

In so far as researchers do attempt to link political orientations to individual experience, their work often suffers from a methodological difficulty. In the tradition of anthropological case studies, the writers merely demonstrate the simultaneous presence, in some one culture, of a certain pattern of child-raising together with some particular set of political orientations.[2] But they do not demonstrate empirically that within the culture they are considering there is a relationship between certain child-raising practices and the individual political orientations. Nor do they use the—however questionable—method of ecological correlations to show that cultures with different child-raising patterns also exhibit different political patterns.

Above selection reprinted from: *The Annals of the American Academy of Political and Social Science*, 361 (September 1965), 59–70.

These limitations reflect the difficulty of the questions we are attempting to answer. It is clear that the link between individual experiences and political orientation is, most often, indirect. Only under the most unusual circumstances will personal experiences, including patterns of socialization, have specific political effects. Given the length of the chain of causation leading from personal experience to political expression, and given the functional equivalence of many different human responses to the same social stimuli, the identification of political socialization patterns is bound to prove an arduous task.

The recent success of Almond and Verba[3] in showing certain connections between social experience and civic competence, that is, the citizen's feeling that he can be politically effective, is therefore particularly impressive. The authors show that civic competence grows out of experience and co-operation, for example, participation in family decisions, the right to complain in home and school, and other similar experiences which raise the individual's confidence that he has some control over his own life and his environment. The evidence for this finding is twofold: not only is civic competence high in those countries in which socialization experiences foster independence (ecological correlation), but the same relationship is found within each country among the individuals sampled (ordinary correlation).

Research Design

In this article, I will use a method similar to that of Almond and Verba. I will attempt to show a relationship between parental overprotection and negative orientations toward political processes and institutions which I will label "political distrust" and "political disaffection." "Overprotection" means here the practice of parents to restrict or control narrowly their children's contacts outside the home and to guide their intellectual and emotional growth with much anxious care. Rhoda Métraux and Margaret Mead, in describing French child-rearing practices, ascribe the pattern here called "overprotection" to the belief that infants and children are too fragile to be exposed to the dangers that lurk outside the safe precincts of the familial "foyer," so that learning by spontaneous experimentation must be discouraged; what is called for is not experimentation but, rather, careful nurture by reliable adults.[4] "Political disaffection" includes the belief that political parties are useless and divisive, and that politicians are immoral. "Political distrust" is a view of the world which holds that politics is conflictful, compromising, and threatening, and that politicians do not have the general welfare at heart.

Our hypothesis is that where young people experience much parental overprotection the transition from the warm protection of the home into the world at large—of which politics is part—is viewed with fear and apprehension. Consequently, youngsters so overprotected will demonstrate political distrust and political disaffection.

The data were obtained by means of paper-and-pencil questionnaires admin-istered in the spring of 1963 to Dutch and Belgian high school and university students. In addition, I will report results for a small group of French students from the Faculty of Letters of the University of Lille.

The Belgian university students were selected from all four Belgian universities —the Free University of Brussels, the Catholic University of Louvain, and the state universities at Liège and Ghent —while the Dutch groups come from only three Dutch universities—the City University of Amsterdam (public and secular), the Free University of Amster-dam (Calvinist), and the Catholic University of Nijmegen. In each of these institutions, as well as at the University of Lille, France, two methods were used for selecting respondents: straight proba-bility sampling of the entire student body and purposive selection of all "leaders." A "leader" was defined as a person occupying an official position in the governing body of a student organi-zation dealing with student problems or public affairs.

The high school student groups in-clude the entire three top grades of six Belgian and three Dutch establishments. The Belgian schools were chosen accord-ing to religious and linguistic affiliation; three of the schools belong to the public and three to the Catholic systems, and within each of these two groups there is one Flemish- and one French-speaking school as well as one from the linguistic-ally mixed Brussels region. Of the three Dutch schools, each belongs to one of the three major school systems: public, Catholic, and Protestant.[5]

In selecting the variables of parental overprotection and of political distrust and disaffection for my investigation, I was guided by what appeared to be, on

Table 1
Loadings[a] on Selected Factors for Walloon, Flemish, and Dutch University Students

ITEMS	Walloons — Social Confinement	Walloons — Guidance	Walloons — Ideological Detachment	Flemings — Social Confinement	Flemings — Guidance	Flemings — Ideological Detachment	Dutch — Ideological Detachment	Dutch — Social Initiation	Dutch — Ideological Opposition
1. My opinions regarding social, economic, and political questions are very different from those of my parents	20	−30	**45**	14	−08	**62**	**62**	−10	**53**
2. My parents do not object to my having friends with political opinions different from mine	01	**35**	38	−25	**31**	−01	−01	26	07
3. Problems that seem important to our parents are not necessarily important to us	08	−02	**72**	08	10	**51**	**51**	05	55
4. I often feel that the state of mind of today's youth is quite different from that of our parents	08	07	**71**	11	02	**61**	**61**	12	**60**
5. In my family, I have often been scolded for reasons that I didn't understand	**57**	−17	16	**53**	−08	37	37	06	**41**
6. Since childhood, I've always known how to please my parents	01	**49**	06	−14	**25**	00	00	06	06
7. My parents can't tell how much money I really need	**57**	−10	12	22	−03	43	43	04	**52**
8. I find it embarrassing to accept money from my parents	**53**	−04	10	04	07	47	47	**28**	**40**
9. Most of the important decisions regarding my future have been made by my family without my being consulted	**56**	−06	05	**44**	08	17	17	02	09
10. I often have problems that my parents are too old to understand	**52**	−08	**40**	36	−24	**41**	**41**	−04	**62**
11. When I have a really serious problem I ask my parent's advice	−24	**62**	−15	−17	**39**	−27	−27	**34**	**−51**
12. It's only with my family that I feel really comfortable	20	**36**	19	03	**53**	−22	−22	20	−13
13. I am surrounded by too much affection in my family	**46**	18	11	**34**	36	07	07	**44**	06
14. My parents often get involved in things that I could very well take care of myself	**56**	15	08	**61**	27	11	11	**44**	11
15. My parents would like me to make friends with people whose social background is different from my own	10	**47**	08	17	**62**	09	09	**50**	04
16. For a long time, my parents did not allow me to meet people of the other sex	**49**	00	11	**71**	−20	08	08	05	18
17. My parents often did not allow me to go out at night	**57**	10	−02	**70**	−09	13	13	13	21
18. My parents have always made sure that they approved of the friends I chose	29	28	−01	**60**	−09	−10	−10	**40**	05
19. My parents often have encouraged me to make new acquaintances	−04	**68**	−03	04	**69**	03	03	**70**	−09

[a] Decimal points omitted.

short inspection, salient and distinguishing characteristics of Belgian culture. The Dutch and French cases were included primarily for the sake of contrast (statistical control).

Since there does not exist any detailed description of Belgian child-rearing practices comparable to the previously cited work by Métraux and Mead on French child-raising, I have relied on the observations of Belgian professionals—social workers, psychotherapists, and sociologists—and on lengthy personal interviews with informants in order to determine to what extent the Belgian pattern is similar to the French one. The reports indicate that the French overprotection pattern prevails, with some slight modifications, in Belgium as well. The major differences appear to be that Belgians seem to prize restrained behavior on the part of children more highly than do the French and, therefore, contrary to French customs, avoid stimulating them. Dutch families are, in contrast, reportedly much more open in the secondary environment and encourage a certain amount of independent exploration among their offspring. Many informants cited certain behavior correlates of these attitudes toward child-rearing. For instance, the Dutch claim that their young people are organization-minded and thus gain much experience outside the home; Dutch young people are said to travel on their own or in groups more frequently and at younger ages than do their Belgian cousins; and Belgian university students prefer to live at home, often commuting over considerable distances in order to attend classes, while Dutch university students will rent a room of their own even if they attend a university in their home town.

Overprotection may lead to political distrust. Métraux and Mead point out that the world outside the "foyer" is made to look threatening to the child, and that fear of open conflict permeates the training of French youth. Since politics is both conflictful and external to the family, it may well generate political distrust among the overprotected. Lucian Pye makes a similar point in his study of Burmese personality and politics.[6] The hypothesis that distrust is one of the main ingredients of Belgian political culture will suggest itself to anyone who follows Belgian political debate for a time. The rather vituperative editorials common even in the more conservative Belgian papers frequently suggest that politicians will work for anything but the common good—although it is rarely clear just what it is they are supposed to be working for. And it is generally assumed in both political discussion and practice that political negotiations can never lead to constructive solutions but only to temporary and probably shaky accommodation.

Patterns of Socialization and of Political Distrust

In view of the hypothesized connection between parental overprotection and political distrust, the questionnaire contained a number of items dealing with family relations and with orientations toward political parties and politicians, toward political compromise and toward the institution of government. Once the data had been obtained, the various sections of the questionnaire were factor-analyzed for the purpose of finding out whether the hypothesized variables actually "exist." This technique makes it possible to ascertain which of the responses are part of some common syndrome describing broad social experiences or orientations. The levels of the correlation coefficients (or "loadings") are taken to indicate the extent to which a given item can be regarded as diagnostic of each syndrome.

Table 1 shows the loadings on those factors which appear to correspond most closely to the hypothesized overprotection variable. Only the data for Belgian and Dutch university students are shown. Since there are subcultural differences between Walloons and Flemings, the corresponding factors for these two groups are shown separately. The boldface numbers are the loadings on those items which I have used for the construction of indices utilized in the analyses to follow.

Of the three Belgian syndromes shown in the tables, two can be regarded as forms of overprotection, while the third represents an ideological reaction to this family pattern. The items which have high loadings on the factor I have labeled "social confinement" all deal with conflicts internal to the family. Those who give positive answers to this set of items are consciously aware of a lack of communication and cooperation between parents and children in their families and of their parents' tendency to restrict their activities and contacts on the outside. A second factor, which I have called "guidance," describes a somewhat different situation. Students who score high on these items indicate a strong attachment to the parents, a certain uneasiness about the world outside the family circle, and a tendency of the parents to encourage outside contacts. Finally, there is an "ideological detachment" factor which, for high scores, reflects the posture of

those who feel that they have ideologically moved away from a family they found too confining.

No factor corresponding to either of the Belgian overprotection syndromes exists among the Dutch students. And the Dutch "guidance" syndrome is different from its Belgian counterpart: there is less of the somewhat infantile attachment to the family we observe among the Belgian students, and perhaps less apprehension about outside contacts. There is also some awareness of parental manipulation which, in Belgium, is part of the "confinement" pattern. Other "confinement" items combine with those which are diagnostic of "ideological detachment" in Belgium to form the Dutch "ideological opposition" factor. This seems to indicate that, in Holland, excessive parental control generates reactions on the ideological level—a development that presupposes at least some level of communication.

The factor analyses of high school student responses (not shown here) support the notion that there is a distinctive overprotection pattern with deficient communication in Belgium. Among the Dutch, excessively controlling parents, while imposing rigid controls on their children's behavior, also favor the making of new social contacts. The reverse is true in Belgium, where overprotective parents appear to discourage such contacts. In Holland, overprotection is linked to deficient communication, while no such relationship exists in Belgium.

If we use a similar factor-analytic procedure in an attempt to identify patterns of orientations toward political institutions and processes, we find no sharp divergences between students

Table 2

Average Scores of Belgian, French and Dutch Students on Items Appraising Political Processes and Institutions [a]

Items	BSL	BSS	BH	FSL	FSS	DSL	DSS	DR
1. Our country would be better off if there were no political parties	−1.7	−0.8	−0.6	−1.8	−0.6	−2.5	−2.0	−1.5
2. Most people have preconceived ideas. There is no point in trying to give them a different point of view	0.3	1.2	1.2	0.1	1.4	−0.2	0.2	0.7
3. Discussions and negotiations between people who hold different opinions never lead to shared views but only to mutual concessions	1.2	1.6	1.3	0.7	1.7	1.7	1.7	1.3
4. It is dangerous to compromise with one's opponents, because the results are always disastrous	−0.6	−0.3	0.0	0.0	−0.6	−1.4	−1.1	−0.5
5. In public life it is dangerous to reach understandings on long-term plans, because men always try to escape their obligations	0.4	1.0	1.3	0.2	0.7	−0.4	0.0	0.6
6. Politicians often betray their voters by making deals with each other	1.5	1.3	1.1	0.9	1.2	−0.3	−0.4	0.2
7. The only decisions that are possible in our country are shaky compromises	1.1	1.1	1.1	0.2	0.2	−0.3	−0.1	0.6
8. In politics, it is better to work for agreements on limited points than on big problems	−0.3	−0.2	0.1	0.7	0.5	−0.8	−1.0	−0.5
9. Most political problems strike me as unimportant, since they are artificially created by our leaders	0.8	1.5	1.6	0.5	1.2	0.1	0.2	0.6
10. Politicians never tell us what they really think	0.8	1.5	1.6	0.5	1.2	0.1	0.2	0.6
11. Politicians only exaggerate the things that divide us	0.1	0.7	0.8	−0.4	0.0	−0.5	−0.6	−0.2
12. To succeed in our country's politics, you must get rid of all morality	−0.1	0.6	0.6	−0.4	−0.2	−1.2	−1.2	0.5
13. Most of our leaders are generous and devoted to the service of our country	−1.5	−1.5	−1.3	−1.3	−0.5	0.1	0.5	0.2
14. Government is:								
a. Capable	−0.8	−1.0	−0.9	0.3	−0.1	−1.0	−0.3	−0.3
b. Just	−0.6	−0.4	−0.3	−1.5	−0.5	1.2	1.0	0.1
c. Generous	0.0	−0.1	−0.1	−1.3	−0.6	0.3	0.4	0.3
d. Consistent	−0.3	−0.7	−0.9	0.1	0.6	0.2	−0.1	−0.1
e. Cultured	0.0	0.1	0.4	0.8	1.6	1.0	1.4	1.6
f. Honest	−0.6	−0.3	−0.3	−1.1	−0.8	−2.0	−1.2	−0.6
Totals	278	676	1124	33	84	82	387	659

[a] Legend: BSL = Belgian Student Leaders; BSS = Belgian Student Sample; BH = Belgian High Schools; FSL = French Student Leaders; FSS = French Student Sample; DSL = Dutch Student Leaders; DSS = Dutch Student Sample; DH = Dutch High Schools.

from the three nations. A political distrust syndrome, consisting in the belief that compromise is dangerous and constitutes betrayal of followers by political leaders, emerges in all the factor analyses. A second syndrome, equally well observable in all three political cultures, can be described as "political disaffection." People who score highly on this factor believe that political parties are useless and divisive and that politicians are immoral. A list of items diagnostic of these syndromes is presented in Table 2. Evidently, the institutional patterns of Western democracies resemble one another sufficiently to generate similar patterns of response.

Political Orientations in Different Political Cultures

If the patterns of political response are similar in the three countries, this does not mean, of course, that they appear with equal frequency. Belgian young people's judgments of political institutions and processes are generally much less favorable than those of their Dutch cousins, with the French occupying a middle position. The average responses to a set of political items are shown in Table 2. The respondents were asked to score these items on a scale going from —3 to +3, so that —3 signifies extreme disagreement, +3 thorough agreement, and 0 the absence of any position on the item.

The data reported in the table indicate, with remarkable uniformity, the relatively low esteem in which government and political processes are held by the Belgians. In assessing the merits of political leadership and of compromise, the Belgian students consistently

give less favorable appraisals than do the Dutch and often exhibit more negativism than the French. In evaluating government, the French exhibit, characteristically, the highest degree of opposition to authority, calling government unjust, dishonest, and ungenerous, even though consistent and cultured. Again, the Belgians are more negativistic with respect to government than the Dutch, particularly in impeaching government for its purported dishonesty.

Observations about possible trends in the development of political orientations can be made by comparing high school and university students (not counting leaders). Among the Dutch, there appears to be greater acceptance of political processes at the university level than in high school. This trend is much weaker among the Belgians, since the Belgian high school student averages are fairly close to those of university students. This may indicate a process of political maturation among the Dutch which is absent among Belgian students.

An analogous difference in political maturity can be noted by comparing the student leaders in each country with the university student samples. The responses to nearly all items show greater acceptance of political processes by the student leaders than by average students. This political-maturation process of leaders is particularly evident in Belgium and France, less so in Holland, so that the gap between the orientations of leaders and students is somewhat smaller in Holland than in the other two countries. In general, while student leaders become more acceptant of political processes, they grow at the same time more critical of government.

Table 3

Average Score of Belgian, French, and Dutch Students on Selected Items Dealing with Family Relations

Items[a]	BSL	BSS	BH	FSL	FSS	DSL	DSS	DH
5. Scolded, didn't understand	−1.5	−1.4	−0.9	−1.2	−1.6	−2.0	−1.8	−1.2
7. Parents can't tell ... money need	−0.7	−0.9	−0.4	−1.0	−1.2	−1.0	−1.1	−1.2
8. Embarrassing to accept money	−0.1	−0.3	−1.2	1.3	1.3	0.2	0.7	−0.9
9. Important decisions taken by family	−2.4	−2.4	−2.0	−2.1	−2.5	−2.3	−2.5	−2.3
10. Parents too old to understand	−0.4	−0.6	−0.5	0.6	0.1	−1.7	−1.4	−1.4
11. I ask parents for advice	−0.4	0.0	−0.3	−0.7	−0.3	0.1	−0.3	0.7
12. Only with family really comfortable	−1.0	−0.6	−0.2	−1.4	−0.7	−1.8	−1.7	−1.0
13. Surrounded by too much affection	−0.5	−0.4	−0.4	−1.1	−0.9	−1.1	−0.8	−0.9
14. Parents get involved	−0.9	−0.5	−0.1	−1.2	−1.0	−1.5	−0.8	−0.5
15. Friends of different social background	−0.3	−0.6	−0.4	−0.4	−0.6	−1.0	−0.8	−1.0
16. Not allowed to meet people of other sex	−1.9	−1.6	−1.4	−1.8	−1.7	−2.6	−2.4	−1.8
17. Not allowed to go out	−1.2	−1.1	−0.3	−1.6	−1.2	−1.9	−2.2	−1.8
Totals	278	676	1124	33	84	82	387	659

[a] For complete text of items, see Table 1 under corresponding item numbers.

Socialization Experiences

What I have called political maturity is, of course, the ability to cope with the world that lies beyond the restricted family circle, particularly with the conflictful and therefore threatening world of politics. The responses of Belgian (and French) young people show that they feel less capable of handling this environment than do their Dutch neighbors. They seem more suspicious and less optimistic, and they find it, therefore, difficult to believe that political compromise can eventuate in constructive solutions to public problems.

Such orientations are likely to develop where the transition from the intimacy of the home into the greater world is experienced as a difficult and fear-arousing step, and where there is little experience in the solution of problems through direct communication. This, it would seem, is the political significance of parental overprotection. Table 3 suggests that both strong attachment to the family and the feeling of being under excessive family control are more common in Belgium than in Holland, with France being somewhat closer to the Belgian than to the Dutch pattern.

The largest differences between means are found on responses to items dealing with direct behavioral restraint, with lack of communication (particularly the feeling that the parents are "too old" to understand one's problems), and with apprehensions regarding the world outside the family. The earlier and greater independence of the Dutch students manifests itself in their embarrassment over accepting money from their parents. The impression thus arises that Belgian students remain psychologically dependent longer than the Dutch, and that they have a harder time in detaching themselves from the family.

A telling pattern of behavior may be cited to support this conclusion. Among the Belgian and French students who have some income from a scholarship or their own work, it is not uncommon to hand all of their money over to their parents and then to receive from them an allowance for their own expenses. If we consider only students who have a separate income, slightly over 41 per cent of the Belgian student leaders and the same proportion of our Belgian student sample turn all of their earnings or stipends over to their parents. For French students, the corresponding figures are 19 per cent and 12 per cent and for Dutch leaders and sample members, only slightly over 2 per cent. This large difference cannot be explained on economic grounds, since the differences in the socioeconomic status distributions of the students' families in the three countries are neglible. And Belgian informants—professors and student leaders—spontaneously indi-

cated that this manner of arranging family finances reflects not economic need but psychological dependency. (Indeed, these observations by informants originally prompted me to include the questions regarding students' contributions to the families' finances in the questionnaire.)

In view of this striking difference in the behavior of students toward their families, the difference in means reported in Table 3 seem small. They may, indeed, underestimate actual differences in the amounts of overprotection present in the three countries. That is, the data may not be strictly comparable: each student group evaluates parental behavior by applying the only standard available to it, that of its own culture. Thus, in a culture where overprotection is the rule, parental behavior will be appraised with reference to what is considered to be normal parental behavior (even though an outsider may regard it as abnormally and excessively protective). To the extent that differences in evaluation can be detected, they reflect either the fact of culture diffusion or a process of change in local norms currently underway, or both. In any event, the discrepancies in responses

Table 4

Average Scores for Selected Political Items by Estrangement from Parents (Item 10; All Students)

ITEMS	Scores on Item 10: "Parents Too Old to Understand"							
	−3	−2	−1	0	1	2	3	r
6. Politicians betray their voters	0.3	0.5	0.6	0.7	1.0	1.3	1.5	.20
7. Only possible decisions are shaky compromises	0.3	0.5	0.7	0.2	0.9	1.0	1.4	.18
11. Politicians exaggerate what divides us	0.0	0.2	0.3	0.0	0.5	0.6	0.8	.14
13. Leaders are generous and devoted	−0.5	−0.7	−1.2	−1.0	−1.1	−1.4	−1.4	−.13
14a Government is just	0.4	0.3	0.0	0.0	0.1	−0.3	−0.5	−.18
14b Government is honest	0.5	0.4	0.1	0.0	−0.1	−0.2	−0.4	−.18

Table 5

Selected Index Correlations *for Belgian, French, and Dutch Students*

	BSL	BSS	BH	FSL	FSS	DSL	DSS	DH
Social Confinement by—								
Political Distrust		16	09		25	29	26	17
Political Disaffection		12	09	39		(19)	22	13
Ideological Detachment	36	32	30	46	22		34	35
Ideological Opposition	46	45	38	56	32		28	33
Guidance by—								
Ideological Detachment	−32	−19	−19	−56	−24	−29	−17	−15
Ideological Opposition	−22	−10	−09	−58		−23	−21	−11

[a] Decimal points omitted. Correlations which are not significantly different from zero on the .05 level have been omitted. The coefficient in parentheses is close to the .05 level.

recorded in Table 3 are probably quite conservative estimates.

Overprotection and Political Distrust

So far, an ecological correlation between overprotection and political distrust has been demonstrated. Where parental overprotection is frequent, distrust of government and political processes is also common. It remains to be shown that this relationship also holds when correlations are computed over individuals. A first impression of this relationship can be gained from Table 4. Here, item 10 in Table 1, which is part of the confinement and the ideological detachment syndromes, has been related to selected political variables. All of the subjects included in the study have been lumped into one group in this table and are thus treated as a large experimental group. This is the item that describes parents as "too old to understand" their children's problems. The means for groups with various scores on item 10 increase in a fairly regular manner from those with low scores on this item to those having high scores.

More specific information about relationships between family relations and political variables appears in Table 5. For this table, I have computed indices, all of which are the simple averages of sets of items having high loadings on some factor. The items used for the indices reflecting patterns of family relations are those shown in boldface in Table 1. The indices of political distrust and political disaffection are based on items shown in Table 2: items 3–7 for the distrust index, and items 1, 9, and 11 for the disaffection index.

The correlations between family and political orientations are all in the expected direction—this also holds for the coefficients omitted from the table because they did not reach the 5 per cent level of significance. Political distrust is positively related to social confinement, and political disaffection shows a similar, although smaller, relationship. But the connection between confinement and ideological detachment or ideological opposition is almost uniformly higher. Possibly parental overprotection generates a certain amount of alienation which, in many cases, expresses itself in conscious differentiation from the parents' ideological position. In so far as the parents' political beliefs are regarded as supportive of

existing institutions and social processes
—which they may or may not be in fact
—ideological detachment may then lead
to political distrust or disaffection. This
is at least one of the possible causative
chains linking political distrust to overprotection. Indeed, ideological detachment correlates positively with political
distrust (.19) and with political disaffection (.16); there is no reason why
this should happen, unless those expressing detachment from their parents'
social and political beliefs perceived
their parents as unduly trustful with
respect to political institutions and
processes.

While confinement within the narrow
precincts of the family spells subsequent
ideological detachment and political
distrust, the guidance index shows the
opposite relationship to ideological detachment. Those who report parental
attempts to lead them safely into the
world beyond the confines of the family
tend to remain ideologically attached
to the parents. This attachment reflects
their concern about social relations
which is part of the guidance syndrome.
It is probably for the same reason—
because of the lingering anxiety about
the world beyond home—that guidance
shows no negative relationships to
political distrust and disaffection. On
the other hand, guidance does show
fairly consistent, and sometimes
relatively high (up to .56) correlations
with political interest on the part of both
the parents and the respondents. Guidance also relates significantly, although
never highly, with various measures of
identification with government. Thus
guidance, which appears to be a milder
form of overprotection, seems to prevent
the kind of disenchantment that we
observe among the socially confined
subjects; it fosters maintenance of beliefs

in authority and even some bystander
interest in political phenomena, without,
however, producing mature positive
orientations toward political processes.

Individual and Cultural Orientations

It remains to be explained why the
reported correlations, although statistically significant, are for the most part
quite low; and why, in particular, the
relationship between social confinement
and political distrust is lowest in Belgium, where relatively high scores on
these two variables are most frequent.

The unexpectedly low correlations for
the Belgian cases may actually contain
a clue to the answer to both parts of the
question. If we suppose, as is likely, that
political distrust and disaffection are
part of Belgian political culture, then
we would have to expect that distrustful
and disaffected responses will be acquired not only by those individuals
who are predisposed by personal experiences to evolve and accept them,
but also by others not so predisposed.
If the means of mass communication
and the daily conversations of citizens
function as carriers of negativistic ideas
about government and politics, then the
expression of distrust would not be
restricted to those whose personal experiences might have generated distrustful orientations.

The same argument holds, of course,
for the expression of views regarding
parental behavior. Any culture generates expectations regarding the role
behavior of its members, and the culturally accepted assumption about
parental behavior may thus become the
common currency of adolescent discourse. Thus, any existing concordance
between reported social experiences

(such as overprotection) and political orientations (such as distrust) may become masked by cultural "noise"— which means lower correlation coefficients. Take, on the other hand, a culture for which the orientations under investigation are not so typical: the relationships between them will stand out more clearly, since there will be relatively few persons who give expression to these orientations unless they are not grounded in their own experiences and personality.

Thus, paradoxically, the low level of the correlation may in part be explained by the presence of cultural beliefs and norms of family relations in the countries studied, and the particularly low correlations in Belgium may, paradoxically, reflect the greater prevalence of these ideas. This raises rather serious questions about the strategy of cross-cultural research in politics.

The most obvious of these questions is whether it is wise to study relationships between orientations in environments for which these orientations are typical. As in medical and psychiatric research, would not the *atypical* cases allow the relationships to stand out more distinctly? In the present instance, would it not have been preferable to study the relationships between overprotection and political distrust in the United States where, presumably, both

orientations are less common? The answer depends on the research objectives to be pursued. If it is a matter of demonstrating a psychological relationship between experiences and resulting orientations, the answer may have to be affirmative. But if we wish to study the mechanisms that account for patterns of political behavior in different cultures, then we cannot afford to analyze psychological relationships apart from the cultural context.

Indeed, in studying the effect of socialization patterns upon political behavior, we must assume the existence of a cultural multiplier effect. Existing patterns of socialization as well as of political belief will be reinforced and maintained by the communication processes, so long as they still reflect some social reality, for example, the child-training patterns of a reasonably large number of parents or the behavior of a reasonably large number of politicians. The multiplier effect will insure that existing patterns remain ideologically the dominant ones even though the behavior and beliefs of the majority of people may have undergone considerable change. As political scientists interested in social-change processes, we must pay particular attention to, and evolve methodologies of detecting, these interactions between cultural and political orientations.

NOTES

1. The methodology of culture and personality studies typically links child-training experiences to social orientations, whereas such studies as *The Authoritarian Personality*, Theodore Adorno *et al.* (New York: Harper, 1949) explain political behavior as a function of personality.

2. Examples of this large literature are Geoffrey Gorer and John Rickman, *The People of Great Russia* (London: Crosset Press, 1949), which tries to explain

revolutionary impulses among the Russians as a reaction to the practice of swaddling. For a review of the numerous attempts to see German political authoritarianism as a consequence of the paternalistic-authoritarian family structure, see Roberta S. Sigel, "What Germans Think And Why," *Commentary*, 12 (1951), pp. 278–284. For a general review of the subject of national character, see Alex Inkeles, "National Character and Modern Political Systems," *Psychological Anthropology: Approaches to Culture and Personality*, ed. Francis L. K. Hsu (Homewood, Ill.: Dorsey Press, 1961).

3. Gabriel Almond and Sidney Verba, *The Civic Culture* (Princeton, N.J.: Princeton University Press, 1963), chap. 12, particularly pp. 347–360.

4. Rhoda Métraux and Margaret Mead, *Themes in French Culture* (Stanford, Calif.: Stanford University Press, 1954), pp. 16 f., 27–35.

5. Although the sampling rates used in the various universities were not uniformly the same, no attempt has been made to correct for the oversampling of certain institutions by appropriate weighting. This would have been possible only in the Belgian universities, where the entire population was used for sampling. Since sampling rates were so determined as to give each subgroup (Flemings, Walloons, various religious groups) adequate representation, the design tends to result in the over-estimation of variances within each nationality group and thus to increase sampling error.

6. Lucian Pye, *Politics, Personality and Nation Building* (New Haven, Conn.: Yale University Press, 1962), pp. 183 f. Note, however, that the permissiveness in Burmese child-rearing and the fickleness of the mother, which Pye describes, are not part of the Belgian pattern. [A selection from the work appears in this volume, pp. 192–200 (ed.).]

PRESIDENTIAL ASSASSINATION: A CASE STUDY IN THE DYNAMICS OF POLITICAL SOCIALIZATION*

- ## Karen Orren and Paul Peterson

How does society transmit political attitudes and orientations to its young? Considerable data have been amassed to demonstrate the importance of the primary group, particularly the family, as a determinant of party identification, political participation, and political beliefs.[1] Other research in political socialization has examined childhood and adolescent information about and attitudes towards the political system, and has traced their development toward mature political behavior.[2] But there is little literature that examines the *dynamics* of the socialization process, that focuses on socializing agencies such as family, school, and mass media in the actual process of directing and influencing the younger political generation.

The following paper is a preliminary inquiry into the dynamics of political socialization. It considers one aspect of the overall process—how and why parents verbally interpret a political event to their children. The data are based on a national modified probability sample of parents with children ages four to twelve.[3] Shortly after the assassination of President Kennedy, these parents were asked by interviewers of the National Opinion Research Center whether and how they explained the assassination to their children.[4]

I

First, a word may be said about the assassination of the President as a subject for research in political socialization. . . . That his assassination had a shocking impact on the child's political world —a world as yet undifferentiated from other aspects of the controlling environment[5]—was reflected in one report of a mother from Houston, Texas: "When my little girl came out of school she told me someone killed the President, and her thoughts were—since the President was dead, where would we get our food and clothes from?"[6] Presidential assassination, therefore, may have been expected to galvanize the process of political socialization. Parents, as well as other socializing agents, were called on to explain, to interpret, to reassure—to perform, in other words, their normal functions in circumstances of special demand.

The extraordinary nature of this political event increased the probability that parents would be aware of their attempts to explain political life to their children.[7] This enabled interviewers to catch a glimpse of the socialization process, permitting the isolation of those variables which determine whether or not parents explained the assassination. Consideration could then be given

Above selection reprinted from: *Journal of Politics*, 29, 2 (May 1967), 388–404.

* The authors wish to thank the National Opinion Research Center, University of Chicago, for making available the data on which this research is based and for staff assistance with various technical operations. They also wish to thank David Easton and Mildred Schwartz for their constructive criticisms of an earlier draft.

to the possibility that factors determining parental interpretation of this event might also be operating when less traumatic political events occur.[8] Furthermore, conscious efforts at interpreting a political event facilitated the generating of data on the content of the explanations given; this enabled us to examine the nature of the attitudes transmitted.

Our data pertain to parents' verbal explanations. But they by no means imply that this kind of communication is the only or most important means of political socialization within the home. Indeed, 65 per cent of the population reported that they did not explain the event to their children beyond telling them that someone had shot the President.[9] The atmosphere of sorrow or anxiety in the home, or a confused and unresponsive parent, might have

had equal if not greater effect on the child's perception of the awesome occurrence. On the other hand, parents who were aware of their attempts to give the assassination meaning were likely to have made greater efforts to interpret it to their children. Those children, moreover, to whom such explanations were given, may have gained a heightened understanding of the assassination. Thus, distinguishing between parents who said they explained the assassination from those who said they did not may reveal what factors help determine whether a parent conveys to the child an increased understanding of political events.[10]

II

What kinds of parents, then, explained the assassination to their children? The

Table 1

Parents' Emotional Involvement and "Explaining": Percentage of Parents Who Explained the Assassination to Their Children by Level of Emotional Involvement

INDICATORS OF EMOTIONAL INVOLVEMENT	LEVEL OF EMOTIONAL INVOLVEMENT[a]		
	High	Medium	Low
	(Per Cent of Parents Explaining Assassination)		
Felt sorrow that a strong young man had been killed at the height of his power	39 (385)	29 (223)	18 (72)
Felt sorry for his wife and children	39 (411)	29 (222)	28 (47)
Felt the loss of someone very close and dear	35 (336)	38 (222)	29 (122)
Felt more upset than most when first hearing the news of assassination	39 (121)	35 (510)	23 (39)
Felt angry that anyone should do such a terrible deed	40 (314)	33 (218)	28 (145)
Felt worried about how his death would affect our relations with other countries	45 (119)	34 (205)	33 (343)

[a] The parent was asked whether the emotion expressed in each statement had been his "very deepest feeling," had been felt "quite deeply," had "crossed my mind" or had "never occurred to me." The first response was considered "high" emotional involvement; the second, "medium," and the last two were considered as showing "low" emotional involvement.

first of two factors differentiating these parents from those who gave no explanation was their level of *emotional involvement*, as measured by responses to the six items listed in Table 1. On every indicator the more emotionally involved parents were more apt to explain the assassination than the less emotionally involved. The "explainers"[11] felt more sorrowful that a strong, young man had been killed at the height of his powers, felt more sorry for the President's wife and children, felt more deeply the loss of someone very close and dear, were more upset at the news of the assassination, were angrier that anyone would do such a terrible deed, and were more worried about the effect of Kennedy's death on United States' relations with other countries. The strongest correlate (.23) with "explaining" among the items measuring emotional involvement was "Felt sorrow that a strong, young man had died at the height of his powers."[12] This item, which in many ways measured the parents' response to the person occupying the White House rather than their response to the loss of a *political* leader, will be used as our indicator of emotional involvement below.

An equally powerful discriminator between those who explained the assassination and those who did not was parent's information as measured by two items included in the questionnaire. One of these asked respondents to recall other assassinations that had occurred within the past year. A sizeable percentage mentioned the assassination of Viet Nam's Premier Ngo Dinh Diem,[13] and this response was used to differentiate parents on *current events information*. Those mentioning Diem were considered high on this index, while those parents who could remember

Table 2

Parents' Political Information and "Explaining:" Percentage of Parents Who Explained the Assassination to their Children by Level of Political Information

TYPE OF POLITICAL INFORMATION	LEVEL OF INFORMATION	
	High	Low
	(Per Cent of Parents Explaining Assassination)	
Current Events	40	29
	(250)	(337)
Historical	38	30
	(210)	(250)

no assassination at all were considered *low*. Table 2 shows that 40 per cent of parents so politically informed explained the assassination of Kennedy to their children, while only 29 per cent of those not so informed were "explainers."

A less powerful predictor of "explaining" was the second indicator of political information, an item asking respondents to name the other presidents who had been assassinated. Those who named all three—Garfield, Lincoln, McKinley—were considered *high on historical information*, while those who could name one or none were considered *low*.[14] As Table 2 shows, 38 per cent who named all three presidents explained the assassination of Kennedy, as compared with only 30 per cent of those who did not have such historical political information.

The question arises whether the emotionally involved and the politically informed were the same parents. Table 3 shows that both emotional involvement and political information had an effect on "explaining" independent of each other. The correlation between emotional involvement and "explaining" remained just as high when either measure of political information was used as a control as when there was no control. The relationship between political information and "explaining" declined slightly when emotional involvement was held constant, but a residual correlation still remained.

Such a summary statement of the relationship among these variables obscures the interesting interaction that exists among them. Table 4 demonstrates the relationship between political information and "explaining" at various levels of emotional involvement. Among parents with strong emotional involvement, the correlation between political information and "explaining" was virtually non-existent, but among those with weak emotional involvement, the correlation was considerable. Among those strongly affected by the assassination, it was not necessary to be politically informed to explain the assassination. On the other hand, those

Table 3

Relationship Among Emotional Involvement, Political Information, and Explaining the Assassination

	Correlation with "Explaining"
I. Emotional Involvement	
No Control for Political Information	.23
Control for Current Events Information	.24
Control for Historical Information	.23
II. Political Information	
A. Current Events	
No Control for Emotional Involvement	.24
Control for Emotional Involvement	.20
B. Historical	
No Control for Emotional Involvement	.12
Control for Emotional Involvement	.07

Table 4

Political Information and "Explaining" by Level of Emotional Involvement

Political Information		Correlation with "Explaining"
A. Current Events		
Information	High	.19
when Emotional	Medium	.20
Involvement is	Low	.62
B. Historical Information		
when Emotional	High	.05
Involvement is	Medium	.12
	Low	.43

who had low emotional involvement tended not to give an explanation unless they were politically informed.

This kind of analysis can be applied equally well to show the relationship between emotional involvement and "explaining" at various levels of political information. Table 5 reveals that when political information was high, the correlation between emotional involvement and conscious explaining of the assassination to children was weak. On the other hand, when political information was low, the correlation between emotional involvement and "explaining" was much stronger. It seems that when political information was present, the parent did not need to be emotionally involved to explain what had happened to his children. But when political knowledge was absent, parents did not explain the assassination to their children unless they were emotionally involved.

In summarizing the complex relationship among these three variables, we can say that both emotional involvement and political information were determinants of parents' explaining Kennedy's assassination to their children. Furthermore, the two variables

Table 5

Emotional Involvement and "Explaining" by Level of Political Information

		Correlation with "Explaining"
Emotional Involvement when Current Events Information is	High	.12
	Low	.29
Emotional Involvement when Historical Information is	High	.07
	Low	.30

tended to compensate for each other. When political knowledge was present, it was not necessary for the parent to be emotionally involved to explain the event to his children. When the parent was emotionally involved, it was not necessary for him to be politically informed in order to take on the socializing task. But if both factors were absent it was highly unlikely that he would give any explanation—only one out of ten such parents explained the assassination to their children.

The relationship that political information had with "explaining" suggested the hypothesis that those persons whom previous research had shown to have a high level of political involvement—persons in high prestige occupations,[15] those who identify with the middle and upper classes, the more educated, and those who vote for the "prestige" Republican party—would have been more likely to explain the assassination.[16]

Table 6 shows that there was a slight relationship between these indicators of social status and "explaining," but the correlation was weaker than the one between current events information and "explaining." Moreover, again it was found that these indicators showed a stronger relationship with "explaining" when the third variable, emotional involvement, was low. On the other hand, when the parent was highly emotionally involved in the event, his social status seemed to have had little impact on whether he explained the assassination.

This relationship between social status and explaining the assassination may be interpreted in one of two ways. It may be argued that upper-status families have gained more information about the political system (and, indeed, we found

Table 6

Parents' Social Status and "Explaining" by Levels of Emotional Involvement

		Occupation	Class Identification	Education	Party
			Indicators of Social Status		
Correlation with Explaining— No control for emotional involvement		.17	.13	.11	.13
Correlation with Explaining When Emotional Involvement is	High	.16	−.03	.14	.18 (385)
	Medium	.14	.36	−.05	.14 (236)
	Low	.36	.44	.42	.26 (72)

a fairly strong correlation [Q equals .36] between occupational prestige and political information), and are more ready to transmit it to their children. An alternate interpretation, which seems to be held by Fred Greenstein, is that these families communicate more with their children independent of their political information and that this leads to more adequate preparation for active participation in politics on the part of their children.

Upper-status parents take the child's opinions seriously, explain the reasons for parental requirements, and discuss family problems with the child. In general, parent-child relationships are more open, less punitive, and more accommodating to the child's individuality. . . .

All of this is certainly relevant to the capacity and desire to raise children who are able to perform the rather intricate manipulation of symbols involved in effective political participation.[17]

Table 7 indicates that the truth may lie somewhere in between these two interpretations. Where political information was present, there was virtually no relationship between status, as measured by occupational prestige, and explaining the assassination. Among those parents of lower status who were politically informed, there was the same willingness to explain as there was among the presumably more communicative higher status parents. On the other hand, the same table indicates that among those having less political information, there was considerably more "explaining" among higher status than lower status parents.[18]

This suggests an interesting hypothesis of both theoretical and practical relevance. Socialization of lower status

Table 7

Parents' Occupational Prestige and "Explaining" by Level of Parents' Political Information

Political Information	OCCUPATIONAL PRESTIGE	
	High	Low
	(Per Cent of Parents "Explaining")	
High[a]	42[b] (120)	40[b] (124)
Low	40[c] (112)	25[c] (247)

[a] Current events information was used as indicator of political information.
[b] Q coefficient for this relationship was .04.
[c] Q coefficient for this relationship was .034.

children into more active political roles may not be entirely dependent on the adoption by lower status parents of middle class family relationships, as Greenstein's argument leads one to conclude. Rather, as lower status parents gain more information about political life this may be in itself sufficient to increase the capacity of lower status families to socialize their young into more active political roles.

III

What kinds of explanations were given to children by parents who did explain the assassination? The content of the explanations was distributed among the following five categories: 1) 3 per cent concentrated on the virtues of the slain President—"Mostly I tried to explain that a great person had been killed," "I told her we had a brave President;" 2) 3 per cent emphasized the tragic or terrible nature of the event—"This was a terrible thing," ". . . it was very tragic;" 3) 11 per cent focused their explanation on the diseased or wicked character of the assassin—"I told him some man mentally ill and sick and didn't know what he was doing at the time, but his sickness was the kind that he probably felt better killing somebody like the President," "I told them a bad man killed our President;" 4) 4 per cent gave a religious significance to the assassination—"I took him on my lap and told him all people were not good, so we will just have to pray for them, and ask God to forgive them," "I just told them we'd better kneel down and pray—the President was just killed;" 5) 6 percent placed the event in a historical or political context for their children: these explanations ranged in sophistication from the mere observation that "history was being made," to a discussion of Lincoln's assassination —"I told her about Lincoln's assassination one hundred years ago and now she was living to see one, and that I thought neither of us would live to see this in our country,"—to explanations of "our form of government," with discussions of presidential succession.[19] It should be noted that none of the explanations suggested that any good, personal or political, could come from the assassination. Rather they indicated admiration for the President, respect or reverence for the American political order, and stern disapproval of the assassin's behavior. In this way, all explanations were supportive of the political system.[20]

Along with transmitting orientations favorable to the political system, there was evidence supporting David Easton's and Robert Hess' suggestion that parents shield their children from the more sordid realities of political life.[21] At the time of the interviewing 62 per cent of the national sample thought that other persons were involved with Oswald in the plot. Twenty-three per cent of the sample volunteered that

Oswald was either paid, ordered, or persuaded to commit the crime, and one-tenth mentioned that Ruby was involved in the assassination (even though this was irrelevant to the question asked by the interviewer).[22] No hint, however, of such an interpretation appeared in the explanations parents gave to their children. No parent told his child about the possibility of a conspiracy. Instead, if they mentioned the assassin, it was to explain that the man who killed the President was wicked or insane.

This attempt at sugarcoating, and its evident success, is indicated in children's reactions to the assassination as reported by Roberta Sigel. She presents evidence on the reactions of 1349 primary and secondary school children in metropolitan Detroit indicating that children, unlike adults, avoided a conspiratorial view of the assassination. Sigel reports, "When asked who was to blame for the President's death," children (in an open-ended question) tended to think exclusively of Oswald. Russia and Communism were mentioned by only four children. No child mentioned Castro, Cuba, or extremists of the right and left.[23]

The kind of explanation given tended to vary with the age of the child.[24] Table 8 shows that the religious explanation was given most frequently to younger children. We may speculate that death itself may be an unfamiliar and preoccupying phenomenon to younger children, requiring an explanation from the religious sphere. Younger children were also told with greater frequency that the event was perpetrated by a wicked or demented individual. Perhaps this fact reflects general tendency of parents in dealing with children of this age to stress the "good" or "bad" aspects of behavior.[25] Or it may be connected to the hypothesis that the idealization of political authority is in part designed to cope with the child's feelings of aggression with regard to superior power.[26] By labelling the deed atypical and immoral, parents tried to restore the child's normal perceptions of a benign political world and pointed to the illegitimacy of acting out agressive impulses toward figures of authority.

The older the child, the more likely that the event would be placed in a historical or political context. Older children are better able to understand the general workings of the political system and are more familiar with American history. This explanation tells the child that the political order is not dependent on the existence of one man, even though that man is the President. It gives the child a broader framework within which he may place the assassination. It conveys information about the political system. Most important, the historical or political explanation (like the other explanations as well) in this particular crisis may have reflected the kind of response given the same child in more usual circumstances. It may be the cumulative impact of a large number of explanations, all of which help to place particular events in a broader context that help some children to be better prepared for participation in the adult political world.

The parents giving the historical or political explanation, therefore, are of peculiar interest to our study. Since the data indicate that the explanation was appropriate only to those children with some knowledge of American history or government, our analysis has been confined to those parents with children who have begun formal education.

Table 9 demonstrates that political information of the parent was the factor most closely associated with giving a historical or political explanation of the assassination. None of the measures of emotional involvement were either positively or negatively related to giving this kind of explanation except to the one concerning worry over how the assassination would affect our relations with other countries. This, the most "political" of the measures of emotional involvement, showed a comparatively

Table 8

Age of Child and Kinds of Explanations

| | Age of Child[a] | | |
EXPLANATION	*4–5 yrs.*	*6–9 yrs.*	*10–12 yrs.*
Tragic Event	3%	6%	7%
Evil or Insane Assassin	14	12	4
Religious	8	2	3
Historic or Political	1	5	7
Miscellaneous, Vague	4	10	6
No Explanation	71	65	74
Total	101%	100%	101%
(N)	(23)	(35)	(26)

[a] In families with only one child age 4-12. See footnote 20.

Table 9

Parents' Political Information, Concern over the Assassination's Effect on International Relations, Occupational Prestige, and Class Identification and Historical or Political Explanation by Age of Child

CHARACTERISTIC OF PARENTS	AGE OF CHILD[a]	
	6–9 yrs.	10–12 yrs.
	(Per Cent of Parents Giving Historical or Political Explanation)	
Concern about International Relations		
High	8	10
	(48)	(51)
Low	2	2
	(57)	(51)
Political Information		
A. Historical		
High	8	8
	(41)	(26)
Low	0	4
	(65)	(78)
B. Current Events		
High	5	14
	(41)	(43)
Low	5	2
	(59)	(52)
Occupation		
High Prestige	8	11
	(40)	(35)
Low Prestige	3	5
	(39)	(57)
Class Identification		
Middle and Upper Class	7	8
	(57)	(30)
Lower and Working Class	2	5
	(44)	(42)

[a] In families with only one child age 4-12, see footnote 20.

strong relationship with the historical or political explanation in both age categories. Finally those employed in the more prestigious occupations and who identified with the middle or upper classes (i.e., those from the demographic groups which tend to have more political information) were also more apt to give this explanation.[27]

Other research has demonstrated that politically informed parents tend to have politically informed children. Political activists often come from families where interest in and knowledge about politics runs high.[28] Our research may have caught a glimpse of the transmission of information about politics from parents to children. Parents who were politically informed were more apt to give an explanation about a political event that would enable their children to place this event in an appropriate context. When many such instances occur, children from these families may well acquire greater interest in politics and eventually feel more competent to participate in the political process. In this way the tendency toward political activism may be passed from generation to generation.

We may summarize our argument as follows:

1) The more emotionally involved the parent, the more likely that he would explain the assassination to his child. The full implications of this finding must await further research on parents' emotional involvement in major political events and the effects of this involvement on the attitudes of their children. Meanwhile, we may speculate that few political events produce the emotional involvement provoked by President Kennedy's assassination. In the more typical political event, the population may look more like the less emotionally involved portion of our sample. It is among this group that political information was the important determinant of explaining.

2) The more politically informed the parent, the more likely that he would explain the assassination to his child. As might be expected, those parents whose own political information reflects their interest or involvement in politics were the ones who were most ready and able to verbally interpret this event to their children.

These same parents, moreover, were likely to give an historical or political explanation to their children. This suggests one reason why the more politically informed parents tend to have politically informed children. The cumulative impact of this readiness to explain and the more adequate nature of explanation given is likely to lead to the child's better preparation for participation in the adult political world.

One qualification of this point is the apparent propensity of upper status groups to explain the assassination even though they may not be politically well-informed. Our findings indicate, however, that when political information is present among lower status parents this compensates for the absence of politically favorable communication patterns hypothesized to be the preserve of upper status parents. Although this finding needs considerable support and elaboration by future research, it suggests that socialization into a higher level of political information and involvement need not depend on basic changes in the interpersonal behavior of lower status families.

3) Explanations varied with the age of the child, with younger children given either religious explanations or told about the wicked or insane character of the assassin, and older children more frequently provided with explanations placing the event in a wider historical or political context. In general, the explanations reinforced children's idealized views of the political system.

4) Finally, parents tended to preserve this positive political picture by avoiding the more sordid aspects of politics. They did not pass on to their children their own suspicions of a conspiracy at work in the assassination. This is, to the best of our knowledge, the first direct empirical evidence that parents are selective in their transmissions of political perceptions and values to their young.

NOTES

1. Bernard R. Berelson, Paul F. Lazarsfeld, and William N. McPhee, *Voting* (Chicago: University of Chicago Press, 1954), pp. 88–117; Angus Campbell *et al., The American Voter* (New York: John Wiley & Sons, 1960), pp. 146–149, 306–310.

2. A summary of research in this field can be found in Herbert Hyman, *Political Socialization* (Glencoe: Free Press, 1959). For studies of pre-adolescent political socialization, see Robert Hess and David Easton, "The Child's Changing Image of the President," *Public Opinion Quarterly*, XXIV (1960), pp. 632–644; [David Easton and Robert Hess, "The Child's Political World," *Midwest Journal of Political Science*, VI (1962), pp. 229–246;] Fred I. Greenstein, "More on Children's Images of the President," *Public Opinion Quarterly*, XXV (1961), pp. 648–654; Fred I. Greenstein, "The Benevolent Leader: Children's Images of Political Authority," *American Political Science Review*, LIV (1960), pp. 934–943 and Fred I. Greenstein, "Sex-related Political Differences in Childhood," *Journal of Politics*, XXIII (1961), pp. 353–371.

3. In addition to the national quota sample, two smaller groups who were administered the same questionnaire are included in the sample. The one is a sample of Negroes living in Detroit, the other sample from Prince George County in Virginia. Because our analysis depends primarily on comparisons of subgroups of the population, these cases were included in order to maintain a higher case base.

4. This was part of a larger study of the adult population's reactions to the assassination. All the interviews were completed within a week of the assassination. For a discussion of the major findings of this survey as well as the details of the survey techniques employed, see Paul B. Sheatsley and Jacob J. Feldman, "The Assassination of President Kennedy: A Preliminary Report on Public Reactions and Behavior," *Public Opinion Quarterly*, XXVIII (Summer, 1964), pp. 189–215.

   After obtaining the age, sex, and degree of upsetness of each child, the interviewer asked the parents: "Did you explain to any of the children what had happened?" If the parent indicated that he had, he was asked, "How did you explain what happened?"

5. See in particular Easton and Hess, "The Child's Political World," pp. 240–241.

6. All quotations are taken from the survey discussed in note 4.

7. Greenstein has argued that "though I have no data based on direct observation, much of the political learning during preadolescent years probably is inadvertant and incidental to normal family activities." Fred I. Greenstein, "The Benevolent Leader," pp. 940–41. These circumstances raise considerable obstacles to empirical research on the dynamics of the socialization process; political events seldom penetrate into the home to the extent that parents become aware of their "inadvertant" transmissions of political knowledge and orientations.

8. That political events can have a great impact on children and that remembrance of these is carried throughout life is indicated in the following discussion of state legislators by Heinz Eulau *et al.*: "Great public events, either of a periodic

character, like election campaigns, or of a more singular though far-reaching nature, like wars or economic depressions, may have a politically mobilizing impact on persons not previously concerned with public affairs. . . . The Presidential campaign, in particular, seems to have a latent socializing function in the American political system. It serves not only to activate voters, but the excitement, the turbulence, the color, the intrusion of the Presidential campaign into the routine existence of a relatively little politicized society seem to make a profound impression on children and adolescents [who later become state legislators.]" "The Political Socialization of American State Legislators," in John Wahlke and Heinz Eulau (eds.) *Legislative Behavior* (Glencoe, Illinois: Free Press, 1959), p. 309.

9. If 65 per cent were unaware of giving an explanation of this traumatic event to their children, it would seem that the awareness of transmitting political orientations and knowledge during "normal" periods would exist among such a small fraction of the population as to preclude research utilizing random samples. This reinforces the argument in note 8. For evidence that this was a traumatic event for the overwhelming majority of the population, see Norman M. Bradburn and Jacob J. Feldman, "Public Apathy and Public Grief," in Bradley S. Greenberg and Edwin B. Parker, (eds.), *The Kennedy Assassination and the American Public: Social Communication in Crisis* (Stanford, California: Stanford University Press, 1965).

10. Nevertheless, this is still only a rough indicator of the dynamics of the socialization process, for it is neither what the parent said to the child (but only what he reported to the interviewer concerning what he has said to the child) nor does it give the child's perception of what the parent told him.

11. If the parent replied that he had not explained or that he had merely given a factual statement of what had happened (which the interviewers were instructed to probe) or that no explanation was needed because the child has heard about the assassination at school or on television, the parent was classified as not having explained the assassination. An example of responses included in this classification is the reply of a Connecticut woman: "I told him the President had been shot. (probe.) That he had died. (probe.) From then on we watched TV together."

12. Goodman and Kruskal's gamma and Yule's Q are the correlation coefficients used throughout this paper. Yule's Q, which is used for dichotomous variables, is but a specific instance of gamma. See Leo A. Goodman and William H. Kruskal, "Measures of Association for Cross Classifications," *Journal of the American Statistical Association*, XLIX (December, 1954), pp. 832–64. We wish to thank Matthew Crenson for his helpful suggestions with respect to the use of correlations in presenting these data.

13. Diem's assassination occurred within a month of Kennedy's; consequently, 30 per cent of the national sample remembered it.

14. The repeated discussions of previous Presidential assassinations on the part of the news media may be the reason for 37 per cent of the national sample naming all three Presidents.

15. The prestige of an occupation is determined by an index developed by Otis Dudley Duncan. See Albert J. Reiss, Jr. *et al.*, *Occupation and Social Status* (Glencoe: Free Press, 1961), pp. 109–161.

16. A summary of studies showing a correlation between socio-economic status and political information, interest, and involvement is given in Berelson *et al.*, pp. 334–44. See also Campbell *et al.*, pp. 175–76, 250, 475–81.

17. Fred I. Greenstein, *Children and Politics* (New Haven: Yale University Press, 1965), pp. 92–94.

18. Emotional involvement was not an intervening variable accounting for these differences. No pattern contrary to the analysis presented in the text emerged when controls for emotional involvement were used in the examination of the relationship among class, political information, and "explaining."

19. Four per cent gave miscellaneous explanations, while 4 per cent were vague or irrelevant in the explanations they gave.

20. The concept of "support" is taken from David Easton, *A Systems Analysis of Political Life* (New York: John Wiley & Sons, 1965).

21. Easton and Hess, "The Child's Political World," p. 244.

22. The question was: "How about the man who killed Oswald—what do you think should be done with him?"

23. Roberta S. Sigel, "An Exploration into Some Aspects of Political Socialization: School Children's Reactions to the Death of a President" [in this volume, p. 152 (ed.).]

24. Since the parent was asked how he explained the event to his children, there was no knowing which child received what explanation. Thus, in order to know whether explanations of the event depended on the age of the child, we had to exclude from the analysis all families in which there was more than one child of age four through twelve.

25. See Jean Piaget, *The Moral Judgment of the Child* (Glencoe: The Free Press, 1965), especially Chapter 2, "Adult Constraint and Moral Realism." Piaget argues that the numerous rules set down by adults preoccupy the moral valuations of children up to 10–11 years.

26. Easton and Hess, "The Child's Changing Image of the President," p. 643.

27. An examination of the inter-relationship between class and political information comparable to the one reported on page 8 produced the following table:

POLITICAL INFORMATION	OCCUPATIONAL PRESTIGE	
	High	Low
	(% giving historical explanation)	
High	11 (44)	6 (36)
Low	4 (28)	4 (78)

In this case, when the effect of political information is controlled, class seemed to have little effect on the percentage giving an historical explanation.

28. The tendency for political activists to come from politically involved families is noted by Dwaine Marvick and Charles Nixon, "Recruitment Contrasts in Rival Campaign Groups," in Dwaine Marvick (ed.), *Political Decision-Makers* (Glencoe: Free Press, 1961), pp. 204–210. A similar finding for state legislators is discussed in Eulau, pp. 306–309. Also see Gabriel Almond, *The Appeals of*

Communism (Princeton, New Jersey: Princeton University Press, 1954), pp. 221–23, and Eleanor E. Maccoby, Richard E. Matthews, and Anton S. Morton, "Youth and Political Change," *Public Opinion Quarterly*, XVIII (1954), p. 29. A useful summary of the literature is presented in Lester W. Milbrath, *Political Participation* (Chicago: Rand McNally & Co., 1965), pp. 110–141. This is related to political socialization in Greenstein, *Children and Politics*, pp. 85–106.

Personality and Politics

3

INTRODUCTION

Woodrow Wilson looked upon the League of Nations as the culmination of his efforts to free the world from war. Why, then, did he reject the few, watered-down amendments that the Senate attached to the peace treaty as its condition for ratification and League membership? Historians have often been at a loss to explain this puzzling intransigence. Recent biographers, notably Alexander and Juliette George,[1] have concluded that no political explanation can be offered for Wilson's behavior and that the explanation has to be found in his particular personality. History abounds with examples of political acts that can be understood better through knowledge of the personalities of the actors involved. Hitler's unhappy youth—especially his having a stern father—is said to have contributed to his paranoid-type, author-itarian personality, which, in turn, sought outlets in military conquests and political persecutions. Feelings of personal unworthiness and isolation seem to have contributed to Catherine the Great's intense desire to establish herself in history; this ambition then contributed to her policy of national expansion.

Knowing about the personality of the actor, even if he is not a great leader, is, of course, always helpful, although perhaps not essential in understanding political behavior.

Gordon W. Allport, the psychologist, said, "The political nature of man is indistinguishable from his personality as a whole . . . . A man's political opinions reflect the characteristic modes of his adjustment to life."[2] While recognizing the validity of the above quotation—we must be careful not to overstate the case.

For one thing, the same political opinion is often held by people of very different personalities; a millionaire and an unskilled laborer may both hold unorthodox political views but may do so from very different personality needs. Also, many political situations have so many constraints built into them that a man's political acts may be more a reflection of these constraints than of his personality. A political prisoner who yields the names of his collaborators when subjected to continued torture acts in response to the stringency of the physical situation and not in response to his characteristic personality patterns. And even under ordinary circumstances, the political scientist usually does not need to know why people act as they do. Rather, he needs to know which people located where engage in what political acts. This is true because the political scientist is concerned not with the actor's underlying motivations but with the effect the actor's political views or behaviors have for the political system. Let us use voting studies as an illustration. The psychologist studying Mr. X sees his non-voting (if he examines it at all) as just another instance of his general behavior. The political scientist is not interested in Mr. X's general behavior; in fact, he is not much interested in Mr. X. Instead, the political scientist wants to know how many nonvoting Mr. X's there are and what effect this nonvoting is apt to have on the political system. He will be interested in the personality dimensions of Mr. X only if and when they offer a key explanation for his nonvoting. Thus, alienation or misanthropy are personality dimensions, but they also become politically relevant when they are among the motivations that keep people from the polls.

Personality, per se is, of course, not a socializing agent or force. Rather, it is itself a product of socialization. Personality develops in the course of interaction of the young organism with the environment and its demands. Since the family is the first group he encounters, it has extraordinary influence over his personality development. But much as the family may try to exert this influence, there are limits to its effects, because the offspring is not putty in the family's hands; rather, the young organism's own unique endowments (biological, mental, etc.) are brought into play. Consequently, no two individuals respond in identical ways to identical parental treatments. The unique way the individual habitually responds to others and to the demands they make upon him and the way he responds to himself and to society, that is, his stable behavior patterns, are what we call his personality. Personality thus comes about when a unique organism interacts with its environment and learns to develop typical response patterns. Personality, once formed, seems to be both stable and patterned and to give rise to predictable behavior.

The study of personality and politics is still relatively young and not always highly regarded by either political scientists or psychologists, although very recently it seems to have met with renewed interest among serious scholars.[3] The first burst of interest emerged just prior to World War II, when scholars were fascinated by the outburst of mass and individual barbarism in advanced and seemingly civilized nations. This fascination found expression in studies of national character and in psychoanalytically oriented studies of some of the major political figures of the time. Although studies of national character have lately fallen into some disrepute, the interest in biography has remained. If one were to classify today's rapidly growing literature on personality and politics, two headings would probably emerge: (1) Biographies of individuals, and (2) analyses of populations.* In the former the biographer makes a depth study of the total personality of a given individual—famous, infamous, or quite obscure—and tries to document how personality determined his political decisions. Some of these biographies are heavily influenced by psychoanalytical theory and emphasize the relationship of the subject's current behavior patterns to childhood socialization experiences and childhood conflicts. The emphasis of the second type of investigation is not on a specific individual but rather on the correlation between certain personalities or selected personality traits and certain political views or acts and the distributions in the population at large. Thus an investigator may wish to study the relationship between misanthropy and hawkishness on a foreign policy issue; another may wish to study the prevalence of authoritarian personalities in a given country We shall return to a discussion of personality and its distribution in large populations. Let us now return to a discussion of the first category, biographies of individuals. Here, too, we can detect two schools of thought; one we might call the hero school and the other the motivational (or antihero) school. Probably no one symbolizes belief in the hero school of

leadership as well as the nineteenth century British writer Thomas Carlyle, who attributed a leader's success to certain divinely inspired heroic qualities. Carlyle can hardly be classified as a psychological biographer, but much of the early psychological leadership research was based on related premises (excepting, perhaps, the assumption of divine inspiration) and desperately tried to isolate a constellation of "traits" said to be characteristic of leaders, an attempt which has been singularly fruitless. The antihero school of leadership is concerned with the motives that drive men to assume positions of power. For our purposes this second school is the more important one because it tends to pay more attention to socialization. The approach is often heavily influenced by psychoanalytical theory, one frequently advanced explanation of leadership being that politicians are driven by an inordinate, if not pathological, power drive—a need to dominate and manipulate others. This need in the leader usually is traced to a desire to compensate for feelings of personal worthlessness and insecurities acquired in childhood as a result of unhappy, harsh, or traumatic socialization experiences. Thus, scholars of this persuasion look upon acts of political leadership as attempts to solve in the public arena what are essentially private conflicts or private ambitions. Harold Lasswell, a leading exponent of this school, thinks

---

* More recently a third type of investigation has gained momentum; David Barber's study of freshmen Connecticut legislators, for example, must be seen as an attempt to erect a typology of political actors which combines both personality and institutional criteria.

The political type is characterized by an intense and ungratified craving for deference. These cravings, both accentuated and unsatisfied in the primary circle, are displaced upon public objects (persons and practices connected with the power process). The displacement is rationalized in terms of public interest. We sum up the political type in terms of the development of motive as follows:

Private Motives
Displaced on Public Objects
Rationalized in Terms of Public Interest.[4]

An example of this approach is furnished in the previously mentioned biography of President Woodrow Wilson. George and George attributed much of Wilson's inability to compromise and his intolerance of criticism to his relationship with his father, a relationship that produced admiration for the father as well as resentment against his steep demands and persistent ridicule of his son. Similarly, in the selection in this volume by Wolfenstein, a persuasive case is made that much of Winston Churchill's need to prove himself powerful and worthy was prompted by his parents' neglect of him during his childhood. In another piece[5] Wolfenstein shows how childhood experiences of neglect and frustration led some people to engage in dramatic behavior in order to attract attention which in turn propelled them into positions of leadership during times of crisis. However, these same persons proved themselves incapable of sustained leadership in times of peace when less dramatic gestures were called for. It is as though the neglected child or the child who feels unloved never outgrows the need to assure himself of the attention and love of others, and the best way he knows of capturing this love and attention is through some dramatic act. Consequently, he will perform superbly in times of crisis, provided he is adequately gifted for leadership, but he will be less successful in times of peace, when patience, tolerance for other people's

point of view, and an ability to compromise may be the qualities most needed to accomplish a given goal.

Persuasive though these biographies seem, there is danger in overpsychologizing and especially in overemphasizing the psychopathology behind political acts. Unless one is willing to accept that all concern for the common good is rooted in childhood conflicts or personality deficiencies, it would seem dangerous to rely too heavily on psychopathology as an explanation for political acts. It is quite conceivable that many people first enter the political fray because of a desire to see certain policies or reforms enacted, for example, more humane treatment of the insane, and use politics as the most likely channel of accomplishing their goals. In other words, acts of political leadership can spring from the needs or talents of a healthy personality as well as from a sick one.* Heavy emphasis on psychopathology in politics also ignores the fact that "power mad" people can find outlets in many other walks of life that afford people the opportunity to exercise power over others. If nonpolitical settings offer better opportunities for the exercise of power—for example, the corporate world or the military—power hungry people will probably prefer these areas to politics. Consequently, we must be skeptical of reasoning that explains political actions almost exclusively in terms of psychopathology, but

---

* Many a young lawyer decides to run for the State House not in order to dominate people but in order to make contacts for a law practice he hopes to establish. Other men become men of power out of a sense of duty and not out of pathology. George Washington apparently did not desire the Presidency and accepted it with great reluctance and only because of a sense of duty.

can accept the notion that personality is one of the variables which explains the motivations and the specific styles of different political leaders.

Reference to leadership styles opens the subject of yet another dimension of leadership, namely, the follower. The net effect of political socialization probably has been greater acceptability of certain leadership styles to some people or to some countries. Woodrow Wilson's popular appeal may well have been due to his lofty, idealistic, quasipuritanical style of oratory, a style well within the American tradition. On the other hand, Adlai Stevenson's oratory, his subtle rather than robust sense of humor, his intellectual approach, may have struck a discordant note. Stevenson's seeming levity offended the political norms and expectations learned by people long ago, while Wilson's seriousness conformed to their expectations. Successful leaders thus act not only in accordance with their own personality needs, but in accordance with the political demands and expectations to which they must conform. Leaders and led alike (with all their psychological and physical needs) are shaped by their environment as much as they shape it. And it is for this reason that it is almost impossible to find a one-to-one relation between personality and politics.

The search for specific political personality structures or typologies perhaps reached its summit with the study of *The Authoritarian Personality*.[6] This monumental work is an attempt to go beyond an examination of the character of a single leader and instead aims to discover a personality structure characteristic of fair-sized populations. The personality is then related to preferences for a specific political ideology, in this case

fascism. Inspired by this model, others have sought (it would seem in vain) for a democratic personality type likely to have democratic political proclivities. So far, political scientists dealing with large populations have not discovered a close connection between specific personality types and political actions. For one thing, it is quite unlikely that there are any "pure" types in real life. But even if there were such types, it would not follow that two people of a type would necessarily share the same ideologies. Their political allegiances would probably be determined more by their group memberships and by the political climate and the political institutions under which they were living than by their personality structures. Because of socialization, most people take their given political environment pretty much for granted and accommodate their political acts to it. In another article, for example, Pettigrew notes that segregationist Southerners are no more authoritarian in personality than racially unprejudiced Northerners. To them racial prejudice is a function not of personality but of political environment. It would seem safe, therefore, to say that there is but slim, if any, evidence that certain personality structures or typologies can be labelled "democratic", "authoritarian", "aristocratic", or what have you and that such personalities in turn can be linked to specific political structures and views. Observations such as these give added weight to Greenstein's caution that "the connection between personality and political belief need to be examined rather than assumed" (pp. 260–276).

We are, however on somewhat firmer ground when we examine the relationship of specific psychological traits to specific political beliefs or opinions. Turning to survey data of national populations, we observe that studies of the American electorate[7] seem to indicate that whether or not a person will take an interest in politics and will vote has much to do with psychological forces. People with low sense of self-worth, people who have feelings of low personal effectiveness also have a low sense of political efficacy. In the reverse, people with a high sense of personal efficacy tend also to score high on political efficacy. Such high scorers generally vote even if their social characteristics (such as low social class status) relegate them to groups with low voting turnouts. Mussen and Warren (pp. 277–292) show that people who are interested in politics and inclined to participate feel differently about themselves and about the world around them and their obligation toward it than do people who are apathetic. Studies of "hippies" currently underway, although still very tentative, seem to indicate that the hippies' withdrawal from political activity and political responsibility may in part be prompted by deepseated feelings of aggressiveness and hostility toward society, glossed over by a thin veneer of love rituals. If this interpretation should prove to be correct, one might well wonder whether withdrawal from a world one hates and against which one would like to aggress is not perhaps the safest way to cope with such hostility. Fearfulness, misanthropy, dogmatism, and several other personality traits have a high correlation with specific political views or acts. Misanthropic people, for example, score higher on political cynicisms and participate less in politics than do people with more positive views of their fellow-

men. People who have trouble tolerating ambiguity favor orthodoxy in speech and press, and support censorship significantly more readily than do people who can tolerate ambiguity better. Dogmatic people, in addition, are attracted to authoritarian political movements of the Right and Left. In general, we can say that links between single traits—as distinct from total character structure—and views on specific political issues have been demonstrated quite convincingly, probably because some views on narrow political questions are closely related conceptually to certain personality traits.

Yet another way of studying whole populations has been the research into "national character." An intriguing question that preoccupied many people during World War II and immediately after (although some serious research on the subject had begun earlier) was whether differences in national socialization practices tended to produce different personalities and whether these differences in turn accounted for the political differences among nations. Some scholars believed they could demonstrated the existence of national character and that it varied from nation to nation. Studies were done which purported to show how the swaddling practices of the Russian peasant led to a "typically" Russian character structure which was said to be a mixture of sentimentality and hostility and which in turn could explain the virulence of much of Russian politics.[8] Other authors thought the German penchant for militarism and authoritarianism in politics was explainable as a natural corollary of the German family's authoritarian structure and childrearing methods.[9] Pye, as we have seen, attributes political troubles in Burma partly to the "Burmese personality," which he sees in turn as being induced by inconsistent socialization practices. Similar studies were conducted in Japan, Norway, and several other countries. On the whole, we probably should discard belief in a very close connection between childhood socialization practices and the political acts of nations—the latter, after all, are dictated by current contingencies and historical forces more than they are by childrearing practices. It may, however, be possible to ask whether cultural uniformity in socialization leads to the development of a modal personality in one country that is noticeably different from that in another country, allowing explanation of at least some residual political actions on the basis of national character.

To summarize, although it is important to spotlight personality, we must also be cautious not to reduce the explanation for all political acts to psychological motivation. Much of what people do or do not do is not related to how they feel about their father or how much idealism they acquired in adolescence, but is dictated by the hard realities of the environment with which they have to cope and the options which are available to them. A prime minister of a small country may have as authoritarian a character structure and as militaristic a credo as is possible, but if the country has little military power and his own power is similarly circumscribed, it is unlikely that such a person could act out his authoritarian or aggressive impulses by embarking on a war policy. Political reality, after all, curtails and often dictates the effect personality can have on politics. Education, native intelligence, health, and other personal or group characteristics also may affect what a person will do about politics. In addition, much may be due to chance. Thus, when we say that personality plays a part in politics, we must always be aware that personality explains but one part of the variance and that the political system, the group-shared beliefs, and many other external factors combined play a larger part. It is only when these factors do not adequately answer all questions in a given political act that we may do well to look to personality for additional explanations.

NOTES

1. Alexander L. and Juliette L. George, *Woodrow Wilson and Colonel House* (New York: Dover, 1956).

2. Gordon W. Allport, "The Composition of Political Attitudes," *American Journal of Sociology*, 35 (1929–1930).

3. Since this manuscript was submitted for publication, several volumes on the subject have appeared. See, for example, LeRoy Rieselbach and George I. Balch, *Psychology and Politics* (New York: Holt, Rinehart and Winston, 1969); also, Vol. XXIV (July 1968) of the *Journal of Social Issues*, Fred I. Greenstein (ed.), was devoted to "Personality and Politics."

4. Harold D. Lasswell, *Power and Personality*, (New York: Viking, 1948), p. 38.

5. E. Victor Wolfenstein, "Some Psychological Aspects of Crisis Leadership," in Lewis J. Edinger, *Political Leadership in Industrialized Societies* (New York: Wiley, 1967), pp. 182–219.

6. Theodore Adorno, *et al.*, *The Authoritarian Personality* (New York: Harper & Row, 1950).

7. Angus Campbell, *et al.*, *The American Voter* (New York: Wiley, 1960).

8. Geoffrey Gorer and John Rickman, *The People of Great Russia: A Psychological Study* (London: Cresset Press, 1949).

9. Bertram H. Schaffner, *Fatherland: A Study of Authoritarianism in the German Family* (New York: Columbia University Press, 1949).

WINSTON CHURCHILL'S CHILDHOOD: TOY SOLDIERS AND FAMILY POLITICS*

• E. Victor Wolfenstein

I

During the course of a long and tumultuous political career Winston Churchill was the advocate of a great variety of causes. Although the causes themselves changed, his style of commitment to them remained constant: each new enterprise received great outpourings of his virtually unlimited energy, each was served with devotion and determination until victory or defeat ensued (or until some new cause beckoned), and each was treated with the militancy and strategic outlook of a general conducting a campaign against a dangerous foe. It was this style that lay behind his most striking achievements and his most stunning defeats. It led him to besiege two anarchists in a house on Sidney Street with over 750 police, several soldiers, and a Maxim gun when he was Home Secretary in 1911. As might be expected, the consequence was public ridicule and a temporary loss of political prestige.[1] But the same traits gave him the perspective and tenacity to fight for and get an enlarged British navy in the months preceding World War I—so that, when war broke out, the British

Above selection has been written especially for this volume.

* Many of the ideas for this paper were generated out of the discussions of the Los Angeles Interdisciplinary Study Group (Robert Dorn, Alexander George, Alfred Goldberg, Herbert Kupper, Ernest Lewy, and Peter Loewenberg) and from conversations with Benjamin G. Williams.

fleet was ready. Similarly, it led him to see in the German glider clubs of the 1930s the rebirth of a dangerous German air force and to warn his nation that its indecision might result in its demise:

> The Government simply cannot make up their minds, or they cannot get the Prime Minister to make up his mind. So they go on in strange paradox, decided only to be undecided, resolved to be irresolute, adamant for drift, solid for fluidity, all-powerful to be impotent. So we go on preparing more months and years—precious, perhaps vital, to the greatness of Britain—for the locusts to eat.[2]

Moreover, this same warlike tenacity enabled Churchill to play with assurance and feeling his role of leader of his people during their darkest—and their finest —hours. It was the wellspring from which he drew the words that enspirited his people during those difficult days:

> We shall go on to the end, we shall fight in France, we shall fight on the seas and oceans, we shall fight with growing confidence and growing strength in the air, we shall defend our Island, whatever the cost may be, we shall fight on the beaches, we shall fight on the landing grounds, we shall fight in the fields and in the streets, we shall fight in the hills; we shall never surrender. . . .[3]

When the fighting ceased, when strident calls to battle were no longer necessary, when the hard and tedious work of reconstruction replaced the defeat of

Germany on Britain's political agenda, then Churchill's martial vigor became a debit, not an asset. He himself sensed the change in spirit that took place in the days following World War II, but he did not know how to react to it. He said to his physician, Lord Moran: "I have a strong feeling that my work is done. I have no message. I had a message. Now I can only say 'fight the damned socialists'! I do not believe in this brave new world."[4] But the British people did not want to "fight the damned socialists," whom Churchill attacked in quite shameful ways during the 1946 electoral campaign; so Churchill led the Conservatives to a resounding defeat.

In short, this fundamental trait of Churchill's personality, this need to have something to defend and something to combat, was both his greatest strength and his greatest weakness. As I shall attempt to demonstrate, its roots are primarily to be found in the attempts of a lonely boy to win the love and respect of his negligent parents.

As the above contention indicates, it is a premise of this essay that early life experiences play a large part in determining adult behavior. Hopefully the reader will find in the data that is presented substantial indications of this connection. One must not, however, make the mistake of the first students of psychobiography and assume that one important early life experience in and of itself accounts for behavior which takes place many years thereafter. Clearly the life history of the individual between his significant early experiences and his adult actions must be taken into account. In short, a pattern of recurrent thoughts and actions, extending from their earliest forms to their most mature expression,

should be sought. This is the orientation that guides the present essay: I hope to indicate the continuities and development of Churchill's first recorded memories, through crucial latency and adolescent experiences, to the political self-conception he expressed in a novel, *Savrola*, which he wrote when he was twenty-five. In the process the critical role of Churchill's family configuration should become clear.

It is a truism that no man or family exists in complete social isolation. Even the most adventurous of pioneering families, even the most reclusive of hermits, maintain some contact with a larger social world. But the fact of social interaction should not lead us to a sociological reductionism any more than the equally palpable fact of the biological basis of the family and individual human life should culminate in a purely physiological explanation of social action. Winston Churchill, like all men, was affected both by his genetic inheritance and his family's elevated position in English social and political life. He appears, for example, to have been both energetic and strong-willed from birth; and his father's spectacular, if ultimately unsuccessful, political career was the critical manifest impetus to Winston's political ambitions. But it was this constitutional energy linked to familial needs and the political world *as embodied in his father*, not simply the existence of the constitutional traits or the political system, that was so important. For whatever view of social causality one chooses, it is an almost inescapable fact that the family is the crucial focus for psychogenetic study. A child's reaction to his school situation, for example, is in many ways a resultant of his experience within the family. He will tend to view teachers as quasi-autonomous extensions of his parents; disruption of relations at home will tend to lead to poor performance at school, and so on. In the present case we will see that Churchill's lack of adaptation to his school environment resulted largely from a displacement of aggression from the family to the school context.

Let me stress that in emphasizing the role of the family in determining childhood and adult behavior patterns I am not arguing for a psychological reductionism to substitute for the two alluded to earlier. It seems clear that any social outcome, such as the political personality of a leader, is influenced by the many and variegated facets of man's social existence. But, on the one hand, the developing child experiences most of these through the mediation of the family and, on the other, basic aspects of personality (which are, after all, our interest here) do seem to be most markedly influenced by the early interaction of the child with his parents and others in his immediate environment. Accordingly, in the present essay, primary attention will be devoted to this sphere.

II

On April 15, 1874, Randolph S. Churchill, member of Parliament from Woodstock, and Jeanette Jerome, daughter of a wealthy New York stockbroker, were married in Paris. The groom, the second surviving son of the seventh Duke of Marlborough, was born into one of Britain's oldest and best established aristocratic families. His election to Parliament shortly before his marriage had been an automatic assumption of a family responsibility, for Woodstock was the traditional Marlborough seat in the

House of Commons. Similarly the leading role he and his bride played in London society was predicated upon his family's social prestige, although their position was augmented by the assiduity and energy with which the young couple devoted themselves to affairs of fashion. It appeared, in fact, that the Randolph Churchills had no concern other than the elegant frivolities of the social whirl; even Randolph's parliamentary duties took a decidedly second place to the delights of the London social season. The birth of their first child, Winston, on November 30, 1874, was accordingly not permitted to distract the Churchills from their social commitments.[5] Winston's needs were quickly put in the hands of servants and nannies, and his mother once again turned her attention to more engrossing pastimes. Indeed, as Sir Winston's son puts it in his biography of his father, "the neglect and lack of interest in [my father] shown by his parents were remarkable, even judged by the standards of late Victorian and Edwardian days."[6]

Because parental neglect and Winston's reaction to it form the underlying themes of this essay, it is all the more important to emphasize that he had one firm basis of love and support in his childhood—his nurse, Elizabeth Everest. His reciprocal love for "Woomany," as he and his brother Jack nicknamed Mrs. Everest, is indicated by his many references to her in his early correspondence, his grief at the time of her death in 1895, and his description of a nanny in a novel he wrote when, as a young army officer in India in 1899, he found himself with some time to kill. The titular character and hero, Savrola, is a brilliant and dashing radical politician in the state of "Laurania." Returning to his rooms after an exhausting day, he is greeted by his faithful nurse. As she tenderly brings Savrola his dinner, the impersonal narrator of the story muses:

She had nursed him from his birth up with a devotion and care which knew no break. It is a strange thing, the love of these women. Perhaps it is the only disinterested affection in the world.[7]

One would guess that Mrs. Everest's "disinterested affection" for Winston, which consisted in small part of providing him with food when the dining rooms of his various schools proved inadequate, was a crucial ingredient of the very considerable self-esteem and confidence he possessed in later life. Whatever affection Winston received from his parents, by contrast, was quite strictly conditional: good behavior was rewarded with at least some expression of love and favor, bad conduct by neglect or angry words.

Such a relationship between parents and child provides little basis for autonomy and healthy self-love, for the child is likely to believe that only his achievements are of any value. It is not *he* but what he *does* that merits love or respect. Although in some cases such a relationship will provide a strong impetus for achievement in order to earn parental esteem, it is just as likely to lead to a sullen apathy and withdrawal. Even when the individual does strive to become the person his parents want him to be, his efforts are likely to be marred by a tendency to devalue whatever he achieves and/or to punish himself and his parents by engineering his own ultimate failure.[8]

Churchill did not entirely escape this fate: some of his actions had a self-defeating character. His striving for power and a place in history was restless and unending; and he frequently fell into profound depressions that he himself termed his "black dog."[9] Yet it is also clear that Churchill possessed a healthy sense of his own worth, which allowed him to weather both the ambivalences and tensions of his relationship with his parents and the pronounced ups and downs of his political career. Because Mrs. Everest, who was more of a mother to him than Jenny Churchill, loved *him* and not just what he did, she helped to provide a reserve of self-esteem that made such resiliency possible.[10]

Mrs. Everest joined the Churchill family early in 1875, and for the next two years the family resided in London or in one of the family country estates. In 1876, however, Lord Randolph became involved in a matter that culminated in the family's temporary "exile" to Ireland and eventuated in his tumultuous political career.[11] The three years the Churchills spent in Ireland saw a slowing down of the hectic pace at which the Churchills had lived. Winston had regular contact with Mrs. Everest and saw more of his parents, although there is no evidence that he benefited by more attention from them. But when the family returned to London, Randolph, after 1880, added the vigorous pursuit of political power to his other interests; and Winston was left to make his solitary way through the boredom and routine of his various schools.[12]

Even under the relatively favorable conditions of life in Ireland, however, it would appear that Winston's life was pervaded by anxiety and fear. Although he appears to have been a bumptious and bold fellow, his memories of the period uniformly concern violent and aggressive activities. His first memory, for example, is of the unveiling of a statue:

I remember my grandfather, the Viceroy, unveiling the Lord Gough statue in 1878. A great black crowd, scarlet soldiers on horseback, strings pulling away a brown shiny sheet, the old Duke, the formidable grandpapa, talking loudly to the crowd. I recall even a phrase he used: 'and with a withering volley he shattered the enemy's line.' I quite understood that he was speaking about war and fighting and that a 'volley' meant what the black-coated soldiers (Riflemen) used to do with loud bangs so often in the Phoenix Park where I was taken for my morning walks.[13]

This memory of a political speech about a military subject points to what was to become a main theme in Churchill's life —how many such speeches would Churchill himself give in the course of his career! Clearly he was identifying himself with a strong and deeply rooted family tradition in selecting for himself a militant political vocation. But the event also tells us that young Winston was much impressed by the glorification of a man of violence. If we treat his recollection as a screen memory, as an event that is remembered because it brings to mind, in disguised form, wishes or fears which are too strong to be thought about directly, then we may perceive a boy who wished for love as a reward for the release of his own aggressive impulses. Although such an inference is speculative, it is consonant both with the memory itself and with the political role Churchill was later to play. To put it in somewhat different terms, the unveiling posed a problem for Winston. Here was a man whose aggressive actions were being honored by

everyone. He was the center of attention. But why? What did one have to do to earn that kind of esteem? It may have seemed to Winston as if the secret of Lord Gough's success were contained in the event—this was, after all, an unveiling, a revealing of something previously concealed. And the message may have been contained in the words, "and with a withering volley he shattered the enemy's line."[14] Bold, active aggression, it would seem, serves to ward off the enemy and to win respect and love.

Churchill's remembering the unveiling of the statue does not imply that he had, at such an early age, mastered the lesson it had to teach. His remembering tells us only that he sensed in the event something important, something that we see in retrospect as one of the major themes of his life. This theme was developed and amplified in the years ahead, as Winston and his environment cooperated in creating for the boy a world of conflict and antagonism, a world from which, when its weight became too heavy to carry, he would fly to the warm comfort of Mrs. Everest (or, when possible, his mother).

His other memories from the Irish period confirm the impression we have thus far gained of Winston's mental life. He tells us of a theatre manager who was killed in a fire: "All that was found of the manager was [*sic*] the keys that had been in his pocket."[15] Winston was disappointed that he was not permitted to see the keys—this time the secret was being safeguarded. He remembers "a tall white stone tower ... [that] had been blown up by Oliver Cromwell."[16] One day, when out for a ride, he reports that Mrs. Everest mistook the local rifle brigade for a group of Irish revolutionists.

In the excitement of this event, Winston was thrown from his donkey and received a concussion. And he remembers that a man who gave him a gift was later killed by a real version of these same rebels.[17] So it seemed that not everyone was Lord Gough or Cromwell. There was a strong likelihood of destruction as well as a chance for love and respect. Winston must have seen life as a risky business indeed.

One figure is conspicuously absent from this picture that Churchill draws of a world of male violence and death. Lord Randolph is mentioned only twice in connection with the Irish period, once in a strictly *pro forma* way and in the following description of Churchill's mother:

My picture of [my mother] in Ireland is in a riding habit, fitting like a skin and often beautifully spotted with mud. She and my father hunted continually on their large horses; and sometimes there were great scares because one or the other did not come back for many hours after they were expected.

My mother always seemed to me a fairy princess: a radiant being possessed of limitless riches and power. . . .

My mother made [a] brilliant impression upon my childhood's eye. She shone for me like the Evening Star. I loved her dearly—but at a distance.[18]

Lord Randolph is seen as preoccupied with the sensuously described pleasure of riding and the aggressive act of hunting, both of which he enjoyed with his wife. The normal resentment of a four-year-old boy of the prerogatives of the father is in this case heightened by the added insult of paternal neglect. But Winston's father was both too awe-inspiring and too inaccessible to be a

suitable object for Winston's aggressive impulses. Only this very muted reproach—this evocation of paternal neglect and monopolization of the mother—and his descriptions of the violence that he saw around him tells of Winston's repressed hostility. For one might speculate that the aggression that Winston attributed to other men largely represents displaced hostility from the arena of father-son conflict. Relations with his father were kept as intact as possible by his giving vent to aggressive feelings in other contexts.

Before turning to the major areas in which, during his childhood, Winston expressed this pent-up hostility—that is, in school and with his toy soldiers—a few words on his relationship with his mother are in order. As can be seen in the passage cited above, Winston had no intimate contact with his mother. Mrs. Everest was his confidant, his mother was a fairy princess who could be worshipped from afar but not embraced. Winston seems desperately to have craved the love of this vain and narcissistic woman, but until his late adolescence his efforts were to no avail. Lady Churchill's attitude toward her son is captured in a letter she sent to her husband when he was visiting London during the Irish exile:

Winston has just been with me—such a darling he is—"I can't have my Mama go—& if she does I will run after the train & jump in" he said to me. I have told Everest to take him for a drive tomorrow if it is fine—as it is better the stables sh[oul]d have a little work . . .[19]

Winston's mother was not completely unfeeling. Then, and later, she was frequently touched by Winston's appeals and sometimes even gave him the favors or attention he desired. But she never realized the importance of granting such favors. She never understood that her son was more important than her horses, that the justification for taking Winston for a drive should have been his pleasure and not the well-being of the stables. It is no wonder that Winston grew up with the feeling that his interests, pleasures, and needs took a back seat to even the most trivial of his parent's preoccupations.

III

The Churchills returned to England in early 1880, and with their return life changed rather markedly for Winston. Just before the departure from Ireland, Lady Churchill gave birth to her second child, Jack; and, once the family was back in London, the intensity of social and political activity increased markedly. Winston accordingly had less contact than ever before with his parents. Typically, in the summer of that year Winston spent his vacation in Ventnor with Mrs. Everest, away from his parents. Any hostility he felt, either toward his parents or his new sibling, was not allowed to show. Indeed, his obedient loyalty to his parents and his brotherly concern for Jack were virtually unbroken throughout his childhood. As a result, however, of this purification of emotion vis à vis the family, one might infer that he was forced to use other figures of authority and peers in his environment in order to release his pent-up animosities. Love was reserved for members of the family, dislike and rebellion for those outside of it. Ultimately this split between family and nonfamily was expressed in Churchill's fierce defense of England against the Nazis.

In the fall of 1882 Winston was sent to school for the first time. The school selected was Saint George's School in Ascot, which was under the direction of a Reverend H. W. Sneyd-Kynnersley. Winston, when he entered, was an impetuous, disorderly, and independent boy with, as we have seen, a penchant for seeing hostility in the world around him. He was not, moreover, eager to leave home:

I was also miserable at the idea of being left alone among all these strangers in this great, fierce, formidable place. After all I was only seven, and I had been so happy in my nursery with all my toys. I had such a wonderful collection of toys: a real steam engine, a magic lantern, and a collection of soldiers already nearly a thousand strong.[20]

It was not only his toys, of course, that he regretted leaving but his mother and Mrs. Everest as well. In the face of these misgivings and his latent hostilities, it would have taken an ingenious school indeed to make Winston a happy and responsible member of the nonfamilial community.

Saint George's was definitely not such a school. The headmaster was a man of great moral rectitude and sadistic temperament. Churchill reports that the floggings that recalcitrant boys received "exceeded in severity anything that would be tolerated in any of the Reformatories under the Home Office."[21] Winston, whose needs to express defiance of male authority were in any case large, received much more than his share of these beatings, which he described in detail:

In the middle of the room [where the punishments took place] was a large box draped in black cloth and in austere tones the culprit was told to take down his trousers and kneel before the block. . . . The swishing was given with the master's full strength and it took only two or three strokes for drops of blood to form everywhere and it continued for 15 or 20 strokes when the wretched boy's bottom was a mass of blood.[22]

Saint George's School thus served to confirm Winston's view that the world of men was a source of danger and pain. He longed for escape from it, from this unequal battle, to home where he could "range [his] soldiers in line of battle on the nursery floor."[23] With his toy soldiers Winston could fight out his wars on his terms. Heading up the British soldiers himself and, as soon as Jack was old enough, leaving the direction of the hostile troops to his younger brother, Winston would fight battle after battle, great military confrontations in which Winston and the British were sure to prevail.

Winston continued to play with his soldiers well into adolescence, supplementing the engagement in the nursery with war games involving his brother, cousins, and other children who were available for such enterprises on the various family estates. In both arenas, moreover, he appears to have worked at developing skills to go along with his interest. He not only found an outlet for his aggressive impulses, but he tried to teach himself the most effective ways to use that outlet. He was a clever and persuasive leader of his young followers, and an earnest student of his toy army's strategic possibilities and limitations. He was careful, for example, to deprive his brother of artillery—in his nursery, no one but Winston would control the big guns. In this manner he prepared himself well for the role of war leader he was eventually to play. Both military and political skills were being developed, albeit in rudimentary form.

While Winston was thus spending two painful years absorbing punishment at Saint George's School and administering it, in sublimated form, at home, Lord Randolph was in the midst of one of the most spectacular climbs in the history of English politics. Upon his return to England he launched a vigorous attack upon both the Liberals and his own Conservative party. He and some of his friends on the Conservative backbenches joined forces under the banner of the Fourth party, and, using the call of democracy within the party as a rallying cry, succeeded in giving the Tories a renewed vigor and popularity that culminated in the Tory electoral victory of 1886. With that victory Randolph became Chancellor of the Exchequer and leader of the party in the House of Commons. But, in December of that year, in a cabinet debate over arms expenditures, Randolph offered his resignation if his arguments for limited funds were not accepted—and, much to his surprise, his resignation was accepted. After that, although he continued to play an active part in parliamentary life, Randolph was a spent force politically. His own declining health and the wealth of enemies he had accumulated during his rise to power together insured that he would be politically impotent. His death in January 1895 came eight years after his effective political life had ended.

Even during his days at Saint George's Winston was following his father's fortunes attentively. When his father was in the midst of a political campaign in Birmingham, he wrote to his mother:

Mrs. Kynnersley went to Birmingham this week. And she heard they were betting two to one that Papa would get in for Birmingham. We all went too a sand pit the other day and played a very exciting game. As the sides are about 24 feet high, and a great struggle, those who got out first kept a fierce struggle with the rest.[24]

Not only was Winston aware of his father's activities but, as the letter indicates, Winston identified himself with Lord Randolph as well. While his father played the game of political control, Winston played the game of sand-pit control. He seems to be telling his mother—"Look, I am engaged in worthwhile combat too. I am as important as my father."

An identification with his father of this kind could serve several purposes for Winston. It provided a legitimate outlet for his own combative feelings, a useful supplement to his toy soldiers and school rebellion. It enabled him to compete with his father for his mother's affections without accentuating unduly the feelings of guilt such activity connotes: he was, after all, paying his father the compliment of trying to be like him. And, less importantly, his vicarious experiencing of his father's career gave him a certain prestige among his schoolmates, whereas his father's career itself served in many ways as a model for Winston's own.

Over the next several years Winston's emotional involvement in his father's political fortunes increased and his adaptation to school improved. This latter change resulted primarily from a shift in schools. Apparently Mrs. Everest saw the wounds Winston had received from Sneyd-Kynnersley's beatings and prevailed upon his parents to find a better school for him. A school run by two spinsters in Brighton was selected and proved to be a fortunate choice. Winston, as might have been expected, proved much less rebellious in a world

run by women than in one run by men. Moreover, the Misses Thomson were solicitous of Winston's whims and, despite a serious encounter with pneumonia, the three and a half years that he spent in Brighton were considerably happier than the two which preceded them.

Although the school situation was now more tolerable, Winston was still viewing family affairs from afar. There are quite frequent references to family affairs and his father's political activities in his letters to his mother; he was obviously eager to be involved in both. But he spent very little time at home; visits from his parents to the school were rare (his father once gave a speech in Brighton without bothering to stop and see Winston); and one would guess that letters to his parents, especially his mother, became a crucial lifeline for the boy. Yet Winston would not readily yield the autonomy he had been fighting to achieve in order to receive those letters or other favors.

At Brighton, and later at Harrow, his work continued to be slovenly. Although manifest rebellion died down, the more subtle protest of not fulfilling the hopes of either his parents or his schoolmasters continued. It is as if Winston were attempting to force his parents to accept him on his own terms, to love him as he was, no matter how far that deviated from what they wanted him to be. Not until he got to Sandhurst, where his games with toy soldiers could be transformed into professional achievement, did Winston really attempt to perform in accordance with his abilities.

Winston entered Harrow during the summer term of 1888. Although he demonstrated his intelligence by memorizing over 1000 lines from

Macaulay's *Lays of Ancient Rome* and did consistently well in English and history, his work in his other classes was never very good. He was constantly being told he must do better, he always reported that his work was improving, and he always remained at the bottom of his form. In this more moderate manner Winston continued the unconscious protest against parental neglect.

The neglect itself did not diminish. One Christmas, for example, Winston's parents went abroad—despite the fact that Winston was lying ill at home.[25] And Lord Randolph did not once visit Harrow during the first year and a half his son was there.[26] Winston's letters to his mother are full of requests for visits, most of which were denied. A common sequence would be a request from Winston for a visit, a denial from his mother, followed by a gift or some money. Winston thus had to content himself with tokens of his parent's affection rather than any very direct manifestation of it; and the most important of these tokens were the letters he received from his mother. It is no wonder that Winston came to attribute almost magical power to the proper use of the English language: the written word was his one way of maintaining emotional contact with his mother; through it he could express his love for her and receive what he could feel to be declarations of love in return. In later years the woman he sought to woo with his words was England. And, like his mother, she was not always ready to listen.

Winston's memorizing of Macaulay appears, in the light of the importance of words to Winston, as another attempt to assure himself and to convince his mother of his worthiness. Characteristically, the lay he chose to memorize was "Horatius," the story of the brave soldier who risked his life to defend his city from an attacking king named Sextus. With Rome under attack, Horatius guarded the bridge into the city until it was destroyed. Then, despite being wounded and wearing heavy armour, he plunged into the Tiber and swam back to safety. Horatius' great gamble with death paid off, and he became a hero. How Winston must have thrilled to such a story, and how he must have responded to lines like the following, which were evocative of so many of his own feelings:

Then out spake brave Horatius,
  The Captain of the Gate:
"To every man upon this earth
  Death cometh soon or late.
And how can man die better
  Than facing fearful odds,
For the ashes of his fathers,
  And the temples of his Gods,

"And for the tender mother
  Who dandled him to rest,
And for the wife who nurses
  His baby at her breast,
And for the holy maidens
  Who feed the eternal flame,
To save them from false Sextus
  That wrought the deed of shame?[27]

Winston found it easy to remember tales of great military valor—from Lord Gough to Horatius—and, as his preoccupation with things military indicates, longed for such glory himself. Then, maybe, his mother would love him; then, maybe, his father would pay attention to him and respect him.

At Harrow Winston joined the Rifle Club and became an excellent fencer; but his performance academically was so mediocre that his father despaired of Winston's chances of making a professional career. Consequently, in the fall of 1889, Winston was entered in the classes that would prepare him to take the entrance examinations for the Sandhurst Military Academy. At the time Winston thought that his father had selected this course for him because he perceived military talent in his son. Only later did he discover that his father thought he was not intelligent enough to practice law or enter politics.[28]

With the added burden of the so-called army classes, Winston's other academic work declined even further. He was constantly in the position of having to apologize to his parents for his poor work and promise to do better. Yet one would surmise that this near failure at school gratified both Winston's rebellious needs and his self-destructive impulses. To some extent Winston must have internalized his parent's low estimation of his abilities and unconsciously felt bound to confirm it. These rebellious and self-destructive elements, as well as his heroic longings, all came together in an event that took place in January 1893.

Over the preceding several months Winston had taken the Sandhurst examinations twice and failed twice. As a consequence his parents took him out of Harrow and prepared to have him sent to a "crammer," a man who specialized in preparing young men for the examinations. Winston was home for vacation before starting this new course. He was playing with his brother and a younger cousin, having them chase him while he sought to escape, when he found himself on a bridge over a gulley—with his brother approaching

from one side and his cousin from another. As Churchill tells it:

One stood at each end of the bridge; capture seemed certain. But in a flash there came across me a great project. The [gulley] which the bridge spanned was full of young fir trees. Their slender tops reached to the level of the footway. 'Would it not,' I asked myself, 'be possible to leap onto one of them and slip down the pole-like stem, breaking off each tier of branches as one descended, until the fall was broken?' I looked at it. I computed it. I meditated. . . . To plunge or not to plunge, that was the question! In a second I had plunged, throwing out my arms to embrace the summit of the fir tree. The argument was correct; the data were absolutely wrong. It was three days before I regained consciousness and more than three months before I crawled from my bed.[29]

In typical fashion Churchill exaggerates somewhat the injuries he sustained. His son reports that he was back at work in less than two months. In any case, the injuries were severe, and one might think that such an event would have a rather sobering effect on the reckless young man. Its consequence, however, was quite the opposite; for Winston, in playing Horatius (a model for his action which might well have been in his mind), gained Horatius' reward. His mother and father rushed to his side when they learned of the occurrence; the best doctors in London were brought to take care of him; and, during his convalescence, he was permitted to attend his parents' dinner parties, go with his father to the House of Commons, and so on. He was treated, more than ever before, as an adult member of the family. Hence by risking all in a suicidal plunge from the bridge he gained what he most desired—the (at least apparent) love and attention of both parents. And, at the same time, whatever self-destructive impulses he possessed were gratified.

Churchill at eighteen was starting to put into practice the lesson that was latent in the unveiling of the Lord Gough statue. Boldness in the face of danger was leading to the expected glory. He still lacked a proper enemy—he would spend the years after Sandhurst looking for one, first in military combat, then in politics, and finally in the war effort that was the grand culmination of his life—but he was coming closer to developing a style of action that promised satisfaction.

Indeed, we can see in the bridge incident a preliminary representation of Churchill's characteristic political stance. As I have put it elsewhere:

From then on, be it in a military or a political context, Churchill would seek out the most dangerous and daring positions, hoping to gain thereby both punishment and praise—the former from an enemy, the latter from his friends. During times of genuine crisis, periods which on a broader stage recreated the situation on the bridge (most notably, of course, during the early days of the Second World War), this need to face danger defiantly, to risk all in the hope of gaining all, perfectly suited the needs of a nation. At other times it led to a rather grotesque searching for enemies to challenge and risks to take where none existed—as, in the example already cited, in the Sidney Street episode in 1911.[30]

It must have seemed, moreover, that this kind of action would lead to a political career, to an alliance and/or identification with his father. "Surely," Winston probably thought, "now that I am growing up, my father will acknowledge my worth and accept me as his aid and heir." To feed this daydream Churchill had the model of Joseph Chamberlain, who lived to see his son Austen become a member of the House of Commons.

But such a resolution to the problems of Churchill's youth was not to be. After his fall from power Lord Randolph had fallen progressively into the grip of what was to prove to be a fatal illness. And with the decline in his physical, mental, and political power came an increased irritability and impatience. Winston bore a considerable part of the burden of his father's irrational vehemence, perhaps most spectacularly in an incident that took place in the summer of 1893. At that time Winston had finally been admitted to Sandhurst, but as a cavalry cadet. His father had wanted him to get into the infantry, which would have cost less money; and when he received the news from Winston that he had only achieved cavalry status, he wrote his son the following:

There are two ways of winning an examination, one creditable the other the reverse. You have apparently chosen the latter method, and appear to be much pleased with your success.

With all the advantages you had, with all the abilities which you foolishly think yourself to possess & which some of your relations claim for you, with all the efforts that have been made to make your life easy and agreeable and your work neither oppressive or distasteful, this is the grand result that you come up among the 2nd rate and 3rd rate class who are only good for commissions in a cavalry regiment. . . . I shall not write again on these matters & you need not trouble to write any answer to this part of my letter, because I no longer attach the slightest weight to anything you may say about your own acquirements & exploits. . . .[31]

One can imagine the blow this must have been for Winston after thinking of himself as an adult member of the family, after being pleased with himself for passing the examination, to receive from his father what amounted to virtually a total condemnation of his whole life. Not unexpectedly, Winston was contrite and promised to work harder in the future. Such promises had, of course, been made in the past; but this time Winston seems to have feared a complete loss of his father's affection; and, when he got to Sandhurst (with an infantry appointment after all), he worked hard and did well.

One of the striking things about the bridge incident and Lord Randolph's response to Winston's examination performance is how very firmly they bound the developing boy to the declining man. Instead of working increasingly at establishing independent goals for himself, Winston was coming more and more to accept his father's judgment in all matters. He was becoming, indeed, increasingly compliant to his father's wishes. What would have happened, given this trend, if Lord Randolph had survived well into Winston's maturity we cannot tell. Perhaps Winston would have outgrown his dependency on his father, perhaps he would have remained subservient to him. But it seems unlikely that he would have had a political career that so radically surpassed his father's in its success. One would guess that Lord Randolph's death, when his son was just twenty years old, set the stamp of political ambition on Winston more firmly than anything else would have done.

In June, 1894, with his health declining rapidly, Lord Randolph set off on a world tour with his wife, hoping for a miraculous restoration of the powers he was losing. His wife and doctor knew the end was inevitable; and, shortly after they left, Winston found out as well. He was shocked by the news but responded to it manfully. Indeed, he responded to it by taking on an air of adult responsibility in his letters to his mother. No longer are they concerned primarily with petty complaints or requests; rather they are full of solicitous concern for his mother. With his father on the verge of dying Winston was preparing himself psychologically to assume his role as head of the family:

Now about yourself, Darling Mummy I do hope that you are keeping well and that the fatigues of travelling as well as the anxiety you must feel about Papa—are not telling on you. I can't tell you how I long to see you again and how I look forward to your return. Do what you can with Papa to induce him to allow me to come out and join you. . . .[32]

As is clear from the tone of this note, Winston was very close to gaining one of his most cherished goals—his mother's love, admiration, and dependence. He could not, of course, undo the psychological consequences of years of neglect; but he was achieving an intimacy with his mother that would not have seemed possible a few years before. It would be my guess that, combined with the underlying confidence he gained from Mrs. Everest, this rapprochement with his mother contributed mightily to the feeling Churchill had that he was destined for success and greatness. The attenuated nature of his relationship with his father, by contrast, created the major problem with which he had to deal in the years ahead.

Winston believed that, just before his father's death, "friendly relations [with his father] were ripening into a Entente."[33] And it is certainly true that relations between father and son improved when Winston started to perform well at Sandhurst. But, as Winston himself observed, his father rejected any suggestion of intimacy; and, when his father died, Winston was left with an unresolved question: How could he, without guilt, without betraying the memory of the awesome man who dominated his mind even in death, be a man? Manhood entailed, given the model of his father, a successful political career. Loyalty to his father, by contrast, connoted a dutiful military career. How was this conflict to be resolved? How could Winston serve both his own needs and his father's memory?

IV

We can see Winston striving to answer these questions, attempting to draw together the strands of his childhood fantasies and adolescent hopes, in the political novel he wrote when he was twenty-four. *Savrola*, which was mentioned earlier in reference to Mrs. Everest, embodies all of the major themes we have been exploring. A fascination with both military affairs and politics, the desire for a beautiful woman whose loyalties are to an older man, a markedly ambivalent attitude toward that man—all are combined in this imaginative effort.

Novels, like the daydreams out of which they grow, are often, if not always, attempts to resolve conflicts, to find solutions. *Savrola* is just such an effort. With it Churchill was trying to make peace with his own past and to build a bridge to the wars, political and other, of the future. An examination of the novel will thus allow us to gain an intimate view of Churchill's state of mind just before he entered upon his political career.

The novel is about three central characters. The first is the head of state of the imaginary land of Laurania, President Antonio Molara. Molara comes to power through his heroic generalship during days when the state was in danger, but he pursues the restoration of order too vigorously and transforms the republic into a dictatorship. He is a good man gone bad, a political leader maintaining power by force or subterfuge instead of by good policy and judicious action.

Molara is married to a woman many years younger than himself, named Lucile. Her family perished in the war that brought Molara to power; and because the general was a friend of the family, she had been entrusted to his care. As the author puts it, "before a month had passed he fell in love with the beautiful girl whom Fortune had led to him."[34] Relations between man and wife are described as "amiable" and "formal:" "even during the first years [of their marriage] there had been something wanting."[35] Lucile was, however, loyal to her husband and involved in his political affairs. She held brilliant soirées for the leading dignitaries of the state and used her feminine charms— within the limits of Victorian sexual propriety—to gain information and advantage for the President.

The third character is Savrola, the young and dashing leader of the political opposition to Molara. He is a moderate, and a man of philosophic bent and cool judgment. Although he is possessed of a keen love of justice and compassion for the sufferings of oppressed humanity and is capable of inspiring men with the same feelings through his great oratorical performances, he recognizes the futility of extremist measures. Accordingly he devotes himself to trying to wrest control of the state from Molara by political means, to restore Laurania's ancient constitution without recourse to violence. His socialist allies, however, who are in contact with exiled Lauranian extremists, are looking for more radical changes.

Churchill's novel, then, reproduces, in only modestly disguised form, his family; there is even an analogue to his brother Jack, in the form of Savrola's friend Moret, as well as the evocation of Mrs. Everest referred to earlier. Indeed, only two major changes have taken place: the family structure has been made to coincide with the political structure, not merely to be connected with it; and Lucile, who is clearly an idealized version of Lady Randolph, is made to be compatible in age with Churchill himself. In short, Churchill has improved upon his family situation by making possible a conquest of the mother by the son and by simplifying the real life situation so that political victory would yield personal victory as well. He has also given himself the satisfaction of recreating the relationship between his mother and father in a more gratifying manner. Instead of a love match between two attractive young people much involved in each other and their social activities, Churchill paints a portrait of an essentially arranged marriage in which the wife never has true feelings of love for her husband. It is easy to see in this transfiguration Winston's wish that he, and not his father, would be the true

and rightful object of his mother's affections.

Having established his cast of characters, Churchill devotes the rest of the novel to bringing about Molara's demise and Savrola's conquest of both the state and Lucile. Savrola's opposition party, as the story opens, has been working for free elections to the Lauranian parliament. Molara, faced with great public pressure, has agreed to hold elections once again; but the wily dictator has attempted to vitiate the effects of his concession by disenfranchising most of those citizens who he feels will oppose him. Faced with this subterfuge, the opposition is disheartened and confused. Its leadership, meeting after they have found out the bad news, cannot agree upon a course of action. Then Savrola enters their meeting room: "he looked around the room, with a face as calm and serene as ever. In that scene of confusion and indecision he looked magnificent."[36] He easily convinces the others not to despair, to elect as many representatives to parliament as possible, and proposes that he and several others go to visit Molara and try to persuade him to take a more reasonable course. Despite his outward calm, Savrola inwardly is aware of the difficulties of his cause. He feels weary and, reflecting on his role in recent events, admits to himself that the people's good provides him with direction, with a manifest goal, but that a personal ambition which he is "powerless to resist" provides the real dynamic for his efforts.[37] In this context the author, standing back to examine his own creation, notes that "the end comes often early to such men. . . ."[38]

Lord Randolph had died at the age of forty-six, after the failure of a political career in which the goal had been the people's good and the engine his driving ambition. Churchill, writing shortly after his father's death, seems to have felt that he, too, was fated to die young and that his achievements must therefore come early. As his correspondence to his mother while he was in India shows, he dreamed of a political career like his father's—but one, presumably, that would end in success and not failure.[39] Like his father, he hoped to be part of a victorious Conservative party; like his father he hoped to win a dominant position in Tory affairs by dint of his oratorical hold upon the electorate and Parliament; and, unlike his father, he hoped to leave no room for betrayal by those within the party whose goals or personal sentiments differed from his own. Thus Savrola resembles both Churchill and his father; for Churchill sought both consciously and unconsciously to mold himself in his father's image. The character Savrola is just one manifestation of this effort. And where Savrola differs from Lord Randolph, there we may surmise that Churchill hoped to differ as well.

Savrola's meeting with Molara yields no concrete results. The two men size each other up, each feeling the other's power, and recognize that a hard fight lies ahead. During his visit to the dictator's palace, however, Savrola has occasion to pass a few words with Lucile, each sensing the other's attractiveness and neither willing to admit the full impact of what is felt. The reader in turn feels that something of an impasse has been reached until Miguel, one of Molara's advisers, proposes an ingenious plan to the dictator. Why not, he suggests, use Lucile as bait to catch Savrola. If Savrola can be caught in

apparently indelicate circumstances with his enemy's wife, his effectiveness as an opposition leader will be destroyed; and, Miguel argues, without Savrola the opposition will be left without effective leadership. Molara does not immediately approve of this clever plan; but he does agree to invite Savrola to the state ball so that Lucile can pump him for information. Lucile, when she is told by Molara that she is to gain what information she can from Savrola, loyally agrees. Thus a problem for the narrative—how to keep Savrola and Lucile in contact with each other—is resolved by having Molara arrange their meetings; or, to reduce the story line to what seems to be its psychological basis, Churchill arranges to have his father's permission to court his mother.

At this juncture, conflict erupts between the private and public spheres of Savrola's life. He receives an invitation to the ball, which he wants to attend in order to see Lucile; but on that same night there is a large public meeting scheduled at which he is to speak. Over the objections of his friends he has the meeting postponed and attends the ball, knowing full well that he is taking a risk, that he will have to overcome popular resentment at this apparent toadying to Molara's power.

Lucile, following her husband's orders, draws Savrola aside at the ball and tries to find out what his plans are. Savrola responds by deluging her with philosophy but tells her little of any immediate relevance. Again, the young couple feel drawn to each other; and Lucile feels a secret delight when Molara later makes her promise to see Savrola again.

Before the ball, Savrola had written his speech for the public meeting. First he prepared the peroration, allowing himself to be completely captured by the flow of the rhetoric. "Presently he rose, and, completely under the influence of his own thoughts and language began to pace the room."[40] Once the speech was written, he carefully rehearsed its delivery. This was the same method of speech preparation that Churchill used in later years. By having Savrola use it as well, he heightened his own consciousness of its basic character and reassured himself of its effectiveness. For when Savrola delivered the speech he had so carefully prepared the results were truly remarkable. In a chapter entitled "The Wand of the Magician," the author describes how Savrola overcomes the intial hostility of his audience and builds slowly to a dramatic climax that leaves him exhausted and his audience exalted. After hearing it, his friend Moret views him as some kind of god; and Lucile, who is in the audience in disguise, finds herself carried away by Savrola's words despite the fact that he was attacking her husband.[41]

The feeling of sensuality in this scene is unmistakable, albeit limited in its impact by the inadequacies of the author's prose. Savrola's words serve him as a phallic wand with which he seduces his audience, especially Lucile, and reaches an emotional climax himself. In the process he also uses his words to undermine Molara's power and prestige. Thus Churchill has Savrola play out in a public context a private drama. And, insofar as we see Savrola as an emanation of Churchill's own impulses and desires, we are given another indication of the dynamic of Churchill's political career: with his words he sought to woo the English people as he would have liked to woo

his mother and to puncture the claims of all rivals for her charms, just as he would have liked to defeat his father in this most fundamental area of competition. The poigance of this fantasy is deepened when we remember that Churchill was considered to be a stupid child, one who did not use words well enough to follow in his father's footsteps and was therefore condemned to a military career. And our sense of the triumph of Churchill's career is heightened when we realize how much of this fantasy he was able to translate into reality, that it was none other than the author of this little story who was to be acclaimed by many as the greatest craftsman of the English language in the history of parliamentary politics.

After Savrola's speech, Lucile is hurt in the crush of the crowd. Savrola, hearing a woman in distress, has water brought to her. Discovering her identity, and realizing she would be in danger if the crowd knew who she was, he has her taken to his dwelling. There, looking at the stars from his rooftop, they recognize their love for each other, although neither admits it in so many words. Just as Lucile is about to leave to return to the palace, a messenger arrives and informs Savrola that the revolutionary exiles have crossed the border and are marching on the city. Thus against his will Savrola is forced into open revolt and, against her will, Lucile is given the information her husband has been seeking. Now she must decide where her loyalties lie: with Savrola or her husband?

The reader and Lucile breathe a sigh of relief together when, upon returning to the palace, she finds out that Molara already knows of the impending attack. Having maintained his heroine's essential integrity, the author at last has Molara give in to Miguel's plot. Telling Lucile only that he wants her to see Savrola in order to get more information, Molara is secretly planning to break in upon his wife and Savrola and to use the situation to discredit his foe. Thus the author has Molara reveal his basically infamous character and, at the same time, legitimize another rendezvous between hero and heroine. Molara is made to take responsibility for what was, in Churchill's real life, a forbidden and unattainable union.

Lucile agrees to see Savrola again, hoping to warn him of the danger that faces him and, by so doing, to serve her husband as well. For if Savrola could be convinced that the odds are against him, he might flee; and if Savrola fled, her husband's chances of victory would be heightened. Savrola, however, has no intention of fleeing and, resigned to losing the woman he loves, he gives her a tender kiss—as Molara bursts into the room. He tells Savrola to fall on his knees and beg for mercy or be shot. Savrola bravely looks down the barrel of his enemy's pistol and refuses. Molara, enraged, is about to shoot when Lucile beseeches him to stop. Thunderstruck, Molara finally grasps the situation. Lucile is really in love with Savrola! Truly maddened now, the President again tries to shoot Savrola, but Miguel, always the shrewd politician, prevents the action he feels would be suicidal for the government's cause. Thus through love and policy Savrola is saved. Or, in other terms, the threatening father is disarmed by his own ambition and his wife's self-sacrificing love for her son. Beneath the waves of melodrama under which the characters almost drown can be seen the plaintive wish of a small boy who longed for his mother's attention and love.

The opponents part, Molara to return to his palace, Savrola to go to revolutionary headquarters. Lucile is left behind in Savrola's apartments, to await the outcome of the struggle along with Savrola's loyal nurse. After some uncertainty, as the rebels clash with government troops, it becomes clear that Savrola's forces have gained the upper hand. Moret goes to the palace to offer the President safe passport out of the country. The message is never delivered, however, for one of Molara's henchmen kills Moret while he is standing exposed under a white flag. The rebels then storm the palace and, inspired by the socialists, kill Molara. Savrola, having received word at his headquarters that Moret had been killed and the palace was being stormed, rushes to the scene in order to save the President's life. But he arrives too late.

The author thus eliminates both Moret (thereby exposing aggressive feelings toward his younger brother that seldom were manifest in life) and Molara without having any blame rest with Savrola. His hero is thus free to live happily ever after with the woman he loves without guilt for having removed the rival claimants for her affection—while at the same time leading his country through difficult days to peace and tranquility. But even Churchill seems a bit uneasy with this all too neatly arranged wish fulfillment. It did not correspond to his father's fate, for his father had won the woman he loved but had been ultimately a failure politically. And, in 1899, Churchill's own political career lay ahead of him. He could hope for, but not feel assured of, eventual success. As a result, the novel ends in a vacillating manner. After Molara's death Savrola has trouble controlling the radical forces in his own movement and is forced into exile, with Lucile at his side. Here, then, Churchill evokes his father's fate. But, not content to end in anything less than full triumph, Churchill tags on an extra paragraph in which he describes how the Lauranian people eventually discover that they need Savrola's wise leadership and summon him and his beautiful wife back to Lauria to take charge of the affairs of state. This coda is the least convincing part of a not very convincing story, however, and reveals the doubts Churchill had about his own ability to be anything like a Savrola in English politics.

We thus see that a marked continuity links the lonely five-year-old boy whose head was filled with images of the violent affairs of men and the unapproachability of women and the young subaltern who, after his father's death, was trying to determine how best to make a political career for himself. This continuity is in part due, one would guess, to the intensity of the original emotional configuration, in part to the neglect that runs as a theme throughout his school years. We have seen young Churchill developing over time the ability to deal with the strength of his own impulses and the coldness of his environment. When *Savrola* was written, that process of growth and struggle was not yet over. Some fundamental questions remained unresolved. As the titular character's attributes reveal, Churchill was bent on a political career in emulation of his father's. Like his father, he would be, in some sense, a rebel. Like Horatius at the bridge or Savrola, Churchill would be willing to take great risks in order to win great rewards. But what would be the result of such gambles? Would he end, symbolically, in exile or at the head of the state? And what could he do to affect his fate? These were the challenges that lay ahead.

NOTES

1. Even a sympathetic biographer has trouble justifying this escapade. See Peter de Mendelssohn, *The Age of Churchill* (London: Thames and Hudson, 1961), I, 502–507.
2. Winston S. Churchill, *The Gathering Storm* (Boston: Houghton Mifflin, 1948), p. 215.
3. Churchill, *Blood, Sweat, and Tears* (New York: Putnam, 1941), p. 297.
4. Lord Charles Moran, *Churchill* (Boston, Houghton Mifflin, 1966), p. 197.
5. Winston's birth less than eight months after his parents' marriage was officially recorded as premature. Whether or not it was, his parents' reaction to it tends to indicate that they were not particularly eager to have a child.
6. Randolph S. Churchill, *Winston S. Churchill* (Boston: Houghton Mifflin, 1966), I, 43.

7. Winston S. Churchill, *Savrola: A Tale of Revolution in Laurania* (New York: Longmans, Green, 1900), p. 44.

8. The best study of a political leader who bore the full consequences of such a childhood is Alexander and Juliette George's, *Woodrow Wilson and Colonel House* (New York: Dover, 1964).

9. See Moran, *op. cit.*, 179–180.

10. As mentioned earlier, Churchill's self-esteem and resiliency were probably developed through genetics as well as environment. And his successes in late adolescence and early manhood, which gradually led to a substantial rapport with his mother, were also involved. One can only speculate on the relative importance of these three factors.

11. The most complete account of this incident is in Randolph S. Churchill, *op. cit.*, pp. 24–32.

12. As was implied earlier, Lord Randolph's political career accentuated for Winston the normal tendency to perceive political authority in familial terms. See Fred S. Greenstein's discussion of this aspect of political socialization in his *Children and Politics* (New Haven: Yale University Press, 1965), pp. 46–50.

13. Winston S. Churchill, *My Early Life: A Roving Commission* (New York: Scribner, 1958), p. 1.

14. That Winston was seeking an answer to a problem is also suggested by the fact that the words in the speech were actually "with a crashing volley the enemy was fiercely beaten back." (Randolph S. Churchill, *op cit.*, p. 36). Winston obviously preferred a more assertive formulation.

15. Winston S. Churchill, *My Early Life, op. cit.*, p. 2.

16. *Ibid.* It might be noted that the consistently phallic quality of the objects that fascinated Winston (a statue, keys, and a tower) points to the oedipal ambition and attendant castration anxiety which one might guess formed a large part of his emotional life.

17. *Ibid.*

18. *Ibid.*, pp. 4–5.

19. Randolph S. Churchill, *op. cit.*, 35–36.

20. Winston S. Churchill, *My Early Life, op. cit.*, p. 10.

21. *Ibid.*, p. 12. When Churchill was Home Secretary he devoted himself to prison reform, a clear reflection of the sympathy for prisoners his own school experiences gave him.

22. Randolph S. Churchill, *op. cit.*, p. 52.

23. Winston S. Churchill, *My Early Life, op. cit.*, p. 12.

24. Randolph S. Churchill, *op. cit.*, p. 55.

25. *Ibid.*, p. 115.

26. *Ibid.*, p. 118.

27. Lady Hannah More Trevelyan (ed.), *The Works of Lord Macaulay* (London: Longmans, Green, 1866), p. 473.

28. Winston S. Churchill, *My Early Life, op. cit.*, p. 19.

29. *Ibid.*, pp. 29–30. Another treatment of the incident can be found in my chapter in Lewis Edinger (ed.), *Political Leadership in Industrial Societies* (New York: Wiley, 1967).

30. Edinger, *op. cit.*, *Political Leadership in the Developed Nations*, p. 167–168.

31. Randolph S. Churchill, *op. cit.*, pp. 188–189.

32. *Ibid.*, p. 228.

33. Winston S. Churchill, *My Early Life, op. cit.*, p. 46.

34. Winston S. Churchill, *Savrola, op. cit.*, p. 27.

35. *Ibid.*, p. 28.

36. *Ibid.*, p. 34.

37. *Ibid.*, p. 42.

38. *Ibid.*, p. 43.

39. See Randolph S. Churchill, chap. 9, *passim.*

40. Winston S. Churchill, *Savrola, op. cit.*, p. 89.

41. *Ibid.*, pp. 150–154.

PERSONALITY AND POLITICAL SOCIALIZATION: THE THEORIES OF AUTHORITARIAN AND DEMOCRATIC CHARACTER

- Fred I. Greenstein*

The socialization experiences which culminate in adult citizenship can be divided into two rough categories: that learning which is specifically about government and politics, and non-political personal development which affects political behavior. My concern here is with a particularly controversial, but intriguing, portion of the topics arising in the second category—the notions of "authoritarian" and "democratic" character. In addition to reviewing theory and research on these character types, I will discuss briefly several of the problems involved in untangling the complex connections among personal character, political beliefs, political action, and the functioning of political and other social institutions. This is an extensive and extraordinarily craggy intellectual terrain. In a brief essay I can only hope, as it were, to engage in high-altitude aerial reconnaissance—that is, to construct a rather abstract and quite selective map of the phenomena which interest us, illustrating rather than demonstrating my assertions.

Above selection reprinted from: *The Annals of the American Academy of Political and Social Science*, 361 (September 1965), 81–95.

* This article was written while I was a Fellow at the Center for Advanced Study in the Behavioral Sciences in 1964–1965. I would like to thank a number of my associates for their thoughtful comments: Christian Bay, Robert Bellah, Miriam Gallaher, Walter Goldschmidt, John R. Seeley, M. Brewster Smith, and Robert Wallerstein.

Put bluntly, the questions which concern us are: "Can we distinguish types of individuals whose personal make-up —apart from their specifically political beliefs—disposes them to act in a democratic or an authoritarian manner?" "What socialization practices produce such individuals?" "What can be said about the circumstances under which the actual behavior of such individuals will be democratic or authoritarian, and about the aggregate effects which individuals with democratic or authoritarian dispositions may have on the functioning of political institutions?"

The Study of Authoritarian and Democratic Character

There is, by far, more literature on authoritarian than on democratic character. One of the wonders of recent social science scholarship has been the profusion of "authoritarianism" research in the past decade and a half. An admittedly selective review of writings on the topic through 1956 contained 260 bibliographical references.[1] Today, anything but the most sparse systematic discussion of the relevant research would require a monograph. Even as interest in this matter begins to fall off, it is rare to find an issue of a journal dealing with personality and attitude research that contains no reference to authoritarianism and no use of the various techniques designed to measure it.

The main immediate stimulus for this explosion of research was the publication in 1950 of a 990-page volume by T. W. Adorno, Else Frenkel-Brunswik, Nevitt Sanford, and Daniel J. Levinson, entitled *The Authoritarian Personality*,[2] which reported the fruits of several years of investigation into the psychology of anti-Semitism. On the basis of a rich but bewilderingly varied and uneven assortment of research procedures, the authors of this work reached a striking conclusion about the psychology of hostility to Jews and other minority groups. Such prejudiced attitudes, they argued, were not simply beliefs which people happened to have acquired. Rather, one could identify what might be called a "bigot personality,"[3] a type of individual with deep-seated psychological needs which manifested themselves in a variety of ways over and beyond ethnic prejudice. *The Authoritarian Personality* is a book dealing more with prejudice than with the problem suggested by its title—psychological dispositions toward authority. "The title," as one of the authors points out, "was not thought of until the writing was virtually finished."[4] But it was the title phrase which came to provide the heading under which subsequent investigation proceeded, and, in general, ethnic prejudice has become a secondary issue in research on authoritarianism.

The term "authoritarian" has at least two shortcomings as an analytical tool. First, it is applicable not only to individual psychological dispositions (our concern here), but also to the content of political belief and to the structure of political systems. Because of this we may easily gloss over the possibility that "authoritarianism" at any one of these levels is not necessarily accompanied by authoritarianism at the other levels. For example, democratic beliefs may be imposed in an authoritarian manner. And, within an authoritarian movement, the leadership may include individuals of nonauthoritarian dispositions, and may even conduct its own deliberations in a democratic fashion.

Secondly, the term seems almost inevitably to be a pejorative. In a liberal democracy "authoritarian" equals "bad." The evaluative connotations of the term interfere with our efforts to use it as a neutral instrument for denoting an empirical phenomenon. A historical note on the work of the Nazi psychologist E. R. Jaensch may help to remind us that the term can have meaning independent of its negative connotations. In 1938 Jaensch described a psychological type with remarkable similarities to the typology presented in *The Authoritarian Personality*. But his evaluation of the type was not at all negative. Rather, he saw it as exemplifying the best virtues of National Socialist manhood.[5]

There is, of course, nothing new in the awareness that some people are more deferential toward authority than others and that the same people often are harsh to their subordinates. The fawning underling is a stock character in fiction, as in the tyrannical superior. It is a safe assumption that the readers of Fielding's *Tom Jones* (1747) had no difficulty recognizing the character of Deborah Wilkins, who "seldom opened her lips either to her master or his sister till she had first sounded their inclinations, with which her sentiments were always strictly consonant," and of whom Fielding says:

It is the nature of such persons ... to insult and tyrannize over little people. This being indeed the means which they use to recompense to themselves their extreme servility and condescension to their superiors; for nothing can be more reasonable than that slaves and flatterers should exact the same taxes on all below them which they themselves pay to all above them.[6]

What *is* new in the twentieth-century literature on authoritarianism is the specification of a constellation of psychological correlates of this tendency and the elaboration of a theory of its psychodynamics and genesis. This theory (which I shall shortly summarize) was woven from a number of strands of contemporary social psychological thought. Some of the formulations in *The Authoritarian Personality* were presaged by research in the 1930's and 1940's into "fascist attitudes."[7] Others can be found in the World War II and cold-war national-character literature, particularly the efforts to diagnose German, Japanese, and Russian character.[8] The discussion of "authoritarian character" in Erich Fromm's widely discussed *Escape from Freedom*[9] seems to have been particularly influential, as were the various efforts in the 1930's by Fromm and others connected with the Institut für Sozialforschung to blend Freud and Marx in an analysis of the role of the family "in maintaining authority in modern society."[10] Underlying all of these discussions was what still is probably the most revolutionary facet of twentieth-century social science —psychoanalysis—and, particularly, several overlapping elements in Freud's thought: the notion of the anal character, his analyses of obsessional neuroses and of paranoia, and his delineation of the mechanism of projection. (The dependence of the conception of authoritarianism upon a personality theory that places such a great emphasis on the significance of childhood experience makes authoritarianism a particularly strong candidate for discussion in a symposium on political socialization.)

The Authoritarian Personality, therefore, served to focus attention on hypotheses which had been in the air for some time, rather than to suggest completely new hypotheses. But it did something more—and this seems to have been especially important in spurring the subsequent research. The section of the book devoted to "measurement of ideological trends" provided a number of "ready-made tests that had already been taken through many of the technical procedures of validation which every [psychological] test must pass,"[11] the most notable and widely used of these being the F- (fascism) scale. The ready-made tests were very conveniently available to subsequent investigators, whereas the fascinating body of theory which guided the research was "in no single place in the volume"[12] conveniently stated. In the long run, this emphasis on certain restricted measurement techniques proved to be most unfortunate, since the authoritarian literature became progressively bogged in what in many respects was a comedy of methodological errors, and a number of the original insights in *The Authoritarian Personality* never received careful attention.[13]

In contrast to the several paragraphs required simply to make peremptory reference to the intellectual history of authoritarian personality study, the state of investigation into democratic personality can be briefly stated. There has been some theorizing on this topic and virtually no research. No one, to my knowledge, has attempted to devise and use a D- (democratic) scale. Our consideration of democratic character, therefore, has far less to go upon. I shall concentrate mainly on what seems to me to be an especially interesting discussion of the topic, an essay by Harold Lasswell which, I think, has not received the attention it merits.[14]

A number of commentators—including the authors of *The Authoritarian Personality*—have expressed skepticism over whether a concept such as "democratic character" corresponds sufficiently to anything found in the "real world" to be worth using.[15] The test of usefulness of a typology—or, in currently fashionable jargon, model—is, however, not merely its correspondence with presently available data. Typologies clarify thinking and guide research. They may serve to summarize aspects of what has already been observed, they may suggest hypotheses for future observations, and they may simply be vehicles for reasoning. What is important is that a typology make sufficient and appropriate distinctions for the purpose at hand.

Authoritarian Character

Three general distinctions appropriate for setting forth a typology of personality are: phenomenology, dynamics, and genesis. In other words, first we may take note of all of the psychological characteristics composing the type which, with a minimum of inferential interpretation, are readily observable. Then we summarize our hypotheses about the processes underlying the observables. How are the observed features related to each other? What ties them together? Finally, we assemble the hypotheses

which are most relevant to the present essay: What accounts for the development of this type of individual? How does he arise in the socialization process?

These distinctions provide us, in effect, with a logical reconstruction of the process of inquiry: We observe that, although each individual we encounter is in many respects unique, individuals resemble some of their fellows more than they do others. If the pattern of resemblances is particularly striking, we begin to reflect on what makes such a type of individual work, on his inner dynamics. Then we endeavor to find out what made him the way he is. The distinctions also often reflect the state of knowledge. Agreement on matters of phenomenology is relatively easy to come by, even among scholars with quite different intellectual orientations. Interpretations of underlying dynamics are more controversial. Given the paucity of good longitudinal research—that is, studies of the same individuals over a period of time—reliable evidence of genesis may be especially rare.

Phenomenology of the Authoritarian

Some of the dozen or so traits appearing in the various conceptualizations of the authoritarian type are of immediate interest to the student of politics since they assume a form which directly parallels activities commonly performed in the political arena. Others would seem to be of more remote interest. Most central for our purposes is the pair of traits labeled "authoritarian agression" and "authoritarian submission"—the dominance-submissiveness tendencies of the authoritarian. Such an individual, like Fielding's Mrs. Wilkins, abases himself before those who stand above him hierarchically, or whom he perceives to be powerful, and lords it over whoever seems to be weak, subordinate, or inferior. "German folklore," Adorno relates, "has a drastic symbol for this"— bicyclist's personality (*Radfahrernaturen*): "Above they bow, below they kick."[16]

Also politically relevant is the tendency of such individuals to *think* in power terms, to be acutely sensitive to questions of who dominates whom. Only at a slightly further remove from politics is the pervasive rigidity in the authoritarian's manner of confronting the world. He is, in Else Frenkel-Brunswik's phrase, "intolerant of ambiguity."[17] He likes order and is made uncomfortable by disorder: where the phenomena he is exposed to are complex and subtle, he imposes his own tight categories upon them, ignoring their nuances. His thinking therefore makes more than the usual use of stereotypes. Another of the traits composing the character type is "conventionalism." The authoritarian, much like Riesman's "radar-controlled" other-directed personality,[18] is described as being particularly sensitive to "external agencies" and, especially, to the prevailing standards of his own social group.

The foregoing authoritarian traits, all of which can be seen to have some rather immediate potential bearing on behavior in the political arena, hang together in a fashion which puts little strain on our common sense: dominance of subordinates; deference toward superiors; sensitivity to power relationships; need to perceive the world in a highly structured fashion; excessive use of stereotypes; and adherence to whatever values are conventional in one's setting. We can easily visualize an individual with these complementary at-

tributes. But what is perhaps most intriguing about the authoritarian syndrome is that several further, less obvious, traits are found as a part of the presenting symptoms.

These rather exotic additional concomitants lead us beyond phenomenology to the psychoanalytically based theory of dynamics. For example, the authoritarian is described as being superstitious. (One of the items of the F-scale is: "Although many people may scoff, it may yet be shown that astrology can explain a lot of things.") He is preoccupied with virility, tending toward "exaggerated assertion of strength and toughness." (While this trait might be juxtaposed with the authoritarian's interest in power, there is the added element here of being hard-boiled and rugged. The equivalent trait in the less well-developed typology of female authoritarianism is "pseudo-femininity" —a preoccupation with being "feminine and soft.") The authoritarian assumptions about human nature are generally pessimistic, and he tends to be cynical about the motives of others. He is disposed to believe that "wild and dangerous things go on in the world"—that "the world is a jungle." He shows a puritanical preoccupation with sex—a "concern with sexual 'goings on'" and "a strong inclination to punish violators of sex mores." And, finally, he shows a trait of which much is made in the theoretical explanation of this pattern— "anti-intraception." This is "an attitude of impatience with and opposition to the subjective and the tenderminded." One of its more conspicious forms is an inability to introspect, to acknowledge one's own feelings and fantasies.

The authoritarian typology, like

Freud's famous juxtaposition of order-liness, parsimoniousness, and obstinacy in the anal personality type, may well have the merit of being less obvious to common sense than most of the formulations with which social scientists work. But what is its basis in reality? Are individuals to be found who exhibit these characteristics, or a sufficient proportion of them, to make the notion of "authoritarian personality" more than an intriguing exercise in reasoning? The answer, I think, is yes, but I cannot even begin to refer to the elements in the tangled body of authoritarian research on which such a conclusion might be based. It can, at any rate, be seen that the question *is* potentially answerable, and much more readily so than the questions arising at the dynamic and genetic levels.[19]

Dynamics of Authoritarianism

While the typology of dynamics which has been proposed to account for this pattern of traits also can be elaborated in considerable detail, we must content ourselves here simply with suggesting its major themes. The authoritarian, it is argued, is an individual with strong, but ambivalent, dispositions toward figures of authority. Denial of the negative side of these feelings is central to such an individual's functioning. The authoritarian is able to conceal from himself his rage toward those in authority only by the massive defense procedure reaction formation, involving a total repression of critical and other unacceptable impulses toward authority and a bending over backwards in excessive praise of it.[20] But repression has its costs and side-effects, and repressed impulses seek alternative outlets. Hos-

tility not only is rechanneled toward whoever is perceived as weak and unauthorative, but also has a more diffuse effect on the authoritarian's generally negative views of man and his works, as well as contributing to his need to scan his environment for signs of authority relationships, his tendency (via projection) to see the world as full of dangerous things and people, and his desire to punish others, for example, sex offenders, who have surrendered to their impulses. Feelings of personal weakness are covered by a façade of toughness. A side-effect of channeling enormous energy into repression and reaction formation is that the authoritarian's emotional capacities and even certain of his cognitive capacities are stunted. He is unable to face the prospect of canvassing his own psyche—for fear of what such introspection may yield—and therefore becomes highly dependent upon external sources of guidance.[21]

This general thesis about authoritarian dynamics might be called the ego-defensive theory of authoritarianism. After the fashion of classical psychoanalysis, the theory places great emphasis on irrationality—on how the self, in seeking to maintain inner equilibrium (that is, to defend against impulses and conscience), is flawed in its perception of and response to the environment. Since the empirical standing of psychoanalysis continues to be controversial, it is not difficult to understand why this aspect of authoritarian theory is less settled than the question of phenomenology.[22]

It is quite possible to accept the phenomenological typology of authoritarianism and reject the ego-defensive thesis of its dynamics. This, in effect, has been done by several commentators who present what might be called a *cognitive* theory of authoritarianism. The cognitive theory holds that the patterns of expression and behavior that have been characterized as authoritarian are based upon simple learning of the conceptions of reality prevalent in one's culture or subculture, and that these patterns also may to some extent be accurate reflections of the actual conditions of adult life faced by some individuals, rather than having the labyrinthine roots in reaction formation suggested by the ego-defensive theory.[23] Recent research suggests that there is some merit in both the cognitive and the ego-defensive formulations. Much of what has been called "working-class authoritarianism" does seem to have its roots in simple cognitive learning, whereas, at the higher socioeconomic levels, authoritarian orientations seem more often to tap less accessible motivational sources.[24]

The Genesis of Authoritarianism

Adorno and his associates, in fact, anticipated the thesis of cognitive authoritarianism by acknowledging that the personality manifestations they were studying could in some instances merely reflect "surface resentment" with a "more or less rational" basis in learning.[25] Subsequent extensions of the cognitive explanation, for example, by Hyman and Sheatsley, have stressed the lack of information available in lower-class subcultures and the lack of opportunity of lower-class individuals to acquire the desire and capacity to manipulate symbols—or, at least, the symbols with which public discourse is conducted—with any degree of sophistication. Such social settings, it is suggested, produce individuals who respond

to the F-scale in much the same fashion as would be predicted by the ego-defensive theory of authoritarianism, but who do not show the pathology described in the theory. Furthermore, the lower-class world may, in many respects, really *be* a jungle. Under such circumstances "authoritarianism" reflects little more than learning from one's exemplars and realistic attempts to characterize one's environment.

The Authoritarian Personality, however, concentrates on elucidating the childhood antecedents of ego-defensive authoritarianism. The typical early determinants of this pattern come as no surprise in the light of the theory of underlying dynamics.

When we consider the childhood situation . . . we find reports of a tendency toward rigid discipline on the part of the parents, with affection which is conditional rather than unconditional, i.e., dependent upon approved behavior on the part of the child. Related to this is a tendency . . . to base [family] interrelationships in rather clearly defined roles of dominance and submission. . . . Forced into a surface submission to parental authority, the child develops hostility and aggression which are poorly channelized. The displacement of a repressed antagonism toward authority may be one of the sources, and perhaps the principal source, of his antagonism toward outgroups.[26]

The authors derived these and similar conclusions about how ego-defensive authoritarianism arises in the socialization process partly from their subjects' retrospective reports of childhood experiences, but also from direct studies by Frenkel-Brunswik of ethnically prejudiced and unprejudiced children. The studies of children suggested that "warmer, closer and more affectionate interpersonal relationships prevail in the homes of the unprejudiced children" and that prejudice was associated with "strictness, rigidity, punitiveness, rejection vs. acceptance of the child."

In the home with the orientation toward rigid conformity . . . maintenance of discipline is often based upon the expectation of external rigid and superficial rules which are bound to be beyond the comprehension of the child. Family relationships are characterized by fearful subservience to the demands of the parents and by an early suppression of impulses not acceptable to the adults.

Since the moral requirements in such a home must appear to the child as overwhelming and at the same time unintelligible, and the rewards meager, submission to them must be reinforced by fear of and pressure from external agencies. Due to the lack of a genuine identification with the parents, the fearfully conforming child does not make the important developmental step from mere social anxiety to real conscience.[27]

I have earlier noted that the authoritarian personality research grew out of an intellectual tradition which drew on both Freudian psychology and Marxian sociology. It is the Freudian emphasis on early childhood socialization that occupies most of the discussion in *The Authoritarian Personality* of how authoritarianism is socialized. But occasionally a Marxian explanation of the genesis of authoritarianism appears, as in the final paragraph of the volume where the authors remark that "people are continuously molded from above because they must be molded if the overall economic pattern is to be maintained."[28] The point being made here is evidently that of Fromm, who in *Escape from Freedom* develops, *inter alia*, a conception of "social character" as

that which "internalizes external necessities and thus harnesses human energy for the task of a given economic and social system;" a conception of the authoritarian character as the energy source in the development of Western capitalism (in contrast to Weber's Protestant Ethic); and a conception of the family as, in effect, mainly a transmission belt providing the system the type of personality it "requires."[29] Apart from whatever merit there may be in Fromm's specific historical argument, we have here a further class of explanatory factors—overlapping the references to culture in the cognitive model—which may be introduced to explain the genesis of authoritarianism, namely, social structure and social role requirements.[30]

From Character Structure to Political Structure

The field of culture and personality research, into which the authoritarian literature falls, is not in especially good repute. Particularly suspect are the attempts—perhaps most marked in the wartime national-character literature—to reason from (often imperfect) evidence about early socialization and personality development, rapidly and effortlessly, to explanations of broad social and historical phenomena, such as the rise of Naziism, Japanese militarism, and so forth. The disparaging label "psychologism" has come to be attached to such inferential leaps. These exercises in reducing politics and sociology to psychology often impress no one less than the psychoanalysts themselves. "Shortly after Pearl Harbor," an analyst relates:

a small group of noted social scientists, intent on studying the cultural roots of German National Socialism, invited a number of refugee scholars and interviewed them about their experiences and ideas on this subject. I was among those invited. I remember that I mentioned among the factors which seemed to me to have disposed the German people for a nationalistic dictatorship, the failure of German nineteenth century liberalism, and the subsequent success of Prussian militarism, in bringing about the much-desired unification of Germany; this experience, I argued, had conditioned the German people to distrust the democratic process and to put their faith in strong-arm methods. I also mentioned the impact of rapid industrialization upon a society still almost feudal in its caste structure, without interceding commercialism and without a strong commercial class such as was already established in Anglo-Saxon countries at the outset of industrialization; such a situation seemed to make people more alert to the possibilities of power, rather than the potentialities of welfare, inherent in industry. I was then interrupted by my host, a noted anthropologist; this was not what I had been expected to contribute. As a psychoanalyst I should point out how Nazism had developed from the German form of child rearing. I replied that I did not think that there was any such relationship; in fact, political opinion did not seem to be determined in early childhood at all. This view was not accepted and I was told that the way the German mother holds her baby must be different from that of mothers in democracies. When we parted, it was clear that my hosts felt that they had wasted their time.[31]

Although there are numerous statements by *Authoritarian Personality* contributors acknowledging that personality factors are neither "the major [n]or exclusive determinants of political or social movements,"[32] it is difficult to gainsay the critics who argue that the

work is shot through with psychologism. For example, by labeling the personality trends we have been discussing "prefascist" and "potentially fascist," they tended to resolve by definition the complex empirical question of how deeper personality trends articulate with specifically political belief and with actual behavior. And their references to the "great . . . fascist potential"[33] in American society seemed to reflect equally naïve assumptions about the relationship between the distribution of psychological dispositions in a society and its over-all political structure. By very briefly indicating some of the many factors which intervene between character structure and political structure, we can touch upon some of the further questions that have arisen in connection with the study of authoritarianism.

Personality and Belief System

As is often pointed out, persons with similar deep psychological characteristics may entertain different political beliefs, and persons with similar beliefs may differ in personality. This is so because there normally are a variety of alternative channels which can express underlying psychic needs, and also because, given the inattentiveness to politics of most citizens, political orientations often are acquired haphazardly, without engaging deeper personality sources. The original authoritarian personality research was influenced not only by the intellectual traditions to which I referred above, but also by the political climate of the 1930's and 1940's and, in particular, the grim history of German national socialism and the presence in the United States of nativistic radical-right movements.

This seems to have been one of the reasons for the insensitivity in the original research to the possibility—which subsequently received a good bit of attention—that authoritarian character traits may be manifested in other than rightist political beliefs.[34] Related to this was a tendency in the original reports to discuss the ethnically prejudiced and politically conservative attitudes of many authoritarians as if these were part of the defining characteristics of the syndrome itself. For some purposes it may be desirable to treat opinions as "an integral part of personality,"[35] but in studying personality and politics we can see that it often is essential to distinguish analytically between character and belief, lest the question of the connections between them be settled in our definitions rather than our research. The research, of course, may well show that authoritarian personality characteristics are associated with authoritarian beliefs, and that these personality characteristics *do* "fit" best with right-wing ideology. But, at best, the relationship is likely to be imperfect.

Effects of Personality and Belief System on Action

The individual with a "potentially fascist" character structure, then, does not necessarily hold "fascist" beliefs. Furthermore, the connections of character structure *and* belief content with action are not necessarily as straightforward as the usage "potential fascist" implies. Action results from the situations in which people find themselves, including the formal and informal roles they are called upon to perform, as well as from their psychological predispositions. The lack of "one-to-one correlation" between psychological dispositions and action is often pointed out. It may be less well appreciated that the correlation can even be negative; in some circumstances an individual's behavior may actually be the *reverse* of what would have been expected if only his predispositions were taken into account. An example of this is to be found in work by Katz and Benjamin on behavior of Northern white college undergraduates toward Negro co-workers. Presumably racially prejudiced "authoritarians were actually more deferential with Negroes than were non-authoritarians," a finding which the investigators felt was "due to the authoritarian's fear of revealing anti-Negro attitudes in a potentially punitive environment."[36] Still further insight into the subtleties of personality-role relationships might have been obtained if the investigators had also looked into whether authoritarians felt more strain in such situations than did nonauthoritarians, or how each group would have responded if sufficient tension and frustration had been introduced to challenge the authoritarians' "inner controls" of their hostile impulses.[37] The point is that we must employ analytic distinctions which attune us to the possible subtleties of our subject.

Aggregate Effects of Individual Predispositions and Actions

So much more than simple addition is involved in moving from the distribution of individual characteristics in a society—for example, its proportion of authoritarians—to questions about overall political structure that some social scientists are led to a kind of vulgar Durkheimianism, which denies on methodological grounds the relevance of psychology to sociology and political science. At the very least, the addition of personal characteristics is a matter of weighted rather than simple sums.[38] It takes a good many authoritarian voters to equal one authoritarian President of the United States. Moreover, "more than one set of personality characteristics" is needed "to make a political movement. . . . Movements and institutions, even if they are authoritarian, require both more and less than authoritarian personality structures," and even "a liberal democratic society itself could probably not function satisfactorily with only 'democratic liberal personalities' to fill all its roles."[39] Here again, the point is not to deny the significance of the sequelae of socialization (personality and political belief), but to suggest the care necessary to make inferences about the matter.

Democratic Character

Lasswell's essay "Democratic Character," like the discussion which has just preceded, is essentially typological. In effect, he elaborates a hypothetical construct, in part from the existing research on the antidemocratic character, in part by deductions from an analysis of the role requirements of democratic society. The main general features of the psychological typology are a "self-system" (the individual's conscious orientations, which consist of his cognitive assumptions, his preferences, and his identifications), an "energy-system" (roughly equivalent to the Freudian unconscious, composed of conscience, ego ideals, and drives), and a special definition of the term "character," as "the self-system of the person, together with the degree of support, opposition or non-support received from the unconscious parts of the personality." "Character" therefore acquires the dimension of strength and weakness, much as in lay usage. "When we say that a man is of steadfast character it is implied that he has sufficient command of the resources of the whole personality to maintain the self-system despite environing conditions which are adverse."[40]

At the cognitive level, the democratic character believes in the benevolent potentialities of mankind, rejecting the authoritarian's more Hobbesian conception of human nature. The democrat's preferences are consistent with the role requirements in the model of the democratic social system—that is, he *wants* to behave in the ways he should behave, if the functioning of the democratic system is to be successful. Furthermore, he is a "multi-valued" moderate who can weigh alternative goals against each other, rather than an absolutist in pursuit of a single value who, because of his inability to compromise, might endanger the stability of the system. And it is especially important that the democratic character be free of the pursuit of power as a single end-in-itself. In addition, the democrat's identifications are broad and comprehensive— Lasswell speaks of the "open ego"— unlike the good guys-bad guys pattern of the authoritarian.

This pattern of conscious perspectives, Lasswell points out, might well be found among individuals who at the unconscious level had antidemocratic inclinations and, particularly, destructive, power-seeking, or self-punishing tendencies. Referring, in effect, to the curiously labeled "rigid low scorer" of the authoritarian studies, Lasswell acknowledges that

democratic responses often arise from motivations which are incompatible with . . . [democracy], and signify that the individual has achieved part of his democratic outlook by 'reaction formation' against tendencies of an opposite kind. Many democrats appear to develop in opposition to anti-democratic parents, for example.

While he grants that "the destructive energies of a person may be directed against enemies of the democratic community," he nevertheless excludes the democrat-by-reaction formation from his typology, since "from the point of view of modern personality research, the characters which are achieved by a complex process of balanced defense are viewed as constituting less enduring formations than those which evolve more directly."[41] On the matter of socialization, Lasswell comments that "there is reason to believe that in some cultures the possibility of developing an outgoing democratic character is excluded at an early period. The prevailing patterns of child care appear to induce early despair that profound gratifications can emanate from other human beings."[42] The concluding sections of the essay are directly addressed to the problem of how to socialize democratic characters.

There is a lapidary quality to Lasswell's essay—his formulation, overly condensed in this review, is itself quite elliptically stated. The formulation does, however, offer promising suggestions for expanding the scope of research on personality and political socialization. And the novel conception of character strength he introduces—the capacity to

withstand environmental pressure adverse to one's values—raises interesting possibilities for bringing together two hitherto largely unconnected strands in the literature on prerequisites of democracy: the psychological writings we have been discussing here and the currently expanding work on the structural features of democracies and the typical belief systems to be found in them.

Summary and Conclusions

In contemporary anthropology the distinction has occasionally been made between the old culture-and-personality literature, which was especially concerned with early childhood socialization and its effects on personality formation, and the new culture-and-personality literature, which focuses on systematic exploration of people's cognitive maps of their environment.[43] I have reviewed what might be called the old political socialization literature—itself a strand of the early culture-and-personality movement—in contrast to the recently burgeoning research on the development of specifically political orientations.

At base, these divisions between old and new are an artifact of the history of research. Human beings, at whatever stage of the lifelong socialization process, are not divided into self-contained compartments of personality versus cognitions, "specifically political" versus "non-political but politically relevant" development. What has been adventitiously separated needs to be pulled together. But in the present instance this will call for a good bit of careful conceptualization. We need sets of distinctions which "carve at the joints" for thinking about what intervenes between personality socialization and political systems.

Some of the distinctions suggested in this essay can be summarized in the following statements: Personality formation may be along ego-defensive or more cognitive lines; the connections between personality and political belief need to be examined rather than assumed; both personality and beliefs must be examined *in situations* in order to understand behavior; the ways in which individual predispositions and actions aggregate and affect the political and social system need to be explicated. And, to turn the circle, it is the political and social systems which provide the socializing environment for "political" and "politically relevant" personal development and the situations within which political action takes place. In a newfangled way, this is to suggest no more than was evident to Plato: that politics needs to be understood (and undertaken) in the light of human nature and human development.

NOTES

1. Richard Christie and Peggy Cook, "A Guide to Published Literature Relating to the Authoritarian Personality through 1956," *The Journal of Psychology*, Vol. 45 (April 1958), pp. 171–199.

2. T. W. Adorno *et al.*, *The Authoritarian Personality* (New York: Harper, 1950), hereafter cited as *AP*.

3. A phrase used in a prepublication report of the study to the general public: Jerome Himelhoch, "Is There a Bigot Personality?" *Commentary*, Vol. 3 (March 1947), pp. 277–284.

4. Nevitt Sanford, "The Approach of the Authoritarian Personality," *Psychology of Personality*, ed. J. L. McCary (New York: Grove Press, 1959), p. 256.

5. E. R. Jaensch, "Der Gegentypus," *Beiheft zur Zeistschrift für angewandte Psychologie und Charakterkunde*, Beiheft 75 (1938). Just as the *AP* was mainly concerned with the type of individual whose dispositions are antithetical to democracy, Jaensch was most concerned with the "anti-type," whose dispositions were incongruent with National Socialism.

6. Henry Fielding, *Tom Jones*, Book I, chaps. 6 and 8.

7. For example, Ross Stagner, "Fascist Attitudes: Their Determining Conditions," *The Journal of Social Psychology*, Vol. 7 (November 1936), pp. 438–454; Allen L. Edwards, "Unlabeled Fascist Attitudes," *Journal of Abnormal and Social Psychology*, Vol. 36 (October 1941), pp. 575–582.

8. For example, Ruth F. Benedict, *The Chrysanthemum and the Sword* (Boston: Houghton, 1946); Henry V. Dicks, "Personality Traits and National Socialist Ideology," *Human Relations*, Vol. 3 (1950), pp. 111–154; and the same author's "Observations on Contemporary Russian Behavior," *Ibid.*, Vol. 5 (1952), pp. 111–175.

9. Erich Fromm, *Escape from Freedom* (New York: Holt, Rinehart & Winston, 1941). The authors also acknowledge their indebtedness to A. H. Maslow's essay "The

Authoritarian Character Structure," *Journal of Social Psychology*, Vol. 18 (1943), pp. 401–411.

10. Max Horkheimer (ed.), *Studien über Autorität und Familie* (Paris, 1936), p. 902.

11. Nathan Glazer, "New Light on 'The Authoritarian Personality,'" *Commentary*, Vol. 17 (March 1954), p. 290.

12. M. Brewster Smith, Review of *The Authoritarian Personality*, *Journal of Abnormal and Social Psychology*, Vol. 45 (October 1950), p. 775.

13. A variety of telling methodological criticisms of *The Authoritarian Personality* appear in the essays of Herbert H. Hyman and Paul B. Sheatsley and of Richard Christie, in Richard Christie and Marie Jahoda (eds.), *Studies in the Scope and Method of "The Authoritarian Personality"* (Glencoe, Ill.: Free Press, 1954), hereafter cited as *SSMAP*. Subsequent investigators may have been discouraged from attending to certain of the original insights because especially severe methodological structures were raised in connection with the sections of the book based on quasi-clinical psychological techniques, precisely the sections which are richest in hypotheses. A vigorous essay by Edward A. Shils in *SSMAP* arguing that the authors had erroneously equated authoritarianism with "right-wing authoritarianism" and that they had fallen victim to naïve sociological assumptions may also have discouraged attention to certain of the broader themes raised by the volume. Somewhat after the publication of *SSMAP*, an extensive series of papers on "response set" in authoritarian research were published, adding further to the methodologically gnarled quality of the literature. Some of these papers were devoted to showing that, at least in part, many of the findings in the authoritarian literature were attributable to a mechanical shortcoming of the psychological test typically used to measure authoritarianism (the F-scale). The test was worded so that a positive response was scored as "authoritarian," but some subjects (especially people of low education) tended to respond "yes" to *any* question, independent of their authoritarian tendencies. Other of the papers were devoted to developing new, "response-set-free" measures. Some of the more interesting of these papers are conveniently reprinted in chapter six of Martha T. Mednick and Sarnoff A. Mednick, *Research in Personality* (New York: Holt, Rinehart & Winston, 1963).

14. Harold D. Lasswell, "Democratic Character," in *The Political Writings of Harold D. Lasswell* (Glencoe, Ill.: Free Press, 1951), pp. 465–525, hereafter cited as *DC*. Also see Karl Mannheim, *Freedom, Power and Democratic Planning* (London: Oxford University Press, 1950), pp. 228–245; Christian Bay, *The Structure of Freedom* (Stanford, Calif.: Stanford University Press, 1958), pp. 155–239; Alex Inkeles, "National Character and Modern Political Systems," *Psychological Anthropology*, ed. Francis Hsu (Homewood, Ill.: Dorsey Press, 1961), pp. 172–209; Robert E. Lane, *Political Ideology* (New York: Free Press of Glencoe, 1962), pp. 400–412.

15. *AP*, p. 1, but see pp. 781–783 for the authors' subtype "the genuine liberal." For a criticism of both the democratic and the authoritarian character typologies in the context of what I take to be the argument that typologies are useless since no individual ever is a pure instance of a type, see David Spitz, "Power and Personality: The Appeal to the 'Right Man' in Democratic States," *American Political Science Review*, Vol. 52 (March 1958), pp. 88–89.

16. T. W. Adorno, "Freudian Theory and the Pattern of Fascist Propaganda," *Psychoanalysis and the Social Sciences*, ed. Géza Róheim, Vol. VII (New York, 1951), p. 291n. My discussion of authoritarian traits is based on *AP*, chap. 7 and *passim* and the Sanford discussion referred to in note 4. The latter is perhaps the single most concise and comprehensive exposition by an *AP* contributor.

17. Else Frenkel-Brunswik, "Intolerance of Ambiguity as an Emotional and Perceptual Personality Variable," *Journal of Personality*, Vol. 18 (September 1949), pp. 108–143.

18. David Riesman, with Nathan Glazer and Reuel Denney, *The Lonely Crowd* (New Haven: Yale University Press, 1950).

19. Christie makes the following statement at the conclusion of an extensive, rigorous review of authoritarianism research. "Both the strength and weakness of *The Authoritarian Personality* lie in its basic assumptions which are rooted in psychoanalytic theory. Such an orientation has led to the uncovering of a host of data which in all likelihood would not have been discovered by investigators with differing theoretical viewpoints. Despite some methodological weaknesses in the original research, subsequent findings have been predominantly confirmatory," *SSMAP*, pp. 195–196.

20. The authoritarian type is described as having repressed sexual as well as hostile impulses, but the significance of repressed sexuality in authoritarianism does not seem to have been fully explicated. At points in the *AP*, the implication seems to be simply that the authoritarian has acceded to parental taboos concerning sexuality. At other points (for example, p. 798), the implication is that the repressed sexual impulses are toward the parents and particularly the father. The latter, more classically psychoanalytic construction, is developed in some detail by Fromm in the work cited in note 9 (pp. 77–135, English abstract, pp. 908–911). See especially his discussion of sado-masochism.

21. Dependence upon external guidance provides the common element in several of the surface manifestations of authoritarianism, which at first glance seem not to be related to each other: conventionality (accepting the prevailing values in one's environment); stereotypy (accepting the prevailing descriptive categories); superstition (belief that we are controlled from without by mysterious agencies); intolerance of ambiguity and use of rigid categories (discomfort when the environment provides few guideposts for thought and action).

22. For two recent discussions designed to reduce polemic and seek empirical clarification of the issues underlying the controversial status of psychoanalysis, see B. A. Farrell, "The Status of Psychoanalytic Theory," *Inquiry*, Vol. 7 (Spring 1964), pp. 104–123; Peter Madison, *Freud's Concept of Repression and Defense: Its Theoretical and Observational Language* (Minneapolis: University of Minnesota Press, 1961). A number of interesting investigations based on the ego-defensive theory of authoritarian dynamics have been reported. For example, Herbert C. Schulberg, "Insight, Authoritarianism and Tendency to Agree," *Journal of Nervous and Mental Disease*, Vol. 135 (December 1962), pp. 481–488.

23. See the essay by Hyman and Sheatsley in *SSMAP* (esp., p. 91 f.); Herbert H. Hyman, *Political Socialization* (Glencoe, Ill.: Free Press, 1959), p. 47; S. M. Miller and Frank Riessmann, "'Working-Class Authoritarianism:' A Critique of Lipset," *British Journal of Sociology*, Vol. 12 (September 1961), pp. 263–276.

I take the ego-defensive versus cognitive distinction from the recent literature on the functions served by opinions for the personality: M. Brewster Smith *et al.*, *Opinions and Personality* (New York: John Wiley & Sons, 1956), chap. 3; Daniel Katz, "The Functional Approach to the Study of Attitudes," *Public Opinion Quarterly*, Vol. 24 (Summer 1960), pp. 163–204.

24. See, for example, Angus Campbell *et al., The American Voter* (New York: John Wiley & Sons, 1960), pp. 512–515. Also the very interesting attempt by Thomas F. Pettigrew to demonstrate that the amount of personality-based (that is, ego-defensive) prejudice toward Negroes is the same in the American North, the American South, and in South Africa, and that the higher level of anti-Negro sentiment in the latter two areas is due to the cognitive learning which occurs in cultures where race prejudice is prevalent. "Personality and Sociocultural Factors in Intergroup Attitudes: A Cross-National Comparison," *Journal of Conflict Resolution*, Vol. 2 (March 1958), pp. 29–42. The question of cognitive versus ego-defensive authoritarianism is complex, however, and a fuller discussion would engage us in technical matters connected with the instruments used to measure authoritarianism (see note 13).

25. *AP*, pp. 753–756.

26. *Ibid.*, pp. 482–483.

27. Else Frenkel-Brunswik, "Further Explorations by a Contributor to 'The Authoritarian Personality,'" in *SSMAP*, pp. 236–237.

28. *AP*, p. 976.

29. See especially the appendix to *Escape from Freedom* on "Character and the Social Process," pp. 277–299.

30. There is, of course, nothing incompatible between explanations of authoritarianism in terms of family socialization and explanations in terms of social structure. Nor need the latter be exclusively in economic terms. Evidence of the effects of the socioeconomic organization of a society on its members' personality characteristics is now becoming available from a study of personality differences between farmers and herders in four East African tribes. Two preliminary reports are Walter Goldschmidt, "Theory and Strategy in the Study of Cultural Adaptability," *American Anthropologist*, Vol. 67 (April 1965), pp. 402–408 and Robert B. Edgerton, "'Cultural' vs. 'Ecological' Factors in the Expression of Values, Attitudes, and Personality Characteristics," *Ibid.*, pp. 442–447.

31. Robert Waelder, *Basic Theory of Psychoanalysis* (New York: International Universities Press, 1960), pp. 53–54.

32. Frenkel-Brunswik, in *SSMAP*, p. 228.

33. *AP*, p. 974.

34. See Shils' discussion of "left authoritarianism" in *SSMAP*. Also see the work of Rokeach, who has attempted to develop a "content-free" alternative to the various approaches to the question of authoritarianism, by stressing the "structure" of people's beliefs. Milton Rokeach, "Political and Religious Dogmatism: An Alternative to the Authoritarian Personality," *Psychological Monographs*, No. 425 (1956) and *The Open and Closed Mind* (New York: Basic Books, 1960). One might say that the Marxian heritage of the original authoritarian research

(by discouraging attention to authoritarianism on the left) hinders awareness of the diversity of belief consistent with common psychological characteristics, whereas the Freudian heritage (by pointing to ego-defensive rather than cognitive explanations) hinders awareness of the diversity of psychological characteristics consistent with common beliefs. For a discussion in *The Authoritarian Personality* of a personality subtype quite like Shils' notion of left-wing authoritarianism, see the treatment of the "rigid low scorer" on pp. 771–773.

35. Smith *et al.*, *Opinions and Personality*, p. 1.

36. Irwin Katz and Lawrence Benjamin, "Effects of White Authoritarianism in Biracial Work Groups," *Journal of Abnormal and Social Psychology*, Vol. 61 (November 1960), pp. 448–456.

37. See the remarks of Riesman and Glazer, in response to criticisms of their psychological explanations of social phenomena in *The Lonely Crowd*. "Although we said in *The Lonely Crowd* that different kinds of character could be used for the same kinds of work within an institution, we emphasized the price paid by the character types that fitted badly, as against the release of energy provided by congruence of character and task." David Riesman and Nathan Glazer, " *The Lonely Crowd*: A Reconsideration in 1960," *Culture and Social Character: The Work of David Riesman Reviewed*, ed. Seymour M. Lipset and Leo Lowenthal (New York: Free Press of Glencoe, 1961), p. 438. The same point (that behavior may be inconsistent with personality, but that some people may nevertheless undergo "distinctive burdens" in conforming to role requirements) is made by Reinhard Bendix in a widely quoted essay criticizing the various "psychiatric" explanations of social institutions. "Compliant Behavior and Individual Personality," *American Journal of Sociology*, Vol. 58 (November 1952), p. 297 and p. 300.

38. A point made by Herbert Hyman in Bjorn Christiansen *et al.* (eds.), *Cross-National Social Research* (Oslo: Institute for Social Research; Mimeographed, 1951), p. 31. On the problem of aggregate effects also see Harry Eckstein, *A Theory of Stable Democracy*, Princeton University Center of International Studies, Research Monograph, No. 10 (April 1961).

39. Shils, in *SSMAP*, p. 45 and p. 48.

40. *DC*, p. 428.

41. *Ibid.*, pp. 506–507. On the rigid low scorer, see note 33.

42. *Ibid.*, p. 497.

43. Anthony F. C. Wallace, "The New Culture-and-Personality," *Anthropology and Human Behavior* (Washington, D.C.: The Anthropological Society of Washington, 1962), pp. 1–12.

PERSONALITY AND POLITICAL PARTICIPATION[1]

• Paul H. Mussen and Anne B. Warren

Democratically oriented social scientists and laymen, realizing that success of a democratic form of government depends upon an actively participating citizenry, have been alarmed by the political lethargy or apathy which seems to characterize the majority of Americans. Barber (2) has examined specific aspects of the social structure which are related to "mass apathy," while Lasswell (3; 4) has suggested that emotional factors may determine the nature of an individual's political activity.

In their excellent analysis of political apathy, Riesman and Glazer (6) discuss many historical, socio-economic, class, and regional factors which are related to political interest or apathy. They also recognize that personality (or character) structure plays an important role in determining whether an individual will be politically interested or apathetic.

According to these authors, the complexity and incomprehensibility of twentieth-century political events so obscures the individual's self-interest that "self-interest, in its variety of traditional meanings, will not suffice to justify, from the standpoint of the individual, his concern with politics today" (6; p. 524). For this reason, active participation in politics requires "energy and courage," as well as "self awareness" and "reflecting on what we are up to." People who feel impotent, dependent,

Above selection reprinted from: *Human Relations*, V (February 1952), 65–82.

or completely occupied with personal problems will not have the "energy and courage" necessary for political activity and, consequently, will be politically apathetic.

Riesman and Glazer also state that activity is related to differences in temperament, by which they mean "such things as native energy level, sanguinity, gregariousness." They describe four types of political involvement or apathy which, they suspect, are "related both to class position and to character structure" (6; p. 537).[2] One of their criteria of apathy or involvement is "criticalness of authority vs. submissiveness." "Of all our criteria, this one is probably most palpably linked to character structure; though conceivably submissiveness toward authorities of state, school, or religion may be the outcome of a rational, though mistaken judgment, we usually expect to trace a basis in personality for the attitude" (6; p. 554).

The works of Lassman and of Riesman and Glazer make it clear that a complete understanding of political involvement can be achieved only if we supplement our knowledge of the social, cultural, and historical factors involved with an examination of the personality characteristics of politically apathetic and active individuals. Although there have been studies of the relationships between political attitudes or opinions and personality structure (8; 9), no systematic studies of the psychological factors

277

involved in political participation have been reported.

The present paper deals with a preliminary study which was designed to determine some of the psychological correlates of political interest (or participation) and disinterest (or apathy). Specifically, we were concerned with investigating the personality differences between politically active and apathetic individuals. We were incidentally interested in checking some of Riesman and Glazer's suggestions about the personalities of these people; that is, with determining whether politically interested and active individuals are as these authors suggest, more self-aware, gregarious, energetic and courageous and more able to criticize authority than politically apathetic individuals who feel impotent, dependent and submissive.

Subjects and Procedure

The subjects of this study were 156 University of Wisconsin undergraduates between the ages of 17 and 27. One hundred and forty-eight of them were volunteers from an introductory psychology course and eight were leaders in campus political organizations such as Young Republicans, Young Democrats or Young Progressives. Although our subjects were generally young and did not constitute a representative sample of the voting population, using such a group had at least two advantages for this study. First, almost all of them had middle-class backgrounds and all of them were well educated; hence any differences between active and apathetic individuals cannot be attributed to differences in socio-economic or educational status. Secondly, such a group is

probably representative of the socio-economic and educational group from which a disproportionately large number of our prominent political leaders come.

Each of the subjects anonymously filled out a lengthy questionnaire which was divided into three sections. The first section consisted of a series of questions of personal information such as age, sex, major subject, vocational objective and political affiliation.

The second part of the questionnaire was designed to measure the subject's attitudes with respect to certain important ideological issues such as anti-Semitism, politico-economic conservatism, ethnocentrism and anti-democratic philosophy. It contained a series of statements about these issues and the subject was instructed to express his degree of agreement or disagreement with each statement. The items were taken from four attitude scales developed and used in the California study of *The Authoritarian Personality* (1): four from the AS scale, measuring the individual's "readiness to support or oppose anti-Semitic ideology as a whole;" ten from the E (Ethnocentrism) scale, measuring attitudes toward groups and group relations; 17 from the PEC (Politico-economic conservatism) scale measuring degree of liberalism or conservatism; and 27 from the F (Fascism) scale, measuring "underlying antidemocratic trends in personality" or "potential for fascism."

The third section of the questionnaire consisted of ten Projective Questions which will be described below.

The classification of the subjects with respect to political interest or apathy was made on the basis of responses to two questions in the personal information section of the questionnaire. These questions were:

To what extent are you now interested in national and local (non-campus) politics (that is, do you vote, belong to political organizations such as Young Democrats, read political news, participate in campaigns, etc.)?

To what extent do you expect to participate in political activities after college (that is, do you expect to join a political party, be active in politics, run for political office, vote, keep up with political news, etc.)?

On the basis of the answers to these two questions, each individual was classified into one of five groups representing different degrees of political interest. The groups, and the criteria for membership in them, are as follows:

Group I. (Active political interest.) Membership in a campus "young" political group, e.g. Young Democrats, or active participation in non-campus, local, state, or national political campaigns.

Group II. (Moderate interest now, more potential interest.) Present interest in political activity includes voting and/or reading about and discussing politics. Expressed desire to participate more actively later: join a party, campaign, and/or run for political office.

Group III. (Moderate interest.) Reading and/or voting, but no expression of interest in more active political participation later. Attitudes toward voting in this group vary from passive acceptance ("the thing to do") to strong feelings that it is everyone's patriotic duty to vote and to attempt to understand politics.

Group IV. (Little interest.) Statement that subject is not now interested in politics, does not read political news and usually does not vote. Expression of a desire to be "more interested" in the future to the extent of reading political news and voting.

Group V. (No interest.) No current interest together with expressed intention to remain uninformed and uninterested. May vote "when necessary." A rather typical response in this group is "I am not at all interested in politics."

The populations of the groups were: Group I, 16 (including the eight officers of campus political organizations); Group II, 29; Group III, 74; Group IV, 29; Group V, 8. It is interesting to note that, although we had no preconceived notions of how many subjects should be classified in each group, about half of the subjects fell into the "moderate interest" group.

For purposes of this study, we considered Group III neutral in political interest. Our attention was focused on the 45 subjects in Groups I and II which we considered the *active* group, and the 37 subjects in Groups IV and V, the *disinterested* or *apathetic* group.

We first compared our active and apathetic groups' attitudes toward the ideological issues mentioned above. *Table 1* presents the means and standard deviations on each of the four attitude-opinion scales used in this study. The two groups did not differ significantly from each other in politico-economic, anti-Semitic, or ethnocentric attitudes, or in "potential for fascism."[3]

These results make it clear that political interest is not directly related to the attitudes measured. Both the active and apathetic groups contain individuals who are politically and economically liberal, middle-of-the-road, and conservative; in each group there are prejudiced and unprejudiced people; subjects who are high and low in "potential for fascism" appear in both groups. In brief, political participation or non-participation seems to be a separate dimension of behavior which is independent of political, economic, or social ideology.

Determining Personality Characteristics

In order to get some understanding of the personality characteristics of our subjects which might be related to membership in the active or apathetic groups, a series of Projective Questions was included in the questionnaire filled out by each of the subjects. According to Levinson, who first used Projective Questions systematically in the California study of *The Authoritarian Personality* (1), "the Projective Question technique is an application of the general principles of projective techniques to the questionnaire method" (5; p. 545). Differences in response to these questions are likely to be due to "personality trends of considerable importance in the individual's psychological functioning" (5; p. 546).

In this study we used ten Projective Questions. The first eight of them were suggested and used by Levinson in the study cited above and the ninth was suggested, but not used, by him. The ten questions were:

1. We all have times when we feel below par. What moods or feelings are the most unpleasant or disturbing to you?
2. We all have impulses and desires which are at times hard to control but which we try to keep in check. What desires do you often have difficulty in controlling?
3. What great people, living or dead, do you admire most?
4. There is hardly a person who hasn't said to himself, "If this keeps up, I'll go nuts!" What might drive a person nuts?
5. What do you consider the worst crimes a person could commit?
6. It seems that no matter how careful we are, we all sometimes have embarrassing moments. What experiences make you feel like sinking through the floor?
7. If you knew you had only six months to live, but could do just as you pleased during that period, how would you spend your time?
8. We get a feeling of awe when something seems to us wonderful, or impressive,

Table 1

Active and Apathetic Groups' Means and Standard Deviations of Scores on Items from Four Attitudes Scales

Scale	No. of Items	Actives Mean	Actives S.D.	Apathetics Mean	Apathetics S.D.
AS (Anti-Semitism)	4	10.78	5.95	11.43	6.84
E (Ethnocentrism)	10	28.42	12.82	31.94	9.74
F (Fascism)	27	80.80	15.85	84.13	13.08
PEC (Politico-economic conservatism)	17	66.84	5.43	66.91	4.99

or really important. What things would give you the greatest feeling of awe?

9. As a parent, what would you try most to instill in your child?

10. If you could change your parents in any way you wanted, what changes would you make in your mother? In your father?

Responses to the Projective Questions were "scored" in a manner similar to that used in the California study (1). The data were thoroughly examined and a set of qualitative categories— many of them adopted, with some modification, from Levinson (5)—was formulated for each Projective Question. These categories were carefully defined and designed to reveal the "primary *psychological content* of the response— what the individual strives for or feels or values or experiences" (5; p. 548). In general, they are interpretive and emphasize the clinical meanings of the responses.

The number of categories in a set varied from four for question 2 to nine for question 10, with a total of 69 for the ten questions. The subject's response to each question was "scored" in terms of presence-absence for each category. A list of categories together with brief descriptions of them is included in *Table 2.*

In order to eliminate any "halo effect" which might carry over from the classification of one response to the classification of another, the responses of all subjects to Question 1 were evaluated and scored before any of the responses to Question 2 were evaluated. It should also be noted that all scorings of responses were made independently of any other data; specifically without knowledge of whether the respondent belonged to the politically active, apathetic or neutral group.

Results and Discussion

The personality characteristics of the politically active and apathetic were then compared by determining which categories of response were characteristic of each group; that is, which categories were chosen with significantly greater frequency by one group than by the other. Since each category was scored only in terms of present-absent, chi-square tests were applied to compare the relative frequencies of occurrence of each category in the two groups. Since the frequencies involved were small, Yates' correction was employed in deriving the chi-square values.

Table 2 presents the 69 categories, the frequencies of occurrence of the response in the two groups, and the chi-square values derived. As this table shows, of the 69 chi-square tests made, 10 were significant at the five per cent level or better. In addition to these 10, 7 chi-square values were significant at between the five and ten per cent levels, and hence may be said to indicate trends in the data.

Analysis of the 17 significant or near-significant chi-square tests reveals the following differences between the groups:

1. In response to Question 1, "What moods or feelings are the most unpleasant or disturbing to you?," the politically active tend to give more responses ($P = .05–.10$) in the category *disappointment in self*, which includes expressed feelings of failure to exercise capabilities and feelings of intellectual inferiority. Examples of responses in

Table 2

Comparison of Active and Apathetic Groups on Frequency of Occurrence of Categories of Response

Definition of Category	Number in Category Actives $N = 45$	Apathetics $N = 37$	X^2 Value	P
1. *What moods or feelings are most unpleasant to you?*				
General self-blame and reproach	12	6	.756	.30–.50
*Disappointment in self due to failure to exercise capabilities	11	3	2.760	.05–.10
Sense of futility, pessimism	4	2	.031	.80–.90
Feelings of rejection	8	2	1.862	.10–.20
Exploitation of, discrimination against, others	6	1	1.735	.10–.20
Lack of support from environment	3	4	.074	.70–.80
Loneliness; fear of being alone	2	5	1.135	.20–.30
Feelings of being victimized	3	5	.443	.50–.70
2. *What desires do you have difficulty in controlling?*				
Expressing dangerous opinions	3	3	.031	.80–.90
Expressing aggression against intolerance	5	2	.274	.50–.70
**Escape studies; quit school	3	10	4.875	.02–.05
Temper outbursts	8	5	.049	.80–.90
3. *What great people do you admire most?*				
Artists and philosophers	21	16	.008	>.90
Physicists and biological scientists	5	5	.000	>.95
**Social scientists and liberal figures	15	4	4.590	.02–.05
Industrial leaders	5	1	1.058	.30–.40
Conservative Americans	5	2	.274	.50–.70
Parents and relatives	7	3	.471	.40–.50
Denial of admiration	4	2	.031	.80–.90
Neutral figures	32	25	.011	>.90
4. *What could drive a person nuts?*				
Frustration, failure, insecurity	17	12	.074	.70–.80
Specific worries; family problems	6	6	.003	>.95
**Inability to adjust to situations; face reality	8	0	5.413	.01–.02
Overwork; study under pressure	8	5	.049	>.95
*Generalized worry; indecision	1	6	3.46	.05–.10
Irritating events	12	9	.000	>.95
Obsessions	5	4	.097	.70–.80
5. *Worst crimes a person could commit?*				
Crimes against society; discrimination, exploitation	5	1	1.058	.30–.40
Crimes against individuals for personal gain	7	4	.091	.70–.80
Aggressive, physical attack	3	7	1.820	.10–.20
Suicide	4	3	.073	.70–.80
Rape	20	20	.415	.50–.70
Stealing	7	5	.003	>.95
6. *Most embarrassing moments?*				
Hurting someone's feelings	7	4	.091	.70–.80
Being ridiculed	12	12	.107	.70–.80
Being personally responsible for mistakes	9	3	1.445	.20–.30
**Social slips; violations of rules of etiquette	4	11	4.59	.02–.05
Having social faults exposed	11	12	.307	.50–.70

Table 2—continued:

Definition of Category	Number in Category		X^2 Value	P
	Actives $N = 45$	Apathetics $N = 37$		
7. *How would you spend your last six months?*				
**Social contribution	12	2	5.07	.02–.05
Being with loved ones	12	12	.107	.70–.80
Sex and sensual pleasures	6	6	.003	>.95
Specific travel plans	11	15	1.743	.10–.20
Keeping busy; accomplishing personal goals	16	11	.104	.70–.80
Straightening out affairs	5	3	.007	>.95
*Social events, good time	3	8	2.73	.05–.10
8. *Most awe inspiring experiences?*				
*Intellectual, aestetic, scientific achievements	17	6	3.665	.05–.10
Mass Emotion; people unified	8	2	1.862	.10–.20
Being recognized and loved	6	2	.689	.40–.50
Power conceived in socially useful terms	9	6	.024	.80–.90
Nature experiences	17	20	1.565	.20–.30
Achievement of conventional goals, e.g. graduation	6	2	.689	.40–.50
Meeting a famous person	4	3	.074	.70–.80
Seeing power	11	9	.060	.80–.90
9. *Instill in children?*				
*Intellectual, aesthetic, and social values	17	6	3.665	.05–.10
**Social consciousness	15	3	6.140	.01–.02
**Striving for maturity and independence	9	1	4.173	.02–.05
Ability to love and be loved	4	9	2.56	.10–.20
**Good manners and obedience	6	16	7.79	>.01
*Good morals	13	19	3.41	.05–.10
**"Successful" interpersonal relations	0	8	8.463	>.01
10. *Changes in parents?*				
*Greater happiness	17	7	2.844	.05–.10
More social consciousness and tolerance	7	2	1.228	.20–.30
More warmth, friendliness	11	13	.664	.40–.50
Less aggressiveness, ambition, domination	4	3	.073	.70–.80
Greater conformity to conventional standards	7	3	.471	.40–.50
Improved physical status	9	5	.232	.50–.70
More independent	9	4	.689	.40–.50
Improved personality, e.g. calmer	10	12	.621	.40–.50
**Denial of need to change; parents perfect	3	12	7.381	>.01

* Significant at between 5 and 10 per cent level.
** Significant beyond 5 per cent level.

this category, taken from records of politically active individuals, are:

feelings of inadequacy to solve certain problems, e.g. write a good book review
being frustrated by lack of training in art and not accomplishing what I want

Levinson classified responses of this sort with those revealing "conscious conflict and guilt," and, according to him, they indicate a "well internalized set of ethical standards" and "a concern with self-understanding and an acceptance of personal moral responsibility for one's actions" (5; p. 550). These traits, then, appear to be more characteristic of politically active than politically apathetic people. This finding tends to support Riesman and Glazer's suggestion that participants in political activity are more "self-aware."

2. In response to Question 2, "What desires do you often have difficulty in controlling?," responses in the category *escape studies, quit school* are more characteristic of the politically apathetic than of the politically active. Typical responses are:

Skipping classes
Desire to quit school. Desire not to study

Although these responses also indicate disappointment, there is a distinct and psychologically important difference between responses of this sort and those indicating disappointment in self which we find more frequently among the actives. In the latter, self-understanding and examination of felt insecurities, as well as the recognition of personal responsibility are involved. In the former, however, there is no recognition of personal responsibility and no examination of feelings and emotions. With the politically apathetic, there is a generally external orientation. The situation is considered intolerable, but they are apparently afraid to acknowledge—or even examine—the possibility that their own inadequacies may be contributing factors. People who give this kind of response give no evidence of having attempted to analyze the factors underlying their dissatisfactions. They are aware only of their strong desire to escape from what is probably their most important current responsibility.

Their unhappiness with their present occupation and status may also indicate a low frustration tolerance and an inability to evaluate their present work in terms of its broader, long-time implications. Moreover, it seems quite likely that dissatisfaction in an area as important as work adjustment—especially when it is not fully understood and cannot be adequately handled—may become a preoccupying problem. In this sense, the finding that such dissatisfaction is more frequent among the inactives supports the suggestion that political apathy may be related to preoccupation with one's own problems.

3. *Social scientists and liberal political figures* (Brandeis, Veblen, Bunche, Paine, Nehru) are named more frequently by the active group as the great people they admire (Question 3.) Apparently the active group has a great admiration for those who have made social contributions and have advocated democratic social change. Their general orientation is social and they identify with great people who have been socially, rather than power or personal-success, oriented. This finding is particularly interesting, since, as we noted earlier, our active and apathetic groups do not differ significantly in politico-economic attitudes.

4. The active group's concern with inner psychological states and their awareness of the importance of conflict and personal frustration is again revealed in the responses to Question 4 (What might drive a person nuts?). Compared with the apathetic group, the active group gives a significantly greater number of answers in *the inability to adjust to situations and/or face reality* category. Typical of responses to this question is this one from a politically active student:

a conflict situation arises in which you find
it difficult to cope with a problem

Statements of this sort give further evidence of the active group's tendency to examine and face their deeper feelings.

In this group, more than in the apathetic, keen awareness of personal problems is accompanied by an attempt to understand the factors involved in them and a realization that they have some inadequacies in handling these problems.

5. The inactive group, on the other hand, tends to be more concerned with diffuse worry, without elaborating this worry or thinking of it in terms of inner insecurities or feelings. Many responses (P = .05–.10) of this group to Question 4 fall into the category *worry, indecision,* exemplified by these responses:

a constant worry
when everything goes wrong

As the last example illustrates, many of the statements indicated an external orientation and a lack of analysis of the emotional factors involved, i.e. an absence of self-awareness. None of the responses in this category referred to affective states or conflicts.

Moreover, undifferentiated worry and indecision, without any understanding of their source or meaning, may have their roots in vague, but deep, feelings of insecurity in the face of what appears to be a generally threatening environment.

6. The apathetic group's concern with conventional ways of behaving is made clear by their responses to Question 6 (most embarrassing moments). More frequently than the active group, the apathetic group answers in terms of *making social slips*. Examples are:

social blunder—making a wrong remark at a wrong time
spill gravy at an important dinner

This concern with "social blunders" reveals a highly rigid, formalized approach to the world. Sensitivity to one's own or another's feelings does not seem to concern the apathetic group. Instead, they seem entirely accepting of, and submissive to, authority and its code, as this is reflected in rules of etiquette. There is, then, in the apathetic group a dependence on prescribed standards. This attitude may again reflect basic feelings of insecurity which may be somewhat overcome by the individual's having a rigid set of conventions to follow. The insecure, dependent individual needs sets of rules to help him cope with the environment which seems generally threatening. Because he does not accept his real feelings, he lacks spontaneity in social situations, and established rules provide the major basis for maintaining interpersonal relationships; hence he is distressed (embarrassed) when he violates these rules.

7. The social and personal orientation of the active group is again aparent in the responses to Question 7 (How would you spend your last six months?) *Social contribution* responses occur more frequently in the records of this group than in those of the apathetic group. Examples, taken from the records of politically active individuals, are:

do as much as I could for the betterment of humanity
work for some important cause—world peace or race relations if I felt I could accomplish something

A concern for the welfare of others, as well as with oneself, seems to be characteristic of the politically active. This is entirely consistent with Riesman and Glazer's criterion of "concern with self and others" (6; p. 551). The emphasis on "doing things for humanity" may also be evidence of the "energy and courage" which those writers say characterize the politically active individual.

8. The political apathetic's "conventionalized, emotionally shallow" thinking is revealed in this group's answers to Question 7. More frequently than the active group (P = .05–.10) this group responds with *travel, social events, good times.* Examples include:

go to various parties, social events
read plays and novels, travel

The complete absence of deep feeling which is obvious in these responses is entirely consistent with the lack of self-awareness and examination of emotions noted in the apathetic group's answers to the questions discussed earlier.

Speaking of responses such as these, which he calls "dilute pleasures," Levinson says, "Interpretively, the individual is seeking satisfaction but his moral facade prevents the free, intense, ego-accepted expression of underlying impulses" (5; p. 574). In this sense, inability to accept his own impulses and emotions is characteristic of the politically apathetic individual, and may underlie the "feelings of impotence" which Riesman and Glazer suggest are characteristic of this group.

9. Responses to Question 8 (What experiences would be most awe-inspiring?) again demonstrate the sensitivity of the actives and their concern with self-expression and feelings. More frequently than the apathetics (P = .05–.10), they give answers in the *intellectual, aesthetic and scientific achievement* category, such as:

Beethoven's Ninth Symphony
seeing birth

Responses like these are evidence of the active individual's ability to accept and enjoy intense emotional experiences. This is in contrast to the apathetics' emotional shallowness revealed in their answers to Question 7 discussed above.

The next differences between the groups involve their responses to Question 9 (What would you try to instill in your child?). The active group, significantly more frequently than the apathetic, emphasizes human, ego-satisfying, and pleasure-giving values. The following categories of response are characteristic of the actives:

10. *Productive living* (P = .05–.10). Responses in this category include an enriched life, achieving happiness, intellectual curiosity and aesthetic sensitivity. Examples are:

enrichment of life by enlargement of aesthetic capacities
artistic and music appreciation, a sense of humor

11. *Social consciousness.* This category is concerned with love and respect for humanity generally and regard for others' feelings and rights. For example:

I would like to teach my child to respect individuals as individuals and not as sterotyped members of groups.

12. *Striving for maturity and independence.* In making these responses, respondents sometimes acknowledge that conscious conflict and rebellion against group standards—and, consequently, personal suffering—may be involved. Despite this, these traits are valued so highly that the group feels they wish their children to have these traits. Examples:

humility but self-confidence
a willingness to think for himself and to be different from his associates if necessary

In brief, the traits which the politically active individual would instill in his child are reflections of his own personality structure as revealed in his responses to the other Projective Questions—his fundamentally social orientation and social consciousness, his awareness of the importance of his own and others' emotions, and his relative freedom from conventional thinking. The kinds of traits and characteristics the apathetic group more frequently chooses to instill in their children contrast sharply with these:

13. *Obedience and good manners.* These responses show the group's concern with conventional values such as:

respect for other people
obedience and discipline

The strong emphasis on these values gives further evidence of the politically apathetic individual's defense mechanisms: by complying with group standards and being submissive to authority he attempts to deny his feelings of insecurity and hostility. Worry, anxiety, and indecision, which are extremely intolerable to the apathetic individual, can be reduced by obeying authority and following prescribed rules.

14. *Good morals and religious training* (P = .05–.10). Conventional values, conformity, fear of challenging constituted authority and submissive attitudes toward power—in this case, of a religious nature—are again stressed as they have been in other responses given by this group. Examples:

right and wrong, honesty, courtesy
existence of God

15. *"Successful" relations with other people.* The responses in this category are concerned with social contacts, but they stress the superficial, rather than the emotional, aspects of these relationships. No social consciousness or genuine social orientation is involved; on the contrary, motivation toward personal success and accomplishment is emphasized. Many of the responses reveal a basically hostile attitude toward people, interpersonal relationships being evaluated in terms of getting along with others because one has to. Examples:

how to get along with others
learn to be careful who you trust

The traits which the politically apathetic groups would instill in their children give further evidence of their own characteristics, values, and orientations—conventionality, submission to authority, vague sense of threat, lack of emotional awareness or involvement, and success orientation.

16. The sensitivity of the politically active group to the feelings, emotions, conflicts, and anxieties of others, is re-emphasized in their responses to Question 10 (What changes would you make in your parents?). More frequently than the apathetic group (P = .05–.10), this group gives responses in the category of *greater personal happiness.* Included in this are responses showing concern with enjoyment of life and rich emotional and intellectual expression. Examples:

the ability to take life more lightly
make my mother happier and less lonesome

The active individual's awareness of the importance of emotions and ego-satisfactions (rather than conventional values) which is evident in these responses may be another reflection of his self-awareness. In any case, these responses again demonstrate the social orientation of the active group, and seem to indicate a warm and understanding attitude toward their parents.

17. Submission to authority and inability to challenge this authority are revealed again in the responses of the apathetic group to Question 10. Many of this group give answers which we categorized *glorification of parents*, or denial of need for change. Examples:

my parents are as wonderful as they could possibly be

no sense in changing anything that has been perfect right along

This lack of awareness of any deficiencies is probably indicative of the respondent's fears of facing shortcomings in the parents. He is so completely submissive to parental authority that he cannot challenge his parents in any way or admit they are not perfect. Such complete submissiveness very likely results from the parents' overly rigid and punitive treatment of the child, which prevents any expression of agression or independence of thought or action. Interpretively, such adulation of the parents may be regarded as an overcompensation for deep-lying hostile attitudes toward them.

When the eight categories of response given more frequently by the apathetics and the nine categories given more frequently by the actives are viewed together, two characteristic, but contrasting, patterns seem to emerge.

The apathetic's characteristics—inability to recognize personal responsibility or to examine—or even accept—his own emotions and feelings; vague, incomprehensible feelings of worry, insecurity, and threat; complete, unchallenging acceptance of constituted authority (social codes, parents, religion) and conventional values—form a self-consistent pattern which, in a clinical situation, would be labelled *passivity*. The deep and persive nature of this passivity is demonstrated further by the relative absence of responses emphasizing self-expression, ego-strivings and satisfactions or warm interpersonal relationships.

From this point of view, political apathy itself may be regarded as one aspect of the individual's fundamentally passive orientation. Political events may be evaluated in the same way as authority and conventional standards are; that is, they must be accepted and cannot be challenged. Expression of political opinions, like any other kind of self-expression, is not part of the passive pattern.

Although the genesis of this passive orientation is not clear, it may be assumed that, since it is a basic aspect of the individual's personality, it has its roots in early familial relationships. The apathetic's glorification of his parents, together with his basic hostility toward people and his view of the world as hostile and threatening, suggests that the parents may have been rigid and severely punitive, discouraging independence of thought or action and encouraging passive acceptance of authority from early childhood.

An over-view of the response categories used frequently by the politically active group demonstrates that its orientation—in sharp contrast to the orientation of the politically inactive— is *active* with respect to both self and others. We find no evidence of passive acceptance of authority and conventional values in this group. On the contrary, there is an emphasis on strivings for ego-satisfactions, independence, maturity, and personal happiness. Instead of vague, unmanageable feelings of threat which form part of the passive pattern, active attempts to achieve self-understanding (many responses in categories pertaining to self-examination, self-awareness, and consciousness of shortcomings) are characteristic of the politically interested group.

The sensitivity to others' feelings, emotions, and conflicts which is revealed by the politically active may also be interpreted as part of a generally active orientation, since it may represent an outgoing response: an attempt to understand, and emphasize with, others. The final aspect of this coherent pattern, the active group's great social consciousness and emphasis on social contribution and love-giving, involves a positive, active relationship with society generally.

Political activity may be regarded as one aspect of the politically interested subject's outgoing social responses and social consciousness. Political participation may be seen as a means of acting constructively in promoting the general welfare and thus, indirectly, making a social contribution.

It is important to note, however, that the desire to make social contributions is not in itself sufficient to stimulate political activity. The basically insecure, threatened individual cannot act in accordance with his desires. Social consciousness must be accompanied by a relative freedom from these feelings if the individual is to be politically active. The relative absence of feelings of threat and insecurity, together with the emphasis on self-expression, independence, and personal responsibility, in the records of the politically active provide evidence that the active group has the freedom (Riesman and Glazer's "courage and energy") necessary for political participation.

One other aspect of our findings merits further discussion. It will be noted that there are some striking resemblances between the personality of the politically apathetic individual and the authoritarian personality described by the California researchers (1); and between the personalities of our politically active group and the non-prejudiced group of the California study. Yet, as we saw earlier, our politically interested and politically apathetic groups did not differ significantly in ethnocentrism, anti-Semitism, or "potential for fascism" as measured by the California scales.

There are several possible explanations of the differences between our findings and those of the California study. First, all our subjects were well-educated and were living in a cultural milieu in which ethnic prejudice is generally discouraged and liberal thinking about social problems is encouraged. Hence, ethnic prejudice and generally intolerant attitudes are intellectually unacceptable to these subjects. The AS, E, and F scales—or at least, the items we used—may not be sufficiently sensitive to discriminate between "highs" and "lows" in prejudice and "potential for fascism" in such a group.

Secondly, we were measuring political

behavior, whereas the California scales measure "dynamic potential." An investigation of the differences between those who actually behave in a prejudiced or fascist way and those who merely hold prejudiced or fascist attitudes might reveal significant personality differences between these two groups.

Finally, there is the possibility that there are two different, though not mutually exclusive, defense mechanisms which threatened, insecure, hostile people may employ. One is to project their own hostilities and inadequacies on to others and thus become ethnically prejudiced and intolerant of others. The other defense mechanism may be to withdraw generally and thus not to participate in activities such as politics which affect the society as a whole. Among the well-educated, the latter type of defense may be more widely prevalent because the former, being generally discredited in their social milieu, has become intellectually unacceptable.

Summary and Conclusions

Our analysis of the responses to the ten Projective Questions demonstrates that there are many meaningful and consistent differences between the politically interested and disinterested groups. We find constellations or patterns of traits and attitudes which enable us to formulate brief composite pictures—"ideal types"—of politically active and politically apathetic individuals.

Stated very generally, our findings lead us to conclude that political apathy and activity are specific manifestations of more deep-lying, and pervasive passive and active orientations. Thus, one of the outstanding characteristics of the politically active individual is his attempt to understand himself, i.e. his awareness, examination, and acceptance of his own emotions, conflicts, and feelings, including feelings of inadequacy and inferiority. He is concerned with ego-satisfying personal experiences and emotional and intellectual expression rather than with conventional values and general social standards. His social consciousness and orientation are apparent in his emphasis on love-giving and social contribution, his respect for the rights and feelings of others, and his admiration for social scientists and liberal political leaders.

The politically apathetic individual, on the other hand, seems to be generally passive, dissatisfied and generally threatened. Although he gives evidence that he is fundamentally hostile, he cannot accept his hostile impulses. Instead he appears to be completely submissive and unchallenging to authority, rigid, and incapable of enjoying deep emotional experiences. He emphasizes conventional values such as obedience, good manners, and social etiquette. Conformity with social conventions, refusal to become aware of deep feelings, and submissiveness may all be devices which aid the apathetic individual to cope with basic insecurities in what he sees as a threatening environment.

It is as though the active individual who can accept himself and his conflicts has a positive approach to people and "free energy" which he can expend in concern with humanity generally, and, as part of this, concern with political events which affect the general welfare. The dissatisfied and hostile apathetic individual, however, must devote his energies to repressing his hostile feelings and conforming to conventional standards; hence he cannot become genuinely concerned with others or with the general welfare.

This does not mean that the active individual is necessarily a better adjusted individual than the politically apathetic one. His self-awareness, consciousness of conflict, and feelings of inferiority must cause him much tenseness and unhappiness. Apparently they do not lead to bitterness toward society or dissatisfaction with his work or status, however, perhaps because his generally active orientation leads to many emotionally gratifying experiences. The rigidity and conventionality of the apathetic individual, together with his repression of feelings of hostility may keep him from experiencing a great deal of conscious conflict and make him appear well-adjusted. Despite such superficial appearances, the apathetic

individual often harbors deep-lying feelings of aggression and dissatisfaction which he does not understand and which probably makes him a basically unhappy person.

In conclusion, we wish to state explicitly that we are not assuming any direct cause-effect relationship between personality structure and political apathy and activity. It would be meaningless, for example, to maintain that the politically active individual's social consciousness *causes* his political interest, since this interest may be regarded as one aspect of his social consciousness. Nevertheless, our findings make it clear that the individual's interest and participation in politics are not independent of basic aspects of personality. Political activity or apathy are not functions *only* of the general social structure and current historical events. The personality of the individual operating within the social-historical context must also be considered.

NOTES

1. This study was supported by grants from the Social Science Research Council and the Research Committee of the Graduate School of the University of Wisconsin.

2. This typology and the relationship between character structure, its determinants, and political apathy, have been elaborated further in Riesman's *The Lonely Crowd* (7) which appeared after the present study had been completed.

3. Comparison of our subjects' mean/person/item scores on each scale with those (based on the same items) of the total population used in the study of *The Authoritarian Personality* (1) show that the two subject populations are very similar with respect to politico-economic attitudes, but that the subjects of the present study show less "potential for fascism" (lower F scores), less anti-Semitism (lower AS scores), and less ethnocentrism (lower E scores) than the subjects in the California study. Our group differs in several important respects from the groups used in the study cited, however.

REFERENCES

1. Adorno, T. W., Frenkel-Brunswik, E., Levinson, D. J., and Sanford, R. D. *The Authoritarian Personality*. New York: Harper, 1950.

2. Barber, Bernard. "Participation and Mass Apathy in Associations" in Gouldner, A. W. (ed.) *Studies in Leadership*. New York: Harper, 1950.

3. Lasswell, H. D. *Psychopathology and Politics*. Chicago: University of Chicago Press, 1930.

4. Lasswell, H. D. *Power and Personality*. New York: Norton and Co., 1948.

5. Levinson, D. J. "Projective Questions in The Study of Personality and Ideology" in Adorno, T. W., Frenkel-Brunswik, E., Levinson, D. J., and Sanford, R. D., *The Authoritarian Personality*. New York: Harper, 1950.

6. Riesman, D., and Glazer, N. "Criteria for Political Apathy" in Gouldner, A. W. (ed.), *Studies in Leadership*. New York: Harper, 1950.

7. Riesman, D. *The Lonely Crowd*. New Haven: Yale University Press, 1950.

8. Stagner, R. "Fascist Attitudes: An Exploratory Study." *J. Soc. Psychol.*, 1936, 7, 309–319.

9. Stagner, R. "Fascist Attitudes: Their Determining Conditions." *J. Soc. Psychol.*, 1936, 7, 438–454.

POLITICAL IMPLICATIONS OF THE MODERN GREEK CONCEPT OF SELF

- Adamantia Pollis

. . . This paper shall deal with the political implications of a given set of self attitudes. Using modern Greece as a case study, an effort shall be made to show that the view of self which a people holds, by determining an individual's conception of his relationship to the world around him, significantly affects the functioning of a political system. If the interrelationship of the view of self, cultural patterns, social structure and political institutions can be more clearly delineated, then the processes of modernization, political development and democracy may become better understood.

Writers argue that in addition to the obvious need for technological changes and for the adoption of 'western' political and economic institutions, modernization requires changes in values and attitudes.[1] The problem of altering values in the direction of modernization may be more complex than usually assumed and apparent changes in value systems and cultural patterns may not assure the development of a 'modern' nation-state or of democracy. Changes in behaviour may take place without a parallel change in basic dimensions of ego structuring; and a new value complex may become a new way of asserting the traditional

Above selection reprinted from: *British Journal of Sociology*, 16 (1965), 29–47. Deletions have been made by the editor in the interest of brevity.

self. In such instances, it may well be that political institutions and political processes which superficially resemble their Western counterparts perform different functions and hold a different meaning.

In analysing the modern Greek concept of the self the writer is not concerned with the self *per se*, but with those aspects which are relevant in providing insight into Greek political processes. The Greek view of the self will be contrasted with the view prevalent in the West. The persistence of the former despite the stresses encountered as a result of socio-economic changes and the assimilation of Western political doctrines will be discussed. And finally, tentative conclusions will be drawn regarding probabilities for the emergence of a modern nation-state, and for the development of democracy.

Greek Vs. Western View of Self

The Western, or Anglo-Saxon, concept of freedom is predicated on a particular set of views regarding human nature. The complex of assumptions regarding the person, his relatedness to others and to society, are summated in what is referred to as individualism. . . . What is most significant is the fact that these doctrines, instead of remaining the philosophy of an intellectual elite, took root and markedly altered the psychological functioning of individuals. The

Protestant view of individual related-ness to God and individual responsi-bility was expanded into a total view of man, his relationship to himself and to society. Man became an autonomous being. Economic and political, as well as religious behaviour became atomized, although regulated by individual re-sponsibility. It is from these underlying precepts that the bulk of Western intellectual thought has stemmed—classical and neo-classical economics, and liberal political thought. Even much totalitarian ideology, while rejecting the validity of individualism, neverthe-less uses it as the common referrent.

The Western tradition justifies free-dom on the grounds that society exists for the fulfilment of the individual. Social, political and economic institu-tions are created by man as a necessary institutional framework within which the individual formulates and pursues his own goals. The much vaunted free-dom of choice characteristic of Western society is grounded, therefore, in a concept of self according to which an individual decides intra-individually; what an individual will be and do is not prescriptive, but is determined by the individual for himself. The counter-part of freedom of choice and personal-ized goals is individual responsibility for one's decisions and actions. The very psychological device employed by Western society to ensure conformity to ethical standards, individual guilt, is a personal feeling independent of external social sanctions. As responsibility for one's actions cannot be shifted to God, to forces of nature, or to anything ex-ternal to the person, so the penalty for transgression of one's values is self-inflicted.

The Western view of self, although, as

Fromm dramatically states, divesting man of his security and certainty, never-theless has governed man's behaviour to a greater or lesser extent. The whole complex of behaviour contained within the notions of individual freedom, personal goals, and individual guilt part of the socializing process. And whereas in the nineteenth century the extremes of individualism led to the theories of Social Darwinism, the central theme of much contemporary literature and critique of American society is the loss of individuality, e.g., Riesman's concern with the 'outer-directed' man[2] and Whyte's concern with the 'organi-zation man.'[3]

Turning to Greece, by the early nineteenth century both within and without the Ottoman Empire, 'Greeks' had been influenced by the intellectual ferment of Western Europe. The Renais-sance itself had formulated the doctrines of Greek nationalism, presenting Greece with a ready-made national history. Accompanying the dissemination of nationalist doctrines was the dissemina-tion of democratic ideas and the theories of natural rights. Democracy and nationalism had a more or less simultaneous development in Western Europe— the French Revolution having been both nationalist and democratic— but a distinction was retained between the political legitimacy of nationalism and a democratic domestic political system. The former was based on loyalty to a nation-state and individual related-ness to the state, the latter on a new concept of man and of man in society. In Greece, questions of freedom and of national sovereignty became con-founded and the attainment of the two became interdependent. Freedom as a personal attribute of man stemming from a new view of the self was lost in the fight for independence and national sovereignty.

To understand how a society can take a concept such as the Western doctrine of freedom, confound it with national sovereignty, use the vocabulary of democracy but ignore individualism, it is necessary to investigate the Greek concept of self—the Greek view of who he is. The Greek view of self is such that it can apparently operate within a wide range of institutional patterns. And if it is true that traditional Greek self-attitudes at the level of fundamental ego involvement can remain relatively intact under divergent political, social and economic systems, then Western ideologies become vitiated.

The Western concept of individualism has been as irrelevant to traditional Greek society as it has been irrelevant to African tribal societies. Setting aside for the moment the problems of urbanization, an individual's life, as in many 'traditional' societies, has been circumscribed by the membership groups into which he was born—the family, the village, and the local church—and these in turn have determined individual relatedness. Only the Eastern Orthodox religion may have served as a reference group extending beyond the village.

Also as in all traditional societies in which experience has operated within the framework of a personalized system of loyalties, behaviour governed by abstract concepts, independent of personal relationships has had little meaning. In the West one values justice, equality and uniform laws applied independent of personal relationships. In Greece it is with reference to specific people, and to groups composed of specific individuals, that attitudes and modes of behaviour operate. Greek speech and conversation is replete with abstract concepts, but they are relevant only with regard to specific persons or things. The application of the law impartially to 'the people' has been as experientially meaningless as is the idea of justice independent of the individuals involved in a particular situation. Objectivity and impartiality are rarely used words, and their role in Greek life is negligible. Quite the contrary, when objectivity and impartiality deflect from the fulfilment of one's personal obligations, the virtues to strive for are subjectivity and partiality.

In the case of Greece, the priority of loyalty owed to membership groups is more than a statement about values; the very person exists only because of these groups. Self-definition is in terms of group relatedness and not as an individual; existence as an individual separate from these groups is inconceivable. Nothing demonstrates more dramatically the absence of the notion of an autonomous individual than the absence of a word in Greek for privacy. One of the basic rights of an individual in the West, the right to privacy, is lacking as a concept and is not part of the cultural pattern of Greece.[4] The frequently heard statements of pity regarding individuals bereft of family and/or far from their village reflect the belief that such a person is incomplete. It is interesting to speculate whether these attitudes are a continuation of the Aristotelian concept that a man outside the *polis* is 'either beast or God.'

A view of self inter-individually defined, precludes the very idea of personal goals or aspirations. Who and what one is, is answered by referring to one's position within membership groups. 'Who am I?' will elicit a response stating family, clan, village and specific status within these groups. Self-worth is judged by the person and by others in terms of how well the pre-scribed obligations and loyalties are fulfilled, and self-fulfilment is attained by performing well the assigned role within membership groups. Such a concept of 'self' does not enable an individual to choose or to set up personal goals. Freedom of action is restricted to a choice among alternative methods for effectively implementing prescribed roles.

Reinforcing the concept of self, ex-perientially defined in terms of a particular pattern of inter-personal relationships, is the psychological mech-anism which is employed for imposing sanctions. In the West an individual is his own critic, judge and at times executioner. Guilt is the punishment meted out for the transgression of internalized values. Since one is re-sponsible to oneself, guilt operates psychologically whether or not the un-desirable behaviour is known to or affects others. In Greek culture, shame is the psychological device employed to ensure conformity, and shame is the emotion a person's transgressions en-gender in him.[5] A Greek is not re-sponsible to himself, but to the group of which he is an integral part. And shame is the psychological penalty for behav-iour inappropriate vis-a-vis the group. Deviant behaviour which does not affect the fulfilment of obligations and does not create doubt as to loyalties does not engender feelings of shame. The irrelevance of the psychological variable 'guilt,' despite Freudian analysis, is evident in the restrictive meaning of

the word in Greek. Except among the bi-cultural and westernized elite, 'guilt' (enohos) is used within a legal context. The words 'fault' (fteo) or 'responsible for' (epephthinos) are somewhat com-parable to the Western use of 'cause' or 'blame' and do not connote feelings of guilt.[6]

A closely related socializing device is the use made of ridicule. A child is either admonished with the phrase 'have you no shame?' (entrope) or ridiculed as unworthy.[7] For adults, group relatedness and group identi-fication is reinforced by evaluating actions in terms of whether they will bring ridicule (rezilepsun) upon the individual and hence the entire group. It is difficult to develop individual autonomy when individual behaviour is perceived as group action and derision is a weapon for ensuring conformity.

Concomitant with the absence of the idea of an autonomous individual, and hence of freedom to choose goals, is the absence of the very notion of individual responsibility. In the West the counter-part to freedom of choice is individual responsibility. An individual is re-sponsible for himself and to himself. In Greek culture, responsibility has meaning only within the context of fulfilling one's obligations and pre-serving one's loyalties. Behaviour ap-propriate for the attainment of these ends, frees a Greek from other pangs of responsibility. A Greek does not feel that he has control over his destiny, but he is 'responsible' for fulfilling his role obligations as traditionally defined. 'Freedom of choice' exists among al-ternative means for fulfilling role obliga-tions. Whether one becomes a doctor, lawyer, politician, sea captain, or farmer is immaterial, so long as the basic pattern of group relatedness is not disrupted.[8] Thus personality factors, for men at least, can be taken into account in choosing an occupation, subject of course to limitations imposed by group interests. If a person manifests considerable drive and effectiveness in the means exercised for fulfilling his role, he is judged to be *prokomenos*.

Summarizing the above, self-fulfilment in the West is attained through success in achieving personally defined goals within a particular ethical system. In Greece, self-fulfilment is attained through the successful implementation of one's role within a greater whole. In the West, self attitudes tend to be anchored intra-individually (in terms of the concept of individualism). In Greece, self attitudes tend to be anchored inter-individually (in terms of reciprocities among clan members, village members). Therefore, in the West, one experiences guilt, whereas in Greece one experiences shame.

The specifically Greek configuration of self functioning within and inter-related with a normative system containing given values in a particular social structure does not have any counterpart in the Anglo-Saxon tradition. The Greek term for the experiencing of oneself as part of a system of group relatedness is *philotimo*. The absence of a comparable English word in itself signifies the absence of an equivalent concept.[9] *Philotimo* is the dominant Greek value; it integrates all other values and norms, defines appropriate behaviour both toward other group members and toward foreigners (*kseni*). Literally the term means 'love of honour,' with honour interpreted within a medieval context. Even this definition, however, does not convey either

the emotional tone of *philotimo* or its behavioural requirements. Dorothy Lee explains *philotimo* as 'self esteem.'[10] Although 'self esteem' or 'self worth' is lacking without *philotimo*, the terms are not synonymous. Behaviour which in the West brings self esteem may be a clear violation of the behaviour required by *philotimo*. The importance of *philotimo* in Greek life is reflected in the oft-heard remark that 'without *philotimo* life is worthless.'

The Anglo-Saxon value system places a high priority on individual integrity, and the latter is frequently used as a criterion for judging individuals. In Greece the concept of individual integrity does not exist (nor is there a word for integrity) just as the concept of *philotimo* is absent in the West. Functionally, however, *philotimo* and individual integrity are comparable. Whereas in the West individuals are evaluated as to whether they possess integrity, in Greece they are judged as to whether they possess *philotimo*. The difference lies in that integrity refers to the consistency of an individual's behaviour with his self-definition as an autonomous individual, whereas *philotimo* refers to the consistency of an individual's behaviour with his assigned role as an integral part of a greater entity, and with the preservation of the public image this demands. Behaviour which violates *philotimo* brings shame upon the individual and hence upon his membership groups.[11]

Man's most precious possession is his *philotimo*—it is this attribute which distinguishes man from beast.[12] The Greek social order is predicated on a Hobbesian view of the nature of man.[13] The arena for struggle, however, has been shifted from the individual to the group level.[14] The absence of the Western view of individualism and the shifting of 'individual' attributes to the 'group' is accompanied by intense inter-group rivalry in which each group manipulates and manoeuvres to win at the expense of all other groups. The struggle takes the form of a continuous battle for preserving *philotimo* and thwarting its molestation (preventing its violation). A commonly used Greek phrase is 'you molested my *philotimo*' ('*mou ethikses to philotimo*'). A Greek is ever on guard against the threats to his *philotimo* which are ever present in the hostile world surrounding him. To ignore these threats, to refuse to respond to the challenge, involves the risk of losing *philotimo* and, thereby, the reason for one's existence. Inter-group conflicts, therefore, regardless of the specific issue, are formulated in terms of *philotimo*.

Foremost, *philotimo* demands that the 'group' remain inviolate and that no infringement of its autonomy be permitted. To the outside world, a picture of perfection and harmony is presented; there is no word of discord or dissention and there is no admission of problems or difficulties confronting the groups. If the 'true state of affairs' is revealed one is overwhelmed by feelings of shame. The virtues of the family-clan are perennially extolled. Just as one will go to extreme lengths to preserve one's *philotimo*, starving rather than publicly admitting need, so any inference by an outsider doubting one's *philotimo* is deeply resented and can easily lead to violence.[15] This does not preclude manipulation and exploitation of one's environment and of people in order to obtain food by subterfuge; it is the admission and the confrontation of the need that is precluded. The range of statements that might be perceived as molesting one's *philotimo* are infinitely diverse—anything which casts aspersions on one's fulfilment of role obligations and/or loyalties, or which accuses one of personal behaviour in violation of the role image to be projected.

Ordinary conversation, or to use the Greek term, *couvenda*, is the sophisticated substitute for armed tribal feuding. What is at issue is not the substantive merits of the topic under discussion, but the ability of the constestants to outwit each other, thus 'proving' their superiority by emerging from the arena with their *philotimo* intact, while possibly molesting that of their adversary. It is this pattern which creates the impression of Greek individualism. However, it is not disagreement on content, but the necessity of preserving *philotimo* that makes verbal disputation mandatory, regardless of reasoned beliefs.

It is quite probable that the existence of 'autonomous group individualism' in Greek society engenders personal psychological tensions which are manifested in deviant behaviour as viewed from the perspective of the Greek cultural framework. Although the problems of psychological adjustment are beyond the scope of this paper, the degree to which the concept of group inviolability is operative in personalized behaviour does have considerable significance. The same unwillingness to reveal himself which governs a person's inter-group relations governs intra-group relations. At all costs he avoids exposure, or in other words, 'the naked truth.'[16] Any revelation of the self in autonomous terms prompts the same, if not greater, feelings of shame, as does exposure of the group. The psychological feasibility of answering the question 'who am I?' in intra-personal terms, given the obstacles existent in Greek society, is well-nigh precluded.

The Self and Greek Democracy

Philotimo, grounded in the Greek view of self, seems far removed from the difficulties encountered by the political system of Greece. But it is how individuals relate to others and to society that gives substance to the institutional framework, and influences conceptions of authority and legitimacy, thereby profoundly affecting political processes. Historically, the modern Greek state dates from the attainment of independence in 1830. Two interdependent sets of problems can be posed regarding Greece's subsequent political development: (1) those revolving around the establishment of national consensus and the foundations of national unity and (2) those revolving around the establishment of a democratic political system. It is primarily in relationship to the latter that the Greek conception of self will be discussed.

Constitutional and political instability has characterized the modern Greek state. In part, the absence of consensus on national norms and values—in short, the absence of national unity—has thwarted the effective functioning of a democratic political system, and in turn the absence of the requisites for democracy has hampered the emergence of individual relatedness to the state, national level leadership, and the primacy of loyalty to the nation-state.[17] In addition to the absence of national consensus, a multiplicity of other interrelated factors have blocked democratic political development: a rigid class structure, an authoritarian elite, the kinship system, a non-industrial society, an authoritarian and inadequate educational system.[18] Underlying the specific factors that account for political instability in Greece is the problem of reconciling a group-oriented society, lacking the concept of an autonomous individual, to democratic polity predicated on this very concept.

From the establishment of constitutional monarchy in 1863 Greece has oscillated between monarchy and republic, dictatorship and formal democracy. By and large, just as constitutional changes in France have not resolved basic cleavages, constitutional changes in Greece have brought neither stability, democracy nor effective government. The adoption of the trappings of democratic political institutions and the conduct of political controversy in democratic verbiage has beclouded the issues, while possibly strengthening anti-democratic values. In the assimilation process, Western concepts of freedom have been reinterpreted so as to be harmonious with Greek cultural values—a reinterpretation further facilitated by confounding the term 'freedom' with 'national independence.'[19] Freedom from alien, Ottoman rule, it was argued, would free one to pursue traditional goals and preserve traditional values. Thus individual rights and freedom of choice were perceived as the rights of traditional groups or of the newly formed groups. Such an interpretation of freedom sanctions group autonomy and group exclusiveness and enables individuals to behave with *philotimo* in the name of freedom. Restraints, controls, submission to national political authority, obedience to the law, can and have been viewed as infringements of democratic rights. Just as the Hobbesian view of man in the state of nature was transposed to the group level, in Greece liberal political thought ignored the individual and became the conceptual basis for group autonomy.

Lack of the system of norms and values critical to a democratic society is reflected in the constitutional implementation of the idea of limited government. The absence of the notion of inherent individual rights can be seen in the primacy repeatedly given to state and group interests and needs;[20] thus it is constitutional to seize a newspaper issue for several reasons, including claims that the contents of an article are insulting to the Christian religion or are 'rebellious.' The constitutional provision prohibiting the death penalty, except in cases of compound offences, allows for the holding of political prisoners. Although freedom of religious conscience is claimed, the restrictions placed by the constitution on the expression and dissemination of any religion other than the established state religion, Eastern Orthodoxy, make a mockery of such claims.[21] To the extent that civil liberties are guaranteed, they define a legal relationship between a Greek citizen and the national government, which on the one hand posits the group autonomy of the state and on the other gives legal sanction to individual behaviour designed to uphold subgroup rights and preserve their inviolability.

The continual charges and countercharges of violations of constitutional guarantees of civil liberties, well founded as they frequently are, have a psychological basis distinct from comparable charges made in Great Britain, Switzer-

land or the United States. Whereas in the latter cases it is the autonomous individual who is threatened, in Greece it is the traditional or newly formed groups which are at stake—they feel threatened by the surrounding hostile world and fear infringement or molestation of their inviolability. In recent decades democracies have struggled with the problem of reconciling individual rights and the national interest or the general welfare; in Greece the conflict is between autonomous group interests and the national interest or the general welfare.

Particularly in the post-World War II period, however, changes—stemming from the dislocations caused by the War and Civil War—have taken place in the Greek social structure and in cultural patterns. The mass migration to Athens, in particular, has given rise to a whole galaxy of apparently voluntary associations. Greece's experience raises serious doubts about the validity of frequently made assumptions that the formation of voluntary groups is a precondition for democratic development. The new reference groups, while affecting the behaviour of individuals, may be assuming the attributes of traditional membership groups.[22] Those new associations that represent attempts to transpose village life to urban centres, thus perpetuating village values and norms, may provide psychological anchorages but obviously do not facilitate changes in the traditional view of self or in traditional loyalties. More fundamentally, the voluntary associations may be no more predicated on notions of individual autonomy than traditional membership groups, hence their internal processes may be equally undemocratic and the view of self may continue to be inter-individually defined. If such is the case, then these associations mark the development of a new structural framework within which traditional loyalties are fulfilled, and/or become psychological substitutes for traditional membership groups. The Greek view of self which rejects individual autonomy remains intact. This is not to argue that there is no change in ego involvement. Changes in environmental conditions must be attended to, and change in occupation from a village farmer to unskilled worker in an urban factory, will affect the individual's ego involvement. The process of reintegration, of coping with new conditions, will modify the view of self, but may leave the basic layer intact; loyalties may become attached to new individuals, a whole range of 'superficial' behavioural patterns may be modified, but the basic pattern of one's relationship to oneself and to the world around one remains unchanged. Unfortunately no investigations or analyses of voluntary associations have been made, hence it is impossible to assess accurately their intra-group structure.

A democratic system presupposes a pluralistic society, predominantly but not exclusively composed of voluntary organizations representing conflicting interests. The political process aggregates the competing claims of these interest groups in accordance with a set of commonly accepted rules of the game. Decision-making in a democratic or open society, reflecting the changing composition of interest groups and changing goals and aspirations, registers the reconciliation of new conflicts and the evolving 'consensus' measured by some form of numerical majority. A consensus on the rules of the game—

such as minority rights, and the procedures for making decisions and the binding quality of those arrived at—enables the system to function effectively.

In Greece, interest aggregation of non-associational and associational group demands is not possible through the operation of democratic political processes, since each group considers its interests exclusive and not subject to common ground rules. Nationalism, which made politics and policy-making the legitimate concern of the citizen, created in the modern Greek state a new arena within which to conduct traditional and associational or voluntary group rivalries. The behavioural requisites of viewing the self as an integral part of a group, the need to preserve the inviolability of the group, the viewing of other groups and their claims as a threat to one's own survival, have distorted democratic institutions.

The nature of inter-group rivalry, as described for interest groups, also applies to the Greek political party system—a multi-party system characterized by fragmentation, factionalism and splintering, except for the duration of the Metaxas dictatorship. Traditionally, the parties have been patron parties,[23] the national organization consisting of a loose alliance of the various factions. Since the formation of new reference groups in urban centres does not seem to have altered the individual's self-view, no basic transformation has taken place in the nature of Greek parties. Competing political parties are vital to the existence of a democratic political system, since they allow for alternative choices while permitting orderly changes in political leadership; but their existence does not assure democracy. The development of mass parties, concurrent with the extension of democracy, has been well well documented by Maurice Duverger.[24] Mass parties within a democratic framework imply individual relatedness, which in turn presupposes individual autonomy. In Greece, attempts by Venizelos and by the Communists to form mass parties seem to have failed.[25] The absence of mass-membership parties, in addition to being indicative of the continuation of traditional social structure, reflects the continuation of the notion of self inter-individually defined, even where urbanization is taking place. Hence, political participation is not a matter of individual choice, but is group determined. Political activity is dependent upon group role, regardless of whether the group is non-associational or associational; and voting becomes a vehicle for implementing group obligations and protecting group survival against perceived external threats.

Thus the group-oriented Hobbesian view of the world historically operative among traditional groups in villages, has been transposed to the political sphere, vitiating democratic norms and institutions. Objectivity and impartiality, as noted earlier, violate the value system, and exposure of the facts or truth engenders feelings of shame since it constitutes betrayal of group loyalty. In democracies, although interest groups and political parties may attempt to keep 'facts' hidden for tactical reasons, ascertaining the facts is vital to decision-making; in Greece, however, it is unethical. Similarly, compromise, essential for the effective functioning of democracy, is seen as a betrayal of group loyalties, since it destroys the inviolability of the group.

Majority rule, the device for registering the outcome of the decision-making process in a democracy, is likewise ineffective in Greece. Democratic majority rule presupposes a commonality of interests superior to the subordinate interests of minority groups, acceptance of the decisions and policies emanating from democratic processes, a commitment to the rules of the game, and the psychological relevance of the autonomous individual. Although a conception of national interest is evolving, inter-group rivalry—in which victory by one group is perceived as destructive to the loser and as an ego defeat—together with the absence of democratic processes within the group, has transformed majority rule from an expression of popular will into a device for imposing, by authoritarian means, the will of the temporary victor upon the entire population. The political victors frequently behave as if their 'mandate,' whether achieved honestly or through election fraud, frees them from continuing responsibility to the general electorate and sanctions the imposition of their will, ignoring opposing claims and violating the rights of the opposition.

Underlying the ineffectiveness of democratic mechanisms is the lack of consensus on the rules of the game. Each interest group, each political party presumes, psychologically, that the existing political machinery has been structured by those in power for their self-interest and is by definition inimical to the interests of those out of power.[26] More often than not, the opposition's claims are substantiated by the actions of those in political control, who feel little commitment to democratic rules of the game.[27] Inevitably, the exercise of political power by any one party or interest group alienates those excluded from leadership, who frequently react by refusing to abide by the decisions or policies of the political leadership. The façade of majority rule within a democratic framework is further evident in the attitudes of the political leaders, whose norms of behaviour do not alter with their role change from party leaders to government officials. The British conception that a party leader who becomes Prime Minister is responsible primarily to the nation, not the party, or the American conception of the President as the national leader, is incomprehensible to and inapplicable in Greece. The Premier of Greece remains a representative of his group interests, and both behaves in terms of, and is expected to behave in terms of, these group interests. To the extent that the concept of the Premier as a 'national' leader exists, it is equated with the group interests of the ruling elite.

There is nothing inherently incompatible between a society organized along group lines, in which interest groups are highly competitive—as in Greece—and a democratic political system which preserves group freedoms. The essentiality of interest groups for democracy has often been argued. The preceding sections have indicated, however, that democratic processes are determined not by the existence of groups (characteristic of all social systems) and inter-group rivalry, but by the norms and values which govern the behaviour and the actions of group members.

The absence of a normative structure and a system of values supporting 'democratic' inter-group processes is equally true for intra-group processes in Greece. The authoritarian nature of

traditional membership groups seems to have been transposed to newly forming membership groups stemming from socio-economic changes. On the one hand, as discussed above, the flexibility in means for fulfilling group goals can accommodate altered occupational and social rules without necessitating a basic redefinition of the self. On the other hand, new membership and reference groups seem to manifest a similar authoritarian structure, and whereas specific values (e.g. the value placed on wealth and its symbols) and the specific individuals to whom one relates may change, the self is still defined inter-individually and the pattern of personalized loyalties and obligations is retained.

The irrelevance of democratic normative behaviour for Greeks is highlighted by the development within newly formed groups—be they political parties or voluntary associations—of the same deferential attitudes traditionally exhibited (in the family, clan, village)— toward those of higher status. Reciprocal duties and obligations determined interpersonally accord the authoritative figure—be he a village elder or a national political leader—deference on the part of those of inferior status. Inevitably, Greek political leaders are constantly subjected to criticism for failure to fulfil obligations commensurate with their authoritative roles. Political issues are discussed in terms of political personalities; rewards and punishments are meted out in terms of 'personal' evaluations rather than policies or programmes. Press, and public, conduct vituperative campaigns of accusations, counter-accusations, and exposés, attacking individuals for betrayal, disloyalty and compromise.[28]

A concomitant of the population's submissive attitudes toward authority and the expectations of fulfilment of the leaders' obligations toward them, is the absence of a sense of participation in the political processes and hence of responsibility for the government's actions. Although some of the more urbanized, sophisticated citizens feel politically alienated, within the meaning the term has acquired in the United States, the pervading sense is not one of alienation, but one of despair at the failure of the authorities to fulfil their roles in an appropriate fashion; and authority is not dependent upon delegation of power by a participating citizenry. The government is viewed as composed of personalities on whom one is dependent. And political personalities are judged in terms of expectations of role fulfilment by those in authority. Such attitudes toward authority are a strongly imbedded deterrent to the development of the attitudes which underpin a political system composed of participating citizens responsible for the policies their government adopts.

It should be noted that the behaviour of the political elite of Greece, as that of traditional political elites of many Middle East, South and Southeast Asian countries, is governed by norms and values at variance with those of the population in general. From the perspective of the Greek value system the elite is immoral. It is equally immoral judged by the standards of the Western value system. The socio-politico-economic elite of Greece seems to constitute a reference group with its own set of stable norms. The 'amorality' of the Greek elite from the Western and Greek viewpoints, accompanied by intellectual awareness of both value systems, enables them to exploit and manipulate both systems. The Greek politician can function within the Western normative pattern under certain conditions and shift to a Greek behavioural pattern when dealing with the Greek populace. This characteristic dexterity, stemming from the political elite's lack of commitment to either ethical system, enhances the perpetuation of undemocratic attitudes internally, while creating the illusion of democracy, internationally.[29]

Political Prospects

Post-World War II developments in Greece do not augur well for democratic development. It is dubious whether the superficial stability evidenced by the eight-year rule of former Premier Karamanlis[30] is indicative either of fundamental political and social stability or of the evolution of democratic political processes. National relatedness may well be evolving; particularly in urban centres, the concept of the nation is acquiring psychological relevance. The retention of ties between urban dwellers and clan members in the village in turn may be transmitting the concept of the nation to the villagers, thus facilitating its emergence as a reference group. However, that these trends reflect democratic tendencies is questionable.

In forecasting the future—always a dangerous undertaking for a social scientist—several trends seem discernible. Accelerated urbanization and the incipient beginnings of industrialization do not seem to be accompanied by the development of normative behaviour characteristic of the autonomous individual. Although as a consequence of socio-economic changes, tensions and stresses have been engendered, and although the fundamental role of traditional norms and values have become 'corrupted' and new values and norms are emerging, the fundamental core of one's view of self remains intact. Traditional cultural patterns which once served a regulative function, such as the dowry system,[31] have become distorted, particularly in urban centres. Instead of regulating the Greek Hobbesian conception of human nature, the dowry system, for example, frequently becomes an exploitive mechanism for the acquisition of wealth, reinforcing the jungle conception of society and social relations. Simultaneously, particularly in Athens, while one may relate to occupation (in addition to or in competition with kin) rather than to the village, nevertheless the processes of inter-personal relations follow those of traditional membership groups. And, whereas in more traditional Greece groups were relatively autonomous and isolated, their limited contacts governed by established norms, the influx of population into urban centres and the continual contact among groups (both traditional and new) is not marked by established norms regulating inter-group processes. Consequently, the relations among autonomous groups thrown together in an urban environment is marked by an intensification of behaviour characteristic of struggle, warfare and conflict. In intra-group relations a Greek is submissive and does not express individual autonomy. In contemporary intergroup relations behaviour is governed by the struggle for survival, thus reinforcing the illusion of Greek individuality. It seems apparent that these trends do not augur well for the emergence of the concept of individual autonomy; and if this concept is funda-

mental to democracy, then the current socio-economic changes in Greece do not necessarily presage democratic development.

Despite urbanization and the formation of voluntary associations, the kinship system seems to have remained relatively intact. Rather than developing a rural-urban split, the kinship system is retaining its viability through the distribution of individual members throughout the socio-economic structure.[32] Thus, each family-clan will attempt to have within its ranks both rural and urban dwellers, and members of various occupations—farmers, doctors, lawyers, politicians, skilled and possibly unskilled workers, teachers, etc.—all of whom maintain close interpersonal ties, thereby maintaining traditional group relatedness and loyalty without erecting barriers to occupational mobility. It should be remembered that traditionally Greek culture has been sufficiently flexible within the confines of a fundamentally binding structure to survive the geographic diffusion and the passage of time characteristic of the seafaring tradition. The ability of the kinship system to absorb new developments with few deleterious consequences may well vitiate even further the psychological and political relevance of the newly forming voluntary associations.

The formation of the modern Greek nation-state was accompanied by transposition of traditional attitudes to new institutions and new relationships. Whereas in traditional Greek society, *philotimo* was operative for the membership groups into which one was born, in the new state *philotimo* became operative for the new reference group, Greek nationality. And if *philotimo*, and in particular the 'public' image such a notion demands, becomes relevant for new reference and membership groups, then inter-group interaction will operate as it has among traditional groups. Rationality, impartiality, objectivity, and the validity of compromise will remain alien to Greek politics.

A further deterrent to democratic political development, as discussed above, is the Greek attitude toward authority. The followers of a 'national' political leader, the professionals of an administrative office, exhibit the same behaviour toward authority as a peasant toward the village elder. If the authority is accepted, loyalty is unquestioned; when authority is considered legitimate, as with the head of a family-clan or a village elder, rebellion or individual disagreement is psychologically out of bounds. The much vaunted refusal of Greeks to submit to authority is a refusal to submit to an authority whose legitimacy is not accepted; if it is accepted, challenges or disputation violate the value system. Since respect for the individual *per se* is lacking, the norms that govern behaviour *vis-a-vis* those toward whom no established interpersonal relations exist and who are not authoritative figures, sanction aggressiveness, hostility, and disregard of others' rights. Thus, in modern Greek history the central government has had difficulty in asserting its authority when it has been viewed as alien interference. Almost equally prevalent, especially in more recent years, has been a refusal to undertake activities through individual or group initiative if the sphere concerned is considered an obligation of governmental authorities.[33]

Underpinning any political system is the society's assumptions regarding human nature. The view held of the self, the individual's relatedness to others and to the social institutions within which he functions, determines the manner in which political systems operate and the form which political processes take. Apparently, the view of self held by some cultures, such as the Greek, permits drastic socio-economic changes and institutional arrangements with relatively few stresses on the basic processes of individual relatedness. Industrialization, urbanization, and democratic political machinery, therefore, do not necessarily presage democracy if the concept of self held is opposed to the concept essential for democracy.

In fact, the probable emergence of the nation-state as a major reference group to which primary loyalty is owed, may well lead to some form of authoritarian or totalitarian political system in Greece. As of now, primary loyalty to the abstract concept of a nation-state is insufficiently developed to lead to a totalitarian political system founded on consensus. But if prevailing attitudes toward authority remain intact, and if a Western or equivalent notion of individuality does not emerge, the prospects for democratic development are dim. The nation could become the 'group' which defines one's existence just as easily as the village, clan or professional association.

NOTES

1. See, for example, Seymour Martin Lipset, "Some Social Requisites of Democracy: Economic Development and Political Legitimacy," *The American Political Science Review*, 53, No. 1 (March 1959), and Bert F. Hoselitz, "Nationalism, Economic Development and Democracy," *The Annals of the American Academy of Political Science*, 305 (May 1956).

2. David Riesman, *The Lonely Crowd* (New Haven: Yale Univ. Press, 1950).

3. William H. Whyte, Jr., *The Organization Man* (New York: Simon and Schuster, 1956).

4. Ernestine Friedl, "The Role of Kinship in the Transmission of National Culture to Rural Villages in Mainland Greece," *American Anthropologist*, 61, No. 1 (February 1959), p. 34. The same author's field study of the Greek village of Vasilika also substantiates the claim that there is no awareness of the notion of privacy.

5. Ruth Benedict, *The Chrysanthemum and the Sword* (Boston: Houghton, Mifflin, 1946); Japanese culture is described as shame-oriented, American culture as guilt-oriented. These two categories are not mutually exclusive. Societies obviously contain elements of both shame and guilt. See also Riesman, op. cit., p. 25, where he argues that the sanction in societies producing tradition-directed persons is shame, whereas guilt is the sanction for inner-directed persons.

6. Ethnocentrism unfortunately characterizes judgments and evaluations even of the literary products of cultures. See, for example, W. H. Auden's remark that Cavafy's poetry is free of any feelings of guilt, despite the poet's homosexuality. ("Introduction" to *The Complete Poems of Cavafy*, translated by Rae Dalven (New York: Harcourt, Brace and World, 1961), ix.) Cavafy's poetry, however, does reflect and reveal feelings of shame. He may not be concerned with freeing himself from guilt, but he is with freeing himself from shame.

7. For a discussion of ridicule as part of the socializing process of children, especially its role in developing attitudes of distrust toward others, see Ernestine Friedl, *Vasilika—A Village in Modern Greece* (New York: Holt, Rinehart and Winston, 1962), p. 77.

8. As a social psychologist, Nicholas Pollis, has commented, this may explain the peculiar lack of professional involvement often characteristic of Greeks.

9. Pioneering work on the relationship of language to culture was done by Edward Sapir. See in particular "Language" in David G. Mandelbaum, (ed.), *Selected Writings of Edward Sapir*, pp. 26–8.

10. Dorothy Lee, "View of the Self in Greek Culture," in *Freedom and Culture* (Englewood Cliffs, N.J.: Prentice-Hall, 1959), pp. 141–3. The discussion of the inviolability of *philotimo* is excellent. However, inviolability is erroneously identified with freedom, in part because the relationship of *philotimo* to group loyalties and the absence of autonomous individuality in Greece are overlooked.

11. Lee, ibid., p. 141, discusses, by inference at least, the Greek concept of 'equality.' It is *philotimo* which makes one man as good as another.

12. The requisite behaviour for women to act with *philotimo* differs from that expected of men. A discussion of the view of self held by women and behaviour appropriate for their sex is beyond the scope of this paper.

13. See Friedl, op. cit., pp. 75–6, for an excellent discussion of the Greek attitude that human relations are battles filled with tensions in which one is continuously pitting himself against all others and against fate.

14. The fact that membership groups constitute a single entity militates against intra-group relations assuming the complexion of a battle marked by constant tension. However, the writer tends to believe that the complex of obligations and loyalties binding individuals to each other are devices for restraining potential conflict. The vituperativeness, vindictiveness and intensity of conflict among family members when the system of reciprocities breaks down tend to substantiate this contention.

15. Illustrative in a humorous vein is the incident in the Greek film *Never on Sunday*, in which a Greek, whose love for his mother is questioned by the American 'boy scout' who hypothesizes in Freudian fashion that the Greek 'really hates her' thus explaining his predilection for prostitutes, socks the American. A violent reaction on the Greek's part was the only possible response.

16. Lee, op. cit., pp. 142, 147. Lee uses the phrase 'the naked fact,' and gives an excellent account of the prohibition against exposing one's inner core. Possibly rejecting the Western mind-body dichotomy, the same attitudes exist *vis-a-vis* covering the body; both mind and body are to be hidden.

17. The beginnings of national level political leadership were exhibited by Eleutherios Venizelos in 1909. See Adamantia Pollis, *The Megali Idea: A Study of Greek Nationalism* (unpublished Ph.D. dissertation, The Johns Hopkins University, 1958), p. 280 ff.

18. It is too early to evaluate the success of the Papandreou government's educational reform programme, which includes revision of teaching methods, drastic curricula changes, and the creation of a new university at Patras—all designed to eradicate the nineteenth-century Germanic tenor of Greek education.

19. Confounding sovereignty and freedom has been characteristic of nationalist movements. Nineteenth-century European nationalisms frequently equated the two—an error which Woodrow Wilson did little to dispel. Contemporary anti-colonialist nationalisms hold similar views, or at best equate democracy with institutional arrangements. See, for example, Kwame Nkrumah, *I Speak of Freedom* (London: Pall Mall Press, 1961).

20. Constitution of Greece, 1952, Articles 3–20, list 'undivided public rights.'

21. Ibid., Articles 1–2.

22. Somewhat comparable are associational groups in India which seem to function autonomously, outside the political system; see Myron Weiner, *The Politics of Scarcity: Public Pressure and Political Response in India* (Chicago: University of Chicago Press, 1962).

23. Ruth Schachter, 'Single Party Systems in West Africa,' *American Political Science Review*, 55, No. 2 (June 1961). The description of patron parties in West Africa is applicable to Greece if one substitutes village elder, local notable, or urban leader, for 'the chief.' See also, William Hardy McNeill, *The Greek Dilemma*

(New York: J. B. Lippincott Co., 1947). Chapter I contains pertinent observations and insights into Greek political parties, There is no adequate history or analysis of Greek political parties: However, see Grigoriou Daphnis, *Ta Ellinika Politika Kommata* (*Greek Political Parties*) (Athens: Galaksia, 1961).

24. Maurice Duverger, *Political Parties: Their Organization and Activity in the Modern State* (New York: Wiley, 1954).

25. There is some evidence that in the rural areas during the guerilla warfare of 1946–49 communism, which depends upon individual mass support, was in part subverted by traditional clan and village loyalties and rivalries.

26. Note the widespread insistence for alteration of the electoral system prior to the holding of new elections subsequent to the resignation of the Karamanlis government in June 1963.

27. Illustrative of the misconceptions regarding democratic precepts is the comment made by a National Radical Union delegate to the Boule (Assembly) in response to the writer's observation that the objective of the delegates in the legislature seemed to be to prevent their opponents from speaking, by any means at their command. The delegate's response was, 'That's democracy'.

28. A perusal of the contemporary Greek press substantiates this observation. As an 'opinion' press it is distinguished by its vituperative writings and personalized attacks.

29. A more detailed analysis of the view of self held by the elite of Greece, and of their norms and values, would constitute a separate study and is beyond the scope of this paper.

30. Premier Constantine Karamanlis resigned in June 1963, ostensibly over a dispute with the monarchy regarding a forthcoming royal visit to Great Britain. After the interim caretaker government of Premier Pipinelis, elections in November 1963, brought to power Premier George Papandreou and the alliance of opposition factions known as the Centre Union.

31. Ernestine Friedl, 'Dowry and Inheritance in Modern Greece,' *Transactions of the New York Academy of Sciences*, 22 (1959), pp. 49–54.

32. Ernestine Friedl, 'The Role of Kinship in the Transmission of National Culture to Rural Villages in Mainland Greece,' *The American Anthropologist*, 61, No. 1 (February 1959). It can be inferred that the preservation of the kinship system deters both the emergence of the concept of an atomized individual and the shift of primary loyalties to organizations and institutions other than the clan.

33. Subsequent to the severe earthquakes in the Ionian Islands in 1952, the villagers refused to co-operate and take local initiative for rebuilding homes, etc.; Friedl, *Vasilika*, p. 104, points out that several reasons 'prevent the life-long daily associations of the men in the village from producing a driving force for enthusiastic joint action for village-wide goals.' Initiative, even by the clan, disappears to the extent that a particular function is viewed as the appropriate obligation of another authority.

4

The School

INTRODUCTION

Recent research strongly suggests that the public schools are close rivals to the family as major agents of political socialization. This should not be surprising since socialization is one of the main functions for which governments set up schools. Since the best guarantee for political loyalty in adulthood lies with its establishment in childhood, if the schools can succeed in making loyal Americans or loyal Chinese out of their pupils, the government's task will be considerably eased later on. No wonder then that from time immemorial governments have used education for propaganda purposes (paradoxical as that may sound) in order to mold youth into adults who would be useful and loyal to the system. Such practices rest, of course, on the belief that formal instruction is the royal road by which to reach this goal. Nowhere in our day is this faith in education more pronounced than in the new African nations, and

likewise in the establishment of revolutionary regimes of this century the place of the schools in the political order has been glaringly visible. One of the first tasks of new rulers has been to rewrite textbooks and to purge the school system of adherence to the old ways in order that memories of the old society might be erased and that the educational machine might be used to imprint the goals of the new order upon the plastic minds of the youth of the land.[1]

Although the heavy hand of the political regime is perhaps not quite as visible in older and more democratic nations as it is in revolutionary regimes (see, for instance, the Cuban arithmetic primer below, pp. 318–320), there is no doubt that even in them the entire school curriculum and often the atmosphere of the school as well tend to reflect the characteristic national values. The schools discharge their socialization responsibility in several ways: first through formal quasi-political instruction and secondly through the atmosphere that prevails in the school, not only during instruction but also in the interaction between pupil and pupil and between pupils and school authorities. The first function is exercised through political indoctrination, which is usually offered in formal courses, such as citizenship, history, and so forth, not to mention rituals and observations of national holidays. In the United States, classes in citizenship (often called civics) are designed to acquaint the young with the institutions of government and the principles on which they are based (although, unfortunately, less effort goes into the latter). In many schools the thrust of such teaching is to instill acceptance of the status quo rather than its critical evaluation. This tendency is beginning to disappear from textbooks, but at a faster rate than in actual classroom instruction. In imperial Japan some indoctrination was accomplished in the daily "moral instruction," morality being equated with chauvinism and emperor worship. Little wonder that elimination of this instruction was one of the first educational reforms demanded by the American occupation.* Civic training in all countries probably aims at creating (1) some knowledge of one's government, (2) expectations as to behavior it is likely to engage in and to accept from its members, and (3) love

* Currently such instruction has found its way back into the curriculum, and in 1967 proposals were made for making "national defense-consciousness" an integral part of moral training.

and loyalty for it. Thus, via cognitive and affective processes the child is expected increasingly to internalize as his very own the country's political norms (always, of course, barring strong pressures to the contrary from other socializing agents)—in short he becomes more and more politically socialized.

Intrinsic to such education is of course a definition of the citizen—what is expected of him, how he can best serve his country, and what political beliefs, expectations, and behaviors are considered desirable. Thus, in one country primary emphasis may be put on an interested citizenry that vitally cares about the way its government conducts affairs and that through writing letters, attending meetings, or voting informs the government of its wishes. In another country the ideal citizen will be one who discharges his civic duty by working hard in order to increase the country's productivity and by becoming versed in Marxian dialectics in order to bring about socialist people's republics. That there can be differences even within a country, depending on the clientele served by the school, is seen in the selections by Edgar Litt and Rupert Wilkinson.

Teaching about the country's past, its heroes, its traditions, and its contribution to the world further enhances the student's sense of national pride and identity. Countries may no longer demand chauvinistic excesses of their school systems, but they certainly would consider the schools a failure should the students emerge from them with a low opinion of their country. How difficult it is to instill such pride in a nation without history and national heroes can be seen in the case of Uganda, so vividly portrayed by Kenneth Prewitt and Joseph

Okello-Oculi (pp. 607–621). Compare the difficulties of that setting with a school in the heart of Kansas, where children arrive in kindergarten already equipped with some fondness for figures of their historical past, such as Abraham Lincoln and George Washington.

If we were to judge by the United States and some of the Western school systems—for which we have better documentation than for some of the newer nations—we should have to conclude that the schools are extraordinarily successful in creating patriots. This success, however, may be illusory and may not really be due to the schools. Rather, most young people may learn the lessons of patriotism and national identification so well because they come to school already disposed to accept these lessons. In other words, the schools merely have to reinforce predispositions rather than alter prevailing attitudes. This latent predisposition may well account for the schools' phenomenal effectiveness.

Patriotism, or love of country, need not always be synonymous with love of one's country's form of government, although in America it is frequently the case that they are synonymous. The editor asked schoolchildren what made them proud to be Americans, and 69% referred to our form of government and the principles for which it stands. The American nation to them was indistinguishable from the American government. How different is this picture from Laurence Wylie's children in the Vaucluse of France. In school they are taught lessons in citizenship and patriotism not too very different from those learned by American schoolchildren; but although Frenchmen yield to no one in their love of country, they have deep disrespect

for their government. What accounts for the difference? Laurence Wylie argues that at home they are taught nothing but disrespect for the government, especially for the government in far-off Paris. As a result they reject at an early age the notion of the government as inspiring trust or admiration. French children, like American children, may love their native country; but apparently they do not associate their government with their homeland. Perhaps herein lies one of the explanations why France has seen so much political instability since the founding of the first republic. Frenchmen may have found it so very difficult to put aside minor political differences for the sake of cooperating in affairs of government because they simply could not trust politicians.

It is a moot question whether schools are as successful in stimulating political knowledge and sophistication, or an appreciation of underlying political principles, as they are in encouraging patriotism. The studies that have been pursued at the Purdue Opinion Panel, for example (see H. H. Remmers and R. D. Franklin), indicate that American schools have not managed to instill in high-school youths a genuine understanding of some of our very basic civil liberties, whereas the selection in the previous chapter on the children's reaction to the Kennedy assassination (Sigel, pp. 152–172) showed how inadequate the elementary and even the high schools had been in conveying to pupils an appreciation of due process of law. Nor do civics courses help much to increase such understanding. Kenneth Langton and M. Kent Jennings,[2] for example, demonstrated that understanding and internalization of basic democratic beliefs did not increase with the number of civics courses taken. In the next chapter the study by Albert Somit, Joseph Tanenhaus, Walter Wilke and Rita Cooley points to the virtual inability of a college course designed to increase political participation to accomplish this goal.

Findings such as these should not, of course be too surprising because we have long known from studies in mass communication, propaganda, and related fields that there are severe limits to a person's ability to change another's attitude if the other person is not so disposed. With respect to the effectiveness of inducing systems-appropriate values in young people via classroom instruction, one could perhaps say that these efforts are likely to be successful in those areas where they build on existing predispositions to accept the content of instruction but that the effect is minimal, at best, where the efforts defy familial or regional belief systems. This perhaps explains why our public schools had such extraordinary success with the Americanization of pre-World War I immigrants, whereas human relations programs in schools today are often far from successful. The immigrant arrived in school predisposed to believing only the best about the United States, whereas the student of the 1960s who is forced to take a course in "Exploring our Prejudices" or "Human Relations" may arrive in school with regionally and/or familially induced predispositions hostile to the "message" of the course. Consequently the message will not "take." The difficulties of political socialization under incongruous conditions are illustrated by a study of students in American Mennonnite high schools.[3] Given the traditional Mennonite aversion to political participation, one would

expect their youth to be politically more uninvolved than the average American high-school pupil. This, however, was found to hold true only for those Mennonites who have had little exposure to secular socializing agents.[4] The Mennonite high schools were far less successful in socializing those youngsters whose home life had introduced them somewhat favorably to the outside world's contrary values. Congruence of socializing experiences thus increases the power of the school as a political socializer, whereas incongruence weakens it.

Observations such as these have made us lose some of our original faith in the omnipotence of formal instruction as a means of socializing people. Studies of the educational enterprise have, however, alerted us to another quite unexpected source of socialization strength exercised by the schools: the school is a social organism, with a pattern and atmosphere unique to itself, that does much to mold a student's sense of personal effectiveness and that conveys to him a view of the nature of the social world, the power allocation in it, and the student's particular position in this allocation. Thus a student will become politically socialized during his years in school, not only by what the school deliberately teaches him but also by the inferences he makes from his school experiences, which may or may not be related to classroom teaching. Particularly crucial in this context are teaching methods, treatment of pupils by school authorities, the social life (clubs, extracurricular activities, type of student body and its pursuits) and the general ethos of a particular school.

Some school systems may be very authoritarian, may adhere to learning by memory, and may discourage the asking of questions and discussions in class, much less discussions of controversial issues or challenging of teachers. Other schools, on the other hand, priding themselves on their more permissive atmosphere, may encourage class discussion, even student-teacher debates, may sponsor student projects that are unsupervised by faculty, and so forth. Probably few school systems completely adhere to either model, but student behavior will be conditioned by the extent to which the school adheres more to one model than to another. An experimental study conducted in Portland, Oregon, suggests that teachers employing democratic teaching methods had significantly more success in bringing about the curriculum-planned democratic political attitudes in their pupils than did the teachers in the control group.[5] In the previously alluded to study of five nations[6] it was found that schools in the five nations varied considerably from one another in degree of permitted student participation—or at least so it seemed in the recollection of adult subjects—and that the adults in these countries also varied considerably in the extent to which they participated in political life. Generally speaking, politically passive adults recalled very little opportunity to express their opinions while still in school. More active citizens remembered opportunities for class discussion. In this same vein it is clear that experience with student government, student directed clubs, and other activities could give students exposure to speaking up in public and to acquiring, in a rudimentary way, the skills for decision-making, compromising and so forth. That such skills can be extremely helpful upon entering the adult political scene is too obvious to deserve further elaboration.

Nor must it be overlooked that the school, after all, is a social system of its own containing unofficial groups, organizations, clubs, and the like. The ease with which students can have access to these groups, the extent to which the school is run by these groups, or by cliques within them, the extent to which the school is an open system or a closed system all seem to shape profoundly the young person's sense of belonging and his own sense of control over his environment. The article by David Ziblatt shows that impressions of belongingness contribute to the high-schooler's view of government, its trustworthiness and fairness, and of his desire to participate in it later on. Thus the school as a social organism can either bestow or deny to the student some of the very skills and tools that permit him to enter the adult political arena with self-assurance and with trust in government.

Undoubtedly, the schools will be at their maximum effectiveness in political socialization where there is great congruence between the deliberate and the incidental learning that transpires, whereas the school will perhaps fail when students perceive it to teach one lesson but to practice another. This latter observation is being currently borne out over and over again in the reports we receive from inner-city schools, where students are taught in history and civics classes about the dignity of the human being and the essential equality of all but where many teachers treat them with anything but dignity and equality. Native pupils attending schools set up by a colonial power very often found themselves similarly affected by the school's eulogies of the colonial power's libertarian practices and institutions. Hence it was precisely those educated in colonial schools who became most annoyed by the absence of political freedom in the colony itself. Consequently they often became the leaders of the revolt against colonialism, as the biographies of Gandhi and others amply demonstrate. Political socialization took place in the colonial school, but its effect may well have been unanticipated and unintended by the school authorities. In short, school effectiveness as a political socializer is dependent not only on what the schools say but on what the schools do.

The process of becoming educated in and of itself also has socializing effects. The evidence is almost irrefutable by now that people who have had more education tend to approach the political process with a greater sense of personal effectiveness, enhanced notions of civic duty, and considerably less fear of political deviancy than do people with but rudimentary education. It is as though the acquisition of knowledge per se—by no means just knowledge about political phenomena—liberates the mind, permits it to see merits to a variety of contradictory suggestions, increases its tolerance for the unfamiliar and the unorthodox, and lessens fear of the unknown.[7]

The selections below also bear witness to the fact that not only do children develop and change in their appreciation of political phenomena but that school systems themselves change over time. Edgar Litt, for example, notices that schoolchildren in the mid-twentieth

century seem to be free of the blatant chauvinism for which earlier generations were so noted. Edwin Lawson, in comparing his study with one done twenty-five years earlier, found that young children today seem somewhat more sophisticated politically. He attributes these differences in part to the omnipresence of television in the lives of our children. Although evidence for this particular explanation is most tenuous, it is at least suggestive of the external forces that impinge upon even the most tradition-bound of all institutions: the school.

Yet all change notwithstanding, there is probably little doubt that the public schools are a choice transmission belt for the traditional rather than the innovative, much less the radical. As a result they facilitate the political socialization of the main-stream young and tend to equip them with the tools necessary for the particular roles they are expected to play in a given society. One may wish to quarrel with the differential roles the government and the schools assign to students, but it would probably be considerably more difficult to deny the schools' effectiveness.

In the largest sense the educational system is a great mechanism for conserving the values, the institutions, the practices of the political order, as it inculcates from the primary school even through college the memories, the unities, and the norms of the system. Yet, the educational process does not completely embalm the political system. From it there come the political innovators as well as the conservators.[8]

NOTES

1. V. O. Key, Jr., *Public Opinion and American Democracy* (New York: Knopf, 1961) p. 316.

2. Kenneth Langton and M. Kent Jennings, "Political Socialization and the High School Civics Curriculum in the United States," Unpublished, mimeographed manuscript (University of Michigan, 1967).

3. Daniel R. Leatherman, "The Political Socialization of Students in the Mennonite Secondary Schools," *The Mennonite Quarterly Review* (January 1962), pp. 89–90.

4. *Ibid.*

5. Alva Whitcomb Graham, "Do Teachers Who Use Democratic Methods Develop Democratic Attitudes?" *Elementary School Journal*, 47 (1946–1947), pp. 24–27.

6. Gabriel Almond and Sidney Verba, *The Civic Culture: Political Attitudes and Democracy in Five Nations* (Princeton, N.J.: Princeton University Press, 1963).

7. Seymour Lipset, *Political Man* (New York: Doubleday, 1960); Stouffer, *Communism, Conformity, and Civil Liberties* (New York: Doubleday, 1955).

8. Key, *op. cit.*, p. 343.

[EXCERPTS FROM] CUBA: THE POLITICAL CONTENT OF ADULT EDUCATION

- Richard R. Fagen

Problems and Exercises*

Items from page 63

Of the 18 employees of a business, 9 are militiamen, 5 belong to Committees for the Defense of the Revolution, and 4 form part of a Battalion of Voluntary Workers. How many employees of this business are contributing their efforts to the progress of the Fatherland during this period of sacrifices?

A family's bill for electricity used to be $8 monthly, and after the reduction in rates ordered by the Revolutionary Government it is $3 less. What is the family's present monthly expenditure for electricity?

On December 2, 1956, Fidel Castro and 81 other expeditionaries disembarked near Belic, at Las Coloradas beach, facing the Sierra Maestra. By land and by sea the forces of the tyranny bombarded them; 70 men lost their lives. How many expeditionaries from the "Granma" began the epic struggle for the liberation of Cuba?

The Revolution is developing goat raising in the mountainous regions of Cuba in order to increase dairy production.

Above selection reprinted from: Richard R. Fagen, *Cuba: The Political Content of Adult Education*, The Hoover Institution on War, Revolution, and Peace, Stanford University, 1964.

*The items are taken from a Cuban textbook.

If one goat gives 6 liters of milk every day, how many liters will 4 goats give? To defend our Socialist Revolution, we Cubans have organized ourselves into Committees for the Defense of the Revolution. If in one block there are 4 committees, each one made up of 9 citizens, how many people are part of those 4 committees?

Item from page 64

In Mégano, at the mouth of the cauto River, fishermen used to gather 300 oysters in the mangrove swamps, put them in a can, and sell them for one peso to the middlemen. Today, with the elimination of the middleman, they receive three times as much for the same quantity of oysters. How much does a fisherman receive today for the number of oysters which he formerly had to sell for three pesos?

Items from page 66

The Revolution has put books within reach of the people. In a Galiano Street bookstall a railroad worker brought Palevói's work "A Man of Truth" (*Un Hombre de Verdad*) for 1 peso and 10 cents, the "Song of Great Achievements" (*Canción de Gesta*) by Pablo Neruda for 50 cents, and "*Bertillón 166*" by José Soler Puig for 35 cents. How much did his purchase of books amount to?

A peasant who used to earn 70 cents a day before the Revolution now earns 2 pesos and 80 cents. How much more does he earn now?

A medicine which cost $4.75 before the Revolution now can be bought for $3.16. How much less do we pay for this product?

In the battle of El uvero, which took place on May 28, 1957, some 120 rebel soldiers fought against the much superior armed forces of the tyranny (of Batista). About one third of the rebel soldiers were killed or wounded. What were the losses suffered by the Rebel Army in this memorable battle?

In the United States there are six million unemployed workers of which three tenths are white and the rest Negroes. What part of those 6 million unemployed men are Negroes? (Think of the number "one" expressed as ten tenths).

Item from page 67

The economic cooperation and mutual fraternal assistance of socialist countries constitute a new type of international relations, one based on equality of rights and respect for the liberty and sovereignty of nations. From these friendly peoples, Cuba has obtained the following credits for its industrial development: 200 Million (pesos) from the U.S.S.R., 60 million from China, 40 million from Czechoslovakia, 15 million from Rumania, 15 million from Hungary, 12 million from Poland, 10 million from the German Democratic Republic, and 5 million from Bulgaria. How much do the credits from the socialist countries received by Cuba for its economic development amount to?

Items from page 68

There have been 3,000 lynchings in the United States in the last 20 years. What has been the average number of lynchings per year in that country?

Imperialism knows no other type of relations between States except domination and subjugation, the oppression of the weak by the strong. It bases international relations on abuse and threat, on violence and arbitrariness. Between January 3 and June 10 in 1961, North American military airplanes violated Cuban air space 3 times in the month of January, 15 in February, 17 in March, 9 in April, 8 in May and 10 in June. What was the average monthly number of violations of Cuban air space by North American military airplanes?

Items from page 69

On August 6, 1945, a North American military airplane dropped an atomic bomb on the Japanese city of Hiroshima. The effects of this bomb were so awful that the population of 343,962 inhabitants was reduced to 137,197. How many inhabitants of Hiroshima did the atomic bomb dropped by the North Americans kill? How many years have passed since this barbarous act occurred?

Following the thoughtful advice of Fidel, a young peasant girl *(campesina)*, having graduated as a teacher of pattern-making and sewing, made a skirt and a blouse for her mother as soon as she returned home. If she used $1\frac{1}{4}$ meters of cloth for the blouse and $2\frac{3}{4}$ for the skirt, how many meters of cloth did she use altogether?

Item from page 70

The annual per capita income of Latin America is $280. That of the United States, on the other hand, is more than $2000. What is the difference in per capita income between Latin America and the United States? To what do you attribute this contrast in wealth?

DEVELOPMENT OF PATRIOTISM IN CHILDREN—A SECOND LOOK[1]

- ## Edwin D. Lawson

A. Introduction

The study and evaluation of attitudes of patriotism or nationalism has been of concern to the social psychologist in the past and is of continuing concern. Investigations of this dimension of attitudes are relatively few with the exception of Horowitz (1) and Newcomb (2).

The Horowitz study was the first investigation of the development of attitudes of children at elementary school level. He reported the growth of patriotism in 82 children, Grades 1–10 in a rural four-room school in Tennessee. As his measure of patriotism, Horowitz had the children choose which of 24 flags were ranked in the top five on the basis of "best-looking." Lawson (3) and Lawson and Stagner (4) also used reactions to the beauty of flags as a measure of nationalism. College students' responses to a flag scale were shown to have a significant correlation with the Ferguson Nationalism Scale (5), a Thurstone-type attitude scale.

Horowitz in his study reported that:

1. Appreciation of the U.S. flag shows a steady development from 27.3 per cent in Grade 1 to 100 per cent from Grade 7 on. (Score was determined by the percentage of pupils who ranked the U.S. flag among the top five.)

Above selection reprinted from: *The Journal of Psychology*, 55 (1963), 279–286.

2. The best-liked flag by the younger children was the Siamese Merchant flag which showed a white elephant.
3. Flags in some way similar to that of the U.S. (Liberia, China, Cuba) tended to be preferred at higher grade levels.

The purpose of this investigation was to determine with a larger sample:

1. Whether responses 25 years later would be similar; i.e., would there be a steady development of appreciation for the U.S. flag, positive reaction to flags with animals, and a generalization pattern for flags similar to that of the U.S.?
2. What responses would be made to the Soviet flag and the United Nations flag.
3. Whether an emergent perceptual and choice pattern could be identified.

B. Method

1. Subjects

The *S*s were children from two school systems (one urban, Schenectady; one suburban, Averill Park) in upstate New York. Twenty boys and 20 girls, kindergarten through twelfth grade (K-12), were interviewed in each system. Thus a total of 1040 school children was tested.

2. Procedure

The procedure, while similar to that of Horowitz, did have some differences. Twenty flags were mounted separately

Table 1

The Percentage of Students in Each Grade, K–12, Who Ranked Flags in the Top Five*

	K	1	2	3	Grades 4	5	6	7	8	9	10	11	12
United States	73.75	68.75	78.75	81.25	73.75	76.75	78.75	75.00	71.25	72.50	65.00	70.00	68.75
United Nations	25.00	12.50	18.75	15.00	31.25	36.25	52.50	66.25	50.00	60.00	68.75	82.50	60.00
Russia	10.00	6.25	7.50	7.50	2.50	5.00	5.00	0.00	5.00	3.75	3.75	5.00	1.25
Liberia	55.00	47.50	58.75	58.75	50.00	51.25	26.25	48.75	22.50	33.75	21.25	26.25	28.75
Greece	28.00	28.75	32.50	32.50	17.50	23.75	25.00	47.50	25.00	36.25	33.75	33.75	42.50
Israel	26.25	28.75	18.75	16.25	10.00	21.25	16.25	20.00	18.75	36.25	15.00	32.50	12.50
Turkey	26.25	15.00	17.50	10.00	8.75	11.25	12.50	8.75	8.75	11.25	5.00	8.75	7.50
Yemen	13.75	13.75	17.50	16.25	12.50	13.75	11.25	11.25	6.25	22.50	10.00	18.75	10.00
France	23.75	20.00	31.25	17.50	12.50	16.25	16.25	12.50	9.75	22.50	17.50	12.50	17.50
Norway	18.50	12.50	13.75	11.25	12.50	12.50	18.75	15.00	5.00	15.00	6.25	2.50	11.50
China	20.00	29.25	13.75	20.00	13.75	6.25	5.00	5.00	10.00	7.50	1.25	6.25	5.00
Great Britain	15.00	15.00	26.75	30.00	28.75	26.25	31.25	20.00	23.75	26.25	32.50	22.50	28.75
Saudi Arabia	20.00	21.25	20.00	21.25	15.00	16.25	21.25	22.25	22.25	18.75	18.75	18.75	22.50
Brazil	20.00	23.00	22.50	26.25	35.00	16.25	34.25	20.00	28.75	13.75	16.25	22.25	20.00
Guatemala	15.00	26.25	18.75	27.50	52.50	40.00	37.50	30.00	58.75	46.25	51.25	46.25	46.00
Peru	20.00	26.25	17.50	21.25	26.25	28.00	25.00	20.00	28.75	23.75	31.25	22.50	28.75
Iran	25.00	31.25	28.00	31.25	25.00	21.25	17.50	15.00	15.00	12.50	28.75	22.50	13.75
Canada	21.25	20.00	30.00	17.50	33.75	28.75	30.00	30.00	28.75	21.25	40.00	17.50	29.25
Lebanon	27.50	35.00	18.75	23.75	21.25	17.50	18.75	15.00	21.25	20.00	21.25	32.50	11.25
Byelorussia	15.00	16.25	8.75	16.25	13.75	28.75	13.75	10.00	16.25	8.75	20.00	10.00	18.75

* Thus 25 per cent of the children in kindergarten ranked the U.N. in the top five.

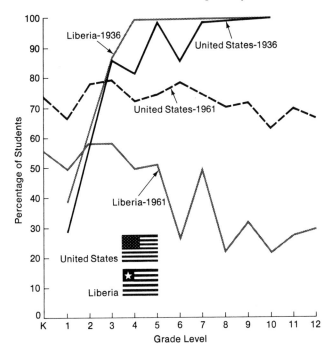

Figure 1 Development of Appreciation of Flags of the United States and Liberia*
*Expressed in percentage of students who ranked these in the first five.

on small masonite rectangles and were randomly presented in a matrix 5 by 4. Each flag was about $1\frac{5}{8}$ inches by $1\frac{1}{8}$ inches and was cut from a chart obtained from the United Nations Office of Public Information. The U.N. flag was slightly reduced in size in order to be equal to the others. *S*s were interviewed separately and were asked to pick out the most attractive flag, then the next most attractive flag, until all of the flags had been ranked and their position recorded by the interviewer. The Ferguson Nationalism Scale was also administered to Grades 10-12. The interviewers were eight graduate students in social psychology.

C. Results

The ranks chosen for each flag were recorded by grade level and sex in each school system. Since the data from the two systems and of boys and girls showed a strong similarity, the data were combined. Following Horowitz (1), Table 1 shows the percentage of pupils, K-12, who included the respective countries among their first choices. Figure 1 is a comparison of the development of appreciation of the flags of the U.S. and Liberia in this study (data obtained in 1961) with that of the Horowitz (data obtained in 1936, reported in 1940). Figure 2 shows the development of attitudes toward the U.S., the U.N., Liberian, and Soviet flags in this study.

1. U.S. Flag

The U.S. flag is rated highest by the 1961 school children at all levels except Grades 10 and 11, but the pattern is quite different from that of the Horowitz study as is shown in Figure 1. In our study, appreciation is fairly constant from kindergarten on with an average percentage of about 70 (indicating that 70 per cent of the children ranked the U.S. flag in the top five). In contrast Horowitz showed a positive acceleration from 27 per cent in Grade 1 to 100 per cent in Grade 7.

2. *Generalization to the Liberian Flag*

Generalization in the Horowitz study is shown in responses to the Liberian flag (this flag was originally modeled after that of the U.S. and is the most similar). While the 1961 children did show an initial preference for the Liberian flag at the kindergarten level (55 per cent) which is substantially above a chance score of 25 per cent but

below that of the U.S., this score did not increase or even maintain this level but dropped to a percentage just above chance in the high school group. While generalization does tend to occur somewhat in the case of Liberia, it is greatest at the elementary school level and then tends to diminish. There is a slight tendency to favor China in Grade 1 in the 1961 sample. This is another flag mentioned by Horowitz as being similar in pattern to that of the U. S.

3. *The Soviet Flag*

The Soviet flag is rejected immediately and has the lowest scores in the study. This is shown in Figure 2. It is chosen by 10 per cent of the children in kindergarten, but declines to 1.25 per cent in Grade 12.

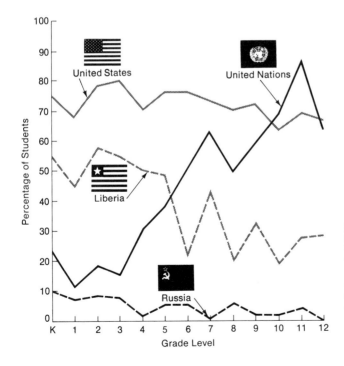

Figure 2   Percentage of Students in Each Grade, K-12, Who Selected the Flags of the United States, United Nations, Liberia, and Russia Among the First Five Choices*

*There were 40 boys and 40 girls at each grade level from two school systems.

4. *The U.N. Flag*

Appreciation of the U.N. flag is initially at chance level (25 per cent) but thereafter increases steadily. At Grades 10 and 11 the U.N. flag is actually higher than the U.S. flag. Thus there is a steady growth in appreciation of the U.N. flag to the point where it is about the same as that of the U.S.

5. *Animal Flags*

There were two flags with animals— Siam, showing elephants, and Iran, showing a lion. Whereas, Horowitz reported the Siamese flag highly chosen in Grade 1, there was no evidence in this investigation that perception of the animals led to a choice of these two flags.

D. Discussion

One question that might arise concerns the validity of choice of flags as a measure of attitude. It is more of a projective measure. Horowitz believed that flag choices would be correlated with attitudes. Our studies with high school and college students tend to confirm this. We doubt whether the average person can be objective when rating the beauty of flags even when the labels are missing. Flags are important symbols of patriotic feeling and often evoke emotional responses even when the immediate purpose of the symbol is no longer served. Thus we note that while most Americans do not associate the Red Cross organization with religion, the counterpart organization in Moslem countries is known as the Red Crescent, and in Israel, the Red Star of David.

In order to strengthen our contention that what is really being rated is indicative of attitudes toward the countries represented, we cite the findings from an earlier study (3) in which a panel of individuals with professional art training ranked the top flags as Greece, Saudi Arabia, Russia, Britain, and Norway. Brazil was rejected. Our *S*s certainly had no ranking approximating this. Because of the results with the art panel and the confirmatory evidence of significant correlations with a standard scale of nationalism (most of the correlations were significant) we feel that the flag scale is a reasonably valid instrument indicating feeling toward the object concerned.

The children in our sample apparently develop their attitudes at a substantially earlier age than those in the 1936 study. This is shown by the early acceptance of the U.S. flag, rejection of the Soviet. That the 1961 group is more sophisticated is shown in failure to generalize positive responses to the Liberian flag and failure to choose flags with animals on them. Perhaps our most interesting result is the steady growth in appreciation of the U.N. flag as the child goes through school until the U.N. flag is in the same range as that of the U.S. indicating a strong positive feeling toward the U.N. But why the crossover effect in Grades 10 and 11? Examination of the social studies offerings of both high schools shows that World History is taught in Grade 10, U.S. History in Grade 11. No unit of history is required in Grade 12. We can only speculate that the students in Grade 10 studying World History developed a positive attitude toward the United Nations which carried over to Grade 11 when U.S. History was being studied. In Grade 12, where history was not required and the instructor's influence was no longer present, the attitudes returned to the previous level.

How can we account for the differences between the two studies? There are several possible factors to be considered.

First, the 1961 sample was in an urban-suburban area in New York, the 1936 in rural Tennessee.

Second, the 1961 sample had a larger number of cases (1040 vs. 82) and covered a greater grade range (K–12 vs. 1–10). It was also based upon two school systems.

Third, the general cultural atmosphere in the country has brought about greater sensitivity to symbols such as flags. Since World War II there has been greater awareness of the position of world leadership and world influence held by the United States. The presence of the United Nations headquarters in New York City is clear evidence that the U.S. is not as remote from world affairs as it would have appeared to a rural Tennessee schoolboy in the mid-thirties. This greater awareness is reflected in the schools, in most homes, and in our organs of communication: newspapers, magazines, television.

On the basis of the three general points raised above we can explain some of the change in attitude. But there is a major question as to why the children in the 1961 sample showed their patterns of acceptance at such an early level, i.e., the rejection of the Soviet flag even in kindergarten. We feel that the best explanation of these early attitudes is in the influence of television. Today, according to one study (6) children watch television from a median of 20 hours a week in kindergarten to a median of 19 hours in the sixth grade. Undoubtedly, much of what the very young child views is over his head but he still takes in a great many values —from Captain Kangaroo featuring Skitch Henderson in a demonstration of classical instruments to Popeye and his inevitable spinach. Some of the children's programs feature a daily pledge of allegiance to the flag. News and other programs give the child of today far greater awareness of the world and of the United States than his father had twenty-five years ago.

E. Summary

Using an adaptation of the Horowitz test of patriotism, 1040 children in Grades K-12 were interviewed in two upstate New York communities. Compared with children interviewed twenty-five years earlier by Horowitz, children recognize flags at an earlier level; the United States flag is liked consistently at a high level, the Soviet rejected. This is apparent from even the earliest grades. Appreciation of the United Nations flag begins at a low level in kindergarten but shows a steady increase. At the high school level it is in the same range as the United States flag, although that of the United States does tend to be slightly higher. Several interpretations were offered to explain the data involving differences in location, size, and year of the two samples. An additional point was made concerning the role of television in helping to shape children's attitudes.

NOTES

1. Revision of a paper read at the annual meeting of the Eastern Psychological Association, April, 1962. This investigation was carried out with the collaboration of Robert J. Cornell, Elizabeth Cunningham, Mary C. Gatzemeyer, Elaine Heidenstrom, Helga Karker, Alvin Rabinowitz, John Ray, and Patricia Wolcott.

REFERENCES

1. Ferguson, L. W. A revision of the primary social attitude scale. *J. of Psychol.*, 1944, **17**, 229–241.

2. Horowitz, E. L. Some aspects of the development of patriotism in children. *Sociometry*, 1941, **3**, 329–341.

3. Lawson, E. D. Attitude shift as related to palmar sweating in group discussion. Unpublished doctoral dissertation, Univ. Illinois, 1954.

4. Lawson, E. D., & Stagner, R. Group pressure, attitude change and autonomic involvement. *J. Soc. Psychol.*, 1957, **45**, 299–312.

5. Newcomb, T. M. Personality and Social Change. New York: Dryden, 1943.

6. Schramm, W., Lyle, J., & Parker, E. B. Television in the Lives of Our Children. Stanford, Calif.: Stanford Univ. Press, 1961.

CIVIC EDUCATION, COMMUNITY NORMS, AND POLITICAL INDOCTRINATION

- Edgar Litt

"All national educational systems," observes V. O. Key Jr., "indoctrinate the coming generation with the basic outlooks and values of the political order."[1] But this indoctrination is not uniform. Do different socio-economic communities, for instance, differ in the kinds of textbooks they employ in civic education? Do differing political attitudes and norms in these communities affect the process of indoctrination?[2] To answer these questions, we analyzed textual material in civic education programs, attitudes of leaders in the school's political and educational milieu, and changes in political attitudes accompanying participation in civic education classes.

Procedure

The study was conducted in the major secondary school in each of three communities in the Boston metropolitan area (to be referred to as Alpha, Beta, and Gamma).[3] The three communities differ in socio-economic and political characteristics: Alpha is an upper middle-class community with much political activity: Beta is a lower middle-class community with moderate political activity; and Gamma is a working-class community with little political activity (Table 1).

Above selection reprinted from: *The American Sociological Review*, 28, 1 (February 1963), 69–75.

A content analysis, described in the Appendix, was made of all textbooks used in the civic education programs in Alpha, Beta, and Gamma schools over the past five years (ten texts were investigated in Alpha, eight in Beta, and seven in Gamma). A random sample of paragraphs was selected in each text and classified, where applicable, along one of the following five dimensions:[4]

1. *Emphasis on citizen political participation* —references to voting, norms of civic duty, political activity, and the effectiveness of citizen action in influencing the behavior of public officials.

2. *Political chauvinism*—references to the unique and nationalistic character of "democracy" or "good government" as an American monopoly, and glorified treatment of American political institutions, procedures, and public figures.

3. *The democratic creed*—references to the rights of citizens and minorities to attempt to influence governmental policy through nontyrannical procedures.

4. *Emphasis on political process*—references to politics as an arena involving the actions of politicians, public officials, and the use of power and influence contrasted with references to government as a mechanistic set of institutions allocating services to citizens with a minimum of intervention by political actors.

5. *Emphasis on politics as the resolution of group conflict*—references to political conflicts among economic, social, and ethnoreligious groupings resolved within an agreed-upon framework of political rules of the game.

A second measure of civic education norms consisted of a series of interviews with a pool of "potential civic and educational influentials" in each of the three communities.[5] The interviews included a sample of all school administrators who were responsible for the school's civic education program; all teachers of civic education; the president and vice-president of each school's Parent and Teachers Association or Home and School Association over the past five years; and the current and most recent presidents and vice-presidents of ten major civic groups in each community. Interviewees included leaders of business, fraternal, labor, patriotic, religious, and civic betterment associations, and the chairmen of the local Republican and Democratic party organizations. A total of 66 leaders were interviewed in Alpha, 57 in Beta, and 63 in Gamma.[6]

The interview schedule was designed to tap the intensity of the respondent's attitudes toward the proper orientation of the community school's civic education program in each of the five political dimensions. The content, reliability and sources of the items are presented in Appendix A.

A third measure involved the affects of exposure to a formal course in civic education.[7] A civic education class in each community was matched with a control group in age, academic attainment, parental social class, parental political affiliation, and ethno-religious affiliation. The control group, which did not take a course in civic education, was used to measure the changes in attitudes along the five political dimensions.

These dimensions were adapted for a questionnaire given to the three civic education classes, and their corresponding control groups, before and after a semester's exposure to the course. (see Appendix A). Thus we can compare attitudinal changes attributable to the school's "official version" of political phenomena, and the differential affects of the course in each community.

Findings

The content analysis of textbooks in the civic education programs of Alpha, Beta, and Gamma schools revealed no substantial differences in references to elements of the democratic creed, or in chauvinistic treatment of American political procedures and institutions. Few references in the material employed

Table 1

Socio-Economic and Political Characteristics of Alpha, Beta, and Gamma

Characteristic	Alpha	Beta	Gamma
Per cent of working force in professions	38%	15%	7%
Median family income	$5,900	$4,250	$3,620
Median voting turnout for five gubernatorial elections	67.8%	43.8%	32.1%

Source: U.S. Bureau of the Census, *General Characteristics of the Population, Massachusetts*, Washington: Government Printing Office, 1960, and Secretary of State, *Compilation of Massachusetts Election Statistics: Public Document 43,* Boston: Commonwealth of Massachusetts, 1950-1960.

by the three schools connoted an insular view of American politics; the isolationist and jingoist orientation of civic education texts observed in Pierce's pioneer study were absent in this sampling.[8] Nor does the textual material differ in references endorsing the political rights of minorities and political procedures available to them. Indeed, the endorsement of the democratic creed far exceeds the other political dimensions. The blandness of the Gamma texts should be noted; they contain a large number of descriptive references (dates of major political events, anatomical presentations of political procedure) that could not be classified along one of the five political dimensions (see Table 2).

Differences do exist in the formal exposure to norms supporting political participation, in the view of politics as process, and in the functions of the political system. Unlike Alpha and Beta texts, Gamma texts contain only a few references to norms that encourage voting, feelings of political effectiveness, and a sense of civic duty. References to

Table 2

References on Salient Political Dimensions in Civics Textbooks

Political Dimension	Alpha	Beta	Gamma
Emphasis on democratic creed	56%	52%	47%
Chauvinistic references to American political institutions	3%	6%	2%
Emphasis on political activity, citizen's duty, efficacy	17%	13%	5%
Emphasis on political process, politicians, and power	11%	2%	1%
Emphasis on group conflict-resolving political function	10%	1%	2%
Other	3%	26%	43%
(Totals)	100%	100%	100%
Number of paragraphs	(501)	(367)	(467)

Table 3

Community Leaders' Support of Political Themes in Civic Education Program

Community Leaders	Democratic Creed	Political Chauvinism	Political Participation
Alpha (66)*	87%**	7%	89%
Beta (57)	82%	16%	89%
Gamma (63)	78%	21%	87%
	Politics As Process, Power	Politics As Group Conflict	
Alpha	72%	68%	
Beta	32%	34%	
Gamma	24%	21%	

* Denotes number of cases.
** Per cent of sample strongly agreeing that theme should be taught in civic education program. See interview items in Appendix A.

the political process as a conduit involving political actors and the use of political power—rather than the workings of an invisible hand of governmental institutions—are also sparse in the Gamma texts.

Both Beta and Gamma texts are short on references to politics as a mechanism for settling competing group demands. Table 2 reveals that only Alpha schools indicate to some degree a political process in which politicians and power are the main ingredients, and through which a political group struggle is periodically ameliorated.

How do the norms of civic education that prevail among the potential civic and educational influentials of each community compare with the formal classroom material designed to shape student political attitudes? Are salient themes in the curriculum reinforced, opposed, or ignored by community norms?

Potential community influentials do support the inculcation of basic democratic principles (the democratic creed) and the avoidance of chauvinistic references to American political institutions—attitudes that were stressed in the texts. They also support material encouraging political activity and competence in young citizens, an attitude that is less reinforced in the Gamma school texts.

Table 3 indicates, however, that the potential influentials in the three milieux differ about the presentation of politics as a process involving the resources of politicians and power, and the conflict-alleviating goal of politics. Alpha leaders endorse these "realistic" political themes; and attempts to impart elements of political reality are present only in the Alpha civic education pro-

gram. In Beta and Gamma the low level of support for these themes reinforce the contextual material of their school programs which ignores or avoids these perspectives on political phenomena.

It would be useless to talk about the effects of civic education programs without considering changes in political attitudes as functions of different textual emphasis and norms of community leaders.[9] Comparisons of attitude changes in the schools do not uncover any reversal of beliefs along the five political dimensions that can be attributed to the school's indoctrination.[10]

Several patterns, however, relate the affects of the civic education program on student attitudes to its material and the community's potential political support. Based on the "before" and "after" questionnaires administered to the three classes and matched control groups, the data in Table 4 reveals that students in the civic education classes were more likely to endorse aspects of the democratic creed and less likely to hold chauvinistic political sentiments than students not exposed to the program. But none of the three "exposed" classes was more likely to favor political participation than their control group. And only in Alpha were perceptions of politics as group conflict involving politicians and political power strengthened through exposure to civic education.

In Alpha, Beta, and Gamma, we observe (Table 4) that exposure to the course strengthened support for democratic processes and negated chauvinistic sentiment, thus reinforcing the material presented in the civic education program and supporting attitudes of community leaders. The result is to level the socio-political differences among the

---

three communities and their school populations. Training in the tenets of democratic fair play and tolerance is sustained by civic education courses within a supporting educational and political milieu.

But civic education does not affect the varying positive attitudes toward citizen political participation manifested by the school population of the three communities. Despite the positive references of civic education material in Alpha and Beta, and the supporting community norms in all three communities, different attitudes—based on socio-political cleavages—remain about the citizen's role in public affairs. Apparently attitudes toward political activity are so strongly channeled through other agencies in each community that the civic education program's efforts have little independent effect.

Attitudes toward political process and function are related to other variables in the classroom and community climate.[11] In Alpha, where community attitudes and texts are supportive, a positive change in views of political process and function occurs among students in civic education. In Beta and Gamma, where

Table 4

Effect of Semester Course in Civic Education on Political Attitudes in Three Communities (in Percentages)

| | ALPHA | | | |
| | Class | | Control | |
POLITICAL ATTITUDE	Before	After	Before	After
Support of democratic creed	62*	89	57	61
Political chauvinism	23	8	19	18
Support of political participation	70	72	79	76
Politics as process of power, politicians	59	72	53	58
Function of politics to resolve group conflict	32	59	39	34
Number of cases	(38)		(44)	

| | BETA | | | |
| | Class | | Control | |
POLITICAL ATTITUDE	Before	After	Before	After
Democratic creed	56	74	53	50
Political chauvinism	31	19	29	27
Political participation	55	56	54	49
Political process	23	21	27	26
Political group conflict	17	21	19	17
Number of cases	(51)		(46)	

| | GAMMA | | | |
| | Class | | Control | |
POLITICAL ATTITUDE	Before	After	Before	After
Democratic creed	47	59	38	44
Political chauvinism	29	10	33	38
Political participation	32	29	31	33
Political process	12	15	16	14
Political group conflict	9	12	8	6
Number of cases	(59)		(63)	

* Denotes per cent of sample strongly holding political attitude. See Appendix A for indices.

attitudes and texts are relatively non-supportive little change in such views occurs; politics is treated and learned as a formal, mechanistic set of governmental institutions with emphasis on its harmonious and legitimate nature, rather than as a vehicle for group struggle and change.

Conclusions

The civic education program does not simply reinforce the prevailing sentiments and political climate of the community.[12] Nor are attitudes about political participation and varying levels of political activity affected by courses in civic education. Even a combination of numerous textual references and support from community leaders fails to result in attitude changes about the role of the citizen in public life.

Nevertheless, without some degree of reinforcement from its material and the political environment, the school system's effort at political indoctrination also fails. The materials, support, and affects of civic education differ in the three communities, and it is the nature of these differences that are crucial in evaluating the political role of citizenship training.

All three classes are instructed in the equalitarian ground rules of democracy. Agreement with the maxims of the democratic creed and rejection of political chauvinism are increased in the civic education programs of all three communities. But the material and affects of the working-class community, Gamma, and its civic education program, do not encourage a belief in the citizen's ability to influence government action through political participation. And only the texts and community

support of Alpha are related through its civic education course to a developed awareness of political processes and functions.

In sum, then, students in the three communities are being trained to play different political roles, and to respond to political phenomena in different ways. In the working-class community, where political involve is low, the arena of civic education offers training in the basic democratic procedures without stressing political participation or the citizen's view of conflict and disagreement as indigenous to the political system. Politics is conducted by formal governmental institutions working in harmony for the benefit of citizens.

In the lower middle-class school system of Beta—a community with moderately active political life—training in the elements of democratic government is supplemented by an emphasis on the responsibilities of citizenship, not on the dynamics of public decisionmaking.

Only in the affluent and politically vibrant community (Alpha) are insights into political processes and functions of politics passed on to these who, judging from their socio-economic and political environment, will likely man those positions that involve them in influencing or making political decisions.

Appendix

The content analysis of the 27 civic education textbooks was conducted in the following manner. A random sample of paragraphs, as the content unit, was selected from each text. The text was entered by use of a random table of numbers to select page and paragraph. Every twentieth paragraph was read and classified by the writer and two other judges. The criteria of classification are noted in the text. In case of disagreement among the judges, a paragraph was classified in the "other" category. Dominant emphasis, based on sentence counts within paragraphs, was determining when a paragraph contained more than one politically relevant theme. In this manner, 1,235 paragraphs were classified.

Five indices were used in the questionnaire administered to the student populations, and the interview with community leaders. Responses ran across a five-point scale from "agree strongly" to "disagree strongly." Unlike the students, the community leaders were asked whether or not each statement should be included in the civic education program. The content, reliability, and source of the political indices follow.

1. *The Democratic Creed:* (coefficient of reliability = .911)

    Every citizen should have an equal chance to influence government policy.

    Democracy is the best form of government.

    The minority should be free to criticize government decisions.

    People in the minority should be free to try to win majority support for their opinions.

    (Adapted from James W. Prothro and Charles M. Grigg, "Fundamental Principles of Democracy: Bases of Agreement and Disagreement," *The Journal of Politics*, 22 (1960), pp. 276–294).

2. *Political Chauvinism:* (cr = .932)

    The American political system is a model that foreigners would do well to copy.

    The founding fathers created a blessed and unique republic when they gave us the constitution.

    Americans are more democratic than any other people.

    American political institutions are the best in the world.

    (Index constructed for this study).

3. *Political Activity:* (cr = .847)

    It is not very important to vote in local elections.

    It is very important to vote even when so many other people vote in an election.

    Public officials do care what people like me think.

    Given the complexity of issues and political organizations there is little an individual can do to make effective changes in the political system.

    People like me do not have any say about what the government does.

    Politics is often corrupt and the interests of the underworld are looked after by some public officials.

    (Adapted from the civic duty and sense of political effectiveness measures of the Michigan Survey Research Center, and Agger's index of political cynicism. See Angus Campbell, Gerald Gurin, and Warren E. Miller, *The Voter Decides*, Evanston: Row-Peterson, 1954, pp. 187–204, and Robert E. Agger, Marshall N. Goldstein, and Stanley A. Pearl, "Political Cynicism: Measurement and Meaning," *The Journal of Politics*, 23 (1961), pp. 477–506.

4. *Political Process:* (cr = .873)

    The use of political power is crucial in public affairs.

    Many political decisions are made by a minority of political activists who seek to secure the agreement of the majority to the decisions.

    Politics is basically a conflict in which groups and individuals compete for things of value.

    Differences of race, class, and income are important considerations in many political issues.

    Governmental institutions cannot operate without politicians.

    (Index constructed for this study).

5. *Political Function:* (cr = .919).
   Politics should settle social and other disagreements as its major function.
   Since different groups seek favorable treatment, politics is the vehicle for bargaining among these competing claims.

Politics is not a means of insuring complete harmony, but a way of arriving at temporary agreements about policies within agreed-upon rules.
The politician is the key broker among competing claims made within society.
(Index constructed for this study).

NOTES

1. V. O. Key, Jr., *Public Opinion and American Democracy*, New York: Knopf, 1961, p. 316.

2. On the relationship between education and politics, consult H. Mark Roelofs, *The Tension of Citizenship*, New York: Holt, Rinehart, 1957, Charles E. Merriam, *The Making of Citizens*, Chicago: University of Chicago Press, 1931, Franklin Patterson, *High Schools for a Free Society*, Glencoe: The Free Press, 1960, James S. Coleman, *The Adolescent Society*, New York: The Free Press of Glencoe, 1961, William Gellerman, *The American Legion as Educator*, New York: Teachers College, Columbia University, 1938, George A. Male, "The Michigan Education Association as a Pressure Group," unpublished Ph.D. thesis, University of Michigan, 1950, Thomas H. Eliot, "Toward an Understanding of Public School Politics," *American Political Science Review*, 53 (December, 1959), pp. 1032–1051, Bessie L. Pierce, *Citizens' Organizations and the Civic Training of Youth*, New York: Scribner's, 1933, Albert Alexander, "The Gray Flannel Cover on the American History Textbook," *Social Education*, 24 (January, 1960), pp.11–14, Robert A. Dahl, *Who Governs? Democracy and Power in an American City*, New Haven: Yale University Press, 1961, pp. 316–318, Herbert Hyman, *Political Socialization*, Glencoe: The Free Press, 1959, Fred I. Greenstein, "The Benevolent Leader: Children's Images of Political Authority," *American Political Science Review*, 54 (December, 1960), pp. 934–943, Herbert McClosky and Harold E. Dahlgren, "Primary Group Influence on Party Loyalty," *American Political Science Review*, Vol. 53 (September, 1959), pp. 757–776, Robert D. Hess and David Easton, "The Child's Changing Image of the President," *Public Opinion Quarterly*, 24 (Winter, 1960), pp. 632–644, Fred I. Greenstein, "More on Children's Images of the President," *Public Opinion Quarterly*, Vol. 25 (Winter, 1961), pp. 648–654, Henry W. Riecken, "Primary Groups and Political Party Choice," in Eugene Burdick and Arthur J. Brodbeck (eds.), *American Voting Behavior*, Glencoe: The Free Press, 1959, pp. 162–183, and Eleanor E. Maccoby, Richard E. Matthews and Alton S. Morton, "Youth and Political Change," *Public Opinion Quarterly*, 18 (Spring, 1954), pp. 23–39.

3. Course titles of civic education instruction vary in the three communities. A control group was available in the same schools of Alpha and Gamma where the civic education course was not required. For Beta, a control group was selected from a school in an adjoining, and comparable community.

4. Based on procedures developed in Bernard B. Berelson, *Content Analysis in Communications Research*, Glencoe: The Free Press, 1952, and Lloyd Marcus, *The*

Treatment of Minorities in Secondary School Textbooks, New York: B'nai B'rith Anti-Defamation League, 1961.

5. The designation "potential civic and educational leaders or influentials" is used because we have no data on overt attempts to influence the school's civic education program. Our immediate concern is with their attitudes toward the political themes in the program. This distinction between manifested and imputed political influence is drawn in Raymond Wolfinger, "Reputation and Reality in the Study of Community Power," *American Sociological Review*, 25 (October, 1960), pp. 636–644.

6. Wherever possible, civic leaders were selected from comparable organizations in each community, such as the Chamber of Commerce and political party organizations. Differences in social structure made complete matching impossible. For example, labor union leaders were included in the Gamma sample, but not in the Alpha or Beta pools. There were 8 non-respondents or 12 per cent of the sample in Alpha, 7 (13%) in Beta, and 11 (18%) in Gamma.

7. On changes in political attitudes through formal civic education or government instruction, see Albert Somit, Joseph Tanenhaus, Walter H. Wilke, and Rita W. Cooley, "The Effect of the Introductory Political Science Course on Student Attitudes toward Personal Political Participation" [in this volume, pp. 404–409 (ed.)], and the extensive literature summarized and evaluated by Neal Gross, "Memorandum on Citizenship Education in American Secondary Schools," unpublished manuscript, Cambridge, Massachusetts: August, 1960.

8. Bessie L. Pierce, *Civic Attitudes in American Schools*, Chicago: University of Chicago Press, 1930.

9. Note James S. Coleman, "Comment on Three Climate of Opinion Studies," *Public Opinion Quarterly*, 25 (Winter, 1961), pp. 607–610.

10. Efforts to relate content, procedure, and environment of civic education instruction to changes in political attitudes are critically reviewed in Gross, *op. cit.* See especially Donald Oliver and Susan Baker, "The Case Method," *Social Education*, 23 (January, 1959), pp. 25–28, Stanley E. Diamond, "Studies and Projects in Citizenship Education," in Franklin Patterson, editor, *Citizenship and the American High School*, New York: mimeographed, 1959, pp. IV, 1–40, and Charles C. Peters, *Teaching High School History and Social Studies for Citizenship Training*, Coral Gables, Florida: The University of Miami, 1948.

11. A comparable investigation of this problem in advancement to college has been made by Natalie Rogoff, "Public Schools and Equality of Opportunity," *Journal of Educational Sociology*, 33 (February, 1960), pp. 252–279.

12. On the influence of "climate of opinion" on socio-political attitudes in the secondary schools, see James S. Coleman, "Comment on Three Climate of Opinion Studies," *op. cit.*, and Martin L. Levin, "Social Climate and Political Socialization," *Public Opinion Quarterly*, 25 (Winter, 1961), pp. 596–606.

POLITICAL LEADERSHIP AND THE LATE VICTORIAN PUBLIC SCHOOL

- Rupert Wilkinson

Between about 1870 and the First World War the Public Schools developed many of the features that make them a controversial topic today. Yet, in the flood of literature that they have inspired, there have been few objective attempts to assess the Victorian Public Schools in terms of their own ends. Even those critics who have charged the schools with defending social inequality and stifling individualism have not generally questioned the schools' efficiency at producing the kind of product they *wanted* to produce.

What, then, was this product? It is the argument here that behind the goal of 'Character-building' the Victorian Public Schools' prime purpose—however tacit and unofficial—was a state purpose, the output of capable public servants.[1] From this point of view, therefore, the best way to judge the Victorian Public School is to ask what qualities of the public servant it seemed to foster. Before we ask this question, however, we should first establish that the schools were indeed bent on the performance of a government 'supply function,' directing their students towards government careers.

The Supply Function

In 1821, Samuel Butler, one-time headmaster of Shrewsbury, could define the

Above selection reprinted from: *British Journal of Sociology*, 13 (1962), 320–330.

Public School as a place where 'boys are educated in the higher department of literature, with a view to their entrance into public life.'[2] Some forty-three years later, the schools were considered enough of a national institution to warrant a Public Schools Act which strengthened the headmasters' appointive powers and called for government approval of each school's controlling body. Despite these straws in the wind, however, the relationship between the Public Schools and the State was unofficial and indirect.[3] As the process of Civil Service reform progressed—a process that culminated in 1870 with the institution of open competition examinations for the Administrative Class—so the Public Schools adjusted their own standards. Uppingham's Edward Thring represented a new era of headmaster reformers who, encouraged by the Clarendon Commission of 1864 and strengthened by the Public Schools Act, widened and intensified the curriculum.

Behind the political role of the Public Schools lay two factors that only came fully into play during the nineteenth century. The first was an improvement in communications, encouraging more and more parents who could afford it to send their sons away to boarding school.[4] Both in speech and outlook the Public Schools began to exert a unifying influence on the upper classes and to create a central pool of leadership trainees.

This pool the schools expanded—and

here lay the second factor in their political influence—by opening their gates to members of the rising middle classes.[5] Thomas Arnold's formula of the 'Christian gentleman' had formed a satisfactory basis for the co-education of the professional man's son and the aristocrat. The Public Schools' new-found emphasis on 'Character' suited the devout respectability of the middle classes; the schools' claim to inculcate gentlemanly manners met the landed classes' requirements of 'good taste' and, at the same time, satisfied bourgeois ambitions.[6]

Despite the advance of the middle classes, opinion in the major Public Schools retained all the prejudices that the landed gentry traditionally felt about careers. Government service and the Church were considered best; Law and Teaching—at the right place—were acceptable, often more so than Medicine; Trade was viewed as a some-what vulgar necessity.[7] School institutions, moreover, propagated the virtues of 'noblesse oblige:' the first school Mission to slum areas was founded in 1869, and in many Public Schoolboys' lives the duties of 'fagging' came long before the privileges of being a prefect. The Public School, in short, made public servants by making gentlemen.

Other facets of school life also played their part in promoting the prestige of government service. There was the network of school custom and etiquette, unwritten rules of behaviour that stressed teamwork and 'House spirit' as well as a hierarchy of rank and privilege.[8] There was the glorified institution of Games, with its colourful train of honours awarded to the heroes who brought prestige upon their community.

And finally, there was the factor of boarding-school hardship itself, ac-climatizing young men to the material drawbacks of working for the government. In their monastic seclusion and their unheated dormitories, the Public Schools surely had a complete counter-part to the family sacrifice and physical discomfort of the military officer and the Imperial administrator.

Character and Organization

What sort of leader did the Victorian Public School in fact tend to produce? How well suited was he to the pattern of British government, how well equipped to deal with its problems?

In Parliament and Public Schools alike, the political process depended on internalized, ethical restraints as much as on coercive law to curb the arbitrary exercise of power. A largely unwritten Constitution and a national executive whose control of the legislature was—as it is today—tempered by custom and usage found their counterparts in the organization of Public School government. By 1880 prefectorial power in many schools had expanded to the point where it really represented an admin-istration, a judiciary and part of the legislature—in conjunction with each housemaster—rolled into one.[9] Despite the absence of formal checks on their actions, however, prefects generally behaved with some self-restraint. Custom and etiquette helped to foster such self-restraint: it prescribed 'fair play' and the 'light touch' in command, and by ordaining a hierarchy of priv-ileges for each age-group it limited the scope of prefectorial legislation.[10] This is not to say that prefectorial abuse of power never occurred. But when one remembers the bullying and virtual anarchy of the pre-Arnoldian Public School, it becomes clear that forces of self-restraint were at work during the Late Victorian period.

If Public School education helped to produce responsible government, it also supported what Walter Bagehot called 'dignified' government, rulers whose authority was enhanced by a differentiated style and the magic of ceremony. The mark of the Public Schoolboy was not only his distinctive accent but the casual assurance of the man who knows he was brought up to lead. In addition to supplying their members with a style of command, the Public Schools also accustomed them to the pomp and circumstance of state. Just as Buckingham Palace Changed the Guards, so Eton held its Procession of Boats; just as the Crown inspired rhapsodies about the historic community, so Clifton Chapel inspired the same.

Even greater than the Public Schools' emphasis on self-restraint and 'style' was the weight the schools placed upon communal loyalties and deference to authority. Here they were perfectly in tune with the requirements of political life: the discipline of the parliamentary party—especially the Tory party; and the loyal reticence and emotional detachment of the civil servant. Although the Victorian period saw a basic standardization of Public School institutions,[11] it was also the time when each school strove to make itself a unique object of loyalty by elaborating its own folklore, language and customs, and—for some—by stressing its own special variant of football.[12] Frequently, there were examinations in the school lore, teaching the entering 'newboy'

to treat the smallest customs as beautiful accoutrements in his reverencing of the community. For, like Edmund Burke, the Public Schools posed their institutions as vehicles of historic wisdom —although in fact some of these vehicles were unknown before the days of Thomas Arnold.

It was against this trend that books like Rudyard Kipling's *Stalky & Co.* were directed. As Kipling pointed out, the Public Schools' new-found attachment to regulation, discipline and group loyalties brooked ill for the schoolboy who might have wanted to go his own way. I say '*might* have wanted' because the system, by playing on aesthetic emotion, usually made its members *want* to conform to a narrowly-prescribed pattern of life and to identify their private desires with a mystical fondness for the community. Only the most resilient individualist would willingly adopt an independent style of behaviour when he knew that etiquette classed such behaviour as showing bad taste. At Winchester, for example, walking to class alone was frowned upon, and the boy who made close friends in a house other than his own was thought by some to be lacking in 'House spirit.'[14]

The division of the Public School into fairly autonomous and constantly competing Houses tended, where this happened, to magnify group loyalties. In the small community it is difficult for the individual to seek freedom in anonymity and to defy the customs that the majority hold sacred. The small community, moreover, can often claim special affection by its nearness to the individual, its ability to appear as a living thing rather than a remote and abstract concept.

Those Public Schools which severely limited individual privacy were in a particularly favourable position for inducing group loyalties and the spirit of close co-operation.[15] Communal living meant that the minority who might have resisted irrational appeals to tradition and 'good taste' were confronted abruptly and constantly by the majority, those who are always content to follow convention. If the Public School dwarfed the individual against the community and made the latter a value in itself, it only did so via public opinion.

In a certain technical sense, therefore, Public School society was *nationalist*. By playing on the individual's very desires, it induced him to seek vicarious pleasure in closely identifying himself with, and subordinating himself to, the group and its aspirations. From this it followed that Public School values supported the British ideal of *voluntary* co-operation —however the voluntary element was induced. It was an ideal that appeared in L. S. Amery's service to the new Commonwealth 'as a co-operative venture—of vivid human interest as well as practical promise.'[16] It appeared in the voluntary service of amateurs—the J.P.'s and village council chairmen— that made a measure of decentralized administration economical. Above all, it appeared in the sensitivity to an informally gauged consensus which marked Cabinet government: the co-operative nature of Cabinet responsibility, and the fact that parliamentary deliberation could only affect executive policy because ministers paid attention to the 'ear' of the House.

Despite the voluntary element, the unquestioning loyalties that Public School life tended to encourage were ultimately hostile to the inquiring mentality. This placed the onus for developing the imagination all the more squarely on the academic curriculum. In the eyes of the authorities concerned, the latter was meant to provide a general, 'non-vocational' education; what it amounted to, in fact, was a syllabus focusing mainly on the classics —a specialist bias that it shared with Oxford and Cambridge as well as the Civil Service examiners. By 1900, admittedly, most leading Public Schools had extended their curricula to languages and science; at Uppingham Edward Thring introduced fine arts; and in many schools Chapel became the Music Master's stronghold. Nevertheless, the classics remained supreme, both in hours devoted to them and in the weighting of marks.

The treatment of the classics themselves hardly fulfilled the ideal of a broad, liberal arts education. For most Public Schoolboys, classical studies usually meant long hours of translation that left little time to consider literary content and meaning. 'They laboriously toiled at the scaffolding and never built the house.'[17] Granted, however, the rigours of Latin translation did provide a general training of the mind, an exercise in logic and analysis. Like Mathematics, Latin demanded a disciplined manner of thought following set rules; it is significant in this regard to note that Eton and Marlborough employed more teachers in Mathematics than in any field except Classics. And even the fact-'cramming' that many schools were prone to could be called a form of general education, an attempt to improve memory-power, an attempt based on the assumption that the memory can be stretched like a muscle.

In general, the Public Schools gave their members an admiration for versatility. They encouraged them to believe that what the leader needed for his job were, primarily, general qualities of mind. Embued with these, the leader might forgo specialized training, the techniques of theorizing in advance. British parliamentary government, for its part, posed a special need for the versatile leader. The Cabinet minister, after all, changes portfolio every few years, he has to debate legislation as well as run a department, and since the Cabinet is a collective entity, he must show quick grasp of problems confronting his colleagues. In the Civil Service, specialists are usually found in advisory roles, away from the command hierarchy; and the bureaucrat respects the political chief, however much of an amateur the latter may be in departmental affairs.

All in all, what intellectual qualities did the Public Schools tend to develop? It is my contention that the schools bred mental flexibility rather than imaginative foresight. Faced with an urgent need to change, the Old Public Schoolboy was usually resourceful in his adjustment; confronted by crisis, he would 'muddle through.' What he frequently lacked was the interest in new ideas that would have helped him to avoid crisis by looking ahead. If he possessed intelligence, he was also apt to be complacent.

Part of the trouble was the way in which moral indoctrination permeated the curriculum. Since most masters beneath the Sixth Form treated Latin as a moral, as well as mental, discipline, it was not surprising that they paid little attention to evoking student curiosity. By the late Victorian era, Samuel Smiles had entered the classroom: hard work —especially unpleasant work, for hardship 'built Character'—was regarded a virtue in itself. In *A Schoolmaster's Apology*, Cyril Alington—one-time headmaster of Shrewsbury and later of Eton —displayed the same moral pre-occupation when he confessed that he was 'more anxious that a boy should have to deal, and know that he is dealing, with gentlemen than that he should be taught the best subjects by the best methods.'[18] Long before he wrote this, Alington's predecessors had downgraded the pursuit of learning for its own sake by permitting the glorification of Games. During the 1870's and 1880's, prefectorial power passed from the scholar to the athlete, and the playing field surpassed Chapel as the guardian of manly virtue.

But Games provided only one way by which the schools claimed to instil Character. Etiquette and custom roped off great sections of a schoolboy's life from the exercise of individual reason; they demanded an unquestioning faith in tradition and instinctive obedience to authority. 'The business of a school,' wrote a Harrow headmaster, 'is to work and to get on with its life without bothering about whys and wherefores and abstract justice and the democratic principle.'[19] Isolation from the contrasts of the outside world fostered intellectual conformity by the same token that it cemented the rule of custom. Politically, this phenomenon was very noticeable. According to one witness, the Wellington headmaster who married Gladstone's daughter found that his alliance 'was not an advantage to the Master of a school whose boys came from largely conservative families, to whom distrust and dislike of the great Liberal leader was almost an article of faith.'[20] Somewhat earlier, a headmaster of Clifton who was himself a Liberal incurred similar unpopularity.

To the extent, therefore, that conflict of ideas develops the imagination, the Late Victorian Public School bred complacence—in thought, if not in action. It would be wrong, on the other hand, to charge the schools with doing nothing whatever to produce adaptability when conditions obviously required it. The unwritten nature of Public School tradition did enable it to change gradually, to invest new institutions with a false aura of antiquity. Criticism and minor reform did stem from internal sources: Old Boy rebels and strong headmasters. And certain features of extracurricular life—student publications, for instance, and debate clubs—probably induced flexible thinking. But sometimes it seemed as if those very qualities of adaptability, added to vast reserves of self-assurance, discouraged the Public Schoolboy from showing imaginative foresight. The confidence that he could handle crises when they came along reduced his efforts to avoid them in the first place. (Hence the pride underlying such popular sayings as 'the Englishman loses every battle but the last' and 'Britain somehow muddles through.')

Behind the civil service ideal of the generalist, after all, lay the belief that a properly educated man didn't need to indulge in advance theorizing; a developed memory and a quick mind should enable him to grasp the practical essentials of each problem as it arose.

This assumption comes out in the speeches of Stanley Baldwin. It is significant that Baldwin, with his unusual ability to sense national moods and attitudes, should feel that he could express such opinions in public—and with such obvious relish:

> The English schoolboy, for his eternal salvation, is impervious to the receipt of learning, and by that means preserves his mental faculties further into middle age and old age than he otherwise would . . .
>
> The Englishman is made for a time of crisis and for a time of emergency. He is serene in difficulties but may appear to be indifferent when times are easy. He may not look ahead, he may not heed warnings, he may not prepare, but when once he starts he is persistent to the death and he is ruthless in action. It is these gifts that have made the Englishman what he is, and that have enabled the Englishman to make England what it is.[21]

No one could deny that the men who came from the Late Victorian Public Schools, men who dominated the national leadership at least until the Second World War, showed general adaptibility to the requirements of change. At home, the Conservative party, like the Constitution itself, *did* adjust to the implications of political and economical democracy; abroad, empire *did* give way to commonwealth. Throughout these immense changes, Britain retained stable and effective government.

Nonetheless, there were two great failures of the national leadership during this period: the military policy of World War One, with its terrible human cost, and the failure to arm against Hitler in the 1930's. From the educationist's viewpoint, both cases have something in common. In both, entirely novel conditions appeared so rapidly that only the most vigorous imagination could have appreciated them in time to avert disaster. In both cases, too, attitudes engendered by Public School education reinforced rather than offset a short-sightedness that British leadership may have possessed anyway. To put it differently—the intellectual shortcomings of the Public Schools comprised one factor, and only one, in the two great failures of British national leadership.

At this point, it may, of course, be argued that the Public Schools did produce outstanding minds, frequently among those who reacted against their schooldays. The answer to this is that the truly inventive few will indeed survive most education systems. What counts, however, is the number of leaders ready and able to *implement* the ideas of this truly inventive few. And it is here that Public School limitations were most felt.

In World War One, for example, few of the top commanders possessed the imagination to understand new technological conditions. The convoy system, the machine-gun, the tank and the mortar—key innovations all—were implemented *against* the advice of the senior professionals by Lloyd George himself, sometimes aided by his Cabinet Secretary Maurice Hankey, sometimes by an energetic temporary soldier or a few junior officers.[22] Unfortunately for the senior commander, the techniques he had once learned in the field suddenly became obsolete with the advent of war. His reluctance to discard these techniques, moreover, was not likely to be lessened by a Public School outlook. The O.T.C., the Public School's one

exception to the rule prescribing non-technical education, taught an old-fashioned brand of warfare, and the school curriculum did little to teach respect for Science.

Then again, the Public School characteristic of unquestioning loyalty and fondness for tradition found its counterpart in similar attitudes that the military profession tends to instil anyway. (Thus, before the Somme offensive, considerations of loyalty seem to have inhibited Haig's army commander, General Rawlinson, from strongly criticizing the plans of attack, though 'privately he was convinced that they were based on false premises.'[23] Please note, however, that we are not singling out the Public Schools as the sole source of World War folly. All we can say is the education system failed to offset the intellectual shortcomings that military habits tend to breed. This failure was particularly unfortunate in the First World War where the British generals and admirals wielded more power *vis-à-vis* than they did in the Second.

During the 1930's, the threat of Naziism called for a special display of imagination by the British Government since England herself had not known a dictator since Cromwell. Here again, attitudes which the Public Schools endorsed formed a fatal combination with other beliefs and values. To the latter—the pacifist principles of a George Lansbury, for example, and the desire for comfort of a war-sickened people—were added opinions more typical of a Public School outlook: the over-confidence and narrow vision created by what Sir Arthur Salter termed the 'psychology of island immunity;' the premium placed by some leaders on discipline and political stability and, consequently, their respect during 1934 and 1935 for German rebuilding; the Conservatives' tendency to fear Communism more than Fascism.[24] At crucial points the Public School set of values failed to perform a 'countercyclical'[25] function that might have produced a quicker national response to the German threat. In other words, attitudes fostered by Public School life reinforced rather than countered trends of opinion that sprang from other factors in the social environment. The 'psychology of island immunity' could originate with monastic schooldays no less than with the facts of national geography and a proud naval tradition. Likewise, the penchant for *voluntary* co-operation that delayed the introduction of conscription and consumption controls characterized Public School life as much as it did the values of democracy and the whole British national character.[26]

Conclusion

The danger that any government faces when it dominates education is twofold. First, it runs the risk of starving professions that nourish the state materially and intellectually. It may do this both by luring able youth away from these professions and by developing unsuitable characteristics in those who do enter them. The Victorian Public School, for example, did little to help commerce and technology: a forum for anti-trade and even anti-Science snobbery, it instilled attitudes which were not generally sympathetic to risk-taking individualism and technological innovation.[27] Likewise, the Public School champion-

ing of the traditional English gentleman figure, with his love of customary procedure and the amateur style, was not friendly to new, expert methods of getting things done. This applied to the civil service—e.g. the Treasury accounting system,[28] and the tepid attitude toward jet engine development—as well as to British industry.

The second liability in making education a political device is that it easily tends to produce unimaginative policy-makers. The easiest way to inspire government-orientation in a majority of students is to employ methods of sub-rational indoctrination and to instil an unquestioning brand of group loyalty. And if particular stress is laid on the magical function of government, the education system will be specially prone to make the aesthetic taste of the group, rather than rational explanation and individual reason, the basis for student behaviour.

For all their intellectual weaknesses, the Public Schools did avoid the worst effects of these two liabilities. They were always able to supply several, quite distinct professions—within government, as well as outside it. Their curriculum, despite Samuel Smiles and the obsession with adversity, never had to take the main brunt of moral indoctrination; and, as a result, the academic side to Public School life tempered somewhat the anti-individualist characteristic of the social side. The leaders the system produced were intelligent, hardworking, honest and responsible. It was only sometimes that events challenged their ability to imagine bold schemes, little related to past experience. It was only then that one could wonder, 'Were their boyhood sacrifices really worth it?'

NOTES

1. Including Churchmen. Just as the state maintained close ties with the Church of England, so the Public Schools could claim many churchmen not only among their Old Boys but among dons and headmasters.

2. Samuel Butler, *Letter to Henry Brougham*, Shrewsbury, Eddowes, 1821.

3. In this respect, the comparison between the Public Schools and Confucian education (after the *Han* dynasties) is particularly interesting. Although the state function of Confucian education was much more explicit, it resembled the Public Schools very closely in the way it made public service part of a gentleman ideal, in the way it used *aesthetic* devices to promote that ideal, and in the way its classical curriculum prepared students for civil service examinations.

4. Vivian Ogilvie, *The English Public School*, London, Batsford, 1957, p. 123. Cf. Asa Briggs, *Victorian People*, Chicago U.P., 1955, p. 141.

5. R. Lewis and M. A. Maude, *The English Middle Classes*, New York, Knopf, 1950, pp. 16–17. Asa Briggs, op. cit., pp. 144–5.

6. Cf. 'synthetic gentility,' E. Wingfield-Stratford, *The Squire and His Relations*, London, Cassells, 1956, p. 389.

7. Cf. R. Lewis and A. Maude, op. cit., pp. 44–5. There is some evidence that the 'private professions' occupied a middle ground in prestige between public service and commercial enterprise. T. H. Pear's description of social attitudes towards and within the professions is relevant here. T. H. Pear, *English Social Differences*, London, Allen & Unwin, 1955, pp. 22, 37, etc.

8. Cf. E. H. Pitcairn, *Unwritten Laws & Ideals of Active Careers*, London, Smith Elder, 1899, pp. 286–9.

9. F. B. Malim, *Almae Matres*, Cambridge University Press, 1948, p. 21.

10. C. E. Pascoe, *Everyday Life in Our Public Schools*, London, Griffith & Farran, 1881, p. 23. T. H. Escott, *England: Its People, Polity and Pursuits*, London, Chapman & Hall, 1885, pp. 295–6.

11. Both the Public School Act and the Headmasters' Conference (established 1869) helped to standardize the Public Schools. In style and outlook, there were shared characteristics despite 'differences in superficial fashion.' Wingfield-Stratford, op. cit., pp. 396–7.

12. Edward Mack, *The Public Schools and British Opinion Since 1860*, London, Methuen, 1938, pp. 122–4. C. E. Pascoe, op. cit., pp. 115, 244. Vivian Ogilvie, op. cit., pp. 181–3.

13. Vivian Ogilvie, ibid., p. 181. G. F. Lamb, *The Happiest Days*, London, Michael Joseph, 1959, pp. 19–26.

14. G. F. Lamb, ibid., p. 20.

15. Bernard Darwin, *The English Public School*, London, Longmans, Green, 1929, p. 88.

16. L. S. Amery, *My Political Life*, Vol. II, London, Hutchinson, 1953, p. 352.

17. Malim, *Almae Matres*, op. cit., p. 124.

18. Edward Mack, quoted by, op. cit., pp. 299–300.

19. T. C. Worsley, quoted by, *Barbarians & Philistines,* London, Hale, 1940, p. 133.

20. Malim, *Almae Matres,* op. cit., p.83.

21. Speech to Royal Society of St George, 1924. See this and other speeches in *On England,* by Stanley Baldwin, London, Allan, 1926.

22. L. S. Amery, op. cit., 119–20, 122–3. J. F. C. Fuller, *The Army in My Time,* London, Rich & Cowan, 1935, pp. 135–40. B. H. Liddell Hart, *Outline of the War,* London, Faber, 1936, pp. 127, 168–70.

23. B. H. Liddell Hart, ibid. p. 122, quoting *The Official History of World War One.*

24. J. F. Kennedy, *Why England Slept,* London, May Fair, 1962, pp. 27, 28, 52, 172–3.

25. David Riesman uses the word 'counter-cyclical' mainly in connection with a school system's position on academic freedom. David Riesman, *Constraint & Variety in American Education,* New York, Doubleday, 1958. Nevertheless, it can be used in other contexts as well. If the Public Schools have served to counter potentially dangerous trends in British society, they have served on the side of conservatism and stability rather than that of intellectual criticism and theoretical imagination.

26. J. F. Kennedy, op. cit., p. 112. Escott, op. cit., p. 441.

27. For an account of the way in which technical specialization was considered ungentlemanly, see Eric Ashby, *Technology and the Academics,* London, Macmillan, 1958, especially Chapter 3.

28. Hugh Massingham, 'Our Man in Threadneedle Street', *The Queen,* London, Stevens Press, Feb. 6th, 1962.

SWEET LAND OF LIBERTY

• H. H. Remmers and R. D. Franklin

Congress shall make no law respecting an establishment of religion or prohibiting the free exercise thereof; or abridging the freedom of the press; or the right of the people peaceably to assemble; and to petition the government for a redress of grievances.

—Article I, Bill of Rights

Possibly because applications of the First Amendment of the United States Constitution are "controversial," they are not well taught by the agencies primarily responsible—the home and the school—for the meaning of this amendment is rejected by many who will shortly be voting citizens, i.e., teenagers. A very reasonable inference is that this general proposition holds for the adult population, too, as will appear below.

Beginning early in the McCarthy era (1951) the Purdue Opinion Panel in its regular operations has at various times polled a nationally representative sample of high-school students regarding their attitudes toward relevant current applications of the Bill of Rights. The results have not been reassuring.

Before presenting them, however, in view of fairly widespread suspicions of polls and their results, perhaps a bit of legitimatizing of such results is in order.

Predictions of election outcomes based on pre-election polls constitute the most convincing evidence of the validity of adult poll results. Here the Purdue poll, based on representative samples of 2,000

to 3,000 individuals, have come off at least as well as the Gallup, Roper, and other polls. We have asked, at about mid-October, "If the coming election were being held today and you could vote in it, for whom would you vote?" Our results predicted the winners and the popular vote with less than one per cent error. For example, our figures in the 1960 election were:

Kennedy-Johnson	47.1%
Nixon-Lodge	46.6%
Some other candidate	1.0%
I wouldn't vote	4.0%
No response	1.3%

Our pre-election polls of 1952 and 1956 were similarly accurate. Apparently, youngsters faithfully reflect their parents' political orientation. Further evidence of close correspondence between many parents' and children's attitudes has been presented elsewhere.*

Abridgment of the freedom of the press is by no means abhorrent to many if not most of our young citizens. In fact, it is less so now than it was ten years ago, as these figures show in response to the statement: "Newspapers and magazines should be allowed to print anything they want except military secrets."

	1951	1960
Agree	45%	29%
Disagree	41%	51%
Undecided	14%	19%
No response	0	1%

* H. H. Remmers, Chapter 4, "Early Socialization," in *American Political Behavior.* Burdick and Brodbeck (editors). Glencoe, Ill.: Free Press, 1959.

Above selection reprinted from *Phi Delta Kappan*, 44, October, 1962, 22–27.

347

The above is clearly a very general statement of the meaning of "freedom of the press." When the issue is made more specific, only 11 per cent vote for no limitation on "the sale and distribution of 'objectionable' printed matter." "Objectionable" was defined as material that many or most people consider "sexy, profane, obscene, immoral, filthy, etc." How should it be limited?

	Total	Boys	Girls
Prohibited entirely	40%	27%	52%
Limited to adults	27%	31%	23%
Limited to adults and teen-agers	19%	25%	13%
Not prohibited or limited at all	11%	13%	8%
No response	3%	4%	4%

"Objectionable" movies fare about the same as printed matter. Only 8 per cent vote for no prohibition or limitation.

More than three-fourths (77 per cent) of our teen-agers say that the U.S. Post Office should continue to prosecute "persons who use the mails to send obscene materials." Further probing of the issue of who should censor printed matter, movies, TV programs, etc., revealed that the federal government is the clear favorite to act as censor:

A federal board or committee set up by Congress	41%
Public opinion	32%
A national Committee of religious leaders from all faiths	27%
A state group	23%
A local citizens committee	23%
Parents	20%
Whoever publishes or produces the material	13%
No one	6%

Since instructions were to "Mark as many as you wish," the percentages add to more than 100. Obviously, in the eyes of the teen-ager the federal government is much more trustworthy in defining and limiting what is objectionable than are parents. Fears of federal thought-control through censorship are evidently not very salient.

The occasions or reasons teen-agers list for limiting or prohibiting printed matter, movies, and the like come as no surprise since the advent of Freud. Frequency of choice:

Sex-perversion, sexual promiscuity, pornography, etc.	63%
Irreligion—profanity, atheism, etc.	43%
Political—un-Americanism, radicalism, etc.	35%
Violence—assault, sadism, gore, etc.	28%
They shouldn't be limited or prohibited for any reason	15%

It seems clear that controversy concerning issues of censorship will continue and that freedom of the press is not likely to be the absolute that a strict construction of the First Amendment language appears to make it. The psychological mechanism of projection ("It won't influence me, but think of all those with less character!") will continue to ensure such controversy. As the late Heywood Broun once observed, "To the pure all things are rotten." Thus Anthony Comstock, responsible for most of the federal statutes on use of the mail for obscene purposes, was active shortly after the turn of the century in attempting to obtain federal legislation to prohibit the exposure to view of unclothed wooden manikins used in store window displays.

Further specific probing of attitudes toward freedom of the press yields no comfort to those who would protect this right guaranteed in the First Amendment. The typical teen-ager believes that "police and other groups" should have the power to impose censorship as shown in the following item:

1. "Police and other groups have sometimes banned or censored certain books and movies in their cities. Should they or should they not have power to do this?"

	1951	1960
Should	60%	60%
Should not	27%	24%
Uncertain	13%	15%
No response	0	4%

Obviously, there has been no significant change with respect to this issue over the ten-year period from 1951 to 1960.

One question aimed at another facet of attitudes toward freedom of the press, as follows:

2. "Some cities have passed laws against printing or selling any Communist literature. Do you think such laws should or should not be passed?"

	1951	1960
Should	66%	61%
Should not	21%	21%
Uncertain	13%	14%
No response	0	2%

If this attitude, again substantially unchanged over a ten-year period, were to be implemented, we should indeed be cutting off our nose to spite our face, for we should then be unable to do what James B. Conant once suggested: "We study cancer in order to learn how to defeat it. We must study the Soviet philosophy . . . for the same reason."

Freedom of speech also is not necessarily and always to be protected, according to the mid-century teen-ager. At three different times over a ten-year period the Purdue Opinion Panel polled a national sample on the proposition:

3. "The government should prohibit some people from making public speeches."

	1951	1958	1960
Agree	34%	20%	25%
Disagree	53%	54%	51%
Uncertain	13%	23%	22%
No response	0	3%	2%

Perhaps the most noteworthy aspect of these results is the great increase in uncertainty in the two later periods. Although the decrease in "Agree" is both statistically and socially significant, the "Disagree" response change is neither.

A similar proposition concerning group meetings yielded a similar result:

4. "Certain groups should not be allowed to hold public meetings, even though they gather peaceably and only make speeches."

	1951	1958	1960
Agree	25%	15%	15%
Disagree	60%	61%	64%
Uncertain	15%	23%	17%
No response	0	1%	4%

Here the reduction over time of "Agree" is significant, though hardly a cause for jubilation among those who agree with the Founding Fathers on the rights of free speech and assembly.

Three more questions first asked in 1951 and repeated in 1960 bear further on freedom of speech.

5. "Some of the petitions which have been circulated should not be allowed by the government."

	1951	1960
Agree	34%	30%
Disagree	34%	34%
Uncertain	32%	34%
No response	0	1%

6. "Should or should not a foreigner visiting this country be permitted to criticize our government?"

	1951	1960
Should	56%	52%
Should not	33%	31%
Uncertain	11%	13%
No response	0	4%

7. "In peacetime, do you think that members of the Communist Party in this country should be allowed to speak on the radio?"

	1951	1960
Should	20%	18%
Should not	65%	63%
Uncertain	15%	16%
No response	0	3%

On one of the freedoms guaranteed by the First Amendment, religious belief and worship, there is, happily, agreement by four out of five teen-agers.

8. "Religious belief and worship should not be restricted by laws."

	1951	1960
Agree	79%	83%
Disagree	13%	9%
Undecided	8%	6%
No response	0	2%

Answers to another proposition on which teenagers were polled four times during the ten-year interval also strongly corroborate this freedom and shows that, ideologically at least, it is safe with our young citizens.

9. "Some religious groups should not be allowed the same freedom as others."

	1951	1956	1958	1960
Agree	7%	6%	5%	4%
Disagree	87%	86%	84%	90%
Uncertain	6%	6%	8%	5%
No response	0	2%	3%	1%

No person shall . . . be deprived of life, liberty or property without due process of law; nor shall private property be taken for public use without just compensation.
—from Article V, Bill of Rights

A series of poll times asked two or more times over the ten-year period show that the right to trial by jury, protection against arrest without formal charge, and protection against search without a warrant are reasonably safe.

10. "In some cases, the police should be allowed to search a person or his home, even though they do not have a warrant."

	1951	1958	1960
Agree	26%	29%	33%
Disagree	69%	58%	57%
Uncertain	5%	13%	8%
No response	0	0	2%

11. "Some criminals are so bad that they shouldn't be allowed to have a lawyer."

	1951	1960
Agree	15%	6%
Disagree	79%	88%
Uncertain	6%	5%
No response	0	1%

12. "Foreigners in this country should always be allowed the same basic freedoms that citizens have."

	1951	1960
Agree	54%	42%
Disagree	32%	32%
Uncertain	14%	23%
No response	0	3%

13. "Local police may sometimes be right in holding persons in jail without telling them of any formal charge against them."

	1951	1958	1960
Agree	17%	17%	13%
Disagree	76%	66%	73%
Uncertain	7%	16%	8%
No response	0	0	6%

14. "In some criminal cases, a trial by jury is an unnecessary expense and shouldn't be given."

	1951	1960
Agree	12%	10%
Disagree	76%	78%
Uncertain	12%	7%
No response	0	5%

15. "In some cases, the government should have the right to take over a person's land or property without bothering to go to court."

	1951	1958	1960
Agree	8%	6%	6%
Disagree	88%	82%	86%
Uncertain	4%	11%	5%
No response	0	1%	3%

16. "The police or F.B.I. may sometimes be right in giving a man the 'third degree' to make him talk."

	1951	1958	1960
Agree	58%	37%	42%
Disagree	27%	33%	32%
Uncertain	15%	28%	23%
No response	0	2%	3%

17. "Persons who refuse to testify against themselves (that is, give evidence that would show that they are guilty of criminal acts) should either be made to talk or severely punished."

	1951	1958	1960
Agree	33%	16%	14%
Disagree	47%	55%	61%
Uncertain	20%	28%	23%
No response	0	1%	2%

It is not reassuring that while in 1951 only one in four (26 per cent) would forego the right of search without a warrant, ten years later one of every three (33 per cent) would yield this right.

The attitude toward the rights of foreigners in this country, in the light of constitutional guarantees, has clearly deteriorated over the ten-year period. Xenophobia appears to be significantly on the increase, with 54 per cent in 1951 and only 42 per cent in 1960 willing to allow "the same basic freedom that citizens have" to foreigners.

The right of private property is in no danger, as shown by the disagreement with the proposition that the government should have the right to dispossess persons without due legal process.

. . . . nor shall be compelled in any criminal case to be witness against himself . . .
—from Article V, Bill of Rights

Physical and psychological torture via the "third degree" is significantly less favored in 1960 than in 1951, but the proportions who would condone this practice—from more than a third in 1958 (37 per cent) to more than a half in 1951 (58 per cent)—constitute cause for serious concern. Doubtless the revulsion against "McCarthyism" accounts for the very significant change in the attitude concerning refusal to testify against oneself; while less than half (47 per cent) disagreed in 1951 with the proposition that such individuals should "either be made to talk or severely punished," in 1960 (61 per cent), disagreed.

No state shall make or enforce any law which shall abridge the privileges or immunities of citizens of the United States; nor shall any state deprive any person of life, liberty, or property without due process of law; nor deny to any person within its jurisdiction the equal protection of the law.
—from Article XIV, Amendments to the Constitution

A series of items aimed at exploring attitudes relevant to protection of the rights of minorities are the following:

18. "Pupils of all races and nationalities should attend school together everywhere in this country."

	1951	1958	1960
Agree	41%	52%	49%
Undecided; probably agree	20%	13%	18%
Undecided; probably disagree	9%	9%	8%
Disagree	29%	26%	24%
No response	1%	0	1%

19. "There should be laws against marriage between persons of different races."

	1958	1960
Agree	38%	35%
Undecided; probably agree	12%	13%
Undecided; probably disagree	12%	15%
Disagree	36%	36%
No response	2%	1%

20. "People who have wild ideas and don't use good sense should not have the right to vote."

	1958	1960
Agree	31%	28%
Undecided; probably agree	16%	13%
Undecided; probably disagree	14%	15%
Disagree	38%	43%
No response	1%	1%

21. "People should not be allowed to vote unless they are intelligent and educated."

	1958	1960
Agree	22%	18%
Undecided; probably agree	11%	8%
Undecided; probably disagree	17%	11%
Disagree	50%	60%
No response	0	3%

22. "Do you think that a person suspected of being a Communist should be fired from his job even if there is no proof that he is actually a Communist?"

	1951	1960
Should	9%	11%
Should not	79%	68%
Uncertain	12%	18%
No response	0	3%

23. "Do you think that some racial or religous groups should be prevented from living in certain sections of cities?"

	1956	1958	1960
Agree	21%	24%	18%
Undecided	15%	21%	22%
Disagree	63%	55%	56%
No response	1%	0	4%

24. "Would you favor a law in your state which requires employers to hire a person if he is qualified for a job regardless of his race, religion, or color?"

	1956	1958	1960
Agree	65%	64%	63%
Undecided	7%	16%	12%
Disagree	22%	17%	22%
No response	6%	3%	3%

Nationally, we are rather clearly in favor of desegregation of schools, as shown by the fact that approximately two-thirds, over a five-year period, "agree" or "probably agree" that "pupils of all races and nationalities should attend school together everywhere in this country." However, to no one's surprise, we find large regional differences in the East, 90 per cent; Midwest, 78 per cent; West, 85 per cent; and South, 29 per cent. Laws against marriage between persons of different races again show regional differences:

East, 39 per cent; Midwest, 44 per cent; West, 33 per cent; and South, 67 per cent.

Protection of a person suspected of being a Communist in his right to a job is fairly staunchly supported. Presumably, these teen-agers would not approve of blacklists for what in a recent unhappy period of our history came to be labeled "fifth amendment Communists," particularly by the late junior senator from Wisconsin, Joseph McCarthy.

Segregation in housing—perhaps an even more basic problem than segregation in education—is definitely disapproved by a majority and shows little change over time. The same holds for attitudes toward a proposed fair employment practices law.

In summary, teen-agers—and inferentially the adult population back of them—accept the Bill of Rights with respect to religious freedom, trial by jury, and the rights of property. Refusal to testify against oneself has lost much of its odium over a decade beginning in 1951.

On the debit side of the ledger are attitudes toward the constitutionally guaranteed rights of foreigners and of minorities generally. The world's image of the world minority in skin color (only about one-fourth of the world population is white) needs much improvement. Supreme Court Justice William O. Douglas has phrased it succinctly:

We cannot glorify Little Rock, anti-Semitism, supremacy of the police, downgrading of education at home, and at the same time be strong abroad. We are the same people in Guinea as we are in Boston. We cannot be leaders of people abroad unless we honor at home the democratic ideal in race relations, in labor relations, in community development.

SOCIAL CLIMATES AND POLITICAL SOCIALIZATION

* Martin L. Levin*

Every individual in a society is, at one time or another, a part of a family, a participant in a peer group, a resident of a neighborhood or a community, and a member of numerous other social subsystems. The part played by these subsystems in the political socialization of the adolescent is the primary concern of this paper. Specifically, an attempt will be made to assess the influence of the climate of political opinion present in the family, the high school community, and the larger social system or the country as a whole in determining the party preference of the high school adolescent.[1]

The data to be analyzed comprise a section of a study of value climates among Illinois high school students.[2] Written questionnaires were administered to every student in ten selected high schools in the autumn of 1957 and again in the spring of 1958. In addition, their parents were polled by means of a mailed questionnaire, providing an index of the political climate of the nuclear family independent of the perceptions of their children.

The Family Climate

The literature on the political socialization of adolescents has shown that the

best predictor of an adolescent's choice of a political party is his parents' party preference.[3] The data from this study support this proposition (Table 1). Ninety-three per cent of those adolescents whose parents are Republican in party preference are Republicans themselves, while 75 per cent of those adolescents with Democratic parents are Democrats.[4] Furthermore, the powerful effect of the climate of political opinion in the family is illustrated by the relationship between the party choice of the adolescent and a variable which has been considered to be a crucial determinant of voting behavior—social status.[5] It was found that 74 per cent of the adolescents with white-collar backgrounds chose the Republican Party, compared with 57 per cent of those with blue-collar backgrounds. However, when social status is controlled by the preference of the parents, as in Table 2, the correlation between social status and the party preference of the adolescent disappears.

Table 1

Family Party Choice, Social Status, and the Party Choice of the Adolescent, Autumn 1957

Parents	Per Cent Adolescents Republican	(N)
Democratic	25	(1,211)
Republican	93	(1,543)
Blue collar	57	(963)
White collar	74	(1,030)

Above selection reprinted from: *Public Opinion Quarterly*, 25 (1961), 596–606.

* The author is in the Department of Social Relations at The Johns Hopkins University. The author would like to thank James S. Coleman and Bernard Levenson for their helpful comments.

Table 2

Social Status and the Party Choice of the Adolescent by Family Party Choice, Autumn 1957

Parents	Per Cent Adolescents Republican	(N)
Blue collar:		
Democratic	24	(511)
Republican	91	(452)
White collar:		
Democratic	25	(317)
Republican	96	(713)

Certain multivariate indices are used to measure the proportion of the variation in the dependent variable explained by each independent variable.[6] Social status explains 17 per cent of the variation in the party preferences of the adolescent. Controlling by the preference of the parents reduces this 17 per cent to only 3 per cent. On the other hand, the party preference of the parent accounts for 68 per cent of the variation in the zero-order relationship and 69 per cent of the variation in the first-order relationship. Thus, it appears that the original correlation between social status and the party preference of the adolescent occurred because of a relationship between social status and the party preference of the parents. Apparently, social status affects the party choice of the adolescent only indirectly, by influencing, in some way, the political climate of his family. The family, however, appears to be the actual *transmitter* of political values.

Despite the strong relationship between the political climate of the family and the party preference of the adolescent, a sizable proportion of the variation remains unexplained. A closer scrutiny of Table 1 reveals that, among adolescents whose parents are Democrats, the proportion who deviate from the choice of their parents is appreciably greater than the corresponding proportion with Republican parents. More precisely, 25 per cent of the adolescents exposed to a Democratic family climate choose the Republican Party; only 7 per cent of the adolescents with Republican parents choose the Democratic Party.

Why should the rate of deviation be greater for the adolescent with Democratic parents? The next two sections will attempt to answer this question by examining the roles of the *high school* and the *national* political opinion climates in influencing the party choice of the adolescent.

The High School Community Climate

To examine the effect of the political climate of the high school community upon the preference of the individual adolescent, each community was first classified in terms of the percentage of parents who are Republicans. Then within each school community the relationship between the opinion climate of the family and the party preference of the adolescent was re-examined.[7] This re-examination was accomplished by indexing the extent to which the children in each school deviated from their parents' political preferences.

The index of deviation rests upon the notion of unexplained variation, as formulated in the technique of multivariate analysis referred to above. We saw in the previous section that the opinion climate of the family, in the zero-order relationship, accounts for 68 per cent of the variation in the party choice of the adolescents. Thus, 32 per cent of the variation remains un-accounted for. This *unexplained variation* has two components, one in the Republican direction and one in the Democratic direction. The index of deviation characterizing each school is based upon these two components: it is the proportion of the *total* unexplained variation in the Republican direction, after the party preference of the adoles-cents has been controlled by the prefer-ence of their parents, i.e., the proportion of unexplained variation in the Repub-lican direction (R) divided by the sum of the proportion of the unexplained variation in the Republican direction (R) and the proportion of the un-explained variation in the Democratic direction (D). For the case at hand—one independent variable—the con-struction of this index is rather simple: the proportion of the adolescents of Democratic parentage who are them-selves Republican (R) divided by the sum of this same proportion (R) and the proportion of the adolescents of Republican parentage who are them-selves Democrats (D).

$$\text{Index of deviation} = \frac{R}{R + D}$$

This index ranges between 0 and 1. The greater its magnitude, the greater are the forces toward the Republican Party within the school it characterizes. Conversely, the lower the index value, the greater the relative proportion of forces toward the Democratic Party.

The observed relationship between the index of deviation and the climate of opinion in each individual school is perhaps best illustrated in graphic form. In Figure 1 the index of deviation for each school has been plotted on the vertical axis against the proportion of

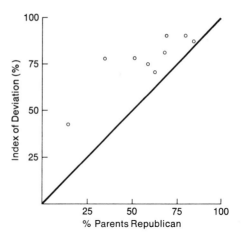

Figure 1.   Index of deviation toward the Re-publican Party, by political climate of the high school community, autumn 1957. (One school was omitted from this analysis because of its small size.)

the parents who are Republican (the operational measure of the climate of opinion in the high school community). The trend of the points is upward and to the right, i.e., the index of deviation tends to increase in magnitude as the proportion of the parents preferring the Republican Party increases.

In substantive terms, the configura-tion of the points in Figure 1 indicates that, as the climate of opinion in the high school community becomes more Republican, the deviation in the Repub-lican direction increases in proportion to the deviation in the Democratic direction. This result supports the contention that the climate of opinion in the community impinges upon its membership to hold attitudes consistent with the majority opinion. For those members whose predispositions were congruent with the climate (i.e., their parents "voted" with the majority in that school), these pressures increased the probability that they would act in accordance with their predispositions, while for those members whose predispositions were incongruent with the climate, this probability was reduced. In the present case, the climate of political opinion in the high school community appears to be exerting influence on all the students within the community to choose the political party that *had already been chosen* by the majority of the adult members, regardless of the party preferences of their own parents. It is noteworthy that this process seems to be operating even though politics is probably not salient to the school community and certainly is not a criterion for membership.

The Tenor of the National Political Scene

The socializing effect of the political tenor of the larger society will be demonstrated only through general inferences. These inferences rest largely upon the assumption that such an effect would operate to increase the forces in the direction of the party in power when the data were collected—in this case, the Republican Party. Previous research on the political socialization of adolescents supports this assumption, showing that a generation tends to affiliate itself with the party in power during the period of its socialization or upon its coming of voting age.[8]

Figure 1 is consistent with the notion that the political tenor of the larger society—the country as a whole—impinges upon the adolescent's choice of a political party with which to identify. The diagonal line drawn across the graph represents all those points where there is a direct correspondence between the proportion of the parents

who are Republican and the proportion of the unexplained variation in the Republican direction (the index of deviation). In other words, when a point lies on the diagonal, the relative amount of unexplained variation in the Republican direction equals the proportion of Republican parents.

All the points lie to the left of the diagonal, indicating that there is a greater force in the Republican direction than would be expected if each additional parent increased the community effect proportionally, i.e., under the hypothesis of a direct correspondence between the climate of opinion of the high school community and the deviation index.[9] This finding is interpreted here to imply that the political climate of the larger social system—the Republican tenor of the country at the time these students were polled—caused the preponderance of variation in the Republican direction.

Data collected from these same students in the spring of 1958 (see Table 3) provide additional, though somewhat weak, support to the notion that the political tenor of the national climate influences the adolescent in his party choice. Over the nine-month period starting in the autumn of 1957, when the adolescents were first interviewed, there was a net shift among all the adolescents of 1 per cent toward the

Table 3

Family Party Choice and the Party Choice of the Adolescent, Spring 1958

Parents' Party Choice	Per Cent Adolescents Republican	(N)
Democratic	22	(1,020)
Republican	92	(1,311)

Democratic Party. Moreover, the direction of this shift is consistent when the party preference of the family is controlled.[10] In fact, the net shift in the direction of the Democratic Party is 1.2 per cent among the adolescents from Republican family climates and only 0.8 per cent for those from Democratic climates.[11] The shift toward the Democrats is further reflected in the multivariate indices for the marginal distributions. In the spring, the political climate of the family explains 70 per cent of the variation, an increase of 2 per cent from the autumn, indicating, as one might expect, that the preferences of the adolescents are becoming more consistent with those of their parents. However, analysis of the unexplained variation reveals that the proportion of the unexplained variation in the Democratic direction *increased* 1 per cent, while the proportion in the Republican direction *decreased* 3 per cent. This results in a reduction of the index of deviation in the Republican direction from 78 to 73 per cent, or a net decrease of 5 per cent. These measures indicate that the over-all increase in consistency of party between the adolescents and their parents was the result of more adolescents from Democratic families choosing with their climates, and less from Republican climates choosing with theirs, than was the case in the autumn. Phrased simply, the Democrats are making a comeback.

At first glance, it might appear that this finding casts doubt upon the contention that the national climate influences the adolescent, for according to the initial argument the shift should have been in the Republican direction. However, it must be remembered that during the spring of 1958 the country was preparing for a Congressional election—an election won by the Democratic Party. The observed shift in the party preferences of the adolescents, then, may have reflected the changing tenor of the national scene.[12] This interpretation, taken in conjunction with the earlier finding that the preponderance of variation was in the Republican direction, supports the contention that the political climate of the national scene affects the political socialization in much the same way, though perhaps not to so great an extent, as the climates of the family and the high school community.

Political Differences Between the Sexes

Up to this point the analysis has remained on the aggregate level, merely attempting to demonstrate that the various social climates to which the adolescent is exposed influence his choice of a party. This final section will try to uncover some clue to the operating mechanisms by analyzing the contexts

Table 4

Family Party Choice and the Party Choice of the Adolescent, by Sex of Adolescent, Autumn 1957*

Parents' Party Choice	Per Cent Adolescents Republican	(N)
Democratic		
Boys	27	(490)
Girls	26	(497)
Republican		
Boys	92	(755)
Girls	95	(749)

* The one school which was not coeducational was omitted from the analysis of political differences between the sexes.

in which influence can flow within each of the climates discussed earlier.

When the relationship between the party of the parent and that of the adolescent is examined separately for boys and girls, it is found that boys are slightly less likely than girls to adhere to the party of their parents (see Table 4). (The proportion of the variation accounted for by the preference of the parents are 65 and 69 per cent, respectively). Moreover, when the index of deviation is plotted separately for each sex within each school against the climate in that school (Figure 2), it is observed that a regression line drawn through each set of points would slope upward and to the right for the boys, while remaining more nearly horizontal for the girls. This suggests that boys are relatively more influenced by the climate of opinion in the high school community than are girls, since the magnitude of the deviation index appears to be dependent upon the climate of the school for them while independent of

the climate for the girls. Finally, in all cases but one the points for the girls fall above the corresponding ones for the boys; thus, according to the argument in the preceding section, it appears that girls are more influenced than boys by the national climate.

These findings—that boys are less influenced than girls by the family and the national political climate and more influenced by the high school community—can be reinterpreted in the light of the literature on the political socialization of adolescents, which has shown that boys are generally more interested in politics than are girls.[13] Viewed in this way,[14] it appears that the more interested adolescents are (1) less likely to go along with their family's party choice, (2) less likely to be influenced by the national climate of opinion,[15] and (3) more likely to be influenced by peers.

These results not only help to specify the effect of *interest* as an intervening variable, but also provide some insight

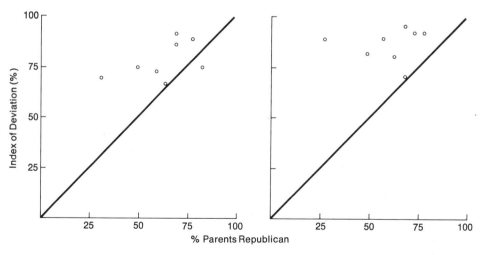

Figure 2. Index of deviation toward the Republican Party, by political climate of the high school community, for boys (left) and girls (right) separately, autumn 1957.

into differential processes of influence transmission in varying social contexts. In the nuclear family, political influence usually flows in only one direction, taking a passive form from influencer to influenced.[16] The politically uninterested adolescent may only *hear* a parent say he is a Democrat or voted for the Democratic Party in the last election, with no interchange of political views. When this adolescent comes into the interview situation or, indeed, when he is ultimately called upon to cast his vote, he also will tend to choose the Democratic Party. Similarly, the tenor of the larger society is communicated passively through the mass media. The uninterested adolescent is not likely to discuss politics with his peers or with any of the influencing agents.

The interested adolescent, on the other hand, is more apt to exchange political opinions in face-to-face interaction. By virtue of his interest, he is more sensitive to the political opinions of his peers, more likely to discuss politics with them, and consequently more likely to be influenced by them. In other words, interest intensifies influence in those social situations where interaction of a political nature is likely to take place and reduces influence in those where the communication is one-way.

Summary and Conclusions

This paper has attempted to assess the extent to which the political climates of opinion in the various social subsystems of which the adolescent is a member contribute to his political socialization and his choice of a political party. Specifically, it was shown that the nuclear family, the high school community, and the larger society each plays a part in impelling the adolescent to choose the political party which represents its consensus.

The second major point discussed was the role of political interest as an intervening variable in the analysis of the socializing effectiveness of the various social subsystems. It was conjectured that adolescents to whom politics is salient will be most influenced in social situations involving bilateral communication of political opinions, while the uninterested adolescent will be more likely to be influenced in a unilateral situation where he assumes a passive role under pressure to conform. That is to say, depending upon their political interest, adolescents are differentially influenced by their membership groups.

It is only a short conceptual jump from the notion that interest in a given area leads to acceptance of certain sources of influence and independence from others to the realization that people are differentially attached to these influenced sources. For example, it would be reasonable to expect that the adolescent who is psychologically dependent upon his family would be more likely to adopt his family's party preferences than would an adolescent alienated from his family. It seems promising, therefore, to take account of the *strength of attachment to the social subsystem* as still another intervening variable which determines in part, the social contexts under which influence will flow effectively.

The relationship between these two variables—political interest and strength of attachment to a social system—portends interesting findings in future research. Take the socializing effect of the family, for example. The data analyzed above indicate that the un-interested adolescent is more likely to choose the same party as his family than is the interested adolescent. Intuition, to say nothing of volumes of sociological literature, suggest that the alienated adolescent will be less likely to choose with his family than the integrated one. But what about the uninterested, alienated adolescent, or the interested, integrated one? Which of these will be most likely to choose with the family climate? That is to say, does the alienated adolescent "rebel" on issues which are not salient to him? Conversely, does the integrated adolescent find that his interest in a certain area is so pervasive that he just can't bring himself to deviate from the attitudes of of his family? Or could it be that salience of the issue in question to the social system is the key to understanding the behavior of these adolescents? Any attempt to answer these questions at this point would be nothing more than pure speculation.

NOTES

1. Those studies of the political socialization of adolescents which have recognized that the climate of opinion in the adolescent's various membership groups affects his party preference have tended to concentrate on only two of these "system effects"—that of the nuclear family and that of the larger social system. For a review of these studies, see H. Hyman, *Political Socialization*, Glencoe, Ill., Free Press, 1959, especially Chaps. IV and VI.

2. For a complete description of these high schools and a broader perspective on their value climates, see J. S. Coleman, *Social Structures and Social Climates in High Schools*, Washington, D.C., U.S. Office of Education, Sept. 1, 1959.

3. Hyman, *op. cit.*

4. The directions on the parents' questionnaire did not specify which parent was to complete it. For purposes of this analysis, the reply to the question on party preference will be taken as an index of the political climate of the nuclear family as a whole, regardless of which parent completed the questionnaire.

5. P. F. Lazarsfeld, B. Berelson, and H. Gaudet, *The People's Choice*, New York, Columbia University Press, 1948; B. Berelson, P. F. Lazarsfeld, and W. McPhee, *Voting*, Chicago, Ill., University of Chicago Press, 1954; A. Campbell, P. E. Converse, W. E. Miller, and D. E. Stokes, *The American Voter*, New York, Wiley, 1960; and others.

6. Limitations of space preclude a complete exposition of the assumptions of this technique. Because such a presentation is as yet unpublished, the reader is asked to bear with the author and assume that the indices employed really perform all that is claimed of them. The complete exposition of the technique will appear in J. S. Coleman, *Introduction to Mathematical Sociology*, Glencoe, Ill., Free Press (forthcoming).

7. This type of analysis has been given various designations—climates of opinion, contextual effects, structural effects, etc. Probably the best statement of the

assumptions and techniques of this approach may be found in Peter Blau's "Structural Effects," *American Sociological Review*, Vol. 25, 1960, pp. 178–193.

8. Hyman, *op. cit.* It is also possible that this effect stemmed from the tenor of the subsystem of the state of Illinois, which, like that of the larger social system, was Republican. Since the present data preclude the possibility of separating the components of influence from each system, it was arbitrarily decided to think of the process as stemming from the national scene. Morever, Parsons, to cite one example, supports the conception that the tenor of the larger society impinges upon the individual the same way the social system of the family does. He asserts that ". . . it is legitimate to consider the voting process by which Presidents are elected as authentically a *social system*. It is a set of processes of action and interaction which may be treated in terms of specific modes of interdependence which can be analytically separated from other influences" (italics in original). T. Parsons, "'Voting' and the Equilibrium of the American Political System," in E. Burdick and A. J. Brodbeck, editors, *American Voting Behavior*, Glencoe, Ill., Free Press, 1959, p. 87.

9. There is no a priori reason for assuming that the relationship operates directly. However, if a greater than direct relationship were operating, then the point for the one school in which the majority of the parents were Democrats should have fallen *below* the diagonal. It is not the contention here that none of the distance above the diagonal is attributable to a greater than direct effect of the structure; rather, it is felt that at least some, if not most, is the result of the forces stemming from the larger social system.

10. This finding might be the result of a shift in the party preferences of the parents, leading to a shift in the adolescents' preferences. Unfortunately, this cannot be tested, since data were collected from the parents only once.

11. It is interesting to compare this finding with Lipset's statement that during shifts in the balance of political power from one party to the other, support for the incoming party is gained from all strata, not merely from those whose initial predispositions are for the incoming party. See S. M. Lipset, "Political Sociology," in R. K. Merton *et al.*, editors, *Sociology Today*, New York, Basic Books, 1959, p. 96.

12. Admittedly the net change in favor of the Democrats is small. Nonetheless, it is consistent, holding generally when the schools are examined separately. It takes on still greater significance when it is realized that a shift of 1 per cent over a nine-month period can have a dramatic effect on the outcome of an election.

13. Hyman, *op. cit.*

14. The study from which these data were taken was not designed to explore the political socialization of adolescents. Consequently, no data were collected about the students' interests in politics. It thus becomes necessary to rely on sex as a rough indicator of political interest.

15. Lipset, Trow, and Coleman reported a similar finding in their study of the International Typographical Union. It was found that within shops, printers with a low level of knowledge concerning the campaign issues (which may be taken as a rough index of interest) were more likely to vote with the majority in an election regardless of their predispositions. By the same token, those with a high level of interest in the campaign exhibited more independence and a greater

likelihood of voting in accord with their initial predispositions. See S. M. Lipset, M. A. Trow, and J. S. Coleman, *Union Democracy*, Glencoe, Ill., Free Press, 1956, pp. 346–347.

16. For the purposes of this analysis it is assumed that the flow of influence in the family is one-way and passive. Obviously, in some cases this is invalid. If the data were available, the nature of the flow could be controlled as a variable, with the expectation that interested adolescents in situations where the flow is two-way would be more influenced by the nuclear family than those in situations where the flow is one-way.

HIGH SCHOOL EXTRACURRICULAR ACTIVITIES AND POLITICAL SOCIALIZATION

- ## David Ziblatt

The American high school is both an educational institution and the site of an intensive round of social life. A typical high school is a complex network of cliques and officially supported extracurricular activities. In this paper I begin with a brief discussion of high school extracurricular activities and American secondary education. Then I consider the extracurricular activity system as an analogue of the adult voluntary association. Finally, I report some research on the relationship between participation in high school extracurricular activities and attitude toward politics.

Extracurricular Activities and Secondary Education

Educators are not in complete agreement about the origin of extracurricular activities in American secondary schools. Some argue that a version of today's student activities existed in the first free public schools, while others insist that extracurricular activities are solely the creation of educational policy.[1] These views reflect disagreements about the value of extracurricular activities for education. Those who believe that they always existed argue that it was necessary to stimulate and relate activities to educational goals. Those who see extra-curricular activities solely as creations

Above selection reprinted from: *The Annals of the American Academy of Political and Social Science*, 361 (September 1965), 21–31.

of school bureaucracies are more free with criticism.[2] There is little disagreement that by the 1920's it was considered legitimate policy to commit scarce educational resources to both the promotion and the organization of extracurricular activities. Teachers were given responsibilities outside the classroom. Full-time professional directors were employed. Schoolrooms, time, equipment, and materials were provided. Experts began to appear. Forty books were published between 1925 and 1940 explaining the role of extra-curricular activities in the secondary school.[3] In a burst of organizational enthusiasm, school administrators began to speak of "curricularizing" extra-curricular activities. The existence of a monthly journal, *School Activities: The National Extracurricular Magazine* is clear evidence of this process of professionalization.

Some of the values actually promoted by extracurricular activities depart drastically from idealized descriptions. In practice, athletics and social success came to dominate, despite frequent rationalizations. The local football coach addresses the benevolent, protective, and hearty members of local voluntary associations and tells them that athletics is the crucible of democracy because it teaches fair play and teamwork.

It remained for James Coleman to document the impact of the entire system on educational ideals.[4] The ten high schools that Coleman investigated varied from one another, but in all cases the "leading crowds" with their emphasis on athletics and social success shaped the values of the rest of the student body. One school in particular is of some interest because of the apparent changes now going on in primary and secondary education. "Executive Heights" High School, located in a wealthy suburban area, was said to rank academically among the first ten in the country. Pressures for the placement of graduates in outstanding colleges were described as intense.[3] Yet even in this school the "all-round" boy was rewarded and the brilliant student shunned by fellow students.[6] In practice, it appears that the value climate which grows up around extracurricular activities discourages intellectual concerns.

These findings led Coleman to argue that the American teen-ager develops a subculture of his own, a subculture whose norms deflect the educational goals of the larger society. This argument remained an assumption throughout the study and was never adequately tested.[7] It is an assumption based upon some very flattering ideas about the central educational values of teachers, school administrators, and the general adult population. For it can be argued that the values fostered by extracurricular activities reflect the concerns of adult society. As long as important elements in adult society value education primarily for its instrumental power, how much can be expected from teen-agers? The ultimate direction of current educational change is not clear. The name of Bruner may be cited more frequently than Dewey in educational reports. Creativity tests take their place alongside intelligence tests. Curriculum

revision proceeds at a rapid pace. Yet it is still not certain that this represents a change toward valuing education for its *intrinsic worth* rather than its *instrumental power*.[8] It is this fundamental distinction that makes it impossible to assess the cost to education resulting from the present organization of extracurricular activities without also taking into account the entire society, adults as well as teen-agers.

These different orientations toward education have implications for political socialization. Educational attainment has shown up time and again as a major factor in shaping political perspectives. We would prefer to believe that education leads to supportive beliefs toward civil liberties, for example, through increased intellectual awareness. Yet in many instances the beliefs can be explained by the rise in socioeconomic status that accompanies educational attainment. Supportive beliefs toward civil liberties based upon increased intellectual awareness may be internalized and difficult to change even in crisis situations. Supportive beliefs toward civil liberties based upon social pressures in the immediate environment may be easily dislodged if the environment changes in times of crisis.[9] The more education is valued for its intrinsic worth, the more likely it is that political beliefs derived from educational experiences will serve reality functions rather than social-adjustment functions.

Extracurricular Activities as Voluntary Associations

The educational theorists who promoted extracurricular activities in American high schools emphasized citizenship benefits, not costs. These benefits derived from a vision of the classroom and the school as miniature democracies shaping the student in the "here and now" to live in a democratic society. Statements such as the following often appeared.

The student is not a subject or a slave, but a citizen with rights and privileges as well as duties and obligations. If this point is not admitted, all the framework of our school system must topple, for if the school does not prepare the child for efficient citizenship in the community which supports it, it cannot be justified. Attempting to prepare the student for membership in a democracy by training him in an autocracy or oligarchy is incongruous and unsuccessful.[10]

The ideal of displacing autocratic school traditions inherited from western Europe became policy. Some evidence of the long-run effects of the policy appears in Almond and Verba's report on the attitudes of national samples of adults in the United States, England, Germany, Italy, and Mexico. A higher proportion of Americans said that they both felt free to complain to a teacher if they believed they were treated unfairly and actually recalled complaining.[11]

The extracurricular activity was given an important position in the philosophy of the democratic school. High school extracurricular activities were to be analogous to adult voluntary associations. Just as a membership in a voluntary association was believed to have positive effects on an adult's citizenship competence, so would the extracurricular activity have positive effects on the teen-ager. Participation would give him insight and awareness into social processes. He would acquire an ability to manipulate these processes. He would have a greater understanding

of how things get done in the larger political system. He would have a more positive orientation toward political phenomena. So the argument went.

This optimistic view was certainly consistent with the image of the American as a joiner. Indeed, ever since Alexis de Tocqueville observed that in the United States "there is no end which human will despairs of attaining through the combined power of individuals united in a society," we have thought of ourselves as joiners.[12] Recent national surveys qualify this claim. Americans join voluntary associations if they have a high educational level, a high income, and a white-collar job.[13] However, Americans do have a higher rate of membership in voluntary associations than English, Germans, Italians, or Mexicans.[14]

The political effects of this pattern are displayed when Almond and Verba's respondents in the same five nations were asked what they would do to change an unjust governmental regulation. In the United States, 59 per cent spontaneously mentioned enlisting the aid of others rather than acting alone. In England only 36 per cent did so. Twenty-eight per cent of the Mexican respondents, 21 per cent of the German respondents, and only 9 per cent of the Italians mentioned enlisting the aid of others.[15] In all five nations, members of voluntary associations (in contrast to nonmembers) were more likely to feel confident in their ability to influence government, to be more active in politics, and to be more open with their political opinions. The relationship held even when formal education was controlled.[16]

Participation in voluntary associations apparently does have an independent effect upon citizenship competence. Is this also true of participation in high school extracurricular activities? Is this a benefit of the current system? Do high school students have a more positive attitude toward politics if they participate in many extracurricular activities? The remainder of the paper will be concerned with this problem.

Extracurricular Activities and Attitude Toward Politics

There has been very little investigation into the political consequences of the informal side of the high school.[17] One recent study carried out in the high school of a small Michigan community reports positive relationships between the degree of participation in high school extracurricular activities and responses showing a sense of political efficacy, political-party appreciation (whether parties exist to mediate conflict or are conspiracies), legitimacy of political institutions (cynical versus trusting response options), and expectations of future political participation.[18] However, these results were not attributed to the direct effects of participation itself.

Students who participate have a clearer image of what is conventionally regarded as good citizenship and have reproduced this in the questionnaires just as they do by high school participation. . . . In short, they are giving socially appropriate responses and have a better idea of what responses are socially appropriate.[19]

The research to be reported here is part of a larger study of teen-agers conducted in the Spring of 1963 in Springfield, Oregon, an industrial blue-collar community of 22,000. The entire sophomore and senior class of Springfield High School (526 respondents) filled out a questionnaire in their classes. Seventeen per cent of the students reported that their fathers had eight grades or less of formal schooling, the fathers of 35 per cent attended high school; 23 per cent had fathers with some college training, and 5 per cent failed to reply.

I am concerned here with the student's attitude toward politics. I define attitude as a response disposition toward an object along a favorable-unfavorable dimension. Under certain conditions a negative attitude toward politics, the evaluation of politics as corrupt or dirty, undermines continuous and competent adult political participation.[20] An earlier survey of adults in the same community showed that cynicism toward politics was associated with educational level, age, and sense of personal efficacy.[21]

Attitude toward politics was measured by the five-item evaluative factor of the semantic differential. The respondents were faced with seven choices for each of the five empirically determined bipolar adjectives ranging from strongly positive through strongly negative. The adjectives composing the factor were harmful-beneficial, wise-foolish, dirty-clean, good-bad, and positive-negative.[22]

If participation in extracurricular activities leads to a more positive orientation toward political phenomena, then there should be an association between the rate of participation and attitude toward politics. Table 1 indicates that no such relationship exists.[23] This is also true when the data are re-examined by age, sex, and party identification. How should this finding be assessed? One way is to entertain a different line

Table 1

The Relationship of Participation in Extracurricular Activities to Attitude Toward Politics by Father's Educational Level

FATHER'S EDUCATIONAL LEVEL PARTICIPATION RATE	ATTITUDE TOWARD POLITICS			(N)
	Positive	Neutral	Negative	
	(In Percentages)			
Low Education				
Low Participation	42	22	36	(70)
High Participation	47	13	40	(15)
Medium Education				
Low Participation	38	24	38	(216)
High Participation	32	32	36	(69)
High Education				
Low Participation	35	33	32	(74)
High Participation	36	27	37	(45)

of reasoning. The idea that participation in extracurricular activities leads to an appreciation of social processes such as politics, may be true, if at all, only under very special conditions. The system of extracurricular activities is also a status hierarchy. A student earns varying degrees of status from his peers by his participation. The student who belongs to various clubs and teams is integrated into a status network, and is spared the development of a junior version of social alienation. What is directly learned by participation may not be important in shaping the teen-ager's attitude toward politics. The important factors may be the psychological consequences that follow from having high or low status in the high school social system. Those on the outside of the status network are both alienated and indignant, and they generalize their indignation to more distant conceptual targets such as politics. A straight unweighted count of the number of activities might be too gross an indicator of this process. For purposes of status, participation in one prestigeful

activity might be equal to participation in five or six less prestigeful activities.

To make the assumptions behind this reasoning explicit, it is assumed that the students on the outside will "blame the system" for their position. They will view high school activities as dominated by a small group who have something in common, such as coming "from the right side of the tracks." They will believe that being "in" is determined by ascriptive criteria, and not by achievement, and they will view the status hierarchy as relatively closed. This explains their indignation toward immediate social processes. It is further assumed that this disenchantment with social processes in the high school will be generalized to social processes such as politics.

The teen-agers were confronted with an item on the questionnaire composed of a series of concentric circles whose center represented "being in the center of things." They were asked to indicate how far out from the center of things they felt they were and then to designate where they would like to be.[24]

Twenty-eight per cent indicated that they were on the inside or in the center of things, while 56 per cent indicated that *they wanted to be* on the inside. Thirty-four per cent placed themselves in a middle position, while only 24 per cent indicated that they wanted to be in this position. Thirty per cent placed themselves on the outside, while only 13 per cent said that this was where they wanted to be. These figures show that a sizable proportion of students were dissatisfied with their perceived position in the high school social system. If all the assumptions are correct, then the further outside a student feels he is, the more likely he will be to have a negative attitude toward politics.

Table 2

The Relationship Between Perceived Position in the High School Social System and Attitude Toward Politics

PERCEIVED POSITION	ATTITUDE TOWARD POLITICS			(N)
	Positive	Neutral	Negative	
	(In Percentages)			
Inside	36	29	35	(149)
Middle	36	30	33	(177)
Outside	38	24	35	(200)

Table 3

The Relationship of Father's Educational Level to High School Participation

FATHER'S EDUCATIONAL LEVEL	NUMBER OF HIGH SCHOOL ACTIVITIES			(N)
	0	1–3	Over 3	
	(In Percentages)			
Low	43	40	17	(88)
Medium	30	45	25	(286)
High	13	50	38	(119)

However, the data in Table 2 do not support this hypothesis. Which of the earlier assumptions was incorrect? It was assumed that the students on the outside would blame the system for their position, that disenchantment with immediate social processes become generalized, and that the basis for their indignation is the belief that "being in the center of things" is dependent upon social background. However, in this particular school, extracurricular activities may not be dominated by students from higher socioeconomic backgrounds. The relationship between father's educational level and rate of participation in extracurricular activities is examined in Table 3. From this it is possible to get some idea of how important background factors actually are.

In fact, social background does play an important part in participation. Students whose fathers have never gone beyond the eighth grade are more than three times as likely as students with college-educated fathers to participate in no activities at all.

It was assumed that feeling inside or outside the status system was associated with the rate of participation in extracurricular activities. However, where a student places himself might have little to do with his participation rate. This self-assessment might be related to some other factor that has not been accounted for. This can be studied by looking at the association between participation and perceived position in the high school social system. These data are presented in Table 4, by father's educational level.

Although the number of respondents is quite small in one of the cells, one general picture emerges. The more frequently a student participates in

Table 4

The Relationship of High School Participation to Perceived Position in the High School Social System

FATHER'S EDUCATIONAL LEVEL	PERCEIVED POSITION IN HIGH SCHOOL SYSTEM			(N)
	Inside	Middle	Outside	
PARTICIPATION RATE	*(In Percentages)*			
Low Education				
0–3 Activities	22	35	43	(72)
Over 3 Activities	47	40	13	(15)
Medium Education				
0–3 Activities	21	32	47	(216)
Over 3 Activities	53	36	11	(70)
High Education				
0–3 Activities	23	41	36	(75)
Over 3 Activities	52	39	9	(44)

extra-curricular activities, the more likely he is to feel on the inside of the status system of the school whatever the level of his father's education. A final assumption left unaccounted for is the idea that the students who feel on the outside will not only blame immediate social processes for their position, but they will also be disenchanted with these processes. The teen-agers were confronted with the two following statements on the questionnaire.

In some schools, there always seems to be one group that more or less runs things among students. What about here? Is there one group that seems always to be in the middle of things or are there several groups like that?

How important would you say coming from the right family and neighborhood is to get in with the leading crowd in this school?

If there is disenchantment, it should show up on the answers to these questions. The questions ask to what extent the school is dominated by a single

group, a group difficult to enter if the student does not come from the right family and neighborhood. Tables 5 and 6 present the responses by father's educational level.

Those students whose fathers have eight grades of education or less are most likely to de-emphasize the importance of background factors for entry into the leading crowd. They are also most likely to see more than one group dominating school activities. Students whose fathers have been to college are most likely to participate and are also more likely to view entry into the leading crowd as determined by background factors. Teen-agers from this stratum see one group dominating.

It has been argued that Americans place a peculiar emphasis on individual responsibility. One observer commenting on the world-wide reaction to the Kennedy assassination said that Europeans invent conspiracies to take responsibility for social events, but Americans invent individuals. That the very students who are most likely to be on the outside are also most likely to see that status system as open has to be explained in these terms.

In his study of political ideology, Robert Lane found that working-class men, rather than feeling powerless, believed that anyone could become more powerful if he wanted to badly enough, "just as anyone who wanted to and had the skills and got the breaks, could be rich."[25] Lane goes on to characterize their beliefs as follows:

Power is dependent on organization and effort; those whom the Gods would make powerful they first must organize. But the decision is your own; you have the right to organize, protected by freedom of association. This view offers a political principle of some importance to these men. Freedom of association provides in the political field the basis for a rationale of relative power positions, just as free enterprise provides this basis for relative wealth in the economic field. If one has little power at any given time, *it is his own fault* for failing to organize his interests. . . . Whatever the game that we are playing may be in this earthly life, it is not a zero-sum game.[26]

Beliefs like these may be learned by adolescence. Certain notions about equality of economic opportunity carry over into thinking about equality of opportunity for power and equality of opportunity for status in the high school, and tend to preclude direct disillusionment with high school social processes. A student on the outside does not blame an impersonal system; he blames himself. Thus, there is no conscious indignation to be generalized to social processes outside of the high school.

The foregoing argument assumes a certain amount of student self-consciousness relative to the actual distribution of opportunities in the high school status system. However, the consequences of this system could still relate to other politically relevant predispositions which mediate the experiences of being inside or outside the status system and attitude toward politics. One such factor is social trust or faith in human nature. Social trust is a set of highly generalized beliefs about human nature. Some people assume that human beings are basically self-interested and exploitative while others believe that altruism and co-operation are fundamental facts of human nature. Morris Rosenberg developed a measure of this factor and tested it on students from eleven American universities. He found that irrespective of party affiliation or social-class origin, students with a low level of trust

Table 5

How Many Groups Run Things

Father's Educational Level	One Group	More Than One Group	(N)
	(In Percentages)		
Low Education	49	51	(88)
Medium Education	54	46	(286)
High Education	70	30	(119)

Table 6

Importance of Coming from Right Family and Neighborhood

Father's Educational Level	Important	Not Important	(N)
	(In Percentages)		
Low Education	52	48	(88)
Medium Education	60	40	(286)
High Education	77	23	(119)

Table 7

The Relationship Between Perceived Position in the High School Social System and Social Trust by Sex

SEX / PERCEIVED POSITION	SOCIAL TRUST			(N)
	Trusting	Medium Trust	Mistrustful	
	(*In Percentages*)			
Boys				
Feel Inside	30	31	38	(73)
In the Middle	15	31	54	(85)
Feel Outside	20	28	52	(90)
Girls				
Feel Inside	46	26	28	(69)
In the Middle	35	31	34	(83)
Feel Outside	20	32	48	(69)

were likely to think that the public is not qualified to vote and that war is inevitable.[27] The same factor was found to relate to political predispositions in the Almond and Verba five-nation study.[28]

Is there any association between perceived position in the high school status system and social trust? If there is, then it would be impossible to assign the direction of causality with these data. Some students may have already entered the system holding mistrustful beliefs, while the beliefs of others may be a direct outcome of their experience in the high school. However, even if students come into the high school holding mistrustful beliefs, these could be continually reinforced by the experience of being in the outside of the status system. Students who feel on the outside, while manifestly blaming themselves for not being further involved and not becoming indignant at the opportunity system could simultaneously be more mistrustful of others. The psychodynamics of such a condition remains to be investigated.

The teen-agers were located on a five-item index of social trust.[29] The relationship between perceived position in the high school status system and social trust is presented in Table 7.[30] The data in Table 7 support the hypothesis. Teen-agers on the outside of the status system show more mistrust than those on the inside. The final step in this analysis is to examine the relationship between social trust and attitude toward politics. The teen-agers who are more mistrustful of others should also have a more negative attitude toward politics.[31]

The data in Table 8 support this hypothesis.

The foregoing analysis can now be summarized by four propositions:

(1) The higher the father's educational level, the more frequently students participate in extracurricular activities.

(2) The more frequently students participate, the greater their feeling of integration into the high school status system.

(3) The greater the students' feeling of integration into the high school status system, the greater their social trust.

Table 8

The Relationship of Social Trust to Attitude Toward Politics

Social Trust	Attitude Toward Politics			(N)
	Positive	*Neutral*	*Negative*	
Trusting	44	33	23	(117)
Medium Trust	36	30	34	(144)
Distrustful	29	25	46	(194)

(4) The greater the student's social trust, the more positive his attitude toward politics.

Conclusion

High school extracurricular activities are a source of the informal status networks in American high schools. The status networks and the norms upon which they are based do not inculcate those values which stress the intrinsic worth of education. The genesis for this failure probably rests with the adult society. However, educational theorists have stressed the beneficial aspects of extracurricular activities. They have argued that extracurricular activities, like adult voluntary associations, produce more competent citizens. This view has been subjected to an empirical test in one high school and with only one indicator of competence, attitude toward politics.[32] This limits any final conclusions about the role of extracurricular activities in political socialization. The data presented in this paper indicate that a feeling of integration into the high school status system is associated with social trust. It is this social trust and not the direct experience of extracurricular participation which is linked with a positive attitude toward politics. Furthermore, the students who are most likely to benefit from the experience of joining, those from the working class, are least likely to belong. It was inferred that these students were insulated from a direct awareness of how the status system actually operates by a belief in equality of opportunity. Future studies should not only investigate how high school participation relates to other politically relevant variables, but should also attempt to incorporate these findings into a developmental theory of political alienation.

NOTES

1. These two views are developed in H. C. McKown, *Extracurricular Activities* (New York: The Macmillan Company, 1952), pp. 2–6. For a more recent history see Edward A. Krug, *The Shaping of the American High School* (New York: Harper and Row, 1964).

2. The debate continues. See Herbert Stroup, *Toward a Philosophy of Organized Student Activities* (Minneapolis: University of Minnesota Press, 1964).

3. McKown, *op. cit.*, pp. 3–4. An example of this material is T. M. Dean and O. M. Bear, *Socializing the Pupil Through Extracurricular Activities* (New York: Sanborn, 1929).

4. James Coleman, *The Adolescent Society* (Glencoe, Ill.: Free Press, 1961).

5. *Ibid.*, pp. 66–68.

6. *Ibid.*, p. 315.

7. For an extended discussion of this point, see Marie Jahoda and Neil Warren, "The Myths of Youth," *Sociology of Education*, 38 (Winter 1965), pp. 138–150. D. C. Epperson, "A Reassessment of Indices of Parental Influence in the Adolescent Society," *American Sociological Review*, 29 (February 1964), pp. 93–96.

8. This distinction is brilliantly captured in John Hersey, *The Child Buyer* (New York: Alfred A. Knopf, 1960).

9. This hypothesis follows from the discussion of compliance identification, and internalization in Herbert C. Kelman, "Processes of Opinion Change," *Public Opinion Quarterly*, 25 (Spring 1961), pp. 57–78.

10. McKown, *op. cit.*, pp. 17–18. While these ideas were emphasized, educational theorists also developed an elitist conception of the proper administrative and political organization for public education. John F. Gallagher, "Implications of the Literature of American Public School Administrators for Public Administration and Democratic Politics" (Unpublished Ph.D. dissertation, Department of Political Science, UCLA, 1964).

11. Gabriel Almond and Sidney Verba, *The Civic Culture* (Princeton, N.J.: Princeton University Press, 1963), pp. 332–333.

12. Alexis de Tocqueville, *Democracy in America*, Vol. 1 (New York: Vintage Books, 1954), p. 199.

13. Murray Hausknecht, *The Joiners* (New York: Bedminster Press, 1962).

14. Almond and Verba, *op. cit.*, pp. 302–303.

15. *Ibid.*, p. 191.

16. *Ibid.*, pp. 307–322.

17. An exception is Martin L. Levin, "Social Climates and Political Socialization" [in this volume, pp. 353–362 (ed.)].

18. Helen Sonnenburg Lewis, "The Teen-age Joiner and His Orientation Toward Public Affairs: A Test of Two Multiple Group Membership Hypotheses" (Unpublished Ph.D. dissertation, Department of Political Science, Michigan State University, 1962).

19. *Ibid.*, pp. 171–172.

20. Robert Agger, Marshall Goldstein, and Stanley Pearl, "Political Cynicism: Measurement and Meaning," *Journal of Politics*, Vol. 23 (August 1961), pp. 477–506. Edgar Litt, [in this volume, pp. 328–336 (ed.)].

21. Agger, Goldstein, and Pearl, *op. cit.*

22. The respondents' position on the measure was determined by their mean score over the five items. The problem of construct validity was investigated by using the same factor to measure attitude toward family, Congress, high school, and the Soviet Union. See C. E. Osgood, G. J. Suci, and P. H. Tannenbaum, *The*

Measurement of Meaning (Urbana, Ill.: University of Illinois Press, 1957), pp. 76–124.

23. In this and the following tables, low participation refers to those who listed fewer than four extracurricular activities unless otherwise noted. The same results were obtained when participation rate was trichotomized. Low education refers to eight grades or less, medium education to some high school or high school graduates, and high education refers to some college or beyond. Tests of significance are not reported because the research design does not meet the necessary conditions. See H. Selvin, "Critique of Tests of Significance in Survey Research," *American Sociological Review*, 22 (October 1957), pp. 519–527.

24. This item appears in Coleman, *op. cit.*

25. Robert Lane, *Political Ideology* (Glencoe, Ill.: Free Press, 1962), p. 172.

26. *Ibid.*, p. 143. The italics are mine.

27. Rose Goldson, Morris Rosenberg *et al.*, *What College Students Think* (New York: Van Nostrand, 1960), pp. 97–153.

28. Almond and Verba, *op. cit.*, pp. 267–273, 284–288.

29. Trusting responses were given a score of 1. Mistrustful responses were given a score of − 1. The cutting points were 2 to 5 trusting, 0 and 1 neutral and − 1 to − 5 mistrustful. Fifty-eight respondents who failed to answer one or more of the questions were excluded from the analysis and re-examined by father's education, attitude toward politics, alienation from high school system, and participation rate. The distribution of trusting responses for Springfield students and the United States national adult sample reported in Almond and Verba differed by no more than five percentage points on any one item. This raises some questions about the validity of those views which stress the peculiar idealism or cynicism of youth.

30. Sex rather than education is controlled here, because girls were found to more trusting than boys.

31. This hypothesis was also tested by age, sex, and political-party identification. Social trust was also found to be related to attitude toward Congress and high school.

32. Size of school might be a significant variable not taken into account in this study. Barker demonstrates the different meaning extracurricular activities have in large and small high schools. Roger Barker, *Big School–Small School: Studies of the Effects of High School Size Upon the Behavior and Experiences of Students* (Stanford, Calif.: Stanford University Press, 1962). The class composition of the schools is still another variable. See Coleman, *op. cit.*,

College and University

5

INTRODUCTION

College students' political views and activities make front page news almost every day in the 1960s. We no longer think of them as the apathetic generation, much less the "silent generation." Some of their elders bemoan the new lack of silence and declare every college campus a hotbed of radicals, whereas others find solace in the thought that the radicals constitute only a vociferous minority, and yet others welcome what they consider to be an "awakening" among our youth. Whatever one's interpretation of the desirability, the magnitude, or the newness of a politically alive campus, there seems little doubt that something happens to some students at some colleges that must be attributed to the college they attend and that probably would not have happened to them had they stayed at home. No wonder that study after study points to the political socializing function of college.

Why should this be so? Studies show that high school seniors tend to hold similar party identification, issue orientation, and so forth, that they held as entering freshmen. But the literature on colleges (see Theodore Newcomb and Alex Edelstein below) points to great changes occurring between the freshman and the senior year—generally in the direction of greater liberalization, although, perhaps, not greater liberalism. Why should so much happen to students in college when so little happened to them between their freshman and senior year in high school?

In Chapter 1 we offered one explanation, namely, that the new environment itself induces change and engagement in the new arrival: "Factors inherent in the ecological structures of universities

375

. . . facilitate collective action" and "social dislocation, changing from one significant environment to another, predisposes individuals to accept new values, ideologies and affiliations in the religious and political spheres."[1] The ever-ready availability of age cohorts the joint enterprise of living and working together in close proximity perhaps further encourage the formation of a youth culture all its own.

Nor must it be overlooked that for many young people this is the first opportunity for prolonged, sustained life away from home and family. The opportunity has come at last for many to assert their independence—which may also include their political independence. As the Bennington study shows, many a liberal coed from a conservative home did not really change her political ideas much; college just afforded her the opportunity to be open about her political stand without fear of parental ridicule or disapproval. For some other students college is the long-searched-for opportunity to rebel not only against parental control but against societal control and society in general.

Other students begin to look upon the college community (or a specific group in it) as a substitute for the family group. The greater the need to find a substitute, the greater the likelihood that the young person will take on the political patterns and behaviors of the group. The more the student wants to be part of the "in-group," the more he will take on its political colorations. For some this will amount to reinforcement —studies of some fraternities disclosed that conservative boys became more so when living in fraternity houses—and for others to conversion—some Southern

students, for example, became noticeably less prejudiced against Negroes while attending Northern colleges.

Social and psychological factors such as the above, rather than course content, seem to explain the ideological changes that occur in college youth. All the data currently available on the effectiveness of political "conversion" or even "activation" via a specific course seem to point to the futility of such an undertaking (see Somit, Tanenhaus, Wilke, and Cooley, below). Although a complete turnabout in political attitudes is rare, politically relevant courses in government, history, and sociology may well cause changes in student beliefs because they function as an antidote to the bland, uncritical type of instruction students had received in high school. The net effect may thus be to make students more critical of some current political institutions or practices. It may also increase their awareness of the complexity of most social and economic problems and thus may make them slightly less prone to accept simplistic explanations. Chances are, however, that such courses will not shake their basic political belief systems, it will merely rob them of some of their naïvety and dogmatism. In all likelihood an increase in sophistication and critical awareness is predicated on a curriculum conducive to analysis and challenge. A highly specialized or technologically oriented curriculum probably does little to affect political attitudes because it never examines, much less shakes, prevailing attitudes, whereas a broad liberal arts curriculum ought to have liberalizing effects.

In this context a word is perhaps in order on the perennial question: Just how conservative or radical is today's college youth? Different scholars answer that question differently because they employ different yardsticks. If one compares students to their parents, one must conclude that today's college youths are more liberal because they accept social welfare and civil rights legislation, for example, far more readily than did the class of 1935 or even 1945. Is this, however, a sign of increased liberalism or is it an acceptance of the *Zeitgeist* and the status quo? In 1935 social security was seen as a dangerous departure from the American way of life and an embarkation on the road to socialism; in 1965 it has become part of the American landscape.

If college youths are compared to one another and not to their parents, it generally turns out that they are somewhat less dogmatic than high school and grammar school educated youths on such issues as communism, civil rights, and free speech, although they are often quite conservative economically. Here again we may refer to the liberating power of education discussed in Chapter 4.

More important, however, these effects of college seem to be lasting. Newcomb,[2] upon reinterviewing the Bennington graduates twenty-five years later, still found them more liberal than their non-Bennington-educated counterparts. Stouffer[3] similarly found college educated people generally to be more tolerant than non-college-educated people, especially in their dedication to civil liberties (freedom of speech, press, assembly, etc.) and less vociferous in their denunciation of communism— observations all of which point to the socializing effect of a college education.

But what about the relatively new phenomenon of American student activ-

ism?* The post-World War II period has seen an unprecedented rash of student protest movements, demonstrations, and at times even violence in connection with a number of political issues. Many observers have concluded that these student activists—whether they are on the right or the left of the political spectrum—can only be classified as radicals bent on profoundly altering or actually destroying the current academic and/or political establishment. The intensity of their political engagement is relatively novel for United States universities. Commonly, American students look upon college as a place for learning (or sports or fun) but not as a political arena. Nor is the bitterness and violence of activism typical of American political behavior in adult or youth. Draft card burning, stoning of recruiters' cars, seizure of university buildings, confrontation with the police, and so forth are indicative of the alienation and desperation felt by some of today's young people, an alienation brought about by deep disenchantment with the materialism of our society, the war in Vietnam, and the persistence of racial discrimination in the United States.[4] These youths are more active and more radical precisely because they care more.

Activists' home backgrounds may offer one clue to their involvement. Studies of activists offer little support to the notion that activism is a form of rebellion against parents (the "generational revolt") but rather tend to indicate that leftism or rightism is to

* This section was written before the more violent confrontations, but it does describe the essential operant processes, although it might have underestimated the frequency and intensity with which such encounters were to occur.

a substantial part an extension of childhood socialization.* Richard Flacks refers to their activism as an extension of parental preferences and not a revolt —generally they tended to come from politically liberal homes. College does not so much socialize them to become politically active as it provides them with the proper arena for it since it gathers on its campus sufficiently large numbers of like-minded people of different persuasions. Closer observation of leftist student activists and the places where they are often found points to two other important preconditions for the intensified radical agitation (1) a relatively permissive environment and (2) sufficient personal economic security. Orbell's analysis of southern Negro student activists[5] discovered they came disproportionately more often from families with higher than average incomes and attended Negro colleges where faculty and administration were favorable (or at least not hostile) to their activities. The colleges also were located close to urban centers rather than in more hostile all-rural areas. State-controlled, rurally located Negro colleges with an economically poorer student body had few activists in their ranks, illustrating once more the socializing force of the environment.

The civil rights movement seems to have been the initial cause that transformed many of the so-called "silent generation" into political activists. As they organized sit-ins, freedom rides, and protest marches, they left a legacy not only to their less active fellow

* It is open to question whether what was written in 1967 holds with equal force three years later. As student protests begin to involve larger number of students, it appears, at least on the surface, that a good deal of rebellion against parents is involved.

students but to the nation at large; a heightened sensitivity to and impatience with the more blatant forms of racial injustice. It is perhaps on this issue more than any other that today's young people differ from their parents. Lest the above create the erroneous impression that all of today's college youth are vitally concerned about politics and forever joining picket-lines, let it be recalled that the majority are not so involved and that the most frequent cause for student protest in the mid-1960s was bad food in college dining halls rather than civil rights or Vietnam.[6]

Student political activism, so novel in the United States, is quite customary in other parts of the world, notably in Latin America and in the underdeveloped nations. Students—along with other intellectuals—were in the vanguard of revolutionary movements, notably in czarist Russia and nationalist China, whereas more recently they have played a major role in attempts to liberalize the communist regimes of Central Europe. But it is in Latin America particularly that students often spend more time on political activities than at their studies. Drawn heavily from the country's elite, they are often less concerned with using the university to prepare for a professional career and more with participating in political movements that can assure them the contacts and publicity for the public career to which they aspire. The very lack of national development further contributes to political agitation on campus. Some of these universities foster a unique student culture that pits itself self-consciously against the prevailing political culture around them and draws youth into a new set of social and political norms. Political activity is thus an outlet for discontent, a way of preparing a more congenial world for oneself, and also perhaps a means of attracting personal publicity.* Even in these nations though it must be pointed out that the intensive political activism at the expense of professional preparation is perhaps again more prevalent among the socially and economically secure than among the upward bound. Studies in progress among students coming from poor peasant and laboring backgrounds give the impression that such youth are quite supportive of the status quo because they hope to become its beneficiaries in the near future. They are generally quite uninterested in politics and their personal and social needs prevent them from participating in the political and intellectual university ferment that so attracts the socially and economically more secure.

In summary, then, it might be well to speculate whether or not college fulfills different socializing functions for different students. Maybe it provides the already concerned student with an arena in which to act out his concern, whereas it provides the less involved student with a ready-made group and an ethos whose norms he may internalize or reject depending on the intensity of his need to belong, the nature of the group ethos, the saliency of his career goals, and the permissiveness of the political atmosphere.

* Some people have commented on the fact that in the underdeveloped nations the two most likely avenues to political leadership for the ambitious youth are the military and the universities.

NOTES

1. Theodore Newcomb, Kathryn Koenig, Richard Flacks, and Donald Warwick, *Persistence and Change: Bennington College and its Students After 25 Years* (New York: Wiley, 1967).

2. *Ibid.*

3. Samuel Stouffer, *Communism, Conformity, and Civil Liberties* (New York: Doubleday, 1955).

4. David Whittaker and William A. Watts, "Personality and Value Attributes of Intellectually Disposed, Alienated Youth" (paper presented at National American Psychological Association meeting, September, 1966); William A. Watts and David Whittaker, "Students of Life: A Study of the Berkeley Non-Student" (paper prepared for Research Group on the Sociology of Education, Sixth World Congress of Sociology, Evian, France, September 4th–11th, 1966); Christian Bay, "Student Political Activism: Here to Stay?" (paper prepared as basis for address to symposium on Comimtted and Alienated Youth, presented at 1967 Annual Meeting of The American Orthopsychiatric Association in Washington, D.C.).

5. John M. Orbell, "Protest Participation Among Southern Negro College Students," *The American Political Science Review*, 61 (1967), 446–456.

6. Richard E. Peterson, *The Scope of Organized Student Protest in 1964–1965* (Princeton, N. J.: Educational Testing Service, 1966).

ATTITUDE DEVELOPMENT AS A FUNCTION OF REFERENCE GROUPS: THE BENNINGTON STUDY

- Theodore M. Newcomb

Membership in established groups usually involves the taking on of whole patterns of interrelated behavior and attitudes. This was one of the hypotheses pursued in the study which is reported here in part. The group selected for study consisted of the entire student body at Bennington College—more than 600 individuals—between the years 1935 and 1939. One of the problems to be investigated was that of the manner in which the patterning of behavior and attitudes varied with different degrees of assimilation into the community.

Not all of the attitudes and behaviors that are likely to be taken on by new members, as they become absorbed into a community, can be investigated in a single study. A single, though rather inclusive, area of adaptation to the college community was therefore selected for special study, namely, *attitudes toward public affairs*. There were two reasons for this selection: (1) methods of attitude measurement were readily available; and (2) there was an unusually high degree of concern, in this community at this time, over a rather wide range of public issues. This latter fact resulted partly from the fact that the college opened its doors during the darkest days of the depression of the 1930's, and its

Above selection from: *Readings in Social Psychology*, Third Edition, edited by Eleanor E. Maccoby, Theodore M. Newcomb, and Eugene L. Hartley, Copyright 1947, 1952, © 1958 by Holt, Rinehart and Winston, Inc. Reprinted by permission of Holt, Rinehart and Winston, Inc.

formative period occurred in the period of social change characterized by the phrase "the New Deal." This was also the period of gathering war clouds in Europe. Underlying both of these circumstances, however, was the conviction on the part of the faculty that one of the foremost duties of the college was to acquaint its somewhat oversheltered students with the nature of their contemporary social world.

In a membership group in which certain attitudes are approved (i.e., held by majorities, and conspicuously so by leaders), individuals acquire the approved attitudes to the extent that the membership group (particularly as symbolized by leaders and dominant subgroups) serves as a positive point of reference. The findings of the Bennington study seem to be better understood in terms of this thesis than any other. The distinction between membership group and reference group is a crucial one, in fact, although the original report did not make explicit use of it.

The above statement does not imply that no reference groups other than the membership group are involved in attitude formation; as we shall see, this is distinctly not the case. Neither does it imply that the use of the membership group as reference group necessarily results in adoption of the approved attitudes. It may also result in their rejection; hence the word *positive* in the initial statement. It is precisely these variations in degree and manner of relationship between reference group and membership group which must be known in order to explain individual variations in attitude formation, as reported in this study.

The essential facts about the Bennington membership group are as follows: (1) It was small enough (about 250 women students) so that data could be obtained from every member. (2) It was in most respects self-sufficient; college facilities provided not only the necessities of living and studying, but also a cooperative store, post office and Western Union office, beauty parlor, gasoline station, and a wide range of recreational opportunities. The average student visited the four-mile-distant village once a week and spent one week end a month away from the college. (3) It was self-conscious and enthusiastic, in large part because it was new (the study was begun during the first year in which there was a senior class) and because of the novelty and attractiveness of the college's educational plan. (4) It was unusually active and concerned about public issues, largely because the faculty felt that its educational duties included the familiarizing of an oversheltered student body with the implications of a depression-torn America and a war-threatened world. (5) It was relatively homogeneous in respect to home background; tuition was very high, and the large majority of students came from urban, economically privileged families whose social attitudes were conservative.

Most individuals in this total membership group went through rather marked changes in attitudes toward public issues, as noted below. In most cases the total membership group served as the reference group for the changing attitudes. But some individuals changed little or not at all in attitudes during the four years of the study; attitude persistence was in some of these cases a function of the membership group as reference group and in some cases it was not. Among those who did change, moreover, the total membership group sometimes served as reference group but sometimes it did not. An oversimple theory of "assimilation into the community" thus leaves out of account some of those whose attitudes did and some of those whose attitudes did not change; they remain unexplained exceptions. A theory which traces the impact of other reference groups as well as the effect of the membership group seems to account for all cases without exception.

The general trend of attitude change for the total group is from freshman conservatism to senior nonconservatism (as the term was commonly applied to the issues toward which attitudes were measured). During the 1936 presidential election, for example, 62 percent of the freshmen and only 14 percent of the juniors and seniors "voted" for the Republican candidate, 29 percent of freshmen and 54 percent of juniors and seniors for Roosevelt, and 9 percent of freshmen as compared with 30 percent of juniors and seniors for the Socialist or Communist candidates. Attitudes toward nine specific issues were measured during the four years of the study, and seniors were less conservative in all of them than freshmen; six of the nine differences are statistically reliable. These differences are best showed by a Likert-type scale labeled Political and Economic Progressivism (PEP) which dealt with such issues as unemployment, public relief, and the rights of organized labor, which were made prominent by the New Deal. Its odd-even reliability was about .9, and it was given once or more during each of the four years of the study to virtually all students. The critical ratios of the differences between freshmen and juniors-seniors in four successive years ranged between 3.9 and 6.5; the difference between the average freshman and senior scores of 44 individuals (the entire class that graduated in 1939) gives a critical ratio of 4.3.

As might be anticipated in such a community, *individual prestige was associated with nonconservatism*. Frequency of choice as one of five students "most worthy to represent the College" at an intercollegiate gathering was used as a measure of prestige. Nominations were submitted in sealed envelopes by 99 percent of all students in two successive years, with almost identical results. The nonconservatism of those with high prestige is not merely the result of the fact that juniors and seniors are characterized by both high prestige and nonconservatism; in each class those who have most prestige are least conservative. For example, ten freshmen receiving 2 to 4 choices had an average PEP score of 64.6 as compared with 72.8 for freshmen not chosen at all (high scores are conservative); eight sophomores chosen 12 or more times had an average score of 63.6 as compared with 71.3 for those not chosen; the mean PEP score of five juniors and seniors chosen 40 or more times was 50.4 and of the fifteen chosen 12 to 39 times, 57.6, as compared with 69.0 for those not chosen. In each class, those intermediate in prestige are also intermediate in average PEP score.

Such were the attitudinal characteristics of the total membership group, expressed in terms of average scores. Some individuals, however, showed these characteristics in heightened form and others failed to show them at all. An examination of the various reference groups in relation to which attitude change did or did not occur, and of the ways in which they were brought to bear, will account for a large part of such attitude variance.

Information concerning reference groups was obtained both directly, from the subjects themselves, and indirectly, from other students and from teachers. Chief among the indirect procedures was the obtaining of indexes of "community citizenship" by a guess-who technique. Each of twenty-four students, carefully selected to represent every cross section and grouping of importance within the community, named three individuals from each of three classes who were reputedly most extreme in each of twenty-eight characteristics related to community citizenship. The relationship between reputation for community identification and nonconservatism is a close one, in spite of the fact that no reference was made to the latter characteristic when the judges made their ratings. A reputation index was computed, based upon the frequency with which individuals were named in five items dealing with identification with the community, minus the number of times they were named in five other items dealing with negative community attitude. Examples of the former items are: "absorbed in college community affairs," and "influenced by community expectations regarding codes, standards, etc.;" examples of the latter are: "indifferent to activities of student committees," and "resistant to community expectations regarding codes, standards, etc." The mean senior PEP score of fifteen individuals whose index was +15 or more was 54.4; of sixty-three whose index was +4 to —4, 65.3; and of ten whose index was —15 or less, 68.2.

To have the reputation of identifying oneself with the community is not the same thing, however, as to identify the community as a reference group for a specific purpose—e.g., in this case, as a point of reference for attitudes toward public issues. In short, the reputation index is informative as to degree and direction of tendency to use the total membership group as a *general* reference group, but not necessarily as a group to which social attitudes are referred. For this purpose information was obtained directly from students.

Informal investigation had shown that whereas most students were aware of the marked freshman-to-senior trend away from conservatism, a few (particularly among the conservatives) had little or no awareness of it. Obviously, those not aware of the dominant community trend could not be using the community as a reference group for an attitude. (It does not follow, of course, that all those who are aware of it are necessarily using the community as reference group.) A simple measure of awareness was therefore devised. Subjects were asked to respond in two ways to a number of attitude statements taken from the PEP scale: first, to indicate agreement or disagreement (for example, with the statement: "The budget should be balanced before the government spends any money on social security"); and second, to estimate what percentage of freshmen, juniors and seniors, and faculty would agree with the statement. From these responses was computed an index of divergence (of own attitude) from the estimated majority of juniors and seniors. Thus a positive index on the part of a senior indicates the degree to which her own responses are

more conservative than those of her classmates, and a negative index the degree to which they are less conservative. Those seniors whose divergence index more or less faithfully reflects the true difference between own and class attitude may (or may not) be using the class as an attitude reference group; those whose divergence indexes represent an exaggerated or minimized version of the true relationship between own and class attitude are clearly not using the class as an attitude reference group, or if so, only in a fictitious sense. (For present purposes the junior-senior group may be taken as representative of the entire student body, since it is the group which "sets the tone" of the total membership group.)

These data were supplemented by direct information obtained in interviews with seniors in three consecutive classes, just prior to graduation. Questions were asked about resemblance between own attitudes and those of class majorities and leaders, about parents' attitudes and own resemblance to them, about any alleged "social pressure to become liberal," about probable reaction if the dominant college influence had been conservative instead of liberal, etc. Abundant information was also available from the college personnel office and from the college psychiatrist. It was not possible to combine all of these sources of information into intensive studies of each individual, but complete data were assembled for (roughly) the most conservative and least conservative sixths of three consecutive graduating classes. The twenty-four nonconservative and nineteen conservative seniors thus selected for intensive study were classified according to their indexes of conservative divergence and of community reputation. Thus eight sets of seniors were identified, all individuals within each set having in common similar attitude scores, similar reputations for community identification, and similar degrees of awareness (based upon divergence index) of own attitude position relative to classmates. The following descriptions of these eight sets of seniors will show that there was a characteristic pattern of relationship between membership group and reference group within each of the sets.

1. *Conservatives, reputedly negativistic, aware of their own relative conservatism.* Four of the five are considered stubborn or resistant by teachers (all five, by student judges). Three have prestige scores of 0, scores of the other two being about average for their class. Four of the five are considered by teachers or psychiatrist, or by both, to be over-dependent upon one or both parents. All of the four who were interviewed described *their major hopes*, on entering college, *in terms of social rather than academic prestige;* all four felt that they had been defeated in this aim. The following verbatim quotations are illustrative:

E2: "Probably the feeling that (my instructors) didn't accept me led me to reject their opinions." (She estimates classmates as being only moderately less conservative than herself, but faculty as much less so.)

G32: "I wouldn't care to be intimate with those so-called 'liberal' student leaders." (*She claims to be satisfied with a small group of friends.* She is chosen as friend, in a sociometric questionnaire responded to by all students, only twice, and reciprocates both choices; both are conservative students.)

F22: "I wanted to disagree with all the noisy liberals, but I was afraid and I couldn't. *So I built up a wall inside me against what they said. I found I couldn't compete, so I decided to stick to my father's ideas. For at least two years I've been insulated against all college influences.*" (She is chosen but once as a friend, and does not reciprocate that choice.)

Q10: (who rather early concluded that she had no chance of social success in college) "It hurt me at first, but now I don't give a damn. *The things I really care about are mostly outside the college.* I think radicalism symbolizes the college for me more than anything else." (Needless to say, she has no use for radicals.)

For these four individuals (and probably for the fifth also) the community serves as reference group in a *negative* sense, and the home-and-family group in a positive sense. Thus their conservatism is dually reinforced.

2. *Conservatives, reputedly negativistic, unaware of their own relative conservatism.* All five are described by teachers, as well as by guess-who judges, to be stubborn or resistant. Four have prestige scores of 0, and the fifth a less than average score. Each reciprocated just one friendship choice. Four are considered insecure in social relationships, and all five are regarded as extremely dependent upon parents. In interviews four describe with considerable intensity, and the fifth with more moderation, precollege experiences of rebuff, ostracism, or isolation, and all describe their hopes on entering college, in terms of making friends or avoiding rebuff rather than in terms of seeking prestige. All five felt that their (rather modest) aims had met with good success. Each of the five denies building up any resistance to the acceptance of liberal opinions (but two add that they would have resented any such pressure, if felt).

Three believe that only small, special groups in the college have such opinions, while the other two describe themselves as just going their own way, *paying no attention to anything but their own little circles and their college work.* Typical quotations follow:

Q47: "I'm a perfect middle-of-the-roader, neither enthusiast nor critic. I'd accept anything if they just let me alone. . . . I've made all the friends I want." (Only one of her friendship choices is reciprocated.)

Q19: "*In high school I was always thought of as my parents' daughter.* I never felt really accepted for myself. . . . I wanted to make my own way here, socially, but independence from my family has never asserted itself in other ways." (According to guess-who ratings, she is highly resistant to faculty authority.)

L12: "What I most wanted was to get over being a scared bunny. . . . I always resent doing the respectable thing just because it's the thing to do, but I didn't realize I was so different, politically, from my classmates. At least I agree with the few people I ever talk to about such matters." (Sociometric responses place her in a small, conservative group.)

Q81: "I hated practically all my school life before coming here. I had the perfect inferiority complex, and I pulled out of school social life—out of fear. I didn't intend to repeat that mistake here. . . . I've just begun to be successful in winning friendships, and I've been blissfully happy here." (She is described by teachers as "pathologically belligerent;" she receives more than the average number of friendship choices, but reciprocates only one of them.)

For these five individuals, who are negativistic in the sense of being near-isolates rather than rebels, the com-munity does not serve as reference group for public attitudes. To some extent, their small friendship groups serve in this capacity, but in the main they still refer such areas of their lives to the home-and-family group. They are too absorbed in their own pursuits to use the total membership group as a reference group for most other purposes, too.

3. *Conservatives, not reputedly negativistic, aware of their own relative conservatism.* Three of the five are described by teachers as "cooperative" and "eager," and none as stubborn or resistant. Four are above average in prestige. Four are considered by teachers or by guess-who raters, or both, to retain very close parental ties. All four who were interviewed had more or less definite ambitions for leadership on coming to college, and all felt that they had been relatively successful—though, in the words of one of them, none ever attained the "really top-notch positions." All four are aware of conflict between parents and college community in respect to public attitudes, and all quite consciously decided to "string along" with parents, feeling self-confident of holding their own in college in spite of being atypical in this respect. Sample quotations follow:

Q73: "*I'm all my mother has in the world. It's considered intellectually superior here to be liberal or radical. This puts me on the defensive,* as I refuse to consider my mother beneath me intellectually, as so many other students do. Apart from this, I have loved every aspect of college life." (A popular girl, many of whose friends are among the non-conservative college leaders.)

Q78: "*I've come to realize how much my mother's happiness depends on me, and the best way I can help her is to do things with her at home as often as I can.* This has resulted in my not getting the feel of the college in certain ways, and I know my general conservatism is one of those ways. But it has not been important enough to me to make me feel particularly left out. If you're genuine and inoffensive about your opinions, no one really minds here if you remain conservative." (Another popular girl, whose friends were found among many groups.)

F32: "*Family against faculty has been my struggle here.* As soon as I felt really secure here I decided not to let the college atmosphere affect me too much. Every time I've tried to rebel against my family I've found out how terribly wrong I am, and so I've naturally kept to my parents' attitudes." (While not particularly popular, she shows no bitterness and considerable satisfaction over her college experience.)

Q35: "I've been aware of a protective shell against radical ideas. When I found several of my best friends getting that way, I either had to go along or just shut out that area entirely. I couldn't respect myself if I had changed my opinions just for that reason, and so I almost deliberately lost interest—really, *it was out of fear of losing my friends.*" (A very popular girl, with no trace of bitterness, who is not considered too dependent upon parents.)

For these five the total membership group does not serve as reference group in respect to public attitudes, but does so serve for most other purposes. At some stage in their college careers the conflict between college community and home and family as reference group for public attitudes was resolved in favor of the latter.

4. *Conservatives, not reputedly negativistic, not aware of their own relative conservatism.* All four are consistently described by teachers as conscientious and cooperative; three are considered overdocile and uncritical of authority. All are characterized by feelings of inferiority. All are low in prestige, two receiving scores of 0; all are low in friendship choices, but reciprocate most of these few choices. Two are described as in conflict about parental authority, and two as dependent and contented. All four recall considerable anxiety as to whether they would fit into the college community; all feel that they have succeeded better than they had expected. Sample statements from interviews follow:

D22: "I'd like to think like the college leaders, but I'm not bold enough and I don't know enough. So the college trend means little to me; I didn't even realize how much more conservative I am than the others. *I guess my family influence has been strong enough to counterbalance the college influence.*" (This girl was given to severe emotional upsets, and according to personnel records, felt "alone and helpless except when with her parents.")

M12: "It isn't that I've been resisting any pressure to become liberal. The influences here didn't matter enough to resist, I guess. *All that's really important that has happened to me occurred outside of college,* and so I never became very susceptible to college influences." (*Following her engagement to be married, in her second year, she had "practically retired" from community life.*)

Q68: "If I'd had more time here I'd probably have caught on to the liberal drift here. But I've been horribly busy making money and trying to keep my college work up. *Politics and that sort of thing I've always associated with home instead of with the college.*" (A "town girl" of working-class parentage.)

Q70: "Most juniors and seniors, if they really *get excited about their work, forget about such community enthusiasms as sending telegrams to Congressmen.* It was so important to me to be accepted, I mean intellectually, *that I naturally came to identify myself in every way with the group which gave me this sort of intellectual satisfaction.*" (One of a small group of science majors, nearly all conservative, who professed no interests other than science and who were highly self-sufficient socially.)

For none of the four was the total membership group a reference group for public attitudes. Unlike the non-negativistic conservatives who are aware of their relative conservatism, they refer to the total membership group for few if any other purposes. Like the negativistic conservatives who are unaware of their relative conservatism, their reference groups for public attitudes are almost exclusively those related to home and family.

5. *Nonconservatives, reputedly community-identified, aware of their relative nonconservativism.* Each of the seven is considered highly dependent by teachers, particularly in intellectual activities; all but one are referred to as meticulous, perfectionist, or overconscientious. Four are very high in prestige, two high, and one average; all are "good group members," and all but one a "leader." None is considered overdependent upon parents. All have come to an understanding with parents concerning their "liberal" views; five have "agreed to differ," and the other two describe one or both parents as "very liberal." All take their public attitudes seriously, in most cases expressing the feeling that they have bled and died to achieve them. Interview excerpts follow.

B72: "*I bend in the direction of community expectation*—almost more than I want to. I constantly have to check myself to be sure it's real self-conviction and not just social respect." (An outstanding and deeply respected leader.)

M42: "My family has always been liberal, but the influences here made me go further, and for a while I was pretty far left. Now I'm pretty much in agreement with my family again, but it's my own and it means a lot. It wouldn't be easy for me to have friends who are very conservative." (Her friendship choices are exclusively given to nonconservatives.)

E72: "I had been allowed so much independence by my parents that I needed desperately to identify myself with an institution with which I could conform conscientiously. Bennington was perfect. I drank up everything the college had to offer, including social attitudes, though not uncritically. I've become active in radical groups and constructively critical of them." (Both during and after college she worked with C.I.O. unions.)

H32: "I accepted liberal attitudes here because *I had always secretly felt that my family was narrow and intolerant, and because such attitudes had prestige value.* It was all part of my generally expanding personality—*I had never really been part of anything before.* I don't accept things without examining things, however, and I was sure I meant it before I changed." (One of those who has "agreed to differ" with parents.)

Q43: "It didn't take me long to see that liberal attitudes had prestige value. But all the time I felt inwardly superior to persons who want public acclaim. Once I had arrived at a feeling of personal security, I could see that it wasn't important—it wasn't enough. *So many people have no security at all. I became liberal at first because of its prestige value.* I remain so because the problems around which my liberalism centers are important. What I want now is to be effective in solving the problems." (Another conspicuous leader, active in and out of college in liberal movements.)

The total membership clearly serves as reference group for these individuals' changing attitudes, but by no means as the only one. For those whose parents are conservative, parents represent a negative reference group, from whom emancipation was gained via liberal attitudes. And for several of them the college community served as a bridge to outside liberal groups as points of reference.

6. *Nonconservatives, reputedly community-identified, not aware of their own relative nonconservatism.* The word *enthusiastic* appears constantly in the records of each of these six. All are considered eager, ambitious, hard-working, and anxious to please. Four are very high in prestige, the other two about average. None is considered overdependent upon parents, and only two are known to have suffered any particular conflict in achieving emancipation. Each one came to college with ambitions for leadership, and each professes extreme satisfaction with her college experience. Sample quotations follow:

Qx: "Every influence I felt tended to push me in the liberal direction: my underdog complex, *my need to be independent of my parents, and my anxiousness to be a leader here.*"

Q61: "I met a whole body of new information here; I took a deep breath and plunged. When I talked about it at home my family began to treat me as if I had an adult mind. *Then too, my new opinions gave me the reputation here of being open-minded and capable of change.* I think I could have got really radical but I found it wasn't the way to get prestige here." (She judges most of her classmates to be as nonconservative as herself.)

Q72: "I take everything hard, and so of course I reacted hard to all the attitudes I found here. I'm 100-percent enthusiastic about Bennington, and - that includes liberalism (but not radicalism, though I used to think so). Now I know that you can't be an *extremist if you're really devoted to an institution,* whether it's a labor union or a college." (A conspicuous leader who, like most of the others in this set of six, *judges classmates to be only slightly more conservative than herself.*)

Q63: "*I came to college to get away from my family,* who never had any respect for my mind. Becoming a radical meant thinking for myself and, figuratively, thumbing my nose at my family. *It also meant intellectual identification with the faculty and students that I most wanted to be like.*" (She has always felt oppressed by parental respectability and sibling achievements.)

Q57: "It's very simple. *I was so anxious to be accepted that I accepted the political complexion of the community here.* I just couldn't stand out against the crowd unless I had many friends and strong support." (Not a leader, but many close friends among leaders and nonconservatives.)

For these six, like the preceding seven, the membership group serves as reference group for public affairs. They differ from the preceding seven chiefly in that they are less sure of themselves and are careful "not to go too far." Hence they tend to repudiate "radicalism," and to judge classmates as only slightly less conservative than themselves.

7. *Nonconservatives, not reputedly community-identified, aware of own relative nonconservatism.* Each of the six is described as highly independent and critical-minded. Four are consistently reported as intellectually outstanding, and the other two occasionally so. All describe their ambitions on coming to college in intellectual rather than in social terms. Four of the five who were interviewed stated that in a conservative

college they would be "even more radical than here." Two are slightly above average in prestige, two below average, and two have 0 scores. Three have gone through rather severe battles in the process of casting off what they regard as parental shackles; none is considered overdependent upon parents. Sample interview excerpts follow:

q7: "*All my life I've resented the protection of governesses and parents*. What I most wanted here was the intellectual approval of teachers and the more advanced students. Then I found you can't be reactionary and be intellectually respectable." (Her traits of independence became more marked as she achieved acedemic distinction.)

q21: "I simply got filled with new ideas here, and the only possible formulation of all of them was to adopt a radical approach. *I can't see my own position in the world in any other terms. The easy superficiality with which so many prestige-hounds here get 'liberal' only forced me to think it out more intensely*." (A highly gifted girl, considered rather aloof.)

c32: "*I started rebelling against my pretty stuffy family before I came to college*. I felt apart from freshmen here, because I was older. Then I caught on to faculty attempts to undermine prejudice. I took sides with the faculty immediately, against the immature freshmen. I crusaded about it. *It provided just what I needed by way of family rebellion*, and bolstered up my self-confidence, too." (A very bright girl, regarded as sharp tongued and a bit haughty.)

j24: "*I'm easily influenced by people whom I respect*, and the people who rescued me when I was down and out, intellectually, gave me a radical intellectual approach; they included both teachers and advanced students. *I'm not rebelling against anything*. I'm just doing what I had to do to stand on my own feet intellectually." (Her academic work was poor as a freshman, but gradually became outstanding.)

For these six students it is not the total membership group, but dominant sub-groups (faculty, advanced students) which at first served as positive reference groups, and for many of them the home group served as a negative point of reference. Later, they developed extra-college reference groups (left-wing writers, etc.). In a secondary sense, however, the total membership group served as a negative point of reference—i.e., they regarded their non-conservatism as a mark of personal superiority.

8. *Nonconservatives, not reputedly community-identified, not aware of own relative nonconservatism*. Each of the five is considered hard-working, eager, and enthusiastic but (especially during the first year or two) unsure of herself and too dependent upon instructors. They are "good citizens," but in a distinctly retiring way. Two are above average in prestige, and the other three much below average. None of the five is considered overdependent upon parents; two are known to have experienced a good deal of conflict in emancipating themselves. All regard themselves as "pretty average persons," with strong desire to conform; they describe their ambitions in terms of social acceptance instead of social or intellectual prestige. Sample excerpts follow:

e22: "*Social security is the focus of it all with me*. I became steadily less conservative as long as I was *needing to gain in personal security, both with students and with faculty*. I developed some resentment against a few extreme radicals who don't really represent the college viewpoint, and that's why I changed my attitudes so far and no further." (A girl with a small personal following, otherwise not especially popular.)

D52: "*Of course there's social pressure here to give up your conservatism*. I'm glad of it, because for me this became the *vehicle for achieving independence from my family*. So changing my attitudes has gone hand in hand with two *very important things: establishing my own independence and at the same time becoming a part of the college organism*." (She attributes the fact that her social attitudes changed, while those of her younger sister, also at the college, did not, to the fact that she had greater need both of family independence and of group support.)

Q6: "I was ripe for developing liberal or even radical opinions because so many of my friends at home were doing the same thing. So it was really wonderful that I could agree with all the people I respected here and the same time move in the direction that my home friends were going." (A girl characterized by considerable personal instability at first, but showing marked improvement.)

QY: "I think my change of opinions has given me *intellectual and social self-respect at the same time*. I used to be too timid for words, and I never had an idea of my own. As I gradually became more successful in my work and made more friends, I came to feel that it didn't matter so much whether I agreed with my parents. It's all part of the feeling that I really belong here." (Much other evidence confirms this; she was lonely and pathetic at first, but really belonged later.)

These five provide the example *par excellence* of individuals who came to identify themselves with "the community" and whose attitudes change *pari passu* with the growing sense of identity. Home-and-family groups served as supplementary points of reference, either positive or negative. To varying degrees, subgroups within the community served as focal points of reference. But, because of *their need to be accepted, it was primarily the membership group as such which served as reference group for these five*.

Summary

In this community, as presumably in most others, all individuals belong to the total membership group, but such membership is not necessarily a point of reference for every form of social adaptation, e.g., for acquiring attitudes toward public issues. *Such attitudes, however, are not acquired in a social vacuum. Their acquisition is a function of relating oneself to some group or groups, positively or negatively*. In many cases (perhaps in all) the referring of social attitudes to one group negatively leads to referring them to another group positively, or vice versa, so that the attitudes are dually reinforced.

An individual is, of course, "typical" in respect to attitudes if the total membership group serves as a positive point of reference for that purpose, but "typicality" may also result from the use of other reference groups. It does not follow from the fact that an individual is "atypical" that the membership group does not serve for reference purposes; it may serve as negative reference group. Even if the membership group does not serve as reference group at all (as in the case of conservatives in this community who are unaware of the general freshman-to-senior trend), it cannot be concluded that attitude development is not a function of belonging to the total membership group. The unawareness of such individuals is itself a resultant adaptation of particular individuals to a particular membership group. The fact that such individuals continue to refer attitudes toward public issues primarily to home-and-family groups is, in part at least, a result of the kind of community in which they have membership.

In short, the Bennington findings seem to support the thesis that, in a community characterized by certain approved attitudes, the individual's attitude development is a function of the way in which he relates himself both to the total membership group and to one or more reference groups.

SINCE BENNINGTON: EVIDENCE OF CHANGE IN STUDENT POLITICAL BEHAVIOR

• Alex S. Edelstein*

In contrast to students in other countries American college students seem politically apathetic. Yet their college experience does influence their attitudes and a sequence of studies has attempted to determine how much they change and in what ways.

Alex S. Edelstein is Associate Professor in the School of Communications at the University of Washington. This article is based on a paper he presented to the Annual Conference of the American Association for Public Opinion Research in May 1962.

Every decade since the 1930's has seen a major inquiry into college youth and its beliefs. The college student of the 1930's, as portrayed in the Bennington study, was an individual thoroughly socialized into liberal political norms.[1] The need for general education was emphasized in the 1940's, and students of the 1950's were characterized as the "silent generation." Now, in the 1960's, we are being told that conservatism is the new college mood, and that Barry Goldwater and William F. Buckley, Jr., are its symbols.[2]

While there is convincing empirical evidence of the liberalism of the 1930's, due largely to the Bennington study, and studies of the 1940's persuaded us

Above selection reprinted from: *Public Opinion Quarterly*, Vol. 26, No. 4, Winter, 1962. Revised by author, 1967. Deletions have been made by the editor in the interest of brevity.

* I wish to express my indebtedness to Mrs. Nancy F. Spitzer, research assistant in the School of Communications, for valuable suggestions and assistance, and to Mr. Herbert Blisard, research assistant, for help in developing and administering the questionnaires and conducting the intensive interviews.

that more general education *was* needed, there is no empirical evidence of the existence of or the explication of a "silent generation" of the 1950's or that conservatism is "sweeping" the campuses today.[3] If anything, a liberalizing, if not liberal, trend, *less* extreme and ideologically centered, has continued steadily in the past three decades. College students are still being socialized into the college culture, but the basis for political socialization appears to be shifting from ideology to intellectualism as the means to the end. The outward character of the "silent generation" might well be viewed in retrospect not as one of apathy but as a search for reality.[4]

The thesis to be offered here is this: If there has been a trend, it has been one of decreasing conservatism *and* liberalism in the ideological sense. This is reflected in a less emotional or doctrinaire commitment to a position on given political, social, and economic issues and an independence of thought from prescribed liberal and conservative doctrine; yet it is marked also by political awareness, knowledge, and party identification. It is in the nature of an intellectual commitment.[5]

Evidence of this will be offered from a selection of studies over the past thirty-five years in which (1) the socialization of the college student, (2) the influence of courses and curriculum, (3) the impact of faculties, and (4) patterns of personality development of students all point to the continuing liberalizing trend in our colleges.

The Socialization of the College Student

The Bennington study continues as the benchmark for the study of political socialization in college. The impact of the small liberal political environment upon students from wealthy and politically conservative families was noted by Newcomb.

o   o   o

Studies since Bennington have continued to stress the socialization function of the college. The Vassar study, reported in 1956, concluded that the student culture was the prime educational force at work in the college, and assimilation into it was the primary concern of most students.[6] The study of "button-down" culture by Davies and Hare went so far as to conclude that the subculture in a men's college operated to *limit* the amount of intellectual activity through the value it placed on the "well-rounded man."[7] Freedman, in his discussion of the "passage through college," said that educational experiences were relatively independent of formal academic influences and identified the characteristics of each passing year:

1. Freshmen: Acceptance by their fellow students; a few seek academic approval.
2. Sophomores: The year of choice of major subject and thus of "commitment." Most major subjects are selected so as to minimize conflict with existing values.
3. Juniors: Maximum educational and social solidarity. "The torchbearers of the culture."

4. Seniors: A transitional year between college values and graduation expectations. One foot is in the "after life."[8]

An unpublished study by Hayes at the University of Washington demonstrates the increasing homogeneity of student friendships, which become stronger and more like-minded from the freshman to the senior year.[9] Rose, in his Cornell University study, pointed out that those students with Stevenson friends voted for Stevenson 2 to 1 and those with Eisenhower friends voted for Ike 3 to 1, both proportions being significantly greater than the vote of the total student body.[10]

A series of intensive interviews with students at the University of Washington reveals numerous references to the influence of socialization into peer groups in bringing about reinforcement, change, and in some cases political conversion. A few examples:

1. Reinforcement: A freshman pre-law girl student, from a close-knit Republican family, worked in the Young Republican Club and in her sorority, participated in mock elections, and argued vociferously with the daughter of the Democratic Governor of the State of Washington.
2. Change: A strongly Republican sophomore girl, from a solidly Republican family, felt she had become "more liberal" as a result of her association with fellow political science majors.
3. Conversion: A twenty-six-year-old male student in chemistry, who had childhood memories of anti-Democratic parents, felt deeply influenced by a Democratic political science roommate. Ultimately, he himself became a Democratic precinct committeeman.

Objections to the socialization theory have been expressed in two forms: one sees college attitudes as only a reflection of outside forces; the other doubts the validity of measurements of college students on political ideology.

An example of the first type is the Jacob report, published in 1957, financed by the Hazen Foundation to evaluate the impact of general education.[11] The Jacob report asserted that rather than working against the grain of "outside" influences, the college culture worked with the grain and became merely a "medium of communication" for newly prescribed social values. Others would agree.[12] Before World War II, Jacob said, studies of attitudes in college toward racial prejudice showed little or no change, and only a major ideological campaign by the government against discrimination (an "outside" force) brought about a shift in college attitudes.

As an example of the second type of objection, Smith has doubted the validity of many college studies, declaring that at least in certain academic departments there are students who:

...learn their liberalism as an accommodation to professors and absorb it from assigned readings in the same enterprising way that they learn French and history. They may, in fact, become "attitude-scale wise" just as they become "test-wise" and learn to make the expected answers. On certain campuses the social climate is liberal, and one may judge that the abler students make the best adjustment to this situation.

...If, for instance, the system is one which offers prestige and approval for being liberals, as at Bennington, doubtless the abler people will join those ranks; if the rewards seem to be available along traditional, conservative lines, our evidence suggests that the abler people—within a given occupation—will accept this challenge, leaving among the uninformed many embittered "liberals" to flirt with thoughts of a new deal.[13]

Newcomb also noted student types who did not perceive politics as an important means of socialization. They were seemingly unaware of the political norms of the groups around them. For them, politics was seen as neither relevant nor meaningful. Students with firmly held beliefs, on the other hand, resisted group influences, and in some cases were characterized by perception biases that operated to distort the values of the group. In this sense, political socialization was dysfunctional. In some cases, the group adjusted to the individual because of his value to the organization at that particular time. Such factors operated to limit the impact of the college culture in modifying student attitudes and beliefs, as illustrated by these brief profiles of University of Washington political "inactives."

1. An undergraduate music student, with a Republican father and a Democratic mother. She was, in her own terms, "a middle-of-the-roader." There was little discussion of politics in her home, never discussion among her sorority friends. "Not deeply interested in anything, she went along with the group."
2. A male architecture student. The boy had his own Cadillac in high school. The voting pattern of his parents was mixed. The boy had no close friends, generally stayed out of political discussions. He disliked his government teacher in junior high school and wonders if this had an influence on him. He is now less interested in money, is developing interests and ability in architecture.
3. A business-education major. Her father is a doctor, her mother holds a master's degree. She felt "forced" by her parents into college as well as into other activities.

A member of the Young Republicans in both high school and college, she was nevertheless inactive in each. Her parents and close friends never were very interested in politics. She never reads political news, says she distrusts both politics and politicians.[14]

The cases just cited, however, represent only a minority of students. The generalization that peer-group socialization is a powerful influence on the student is generally upheld.

The Influence of the Curriculum

The condemnation of the "silent generation" probably owes its genesis to the indirect as well as direct influence of the editorial policies of *Time* magazine. In 1940, curious as to the status of the "college bloc," *Time* underwrote a statistical report on United States college graduates. Designed as a circulation and prestige builder, it also had a slight philosophical perspective. Its editor, Lawrence F. Babcock, wrote:

The management of *Time, Inc., does* believe that education is the hope of democracy. And it believes that at this time, when two antithetical philosophies of government are competing for the control of civilization, the existence of a group of 2.7 million college graduates is one of the most important factors in the preservation of the American way of life. This study was undertaken ... to test these assumptions for the first time by newly determined dependable data.[15]

The Babcock study led *Time* to lend its resources to a second study in 1947, which reflected prevailing concern over the "kinds of citizens being turned out by our colleges."[16]

On the basis of a 60 per cent return to 17,000 mail questionnaires addressed to graduates of 1,000 accredited institutions, it concluded that:

Most college graduates read, talk, listen, and vote in national elections, some 79 per cent as compared with 55 per cent of the public.

Less than one-third, however, signed petitions; less than one-fourth sent letters or telegrams to their representatives; less than one-fifth contributed money to a political cause.

Furthermore, of eleven most likely political activities, college graduates engaged in only five.

The Jacob report cited the Pace report of graduates as evidence that students (not graduates) were largely apathetic and ignorant, and gave only "lip service" to democratic responsibilities. Jacob documented this by the "fact" that only 1 student in 10 gave a high priority to national and international problems. However, this turned out to be higher than the percentage reported by Stouffer for the general population on the same question,[17] as noted by Riesman in his review of the Jacob report.[18]

Pace's study of the consequences of general education was valuable, however, in many respects. It provided needed evidence of the effect of the curriculum in broadening and liberalizing students' views. For example, Pace discovered that students in general education were more liberal on socioeconomic questions than were students in the technical-professional departments, and that graduates of Ivy and Big Ten schools were far more liberal in their views than graduates of seventeen leading technical schools.

The following are examples of the liberalizing function of the curriculum:

In a test of attitudes toward segregation, Holtzman found that students in education, the social sciences, and the humanities were more tolerant than those in business, engineering, and natural science.[19]

Nogee and Levin reported the least change in political outlook in business students, and the most change (in a liberal direction) in those studying for the ministry at Boston University.[20] A University of Washington study found students in the general education area more liberal (self-assertion validated by reaction to issues) than those in the technical - professional - vocational areas.[21]

Drucker and Remmers, in an effort to solve the cause-effect riddle (do more tolerant persons go into general education or does general education make persons more tolerant?), controlled factors of parental and cultural orientation.[22] Using a modified set of scale items adapted from the Pace study, they compared engineers (exposed to a total of twenty-seven hours of English, economics, psychology, etc., in their four-year program) to science majors who had been exposed to a broad liberal arts curriculum. Holding the two factors constant, engineering students still demonstrated a less political outlook at the end of the four years.[23]

A number of studies have also measured the amount of change in political ideology occurring as a result of exposure to one or more specific courses in a curriculum. Here, too, the direction has been toward increasing liberalism. For example, the very early experiment by Kornhauser demonstrated extensive changes from quarter to quarter during a two-year course in attitudes and opinions regarding economic theories.[24] Of those who changed

their attitudes during the first year, 3 out of 4 became more liberal: By the second year the proportion had increased to 5 out of 6.

In these studies, too, the liberal trend correlates with passage through the college years. In the University of Washington study, of those students who said they had changed their political outlook in college, 2 out of 3 said they had become "more liberal."[25] These "liberal" responses were validated by responses to conservative-liberal issues. Nogee and Levin reported precisely the same rate and direction of change at Boston University.[26]

The Jacob report concedes that this tendency varies little from school to school. The majority of students, Jacob says, have commitments to such issues as civil rights at the time that they enter college, and these become stronger as they proceed through college. Jacob said seniors were generally less anti-Communist, less unqualifiedly committed to the American way of life, and more likely to reject such views as "Liberals are soft-headed, gullible, and potentially dangerous." Seniors also were less ethnocentric; morally more permissive in religion, literature, books, and sex; and more skeptical of the supernatural.

There are, of course, conservative influences at work in the colleges that account for the 1 out of 3 students who reports he is developing a more conservative outlook, but, as will be discussed later, one must doubt if this conservatism is as deeply ideological in nature as *Time* magazine would imply.

The Cornell study, for one, reports increasing conservatism through the college years in 10 out of 11 schools on a series of economic and political *attitude* questions. The University of Washington study was concerned with *specific issues*. If attitudinal structure is thought of as "ideological," for purposes of discussion, and issues as impinging on this structure, it would suggest that specific issues challenge the attitude structure to engage in a variety of adaptive processes. For example, one can agree that the "welfare state" tends to destroy individual initiative, government planning inevitably results in the loss of individual liberties and freedom, and the best government is the one which governs least—all of which were Cornell Values Study items—but at the same time support medical care for the aged through social security, Federal aid to education, and foreign aid. The authors of the Cornell study acknowledge this in what they call "the contrast between the abstract and the concrete" in matters of religious tolerance, the issue that produced the contradiction in attitude and behavior.

Influence of the College Faculty

Little will be reported here on the influence of the college faculty as agents of political socialization, for the ground has been well covered by Lazarsfeld and Thielens, limited as their study may have been to social scientists.[27] However, since a number of references have been made to studies of the political behavior of University of Washington students, it might be appropriate to report the results of studies done by Gottfried on faculty political behavior at the University of Washington.[28]

In 1960, 26 per cent of the Washington faculty said they generally thought of themselves as Republicans, 43 per cent

Democratic, and 28 per cent independent. The 1956 findings were similar. As reported earlier by Lazarsfeld and Thielens, Republicans were most likely to be found among older, senior professors. The most pronounced Democratic preference was found at the assistant and associate professor ranks.

Of arts and science departments, all but two in 1960 voted for Kennedy, many heavily; the two split their vote evenly. Nixon carried all the professional and vocational departments, but by less margin than Kennedy in his areas.

In what Gottfried termed the "iron test of financial contribution," there were eight times as many contributions to Stevenson as to Eisenhower; where the contribution was $25 or more, the ratio was 12 to 1 Stevenson. Gottfried commented, "Perhaps no clearer indication than this last comparison can be given of the high degree of identification of academic voters with the prototype of 'egghead.'"[29]

The admiration of some students for certain of their professors is as well known a phenomenon as the indifference exhibited toward others. Brown, in the Vassar study, classified students into five types.[30] Several of these were marked by either high or low "faculty ideology," which expressed the degree of their identification with faculty values and, inferentially, personalities.[31] A review of the intensive interviews with University of Washington students—with their numerous testimonials to the influence of professors and courses—shows clearly that there are important things to be learned about the emotional, intellectual, and ideological functions served by student-professor relationships. For the purposes of this study, it can be fairly well asserted that a predominantly liberal faculty culture has had its liberalizing impact upon college youth.

Studies of Personality Development

Here, too, studies as early as the late 1920's provide suggestions as to the patterns of political behavior of college students. While the early studies were intended to study the radical personality per se, not the political behavior of students in a college setting, two of these, nevertheless, offer theoretical concepts of the radical personality that are seen in later studies of student political behavior.[32]

Moore found among Yale and Dartmouth undergraduates what he called "radical" and "conservative" temperaments.[33] The radical was more ready to break old habits, to sacrifice accuracy for speed, and to make snap judgments; however, he also tended to be more original in his thinking and relatively independent in the face of majority influences.

Allport and Hartman concluded from a study of Syracuse University students that there were more similarities between reactionaries and radicals than between either of these two groups and middle-of-the-roaders.[34] Both had greater difficulty than the middle group in accepting established conventions; both were less willing to answer questions on their attitude toward sex, and both were guided in their opinions more by wishes than by reason.

In the Bennington study, Newcomb sought through a system of classification to identify elements of personality as correlates of liberal and conservative political belief. If "personality" was a predictable pattern of response to

events and ideas, evidence of personality development in college would provide suggestions as to present and even future political behavior.

The Vassar College study adopted this approach, Sanford, one of the investigators, commenting:

The kinds of intellectual, moral, social and emotional character which the liberal college usually seeks to develop or to foster, and those which it seeks to reduce or eliminate, are much like those which concern the psychologist when he thinks about the maturity or health or the optimum functioning of the individual.[35]

What suggested by Sanford and his associates was that personality development proceeded with maturation, and that this was accompanied by liberalizing attitudes and opinions toward political ideology and public affairs.

Webster, one of Sanford's colleagues, demonstrated that seniors scored lower than freshmen on authoritarianism scales and higher on the development scales devised by the author.[36]

The freshman syndrome was made up of such characteristics as impulsiveness, conventionality, religious fundamentalism, lack of self-confidence, projectivity, and romanticism. The seniors were more self-confident and self-critical, less passive, and less conventional, and they sought more diversity and complexity.

Again, with respect to the developmental scale, seniors possessed more flexibility and tolerance of ambiguity. They were more tolerant and held less punitive attitudes toward others. They were more critical of parents and family. They were characterized by religious liberalism, more subjectivity in interaction, more mature interests. They were less conventional and conformist, more realistic, and, very importantly, attached more value to intellectual processes.

It is noteworthy that *successive senior classes demonstrated a progressive increase in these attributes.* Less willingness to accept social responsibility, much lamented, might be interpreted as less identification with ideology and a more abstract and intellectual concern with consequences. An element of alienation from "outside norms" also seems present.

Brown's educational types at Vassar provided similar evidence of the relationship of personality development to political attitudes.[37] As indicated, only one of his four personality types—the so-called "over-achievers"—maintained a conservative social and political ideology through college. Brown attributes this to an attitude of submission to authority. He comments, apparently seriously, "This . . . tends to support the often-heard complaint that grades can to some extent be achieved with only a reasonable capacity, little deep intellectual curiosity, and a good deal of 'proper' behavior, accompanied by some careful choice of content from the curriculum."

Significantly for this thesis, Brown's liberal groups were characterized both by low authoritarianism and high intellectual interest and tended to identify strongly with "faculty ideology."

Thus, a variety of studies of personality development show the same liberalizing forces at work in the college culture. If, as it appears, personality maturation accompanies the socialization of the college student, a liberalizing of political behavior can be predicted inside *and* outside the college environment.

The studies cited have also reported a continuing shift by most college students, particularly in the general education areas, toward more tolerant and flexible attitudes toward politics and the political process. This serves to explain the unanticipated tolerance for the radical conservative movement on college campuses and accounts also for the many curious spectators on the scene. There is very little in the studies to show a trend toward ideology of the extreme right or left. If anything, the "id" may be said to have been taken out of "ideology." A few examples: Webster's "highest development" freshmen showed independence on political issues and low scores on political ideology; Nogee and Levin similarly reported most change toward independence and issue orientation; Maccoby reported "conscious selection processes at work" among students in her sample;[38] Rose said there was evidence of "accurate perception processes" among Cornell students— they agreed on what the issues were; at the University of Washington, the more knowledgeable the student, the less he distorted the source of the controversial statement. Even Jacob noted, after his nationwide study, that students are "less rigid, dogmatic and absolute in the standards and beliefs they hold, more critical of authority per se, more self confident . . . and/reliant . . . less prejudiced, and more tolerant of deviation. . . ."

Discussion

These findings tend sometimes to be obscured by comparisons of college students with college graduates. There are numerous illustrations of students who become more liberal in college but later revert to originally held beliefs. This is particularly true of those who placed a high value on peer-group orientation in college without an equivalent intellectual commitment. Maccoby reported that graduate students at Cambridge in a strongly Republican year (1952) were far more Stevenson-minded than their parents, but after leaving Cambridge there was almost an inversion effect. Havemann and West, in a well-known study, report similar findings.[39]

The foregoing is not meant to suggest that college graduates all become more conservative. The longer college graduates are out of school, the more conservative they *seem* to be. What is accepted by a later generation (the graduated income tax, social security, or the governmental role in supporting university research) was at an earlier time an innovation. An extreme example of this is a comparison, offered by some writers, of college graduates of the thirties and the twenties. Yet even the innovations that characterized the thirties (social security, unemployment compensation, collective bargaining, etc.) were becoming accepted institutions in the forties and are scarcely questioned today. This would not necessarily make this generation more

"liberal" than the past one. Most of the ideological meaning is gone.

Some writers are speaking of the "end of ideology" and of an age of "pluralism."[40] If, as Jacob has expressed it, "the stream of society" continues to run a substantially pragmatic course, we can expect intellectualism or choice making to assert itself even more strongly. This should become a factor in the examination by students of liberalism *and* conservatism. Few students have been fooled by the claims and protestations of the Left or the Right. Those who have demonstrate a need for identity and reassurance and do not give evidence of strength.

A final note: It is curious that *Time* should have used such care in inquiring into college values in the 1940's and been so superficial in its characterization of the college students of the 1950's and the 1960's. There are limits to the "self-fulfilling" prophecy suggested by Riesman (being told that they are "silent" by the *Nation*, or "conservative" by *Time*, the students will conform to the prophecy).[41] The findings of social research lend themselves increasingly to the important task of confirming intuition or denying horseback opinion. This auditing of our knowledge of student political behavior represents one such effort.

NOTES

1. The abbreviated version of the book-length study is found in Theodore M. Newcomb, "Attitude Development as a Function of Reference Groups: The Bennington Study," in Theodore M. Newcomb, Eleanor E. Maccoby, and Eugene Hartley, *Readings in Social Psychology*, 3rd ed., New York, Holt, 1958, pp. 265–275.

2. "Campus Conservatives," *Time*, Feb. 10, 1961, p. 34. See also, "A Wave of Conservatism," *Time*, Mar. 10, 1961, p. 21; "The Need to Speak Out," *Time*, Feb.

23, 1962, p. 74; and "Organizations: Convincing the Convinced," *Time*, Mar. 16, 1962, p. 20. Although in one place *Time* says that the radical right is a tiny minority (Mar. 10, 1961), the implication is that they are merely the more enthusiastic and more articulate members of a growing majority.

3. As late as May 1959, the *Nation* charged that college youth were "apathetic, conformist, indifferent, confused."

4. Goldsen *et al.*, noting the reluctance of college students to get "worked up" about political matters, commented: "It is very tempting to interpret this sort of lack of involvement and apparent disinterest . . . as indicative principally of apathy, complacency, and unquestioning contentment. . . . Undoubtedly such an interpretation is justified in many cases. But we have found that what seems to be aloofness in political matters may sometimes be coupled with a certain realistic disenchantment with issues and causes. . . ." [See Rose K. Goldsen *et al.*, *What College Students Think* (The Cornell Values Study), Princeton, N.J., Van Nostrand, 1960, p. 98.] The same point is made by Peter Schrag, "Stirrings on Campus," *New Republic*, Apr. 27, 1961, pp. 9–11.

5. See Milton Rokeach, *The Open and Closed Mind: Investigations into the Nature of Belief Systems and Personality Systems*, New York, Basic Books, 1960. It is true that differentiation must be made on issues. Some students hold conservative views on economic policies and liberal views on social legislation. The concern here is how they arrive at their views, through the maintenance of an "open" or a "closed" belief system.

6. Nevitt Sanford, editor, "Personality Development during the College Years," *Journal of Social Issues*, Vol. 12, No. 4, 1956. Much of the data is given fresh interpretation in a collection of readings edited by Sanford. See *The American College: A Psychological and Social Interpretation of the Higher Learning*, New York, Wiley, 1962. All references to Sanford in subsequent footnotes are to the earlier collection.

7. James S. Davies and Paul A. Hare, "Button Down Culture: A Study of Undergraduate Life at a Men's College," *Human Organization*, Vol. 14, Winter 1956, pp. 13–20.

8. Mervin B. Freedman, "The Passage through College," in Sanford, *op. cit.*, pp. 13–28.

9. Donald Hayes, Seattle, University of Washington, 1962, unpublished paper.

10. Peter I. Rose, "Student Opinion on the 1956 Presidential Election," *Public Opinion Quarterly*, Vol. 21, 1957, pp. 371–376.

11. Philip E. Jacob, *Changing Values in College: An Exploratory Study of the Impact of College Teaching*, New York, Harper, 1957.

12. "The College Scene," *Harper's*, October 1961, supplement. See Philip Rieff, "The Mirage of College Politics," pp. 156–163. He agrees that there have been no major "movements" (i.e., unsilent to silent, liberal to conservative) but progressive change. He sees students' political activity as a protest largely against outside control and management of their lives—including parents and institutions of government. The conservatives, he says, are pledging their support to Barry Goldwater merely as the symbol of their faith in a *business* society.

13. George Horsley Smith, "Liberalism and Level of Information," *Journal of Educational Psychology*, Vol. 39, 1948, pp. 65–81. See also Hadley Cantril, "The Place of Personality in Social Psychology," *Journal of Psychology*, Vol. 24, 1947, pp. 19–56.

14. Alex S. Edelstein, "Student Political Behavior in the 1960 Presidential Campaign," Seattle, University of Washington, 1962, unpublished paper.

15. Lawrence F. Babcock, *The U.S. College Graduate*, New York, Macmillan, 1941.

16. C. Robert Pace, "What Kind of Citizens Do College Graduates Become?" *Journal of General Education*, Vol. 3, 1949, pp. 197–202.

17. Samuel A. Stouffer, *Communism, Conformity, and Civil Liberties*, New York, Doubleday, 1955, p. 59. Only 1 per cent, "by a generous estimate," were interested in civil liberties, and only 8 per cent were interested in world problems, *including the threat of war*.

18. Davis Riesman, "The Jacob Report," *American Sociological Review*, Vol. 23, 1958, pp. 732–738.

19. W. H. Holtzman, "Attitudes of College Men toward Non-segregation in Texas Schools," *Public Opinion Quarterly*, Vol. 20, 1956, pp. 559–569.

20. Phillip Nogee and Murray B. Levin, "Some Determinants of Political Attitudes among College Voters," *Public Opinion Quarterly*, Vol. 22, 1958, pp. 449–463.

21. Edelstein, *op. cit.* According to the U.S. Office of Education, 3 out of 5 students get technical-professional degrees (1959–1960).

22. A. J. Drucker and H. H. Remmers, "Citizenship Attitudes of Graduated Seniors at Purdue University, U.S. College Graduates and High School Pupils," *Journal of Educational Psychology*, Vol. 42, 1951, pp. 231–235.

23. Harold Webster, "Some Quantitative Results," in Stanford, *op. cit.*, pp. 29–43, has said that, with respect to personality, mathematics and science majors tend to differ from social science majors. They have more of an aversion to direct communication with people. There is higher self-discipline and lower hostility, but these are accompanied by less tolerance of individual differences and of ambiguity.

24. Arthur W. Kornhauser, "Changes in the Information and Attitudes of Students in an Economics Class," *Journal of Educational Research*, Vol. 22, 1930. pp. 288–308.

25. Edelstein, *op. cit.*

26. *Op. cit.*

27. Paul F. Lazarsfeld and Wagner Thielens, Jr., *The Academic Mind*, Glencoe, Ill., Free Press, 1958. Lazarsfeld and Thielens point out that there is greater "permissiveness" (liberal orientation) at private colleges, particularly small private colleges, than at state universities, and that state universities, in turn, are more permissive" than teachers colleges. The Catholic colleges are the least "permissive" (Figs. 5–6, p. 128).

28. Alex Gottfried, "Professor and Politics," *Western Political Science Quarterly*, Vol. 14, September 1961, pp. 43–44.

29. Comparisons for 1960 were not available.

30. Donald Brown, "Some Educational Patterns," in Sanford, *op. cit.*

31. Brown's variables may be summarized as (1) social orientation into the peer group, (2) orientation to career objectives, (3) internalization of faculty ideology, (4) orientation to future family responsibility, (5) seeking of new identity—wherever college values produced social and cultural "discontinuities" for the student. Where there was change in the student as a result of adopting new identity, change tended to be radical.

32. This should concern us with the extensive literature on the authoritarian personality, but a review of it would be beyond the scope of this paper.

33. Henry T. Moore, "Innate Factors in Radicalism and Conservatism," *Journal of Abnormal Psychology*, Vol. 20, 1925, pp. 234–244.

34. Floyd H. Allport and D. A. Hartman, "Measurement and Motivation of Atypical Opinions in Certain Groups," *American Political Science Review*, Vol. 19, 1925, pp. 735–760.

35. Sanford, *op. cit.*

36. Webster, *op. cit.*

37. Brown, *op. cit.*

38. Eleanor E. Maccoby *et al.*, "Youth and Political Change," *Public Opinion Quarterly*, Vol. 18, 1954, pp. 23–39.

39. Ernest Havemann and Patricia Salter West, *They Went to College: The College Graduate in America Today*, New York, Harcourt, Brace, 1952.

40. See Daniel Bell, *The End of Ideology: On the Exhaustion of Political Ideas in the Fifties*, Glencoe, Ill., Free Press, 1960; and William Kornhauser, *The Politics of Mass Society*, Glencoe, Ill., Free Press, 1959.

41. In a recent letter, David Riesman comments that *Time* did make one "effort at a study" in the 1950's, the results of which were summarized by Riesman but not available to this author. Commenting on the thesis of this paper, Riesman sees conservatism making inroads into college campuses in response "precisely" to the forces described, i.e., the liberalizing influences in the college. Thus intellectualism faces the challenge of asserting itself as a "third force." [Five years later, reviewing Riesman's comment for the present volume, the writer would again emphasize the challenge to intellectualism as a "third force" on college campuses and note that the "cool generation" of the middle 1960's is an expression of that force. The "hippie" movement seems to represent a "hot" version of the "cool generation."]

THE EFFECT OF THE INTRODUCTORY POLITICAL SCIENCE COURSE ON STUDENT ATTITUDES TOWARD PERSONAL POLITICAL PARTICIPATION*

- Albert Somit, Joseph Tanenhaus, Walter H. Wilke, and Rita W. Cooley

In its analysis of the introductory course in *Goals for Political Science*, the APSA Committee for the Advancement of Teaching some years ago reported almost universal endorsement of at least one objective—"training for citizenship." Sharp differences divided the profession, however, as to the pedagogical means to that end. A majority felt that a better understanding of governmental institutions and political processes would produce more sophisticated, and hence better, citizens. But to other political scientists good citizenship does not exist *in vacuo;* it implies active personal political participation. They felt, therefore, that the introductory course should be "organized and conducted for the sole purpose of developing effective, participating citizens." Some political scientists even contended that "preparing students for participation in politics should be a primary objective of every American college." The courses favored by these last two groups reflected the belief that "book learning" alone is not sufficient to arouse interest in political participation. Rather, traditional library and classroom work should be supplemented by direct student contact with politics, politicians, and party organizations.[1]

The effectiveness of courses designed to improve student understanding of political institutions and processes can be satisfactorily measured by the traditional course examinations. But evaluating courses which seek to develop effective, participating citizens is more difficult. The ultimate criterion of effectiveness must be actual participation in political affairs. Since candidacy for office, active work within a party organization, or even voting, normally do not occur until after the student finally leaves college, only a study of later political behavior can pass final judgment on the participation-oriented introductory courses. Nevertheless, given the importance of the issue, it is remarkable that the APSA Committee found so little evidence of any effort to evaluate these courses, or even to develop satisfactory testing instruments.[2]

Until data permitting the correlation of undergraduate exposure to participation-oriented introductory courses with subsequent adult political behavior become available,[3] alternative methods of evaluating these courses must be employed. One such is a measure of the impact of various types of introductory courses on student *attitudes* toward participation. Expressed attitudes do not correlate perfectly with immediate overt

Above selection reprinted from: *The American Political Science Review*, 52 (1958), 1129–1132.

* The authors are indebted to the Maurice and Laura Falk Foundation for its financial support of the Research Project in Political Motivation, of which the study here reported is a part.

behavior, and may be an even less dependable basis for predicting future behavior. These limitations notwithstanding, it seems reasonable to assume that undergraduates who express favorable attitudes toward personal political participation are more likely to play an active political role in later life than their fellow students who manifest indifferent or unfavorable attitudes.

This article reports a three-year study which sought to determine what changes in student attitudes, if any, toward personal political participation were produced by several kinds of introductory courses in political science. We shall first describe the nature of these courses; second, the attitude measure; third, the results obtained; and last, the implications of these findings.

Nature of the Courses. Four kinds of introductory political science courses were studied—one standard and three participation-oriented offerings. All four met for three hours weekly in sections small enough to permit considerable student discussion. With a single exception, all were taught by faculty members of professorial rank. Students were undergraduates at New York University's Washington Square College, a great majority of whom live in the New York metropolitan area.

Given in 1953–56, the standard course (designated No. 1 in the Table below) was the established two-semester introduction to government then required of almost all students other than those who enrolled in the "integrated" social science sequence

Table 1

Effect of Standard and Participation-Oriented Introductory Courses in Political Science on Student Attitudes toward Personal Political Participation

Year	Course	N (cases)	N (sections)	Average Initial Score	Average Final Score	Difference	Critical*	P†
1953–54	No. 1 (standard)	60	2	72.48	72.13	−.35	.31	.76
	No. 2 (P-O)	17	1	76.12	74.24	−1.88	.75	.45
1954–55	No. 1 (standard)	95	3	70.78	72.03	1.25	1.41	.16
	No. 2 (P-O)	45	2	69.33	70.51	1.18	.83	.40
1955–56	No. 1 (standard)	24	1	74.08	74.88	.80	.33	.75
	No. 3 (P-O)	22	1	64.86	70.27	5.41	2.04	.04
	No. 4 (P-O)	35	1	68.94	71.31	2.37	1.06	.29

* The critical ratio is "a measure of statistical significance or stability, of how likely it is that the obtained statistic is materially affected by chance. The most commonly used is the C R of a difference. A difference is usually regarded as not sufficiently stable unless the C R is about 3.00." It is computed by dividing the difference (between initial and final scores) by the standard error of the difference.

† The P column is "a measure of the risk that the value of a statistic is affected by chance." A P value of .01 or .05 is usually regarded as a reasonable minimum, indicating that the obtained result would be likely to occur by chance (due to variations in sampling) only one or five times in 100, respectively. Horace B. English and Ava Champney English. *A Comprehensive Dictionary of Psychological and Psychoanalytical Terms* (New York, 1958).

described below. Fundamentally traditional in approach, it placed a major stress on American government, with some attention devoted to political theory and foreign political institutions. The same syllabus and textbooks were used in all sections, although the instructors were permitted (and exercised) considerable latitude in developing the material and in assigning additional readings.[4]

The three participation-oriented courses had a number of common features. All were components of an "integrated" three-semester social science sequence which covered psychology, sociology, economics and political science. In each, approximately twelve weeks were spent in the formal classroom presentation of the political science segment of the sequence. Another common feature was the effort made in all three to expose the students to practical politics and practicing politicians. Prominent public personages and local Democratic and Republican party officials discussed their experiences with the students. Other politicians, including members of the United States Congress, recorded interviews for use during class hours. Students were urged to participate in workshops of the local Citizenship Clearing House and, for the benefit of those who could not attend, the more important proceedings were tape-recorded. In addition, arrangements were made for course members to work actively during election campaigns with party organizations of their choice, although, unfortunately, not everyone was able to do so.

The differentiating characteristics of the three participation-oriented courses were as follows: Course No. 2, given in

1953–55, was concerned almost exclusively with American government.[5] Course No. 3, given in 1955–56, placed major emphasis on political science rather than American government materials.[6] Course No. 4, also given in 1955–56, used the same materials as No. 3. But in No. 4 a deliberate and sustained attempt was made by the instructor and by visiting guest speakers to stress the desirability of active personal political participation. No similar "selling" attempt was made in the standard course or in the other two participation-oriented courses.

Attitude Measurement. To measure student attitudes toward personal political participation, a 22-item Likert-type scale was devised,[7] which is reproduced in the Appendix. The favorable extreme was defined in terms of participation in the affairs of a political party, rather than purely individualistic political activity, consonantly with the general position of those who advocate training for political participation. Responses to a five-point scale for each item (Strongly Agree, Agree, Undecided, Disagree, Strongly Disagree) were scored from 1 to 5, the highest score representing the most favorable attitude toward participation. The possible range of scores thus runs from 22 to 110, with the mid-point of 66 indicating an undecided or neutral position. Davis discrimination indices were computed and were considered sufficiently high to warrant retention of all items.[8] The test-retest reliability of the scale was determined for five groups ranging in size from 17 to 95 students. The reliability coefficients obtained (.694; .750; .689; .834; and .704) indicate adequate consistency of measurement for a comparison of group scores.

The validity of the Likert-type attitude scale has been repeatedly demonstrated by obtaining scores differing in the expected direction from groups known to hold contrasting attitudes. The setting in which the instant study was conducted and the subject-matter of the scale were considered favorable for eliciting candid responses. As an additional check, independent estimates based on detailed personal interviews were made of the attitudes of twenty-two students. These estimates corresponded closely with the students' attitudes as measured by the scale.

Results. Average group attitude scores for each type of course are indicated by year in Table I. In each case the average initial score was obtained by administering the scale at the beginning of each course. The scale was again administered at the end of the second semester of the standard course and at the end of the third semester of the participation-oriented courses. Two generalizations are suggested by these data.

First, it is quite apparent from Table I that at the outset of all four courses the typical student attitude toward personal political participation was close to the neutral or indifference point represented by a score of 66. For no group during any year was the average initial score higher than 76.12. A clearly favorable attitude as measured on the scale requires an average score of approximately 90.

Second, no significant change of attitude was produced by any of the courses. The criterion of statistical significance here is the usual .01 level of confidence. Only in one case, course No. 3, was the difference between the average initial and average final scores sufficient to reach significance at the .05 level. And in this instance, as can be seen from Table I, the average initial score (64.86) was appreciably lower than the average initial score for any of the other groups studied over the entire three-year period, whereas the average final score for course No. 3 was well within the range of the other average final scores.

Conclusions. Only future research can establish whether the findings of this study would be duplicated at other educational institutions. It is quite possible, for example, that the results obtained were significantly influenced by the prevailing climate of opinion during 1953–56, by the nature of Washington Square College as an educational institution, and by the socio-economic, religious, and regional composition of its student body.

Nevertheless, many political scientists will probably not be surprised to learn that repeated measurements of student attitudes reveal general indifference toward personal political participation. Undergraduates might well be expected to mirror the apathy of their elders toward politics, evidenced by widespread disinterest in civic affairs, poor voting turnout, and the unfavorable opinions of politicians so often noted by commentators on the American political scene. This reflection of adult attitudes was in fact further demonstrated, in the larger study from which the data here presented were drawn, by an indifferent attitude toward politicians and a low level of interest in political news.[9]

Student disinterest in personal political participation is but one aspect of our findings. No less important are the data which challenge the frequent assumption that the participation-oriented introductory course so alters student attitudes as to stimulate increased political participation in later life. It cannot be concluded from the results of the present study that all participation-oriented courses fail in their goal. However, it does seem clear that future claims for them must be demonstrated rather than assumed.

NOTES

1. Report of the Committee for the Advancement of Teaching, American Political Science Association, *Goals for Political Science* (New York, 1951) pp. 169–219.

2. *Ibid.*, pp. 205–207.

3. The Political Motivation Research Project has in its files data which, it is hoped, will make such a follow-up study possible within a few years.

4. The textbooks used in the standard course were Ferguson and McHenry, Roche and Stedman, and the volume of readings edited by Harvey, Skinner, Somit, and Nealon (brought up to date by more recent materials). Supplementary readings assigned by section leaders ranged from Barth, *The Loyalty of Free Men*, to Koestler, *Darkness of Noon*, and Orwell, *1984*.

5. The text was Burns and Peltason. Additional readings were assigned from Riordon, *Plunkitt of Tammany Hall*, Lubell, *The Future of American Politics*, and the volume of readings by Bishop and Hendel.

6. Readings were drawn from Gettell, *Political Science*, Ebenstein, *Man and The State*, Appleby, *Big Democracy*, and Bishop and Hendel.

7. A somewhat similar scale was independently devised by the staff of the Ben A. Arneson Institute of Practical Politics at Ohio Wesleyan University in an attempt to measure the extent to which students' college experiences affect their attitudes toward practical politics. See Ruth M. Larson and Chester O. Mathews, *Changes in Students' Attitudes Toward Practical Politics Over a Four-Year Period* (Delaware, Ohio, 1958). None of the Institute's work seems directly comparable with the study here reported.

8. The Davis discrimination index is a linear scale from 0 to 100. See Frederick B. Davis, "Item Analysis Data: Their Computation, Interpretation, and Use in Test Construction," *Harvard Education Papers*, No. 2 (Cambridge, 1946).

9. The three scales used to measure (1) attitudes toward politicians (2) interest in political news, and (3) attitudes toward personal political participation were largely independent instruments. Their intercorrelations, based on a sample of 354 students, were as follows: attitudes toward politicians and interest in political news ($r = .141$); attitudes toward politicians and attitudes toward personal political participation ($r = .177$); interest in political news and attitudes toward personal political participation ($r = .202$). These results are not dissimilar to those in a recently reported study, where students at the University of Western Australia selected from a list of 84 adjectives best describing the politician the following five: ambitious, argumentative, power-seeking, talkative, and evasive. See K. F. Walker, "A Study of Occupational Stereotypes," *Journal of Applied Psychology*, Vol. 42 (1958), pp. 122–124.

Appendix

Personal Political Participation Attitude Scale

Directions

This is not a test, but a request for your honest opinion on the subjects indicated below. Read each statement carefully. To indicate your opinion, circle the word or phrase on the answer sheet that describes your opinion most accurately. When you have finished, please look over the paper to make sure you have recorded your opinion for all of the statements.

1. I like to discuss, with people I know, recent or proposed actions by our city officials.
2. I pay very little attention to speeches and decisions by the Governor and other state officials.
3. I am intensely interested in discussions as to the merits of the policies advocated by the President and other members of the national administration.
4. I would like to run for the position of United States Congressman.
5. I would not care to be a member of the State Legislature.
6. I would like to run for the job of City Councilman.
7. I can't imagine myself ever being a candidate for any political office.
8. I have no hesitation in letting my acquaintances know my opinions about political parties and candidates.
9. I don't see any reason why I should keep my political views a secret from my business associates, present or prospective.
10. I think that I could make a useful contribution to good government by taking an active role in that political party which best represents my ideas.
11. Even though I think a given candidate should be elected, I would be unwilling to speak on his behalf before a group of people.
12. I do not think I would contribute money to help a candidate or political party win an election, even if I favored that candidate or party.
13. I would voluntarily give some of my spare time during election campaigns to work for the political party that I favor.
14. I would not risk jeopardizing my position with a future employer or business associates by running for public office on a political ticket.
15. I would like to be elected to an office in which I could exercise some influence on important government policies and decisions.
16. I would not regard it as a worthwhile achievement to be elected to a political office, even if I felt qualified for that office.
17. It would be against my principles to do the things that seem necessary in order to be elected to a public office.
18. It is my intention to be independent in politics, rather than a regular supporter of any organized political group.
19. I would run for office on the ticket of some independent or nonpartisan group, but would not run for office under the sponsorship of one of the regular parties.
20. I do not feel that I have the personal qualifications for a successful career in politics.
21. A citizen should be willing to run for public office if numerous responsible and public-spirited citizens urge him to do so.
22. I regard many public questions as so important that I intend to give active support to parties and politicians who favor the same policies that I do.

Relevant Others: The Peer Group

6

INTRODUCTION

One sign of maturing is the ability and desire of the young person to become a more autonomous human being who can function independently of family guidance. As this maturation occurs, the influence of the family diminishes. The process generally reaches its peak during adolescence when it seems—at least for a time—as though fellow adolescents have become the only important reference group and as though the family is unimportant at best. What to parents may seem a shocking disregard and lack of concern for the family is nothing but a necessary preparation for the approaching task of adulthood and independence. Growing up is a process of increasing self-differentiation. As such the process brings with it a struggle with those adults who previously were the one important source of love, control, and approval. In many countries these adults are the child's parents or immediate family. Hence, the proverbial turbulence and conflict that occurs in many families during the period of adolescence when youth fights parents and their ideas and values simply in order to gain a feeling of self, of uniqueness, of independence and individuality.

The degree to which the family is rejected and the peer group becomes the relevant reference group varies with the degree of parental control. In many Western European countries, for example, the family asserts its control over the adolescent for a much longer period; and the peer group, therefore, never assumes quite the all-important role that it does in the United States and in Great Britain. The Pinner article in this volume (pp. 204–216) indicates, for example, that Belgian families hold

411

rather tight control over young people even when they are already attending a university. Observations in France, Germany, and a few other Western and Central European countries seem to indicate that the judgment of the family carries more weight with these adolescents than the judgment of peers.[1]

The extent to which the peer group becomes the political socializer also depends on the extent to which politics is salient to them. In the United States, for example, youth groups are seldom vitally interested in politics. In interviewing adolescents the editor came across many who never talked politics to friends although they did discuss it with parents and teachers.[2] But when politics is salient to the group, then it becomes a powerful political socializer as was shown in the Bennington study. The observations by Murray Seidler and Mel Jerome Ravitz on a Jewish peer group further illustrate how a group of young people can depart from parental politics to the point of rejecting parental ideas on Zionism, race relations, and so forth, once the peer group has superseded the family in its importance to maturing young people.

Bronfenbrenner (below) in a comparison of American and Russian schoolchildren noted the great impact of the peer group in both countries; but he also noted that peer groups had different impacts on antisocial behavior in the two. He found that in the United States children would be more likely to engage in antisocial behavior under the influence of peers than if alone or with adults; whereas in Russia the peer group, rather than encouraging antisocial behavior, would reinforce compliance with societal norms. The hippies in the United States, the provosts in Holland, and similar movements elsewhere show what can happen when peer groups are totally alienated from the society as well as the family. The importance of the peer group, then, lies in the fact that it helps bridge the gulf between dependence on the family for political cue-giving and dependence on oneself for the making of political judgments and choices.

In some societies, however, youth is brought up in a more collective existence—as, for example, Israeli children growing up on Kibbutzim. The family then assumes a less ubiquitous role; and even before adolescence the peer group takes over many of the family's socializing functions. In Russia the peer group is utilized by the school and the state (see article by Bronfenbrenner in Chapter I and below) to help mold the new Soviet man. From a very early age on it therefore becomes the significant other who helps control the young person and to instill in him the idea of right and wrong and of acceptable and unacceptable behavior. Dependence on the good will and esteem of the peer group is so great that the desire to become an individual is muted by the desire to become a functioning member of this collectivity.

The heavy emphasis on the peer group somehow seems to contradict observations made in previous chapters on the continuity through life of values acquired early in the family. In part, the just-observed departure from familial values is merely temporary. Many young people are known to have adopted radically different ways of thinking about politics and other social matters during adolescence, only to revert to familial ways during adulthood. In part the peer group's political influence is not always apparent because its political values are not necessarily in sharp conflict with the family's. Not only is politics of low salience in most adolescent groups but peer groups, at least in the United States, tend to be quite similar to the familial group in many vital characteristics, most notably in socio-economic status, religion, and race. The peer group thus often is a political reinforcer of familial ideas rather than a resocializer. The more stratified or the more static the society, the less the peer group will probably conflict politically with the family. At the moment we do not yet have enough data on peer groups in transitional societies to know whether they play a more active role there as political socializers than they do here. And yet the peer group *is* an important socializer. Its importance lies in the fact that it offers youth the first opportunity to look to a nonfamilial reference group that can teach him how to play his role and to socialize him to new ways of thinking, feeling, and behaving.

NOTES

1. David C. McClelland, *et al.*, "Obligation to Self and Society in the United States and Germany," *Journal of Abnormal and Social Psychology*, 56 (1958) 245–255.

2. Roberta S. Sigel, in a study (in progress) of fourth, sixth, and eighth graders, found only a minority (38%) ever talking politics with friends. 62% would ask their family for political information, but less than 19% would ask their friends.

RESPONSE TO PRESSURE FROM PEERS VERSUS ADULTS AMONG SOVIET AND AMERICAN SCHOOL CHILDREN[1]

- U[rie] Bronfenbrenner[2]

Problem

The experiment to be reported here is part of a more extensive research project investigating the differential impact of adults and peers on the behavior and personality development of children in different cultural contexts. Our earlier studies had pointed to important differences from culture to culture in the part taken by peers *vis-a-vis* adults in the socialization process. For example, in Germany the family appears to play a more central and exclusive role in upbringing than it does in the United States, where children spend a substantially greater proportion of their time outside the family in peer group settings (Devereux, Bronfenbrenner, and Suci, 1960). The influence of peers emerged as even stronger, however, among English children, who were far more ready than their American age-mates to follow the lead of their companions in socially disapproved activities rather than adhere to values and behaviors approved by parents and other adults (Devereux, Bronfenbrenner, and Rodgers, 1965). In other words, the evidence suggested that in both countries —and especially in England—peers often stood in opposition to adults in influencing the child to engage in anti-social behavior.

Above selection from: *International Journal of Psychology*, 1967, 2, pp. 199–207. Reprinted by permission of the International Union of Psychological Science and DUNOD, Publisher, 92 rue Bonaparte, Paris VI⁰.

In contrast, field observations in the Soviet Union (Bronfenbrenner, 1963) indicated a rather different pattern. In that country, in keeping with the educational principles and methods developed by Makarenko (1952), and others, an explicit effort is made to utilize the peer group as an agent for socializing the child and bringing about an identification with the values of the adult society (Bronfenbrenner, 1962). Accordingly we were led to the hypothesis that in the Soviet Union, in contrast to America or England, children are less likely to experience peer pressure as conflicting with adult values and hence can identify more strongly with adult standards for behavior.

Research Design and Procedures[3]

An opportunity to investigate this hypothesis was provided during the author's visits as an exchange scientist at the Institute of Psychology in Moscow in 1963 and 1964.[4] With the cooperation of Soviet colleagues, it was possible to carry out a comparative study of reaction to pressure from peers *vs.* adults in six American (N = 158) and six Soviet (N = 188) classrooms at comparable age and grade levels (average age of 12 years in both countries, 6th graders in US, 5th graders in USSR, where school entrance occurs one year later). To measure the child's responsiveness to pressure from adults *vs.* peers we employed the following experimental procedure.[5] Children were asked to respond to a series of conflict situations under three different conditions: 1) a *base* or *neutral* condition, in which they were told that no one would see their responses except the investigators conducting the research; 2) an *adult* condition in which they were informed that the responses of everyone in the class would be posted on a chart and shown to parents and teachers at a special meeting scheduled for the following week; and 3) a *peer* condition, in which the children were notified that the chart would be prepared and shown a week later to the class itself. The conflict situations consisted of 30 hypothetical dilemmas such as the following:

to +30 with zero representing equal division between behavior urged by peers and adults. Split-half reliabilities for the ten-item forms ranged from .75 to .86 under different experimental conditions; the reliability of the total score (i.e., sum across all three conditions) was .94.[6]

The basic research design involved a double Latin square with experimental treatments constituting the three rows, classrooms appearing in the columns, and forms distributed randomly, with the restriction that each form appear only once in each column and twice in each row. This basic pattern was repeated twice in each culture, once for boys and once for girls, for a total of four

The Lost Test

You and your friends accidentally find a sheet of paper which the teacher must have lost. On this sheet are the questions and answers for a quiz that you are going to have tomorrow. Some of the kids suggest that you not say anything to the teacher about it, so that all of you can get better marks. What would you *really* do? Suppose your friends decide to go ahead. Would you go along with them or refuse?

REFUSE TO GO ALONG WITH MY FRIENDS			GO ALONG WITH MY FRIENDS		
absolutely certain	fairly certain	I guess so	I guess so	fairly certain	absolutely certain

A Russian-language version of the same thirty items was prepared, with minor variations to adapt to the Soviet cultural context. Each response was scored on a scale from —3 to +3, a negative value being assigned to the behavior urged by age mates. To control for a positional response set, scale direction was reversed in half of the items. The situations were divided into three alternate forms of 10 items each, with a different form being used for each experimental condition. Thus under any one condition a child could obtain a score ranging from —30

sets of double Latin squares (three conditions by six classrooms in four sex-culture combinations). In order to equate for varying numbers of boys and girls in each classroom, the individual cell entries used for the primary analysis of variance were the mean scores obtained by all boys or girls in a given classroom under a particular experimental condition. In this model, classrooms and forms were treated as random variables, and culture, experimental treatment, and sex of child as fixed effects. It is of course the latter three which constitute the primary focus of interest in the experiment.

Results

Mean values obtained by boys and girls in each culture under the three experimental conditions are shown in Table 1, relevant mean differences and corresponding significance levels in Table 2. Several findings emerge from this analysis. First of all, there is clear evidence that Soviet children are far less willing than their American age mates to say that they will engage in socially disapproved behavior. The mean scores for Russian boys and girls (Table 1, Col. IV) average about 13 and 16 respectively, values that are clearly on the adult side of the continuum. The corresponding American averages of approximately 1 and 3.5 are barely over the dividing line, indicating that the children are almost as ready to follow the prompting of peers to deviant behavior as to adhere to adult approved standards of conduct. The above cultural difference is highly significant across both sexes (Table 2, Line 1).

Second, the data show that both in the USSR and in the United States, boys are more inclined to engage in socially undesirable activity than girls. The absence of a reliable sex by culture interaction (Column IV) indicates that the sex difference was no larger in one country than in the other. It is noteworthy that despite the differing conceptions of the role of women in the two societies, females in the Soviet Union as in the United States lay greater claim to virtuous behavior, at least up to the age of twelve!

Third, turning to the experimental effects, we learn (Line 3) that in both countries children gave more socially approved responses when told that their answers would be seen by adults than when faced with the prospect of having their statements shown to classmates.

Table 1

Mean Scores Obtained by Boys and Girls in the U.S. and the USSR Under Three Experimental Conditions

Subjects	I. Base	II. Adult	III. Peer	IV. Average across Conditions
Boys				
Soviet	12.54	14.21	13.18	13.30
American	1.02	1.57	.16	.92
Difference	11.52	12.64	13.02	12.38
Girls				
Soviet	15.13	17.02	16.90	16.33
American	3.83	4.35	2.38	3.52
Difference	11.30	12.67	14.52	12.82
Both Sexes				
Soviet	13.84	15.62	15.04	14.82
American	2.43	2.96	1.27	2.22

Table 2

Differences in Total Score and Experimental Effects by Culture and Sex

	Soviet I.	American II.	Effect Across Both Cultures (Soviet plus American) III.	Cultural Difference (Soviet minus American) IV.
Total Scores				
1. Both sexes (Girls + Boys)	14.82	2.22	——	12.60**
2. Sex difference (Girls − Boys)	3.03	2.60	5.63**	.43 n.s.
Shift Scores				
Both Sexes (Girls + Boys)				
3. Adult-peer conflict (Adult − Peer)	.58	1.69	2.27*	−1.11 n.s.
4. Adult shift (Adult − Base)	1.78	.53	2.31	1.25
5. Peer shift (Base − Peer)	−1.20	1.16	−.04	−2.36
6. Adult shift − Peer shift	2.98	−.63	2.35 n.s.	3.61*

Sex differences (Girls − Boys)
None of the shift effects showed a significant interaction by sex.

(Single and double asterisks indicate differences significant at the .05 and .01 level respectively.)

Although American youngsters exhibited a greater shift than their Soviet counterparts, a fact which suggests stronger conflict between peer and adult influences in the United States, this cultural difference is not statistically significant (Line 3, Col. IV). A reliable difference does appear, however, for the remaining independent degree of freedom measuring which shift was greater, that from *base* to the *adult* condition or from *base* to *peer* condition. As indicated in Table 2, Line 6, Soviet children shifted more when subjected to pressure from grown-ups, whereas Americans were slightly more responsive to pressure from peers. The components entering into this difference are shown in Lines 4 and 5 of the same table. Although the cultural differences cannot be subjected to an independent statistical test, since they are incorporated in the single

degree of freedom tested in Line 6, they do provide a more detailed picture of the different reactions of children in the two countries to pressure from grown-ups *vs.* age mates. Thus we see from Line 4 that although both Russian and American youngsters gave more socially acceptable responses in moving from the neutral to the adult condition, this shift was more pronounced for the Soviet children. Moreover, under pressure from peers (Line 5), there was a difference in direction as well as degree. When told that classmates would see their answers, American pupils indicated greater readiness to engage in socially disapproved behavior, whereas Soviet children exhibited increased adherence to adult standards. In other words, in the USSR, as against the United States, the influence of peers operated in the same direction as that of adults.

In summary, our original hypothesis has been sustained in a number of respects. First, in contrast both to American and English children, Russian youngsters showed less inclination to engage in anti-social activity. Second, although pressures from adults induced greater commitment to socially approved behavior in both cultures, Soviet children were more responsive to the influence of grown-ups than of peers, whereas their American age mates showed a trend in the opposite direction. Putting it another way, pressure from peers operated differently in the two countries. In the USSR it strengthened commitment to adult-approved behavior; in the United States it increased deviance from adult standards of conduct.

If, as our data strongly suggest, the social context is a powerful determinant of behavior, then we should expect differences in responses to be associated not only with molar social structures like cultures but also smaller units such as classroom groups. This expectation can be tested from our data by determining whether, in each culture, there are significant classroom effects (the error term for this comparison is the mean square for individual differences within classrooms). Table 3 shows the variance

Table 3

Variances Among Classroom Means Under Three Experimental Conditions

	American	Soviet
Base	36.01**	43.40**
Adult	13.43	9.25
Peer	45.77**	17.01*

(Single and double asterisks indicate differences significant at the .05 and .01 level respectively.)

of classroom means in each country under each of the three experimental conditions. The accompanying significance levels reveal that there are reliable classroom differences in both countries, but only under *base* and *peer* conditions. It would appear that pressure from adults has the effect of dissolving the tendency to conform to peer group norms which operates in the absence of monitoring by parents and teachers. Although the pattern of classroom variances under the three experimental conditions differs in the two countries—the highest mean square occurs under peer condition in the United States and base condition in the USSR—this cultural variation is not significant. Nor were there any reliable classroom differences associated with the sex of the child.

The finding that in both societies adult pressure dissolves group solidarity suggests some opposition between adult values and peer interests in the Soviet Union as well as in the United States. The fact remains, however, that at least in our data, readiness to resist promptings to anti-social behavior, and responsiveness to adult influence were greater among Russian than among American children. In addition, the results showed that in the USSR peer groups exerted some influence in support of adult standards, whereas in America they encouraged deviance from adult norms.

Although these results are in accord with our original hypothesis—indeed perhaps for this very reason—it is important to stress the limitations of the study. To begin with, our samples were rather small, only six classrooms—comprising less than 200 cases—in each culture. Second, both samples were essentially accidental, the American classrooms being drawn from two schools in a small city in upstate New York, the Russian from three *internats*—or boarding schools—in Moscow. The latter fact is especially important since one of the reasons for the widespread introduction of boarding schools in connection with the educational reform carried out in the Soviet Union during the past nine years was to make possible more effective character education in the school environment. It is therefore possible that pupils in the internats are more strongly identified with adult values than those attending day schools. For this reason, the experiment here described is currently being carried out—through the collaboration of the Institute of Psychology—in six other Moscow classrooms in schools of the more conventional type where the students live at home. At the same time, the experiment is also being repeated in a series of classrooms in a large American city more comparable to Moscow.

Even if these further and more relevant replications confirm the trends revealed by the present data, two additional questions remain. First there is the matter of the generalizability of the results outside the experimental setting. Although carried out in school classrooms, the research remains in effect a laboratory study dealing with hypothetical situations rather than behavior in "real life." What evidence is there that in fact American children are more likely than their Soviet age mates to engage in anti-social behavior? None in the present study. The present investigator has reported elsewhere, however—in fact in a paper presented to this same scientific body at its meetings three years ago—some field observations of Soviet children which described a pattern quite in accord with the findings of the present research. For example,

In their external actions they are well-mannered, attentive, and industrious. In informal conversations, they reveal strong motivation to learn, a readiness to serve their society . . . Instances of aggressiveness, violation of rules, or other anti-social behavior appear to be genuinely rare (Bronfenbrenner, 1963).

Finally, we must bear in mind that both the earlier observations and present experimental study were carried out with children at a particular age level—namely late childhood and early adolescence. We are therefore left with the all important question—left unanswered by our data—as to how these same youngsters will behave as adults. Do children who at the age of 12 or 13 yield to peer pressures toward anti-social behavior continue to show such reactions in later years? Does early commitment to the values of adult society endure? Does the presence of such a commitment in adulthood require that the norms of behavior among children be fully compatible with those of grown-ups, or does some conflict of interest further the development of capacities for independent thought and responsible social action? Our results shed little light on these complex questions.

Despite the acknowledged limitations of the study, it has several important implications, both theoretical and practical. With respect to the former, it demonstrates that social pressure can have substantial effects even in such differing social systems as those of the Soviet Union and the United States. At the same time, the research indicates that these effects can vary appreciably as a function of the larger social context.

Where the peer group is to a large extent autonomous—as it often is in the United States—it can exert influence in opposition to values held by the adult society. In other types of social systems, such as the USSR, the peer group—and its power to affect the attitudes and actions of its members—can be harnessed by the adult society for the furtherance of its own values and objectives. This fact carries with it significant educational and social implications. Thus it is clear that in the Soviet Union the role of the peer group is in large part the result of explicit policy and practice. This is hardly the case in the United States. In the light of increasing evidence for the influence of the peer group on the behavior and psychological development of children and adolescents, it is questionable whether any society, whatever its social system, can afford to leave largely to chance the direction of this influence—and realization of its high potential for fostering constructive achievement both for the child and his society.

NOTES

1. This paper was presented at the XVIII International Congress of Psychology held from August 4–11, 1966 in Moscow and was published in *Social Factors in the Development of Personality*, XVIII International Congress of Psychology, Symposium 35, 1966, Moscow. pp. 7–18.

2. This paper was first presented in the United States by Edward C. Devereux, Jr., at the meetings of the American Sociological Association held August 29–September 1, 1966, Miami, Florida.

3. This research was supported by a grant from the National Science Foundation.

4. Grateful appreciation is extended to the Academy of Pedagogical Sciences of the RSFSR, which served as a generous host during the exchange visits, and to colleagues at the Institute for their active and unstinting collaboration in translating, arranging for, and carrying out the experimental procedures in the Soviet schools. Especial thanks are due to Dr. A. A. Smirnov, Director of the Institute, L.I. Bozhovich, Head of the Laboratory of Upbringing, and to all my colleagues in that laboratory, notably E. S. Makhlakh, E. I. Savonko, S. G. Yakobson, and I. G. Dimanshtain, who, despite heavy research commitments of their own, gave so generously of their knowledge and assistance.

5. This procedure was developed by the author in collaboration with the other principal investigators for the project as a whole: E. C. Devereux, Jr., G. J. Suci, and R. R. Rodgers, who also carried out the American phase of the experiment.

6. All reliability coefficients are corrected for attenuation by the Spearman-Brown formula.

A JEWISH PEER GROUP

- Murray B. Seidler and Mel Jerome Ravitz

Abstract

The authors are original and continuing members of a peer group of Jewish boys formed during adolescence. This fact, perhaps, impairs the objectivity of their analysis. On the other hand, it may provide a certain insight which an outsider cannot achieve.

The group began seventeen years ago, when the members were in junior high school. They were ten boys all but one pupils in the same junior and senior high schools. In fact, half of them attended the same elementary school. The number ten is arbitrary, as some boys have belonged peripherally and some others who consider themselves group members are in reality only friends of members. For geographical reasons, some others seem to be sometimes in, sometimes out, but ten comprise the group's core.

The three schools are all large city schools in Detroit. The elementary school had a population of approximately two thousand, while the junior high school and high school each had approximately three thousand students. All are located on a single plot of land in a neighborhood predominantly middle-class and Jewish. The friendships among the group members generally began in school.

The members were all born in the United States. Both parents of all but

Above selection reprinted from: *American Journal of Sociology*, LXI, 1 (July 1955), 11–15 by permission of The University of Chicago Press. Copyright 1955 by the University of Chicago Press.

two group members were born in Europe, for the most part, in Russia or Poland. Most of the fathers are small businessmen. One is a lawyer. In general, the families have enjoyed a comfortable but not lavish standard of living. None can, by any stretch of the imagination, be considered among the elite Jewish families of Detroit; not even the wealthiest belongs to either of the two exclusive local Jewish country clubs. Several of the parents belong to synagogues, but only very few are religious, and some are definitely not interested in religion and religious activities. The commonest of Jewish traits in their homes were Jewish food and an occasional Jewish phrase, often used because the children would not understand.

During adolescence the members' behavior was typical in many ways of American teen-age behavior. Almost all the boys, for example, "dated" extensively. It was more often than not double or multiple dating. There were also innumerable parties, dances, wiener roasts, athletic contests, etc. Most of the boys were very active in organizations in the high school.

In one important respect, however, this group may be considered not typical of American teen-agers: the very deep and live interest they manifested in public affairs. Though the fascinating topics of sex and athletics were not excluded from their conversations, social and economic issues interested them profoundly. One problem, of course, loomed above all others: whether or not the United States should become involved in World War II. All but two were interventionists. These—one a socialist, the other a self-styled anarchist—eventually registered as conscientious objectors.

Grist for their discussions also included race relations, socialism, freedom, and religion—despite the fact that not a single member, not even those whose parents were the most devout, exhibited any real interest in religious worship, then or since. A few attended the synagogue during the Jewish high holidays, but that was because of parental pressure.

As at once a social club, an athletic club, a discussion club, and a friendship club, the group differed little from a variety of similar age groups in the same area and probably elsewhere as well. "The general fact is that children, especially boys after about their twelfth year," Charles Horton Cooley observed, "live in fellowships in which their sympathy, ambition, and honor often are engaged even more than they are in the family."[1] However, a distinctive feature of this group is its longevity, which happily permits an analysis of group influences over a considerable time span.

On the manifest level, then, this particular group was not extraordinary. But latently it functioned as a strong surrogate for the family. It was clearly a primary group, and as such it was a crucial agent of socialization.[2]

Not all adolescent groups may be truly said to be primary groups. Not all of them are sufficiently integrated to have so strong a hold over their members. Indeed, the following hypothesis is offered here for subsequent testing: The greater the integration and cohesion of the peer group, the greater the extent to which it will usurp the role of the family in socialization.

In general, during the high-school years the "we feeling" was very strong. As it was the current ruling student group of the school, holding virtually all the important class offices, membership in it was highly prized and jealously guarded.

The cohesiveness of the group expressed itself in numerous daily telephone calls, in the letters written when on vacation, in vacations spent together, and in the inevitable congregating at one another's homes after school, in the evenings, and on week ends.

Beginning with a high-school "revolt," the group came generally to be spoken of as "the boys" both by themselves and by others. Whether it was the outsiders (parents) perhaps who first gave them the name or whether the members themselves, becoming aware of their unity, began to use the name, no one can say. It is not unlikely, however, that the second possibility followed after the first.

Further proof of extremely high integration, even in the face of a basic crisis, may be seen in the following behavior. "The boys," with two exceptions, were members of the first high-school class to graduate after Pearl Harbor. All but the two who had earlier declared themselves pacifists were inducted into the armed services about a year after graduation. This meant an interruption of college. The boys in service, however, all gave moral support to their two pacifist friends and, furthermore, offered written testimony to the Selective Service authorities as to the sincerity of the latters' convictions. The conscientious objectors were in no way rejected. They all wrote to one another and on leave resumed the intimacy, and old times and the future were discussed with the old feelings of genuine unity.

At the time of writing, the average age of "the boys" is thirty-one. Nine of the ten are married, yet the unity persists: the group has been expanded to include the wives. Of course, this is not to suggest that the group has not been affected by the marriages; it has. But the basic feeling of togetherness still exists. Most of the social activities of the married members, for example, continue to be among "the boys." Moreover, an annual New Year's Eve party at one of the homes has become a tradition. To this gathering come even the peripheral members and those who consider themselves members, as to the annual gathering of the clan to reaffirm fealty.

Thus, the clique seems to have survived at least three threats: graduation from high school, World War II and its ensuing dispersion, and, finally, marriage. Scrutiny of the behavior of "the boys" and their parents should reveal how the group controlled its members' behavior in three main areas of life: courtship and marriage, social and political beliefs and behavior, and occupational selection.

To be sure, the clique did not do all the socializing of "the boys" while they were members. Each family certainly contributed much to the son's personality, enabling him to become and remain a member. Though the families must be held primarily accountable for the characteristics of their sons, paradoxically, once the group originated and developed, it reduced family influence. "The boys" were in one another's company constantly. Sometimes they resented staying at home to greet their family's guests or rebelled at going out

with the family, because it prevented them from being together. The families recognized the effect of the group on the lives of their sons. Several parents occasionally blamed the group for their sons' objectionable behavior, the immediate effect of which, of course, was that "the boys" defended their friends. Sometimes they denied the rather obvious fact that the group had any hold on them at all. In any event the group's hold on "the boys" probably was noticed earlier by the parents than by the "independent and individualistic" young adolescents.

So strongly integrated a primary group curtailed its members with outsiders. Each member was involved in a most satisfying network of relationships and therefore did not seek more than marginal contact with others. Only one new member joined after "the boys" graduated. In short, their outlook was markedly ethnocentric. Symptomatic of their ethnocentrism was the defensiveness of "the boys." They would argue that other groups and other people offered very little of interest; that others were interested in dances, football, parties, and the like, to the exclusion of the important matters of the mind that occupied *their* group.

Limiting contacts with outsiders proved not to be a permanent or serious problem. When a member had to leave for school or the army, he was apparently not at all socially handicapped. The members seemed to make friends with more than average ease, and, though usually these new relationships were not so deep and intimate, some close attachments were established with outsiders— a tendency that appears increasingly prominent. In a way, this moving-out into the world and making outside contacts may be likened to the moving-out of the family by the adolescent and his growing sense of independence and security beyond the confines of family life. With respect to these boys, the clique functioned as a substitute for the family and even retarded the development of the members' outside or foreign relationships. The full consequences of acquiring new friends have yet to be seen.

During their high-school days "the boys" dated Jewish girls (they were the great majority at the school) almost exclusively. After graduation, however, they made almost as many social arrangements with non-Jewish as with Jewish girls, which is unusual behavior in young Jewish Americans. Not that other Jewish boys did not date non-Jewish girls; they did, but, as other in-group males with out-group females, it was to exploit them sexually. What was unusual was the non-Jewish girls they dated were treated as they treated their Jewish girls. These were not clandestine relationships; non-Jewish girls were openly escorted to group parties and were received with cordiality and warmth. They were even introduced to parents. In later years eight of the ten members were to have at least one intense emotional relationship with a non-Jewish girl, in which marriage was a real possibility.

Even more startling is the incidence of outmarriage among "the boys." Of the nine already married, three are married to non-Jews. And, when peripheral group members are counted, there are two more. It is also important to point out again that eight of the ten seriously considered exogamy. Moreover, judging from the dating of the still unmarried member, there is a reasonable likelihood that he, too, may marry outside the religion of his parents. Such

behavior is clearly proscribed by Jewish folkways and mores.

The statistics concerning the intermarriage of Jews in the United States are neither clear nor definite. But there is no evidence to indicate that the rate of intermarriage is greater than 5 per cent. Of the larger groups in the American community, only Negroes exceed Jews in endogamy.[3] It should be noted, however, that more Jewish men than women intermarry.[4] Even so, the rate of intermarriage for this Jewish clique is extraordinarily high. None of their parents intermarried or even contemplated doing so, and in each family the prospect of intermarriage was met with objections. But the integration of "the boys" was strong enough to enable them to defy the mores of their ethnic group.

While hard to substantiate conclusively, it seems clear that certain individuals altered their social outlook, consciously or unconsciously, toward more nonconformity (from the community viewpoint) in order to gain greater acceptance from the clique. One member, for instance, upon first joining the group, argued that Negroes were inferior to whites. It was not long before he became a champion of racial equality, even though his parents still think as he did earlier.

When the second World War ended, "the boys" returned to college. Their social, political, and economic philosophies had become markedly nonconformist. Several had seen very difficult military service; one had been killed. Another vowed he would never fight in a war again. All had deeply resented every aspect of military life, especially its authoritarianism. Most were considerably disillusioned by the disparity between the declared aims of the war and its results, as they interpreted them. Five voted Socialist in 1948, when they had their first opportunity to vote in a presidential election. One refrained from voting on anarchist principles. All became much more interested in social reform in general. They were especially concerned with bettering the lot of minorities in the United States. Emphatically they rejected every form of racism, including Jewish prejudice toward non-Jews. As a group, with one exception, they were either hostile or indifferent to Zionism.

In contrast, several of the parents were decidedly friendly toward the Zionist movement, nine of the ten parents were staunch Roosevelt Democrats, and several harbored at least a perpetual suspicion of Negroes. Moreover, the siblings of the members, on the whole, followed their parents, with, of course, some "next-generation" modification and liberalization.

The wives of "the boys," in general, adopted their husbands' friends and eased away from their former friends. The clique was so strong that in effect it pulled in all intimate associates of its members and left them little time for other relationships. Moreover, of course, "the boys" were more committed to their clique than were their wives, who were involved in the groups in which they had previously participated.

For some members the group may have been influential in reinforcing at least the choice of occupation. In moving all the group members into the professions, it may have been significantly influential. Six of the ten are now physicians, of whom four have decided upon psychiatry as a specialty and at least one other had considered it seriously at one time. Of the others, two are

university social science teachers, one is a lawyer, and, finally, one is totally committed to the idea of becoming a writer. Only one ever gave any thought to the idea of going into business, yet that is an occupation very common among boys of their particular background. But their clique generally condemned business ethics. Further, the physicians among them are highly critical of the status quo in medicine and favor either compulsory health insurance or the outright socialization of medicine. Both the university instructors are members of the American Federation of Teachers.

Inasmuch as medicine ranked very high among Jewish parents as a suitable occupation for their sons, the clique can hardly claim exclusive credit for turning the latter's attention to a medical career. Each of "the boys" would doubtless have been encouraged by his family at least to consider medicine seriously. Three, for example, had brothers who were doctors. The clique reinforced the interest in that profession. Also, their preponderant interest in psychiatry—a branch of medicine viewed with some suspicion even by many doctors—is, very probably, another manifestation of the group's patterned nonconformity: that the four physicians decided to become psychiatrists is surely more than a chance happening. One of the other two decided *not* to specialize in psychiatry only after he had been away from the group for a year while studying in another city. It is likely, too, that the common professional background of "the boys" has helped the group to endure.

To turn to the main hypothesis of this paper, that the clique was so strongly integrated that it became a primary group for its members and took over that role from the respective families—how else can we explain for the group the high incidence of outmarriage, of nonconformist ideas, of professionals—physicians, psychiatrists, and social scientists? There is nothing unusual about the values and beliefs of the parents of these young men which would account for the direction of their ideas and behavior, with one exception. One boy's parents were lifelong socialists, and his attitudes were derived at least in part from his family. However, they were probably strongly supported by the group values. Some seeds of interest in social issues probably stemmed from this source, especially as the group met frequently at this boy's home. The attitudes of the parents were for the most part commonplace, ranging from hearty opposition to reluctant acceptance of intermarriage, from agreement to the more usual disagreement in matters political, social, and economic. There was little parental opposition to the occupational selections; in fact, virtually all the parents were pleased. In keeping with the American promise, the children had surpassed their parents in professional achievement.

James Bossard says: "Each peer group has a culture which is distinctly its own." He goes on to say that peer groups may be considered as primary groups which have a fundamental impact upon the personalities of their members. Moreover he maintains, as did Cooley, that they can exert, exceeding that of their families, a degree of control over their members.[5] More recently, David Riesman theorized about the influence of the peer group, particularly upon what he calls "other-directed" children.[6] Many of the data from the study of "the boys" support Riesman's propositions.

The intense solidarity of the group and its long duration fostered a situation which was extremely favorable to the members' internalization of its culture. Even granting differentials in internalization, it can be safely assumed that all the personalities of "the boys" were fundamentally affected by the group culture.

NOTES

1. *Social Organization* (New York: Charles Scribner's Sons, 1911), p. 23.

2. According to Cooley, "a primary group is characterized by intimate face-to-face association and co-operation. . . . The result of intimate association, psychologically, is a certain fusion of individualities in a common life and purpose of the group. Perhaps the simplest way of describing this wholeness is by saying that it is 'we;' it involves the sort of sympathy and mutual identification for which 'we' is the natural expression" (*ibid.*, pp. 24–25).

3. Ruby Jo Reeves Kennedy, "Single or Triple Melting Pot? Intermarriage Trends in New Haven," *American Journal of Sociology*, XLIX (1944), 331–39.

4. M. C. Elmer, *The Sociology of the Family* (Boston: Ginn & Co., 1945), p. 195.

5. *The Sociology of Child Development* (New York: Harper & Bros., 1948), pp. 504, 508, 516, 519.

6. *The Lonely Crowd* (New Haven: Yale University Press, 1950).

Socialization in Adulthood– The Importance of Role

7

INTRODUCTION

Political socialization literature up to now has paid far too little attention to the important socializing that takes place in adulthood. In part this was no doubt prompted by the awareness that much adult socialization is dependent on the foundation laid in childhood and can be understood properly only if someone knows something about these childhood antecedents. What such emphasis has overlooked, however, is that the family is not in a position to prepare the young person for *all* the demands he has to meet in adult life and for all the circumstances in which he has to function. In other words, the family cannot anticipate the adult roles* that the person will have to play in response to his own changing needs and to the changes in the society around him.

Even though some of the expectations of the society are relatively stable through the life cycle, many others change from one age to the next. We know that society demands that the individual meets these change expectations, and demands that he alter his personality and behavior to make room in his life for newly significant persons such as the family members, his teachers, his employer, and his colleagues at work.

---

* "Roles" are usually defined as prescriptions for "the behaviors expected of people in specified positions operating in specifically defined or standard situations. . . . For every recognized position there is an expectation widely shared by numbers of the community of what *should be* the behavior of persons who occupy that position. What a typical occupant of a given position is expected to do constitutes the *role* associated with that position. Roles are 'families of expectancies.' The expectancies making up a role are not restricted to actions; they also include expectations about motivations, beliefs, feelings, attitudes, and values." David Krech, et al., *The Individual in Society* (New York: McGraw-Hill, 1962), pp. 310–311.

The effectiveness of childhood socialization is certainly greater in relatively unchanging societies. Cultural prescriptions of a powerful nature define the usual sequence of statuses and roles that individuals are to assume during their life span. . . . However, even in such relatively unchanging societies one cannot be socialized in childhood to handle successfully all the roles he will confront in the future. Socialization in later years builds on attitudes and skills acquired earlier, using them as a foundation for later, more demanding learning.[1]

The above quotation makes repeated reference to the socializing and resocializing power of roles that the person has to play upon reaching adulthood and for which he may or may not have been prepared in childhood. Role behavior occurs in the course of a person's interaction with other people or groups and with organizations that he chooses to join or must join. Such associations or groups demand of people certain sets of behaviors and certain perspectives. They socialize people to play a role in certain ways and to avoid behaviors that are considered role-inappropriate. In work-oriented societies such as the United States a man receives his official identity from the work he performs. Consequently he often identifies more with his job-associated role than with many other roles he may be called upon to perform. The more identified he feels with his job and the more worthwhile and gratifying it is to him, the more he is likely to engage in role-appropriate behavior and to adopt role-appropriate values. Once he has played the role over a period of time, it is not uncommon that he begins to so identify with it that the role-associated values and behaviors become second nature to him. In a study of the American Senate, Donald Matthews[2] found that Senators who enjoyed their careers quickly learned the Senate folkways, which put prime emphasis not on winning political floor fights but on "getting along with others." Kent Jennings and Harmon Zeigler (below) note individual differences among social studies teachers but also note great similarities, especially with respect to the inappropriateness of political self-expression in the classroom. They attribute this uniformity in part to the ethics of the profession and the socializing influence of teacher preparation.

The nature of the work experience and the type of work people perform also tend to have profound political influence. By virtue of their physical isolation from the mainstream of society, laborers in isolated, nonmass industries tend to be much more inclined toward political radicalism than are assembly line workers.[3] Among assembly line workers political alienation seems greatest among those performing the dullest, least gratifying, and most unskilled work.[4] Small businessmen caught between big labor and big business are chafing daily under the new ways of doing business; and they become increasingly conservative and nostalgic for the good old days of rugged individualism. On the other hand big business' new role perception of itself is making it increasingly more civic-minded and internationalist. As businessmen play this new role, that is, engage in civic activities and foreign travels, they come into personal contact with an ever-wider variety of people, which in turn enhances their civic-mindedness and internationalism.[5] Studies of the clergy have shown that a given denomination's view of its specific mission in the political arena determines to no small degree the extent to which the clergyman considers himself obligated to become a leader in the community.[6]

The old question as to the extent to which occupational choices and occupational values reflect values first learned in the family is answered in part in the selections by Allan Kornberg and Norman Thomas below. Kornberg and Thomas found that interest in embarking on a legislative career can be just as easily attributed to outside experiences *after* childhood as to familial influences. To be sure, the earlier a person became interested in a political career, the more likely it is that the family was the socializing agent; but there are many people who become actively interested in seeking political office as a result of civic activities, concern over a specific political cause, or as a result of a casual political activity.[7] A study by Garrison,[8] on the other hand, points to the importance of childhood experiences. Lutheran clergy with strong pro-Negro attitudes, but assigned to segregated congregations, would be more likely to become active in civil rights causes if they had had biracial associations in their childhood. In spite of intense pro-Negro feelings, those who had had no such contacts in childhood would become active only in an integrated parish. This article, like the study of schoolteachers, brings out the very important point that people will be more likely to act in accordance with earlier socialization experiences when the community environment is supportive of such norms. Jennings and Zeigler, in a similar vein, point out that teachers in urban communities, where there is less homogeneity of views, will be more likely to engage in classroom discussion of politics, contro-

versy in the classroom, and so forth, than will small-town teachers from very homogeneous communities. In short, the profession alone does not determine the political behaviors a person will feel free to engage in. Rather the community norms, at least as they are perceived by the person, will also weigh heavily and might preclude engaging in some behaviors that a person would otherwise consider to be role-appropriate. We are thus again confronted with the interplay of person (or small group) and larger environment. The group itself may be a powerful socializing agent, as we think the occupational group is, but it is after all anchored in a larger environment which in turn exerts a pull and which, if its pull is contrary to that of the occupational group, may at times attenuate the power of the occupational group unless perhaps, as in the case of the ministers, childhood experiences have built so firm a foundation that they can counterbalance antagonistic community norms.

The great technological and occupational changes that we are witnessing today will also, no doubt, have socializing influences. As demand for manual labor decreases and demand for technical experts increases, more and more sons of blue-collar fathers will join the labor force to become technicians rather than assembly line workers. It is reasonable to assume that their employment will socialize them to the political style congruent with a quasi-professional occupation in spite of their blue-collar home background. This should mean for example that it would further inhibit any propensity to political radicalism but would, on the other hand, encourage political attitudes generally found among professionals, such as concern for improving education, mental-health care, and a variety of related social services. The nature of the twentieth-century business world should have similar socializing effects. Fewer and fewer middle-class youngsters today contemplate going into a business venture of their own but rather think of a managerial or executive career. Recruiting corporations have noticed that—compared to their father's generation—these young people show far less enthusiasm for the political doctrine of rugged individualism and are instead concerned with questions of security, as witnessed by their interest in company-guaranteed fringe benefits, pensions, and lately even union membership. When automobile dealers and football players begin to talk of forming unions in order to bargain collectively, they show that they have been socialized into different political norms than the Horatio Alger norms of their fathers.

Dramatic though these changes may seem, they are probably infinitesimal compared to those experienced by a young African leaving his father's tribe to seek office employment in the new nation's capital. Not much is known as yet about the socializing effect of career in less developed nations; but all the data available on such countries as India, Burma, Egypt and a few others would indicate that it is the modern occupation that contributes greatly to the person's political socialization and accounts for many of the tensions in these more traditional societies.

In most instances occupation is also closely allied to social status. (Physicians are not apt to be of low social status, although the degree of status enjoyed by them will vary over time and across societies.) Yet occupation and social status are not synonymous. Caste and

race, for example, operate independent of the occupational hierarchy. (In the American South, for example, a Negro physician is still first and foremost a Negro.) Social status in turn is accompanied by specific political styles. Persons enjoying high social status, especially in a small town, feel it incumbent upon themselves to appear civic-minded; people on the wrong side of the railroad tracks often feel no such constraint. The extent to which a given social status forces specific role performance is seen in a study of Negro leadership in the South. Daniel Thompson[9] detects three distinct types of Negro leaders: 1) the "Uncle Tom," 2) the racial diplomat, and 3) the race man. These three types of leaders operate very differently from one another in their effort to improve the lot of their Negro constituents; but in each case their behavior was dictated strictly by the nature of the white clientele with whom they had to deal. Thus, Uncle Toms adopt their type of behavior in response to confirmed segregationists, who only tolerate a Negro who will play the bowing, scraping role of an Uncle Tom. Here then we see how role behavior is a function of the interaction between a person's status and the environment with which he has to come to terms.

Social status is a whole way of life not only with respect to shared notions of morality and manners but also with respect to politics. Doing the "correct" thing politically is simply one more way of identifying with a given class, one more way of locating oneself on the status hierarchy. Depending on their social status, people vary from one another with respect to their views on civic duties, public regardingness, and civil rights, to name but three. For example, upper-class people feel more obligated to vote and to become active in the community than do lower-class people. Upper-middle-class people are more willing than are low-status people to tax themselves for social services that they may never draw upon, such as general hospitals or free clinics, because their class ethos dictates such public regardingness.[10] Opposition to civil rights is not only more pronounced in working-class groups but takes on different forms—working-class people might burn crosses in front of the homes of Negroes moving into a formerly all white neighborhood; middle-class people condemn such actions as illegal and un-American but, meanwhile, might move to the suburbs. A host of other political issues are similarly affected by social-class membership. Thus, many white-collar people whose income is barely average and often much below average and who would benefit from the adoption of liberal economic policies will hold conservative political views surprisingly akin to those of affluent business executives. The similarity no doubt is brought on by a feeling of identification with the managerial class or at least with the solid middle class. It has often been observed, for example, that the petite bourgeoisie in Germany, once it felt its social and economic status threatened, was among the most enthusiastic supporters of the new Nazi party, not because the party promised them greater economic gains than, for example, the Socialist party but because it promised them a sense of social importance. The petite bourgeoisie eschewed the Socialist party precisely because the bourgeoisie wanted to maintain its class identity and because it wanted to avoid becoming amalgamated into a classless society. Political radicalism of the right or left is, as David Westby and Richard Braungart point out in this chapter, "most likely to be found among groups that desire to maintain or improve their status relative to other groups in society."

Man, however, plays many roles simultaneously. At times the roles he must play conflict sharply with each other. A study of Southern judges whose task it was to enforce the 1954 Supreme Court decision clearly illustrates this. Their role as federal judge required of them that they enforce the desegregation decision with all deliberate speed. Such role performance, however, was in deep conflict with their role as Southerners and led to personal as well as political tensions in the community.[11] In their study of college students, Westby and Braungart illustrate the political consequences created by conflict due to status inconsistencies. Ziegenhagen (below) further speculates on the implication of role conflict for political socialiation. He seems to feel that it is in the nature of complex industrialized societies to give rise to a good deal of role conflict.

The amount of political socialization that takes place in adulthood varies with the political society under discussion. The more static and simple the society, the fewer new roles have to be learned upon reaching adulthood. The main political task facing a young man in some primitive societies is that of soldier; from early boyhood on he is trained for it; he knew the role well upon reaching adulthood. Even complex but highly stratified, nonmobile societies can do much of their political socializing prior to adulthood.

caste-divided societies are an example. Studies of quasi-feudal and caste societies and studies of the American South show that low-caste children have completed their political role learning early in childhood: from a young age on they are taught political passivity, fatalism, and subservience to those in power.[12] Until perhaps a generation or so ago the political socialization of many a young Negro in the Deep South was completed by adulthood or before because there was no new political role he could aspire to or could assume upon reaching his majority. Although in such societies adult political socialization may be minimal, it plays a much more important part in highly complex societies. There the family, school, and peer group can only engage in anticipatory political socialization by helping with the acquisition of values and skills useful for playing the role of citizen as well as a host of other adult political roles. But in the final analysis, playing the role of voter, precinct captain, taxpayer, union foreman, jury member, officer in the National Guard, state legislator, or even President can only be learned "on the job," that is, upon reaching adulthood.

If in addition the definitions and expectancies of these roles change during one's lifetime, the family can do even less preparatory socialization and even more will depend on adult socialization. Pye, in his discussion of Burma, asserts that modern nations need participatory citizens but that the Burmese generation of parents—who grew up as colonial subjects—still train their young for passivity. American blacks are another case in point: they see their role different from the previous generation. Undoubtedly few young

Negroes living in the South had been prepared in childhood for the role of militant or Black Nationalist. As Robert Mendelsohn and Eliot Luby indicate, middle-aged and older Negroes do not usually value this role; but it is highly respected by many younger Negroes. In summary then, we can say that the greater the discontinuities—as under conditions of rapid political change—between old family values and new political realities, and the larger the number of political roles for which an adult is eligible, the more the adult is likely to learn political lessons not taught by the family.

This chapter concentrates on the importance of role as an adult socializer. There are, of course, many other factors that can account for resocialization, such as dramatic political events, personal trauma. Some of these may involve whole personality restructuring (as exemplified in the experience of some of the concentration camp inmates), others may involve a permanent restructuring of one's political cognitions and preferences (it has been pointed out that the Great Depression constituted such an event, which permanently changed partisan loyalties, voting patterns, and even ways of looking at government.) A long historical tradition also has socializing power. Countries that have experienced occupation or exploitation by other nations, not over years but over generations, tend to adjust their political thoughts and behaviors to this condition so well that the adjustment will persist even when conditions have been changed. Greek citizens' distrust of the state and readiness to deceive authorities can be traced to a time when the state was synonymous with the Turks and, hence, deception was not considered immoral.[13] Nor have we discussed many other adult socializers as, for example, the mass media. Space simply permits no fuller coverage. The illustrations offered in this chapter, however, should suffice to remind us that man does not cease learning political lessons upon reaching adulthood.

NOTES

1. Orville G. Brim, Jr., *Socialization After Childhood* (New York: Wiley, 1966), pp. 18–20.

2. Donald Matthews, *U.S. Senators and Their World* (New York: Random House, 1960).

3. Seymour Martin Lipset, *Political Man—the Social Bases of Politics* (New York: Doubleday, 1959).

4. Lewis Lipsitz, "Work Life and Political Attitudes: A Study of Manual Workers," *American Political Science Review*, LVIII (1964), 951–962.

5. Ithiel de Sola Pool, Suzanne Keller, and Raymond Bauer, "The Influence of Foreign Travel on Political Attitudes of American Businessmen," *Public Opinion Quarterly*, XX (1956), 161–175.

6. Gerhard Lenski, *The Religious Factor* (New York: Doubleday, 1963).

7. Kenneth Prewitt and Heinz Eulau, "Political Socialization and Political Roles on Two Levels of Government," Paper prepared for the Sixth World Congress of the International Political Science Association (Geneva, Switzerland: 1965).

8. Karl C. Garrison, Jr., "The Behavior of Clergy on Racial Integration as Related to a Childhood Socialization Factor," *Sociology and Social Research*, 51 (1967), 209–219.

9. Daniel C. Thompson, *The Negro Leadership Class* (Englewood Cliffs, N.J.: Prentice-Hall, 1963).

10. James Q. Wilson and Edward Banfield, "Public Regardingness as a Value Premise in Voting Behavior," *American Political Science Review*, LVIII (1964), 976–987.

11. Jack W. Peltason, *Fifty-eight Lonely Men: Southern Federal Judges and School Desegregation* (New York: Harcourt, Brace & World, 1961).

12. John Dollard, *Caste and Class in a Southern Town* (New Haven, Conn.: Yale University Press, 1937).

13. Anna Pipinelli Potamianou, "Personality and Group Participation in Greece," Publication No. 24 (Athens: Center for Mental Health and Research, 1965), p. 17.

POLITICAL EXPRESSIVISM AMONG HIGH SCHOOL TEACHERS: THE INTERSECTION OF COMMUNITY AND OCCUPATIONAL VALUES*

- ## M. Kent Jennings and Harmon Zeigler

Teachers have seldom come under the scrutiny of political scientists; and when they have, the examination has been conducted primarily because of the belief that educational establishments socialize children into the acceptance of basic societal norms. In contrast, we are looking at teachers not only because they are agents of political socialization but also because they offer a useful opportunity to measure the intersection of occupational values and community expectations.

The specific attitudinal dimension that we intend to measure is the extent to which teachers believe that they should express themselves freely on political topics to their classes and, by their actions, to the community. We are looking at the teaching occupation as productive of certain expectations and hence can employ the concept of occupation as a *culture*. Social scientists commonly deal with occupation as a measure of status, or with the relationship between work life and attitudes toward the job (such as the correlates of job satisfaction). Looking at occupation as a measure of social status relegates a person's job to a static, rather ecological

concept. Thus, people who hold "high status" or "low status" occupations are said to behave politically in certain ways partially because of their status positions.

We want to investigate occupations in neither sense but rather as factors that can affect perceptions of proper roles, even though these roles might be only peripherally related to the actual performance of the teaching function. This suggests that, although the political roles of teachers in classroom and community might not necessarily be primary roles, they are nevertheless influenced by primary roles. Along these lines, Seymour Martin Lipset has speculated that the monotony and routinization of factory work is partially responsible for the persistent radicalism of European workers.[1] The notion that the requirements of a job might have an effect upon political ideology was confirmed by Lewis Lipsitz.[2] There is some slight evidence, then, that on-the-job performance and off-the-job politics are part of the same system of behavior. However, the evidence is sparse and needs supplementing.

It seems clear that occupations develop ideologies; and persons who are part of an occupational structure become, to a greater or lesser extent, committed to a pattern of thought and behavior. Cottrell's classic study of

The above selection has been written especially for this volume.

* Financial support for the study reported here comes from The Danforth Foundation and the National Science Foundation.

railroad men illustrates how an occupational ideology might develop.[3] Railroad men are isolated and clannish, with a distinct pattern of folkways and jargon. They stand in vivid contrast, for example, to business executives, for whom social life is often the key to success. Undeniably, certain occupations recruit particular personality types, but occupations also socialize their members with acceptable attitudes.[4]

An occupational ideology is formed, therefore, by a combination of selective recruitment and occupational socialization. As a result, compared with other professions, teachers tend to be compliant, noncompetitive, and deferential.[5] Although members of occupational groupings do exhibit distinct modal characteristics, intraoccupational variations undoubtedly occur. Thus, in spite of pressing occupational ideologies it is clear that teachers are by no means a completely homogeneous lot. Some are much more assertive and expressive than others and these variations extend to the political sphere.[6] Various personal, environmental, and suboccupational forces may be reasonably expected to affect the political role perspectives of the teacher.

We propose to examine certain variables related to the teacher's environment and his career, each of which clarify the relationship between occupational ideologies and political role playing. Environmental variables will include region and metropolitanism; career variables will consist of undergraduate preparation, length of time teaching, and level of formal education. These factors are explained in more detail after discussing the study design and measures of expressive role orientations.

Study Design

Social studies teachers are a particularly apt group to study in light of our earlier observations, because they deal with politically relevant content in the classroom. Whereas political socialization undoubtedly occurs in nonsocial studies classrooms also, it is patent that the major thrust of formal civic education rests in the social studies and that affective and cognitive orientations to politics and public affairs serve as foci of instruction in these classes. Social studies teachers, not surprisingly, talk about politics in class substantially more than do teachers of other subjects.[7] We are interested in the extent to which and the conditions under which the social studies teachers perceive certain classroom behaviors as improper, on the assumption that this affects their own behavior and, ultimately, may influence the political orientations of their students. In this respect we are concerned with the teachers as agents of political socialization.[8]

Social studies teachers are intriguing on another count. Not only are they agents of political learning, they are also adult members of the political community. More than teachers in other areas, however, their community political roles are linked to their teaching subject areas. Other things being equal, one would expect social studies teachers to be more attentive to and involved in the political life of the community.[9] On the other hand, because of the tie between classroom content and community life, the political roles of social studies teachers are probably under more scrutiny than are those of other teachers—at least the social studies teachers probably perceive this to be the case. The social studies teachers are thus particularly good subjects for looking at the interaction between occupational norms and political roles.

In pursuing this task we shall draw upon data collected within the context of a larger study of political socialization of American high school students. During the spring of 1965 interviews were held with a national sample of social studies teachers to whom the 1669 students had been most exposed during grades 10–12. A total of 317 teachers were interviewed, 286 of whom were public school teachers. Because public school teachers operate in a milieu with a different set of expectations and constraints than do their counterparts in the nonpublic school, the latter are excluded from the analysis.

Inasmuch as the teacher sample is not a sample of the universe of all social studies teachers, we should be very explicit about how the sample was determined. The investigators in the political socialization study desired a sample of social studies teachers that would reflect the number and variety of course hours taught to their sample of students. Decisions about the relative value of various levels of depth coverage —number of teachers per student— were achieved by means of a selection scheme.[10] A concise definition of the sample is that it represents those social studies teachers bearing the heaviest load of social studies teaching during grades 10 through 12 for a national sample of twelfth graders.

Norms of Expressive Behavior Among Social Studies Teachers

Norms may be descriptive (what is) or prescriptive (what should be) in nature.

Here we shall emphasize prescriptive norms because they are more likely to capture the occupational ideological structure through which the teacher was socialized and because they are more resistant to the environment in which the teacher happens to be at a particular point in time. The line of questioning that elicited the expressiveness norms went as follows:

Now I would like to ask you some questions about some things that a teacher might do in the community and the classroom. I will mention something that a teacher might want to do, and would you tell me if you think a teacher should or should not feel free to do this, assuming that the teacher wanted to?

Eleven activities were cited; the proportions indicating that a teacher should feel free to do the activity are presented in Table 1.

There is a great range in the affirmation of the behavior in question, all the way from the near unanimous opinion that pro-United Nations talk is legitimate, to the less than majority feeling that striking is within the pale. The proportions clearly fall toward the freedom of expression and behavior side, but this is in all likelihood partly artifactual. Tougher, more sensitive activities would generate lower percentages and, as noted earlier, social studies teachers are more expressively oriented than teachers in other fields.

Although possibly subject to the same criticism of item variability, it is also apparent that most of the low-ranking activities (going on strike being the notable exception) involve classroom rather than community deportment. That teachers should have stricter and more conservative norms about on-the-job versus nonjob activities is, however, quite plausible. Career socialization would be stricter concerning job versus nonjob behavior. Assuming that the items represent roughly equivalent forms of community and classroom activities, one would cautiously conclude that the prescriptive norms are more constraining in the classroom than in the community.[11]

We are not so much interested in the problem of differences *between* the normative structures regarding these two domains as in the conditions under which the normative structuring differs *within* each domain. Stated more simply, Why do some teachers prefer a more constrained role than do others? and What are some important corollaries of these differing role orientations?

In answering these questions we found it more convenient and more analytical-

Table 1

Proportion of Social Studies Teachers Agreeing that a Teacher Should Feel Free to Engage in Certain Activities

Speak in class in favor of the United Nations	96%
Join a teacher's union	88
Serve as party precinct worker in preelection activities	87
Run for political office	83
Belong to the NAACP or CORE	81
Speak in class for or against the civil rights movement	76
Publicly criticize local government officials	68
Allow the distribution of anticommunist literature put out by the NAM	63
Allow an atheist to address the class	58
Speak in class favorably about socialism	57
Go on strike to secure higher salaries and other benefits	41
	N = 349*

* This is a weighted *N* made necessary by the use of unavoidably imprecise estimates used in the construction of the sampling frame. All data reported are derived from this weighted base *N*.

ly satisfying to produce index scores for each teacher in the two areas of classroom and community behaviors. To be sure that the items in each index formed a relatively self-contained and highly interrelated cluster, a 10×10 matrix was formed consisting of the gamma correlations between each pair of individual items used in the original question (except for the highly consensual United Nations item). The coefficients were then arranged and rearranged in such a way as to enclose in separate square matrices the various pairs that were most highly interrelated.

As a result of these operations two distinctive clusters emerged. One consists of four community behaviors: joining a teacher's union, belonging to the NAACP or CORE, being a precinct worker, and running for office. The intercorrelations range from .54 to .79, with an average of .67.[12] A second quartet of highly associated items lay in the classroom domain and included allowing an atheist to address the class, speaking in favor of socialism, speaking for or against civil rights, and publicly criticizing local officials.[13] Here the gamma coefficients ranged from .46 to .73, the average being .60.[14] A crucial property of each cluster is that the inclusion of any other item in an expanded square matrix generates one or more coefficients lower than all of those in the original cluster.[15]

Knowing that the items in each cluster are, relatively speaking, highly interrelated, one may then score the responses in the conventional manner of index construction where each item receives equal weight. Summing the scores provided each teacher's score within a range of 0 to 4, from low to high expressiveness. Some collapsing was done so that each index of expressiveness is a trichotomy of low, medium, and high. As might be expected from the raw percentages, the community expressiveness index is somewhat skewed toward the high side; but the classroom index has a more equitable distribution among the three categories.

These distributions and the cross tabulations of the classroom index scores against the community index scores are presented in Table 2. The cross tabulation shows that the two measures are substantially associated with each other. Teachers who subscribe more to expressiveness in the classroom also tend to take the same stance regarding community behaviors, and vice versa. Yet the two measures are independent enough to dictate the utility of preserving their individuality for analytical purposes.

Before turning to an explication of the factors prompting differential role orientations, the question of articulation between prescriptive norms and overt behavior should be examined briefly. It is not necessary that such an articulation exist, but one can make more inferences from the data under

such conditions. The community expression index shows positive relationships to a number of political participation measures: party identification intensity (gamma = .20); talking to people during election campaigns (gamma = .36); doing other campaign work (gamma = .28); talking with colleagues about politics (gamma = .33); and belonging to civil rights groups (gamma = .69).

Behavioral data from the classroom domain are more scarce, but it should be noted that teachers with more expressive classroom norms are also more participative in political affairs. It is also consistent with our assumptions that these teachers are more enthusiastic about using controversial materials in the class (gamma = .19) and they more often disavow that there are topics which they should not discuss in the classroom (gamma = .20). Finally, the more expressive the teacher the less he subscribes to traditional and safe goals of civic education: that the main objective is to teach students to be good citizens (gamma = −.21); that teaching facts is the most important goal (gamma = −.17); and that students should not have access to books which might confuse

Table 2

Relationship Between Expressive Orientations in the Classroom and in the Community

Classroom Expression Index Scores	Community Expression Index Scores			Row Totals	Marginal Totals	N
	Low	Medium	High			
Low	42%	23	34	99%	24%	(83)
Medium	11	23	66	100	41	(144)
High	3	15	82	100	35	(122)
Marginal Totals	16%	20	64		100%	
N	(55)	(71)	(223)			(349)
			gamma = .58			

them (gamma $= -.29$). Considering that these various independent measures are somewhat removed from the items forming the expressivism indexes, the associations may be taken as evidence that the teacher's normative structure has some connection with the way he behaves.

Explanatory Factors: The Impingement of Community Characteristics

The first class of variables are measures of the broader community in which the teacher lives. The holder of a given occupational position is, in addition to being subject to the pressures of his occupational norms, the object of forces that are extraoccupational, forces that we shall call "community characteristics." We shall later argue that certain suboccupational characteristics also differentiate teachers. For the present we are interested in characteristics that may alter the effects of occupational ideologies.

An obvious example of a supraoccupational ideology system is region. Sectionalism has always been considered a significant aspect of the American political scene. However, the most explicit statement of regional values at the mass public level is found in Stouffer's work on tolerance.[16] Stouffer found that Southerners and Midwesterners were substantially less tolerant of nonconformists or deviant behavior than were Easterners or Westerners. Although the South is usually cited as an example of rigid sectionalism, there are other perhaps less distinct but still distinguishable regional cultures.[17] If we inquire about the extent to which teachers, as smaller

subsamples of these larger regional samples, epitomize these regional values, then we should expect to find that Midwestern and Southern teachers are less likely to be expressive than are Western and Eastern teachers. In the analysis teachers will be allocated into the conventional four regions.[18]

Similar hypotheses can be argued for the next variable; size and complexity of community. The teachers in large heterogeneous communities face, according to Stouffer, a relatively tolerant environment and should, consequently, appear as small images of this environment. Conversely, the smaller, more homogeneous communities, which are the least tolerant, should produce the least expressive teachers. Although absolute community size is an obvious measure that could be employed to tap this dimension, we have elected to use a scheme based on the presence and/or nature of the Standard Metropolitan Statistical Area (SMSA) in which the school is located. An advantage to using an SMSA classification is that it incorporates not only population and urban factors in the immediate environment but also includes social and economic dependencies. Using this measure instead of sheer community size means, for example, that the small town in a large metropolitan area is separated from the small town in a remote, rural area; simply using community size would put these two towns in the same cell.[19] The teachers in the sample have divided according to those teaching in schools located in one of the twelve most populated SMASs in the nation, hereafter called large SMSAs; in other SMSAs not among the twelve largest (medium SMSAs); or in areas not part of any SMSA (non-SMSAs). For convenience and variety the terms metropolitanism, community complexity, and urbanism will be used interchangeably when dealing with the SMSA characteristic.

The two independent environmental variables are moderately related to each other (contingency coefficient = .40). The South and Midwest are typified by smaller, more homogeneous communities, whereas the Northeast and West are characterized by more urban, heterogeneous communities. Although the analysis of the relationship between environmental variables and teachers' role perceptions begins with a study of some simple relationships, the intercorrelations among the independent variables make it necessary to establish the existence of an independent effect for each variable.

Let us begin by examining the simple relationship between these independent variables and the teachers' standards of proper classroom and community behavior. Table 3 reveals that both variables seem to affect the way teachers view their roles. Considering region first, the Northeastern and Western teachers are more expressive than the Midwestern and Southern teachers, whether one is speaking of classroom or community norms. Thus, the inferences drawn from Stouffer's research appear to be substantiated in the role perceptions of teachers. This relationship can be approached in one of two ways: either the teachers in the Northeastern and West are expressive because the *communities* in which they teach are less likely to attempt to impose sanctions upon teachers, or these teachers are expressive because they *personally* reflect tolerant and open regional norms.

The first argument can be tested directly from these data. If tolerance of nonconformity (and by inference, tolerance of teachers speaking up in class) is indicated by a lack of sanctioning efforts, then the relationship between the ex-

Table 3

Relationship Between Community Characteristics and Expressive Role Orientations in the Community and Classroom

| | N | Community Expression | | | Classroom Expression | | |
		Low	Medium	High	Low	Medium	High
Region							
South	(84)	20%	28	52	37	36	27
Midwest	(111)	21	20	59	27	47	26
West	(62)	11	14	75	12	44	44
Northeast	(91)	09	17	74	17	36	47
Metropolitanism							
Non-SMSAs	(125)	29	25	46	35	40	25
Medium SMSAs	(121)	09	17	74	19	41	41
Large SMSAs	(103)	08	18	74	17	43	40
			(gamma = .40)			(gamma = .24)	

* Row percentages here and in other tables add to 100% except for occasional discrepancies due to rounding. Gamma coefficients are not used for regional results because region is a nominal-level variable.

pressive perceptions of Western teachers and their perceptions of the community are not congruent. When asked if they could recall criticism of teachers for the discussing of controversial events in class, 68 percent of the Western teachers responded in the affirmative, compared to about one-fourth of the teachers in the other areas. Hence, one of the most expressive groups of teachers lives in an area that is perceived to be heavily laden with attacks upon teachers. Second, and as a partial consequence of the above, there is a slight positive correlation between the perception of criticism and expressive role orientations. Teachers who perceive criticism are more likely to score high on both the classroom (.17) and community behavior (.17) indices in comparison to those teachers who do not perceive criticism. Teacher criticism is not a likely stimulus to expressive behavior. It is just as reasonable to argue that expressive norms sharpen the perception, so that criticism is more easily ascertained. In sum, there is no evidence to suggest that the expressive behavior of Northeastern and Western teachers is related to the benign environment in which they teach. Indeed, in the West the evidence is very much to the contrary.

We are left, then, with the second alternative, that teachers reflect—perhaps exaggerate—their milieus. To consider this argument we need to know the extent to which teachers are mobile between regions, since a high rate of mobility would confuse the argument that teachers behave according to regional norms. However, there is very little regional mobility. The relationship between the region in which teachers were raised and the region in which they teach is extremely high

(contingency coefficient = .84). The argument is not faulted, therefore, since the mobility pattern of teachers is not one that would create tension between their values and dominant cultural norms. This is not to say that the role perceptions of teachers are not more than mirrors of the culture. There is also the questions of values related to occupational choice and role orientation, which will be considered later.

The more urban the environment, the more expressive the orientation of the teacher; but the variation is not clearly monotonic (Table 3). The percentage distributions indicate that there is no difference at all between teachers in the large and medium-sized SMSAs. Concerning classroom behavior, two-fifths of the teachers in large and medium-sized SMSAs are high expressives compared to one-fourth in the non-SMSAs. A similar pattern emerges for the community behavior index, which indicates that three-fourths of the teachers in both the large and medium-sized SMSAs are very expressive compared to four-ninths of the teachers in the non-SMSAs. These rural and small town teachers stand out. Once the threshold of the metro area has been crossed, increasing size of the metro area accounts for little difference in the normative structures.

We can now make the same inquiry that guided us in discussing regional data. Are the role orientations of small town teachers a result of community pressures, or a reflection of the teachers' own norms as generated by the small town environment? There is a positive correlation (contingency coefficient = .39) between the size of the community in which the teacher was brought up and the size of the community in which the respondent teaches. Although the correlation here is not as great as that between regions, (almost necessarily given historical changes in population movements) a majority of the teachers live in areas roughly comparable to those in which they were raised. So the differences among teachers can be interpreted not so much as a result of divergency arising out of mobility patterns but rather as a result of teachers reflecting community norms.

This conclusion is reinforced by the distribution of perceived criticism leveled at teachers. Perception of criticism increases appreciably with community complexity (44 percent of the large metro teachers, report criticism, compared to 29 percent of the nonmetro teachers). Thus, the big city teacher, functioning in a heterogeneous conflict-oriented environment, is expressive, whereas the hinterland teacher living in a homogeneous community with less actual conflict, is more reticent. Of course, these relationships should not obscure the possibility that the potential for conflict is as great in a small town and the sanctioning power of community agents might be more severe in a small town if the teachers were to expand the definition of proper behavior.

Table 4

Correlations Between Teacher Role Orientations and Metropolitanism, by Region

Region	Community Expression	Classroom Expression
	gamma	*gamma*
South	.52	.52
Midwest	.41	.14
West	.43	.20
Northeast	−.02	−.21

The Interplay of Community Factors

Both measures employed so far suggest the conclusion that community homogeneity and reticence are highly related. The next problem to attack is the extent to which each variable has an independent effect upon the normative roles of teachers. Table 4 indicates that holding region constant has a variable effect on the relationship between metropolitanism and role definition with regard to both community and classroom behavior.[20] In the Midwest and West the correlation remains relatively unchanged from the overall gamma (.40 and .24 for community and classroom, respectively). However, in the South the association is somewhat strengthened, whereas in the Northeast it is severely weakened to the extent of a sign change. Overall, in both classroom and community behavior the positive correlation between community complexity and prescriptive norms holds, with the exception of the Northeast. Regionalism reverses the relationship in the Northeast and exaggerates it in the South. Actually, there is a slight tendency for the non-SMSA Northeastern teachers to be more expressive than their large SMSA counterparts, especially when one examines classroom behavior. The evidence suggests that the relationships between regions, community complexity, and role norms are both independent and cumulative. In the case of the South, regional values buttress community values to contribute to a highly reticent posture.

Consistency of Expressivism

An interesting question emerges as to a possible directionality of expressive

Table 5

Selective Expressive Classroom Behavior: Percentage of Teachers Who Are Highly Expressive on " Liberal" and " Conservative" Items, by Metropolitan Characteristics

Metropolitanism	Liberal Item	Conservative Item	Difference	N
Non-SMSAs	49%	59%	+10	(125)
Medium SMSAs	65	64	−1	(121)
Large SMSAs	65	68	+3	(103)

norms. The items in the classroom index all require that the teacher commit an act which, especially in small communities, would reflect a commitment to change. Suppose, on the other hand, we consider a behavioral possibility that is supportive of the status quo? An item not included in the index was the question of whether or not a teacher should allow the distribution of anticommunist literature produced by the National Association of Manufacturers. If the index items are "liberal," surely this item is "conservative." If the small town teachers are making a distinction between types of behaviors, then they should be more willing to allow anticommunist literature to be distributed than they are to engage in the behaviors summarized in the index. Further, they should be at least willing as teachers in large communities to permit this act.

The two items on the index that most clearly require a radical departure from safe behavior are allowing an atheist to address the class and speaking in favor of socialism. Comparing the average expressive responses to these two items with the response to the conservative item not included in the index (Table 5) suggests that the small town teachers are more likely to express themselves when the issue is connotative of main-

tenance of the status quo. In large and medium-sized SMSAs, teachers do not draw a distinction based upon the nature of the item. However, in non-SMSAs substantially more teachers are willing to adopt an expressive position on the distribution of anticommunist literature than they are on the presentation of atheist and socialist points of view in class. Parenthetically, it should be noted that this distinction also characterizes the more conservative regions of the country. The Northeastern teachers do not make a distinction; Western teachers actually make a distinction in favor of the more liberal items, whereas Midwestern and Southern teachers draw a sharp distinction in favor of the more conservative items.

In spite of the increase of expressivism among small town teachers on a conservative item, they still do not become as expressive as the medium and large city teachers. Although the small town teachers are more selective in their expressive role orientations, this selectivity does not erase the difference between these teachers and those in larger communities. The small town teacher reflects a general reluctance to adapt an expressive role, but the reluctance is greatest when the expression requires change-oriented behavior.

Explanatory Factors: The Force of Occupational Characteristics

The preceding section demonstrated the impact of forces extraindividual in nature. But just as the social studies teacher's perspectives are shaped by his environment, so may he also respond to conditions of his occupational training and career patterns. One such variable is length of time teaching. If we conceive of the occupation as a socializing influence, then it is logical to assume that there is a developing congruence of values between the individual and the occupational role he plays. Even though a person may work to change the occupation to suit his conceptions, there is a strong tendency to either leave an occupation or adjust to its demands. It is instructive, therefore, to think of a career in terms of its stages.[21] Also, as he passes through these career stages, the teacher will learn more clearly what the expectations are.[22] Guba and his associates found that such personality characteristics as a need for deference and order are substantially more exaggerated in more experienced teachers.[23] In view of these findings, we can advance a specific hypothesis concerning the relationship between length of time teaching and role orientations: the longer a person remains in teaching the less will he sanction expressive behavior both within the classroom and the community.

Having based one variable upon the assumption that a career socializes its occupant after entrance, we base the next upon the assumption that differential patterns of recruitment and training are operative within a career. With this in mind we will examine the undergraduate backgrounds of teachers, distinguishing among five majors: education, social studies, history, the social sciences, and "other" subjects.[24] The choice of an education major implies that such students have chosen the most direct route to the classroom. Similarly, the social studies majors come primarily from teachers colleges and divisions. Both are more likely to be profession-oriented than those who elect other majors and different types of instruction. In addition, the education and social studies majors probably begin the acquisition of professional norms at an earlier stage. They encounter less of the "fads and frills" of the usual college communities and are exposed to a more unified set of values. Thus, Guba et al. found that teacher's college students had developed a need pattern not unlike that of teachers with at least ten years of service.[25] Although there is no direct evidence, as there was in the case of length of time teaching, it is nevertheless possible to hypothesize that teachers who majored in education and the social studies should be less expressive within the classroom and the community in comparison to teachers who majored in other fields.

We shall also assess the effect of graduate training. It may be argued that having a M.A. versus a B.A. would broaden the teacher's construction of what is legitimate behavior because the teacher will feel more assured of his own status. It is also true that those obtaining an M.A. displayed enough aggressiveness to earn that degree and may, therefore, be disposed to be more aggressive generally. On the other hand, it might be argued that the M.A. holders will be the superrepresentatives of the profession and will consequently be less expressive.

Table 6

Relationship Between Occupational Characteristics and Expressive Orientations in the Community and Classroom

	Community Expression			Classroom Expression			N
	Low	*Medium*	*High*	*Low*	*Medium*	*High*	
Years Teaching							
0–4	19	22	60	17	36	48	(69)
5–9	13	17	70	18	38	44	(89)
10–19	14	22	64	21	49	30	(103)
20+	18	20	61	39	38	22	(88)
		gamma = −.02			gamma = −.29		
Undergraduate Major*							
Social science	08	07	85	13	32	55	(31)
History	06	21	74	12	50	38	(107)
"Other"	14	17	69	30	39	31	(54)
Social studies	19	23	58	26	39	35	(88)
Education	28	25	47	40	41	19	(45)
Education Level							
B.A.	21	23	56	27	40	32	(177)
M.A.	10	18	72	20	42	38	(172)
		gamma = .31			gamma = .13		

* No gamma coefficients are presented because this variable is nominal rather than ordinal.

In examining those variables not specifically related to the community, we nevertheless make the assumption that these variables might interact with community variables to produce a unique relationship. Further, it is possible that each of the occupational variables might relate to the dependent variables by means of other, intervening occupational variables. Thus, we continue the type of analysis begun in the last section, starting first with an overview of the data.

We suggested that the social structure of the school and the community plus the conditioning factors of the classroom situation should increasingly inhibit the expressive orientations of teachers. Such is not the case for community activities, but the argument is vindicated for classroom behavior norms (Table 6). Increasing experience reduces the normative support for expression in the classroom. Whether this pattern comes about because of differential career dropout rates, generational changes in the teaching profession, or the socializing process is not easily resolved with the data at hand. It seems highly unlikely though that more experience *increases* expressivism among individual teachers.

It was initially hypothesized that the educational background of teachers would affect their behavior primarily because of the process of selective recruitment. The aspirations and motivations of teachers with education and social studies undergraduate majors should differ from these with other kinds of majors; and those teachers who have had some graduate training should display attitudes fundamentally dissimilar from those who had none. An examination of Table 6 indicates that the educational background of teachers is strongly related to their role orientations. As predicted, education and social studies majors are substantially more restrained in their orientations, both within the classroom and in the community. By comparison, the social science and history majors, particularly the former, possess a set of very expressive norms.

Although it cannot be demonstrated here, our interpretation is that both the major itself and the type of institution at which the teacher matriculated have a bearing on these sharp differences. To be sure, there are probably self-selection features distinguishing the teachers attending certain schools and adopting certain majors. Our contention is that these differences are likely to be reinforced and elaborated during the college years. Social science and history majors receive more of the liberal arts slants and typically matriculate at liberal arts colleges and universities. Social studies and education majors receive training that reflects the conservatism of the profession and, in addition, are often trained in normals, teachers colleges, and education schools.

What is the effect of graduate training upon the expressive norms of social studies teachers? A first answer to this question comes by simply splitting the sample almost evenly between those with B.A. (or B.S.) degrees only versus those with M.A. (or M.S.) degrees. There is a moderately strong connection between the degree level and community expression (Table 6); those with a Master's are more expressively oriented. But the relationship dwindles considerably for classroom behavior. As we shall see later, educational level bears an interesting configuration to expres-

sivism when length of teaching is taken into account. But for the moment it is sufficient to point out that possessing the M.A. seems to give the teacher more protection, confidence, and aggressiveness in defining the teacher role in public life but that the strengthening is muted in the classroom domain.

The Interplay of Occupational Factors

One question of immediate interest is whether the strong differences according to undergraduate majors are exacerbated or erased by the effects of graduate training. Table 7 indicates the conditions under which the continuation of education serves to increase expressivism. With the exception of history majors, going on to obtain a M.A. degree strengthens both classroom and community expressivism, especially the latter, regardless of major. More degrees make a difference, although it is certainly possible that those who gain the M.A. were more expressively oriented to start with.

As anticipated, the factoring out of those who have graduate training tends to heighten the difference between social science and history undergraduate majors versus social studies and education undergraduate majors. For example, the difference on the community expression index between the social science undergraduate major who has graduate training and the undergraduate education major with no master's is immense. Furthermore, the M.A.s among the education and social studies majors do not attain the levels of the social science M.A.s, although those in the social studies do "catch up" with the history majors. Even if the education major has acquired graduate training, his

Table 7

Role Orientations and Undergraduate Majors, by Highest Degree Obtained

Undergraduate Major and Highest Degree Obtained	N	Community Expression		Classroom Expressions		
		Low	High	Low	Medium	High
Social science						
M.A.	(18)	04%	96	07	39	54
B.A.	(13)	29	70	22	23	56
History						
M.A.	(56)	29	71	15	46	39
B.A.	(50)	22	77	11	53	36
Social studies						
M.A.	(34)	29	71	15	39	45
B.A.	(54)	50	50	32	39	29
Education						
M.A.	(21)	43	57	36	41	23
B.A.	(24)	61	39	41	42	18

orientation is substantially more retiring than that of social science and history undergraduate majors who have not gone to graduate school and of course is even more reticent than the orientation of social science undergraduate majors who have done graduate work.

The situation is most acute in the classroom domain where both categories (B.A. and M.A.) of the education majors are less expressive than all other categories among the other majors. Indeed, further education has precious little impact concerning classroom expression for teachers who start out as collegiate education majors. More so than those with other backgrounds, these teachers receive an outlook on classroom conduct that is highly resistant to change by more education and may, in fact, be reinforced in graduate school if the graduate area is education. We found, in further analysis, that the master's field has a differential effect depending upon the undergraduate field. Teachers who earned B.A.s in history, social science, and the social studies and took their M.A.s in education, continued to hold

more expressive classroom norms than those who took both their B.A.s and M.A.s in education. The B.A.s in education who received M.A.s in that field became as expressively oriented in regard to *community* behavior as did M.A.s with other B.A. backgrounds. Education majors distinguish strongly between the community and the classroom. Overall, being an undergraduate education major seems to impose a powerful set toward restrained norms of classroom behavior, norms that are not appreciably altered by graduate training.

Although the case is perhaps most striking for the education B.A.s, there is a strong hint in the data for all teachers (Table 6) that the M.A. provides a more liberating force in the domain of community versus classroom behavior norms. It is certainly possible that master's training may emphasize the right of the teacher to involve himself in the political life of the community, however controversial. There is another explanation that can be advanced here. Perhaps more education increases self-esteem, so that the most educated teacher feels more confident of his ability to handle a community situation. At the same time, the increase in self-esteem would not necessarily affect classroom behavior that is more tightly under the control of professional norms. Thus, the general repressive or fear-arousing nature of the classroom prevents the release of expressive tendencies that develop with graduate work.

One seemingly paradoxical result from our analysis is the negative relationship between years teaching and classroom expression and the lack of a positive relationship to community expression norms. These findings emerge despite the fact that the longer the teacher's employment, the more likely will he be to have a master's degree.[26] As noted earlier, holders of the master's are a shade more likely than B.A.s to support expressive roles in the classroom and much more inclined to espouse such roles outside the classroom. By controlling for educational attainment, the relationship between years teaching and role orientation is further exposed.

Contrary to what might be expected, increasing teacher experience extracts a greater toll from the expressiveness of the M.A.s than of the B.A.s (Table 8). Expressive behavior support among the M.A.s declines substantially more with

Table 8

Length of Time Teaching Related to Expressive Behavior Support, by Educational Attainment

Highest Degree Obtained	Community Expression	Classroom Expression
B.A.	−.05	−.30
M.A.	−.18	−.42

experience than it does among the B.A.s. Furthermore, the relationship is monotonic among the M.A.s, whereas for the B.A.s there are some irregularities. What these results suggest is that the increasing commitment to the teaching career—represented by lengthening employment as a teacher—serves to erode expressive orientations connected with obtaining the master's degree. These conclusions hold for both classroom and community activities, although the evidence is substantially stronger for the classroom domain.[27]

The Combined and Separate Effects of Community and Occupational Characteristics

We have now considered two major classes of explanatory factors affecting the expressiveness norms of social studies teachers.[28] Each apparently helps account for differing normative structures, or definitions, of proper "political" behavior in the classroom and in the community. But there may be interrelationships between the community and occupational characteristics that confound the apparent contribution of each set of variables. Given the initial sample size, it would be impossible to control simultaneously for even a sizable subset of the two major community and the three major occupational characteristics examined. It is possible to take at least a pair at a time, especially those variables that are most likely to be introducing a spurious note to the initial associations and those that emerged as the most powerful.

It should be observed at the outset that there are few large biases with respect to the distribution of any given occupational characteristic along a community characteristic, or vice versa. The most noticeable, and potentially most important, was the relatively greater incidence of social studies and education undergraduate majors in the South and Midwest and in the medium size SMSAs and the non-SMSAs, and an accompanying greater incidence of majors outside these fields in the West and Northeast and in the larger SMSAs. Bearing these exceptions in mind, the likelihood of spurious relationships is reduced though certainly not eliminated.

It will be recalled that years of teaching was negatively related to classroom expressiveness (—.29). This association holds up remarkably well when community characteristics are controlled one at a time. For example, according to metropolitanism the gamma coefficients are —.27 for large SMSAs, —.31 for medium SMSAs, and —.31 for non-SMSAs. Variations by region are more erratic, but all continue to show a negative sign. By the same token, the strong association between region and metropolitanism with support for expressive behavior remain when length of teaching is controlled. Rather, the effects *tend* to be cumulative. Illustratively, when years teaching and metropolitanism are simultaneously related to classroom norms, the most expressive stratum is novitiate teachers in large SMSAs (68 percent scoring high on the classroom index) and the most reticent are twenty-year or more veterans living in non-SMSAs (9 percent scoring high on the same index).

The occupational characteristic which emerged as most discriminating was that of the undergraduate major. A rough hierarchy of support for expressive behavior placed social science majors first, history majors second, "other"

majors next, social studies majors fourth, and education majors last. Attempting to control for either region or metropolitanism results in embarrassingly small cells, but the overall picture is rather clear. One conclusion is that a social science background makes the teacher more impervious to the vicissitudes of the community environment. Scant differences appear among such teachers regardless of the region in which they live or the degree of community complexity. Another pattern, considerably less strong, is that teachers in the Northeast and West and in large SMSAs tend to be less influenced by the nature of their collegiate majors than their colleagues in the Midwest and South and less urbanized areas. That is, the kind of major (and perhaps the nature of the institution where such majors were available) account for more variation among teachers in the latter regions and areas than in the former.

On the other hand, the independent and cumulative pattern is perhaps the most impressive aspect of the data. Grouped by undergraduate major, teachers in the Midwest and South are virtually always less expressively oriented than Northeastern and Western counterparts; and those in non-SMSAs are consistently less so than those in medium-size and large SMSAs. At the same time as one moves across regions and SMSA types it is clear that the educational background is exerting its effect also. As an example, although 86 percent of the Southern teachers with social science backgrounds score high on the community expression index, the same is true of only 33 percent of Southern teachers with education backgrounds. Both percentages, at the same time, are lower than for the parallel groupings in the

Northeast. Although the insufficiency of sample size prohibits firm generalizations, the evidence is quite strong that expressiveness is accentuated by the convergence of occupational and community characteristics.

Concluding Observations

We began this essay by discussing the importance of occupational culture as a determinant for political orientations. Despite the fact that social studies teachers have a surface homogeneity of suboccupational specialization, there are large-scale and systematic differences among them with respect to their definitions of proper classroom and community behavior. It is clear that the stereotyped teacher, anxious and reticent, is much more abundant among certain strata of the population than others. Regionalism and metropolitanism seem to be community variables accentuating the differences; and years teaching, educational levels, and undergraduate training are occupational factors exerting an effect. When these characteristics are combined the effects tend to accumulate and produce massive differences among the teachers.

Although there may well be canons of proper behavior that set off teachers from other professionals—or social studies teachers from other teachers—it is nevertheless also true that there are strong currents systematically distinguishing the social studies teachers from one another. What results is not a monolithic occupational culture but one rich in diversity. The extremely reticent are superembodiments of a set of norms that, although probably undergoing considerable change at this point, are the precepts by which generations of teachers have been recruited, trained, and advanced. On the other hand, the more expressively oriented teachers are perhaps a portent of the evolving standards, inasmuch as they come from community and occupational strata that are not only more congruent with general population and social shifts in this country but also more congruent with the changing nature of teacher preparation.

The analyses demonstrate how properties in sociopolitical systems influence the political norms of occupational incumbents. This is most evident in the effect of the community level variables. It is also apparent that some factors not immediately recognizable as "political" also condition normative outlooks. These are revealed primarily in the occupational and personal characteristics of the teachers.

But just as the teachers are reacting to forces from their past experience and present environment, it seems equally clear that they in turn constitute a force acting on the students. In this essay we cannot undertake an analysis of the impact of the teachers upon the political orientations of their students. Yet it seems most likely that the impact of teachers with more restrained definitions of proper political expression would produce somewhat different political outcomes among their students than teachers with very expansive constructions. It is debatable how much difference high school teachers make in the political socialization of preadults, but in the measure that they do we are arguing that the variations in norms of expressiveness would affect that difference.

Assuming that there is a connection

between more permissive norms and a tolerance for nonconformity, one can visualize the teachers acting to perpetuate the values of the communities in which they live. If our reasoning about regions and metropolitanism is sound, there are variations in the community political norms along these dimensions. In a sense the teachers aid in the re-creation of the community's values through socializing the adolescents. From this point of view the fact that there are strong normative differences among the teachers assumes importance not only in terms of their own behavior in the community but also in terms of the civic education of new generations.

NOTES

1. Seymour Martin Lipset, *Political Man* (New York: Doubleday, 1960), p. 237.

2. Lewis Lipsitz, "Work Life and Political Attitudes," *American Political Science Review*, 58 (December 1964), 956.

3. W. Fred Cottrell, *The Railroader* (Stanford, Calif.: Stanford University Press, 1940).

4. Morris Rosenberg, *Occupations and Values* (New York: Free Press, 1957).

5. See Rosenberg, *op. cit.*, pp. 18–20; Ward Mason, *The Beginning Teacher: Status and Career Orientations* (Washington: U.S. Department of Health, Education, and Welfare, 1961), pp. 71–72; Franklin P. Kilpatrick, Milton C. Cummings, Jr., and M. Kent Jennings, *Source Book of a Study of Occupational Values and the Image of the Federal Service* (Washington, D.C.: The Brookings Institution, 1964), chaps. 5 and 6, esp. pp. 125–126, 162–163; Theodore Caplow, *The Sociology of Work* (Minneapolis: University of Minnesota Press, 1954), p. 126: and Egon G. Guba, Philip W. Jackson, and Charles E. Bidwell, "Occupational Choice and the Teaching Career," in W. W. Charters, Jr., and A. L. Gage (eds.), *Readings in the Social Psychology of Education* (Boston: Allyn and Bacon, 1963), pp. 271–278.

6. Harmon Zeigler, *The Political Life of American Teachers* (Englewood Cliffs, N.J.: Prentice-Hall, 1967), pp. 99–119.

7. *Ibid.*, pp. 116–17.

8. Little systematic knowledge exists about the teacher as a political socialization agent. Subsequent writings based on data from which this paper is drawn will examine that question.

9. Zeigler, *op. cit.*, pp. 142–143.

10. In a number of small schools an obvious choice existed, since there was only one main social studies teacher. In order for another teacher to be chosen in these schools, he had to have taught at least three students. Among the other schools automatic selection went to the top two teachers in terms of the number of sample students taught. Additional teachers were chosen by assigning scores that gave most emphasis to coverage of a wide number of sample students and next most for achieving depth coverage of the sample students.

Balance among subject areas was, of course, weighted toward the more frequently given courses. For example out of all courses taught by the teachers during the past three years 32% were American history; 23% in- American government, problems of democracy, and other "political science" courses; 22% in world history; 10% in economics; and the rest were distributed among sociology, geography, psychology, general social science, and a smattering of miscellaneous titles.

11. This is a major finding in Zeigler, *op. cit.*, pp. 98–99.

12. Omitted from this cluster is the "going on strike" item, which correlated quite highly with the reaction to union membership (.95) but rather poorly with the other items in the cluster.

13. This item could also be considered in the community domain, but the word "publicly" and the pattern of intercorrelations augur for inclusion in the class-room category.

14. Excluded from this cluster is the item on passing out anticommunist literature in class. Although responses to that item were moderately related to those on the civil rights statement (.55), they were quite poorly associated with those for the three remaining items in the field.

15. The only exception to this is that the item on belonging to the NAACP or CORE could have qualified for the classroom cluster, but the correlation with items in that cluster are considerably lower than with other items in the community cluster.

16. Samuel Stouffer, *Communism, Conformity, and Civil Liberties* (New York: Wiley, 1966). A more recent study has corroborated Stouffer's findings. See Norval D. Glenn and J. L. Simmons, "Are Regional Cultural Values Diminishing?" *Public Opinion Quarterly*, 31 (Summer 1967), 176–193.

17. John Gillin, "National and Regional Cultural Values in the United States," *Social Forces*, 34 (December 1955), 107–113.

18. Regional groupings follow Census Bureau classifications: Northeast comprises New England and Middle Atlantic states; Midwest comprises East North central and West North central states; South comprises South Atlantic, East South central, and West South central states; and West comprises mountain and Pacific states.

19. The number of schools in the sample prohibits the simultaneous case of both size and SMSA characteristics.

20. When controls are introduced the community expression index, because of its rather skewed distributions, will be collapsed from a trichotomy into a dichotomy.

21. See, for example, Oswald Hall, "The Stages of a Medical Career," *American Journal of Sociology*, 52 (March 1958), 327–336.

22. Howard Becker, "The Teacher in the Authority System of the Public Schools," *Journal of Educational Sociology*, 27 (November 1953), 129–141.

23. Guba, et al., *op. cit.*, p. 273. See also Zeigler, *op. cit.*, pp. 28–29.

24. The distinction between the social science majors and "social studies" majors is crucial. Among the former would be the classic social science disciplines of

political science, economics, sociology, psychology, and anthropology. Teachers with social studies backgrounds ordinarily majored in that area—versus, e.g., mathematics or English—as a specialty in their preparation for a teaching career.

25. Guba, et al., *op. cit.*, p. 275.

26. Percentages of teachers holding M.A.s at various levels of experience are as follows: 0–4 years = 17%; 5–9 years = 45%; 10–19 years = 58%; and 20 or more years = 67%.

27. This should not obscure the fact that M.A.s are still more expressively-oriented than are B.A.s.

28. We also considered the effects of variables other than the ones presented here. Expressiveness is not related in any strong fashion to the academic quality of the school (in terms of percentage of graduates going on to a four-year college) or to the proportion of parents who were P.T.A. members. The religious composition of the school does seem to affect expressiveness, a finding to be reported in another place. School size (as expressed by senior class enrollment) shows the same pattern as does SMSA type, but the latter is the more fruitful explanatory variable, both statistically and empirically.

THE POLITICAL SOCIALIZATION OF NATIONAL LEGISLATIVE ELITES IN THE UNITED STATES AND CANADA

- Allan Kornberg and Norman Thomas

The concept of socialization has been most widely employed by social psychologists seeking an explanation of how the individual is acculturated with particular emphasis on how this is accomplished among the very young. Social psychologist Herbert Hyman's ambitions were somewhat more modest in that he sought, through an extensive review of the literature, a general formulation of political behavior as a product of early learning or socialization. The bulk of the research he reviewed suggested that the average American has accepted most of his political values and attitudes by age sixteen.[1] Sociologist Seymour Lipset and his colleagues were also inclined to cite the pre-adult period, particularly adolescence, as the time at which the political process first becomes meaningful to the individual.[2]

On the other hand, political scientists Gabriel Almond and Sidney Verba, although recognizing that the individual's early socializing experience in the family exerts an important influence upon his later political attitudes and participation, also suggest that numerous other factors intervene between the early experiences and subsequent political behavior. These later experiences may be equally and in some cases more important determinants of political participation and behavior than the early primary group influences. In other

Above selection reprinted from: *Journal of Politics*, 27 (1965), 761–775.

words, they suggest that the family may not be as important an agent in the process as previously assumed.[3]

The studies reported on by Hyman and Lipset as well as the data presented by Almond and Verba deal with mass political socialization. Heinz Eulau, however, was among the first to study systematically and report upon the political socialization of an elite group—the members of four American state legislatures. Eulau's data indicated that about one-third of the respondents he studied became interested in politics as children; an additional fifteen percent traced their first interest to adolescence; the remainder did not become oriented toward politics until they first actively *participated* in politics. Eulau concluded, therefore, that even among an important group of actors engaged in the legislative process at the state level, the time of political socialization was not confined to the pre-adult period of the life cycle, but rather that it could "occur at almost any phase of a person's development."[4]

Our research was in part inspired by a desire to ascertain whether Eulau's findings extended to an even more elite group of legislative actors—the leaders in two national legislatures. Second, we wished to determine whether cultural variations and individual differences would manifest themselves in a difference in the socialization patterns of national legislative elites in two polities. For example, we suspected that societies might differ in terms of the conscious efforts made within them to socialize politically[5] and that differences in the social backgrounds of individual legislators might also affect the manner in which they were socialized. Thus, we were interested not only in the time of socialization, but also in the process itself. To help ascertain both the time and the manner in which a political elite is socialized, the following open-ended question was asked a group of Canadian Parliamentary leaders and American Congressmen: "How did you first become interested in politics?"[6]

Our intention in this report is to show that there is a very strong relationship between the times and "agents" of political socialization; that even among the elite groups we studied, a substantial proportion did not recall becoming interested in politics until they were adults; and that variations in the socialization process do appear to be related to differences in the legislator's national and personal backgrounds.

The Sample

In 1962 interviews were carried out with a random sample of 165 members of Canada's 25th Parliament. Thirty-nine of the respondents who fell within the sample make up our Canadian leadership panel. Included are two national party leaders, two deputy-leaders, a number of then-Cabinet ministers and then-Parliamentary assistants, former Cabinet ministers, party whips and caucus chairmen. Our sample thus includes: leaders chosen by the parties outside of Parliament in national party conventions (e.g., party leaders and deputy-leaders); those leaders elected in parliamentary caucuses by the parties

in Parliament (e.g. party whips and caucus chairmen); as well as the heads and former heads of some of the major departments of government (e.g. Conservative Cabinet ministers, parliamentary assistants and Liberal ex-Cabinet ministers).[7]

In October 1963, questionnaires soliciting data on demographic characteristics such as age, religion, father's primary occupations, as well as career patterns and also containing the above question regarding political socialization, were sent to forty-two elective and seniority leaders in both houses of the 88th Congress. Since we wished the American panel to approximate the size of the Canadian one, we could not, of necessity, include all of the committee chairmen and ranking minority members in each houses. Consequently, we selected only those committees which play a major role in congressional policy-making, or which deal with important substantive policy areas and upon which membership is highly desired.[8] We did, however, include all of the elective leaders since we felt that they manifested the influence of party in congressional policy-making. After three follow-up letters, responses were eventually secured from forty of the forty-two members of the original panel. Four of the respondents, three Senators and a Congressman, sent rather long and detailed biographies (together with covering letters) from three of which we were able to extract the required information. The other was excluded from the analysis.

We realize that we are comparing the responses of a group of leaders selected randomly with another group deliberately chosen and that the latter group is thus not as representative of the universe of leaders from which they were drawn as is the former. Furthermore, we recognize that our results may have been affected by the fact that replies to open-end questions on mailed questionnaires are generally neither as rich nor meaningful as responses obtained from interviews. Despite these shortcomings, we are reasonably confident that both "pots" of data are comparable enough to shed light upon the political socialization of legislative leaders in the two countries.

The Findings

Respondents were first classified in terms of the time of socialization. There were three codes: childhood or grammar school (1); adolescence or high school (2); and adult (3). The latter code included all those legislators who cited the post-adolescent period of the life space (i.e., college or equivalent period, after college, entry into political or civic life) as the time of their first interest in politics. An interesting finding, therefore, is that despite their more elite positions, the national legislative leaders in our panel did not differ appreciably from the state legislators Eulau studied in terms of the time of socialization. (See Table 1).

Table 1

Time of Socialization for National Legislative Leaders and Members of American State Legislatures

	State Legislators	National Legislators
CHILDHOOD	37%	46%
ADOLESCENCE	15	13
ADULT	48	41
Total		
	100%	100%
	(N=421)	(N=78)

Table 2

The Relationship Between Time and Agent in the Political Socialization Process

	Childhood	Adolescence	Adult
FAMILY	88%	0%	0%
SELF	6	100	0
EXTERNAL EVENTS AND CONDITIONS	6	0	100
Total	100%	100%	100%
	(N=36)	(N=10)	(N=32)

Gamma=.98[10]

It was considerably more difficult to classify the respondents in terms of the agent in the socialization process. As did Eulau, we found that the family, personal predispositions, actual political participation and certain events, individuals, or conditions all acted as socializing agents. Although those socialized by the family or by self were easily classified, it was almost impossible to distinguish analytically among those whose socialization occurred because of an event (i.e., participation in a political campaign, exposure to a charismatic individual, attendence at a college or university) and those who cited conditions such as war, the depression and so forth as the source of their interest. Consequently we collapsed these into a single code which we have termed "external events and conditions."[9]

Accordingly, our three "agent" codes were: family (1); self (2); and external events and conditions (3). Analysis indicated that there was an extremely high correlation between the time and agent of political socialization. (See Table 2).

Indeed, so strong was this correlation that we have arrayed the legislators along a bi-dimensional continuum schematized below, ranging from those who were socialized early (childhood or grammar school) by the family, through those socialized as adolescents by self (self-starters), to those whose socialization was delayed until the post-adolescent (adult) period and occurred because of external events and conditions. (See Figure 1).

Figure 1. *A political socialization*
            continuum

Early	Adolescent	Adult
Family	Self-Starter	External

The four legislators who recalled being socialized as children, but who said it was through their own efforts or because of some external event or condition will be excluded from further analysis.[11]

Responses typical of those who said they had been socialized by the family as children were:

Both of my parents were extremely active in politics. I can remember going to party conventions with them when I was very young, so you might say I've always been interested in politics, even at the school board level. (A Canadian)

or,

I have had a lifetime interest in politics. My family participated in politics over many, many years. (An American)

or,

My family were always Conservatives, strong Conservatives. I was told very early that my politics were Conservative politics. My father believed in discussing public affairs at home. He took me to political meetings with him from my earliest years. (A Canadian)

or,

My father was very active in the organizational end of politics. I grew up in an atmosphere that was charged with political electricity. Politics have always fascinated me. I joined the Liberal party organization quite young and worked my way up until I became ———. (A Canadian)

Some typical responses from those whom we have termed adolescent self-starters were:

From the time I was a boy I would mainly read books in history and government. Since then I have been a student of history and government so I think it was natural for me to be interested in public life. (An American)

or,

As a teen-ager. I had to leave school when I was very young. I was studying by myself at night so that I could return to school. It was during that time I started to take an interest in politics. (An American)

Finally, those who did not become interested in politics until they were adults typically said:

I became interested in politics when as a young man I worked for Senator ——— on the old ——— committee. At the same time I attended law school here in Washington. (An American)

or,

As a result of my studies during law school. (An American)

or,

When I was an undergraduate at the University of ———, I became interested in drafting the constitution for the student government association. I ran and was elected first President of the association and have been very much interested in politics ever since. (An American)

or,

Primarily because of the poverty, the terrible socio-economic conditions of the thirties. I was studying for the ministry at the time and this probably made me more aware of things and made me want to do something to help relieve those conditions. (A Canadian)

Two things stood out in the responses of the legislators. First, among those socialized early by the family, the responses of the Canadian leaders reveal a much more conscious effort on the part of the family to indoctrinate. Although the American congressmen in this group generally professed a life-long interest in politics, there is no indication in their responses that the family tried to develop partisan values and attitudes in them. Furthermore, in the responses of the Canadians we find socialization linked with the development of a partisan identification. There is no equivalent attempt by the family to make "good" Democrats or Republicans out of our embryo American legislators. Only in the responses of the small number of Canadians who developed an interest in politics during adolescence do we find the lack of ideological content characteristic of the responses of most Americans.

Second, among the legislators in the Adult-External position of the continuum, the Americans tend to cite a law school education as the socializing agent much more often than do the Canadians. The latter generally became interested in politics because of the great Depression of the 1930's.

The differences between the two groups of leaders also extended to the time of their socialization in that a considerably larger proportion of the Canadians were on the Early-Family end of the continuum. (See Table 3).

Such variations between our two leadership panels are, we suggest, at least in part a function of differences in the nature of the party struggles in the two countries.

The conflict between American parties, although indeed bitter at times, tends to be less programmatic and

Table 3

The Relationship Between Political Socialization and National Background of Legislative Leaders

	Canadian Leaders	American Leaders
EARLY-FAMILY	54%	32%
ADOLESCENT-SELF-STARTER	11	27
ADULT-EXTERNAL	35	41
Total	100% (N=37)	100% (N=37)
		Gamma = .34

ideological in its content than is the case in Canada.[12] Both inside and out of the legislature American parties (in addition to being non-cohesive and loosely disciplined) are generally assumed to function better as consensus builders and compromisers than as promulgators of party programs based upon party doctrine.[13]

In Canada, on the other hand, the presence of two left-wing parties[14] which have consistently placed a definite program before Parliament and the people has meant that the ideological differences between left and right have been something more than differences between "Tweedledum and Tweedledee." Even before the formation of the New Democratic and Social Credit Parties, party lines between Liberals and Conservatives were consistently and sharply drawn[15] over such issues as tariff rates, the scope of governmental activity, relations with the United States and Great Britain and attitudes toward French Canada. As in other western democracies, the left wing in Canada has tended to play an innovative role, introducing into the system a majority of the issues whose debatable limits define the ground over which the political battle has been waged.[16] Due to the requirements of a parliamentary system patterned after the British model, there has been very infrequent crossing of party lines. Consequently, tensions between the parties tend to remain high and are manifested frequently in vituperative parliamentary debates.[17] This has been particularly true in this century as a series of Liberal Governments has introduced a fairly comprehensive program of social legislation (i.e., Family Allowances, National Unemployment Insurance Grants, Old Age Pensions and so forth).

What we are suggesting, then, is that the intensity and frequent bitterness of the party struggle in Canada may have created a situation in which partisans in that struggle actually engaged in the active political indoctrination of their young. As was previously pointed out, the responses of many of the Canadian legislators suggest both that their parents *were* actively engaged in party politics and that they were deliberately and formally socialized by them rather than indirectly, as for example, through chance exposures to dialogues with a political content.

The importance American legislators attributed to law schools may simply reflect the fact that 46 percent of the American panel held law degrees as compared to only 30 percent of the Canadian. However, research by Joseph Schlesinger,[18] among others,[19] suggests that this tendency to cite law schools as agents of political socialization may well be a function of societal differences between the United States and Canada. Schlesinger points out that lawyers in the United States enjoy a monopoly of the public offices involved in the ad-

ministration of laws through the courts. Furthermore these offices have frequently served as major vehicles for the advancement of the careers of political leaders. In Canada, however, there are both proportionally fewer of such offices and most of those that do exist are appointive rather than elective. Consequently the law schools play a less important part as socializing agents in Canada, both because there are fewer of them (law schools) and because a political and legal career are apparently less compatible than in the United States. The dominance by lawyers of public offices involved in administering law in this country suggests that the embryo American legislative leader probably found himself in an environment in which politics and the political process were salient topics of conversation. He soon realized, or was made to realize, the possibilities inherent in combining a legal with a political career. Small wonder, then, that such a substantial proportion of American leaders recalled first becoming interested in politics while in law school.

In addition to being related to the national backgrounds of legislators, differences in the political socialization process were also related to differences in their socio-economic backgrounds (as measured by the occupations of their fathers). The data showed that the higher this background, the more likely the legislator was to be socialized earlier in life by the family than later by external events and conditions. (See Table 4).

The fact that fully 91 percent of the legislators whose fathers held low status occupations were socialized as adults would certainly support the findings of voting studies as to the impact of socio-economic background and social class upon political interest and participation.[22] Very briefly stated, these studies present empirical evidence that voting turnout, the frequency with which one discusses political affairs and one's interest and involvement in the political process all vary quite strongly with one's socio-economic and social class backgrounds.

Their father's occupations were particularly salient for the manner in which the Canadians were socialized, the magnitude of the correlation for them being approximately three times as great as for the Americans. (See Table 5).

The fairly large proportions of legislators in both societies with farm backgrounds who were on the early-family end of the socialization continuum would at first blush appear to be somewhat unusual. According to Angus Campbell and his colleagues at the Survey Research Center, American farmers *at the mass level* tend to be among those least interested in politics or political campaigns.[24] Why, then, should 45 per cent of the legislators with farmer-fathers be on the early-family end of the continuum? Again, Campbell and his colleagues suggest an answer—they state that at the *elite level* farmers *do* indeed show an unusual

Table 4

The Relationships Between Political Socialization and Economic Background [20]

	Business-Professional[21]	Farmer	Low Status
EARLY-FAMILY	55%	45%	0%
ADOLESCENT SELF-STARTER	7	30	9
ADULT-EXTERNAL	38	25	91
Total	100% (N = 42)	100% (N = 20) Gamma = .42	100% (N = 11)

Table 5

The Relationship Between Political Socialization and Economic Background Compared for American and Canadian Legislative Leaders

	American Legislators[23]			Canadian Legislators		
	Business-Professional	Farmers	Low Status	Business-Professional	Farmers	Low Status
EARLY-FAMILY	41%	33%	0%	70%	54%	0%
ADOLESCENT-SELF-STARTER	9	33	20	5	28	0
ADULT-EXTERNAL	50	33	80	25	18	100
Total	100% (N = 22)	100% (N = 9) Gamma = .24	100% (N = 5)	100% (N = 20)	100% (N = 9) Gamma = .61	100% (N = 6)

Table 6

The Relationship Between Political Socialization and Age Level

	Age 50 Years or Less	Age 51–64 Years	Age 65 Years and Over
EARLY-FAMILY	53%	54%	15%
ADOLESCENT-SELF-STARTER	10	8	25
ADULT-EXTERNAL	37	38	60
Total	100% (N = 19)	100% (N = 35)	100% (N = 20)
		Gamma = .34	

interest and are intensely involved in political affairs.[25] The fact that 65 per cent of the legislators in our panel whose fathers were farmers had *at least one university degree* would seem to indicate that their families were at the elite rather than at the mass farmer level, since a higher education is in no small way a function of economic well-being.

Finally, we found that variations in socialization were also related to differences in the legislators' ages.[26] (See Table 6).

In part this correlation was a manifestation of differences in national backgrounds, since all but two of the youngest group of legislators were Canadians, while the reverse was true of the oldest group of legislators. Further analysis then revealed that age was not a discriminating variable for Canadians since among them there was a correlation of only .11 between age and socialization. Among the two older groups of Americans, however, the magnitude of the correlation increased to .44. The Americans aged 51–64 were distributed along the socialization continuum in a manner which did not differ appreciably from the Canadians. It was among the group of Americans over 65 years of age that we found the heaviest

incidence of socialization occurring late in life as a result of some external events or conditions. (See Table 7).

Table 7

These variations between the two groups of American legislative leaders, together with the modest differences between the younger group of American leaders and the Canadians considered as a whole, are intriguing. Unfortunately, we can only point out rather than offer a reasonable explanation for their existence.

Summary and Conclusions

The finding, even among an elite group such as our panel of national legislative

A Comparison of the Socialization Process Among Americans Only in Terms of Age Differences

	Americans Age 51–64	Americans Age 65 and Over
EARLY-FAMILY	47%	16%
ADOLESCENT-SELF-STARTER	12	23
ADULT-EXTERNAL	41	61
Total	100% (N = 17)	100% (N = 18)
	Gamma = .44	

leaders, that political socialization is a phenomenon which can occur at various stages of the life cycle rather than primarily in the pre-adult period is consonant with the conclusions drawn by Heinz Eulau from a study of American state legislators. The fact that over half of the leaders did not cite the family as the socializing agent tends to support the position taken by Almond and Verba on the relative importance of the family group as opposed to other socializing agents. Equally comforting is the finding that the socialization process varies with the socio-economic background of the legislators. Voting studies report a similar relationship at the mass level between political interest and social background. These results tend to increase our confidence in the validity of that half of the data gathered by the use of a questionnaire.

A cross-tabulation of the legislators' positions on the socialization continuum with their national background revealed that a considerably larger proportion of the Canadians were in the early-family position. As well, the Canadians' responses reveal a conscious effort on the part of their families to indoctrinate them. This was not apparent among the Americans. It was felt that this could in part be explained by the more programmatic, ideological and consistently acrimonious nature of Canadian party politics. Similarly, the apparent greater importance of the law school as a socializing agent in the United States may be related to the compatibility of law and politics as careers in that country. This is not to suggest, of course, that these two careers are incompatible in Canada.[27]

Nor do we suggest that the failure of the Americans to link in their responses the process of socialization with the development of a partisan identification (as did many of the Canadians) indicates that party identification is part of the process of socialization in one country and not in the other. In fact, the aforementioned findings of Campbell and his colleagues and Fred Greenstein[28] suggest that in the United States a partisan identification may very well develop antecedent to any attitudes toward or interest in politics. A comparative study fully delineating the relationship between political socialization and partisan identification would certainly be worth considering. Also worth exploring in greater depth cross-culturally are the relationships between chronological age, social background and political socialization. Unfortunately in this study we were able only to bring out that the strength of such correlations varied with national background rather than to suggest why this should have been the case.

NOTES

1. Herbert H. Hyman, *Political Socialization* (Glencoe: The Free Press, 1959), pp. 51–68.

2. Seymour M. Lipset, Paul F. Lazarsfeld, Allen Barton and Juan Linz, "The Psychology of Voting: An Analysis of Political Behavior," in Gardner Lindzey, ed., *Handbook of Social Psychology*, II, (Cambridge: Addison-Wesley Publishing Co., Inc., 1954), pp. 1124–1177.

3. Gabriel A. Almond and Sidney Verba, *The Civic Culture*, (Princeton: Princeton University Press, 1963), pp. 323–374.

4. Heinz Eulau, "Recollections," in John C. Wahlke, Heinz Eulau, William Buchanan, and LeRoy Ferguson, *The Legislative System*, (New York: John Wiley and Sons, Inc., 1962), pp. 77–95.

5. Political socialization may occur either "directly" or "indirectly." By directly is meant the formal conscious attempts by individuals or groups to inculcate certain political values, attitudes, and expectations in others. Examples of this direct type of political socialization in democratic polities such as Canada and the United States include the efforts of families to develop partisan attachments in children, the "training for citizenship" carried on in schools and by good government groups, and the "political education" campaigns undertaken by unions, business and other socio-economic groups. Indirect socialization occurs informally and more subtly, not as a result of any conscious, rationally devised process of indoctrination, but rather as a consequence of individual exposure to the social and cultural mechanisms, by which people are integrated or acculturated into a political system.

6. This question is a condensation of the two questions employed by Heinz Eulau. The legislators in the four states studied were asked: "How did you become interested in politics?" and "What is your earliest recollection of being interested in it?" Eulau, *op. cit.* p. 79.

7. When this study was undertaken the parties in Canada fell rather naturally along a left-right political continuum. On the far left was the socialist New Democratic Party. The party on the left-center was the Liberal Party while the Conservatives were the party of the right-center. The Social Credit Party occupied the far right. Since then a large portion of the Quebec wing of the Social Creditors has split off and formed a fifth party in the 26th Parliament, Le Ralliement des Creditistes. Presumably the split resulted because Mr. Real Caouette was able to convince eleven of his colleagues representing Quebec constituencies that the parent party was not adequately articulating the interests of Quebec.

8. In distinguishing between elective and seniority leaders we used the criteria laid down by David B. Truman in *The Congressional Party* (New York: John Wiley and Sons, Inc., 1959), pp. 99–134 and 197–246. George B. Galloway classified committees in terms of prestige as "top," "interest," "pork" and "duty." See *The Legislative Process in Congress* (New York: Thomas Y. Crowell Co., 1953), pp. 278–279. Our panel included all of the top and interest committee chairmen and ranking minority members.

9. Unfortunately we cannot compare our panel of leaders in this respect with the state legislators studied by Eulau because his columns total more than 100%. See Eulau, *op. cit.*, p. 79.

10. This is a statistic proposed by Leo A. Goodman and William H. Kruskal in "Measure of Association for Cross-Classifications," *Journal of the American Statistical Association*, Vol. 59 (Dec., 1954).

11. The four include two Democrats, a Senator and a Congressman, a former Liberal Cabinet Minister and one of the elected leaders of the Conservative party.

12. For the view that Canadian political parties are no more programmatic than those in the United States, see Leon D. Epstein's excellent article, "A Comparative Study of Canadian Parties," *American Political Science Review*, Vol. 50, (June, 1956) pp. 360–77. However, data gathered by one of the authors which deal with the M.P.'s motives for maintaining party cohesion indicate that party policy goals and their achievement are important considerations for a considerable proportion of them.

13. See, for example, Austin Ranney and Willmoore Kendall, *Democracy and the American Party System* (New York: Harcourt, Brace and Co., 1956).

14. The remark generally attributed to former Liberal Prime Minister Louis St. Laurent that "They [the New Democrats] are nothing but Liberals in a hurry" would seem to indicate that there is little ideological difference between the two left-wing parties. Data we have concerning the ideological positions of M.P.'s on certain welfare-state policy issues indicate that the differences between the two left-wing parties as a group are minimal. This was also true of the two right-wing parties. However, differences between right and left were indeed substantial.

15. See Frank Underhill, *In Search of Canadian Liberalism*, (Toronto: The Macmillan Co., 1960).

16. See, for example, V. O. Key's discussion of the innovative function performed by the Democratic Party in the United States. *Politics, Parties and Pressure Groups*, 5th ed. (New York: Thomas Y. Crowell Co., 1964), pp. 200–222.

17. See, for example, the Hansard reports of debates over their new flag, the new Pensions legislation, the alleged immorality of the Liberal Cabinet and the "repatriation" of the Canadian constitution in the current (26th) Parliament. For editorial comments on the quality of House of Commons debates see the 1965 editorial columns of a leading Canadian newspaper such as *The Winnipeg Free Press*.

18. Joseph A. Schlesinger, "Lawyers and American Politics: A Clarified View," *The Midwest Journal of Political Science*, Vol. 1 (May, 1957) pp. 26–39.

19. See, for example, Donald R. Matthews, *The Social Background of Political Decision-Makers* (Garden City, New York, 1954) p. 30.

20. Low status occupations include blue collar and low level white collar jobs such as clerks, salesmen, etc. Business-professional include those who were proprietors of their own business, executives of large businesses and professionals such as doctors and lawyers.

21. Data for one American respondent not ascertained.

22. See: Angus Campbell, Philip E. Converse, Warren E. Miller and Donald E. Stokes, *The American Voter* (New York: John Wiley and Sons, 1960), pp. 333–380; Bernard Berelson, Paul Lazarsfeld and William McPhee, *Voting*, (Chicago: University of Chicago Press, 1954); and Paul Lazarsfeld, Bernard Berelson and Hazel Gaudet, *The People's Choice* (New York: Duell, Sloan and Pierce, 1944). For works which have made use of many of these empirical findings see Seymour M. Lipset, *Political Man* (New York: Doubleday Anchor Books, 1963); and Robert E. Lane, *Political Life* (Glencoe: The Free Press, 1959).

23. Data for one American respondent not ascertained.

24. Angus Campbell et al., *loc. cit.*, pp. 402–440.

25. *Ibid.*, pp. 409–410. This would be particularly true for Canadian leaders from Western Canada with farmer fathers. For two good accounts of the part played by farmers in party politics in this region, see Seymour M. Lipset, *Agrarian Socialism* (Berkeley and Los Angeles: University of California Press, 1950), and William Morton, *The Progressive Party in Canada*, (Madison: University of Wisconsin Press, 1952).

26. Since such a large proportion of the legislators were at least second generation Americans or Canadians and since they were also overwhelmingly of Anglo-Saxon or French descent we did not employ these factors as independent variables. We did, however, cross-tabulate differences in political socialization with the respondents' religious affiliations and urban-rural backgrounds. There was a correlation of only .11 between the latter and political socialization and an even smaller correlation (.08) between religious affiliation and the dependent variable.

27. The fact that slightly less than a third of our panel of Canadian leaders held a law degree indicates that law and politics are also congenial vocations in Canada. Lasswell, Lerner and Rathwell, *The Comparative Study of Political Elites* (Stanford, 1952) show that lawyers are well represented in the legislatures of most western democracies. However, Matthews' study, *The Social Background of Political Decision-Makers* shows the proportion of lawyers is greatest in the Congress.

28. Fred I. Greenstein, "The Benevolent Leader: Children's Images of Political Authority," *American Political Science Review*, Vol. 54, (December, 1960) pp. 30–34 and *The American Party System and The American People* (Englewood Cliffs: Prentice-Hall, 1963) pp. 3–34. Greenstein found that a majority of the nine year old children whom he studied had party preferences and were familiar with the names of a few conspicuous public officials.

POLITICAL SOCIALIZATION AND ROLE CONFLICT: SOME THEORETICAL IMPLICATIONS

- Eduard A. Ziegenhagen

The study of political socialization has involved (1) descriptions of the agencies of political socialization, in particular the family,[1] the peer group,[2] and occupational work groups,[3] (2) evolution of stages in the socialization process,[4] (3) changes in the configuration of the substantive elements of political cultures,[5] (4) description of norms, values,[6] and (5) the relationship of the process of political socialization to personality and behavior patterns.[7]

Political scientists have made substantial contributions to the description of political attitudes as a product of the socialization process and are beginning to deal with the relationships of the process of socialization to political attitudes and behavior. Yet political socialization literature remains predominantly descriptive with minimal concern for theory or prediction.[8]

Some studies, however, have dealt with aspects of the socialization process by description of role differentiation, role perception, and role expectations in government organizations.[9] In these studies roles associated with particular organizations, for example, courts, legislatures, military organizations, and so forth, are described in detail; but relatively little attention is paid to processes that may be responsible for the formation of change of political roles.

Political scientists have been equally slow to fully utilize the concept of role conflict for political behavior. For example, Angus Campbell, Gerald Gurin, and Warren Miller's conception of the influence of "cross pressures" on voting behavior is related to role conflict, although the full theoretical implications of role theory have not been explored.[10] Morris Janowitz writes briefly of delays in the assimilation of military roles by those who are subject to the expectations of nonmilitary groups.[11] James Barber deals with expectations of legislative colleagues and constituents and describes four alternative legislative roles.[12] Lucien Pye provides a substantial, although not a theoretically rigorous, account of conflicting conceptions of political roles and modernizing groups in Burma and speculates about probable effects on patterns of political behavior.[13] Gabriel Almond and Sidney Verba dealt with cross-national data ranging from reports of interpersonal relations in the family and school to party identification and levels of political activity. Most attention was focused upon the transfer of patterns of political culture rather than aspects of the underlying process.[14] Therefore, attempts to deal with role conflict as an aspect of socialization and its implications for political behavior do exist, but full utilization of its theoretical components has not been attempted. Yet, substantial theoretical literature and empirical

Above selection has been written especially for this volume.

findings presently exist, respecting the socialization process, that may be utilized for the purpose of making explicit hypotheses about political behavior. It is the purpose of this essay to explore the implications of some aspects of role theory and specifically role conflict for the study of political socialization.

Role Theory and Political Socialization

The symbolic interactionist hypotheses of Charles Cooley, George Mead, and Harry Stack Sullivan are most frequently claimed as the theoretical bases for role theory.[15] Mead's basic hypotheses can be summarized in two parts. First, the perceived responses of others influence how one conceives of oneself; and second, one's conception of oneself and others is developed by taking the attitudes of others toward oneself. The development of one's conception of oneself and others takes place in the context of social interaction. The individual develops his self conception from taking the standpoint of individual members of his social group or from a generalized viewpoint of the group to which he belongs.[16] When the individual becomes involved in social interaction he tends to conceive the "generalized other" or the particular viewpoint of individuals or an organization of roles and attitudes toward specific social undertakings. Mead uses a simple game as an example of this process. A game is meaningless if one is not able to take into consideration the roles and attitudes of other players as a means of determining what kind of behavior would be appropriate under

the circumstances so that he can anticipate what kind of response can be expected from others. As one develops conceptions of the social and political roles of others, one also develops a conception of oneself based upon the role prescriptions of others. In this manner one is able to develop expectations concerning oneself and others appropriate to most situations encountered.

If political socialization is conceived as a process by which one learns appropriate political roles, certain basic features of the socialization process are apparent. (1) Since a multitude of independent variables such as social position, status, culture, and idiosyncratic aspects of the interaction process exist, a high probability for development of conflicting role perceptions and role expectations also exists. (2) Role conflict must be resolved in some manner acceptable to those experiencing the conflict as well as other concerned members of a society. (3) The genesis and resolution of role conflict may have implications for political behavior as well as social behavior.

Orville Brim constructs a theory of socialization upon the symbolic interactionist hypotheses.[17] Socialization is conceived as an aspect of personality development that involves the preparation of the individual to meet the expectations and requirements of other members of the society. Each situation involves demands for appropriate behavior learned through the socialization process, which varies in intensity and direction but is continuous throughout the individual's life span. The behavior expected of a person by others is his prescribed role and its substantive elements are determined by the status or position occupied by the person in question. For example, judges demand highly deferential behavior from attorneys involved in judicial proceedings and may punish improper behavior by fine or imprisonment for "contempt of court." Because persons vary in status or position and because social change effects statuses and positions, the role that an individual is to play differs in respect to the individuals with whom he interacts and roles also differ through time. The judges mentioned above are not likely to expect or receive the same degree of courteous regard when they associate with their fellow judges outside of the courtroom.

Brim contends that the formation and differentiation of roles are related to certain major independent variables, for example, social-structural and cultural-idiosyncratic variables. Social-structural variables refer to the positions and statuses relevant to the individual and the presence or absence of particular socializing agencies. For example, persons of high or low status will be subjected to differing patterns of power, privilege, and deference as well as varying exposure to particular social, economic, and political groups and organizations. Differential treatment by the police of Negroes and white persons is a frequent complaint of the Negro community. The Negro learns to regard the police with suspicion and hostility, whereas white persons may regard the police as protectors of their property and well being. The cultural-idiosyncratic variables refer to variance of the substantive features of a culture. Conceptions of proper social and political roles are directly related to the norms, values, and customs of specific cultures or subcultures. Thus, as cultures vary, so do conceptions of political and social

roles. Additionally, intracultural idiosyncratic patterns of interaction are present and are tolerated in varying degrees in different societies.

Social-structural and cultural-idiosyncratic variables exist in all societies but appear in differing combinations and intensities that are in turn related to the degree to which individuals learn roles appropriate to the social situations in which they participate, that is, the degree to which the socialization process is complete and the roles congruent. A role-congruent situation involves perception of similarities of expectations, whereas a role-conflict situation involves perception of significant differences in expectations. Role conflict appears to have several meanings: (1) expectations of various groups respecting the behavior of a particular individual as mutually exclusive whether perceived by the actor or not, (2) perception of conflicting expectations whether a conflict exists or not, (3) conflicting expectations arising from occupation of two or more social positions, and (4) conflicting expectations arising from occupation of a single position.[18]

Study of socialization processes in areas undergoing comparatively high degrees of social change indicates great discontinuity in the socialization process and accordingly many role conflict situations. Latent stages of the socialization process may provide individuals with conceptions of political roles based upon a traditional political culture unlike that required for political participation in a modernizing political system. In Burma, Pye observed that even the children of the modernizing elite are cared for by older relatives or servants who know only the political norms, values, and customs of the past and consequently pass on perceptions of the political world that no longer may be appropriate.[19] In predominately rural areas there would be even less likelihood that latent socialization would serve as a basis for induction into the political culture of the modernizing state.

Differences in social structure, status, and access to the agencies of socialization produce a variety of conceptions of political roles. Where national socializing agencies have failed to gain access to populations, perpetuation of the traditional sectarian political culture continues, while at the same time others with whom communication has been established learn political roles associated with modern political systems. Additionally, the political roles learned by the population are likely to describe unreliably the behavior patterns actually required. Many Asian, African, and Latin American nations do not have political systems for which modern or traditional versions of political roles are appropriate. An administrator trained at a Western university may find his knowledge inapplicable to the political system in which he must participate. Daniel Lerner describes a group from his sample of political and social attitudes in Syria. It appears that the "young Effendis" have been trained to manage a state that does not yet exist. For example, a judge complained of difficulties in administering Western legal codes among those who still adhere to the Koran. Local persons who appeared before the court did not understand what political-legal role they were to play, and their expectations were not comprehensible to the Western educated Syrian.[20]

Socialization, Role Conflict, and Social Institutions

Speculation about the relationships of role congruency or role conflict to social institutions has taken two forms: (1) role congruency or role consensus aids in the perpetuation of social institutions, or (2) role conflict within limitations provides for adjustment of social institutions to critical changes in social inputs. Goode suggests that attempts to reduce role conflict determine the direction of effort to meet role prescriptions, which in turn determine the degree of support or the lack of it for social institutions.[21] Conflicting demands of institutions require decisions as to which role prescriptions shall be met and to what degree. Allocation of resources such as time, effort, and money to fulfill some institutional expectations reduce the resources available for other institutions. The direction and effectiveness of role performance determine which social institutions shall continue to exist in the society.

Government is generally the most pervasive and authoritative social institution. The demands of social groups acting through government occupy high positions in a hierarchy of role prescriptions and therefore can determine the direction of the allocation of social resources to aid or hamper other social institutions. For example, legal sanctions against members of Jehovah's Witnesses for failure to comply with patriotic rituals forced members of this religious institution to decide whether to accept the role prescriptions of the government and reject those of their religious institution or reject the role prescriptions of the government and suffer the penalties for their action. In role conflict situations such as this, the study of political socialization may encompass an examination of the determinants of the direction of decisions in such situations. Some studies have hypothesized that situational potency, that is, the degree to which an individual is aroused to conform to group expectations in a social situation, is a primary factor in the determination of the direction of decisions. Exploration of the effect of situational factors in socialization processes may be fruitful for the study of politics and decision-making.[22]

Because a role may not be sufficiently in accord with the needs of those concerned, conventialization may be employed. Conventialization involves acceptance of certain attitudes and behavior that normally would not be acceptable. For example, members of the United States Senate may not approve of securing favorable treatment for constitutents in return for financial benefits; but they may take no action because they believe that such behavior is necessary if a Senator is to remain financially solvent. Or perhaps the Senators may have accepted a complex of values, norms, and customs that places protection of the image of Senatorial integrity above actual practices. Further examination of the uses of conventionalization in the judicial opinions, administrative decisions, and legislation may offer a new perspective for students of politics.

Roland Warren has addressed himself to a related issue, that of the implications of role conflict for social instability or disorganization. He hypothesized that social disorganization, that is, "lack of consensus, lack of integration of institutions and lack of social control,"[23] varies directly with social needs that cannot be satisfied by conformity to cultural roles. Warren, unlike William Goode, accepts the proposition that role consensus functions to support social stability and varying degrees of role conflict are indicators of social disorganization. Lack of conformity to cultural roles in politics may be manifested by the rejection of subjectively or objectively inferior political roles. The civil rights movement as well as the reaction to it by those who believed themselves threatened can be considered as a manifestation of role conflict or social disorganization. Role conflict, of course, is merely a part of the socialization process during which some means are developed to learn new roles more appropriate to the social situation.

Lack of specificity of political and social roles also may lead to role conflict. Conceivably, in political systems like that of the Union of South Africa, which explicitly allocates political roles for various segments of the population, ambiguity is minimized and expectations regarding political acts and attitudes are fully understood. Adherence to role prescriptions, however, depends upon other factors such as levels of comparison among those who have dominant and deprived roles, satisfaction of social and physical needs, continuity of role learning, and so forth. For example, the American Negro experiences increasing role ambiguity because restrictive social and political barriers are intermittently rather than continuously imposed during the socialization process. Evidence that some opportunity to escape a less satisfying deprived role contributes to broadening levels of comparison that encompass some aspects of the dominant role of the white community.

Social disorganization may vary with the degree to which roles are achieved rather than ascribed. The opportunity for members of a society to compete for a few prestigeous roles in politics also involves psychic and social costs for those who are not successful in their aspirations as well as for those who must develop new conceptions of roles as they become active political officeholders. In a society having predominantly ascribed political roles individuals have fewer choices but also are more certain of the outcomes.

Social disorganization also appears to vary with the proportion of role clusters in which role conflict exists. As suggested above in societies lacking general continuity in socialization, that is, role learning, a greater opportunity for conflicting roles exists. Persons who perceive conflicting expectations respecting familial, occupational, ethnic, and racial roles may treat these strains as if they were the products of prior colonial status, lack of military power and political influence, and so forth.[24]

Socialization and Resolution of Role Conflict

Although role conflicts function to support social change in a society as a whole, societies ideally maintain some degree of stability although social change is taking place. Jackson Toby contends that the degree to which social stability exists is related to a series of integrative mechanisms.[25] Segregation or redefinition of roles aids the avoidance of role conflict, and involves the differentiation of reciprocal expectations and behavior in accord with situational circumstances. A role of a legislator is separate from a role as head of a family, although the roles are related. Nepotism is not considered to be a legitimate legislative norm, although as head of a family the legislator may provide for his family by employing them at high salaries. Segregation of the occupational from the familial role reduces pressure to indulge in nepotism. Role definition involves the development of a new conception of one's role in a manner that eliminates conflicting situational elements.

Integrative redefinition leads to the development of a hierarchy of role obligations, whereas split-relationship redefinition provides for segregation of roles.[26] In the above example integrative redefinition would result in the development of a hierarchy of role obligations dealing with nepotism. Split-relationship redefinition results in the separation of the individual's role as legislator and familial head. To become a better provider, he may leave his legislative position for a more lucrative one in business, or he may remain a legislator and provide less financial support for his family.

Hierarchies of role obligations may exist with sufficient clarity to insure which role takes precedence over others in certain social situations; in British politics, for example, obligations of a member of Parliament to his party may be greater than his obligations to his constituents. However, hierarchies of role obligations also may be closely related to perception of other factors. For example, in a study by Neal Gross, Alexander McEachern, and Ward Mason it was found that decisions are often made on the basis of noninstitutionalized perceptions of situational factors.[27] Some decision makers may give precedence to the perceived legitimacy of the expectations of others, whereas other decision makers may consider the expected sanctions others will employ if one does not conform to their expectations. Additionally, for some decision makers primacy is given to either legitimacy or sanctions, depending upon which feature is strongest.

Of particular interest to political scientists is the issue of role conflict and role effectiveness. Jacob Getzels and Egon Guba dealt with the relationship of personality and situational variables in the analysis of role conflict.[28] The researchers contend that an individual is judged ineffective by the groups concerned when he acts contrary to their expectations. The propositions investigated involved the identification of role conflict situations in a field situation, description of the relationship of attitudes toward individuals (in this case military instructors), indicative of conflicts, location of relationships between role conflicts, the characteristics of the individuals and the organizations concerned, and the relationships between role conflict intensity and effectiveness in specific roles. The degree to which an individual is effective in meeting the expectations of other groups may be related to effectiveness in the performance of basic political functions such as securing and maintaining electoral support in order to maintain oneself in office or gaining compliance or aid for the purpose of making authoritative decisions. William Mitchell notes that insecurity of tenure, conflict among public roles, conflict of private and public roles, ambiguities in political situations, diffused responsibility and limited control of situations, time and pressure of demands, and status insecurity all contribute to role strain among elected public officials. On this basis one may speculate about role strain and role effectiveness in governmental organizations.[29] Mitchell hypothesizes that different governmental institutions are subject to role strains of differential intensity or frequency and that a relationship may exist between the frequency of role strain and hierarchial position of the office occupied. Speculation could be extended to questions about degree of role strains and the ability of governments to respond to demands from significant social groups, the ability to process these demands, and the ability to allocate resources accordingly.

In conclusion certain implications of the theory and findings respecting role conflict for the study of political socialization can be stated. Most elementary of all the outcomes that may be provided by more attention to the process aspects of political socialization, and apparently a prerequisite for more sophisticated study, is the development of a conception of political socialization as a dynamic process. The utilization of role conflict as a central theoretical component in the study of political socialization constitutes an advance in this direction. The study of role conflict as an aspect of socialization provides for the integration of the description of products of socialization, for example, political norms, values, customs, and behavior, with the study of their possible antecedents, that is, aspects of the socialization process. Possible outcomes that may be provided by this orientation include greater utilization of theory, hypotheses, and findings relevant to the process aspects of socialization for the purpose of prediction rather than mere static description of political phenomena. Conceptualization of political socialization as role learning may also provide a potentially useful theoretical orientation for exploring the relationships between political attitudes and behavior, culture, social structure, personality, and social interaction. Additionally, greater utilization of role theory as an aspect of the socialization process may lead to reexamination of areas of traditional interest to political scientists such as political stability-instability, social bases for political conflict or consensus, and the social functions of political ideology.

NOTES

1. See William A. Glaser, "The Family and Voting Turnout," *Public Opinion Quarterly*, 23 (1959), 563–570; Robert E. Lane, "Fathers and Sons: Foundations of Political Beliefs," *American Sociological Review*, 24 (August 1959), 502–511; Herbert McClosky and Harold E. Dahlgren, "Primary Group Influence on Party Loyalty," *American Political Science Review*, 53 (September 1959), 757–776.

2. See Theodore M. Newcomb, "Student Peer Group Influence," in Robert L. Sutherland, *et al.* (eds.), *Personality Factors on the College Campus* (Austin, Tex.: Hogg Foundation for Mental Health, 1962), 69–91; Robert D. Hess and David Easton, "The Role of the Elementary School in Political Socialization," *The School Review*, 70 (September 1962), 257–265.

3. See Morris Janowitz, *The Sociology of the Military Establishment* (New York: Russell Sage Foundation, 1959); Sanford M. Dornbusch, "The Military Academy As An Assimilating Institution," *Social Forces*, 33 (May 1955), 316–321.

4. See Eleanor E. Maccoby, *et al.*, "Youth and Political Change," *Public Opinion Quarterly*, 18 (1954), 23–39; Kenneth P. Langton, "The Political Socialization Process: The Case of Secondary School Students in Jamaica" (unpublished Ph.D. dissertation, University of Oregon, 1965).

5. See Stephen Dunn and Ethel Dunn, "Directed Cultural Change in the Soviet Union: Some Soviet Studies," *American Anthropologist*, 64 (1962), 328–339; Phillip Jacob, *Changing Values in College* (New York: Harper & Row, 1957); Frederick Yu, *Mass Persuasion in Communist China* (New York: Praeger, 1964).

6. See James D. Barber, *The Lawmakers, Recruitment and Adaptation to Legislative Life* (New Haven, Conn.: Yale University Press, 1965); Donald R. Matthews, *U.S. Senators and Their World* (New York: Knopf, 1960); Ralph Huitt, "A Case Study in Senate Norms," in John C. Wahlke, *et al.*, Legislative Behavior (New York: Free Press, 1959), 284–294.

7. See Alexander George and Juliette George, *Woodrow Wilson and Colonel House: A Personality Study* (New York: Day, 1956); Eunice Cooper and Marie Jahoda, "The Evasion of Propaganda: How Prejudiced People Respond to Anti-Prejudiced Propaganda," in Daniel L. Katz, *Public Opinion and Propaganda* (New York: Holt, Rinehart, and Winston, 1964), 313–319; Dean Jaros, "Children's Orientations toward the President: Some Additional Theoretical Considerations

and Data," *Journal of Politics*, 29 (1967), 368–387; Eduard A. Ziegenhagen, "Perceived Inconsistencies Regarding Self and Ethnocentric Political Leadership" (unpublished, Ph.D. dissertation, University of Illinois, 1964).

8. Writings such as those in groups 1, 3, and 4 compose the greater bulk of the literature and are primarily descriptive, yet renewed interest in the socialization process is indicated by many studies in this volume.

9. Barber, *op. cit.*, Huitt, *op. cit.* See John C. Wahlke and Heinz Eulau, *Legislative Behavior* (New York: Free Press, 1959).

10. Angus Campbell, *et al.*, *The American Voter* (New York: Wiley, 1960).

11. Janowitz, *op. cit.*

12. Barber, *op. cit.*

13. Lucian Pye, *Politics, Personality and Nation Building* (New Haven, Conn.: Yale University Press, 1962).

14. Gabriel Almond and Sidney Verba, *The Civic Culture* (Boston: Little, Brown, 1965).

15. Charles H. Cooley, *Social Organization* (New York: Scribner, 1923); George H. Mead, *Mind, Self, and Society* (Chicago: University of Chicago Press, 1934). Also see Talcot Parsons, *The Social System* (New York: Free Press, 1959).

16. Mead, *op. cit.*, p. 138. For empirical tests of the symbolic interactionist hypotheses see Frank Miamoto and Sandford Dornbusch, "A Test of the Symbolic Interactionist Hypothesis of Self Conception," *American Journal of Sociology*, 61 (March 1956), 400.

17. Orville Brim, "Personality Development as Role Learning," in Ira Iscoe and Harold Stevenson, *Personality Development in Children* (Austin: University of Texas Press, 1960), pp. 127–159. Goffman and Coser both describe socialization as a process of continuous conformity and nonconformity to social roles. For example, as children mature some roles become inappropriate; nonconformity becomes necessary, but conformity to other roles is required. Changes of situational inputs in adult political life can also be conceived in this manner. For example, persons elected to the U.S. Senate are expected to assume the prerogatives and responsibilities of Senators, that is, assume a role consistent with their new position. See Rose L. Coser, *American Journal of Sociology*, 72 (July 1966), 173–187 and Erving Goffman, *Encounters* (Indianapolis: Bobbs-Merrill, 1961).

18. Neal Gross, Alexander McEachern, and Ward Mason, *Explorations in Role Analysis: Studies of the School Superintendency Role* (New York: Wiley, 1958). See also, Howard J. Ehrlich, James W. Rinehart, and John C. Howell, "The Study of Role Conflict: Explorations in Methodology," *Sociometry*, 25 (1962), 85–97.

19. Pye, *op. cit.*, p. 47.

20. Daniel Lerner, *The Passing of Traditional Society* (New York: Free Press, 1958).

21. William J. Goode, "A Theory of Role Strain," *American Sociological Review*, 25 (August 1960), 483–496 for a comprehensive presentation.

22. John French, Jr., and Robert Zajonc, "An Experimental Study of Cross-Cultural Norm Conflict," *Journal of Abnormal and Social Psychology*, 54 (1957), 218–224. See also Simon Herman and Erling Schild, "Ethnic Role Conflict in a Cross-Cultural Situation," *Human Relations*, 13 (1960), 215–227.

23. Roland L. Warren, "Social Disorganization and the Interrelationship of Cultural Roles," *American Sociological Review*, 14 (February 1949), 83–87.

24. Pye, *op. cit.*, p. 47.

25. Jackson Toby has presented all of the integrative mechanisms discussed here in his article "Some Variables in Role Conflict Analysis," *Social Forces*, 30 (March 1952), 323–327.

26. Stewart E. Perry and Lyman C. Wynne, "Role Conflict, Role Redefinition, and Social Change in a Clinical Research Organization," *Social Forces*, 38 (October 1959), 62–65.

27. Gross, McEachern, and Mason, *op. cit.*

28. Jacob Warren Getzels and Egon Gotthold Guba, "Role, Role Conflict and Effectiveness: An Empirical Study," *American Sociological Review*, 19 (April 1954), 164–175.

29. William C. Mitchell, "Occupational Role Strains: The American Elective Official," *Administrative Science Quarterly*, 3 (1958–1959), 210–228.

THE ALIENATION OF GENERATIONS AND STATUS POLITICS: ALTERNATIVE EXPLANATIONS OF STUDENT POLITICAL ACTIVISM

- David L. Westby and Richard G. Braungart

This paper is an investigation into the social and political backgrounds of some active participants in what is referred to today as the "student movement."[1] Evidence will be presented and examined concerning two different, although not necessarily opposed, theories that attempt to explain student political activism on the basis of certain aspects of the social structure existing in modern American society. In order to accomplish this we shall report on findings drawn from a sample of student activists of the right as well as the left, most of whom may be regarded as student political leaders. An earlier study based on a small number of students at one university provided the basis for the refinement of ideas incorporated in the present paper.[2]

Some of the thinking concerning student political activism may be summed up in the idea of the "generational revolt." Probably the most succinct and systematic statement of this theory is found in the work of S. N. Eisenstadt, who maintains that youth movements are reactions against the older generation occurring in institutionally differentiated societies. In a differentiated society, Eisenstadt argues, some degree of incongruity in experience is inherent because the transition from the family, with its particularism,

Above selection has been written especially for this volume.

solidarity, and unqualified acceptance on an ascriptive basis, to the public worlds of economic and political life, with their universalism, competition, and achievement orientation, inevitably creates a conflict of values. It is the function of transitional institutions, especially the school, to progressively orient the individual away from ascriptive family ties and toward the achievement and competitive principles of public institutions.

This process is experienced by youth as one of alienation from the older generation and is greatly exacerbated when they leave home and take up life elsewhere at school. Consequently, the latter have been historically the first targets of collective rebellion.

The tensions inherent in this developmental process result in various reactions by youth, such as the creation of partially autonomous "youth cultures." The schools, as the societal agents generally responsible for inculcating the values and standards of the previous generation and thereby effecting the transition to socially defined adulthood and effective societal functioning, become the objects of generalized hostility and at times the targets of organized rebellion.[3]

These ideas have not, to our knowledge, been applied systematically to recent American experience, although they appear in somewhat truncated form, especially in the polemical literature, where they are more often pressed by writers of antistudent tracts and rejected by students and their defenders. For the latter, to explain political activity on the basis of earlier experiences and socialization comes perilously close to the rejection of the manifest issues of civil rights, university "paternalism," Vietnam, and so forth, as legitimate and sufficient causes of political protest.

One well-known commentator on the university scene has proposed this interpretation specifically for the rebellion at Berkeley in the fall and winter of 1964. Lewis Feuer, professor of social science and philosophy there at the time, writes of "the generational animus which underlies the student uprising," occasioning student beliefs such as, "We have a saying in the movement that you can't trust anybody over 30."[4] The generational animus is of such depth and power that it is capable of uniting ideological extremes in common action. "Generational solidarity carried the day as undergraduate Goldwaterites and graduate Maoists somehow defined a common enemy in Paternalism (a word endlessly repeated) and the System. There were no stepsons; all the activists were sons against the father."[5] Further evidence of this lies in the fact that student leaders use or attempt to use the "ties of generational solidarity" to mobilize protest in specific situations. When charges were brought against Mario Savio, a student leader, for allegedly biting a policeman, "at once all the ties of generational solidarity were brought into play. The student activists no longer were compelled to invent scholastic arguments for an alleged right to organize illegal actions on the campus. Now they could rely on

the elemental reaction of their fellow-generationists against the Cruel Heartless Administration . . ."[6]

We shall assume that the different versions of the generational explanation have in common the principle that student protest and rebellion are fundamentally the result of earlier alienating experiences rooted in structural discontinuities in the basic relationships within the institution of socializations—family, church, and school. Furthermore, since the common ingredient of these relationships is authority based on diffuse generational lines (as well as knowledge, competence, and other bases), we shall define the generational hypothesis as an association between (1) the experience of alienated forms of relationships cutting across institutional spheres during adolescence and (2) active participation in protest groups in college, regardless of the substance, content, or goal of the protest.

In itself, the generational hypothesis suggests little or nothing concerning the location, extent, intensity, or other dimensions of student rebellion. Little is said along these lines, except perhaps the suggestion that rapid social change may produce more protest than periods of relative tranquillity. Generally, it seems fair to say that the generational theory neither states explicitly nor implies that any particular political or politically relevant sector of society would be expected to produce student protest or to be of any relevance in accounting for its forms. But since student rebellion is clearly not a constant but a greatly variable feature of modern society, this becomes an important weakness in the theory. Even if the "generational animus" is a pervasive feature of differentiated societies, it still remains to explain the difference in form and extent exhibited over time by student protest movements.

A second approach to an understanding of student political protest lies within the traditional domain of political sociology. It has always been assumed that various aspects of a society's stratification system are crucial for an understanding of at least certain characteristics of its politics. The most powerful expression of this idea, of course, is Marxism, including its more recent forms. Fundamental to Marxism is the idea that social and political conflict is primarily the result of economically determined classes—groupings of men having in common the forms of their interpersonal relations relative to the means of production. In industrial societies this means that the fundamental division is between the propertied and the propertyless. In more recent times and in societies that have completed the transition to industrialism where Marxist ideas have seemed rather weak tools for political analysis (especially the United States), some have argued that concerns for status rather than economic conditions per se have become increasingly significant factors in politics. In the United States the principal advocates of this view are probably S. M. Lipset, another former professor at Berkeley during the rebellion, and Richard Hofstadter, professor of history at Columbia.[7] Labeled the status politics theory, this idea proposes, as we understand it, that as industrialism creates increasing affluence the necessity for political struggles centering about the allocation of economic benefits wanes. This permits the emergence or quantitatively significant growth of struggles centering about the social ranking and mobility of groups and of the general societal acceptance of their social, political, and economic ideologies. The concept of status politics has been advanced primarily to account for the strong radical right-wing movements of recent times—Coughlinism, McCarthyism, Birchism, as well as the Negro rights movement of the left.[8]

There is rather desultory but well-known evidence suggesting the importance of class and status factors in the student movement. In particular, the large numbers of members with Jewish backgrounds and of students whose fathers were radicals in the 1930s frequently has been noted. Unfortunately, these and similar facts, to our knowledge, have never been subjected to systematic theorizing and analysis. In our research we have raised the question of whether status factors in contrast to sheer intergenerational processes have any utility in understanding the sources of the student movement.

In order to test the power of the two theories, we used samples from the two largest groups on the left and right, respectively, of the college ideological spectrum: the Students for a Democratic Society (SDS) and the Young Americans for Freedom (YAF).[9] With approximately 6,000 members, SDS is by far the largest of the active groups on the left. YAF, claiming 20,000 members nationally, almost completely dominates the right. It seems fair to say that these groups represent, on the major issues— race, poverty, Vietnam—roughly similar degrees of dissent from current (early 1967) middle-of-the-road administration policies. SDS advocates a pull-out in Vietnam, immediate economic and political upgrading of the poor, and full legal, social, and political recognition of Negroes. YAF regards the antipoverty programs as the vanguard of pure socialism, wants an unrestricted "win" policy in Vietnam, and according to some of our data at least, is opposed overwhelmingly to federal involvement in racial integration.[10] Both groups are highly activist and have engaged in organized mass political action of several types—and with at least some degree of success.

We intend to treat SDS and YAF as segments of their generation, or as Mannheim called them, "generation units." The concept of the generation unit is useful to us because it represents, as Mannheim put it, "a much more concrete bond than the actual generation as such."[11] He defined generation and generation unit as follows: "Youth experiencing the same concrete historical problems may be said to be part of the same actual generation; while those groups within the same actual generation which work up the material of their common experiences in different specific ways, constitute separate generation units."[12] The idea of the generation unit is useful here because it avoids misinterpreting the student right as a kind of reaction against the student left and, therefore, as not really a part of the student movement. Aside from the meaning of such terms as "the movement" for those involved as collective symbols, such questions quite obviously reduce themselves to mere terminological quibbling and therefore are to be avoided. Some have preferred to think of the campus right as just such a reaction, but we find the notion unsatisfactory on at least three counts. First, the historical circumstances of the origin of the modern campus right, and

particularly YAF, have little to do directly with the growth of the campus left. Secondly, there are many cases where left and right have acted in concert, one of which is alluded to by Professor Feuer and which is cited earlier. Third, while regarding most of one another's programs as anathema, the groups nevertheless have certain things in common. At the symbolic level, both represent themselves by means of a very similar rhetoric of freedom, although of course, the specific applications are quite different. For example, both SDS and YAF discredit the same programs and policies of the Johnson administration. SDS rejects the federal apparatus, with its "depersonalization" and "amorality," on grounds that it impedes local grass-roots political identification and participation. Similarly, YAF spurns "excessive" federal legislation, maintaining that its increased political hegemony is crushing individual initiative and private enterprise. Both groups, in good generational form, feel that their elders have sold out the old ideals so that their own youth groups have become temporary repositories of these ideals for the future. SDS and YAF, then, constitute major segments of two separate generation units, although both belong to the same actual generation and both are in opposition to the central political and economic thrust of contemporary American society.

Analysis: The Generational Hypothesis

We proposed two kinds of tests for the generational hypothesis. First, we argued that if students were rejecting or rebelling against the older generation, this probably would involve a belief or perception that their political position or identity differs from their parents' and that they would not be likely to believe that their parents approved of their activity. Second, we would expect activist students to have experienced extensive alienation prior to entering college, that is, in high school days.

Table 1 shows that the amount of shifting away from the political identities of their parents differs considerably for the two groups. Although 51 percent of the parents of SDS members were identified as Democrats, only 15 percent of the students so identify themselves. This is a 36 percent change for the group as a whole. Although only 9 percent of their parents were identified as radicals, Socialists, or Communists by SDS members, 36 percent of the group apply these identities to themselves, a 25 percent change. The corresponding percentage shifts among the right-wing YAF, involving "Republican" and "conservative" identities, are much smaller, being only 14 and 7 percent respectively.

The contrast between parental and student "independent" identifications for the two groups further emphasizes the difference. We feel safe in saying,

therefore, that the amount of shift away from parents' political identification for the left-wing SDS members is of much greater magnitude than the corresponding shift among the right-wing YAF. This seems to suggest that the generational hypothesis may apply to the SDS but not necessarily to the YAF.

SDS students, similarly, are much more likely to believe that their parents do not, "generally support or approve" of their political activity. 27 percent of SDS members report this as their belief, whereas the figure for the YAF is only 11 percent (see Table 2). This pattern is consistent with that demonstrated for political identities.

Our data on alienation bear more directly on the question. We argued that if the generational hypothesis is correct, students should not only exhibit high levels of alienation at present (a truism in the light of their actions and the meanings associated with them) but also report generally alienating experiences prior to entering college. Since the generational hypothesis is a societal phenomenon and presumably not restricted to a single sphere or institutional sector, we expected that the experience

Table 1

Political Identities of SDS and YAF Members and Their Parents (percentages)

IDENTIFICATION	SDS		YAF	
	Parents	*Members*	*Parents*	*Members*
Conservative	1%	0%	4%	11%
Republican	18	0	65	79
Independent	20	39	15	10
Democrat	51	15	15	0
Radical, Socialist	8	33	0	0
Communist	1	3	0	0
Other	2	10	1	0
Total	100%	100%	100%	100%
	(130)	(130)	(125)	(125)

Table 2

Perceived Parental Approval of Student's Political Activity

DO YOUR PARENTS GENERALLY APPROVE OR SUPPORT YOUR POLITICAL ACTIVITY?	SDS		YAF	
	N	$\%$	N	$\%$
Generally support or approve	73	56	99	79
Indifferent	16	12	11	9
Generally do not support or approve	35	27	14	11
Other	6	5	1	1
	130	100%	125	100%

$$X^2 = 17.31$$
$$\text{d.f.} = 3$$
$$p < .001$$

of alienation would be general to the principal institutions of socialization—family, school, and church.

Tables 3, 4 and 5 give responses of members of both groups to questions concerning alienating experiences in these situations. In all cases, considerable differences distinguish the two groups, with SDS members reporting significantly more alienation than those in YAF. The differences seem greatest in the relationship with high school and religious functionaries and smallest in the parental relation. In the religious case most of the SDS members in the "No answer" category (52 percent), failing to respond to the question, must be regarded as, at best, experiencing conflict or ambivalence and, in many cases, rejecting religion and its personal or social relevance *in toto*. Some of our other data support this. Table 6 shows that although 81 percent of YAF members regularly attend church or synagogue, this is true of only 26 percent of SDS members. Generally, there are rather marked differences between SDS and YAF members on both the degree of political shift away from parents and on the prevalence of alienation. The generational hypothesis, then, seems to

apply with considerable power to the students on the left but with hardly any strength at all to those on the right.

Analysis: The Status Politics Hypothesis

The status politics hypothesis proposes that political radicalism is most likely to be found among groups that desire to maintain or improve their status relative to other groups in society.[13] In American society there are two not entirely, but still greatly independent, types of status. The first we ordinarily designate by terms "social class," or "social status;" the second is "ethnic status." The cultural evaluation at the root of social class, or social status, lies primarily in the societally determined evaluation placed upon differences in education and occupation. Considerable research has shown rather conclusively that indicators based on amount of education and occupational prestige are consistently valid reflections of social class position. This is less true of the extremes—rich upper classes and impoverished lowers—than of the area lying between them. At the top money and family traditions, and at the bottom

Table 3

Alienation from Parents for SDS and YAF Students

ATTITUDE ITEMS	SDS		YAF	
	N	%	N	%
I feel that I can always go and talk with my parents about personal and emotional problems.				
Agree	34	26	58	46
Uncertain	14	11	17	14
Disagree	82	63	50	40
Total	130	100%	125	100%
	$X^2 = 14.21$	d.f. = 2		p < .001
My relationship with my father is very close with much communication and mutual understanding.				
Agree	34	26	51	41
Uncertain	26	20	26	21
Disagree	70	54	48	38
Total	130	100%	125	100%
	$X^2 = 7.40$	d.f. = 2		p < .05
My relationship with my mother is very close with much communication and mutual understanding.				
Agree	54	42	65	52
Uncertain	19	15	24	19
Disagree	57	44	36	29
Total	130	100%	125	100%
	$X^2 = 6.24$	d.f. = 2		p < .05

Table 4

Alienation from Authority Figures in High School for SDS and YAF Members

ATTITUDE ITEMS	SDS		YAF	
	N	%	N	%
Most high school teachers are more interested in maintaining their status and throwing their authority around than in actually relating to the students and trying to teach them something.				
Agree	72	55	34	27
Uncertain	23	18	20	16
Disagree	35	27	71	57
Total	130	100%	125	100%
	$X^2 = 25.98$	d.f. = 2		p < .001
My experiences in high school were generally frustrating and unpleasant.				
Agree	59	46	27	22
Uncertain	20	15	8	6
Disagree	51	39	90	72
Total	130	100%	125	100%
	$X^2 = 27.76$	d.f. = 2		p < .001

Table 5

Alienation from Religious Authority Figures for SDS and YAF Members*

HOW WOULD YOU DESCRIBE, IN YOUR OWN WORDS, YOUR RELATIONSHIP WITH RELIGIOUS FUNCTIONAIRES WHEN YOU WERE IN HIGH SCHOOL?	SDS		YAF	
	N	%	N	%
Meaningful, personal, satisfactory	21	16	53	42
Superficial, formal, an externally compliant relation	21	16	25	20
Scepticism, rejection, progressive loss of respect	17	13	14	11
Unclassifiable	4	3	11	9
No answer	67	52	22	18
Total	130	100%	125	100%

$$X^2 = 53.69$$
$$\text{d.f.} = 4$$
$$p < .001$$

* Based on content analysis.

Table 6

Religious Practices of Political Activists

DO YOU ATTEND A CHURCH OR SYNAGOGUE NOW AND/OR DID YOU ATTEND A CHURCH OR SYNAGOGUE WHEN YOU WERE IN HIGH SCHOOL?	SDS		YAF	
	N	%	N	%
Yes (now); Yes (H.S.)	34	26	100	81
Yes (now); No (H.S.)	2	2	4	3
No (now); Yes (H.S.)	31	24	8	6
No (now); No (H.S.)	63	48	13	10
	130	100%	125	100%

$$X^2 = 80.57$$
$$\text{d.f.} = 3$$
$$p < .001$$

disorganization and "moral principles," become more decisive determinants of status.

Ethnic status is, in principle, fundamentally different from social class. Classes arise out of the division of labor in society, to which they are usually thought to bear some functional relation; ethnic groups are communal ways of life that exhibit special cultural or subcultural characteristics. Such subcultures typically are the basis of group solidarity and identification. The United States has experienced a historically determined gradation of ethnic groups dependent mainly on relative time of arrival in the New World. Research has shown that a finely distinguished hierarchy of status became established during the later period of great immigration (roughly 1880–1923) with the English and Northern European decendents at the top and the Southern and Eastern Europeans at or near the bottom. Ethnic status and class status are independent systems of evaluation. In the United States they have often provided the basis for profound social and personal conflict, as individuals are forced to orient themselves primarily toward one or the other—outward toward the class system or inward toward the solidarity of the ethnic group.

Tables 7 and 8 present SDS and YAF members in terms of the social class identifications of their families for

Table 7

Father's Occupation of SDS and YAF Members

HOLLINGSHEAD ISP CLASSIFICATION	SDS		YAF	
	N	%	N	%
Higher executive, proprietors of large concerns, and major professionals	47	35	23	18
Business managers, proprietors of medium sized businesses, and lesser professionals	29	22	15	12
Administrative personnel, small independent businesses, and minor professionals	26	20	47	38
Clerical and sales workers, technicians, and owners of little businesses	10	8	14	11
Skilled manual employees	7	5	17	14
Machine operators and semi-skilled	1	1	6	5
Unskilled employees	1*	1	0*	0
Other (deceased, n.a.)	9*	8	3*	2
	130	100%	125	100%

$$X^2 = 29.09$$
$$d.f. = 5$$
$$p < .001$$

* Not included in chi-square analysis.

Table 8

Extent of Father's (Guardian's) Education

LEVEL OF EDUCATION	SDS		YAF	
	N	%	N	%
Partial high school (and under)	20	15	24	19
High school graduate	14	11	31	25
Partial college	23	18	25	20
Standard college graduate	26	20	24	19
Graduate professional training	47	36	21	17
	130	100%	125	100%

$$X^2 = 16.77$$
$$d.f. = 4$$
$$p < .01$$

Table 9

Social Class of SDS and YAF Members as Obtained by Hollingshead Two-Factor (ISP) Index

SOCIAL CLASS	SDS		YAF	
	N	%	*N*	%
I, II (Upper-middle)	78	64	39	32
III (Lower-middle)	24	20	46	38
IV, V (Working, blue-collar)	19	16	37	30
	121*	100%	122**	100%

$$X^2 = 25.70$$
$$\text{d.f.} = 2$$
$$p < .001$$

* Data on 9 S s were insufficient to compute ISP position.

** Data on 3 S s were insufficient to compute ISP position.

Table 10

Annual Family Income SDS and YAF Members

	SDS		YAF	
	N	%	*N*	%
Above median	71	57	56	47
Below median	54	43	62	53
	125*	100%	118**	100%

Median test:
SDS (Med) = $11,533
YAF (Med) = $ 9,682

$$X^2 = 2.12$$
$$\text{d.f.} = 1$$
$$p < .20$$

* Five respondents gave no answer.

** Seven respondents gave no answer.

occupation and education separately, and Table 9 combines the two into the Hollingshead two factor index of social class, which is based on a weighting of occupation and education. All show quite clearly the greatly diverging backgrounds of our two groups—SDS members come predominantly from upper-middle-class families, whereas YAF members' backgrounds are, to a much greater extent, lower-middle and working-class. It should be noted in passing that these considerable differences do not appear to extend to the purely economic factor of income, since Table 10 shows only a small (and statistically insignificant) difference in this respect.

The ethnic status of the families of our students is presented in Table 11. Great differences mark the two groups. Eastern European nationalities are represented overwhelmingly in SDS, with 53 percent having at least one parent of this origin; this is true of only 21 percent of YAF. Correspondingly, YAF members come overwhelmingly from old American backgrounds, 78 percent falling in this category, whereas this is true of only

45 percent of SDS members. In Table 11 the first six categories are exclusively old American. (Although the Irish are not traditionally brought under this category, the great bulk of their immigration by now is well over three generations past, and they have generally taken their place in well-to-do middle-class America.) The striking fact about SDS is that it contains a disproportionate number of second and third-generation sons and daughters of relatively newly arrived immigrants from Eastern Europe.

These two sets of data on the two major types of status in the United States present us with an interesting problem.

Although the high-status backgrounds of SDS members is very un-Marxist, it is nevertheless true that it is consistent with the pattern of increasing anchorage of at least certain aspects of liberalism in the middle classes. Opinion polls and other data demonstrate consistently that on civil rights and foreign policy matters particularly, the middle classes are far more liberal than the working class. This is not true, however, in the case of the so-called "bread and butter" issues of liberalism that provided most of the working-class programs of the 1930s—what we might broadly call "welfare liberalism."

Neither does it seem reasonable to

Table 11

Ethnic Backgrounds of SDS and YAF Members (in percents)

NATIONALITY CATEGORIES (PARENTAL COMBINATIONS)	SDS		YAF	
English, Scot-Irish, Welsh	20%		20%	
German, French, Scandinavian, Dutch	10		17	
English-German	5		22	
		(45)		(78)
English-Irish	3		3	
Irish-North European*	6		13	
Irish	1		3	
English-Eastern or Southern European**	5		3	
Eastern European-German	9		6	
Irish-Eastern or Southern European	2		4	
Italian	1	(55)	1	(22)
Eastern European	37		8	
American Negro, West Indian	1		0	
Total	100%		100%	
	(97)†		(120)‡	

NOTE: Percent with at least partial Eastern European background:
SDS (53%); YAF (21%)
Percent with exclusively Northern European background:
SDS (45%); YAF (78%)

* Includes German, Scandinavian, Dutch, Belgian and French.

** Eastern European includes Russian, Polish, Czech, Bulgarian, Hungarian and all others of Slavic descent. Southern European includes Italians and Greek. No one of Spanish or Portuguese descent appeared in our sample.

† Thirty-three students reported "U.S.," "don't know," et cetera.

‡ Five students reported "U.S.," "don't know," et cetera.

find so many children from relatively low social-class backgrounds embracing the extremely conservative programs of an organization like YAF. Conservatism is traditionally the philosophy of upper classes and is marked by its distrust of the common man. And yet, as public opinion polls demonstrate, the working classes today embrace conservative ideas in foreign policy and civil rights. The social class backgrounds of both student groups, we conclude, are generally consistent with the main trend of the changing anchorage of basic political philosophy in American society.

Combining the two sets of data on status, we may characterize the activists in our sample as follows: left-wing SDS students come from high-class albeit low ethnic status backgrounds, whereas right-wing YAF members come predominantly from the working- and lower-middle class with high, old American ethnic backgrounds. We might say that the modal status position of the members of both groups is inconsistent, since each is characterized by one high and one low status quality. In this they are both alike and unlike.

The status position of our two groups is entirely consistent with the status politics hypothesis. YAF members are mainly low status old Americans—a category the theory would predict to be radicalized in the sense of overconforming. Furthermore, it is precisely this category that would experience most intensely the threat of the upward thrust of the new minorities, because their own identifications are old American. Lower middle-class and working-class old Americans are a group that has probably experienced considerable frustration in keeping up with their ethnic peers, while at the same time observing considerable

movement upward on the part of ethnic "inferiors." This is a situation likely, in terms of the theory of status politics, to produce the resentment and rejection of prevailing arrangements necessary for the degree of conservatism displayed by groups such as the YAF.

The families of SDS members, on the other hand, represent a group that, relative to the great bulk of Americans, undoubtedly have experienced considerable mobility. The fathers of these students have good educations and good jobs. They represent a segment of new American ethnic types that have experienced great upward social mobility. They undoubtedly view themselves as successes, a perspective probably not possible for their inconsistent counterparts—the lower-class, high ethnic status families supplying the bulk of the YAFers. It seems likely that their very success would make improbable the experience of being threatened and of frustration that we believe to be an important source of extreme conservatism of the YAF members.

Finally, it is clear that our findings articulate with the growing body of material in the field of stratification usually designated by the term "status inconsistency." It has been shown in several studies that inconsistent status combinations generally tend to predispose individuals toward changing the status quo. Over a decade ago, Lenski, in a now famous study, demonstrated that individuals possessing "inconsistent" status attributes (i.e., high-low combinations on occupational, educational, income, and ethnic dimensions) tended to support liberal positions on a series of current issues more often than those with "consistent" patterns. This relationship seemed to be strongest for those exhibiting low ethnicity but who were high on the other attributes.[14] More recently, Rush found that extreme right-wing conservatism was related to low education backgrounds in combination with high income and occupational status.[15] The data in our study are consistent with the general research in this field.

Conclusion

Our findings suggest that whereas the generational hypothesis seems to apply rather well to left-wing student activity, it is considerably less powerful when proposed as an explanation for student politics on the right. We find that analysis based on the ideas of the generation unit and stratification theory carry us further in understanding student involvement in politics than is possible if only the generational hypothesis is applied. Thus, our analysis tentatively attempts to bring student political activity within the same explanatory framework as politics in general, a scientifically desirable state of affairs. We hope this line of analysis will prove fruitful in future research.

NOTES

1. The term "student movement" applies to the new style of student protests that have emerged in the 1960s. Unlike the pre- and post-World War II era and the Eisenhower years, the present generation of campus activists is attempting to bring about fundamental changes in the university system and in the surrounding society. We refer to this campus-based phenomenon as the "student movement."

2. See David L. Westby and Richard G. Braungart, "Class and Politics in the Family Backgrounds of Student Political Activists," *American Sociological Review* 31 (October 1966), 690–692.

3. S. N. Eisenstadt, *From Generation to Generation* (New York: Free Press, 1956), p. 315.

4. Lewis Feuer, "Rebellion at Berkeley," *The New Leader*, 47 (December 1964), 6.

5. *Ibid.*, p. 6.

6. *Ibid.*, p. 7.

7. See Daniel Bell (ed.), *The Radical Right*, 2nd ed. (New York: Doubleday, 1963), especially the essays of Lipset and Hofstadter.

8. A recent analysis of American society from this perspective is E. Digby Baltzell's *The Protestant Establishment* (New York: Random House, 1964).

9. Data in our study were collected from the majority of collegiate delegates attending (1) an SDS (Students for a Democratic Society) convention held at Antioch College, Yellow Springs, Ohio, April 1966, and (2) a YAF (Young Americans for Freedom) convention held at Franklin and Marshall College, Lancaster, Pennsylvania, July 1966.

10. Data supporting this point are as follows. Both groups were asked, "If Negroes are not getting fair treatment in jobs and housing, the Federal government

should see to it that they do." 92 percent of the SDS as opposed to 8 percent of the YAF members agreed to this statement. When asked if, "The Federal government should stay out of the question of whether white and colored children go to the same school," 95 percent of SDS members disagreed with the statement, whereas only 21 percent of the YAF members disagreed.

11. See Karl Mannheim, "The Problem of Generations," in Paul Kecskemeti (ed.), *Essays in the Sociology of Knowledge* (London: Routledge & Kegan Paul, 1952), p. 304.

12. *Ibid.*, p. 304.

13. See for instance, Lipset's discussion in, "The Sources of the Radical Right," in *The Radical Right, op. cit.*, pp. 259–312.

14. See Gerhard Lenski, "Status Crystallization: A Non-vertical Dimension of Social Status," *American Sociological Review*, 19 (August 1954), 405–413.

15. Gary B. Rush, "Status Consistency and Right-Wing Extremism," *American Sociological Review*, 32 (February 1967), 86–92.

The Political Environment- Source of Con- formity and Deviancy

8

INTRODUCTION

So far the selections have made only occasional reference to the impact of the political environment itself upon the individual. In this section we shall turn to an examination of the ways in which different political systems by virtue of their structure, their laws, and their distribution of authority impel people to develop specific political attitudes and behaviors. However, before discussing the way in which political structure affects and shapes behavior, let us turn the proposition around and show how behavior affects institutions, at times reinforcing them, at times (as in the illustrations which follow) weakening them.

At one time it had been thought, perhaps somewhat naïvely, that alterations in governmental structure would almost ipso facto engender new political behaviors. Hence the great faith that people put into designing democratic constitutions or searching for the ideal form of government under which people could behave with justice and responsibility. One of the great shocks to many Americans, for example, was the ease with which Germans slipped into fascism while still theoretically living under what was perhaps one of the most democratic systems of government in existence, the Weimar Republic. In a similar vein Robert LeVine shows that governmental structure itself has different effects, depending on the sets of values and expectations people bring to it. In comparing two stateless societies that were otherwise very similar to each other in kinship and tribal patterns, he observed great differences in people's response to newly introduced legal institutions—differences based on the personal values people brought to them. The Gurii had very authoritarian political and personal beliefs and child-rearing practices and could accept the notion of someone imposing heavy penalties or sitting in judgment on them with a fair amount of ease. Consequently they could also, when ordered to do so, give up blood feuds as a way of adjudicating interpersonal conflict. But the Nuers, who were far more egalitarian, found it difficult to accept impersonal adjudication in lieu of blood feuds and even more difficult to sit in judgment upon each other. The author thus argues that exclusive examination of political or prepolitical structures alone will fail to make us understand differences in political behavior inside governments and countries that on the surface look structurally similar. In Chapter 3 Pollis made similar observations when she noted that perhaps the greatest impediment to successful democracy in Greece was the Greeks' notion of self, which seemed incompatible with the type of consensual, individualistic political behavior necessary for the successful functioning of democracy. Edward Banfield shows how responses to a given economic and political situation can gradually become so ingrained that they are transmitted from generation to generation and finally begin to form a permanent value system (in the case of Italy he calls it amoral familialism) whose rigid ethos makes it impossible for people to make a political system work or even to engage in cooperative action by which to bring leverage to bear upon the system. Banfield is most emphatic in pointing out that it is futile to look into any one aspect in isolation; neither the government alone nor the poor state of the economy nor the ignorance and illiteracy of the population alone can account for the lack of political activity and civic cooperation in the Sicilian village. To

him the crucial variable is the political ethos that has developed over time in response to an oppressive government, a poor economy, a society rent by sharp class conflict. Gradually the political ethos now has become so much part and parcel of the villager's way of life that even a change in the political and economic system, Banfield thinks, cannot bring about civic cooperation for the time being. In short, political mores, developed under one set of political circumstances, will persist long after the circumstances that necessitated their arousal have vanished. In other words, adaptive patterns may develop such functional autonomy that they persist even after changes in the political structure have taken place. Observations such as these should alert us once more to the difficulty we have in political socialization when we wish to ascribe causality to any one phenomenon, be it the political system, the social stratification, the schools, or what have you. In political life there is a great interdependence of factors; and the longer these factors persist over time, the more they will become historical forces, the more difficult it is to isolate them, much less to change them quickly.

Although the selections just referred to tend to minimize the importance of structure per se, the selection by Morton Deutsch and Mary Collins and the one by Thomas Pettigrew do point to the importance of political structures and laws emanating from them. The Deutsch and Collins article points out how much the manipulations of the structure (in this case integrated versus nonintegrated housing) and a change of official rules can influence socialization. Tenants who were prejudiced against Negroes prior to moving into a racially integrated housing project tended to decrease in prejudice as a result of prolonged living in integrated government housing projects. The change, however, was only in part a function of the housing arrangement and was in part a function of official rules with respect to what the tenants perceived to be behaviors and values approved by the housing authority. Most tenants interpreted integrated housing arrangements as an indication of the authorities' conviction that such patterns were the desirable ones and that desirable tenants would not be prejudiced, at least not in their overt behavior. Similarly, Pettigrew observed that otherwise unprejudiced Southerners and natives of the Union of South Africa portrayed a great deal of racial prejudice and that this prejudice undoubtedly was a function of long-standing accommodations to the laws of apartheid. Interestingly enough, young people of farming or working-class background who desired upward social mobility tended to be most prejudiced, probably because they hoped by their intense prejudice to find social acceptance in the eyes of the establishment. If one were to draw a generalization from these articles, one would have to say that the very presence of a law in and of itself indicates to those affected by it that the government or those in power conceive the legally prescribed ways of feeling and behaving to be acceptable and other ways to be illegal as well as morally unacceptable. In asmuch as Deutsch and Collins point out that most people tend " to behave as they are expected to behave" (pp. 514–525), it is only logical to assume that the behaviors condoned and encouraged by given political systems would in and of themselves affect the political behaviors, if not actually the feelings, of those living

under their jurisdiction. In other words, a new regime may at first have to coerce certain behavior patterns because initially they seem uncongenial to the citizen; but gradually in accommodation to the regime demands, subsequent generations will have learned the particular accommodation pattern so well that they can teach it unhesitantly to subsequent generations. Presumably, after a given period, the behavior will have been so well internalized that it will have become self-perpetuating. Unfortunately, there is at the moment no short study that could be included in this reader which could systematically demonstrate how the laws, rules, and regulations of a political system socialize citizens to internalize specific political values, attitudes, and behaviors. Anyone, however, who has ever traveled in Europe must have been struck by the observation that in some democratic countries citizens seem less individualistic and somewhat more subservient than they do in the United States. In the same countries the traveler often finds a bewildering number of governmentally imposed rules, regulations, and prohibitions all of which might in part account for the greater subservience of the citizens. Some of these countries, to follow up this line of reasoning, take it for granted that they are entitled to know at all times of the movements and residences of its citizens. As a result, they see nothing amiss—and neither do the citizens—in requiring registration with the local police station as one moves out or into an apartment, elaborate forms on occupation, purpose of visit and so forth, to be filled out upon registering in a hotel, and so on. Hannah Arendt, in her analysis of the Eichmann trial,[1] commented on and deplored the cooperativeness with which German

Jewish community leaders handed over to the Nazi government census data and records of the Jewish community— records that in turn facilitated the Nazi roundup and extermination of the German Jews. Having over many generations become used to government intrusion, it is not surprising that such citizens are more deferential to authority.

But one may also ask the following questions: Should one not expect properly socialized citizens to comply with government demands in a country where every good citizen had become socialized to such obedience to the government and had learned to consider compliance with its myriads of little rules and regulations as the hallmark of a good and civilized citizen? After all, what would look like intolerable invasion of privacy to an American citizen did not look that way to a German. This illustration may be of a particularly extreme nature, but it should give some inkling of the way in which governmental practices tend to socialize citizens, provided they have been in effect over a sufficiently long span of years.

Just how long lasting can be the effects of governmental practices and laws can be seen from the following illustration: Currently there has been much emphasis on the matriarchal nature of the American Negro family and on its corollary, namely, the extent to which the American Negro male seems to be denied his role as head of the household and therefore, indirectly, his masculinity. Family structure on the surface may seem to be a social, not a political, phenomenon. In this context, however, it is well to remember that many political practices (statutes, codes, etc.) have contributed to this social phenomenon. Certainly

plantation practices, sanctioned by the laws of the state, made the breakup of the family and the preferential treatment of the female a matter of legal practice. In our day the social welfare laws, such as ADC, only accentuate this practice, because until recently a destitute family could not get child support unless a father was physically absent from the home. It is easy to see how the nature of this law contributed to the high number of females as head of households. Bradbury Seasholes[2] theorizes how much this state of affairs may have contributed to the low feelings of efficacy and low interest in political participation among young Negroes both North and South.

The treatment of the Negro draws to our attention yet another way in which the political environment has an influence of its own. Every political system is not only a set of institutions and laws but also a way of distributing wealth, power, and deference. In other words, even the most egalitarian of systems treats some people more equally than others. Far more political systems, however, are not egalitarian but rather are stratified; and in them some people clearly command more power and more respect than others. Power allocations, of course, affect leadership opportunities. Most political systems make access to power and leadership positions easier for some people than for others. For example, Donald Matthews,[3] in his study of the United States Senate, pointed out that the Senate draws disproportionately from a relatively small segment of the well-educated American upper-middle class. Other countries open the doors to political advancement to people of the clergy, or the military, or the corporate structure. Very often such preference brings with it not only more power for the "correctly located" individual but prompts in such families a tradition of socializing their children for public service and positions of leadership that set them sharply apart from the socialization experienced by the rest of the population (see Wilkinson pp. 337–346). To be sure, on the surface this is merely the result of family preferences with respect to socialization. But let us not overlook that these preferences are in part prompted by governmental practices and traditions. The selections below dealing with the Irish, the Puerto Ricans, and the Negroes in this country clearly show how differential treatment at the hands of the same political system socializes people very differently and gives them a completely different view of the political system under which they grow up. Witness, for example, how two young New York high-schoolers growing up within two blocks from each other relate very differently to the government of the United States. One, a comfortable middle-class boy from Irish extraction is quite uninterested in politics because he can see very little that the government does that either hurts or helps his comfortably established family. His patriotism and love for country is great; and in addition he has just had the pride of seeing one of his own ethnic group, namely John F. Kennedy, reach the highest zenith of political power in the country. Also the treatment of the Irish in the Bronx and in the nation at large is such that he derives comfort and pride from his group membership rather than shame. He is dimly aware of the fact that there is not only a war going on but also that there are poverty, racial discrimination, and other forms of injustice prevalent in the United States. But rather than feeling shame or anger over these practices, he smugly accepts them as though they were a fact of life that cannot be altered right away. What concern he has with politics deals with relatively selfish and mundane matters, such as the absence of open fields where boys his age could play ball. Compare this with the bitterness and cynicism of the young Puerto Rican, who is convinced that the government is run by the rich for the rich and that Puerto Ricans' participating in it at the present time would be futile and might actually lead to reprisals. Notice his bitterness toward the police, his impatience with the older generation, who are willing to take discrimination and injustice for granted, and his anticipation of violence at the hands of the younger generation, who no longer want to wait for the day when life would be better. His comments on the political scene show a real feeling of despair over the power structure, a sense of urgency and cynicism that bears little resemblance to the picture of strength and pride which the Irish boy has of his government.

John Howard's description of the Black Muslims shows how their political attitudes and practices also have come about as a result of a keen awareness of the unequal distribution of power and wealth but worst of all of denial of respect for the Negro. The militants among them separated themselves from the mainstream of politics precisely because they felt the political system treated them as outsiders and barred them from access to it as well as from personal ascent. Both groups of Black Muslims essentially chose the path they did in response to their perception of the treatment awarded them by the political system and the society. What Howard describes—he calls it "a commitment to deviance"—is essentially a resocialization process by which the Black Muslim first begins to participate in a political system quite different from the larger system and then with the help of the new system gradually becomes insulated from the larger system. The analysis of the Black Muslim leads us to conclude that the political system then socializes not only by its official laws, pronouncements, and institutions but also by its unofficial ways of treating its citizens. The more disadvantaged the citizen, that is, the less access he is given to the values of society and the more he is treated as an inferior, the more likely that he will not become fully socialized into the ongoing political norms and that he will either remain on the outside, passive and alienated, or he will actually, because of this alienation, become resocialized to a different political value system. The latter, in turn, may cause acute political conflict between the political system at large and the smaller political system.

The article below on the children of Appalachia is an eloquent illustration of differences between subculture and political culture at large. The children of Appalachia, perhaps because of historical traditions as well as current economic hardships, apparently do not share the enthusiasm and idealism observed in American school children elsewhere in the country; rather they show a cynicism and lack of faith in government quite akin to that of the Italian and Negro adult discussed in the selections in this book The youth apparently have heard or seen very little about the government that commends it to their respect and love.

Cynicism and disillusionment of a different kind are seen in a group of ultrarightists studied by Ira Rohter in Oregon (pp. 626–651). Their disillusionment stems not so much from the absence of democracy or from lack of egalitarian treatment on the part of government but rather from yearning for the "good old days" when there was more stratification, when their families and other families on the right side of the railroad tracks were accorded more respect and were given more power and position in political affairs than they are today. To be sure, as Rohter points out, there are many other bases for this disillusionment on the part of rightists, notably religious beliefs and personality factors; but their response to current development is mainly prompted by their disaffection for the current government and their yearning for the government of yesteryear.

In summary then, a stable governmental system (its institutions and laws) in and of itself is a socializing force for four main reasons. First, the structure and institutions determine opportunities for leadership, self-government, and individual freedom to which people learn to accommodate. Second, the regime's laws, regulations, and traditions ordain certain behavior patterns that become internalized after they have been practiced long enough. Once internalized, they become transmitted voluntarily from generation to generation, thus further contributing to political socialization. Third, the differential distribution of power, wealth, and deference practiced by each government will convey different pictures of the government, the role of the citizen, and the importance of different groups in the governmental process. These pictures in turn will affect notions of political efficacy, alienation, civic duty, and so forth. From these differential pictures then will follow differential political behavior. Fourth, the extent of the difference and the bitterness arising from it can at times lead to severe political conflicts, which in turn can bring on new ways of behaving politically, which then in turn can become a force for resocialization.

NOTES

1. Hanna Arendt, *Eichmann in Jerusalem: A Report on the Banality of Evil* (New York: Viking, 1963).
2. Bradbury Seasholes, "Political Socialization of Negroes: Image Development of Self and Polity," in William C. Kvaraceus, *Negro Self-Concept* (New York: McGraw-Hill, 1965), pp. 52–69.
3. Donald Matthews, *U.S. Senators and Their World* (New York: Random House, 1960).

PERSONALITY AND SOCIOCULTURAL FACTORS IN INTER-GROUP ATTITUDES: A CROSS-NATIONAL COMPARISON[1]

- ## Thomas F. Pettigrew

I. Introduction

Along the continuum of prejudice theories, two extreme positions have been popular. One strongly emphasizes the personality of the bigot and neglects his cultural milieu; the other views intolerance as a mere reflection of cultural norms and neglects individual differences. Recent evidence lends little support to either pole. As further data are gathered with more refined research tools, it becomes increasingly apparent that the psychological and sociological correlates of prejudice are elaborately interwined and that both are essential to provide an adequate theoretical framework for this complex phenomenon.

Carrying this viewpoint further, Smith, Bruner, and White (38, pp. 41–44) have delineated three functions that attitudes may serve for an individual. First, there is the *object-appraisal* function; attitudes aid in the process of understanding "reality" as it is defined by the culture. Second, attitudes can play a *social-adjustment* role by contributing to the individual's identification with, or differentiation from, various reference groups. It should be noted that both these functions—object appraisal and social adjustment—are important reflections on the personality level of sociocultural conditions. But the most studied function of attitudes, *externalization*, is somewhat unique. "Externalization occurs when an individual, often responding unconsciously, senses an analogy between a perceived environmental event and some unresolved inner problem . . . [and] adopts an attitude . . . which is a transformed version of his way of dealing with his inner difficulty." Such a process may serve to reduce anxiety. The principal psychological theories of prejudice—frustration-aggression (9), psychoanalytic (20), and authoritarianism (1)—all deal chiefly with this third process.

External expression of inner conflict is relatively more independent of sociocultural factors than are the other functions of attitudes. Indeed, a heuristic distinction between externalized personality variables and sociological variables contributes to our understanding of much that is known about intergroup conflict.

Minard's observations of race relations in the coal-mining county of McDowell, West Virginia, serve as a direct illustration of the point (26). The general pattern in this region consists of white and Negro miners being integrated below the ground and almost completely segregated above the ground. Minard estimates that roughly 60 per cent of the white miners manage to reverse roles almost completely; they can accept Negroes as equals in the mines but cannot accept them as equals elsewhere. Furthermore, he feels that, at one extreme, about 20 per cent accept the black miners as equals in both situations, while, at the

Above selection reprinted from: *Journal of Conflict Resolution*, II, 1 (1958), 29–42.

other extreme, about 20 per cent never accept them in either situation. In our terms, the behavior of the majority of these whites studied by Minard can be predicted largely by sociocultural expectations, and the behavior of the consistent minorities can be accounted for largely by externalized personality variables.

The research literature abounds with further examples in which a separation of psychological and sociological factors is helpful. The many papers on interracial contact in housing (7, 40), at work (11), and in the army (39) show the marked effects that can be brought about by certain changes in the social situation between races. But personality factors are still operating. Usually these studies report that some individuals hold favorable attitudes toward minorities even before the contact and that other individuals still hold unfavorable attitudes after the contact. Many of these studies also find that the changes brought about by the contact are quite specific and delimited in nature. That is, the intergroup changes occur only under a narrow range of conditions, since the basic personality orientations of the participants have not changed fundamentally. Thus white department-store employees become more accepting of Negroes in the work situation after equal status contact but not in other situations (11). And the attitudes of white army personnel toward the Negro as a fighting man improve after equal status contact in combat, but their attitudes toward the Negro as a social companion do not change(39).

Desegregation findings furnish further illustrations where the distinction is useful. Social demands for racial desegregation and the irresistible trend of the times are counteracting personality pre-dispositions in many communities. Thus a 1954 public opinion survey in Oklahoma found an overwhelming majority of the residents sternly against desegregation, and yet today mixed schools have become accepted throughout most of the state without incident (17). And in Wilmington, Delaware, two years after successful school integration without apparent public opposition, a poll indicated that only a minority approved of the school desegregation decision of the Supreme Court (17). Indeed, this discrepancy between opinons and demands is a general phenomenon throughout the border states. Hyman and Sheatsley (16) report that only 31 per cent of the white population in those border areas that have already integrated their school systems indorse desegregation.

This conflict between authority-supported cultural changes and personal preferences is underscored by another finding that public opinion polls have uncovered in the South. Several investigators have independently shown that respondents themselves make a distinction between what they individually favor and what they expect to happen in their community. Thus the huge majority of southern whites favor racial segregation, but most of them also feel that desegregation is inevitable (16, 28).

Finally, the work originally done by La Piere (19) in 1934 and more recently replicated in different contexts by Saenger and Gilbert (34) and by Kutner, Wilkins, and Yarrow (18) furnishes further justification for a theoretical separation of social and externalization aspects of intergroup conflict. These investigations illustrate the results of conflicting personality predispositions and actual social situations with minority-group members; frequently the face-to-face conditions override previous practices.

Such work has led several authorities in the field to make the sociocultural and personality differentiation. Psychologist G. W. Allport discusses the two classes of of factors separately in his definitive volume, *The Nature of Prejudice* (2), and sociologist Arnold Rose makes a similar distinction in a recent theoretical article on intergroup relations (33).

The present paper is a summary report on research conducted chiefly to gain cross-national perspective on these two sets of prejudice factors. The studies were made in two parts of the world where racial conflict today is highlighted and cultural sanctions of intolerance are intense and explicit: the Union of South Africa and the southern United States. First, a more detailed report of previously unpublished data will be presented on the South African study. Following this, a comparison will be made with the southern United States based on a summary of data presented in detail elsewhere (29).

II. Racial Prejudice in the Union of South Africa[2]

The limited evidence available supports the general belief that white South Africans are unusually prejudiced against Africans (14, 21, 24). This raises the intriguing question as to whether this increased hostility represents (*a*) more externalizing personality potential for prejudice among South Africans, (*b*) the effects of different cultural norms and pressures, or (*c*) both of these.

To provide a tentative answer, a questionnaire study was undertaken of the racial attitudes of students at the English-speaking University of Natal in the Union of South Africa. A non-random sample of 627 undergraduates—approximately one-third of the entire university—completed an anonymous instrument containing three scales and a number of background items.[3] The three scales are a thirteen-item measure of authoritarianism (F scale) whose statements are shown in Table 2, a sixteen-item measure of social conformity (C scale) whose statements are shown in Table 3, and an eighteen-item measure of anti-African attitudes (A scale) whose statements are shown in Table 8.[4] Background information includes place of birth, political party preference, father's occupation, and ethnic-group membership.

Taken as a group, these students evidence considerable hostility toward Africans, accepting in large degree the white-supremacy ideology so adamantly propounded by the present government of their country. Thus 72 per cent of the sample agree that "there is something inherently primitive and uncivilized in the native, as shown in his music and extreme aggressiveness;" and 69 per cent agree that "manual labor seems to fit the native mentality better than more skilled and responsible work." And yet their F-scale responses are roughly comparable to those of American student populations.[5] Thus these South Africans are sharply prejudiced against blacks without possessing any greater externalizing personality potential for intolerance than peoples in more tolerant areas.

In addition, authoritarianism correlates with anti-African attitudes at a level comparable to relationships between authoritarianism and prejudice in other parts of the world. Table 1 shows that the A and F scales correlate $+0.56$

among the Afrikaans-speaking members of the sample and +0.46 among the English-speaking members. Similar scales typically correlate in the fifties in American college samples.[6] The C-scale measure of social conformity—employed for the first time in this investigation— relates to the A-scale scores significantly, too, in both ethnic groups (Table 1).

More detailed analyses of the F and C scales' relationships with anti-African attitudes are provided in Tables 2 and 3. Each of the thirteen authoritarian statements separates the less and more prejudiced halves of the sample in the predicted direction, seven of the differences proving to be significant at better than the 0.001 level of confidence. The sixteen C-scale items predict almost as well; the more anti-African students in every case agree more often than the less prejudiced. Perhaps the conforming attitude of the bigots is capsuled in the first item of Table 3. While only a third of the tolerant members of the group agree

Table 1

*Correlations Between Anti-African Scale (A) and Authoritarianism (F) and Conformity (C) Scales**

	Ethnic Group†	
VARIABLES	*Afrikaners*	*English*
N.	50	513
A and F	+0.56	+0.46
A and C	+0.42	+0.46

* All four of these product-moment correlations are significantly different from zero at better than the 1 per cent level of confidence. The scale scores that were correlated vary between 0 and 10. They were calculated on the basis of + 4 for agree strongly, + 3 for agree, + 2 for omitted response, + 1 for disagree and 0 for disagree strongly for each item, and then the total scores were collapsed into the 0–10 categories for machine analysis.

† Separate analyses by ethnic group are made necessary by the sharply divergent A-scale means of the two groups (see Table 7).

with the statement, over half the prejudiced students feel that "it's better to go along with the crowd than to be a martyr."

These personality relationships suggest (*a*) that personality factors are as important correlates of prejudice in this sample as they are in other, non-South African samples; (*b*) that social conformity (as measured by the C scale) is a particularly crucial personality variable in this sample's attitudes toward Africans; and (*c*) that personality components do not in themselves account for the heightened intolerance of this sample.

We must turn to sociocultural factors to explain the extreme prejudice of these respondents, and the unusual importance of these variables is made clear by the data. For instance, the 560 students who were born on the African continent are significantly more intolerant of Africans than the remaining 65, but they are *not* more authoritarian. Table 4 shows that those not born in Africa are much less likely to fall into the most prejudiced third of the distribution than other sample members. And yet the two groups do not differ significantly in their F-scale scores. More thoroughly influenced throughout their lives by the culture's definition of the white man's situation in Africa, students born on the Dark Continent are more anti-African without the usual personality concomitants of ethnocentrism.

Another such relationship involves students who support the Nationalist party—the pro-*Apartheid* political faction that is presently in power. Table 5 indicates that these respondents score significantly higher on the A scale than their fellow undergraduates, but these two groups do not differ on the F scale. Again a prejudice difference is not accompanied by a personality potential difference. These relationships with political party preference and prejudice hold for each of the major ethnic groups— Afrikaners and English—considered separately.

Two other comparisons yield statistically significant differences in both authoritarianism and anti-African prejudice. Table 6 indicates that those sample members whose fathers are manually employed are significantly more intoler-

ant of the African than those whose fathers are non-manually employed. The two groups differ in the same manner in their F-scale scores. But when authoritarianism is controlled for, the groups still differ significantly in their attitudes toward blacks.[7] In other words, the children of manual fathers are more prejudiced and more authoritarian than other students, and they remain more prejudiced even after the difference in authoritarianism is partialed out of the

Table 2

Anti-African Prejudice and F-Scale Items

F-SCALE ITEM	Percentage Agreement* Less Prejudiced Half	More Prejudiced Half	$2 \times 2 \chi^2$	p
a) Nowadays when so many different kinds of people move around and mix together so much, a person has to be especially careful not to catch an infection or disease from them	13.6	33.2	33.5	0.001
b) There is hardly anything lower than a person who does not feel a great love and respect for his parents	52.6	70.5	21.2	.001
c) People can be put into two distinct classes: the weak and the strong	23.5	37.8	15.1	.001
d) Most of our social problems would be solved if we could somehow get rid of the immoral, crooked, and feebleminded people	45.4	60.6	14.8	.001
e) The most important thing a child should learn is obedience to his parents	79.8	90.2	13.2	.001
f) Every person should have faith in some supernatural power whose decisions he obeys without question	46.7	60.9	13.0	.001
g) When a person has a problem or worry, it is best for him not to think about it, but to keep busy with more cheerful things	39.4	53.2	11.8	.001
h) Nowadays more and more people are prying into matters that should remain private and personal	63.5	74.5	8.6	.01
i) If people would talk less and work more, everybody would be better off	67.8	78.2	8.3	.01
j) An insult to our honor should always be punished	31.8	40.3	4.7	.05
k) No sane, normal person would ever think of hurting a close friend or relative	67.9	76.6	4.3	.05
l) Science has its place, but there are many important things that can never possibly be understood by the human mind	80.7	85.8	2.9	0.10
m) Some day it will probably be shown that astrology can explain a lot of things	44.4	48.0	0.9	n.s.

* The respondent was given four categories: agree strongly, agree, disagree, and disagree strongly. Percentage agreement is calculated by combining the first two of these replies.

relationship. These upwardly mobile students must be carefully in step with the mores to establish firmly their rise in the social structure, and the mores of South Africa lead to intolerance.

Table 7 shows the sharp difference between the Afrikaner and English subjects in the sample. Afrikaners are both more anti-African and more authoritarian, and, when the F-scale differences are corrected, for, they remain significantly more hostile to the African.[8] These 50 students are directly subject to the national ethos and have no conflicting national reference, as many English-speaking South Africans have in Great

Table 3

Anti-African Prejudice and C-Scale Items

C-SCALE ITEM	Percentage Agreement* Less Prejudiced Half	More Prejudiced Half	$2 \times 2 \chi^2$	p
a) It's better to go along with the crowd than to be a martyr	34.8	53.2	21.8	0.001
b) When almost everyone agrees on something, there is little reason to oppose it	16.6	31.1	18.5	.001
c) Adherence to convention produces the best kind of citizen	31.8	46.8	14.9	.001
d) To be successful, a group's members must act and think alike	45.7	60.0	12.5	.001
e) It is important for friends to have similar opinions	28.5	42.2	12.1	.001
f) It is more important to be loyal and conform to our own group than to try to co-operate with other groups	25.6	38.5	11.7	.001
g) We should alter our needs to fit society's demands rather change society to fit our needs	42.4	55.1	11.4	.001
h) A good group member should agree with the other members	21.2	33.2	11.1	.001
i) It is best not to express your views when in the company of friends who disagree with you	23.8	32.9	6.1	.02
j) Before a person does something, he should try to consider how his friends will react to it	54.6	63.1	4.4	.05
k) To become a success these days, a person has to act in the way that others expect him to act	33.2	41.5	4.2	.05
l) A group cannot expect to maintain its identity unless its members all think and feel in very much the same way	59.3	66.8	3.9	.05
m) It is one's duty to conform to the passing demands of the world and to suppress those personal desires that do not fit these demands	43.7	51.1	3.4	.10
n) A person should adapt his ideas and his behavior to the group that happens to be with him at the time	45.7	52.6	3.1	.10
o) It is extremely uncomfortable to go accidentally to a formal party in street clothes	78.5	83.1	2.0	.20
p) To get along well in a group, you have to follow the lead of others	27.2	31.1	1.1	0.30

* Percentage agreement calculated as in Table 2.

Britain. Like the upwardly mobile, they are in roles that demand unusual conformity.

Table 8 clarifies further the ethnic differences in attitudes toward the African. Sixteen of the A scale's eighteen statements significantly separate the Afrikaners from the English, the former scoring higher in all cases. And, moreover, there is a definite trend in these differences. The five items which discriminate poorest between the ethnic groups (items *n* through *r*) are all stereotyped-belief state-

Table 4

Place of Birth and Anti-African Prejudice*

ANTI-AFRICAN ATTITUDES†	N	Place of Birth	
		On African Continent	Not on African Continent
		560	65
Least prejudiced	176	28%	29%
Medium prejudiced	246	38%	54%
Most prejudiced	203	34%	17%

* 2 × 3 chi-square = 9.33; $p < 0.01$.

† The least prejudiced are the students who rated A-scale scores from 0 through 4 by disagreeing with a heavy majority of the items; the medium prejudiced received scores of either 5 or 6 by agreeing with roughly half of the 18 A-scale items; and the most prejudiced obtained scores of 7 through 10 by agreeing with a majority of the statements.

Table 5

Political Party Preference and Anti-African Prejudice*

ANTI-AFRICAN ATTITUDES	N	Political Party Preference†	
		Nationalist Party	Other Parties
		72	483
Least prejudiced	157	8%	35%
Medium prejudiced	210	26%	36%
Most prejudiced	188	66%	29%

* 2 × 3 chi-square = 38.60; $p < 0.001$.

† Seventy-two of the 627 students did not indicate any political preference.

Table 6

Father's Occupational Status and Anti-African Prejudice*

ANTI-AFRICAN ATTITUDES	N	Father's Occupational Status†	
		Manual	Non-manual
		146	417
Less prejudiced half	280	34%	55%
More prejudiced half	283	66%	45%

* 2 × 2 chi-square = 18.90; $p < 0.001$.

† Sixty-four of the 627 students did not indicate their fathers' occupations.

Table 7

Ethnic Group and Anti-African Prejudice*

ANTI-AFRICAN ATTITUDES	N	Ethnic Group†	
		Afrikaners	English
		50	513
Less prejudiced half	264	14%	50%
More prejudiced half	299	86%	50%

* 2 × 2 chi-square = 23.7; $p < 0.001$.

† Ethnic group is determined by both the student's own ethnic identification and the principal language spoken in his home. Sixty-four of the students identified with other groups (e.g., Jewish, French, German) and are not included in this analysis.

ments; they refer to the standard traits frequently associated with Africans— lazy, primitive, happy-go-lucky, and bad-smelling. Conversely, five of the six best discriminators (items *b* through *f*) are all exclusion-discrimination statements; they deny equal rights to Africans in employment, housing, and voting. Afrikaans-speaking and English-speaking students, then, do not differ sharply in the degree to which they harbor the traditional stereotype of the African, but they do possess markedly divergent views on discrimination against the African. A key to these differences may be provided in the lone exception to this trend, item *a*. Seven out of every ten Afrikaners, as compared with only a third of the English, believe that the "natives will always have a greater tendency toward crimes of violence than Europeans." Strong projection may be operating for those agreeing with this statement, but, in any event, it suggests that physical fear of the black man is especially prevalent among our Afrikaans-speaking respondents and that this may be the fundamental motivation for their emphasis on excluding and discriminating against the African.

All these findings point to the crucial role of the cultural milieu in shaping the attitudes of the white South African toward the blacks in his midst. While externalizing personality factors do not account for the students' unusually prejudiced attitudes concerning Africans, variables which reflect the dominant norms of the white society prove to be important. Students who are especially responsive to these norms—those who were born in Africa, those who identify with the Nationalist party, those who are upwardly mobile, and those who have been molded by the conservative traditions of the Afrikaans-speaking people—tend to be intolerant of Africans to some degree, regardless of their basic personality structure.

III. Racial Prejudice in the Southern United States

Similar considerations led to an earlier comparative study of anti-Negro prejudice in the southern and northern United States. While considerable evidence indicates that white southerners are typically more intolerant of the Negro than white northerners (16, 27, 30, 35, 36, 39), little work has been focused on the factors underlying this difference. But, like the South African data, the scant data available suggest that sociocultural and not externalization factors may be the crucial determinants of the contrasting regional attitudes toward the Negro.

Thus, if the South did have more externalizing personality potential for prejudice than other American areas, it should also be more anti-Semitic.[9] But Roper (31, 32) has twice found in his national polls that the South is one of the most tolerant regions toward Jews, and Prothro (30) has noted that 40 per cent of his adult white Louisiana sample is at the same time favorable in its attitudes toward Jews and highly anti-Negro. Furthermore, there is no evidence that the stern family pattern associated with "prejudiced personalities" (1, 12) is more prevalent in the South than in the North (6, 8). And, finally, the few white southern populations that have been given the F scale have obtained means that fall easily within the range of means reported for non-southern populations (1, 25, 37).

Rose categorically concludes: "There is no evidence that 'authoritarian personality' or frustration-aggression or scapegoating, or any known source of 'prejudice' in the psychological sense, is any more prevalent in the South than in the North" (33). And Prothro adds: "Situational, historical and cultural factors appear to be of considerable, perhaps major, import in addition to personality dynamics" in determining anti-Negro attitudes in the South (30).

In testing these ideas in the two regions, different methods were employed than those used in South Africa. Public opinion polling techniques were utilized with 366 randomly selected white adults in eight roughly matched communities in the North and South. The four small southern towns, located in Georgia and North Carolina, were chosen to have Negro population percentages ranging from 10 to 45 per cent, while the small northern towns, all located in New England, have less than 1 per cent Negroes each.

The interview schedule contained a ten-item measure of authoritarianism (F scale), an eight-item measure of

Table 8

Ethnic-Group Differences on A-Scale Items

A-SCALE ITEMS	Percentage Agreement* Afrikaners	English	$2 \times 2 \chi^2$	p
a) Because of their primitive background, natives will always have a greater tendency toward crimes of violence than Europeans	70.0	34.9	33.6	0.001
b) Native musicians are sometimes as good as Europeans at swing music and jazz, but it is a mistake to have mixed native-European bands	86.0	54.2	18.8	.001
c) Most of the natives would become officious, overbearing, and disagreeable if not kept in their place	80.0	48.3	18.2	.001
d) Laws which would force equal employment opportunities for both the natives and Europeans would not be fair to European employers	74.0	44.2	16.2	.001
e) The natives have their rights, but it is best to keep them in their own districts and schools and to prevent too much contact with Europeans	86.0	63.7	9.9	.01
f) The natives do not deserve the right to vote	64.0	41.3	9.5	.01
g) The natives will never have the intelligence and organizing ability to run a modern industrial society	42.0	23.2	8.7	.01
h) As the native will never properly absorb our civilization, the only solution is to let him develop along his own lines	68.0	46.3	8.6	.01
i) Manual labor seems to fit the native mentality better than more skilled and responsible work	88.0	68.9	8.0	.01
j) Seldom, if ever, is a native superior to most Europeans intellectually	72.0	52.2	7.1	.01
k) The natives tend to be overly emotional	66.0	46.5	7.1	.01
l) Because of his immaturity, the South African native is likely to be led into all sorts of mischief and should therefore be strictly controlled in his own best interests	92.0	75.6	6.9	.01
m) The granting of wide educational opportunities to natives is a dangerous thing	36.0	19.9	6.9	.01
n) Most natives are lazy and lack ambition	60.0	44.1	4.6	.05
o) There is something inherently primitive and uncivilized in the native, as shown in his music and extreme aggressiveness	86.0	72.1	4.4	.05
p) Due to the differences in innate endowment, the Bantu race will always be inferior to the white race	54.0	39.6	4.0	.05
q) Most of the natives are happy-go-lucky and irresponsible	70.0	60.0	1.9	0.20
r) In spite of what some claim, the natives do have a different and more pronounced body odor than Europeans	84.0	81.5	0.2	n.s.

* Percentage agreement calculated as in Table 2.

anti-Semitism (A-S scale), and a twelve-item measure of anti-Negro prejudice (N scale), together with numerous background questions.[10] The poll purported to be concerned with the effects of the mass media upon public opinion, and it seems largely due to this guise that the blatantly phrased prejudice statements caused no interview breakoffs.

Of greatest immediate interest is the striking similarity in these results with those of the South African investigation. First, the southern sample is considerably more anti-Negro than the northern sample but is *not* more authoritarian. Similar to the Afrikaner-English differences (Table 8), the southerners respond in the more prejudiced direction on each of the N-scale statements but are most unique in their extreme attitudes concerning excluding and discriminating against the Negro. That is, southerners and Northerners in the samples both share in large degree the lazy, primitive, happy-go-lucky, and bad-smelling stereotype of the Negro, but southerners far more than northerners wish to deny equal rights to the Negro in employment, housing, and voting. And yet there is no difference in the externalization potential for intolerance; the F-scale means of the two samples are almost identical.

Further similarities to the South African data support the contention that personality dynamics, such as authoritarianism, are not responsible for the sharp North-South divergence in attitudes toward the Negro. When age and education are partialed out,[11] the N and F scales correlate to a comparable degree in the two populations. Moreover, with age and education partialed out again, the N and A-S scales relate at equivalent levels in the two regional samples. In other words, the externalizing prejudiced

personality as tapped by the F and A-S scales does not account for any more of the anti-Negro variance in the southern sample than it does in the northern sample. This finding, combined with the previously mentioned fact that the two groups do not differ in their F-scale responses, indicates that externalization factors do not explain the heightened bigotry of the southerners. As with the South African results, we must turn to social variables in an effort to account for the regional discrepancy in attitudes toward the Negro.

All six of the sociocultural dimensions tested yield meaningful relationships with Negro prejudice in the southern sample: sex, church attendance, social mobility, political party identification, armed service, and education. These variables reflect southern culture in a manner similar to the social variables tested in the South African study. And as in South Africa, those southerners, who by their roles in the social structure can be anticipated to be conforming to the dictates of the culture, prove to be more prejudiced against Negroes than their counterparts. For example, females, the "carriers of culture," are significantly more anti-Negro than men in the southern sample but *not* in the northern sample.

Two other groups of southerners who manifest conforming behavior in other areas are also more intolerant of Negroes.[12] Respondents who have been to church within the week are significantly more anti-Negro than those who have not been within the month, and there is a tendency (though not statistically significant) for the upwardly mobile to be more anti-Negro than others in the non-manual occupational class. The latter result recalls the finding in the South

African study that students whose fathers are manual workers tend to be more anti-African (Table 6). In the northern sample, no such trends appear. Protestant church-goers in the North tend to be more tolerant of the Negro than Protestant non-attenders, and no relationship between upward mobility and attitudes toward Negroes is discernible. Conformity to northern norms—unlike conformity to southern or South African norms—is not associated with hostility for the black man.

In contrast to the conformers, southerners who evidence deviance from the mores in some area of social life tend to be *less* anti-Negro. Non-attenders of church furnish one example. Another example are respondents who explicitly identify themselves as political independents, which also represents a degree of deviance: they tend to be considerably more tolerant of the Negro than are southerners who consider themselves either Democrats or Republicans.[13] Again, no such discrepancy occurs in the northern population.

Downward mobility has been noted by other investigators to be positively related to intolerance in the North (3, 10), and this finding is replicated in the present northern data. But in the southern data a striking reversal occurs. The downwardly mobile in the South are much less anti-Negro than other manually employed respondents, though the two groups do not differ in authoritarianism. Perhaps in a culture that emphasizes status and family background, that makes a sharp distinction between "poor whites" and "respectable whites," and that cherishes its aristocratic traditions (4, 6, 8), the downwardly mobile southerner learns to reject much of his culture. And rejecting the culture's stress on tradition and status makes it easier to reject also the culture's dicta concerning the Negro.

Two groups of southerners—armed service veterans and the highly educated—are potential deviants from southern culture simply because their special experience and study have brought them into contact with other ways of life. And, as we might expect, we find that both veterans and college-educated southerners are considerably more tolerant of the Negro than non-veterans and the poorly educated. Veterans in both regions prove to be more authoritarian than non-veterans,[14] and, consistent with this, northern veterans are less tolerant of Negroes than northerners who had not served. Education is negatively related to N-scale scores in the northern sample, too, but significantly less than in the southern sample. Exposure to non-southern culture leads to deviance from the strict southern norms concerning the Negro; little wonder that southerners who have been out of the region for any considerable length of time are generally viewed as suspect by their neighbors upon return.

These consistent relationships with social factors in the southern data have been interpreted in terms of conformity and deviance from the narrowly prescribed mores of small-town southern life. Evidence for such an analysis comes from a final intrasouthern difference. Southern communities with high Negro population ratios (38 and 45 per cent) have significantly higher N-scale means than the other communities sampled in the South with low Negro ratios (10 and 18 per cent), though they are *not* different in authoritarianism or anti-Semitism. In southern areas with the most intensely anti-Negro norms, prejudice against the black southerner is greater, even though there is not a greater amount of externalizing personality potential for prejudice.

Though limited by the restricted samples employed, this evidence indicates that sociocultural factors—as in the South African sample—are indeed the key to the regional difference in attitudes toward the Negro. In spite of the marked contrast in samples and method between the two investigations, both the South African and the southern results underline the unique importance of social variables in prejudice that is sanctioned by the cultural norms.

IV. Summary and Conclusions

Finely interwoven personality and sociocultural variables together form the foundation upon which a broad and satisfactory theory of racial prejudice must be built. Neither set of factors can be neglected, but a heuristic separation between the relatively culture-free externalization factors and social factors aids analysis. The present paper uses this distinction to interpret prejudice data from two parts of the world with tense racial conflict—the Union of South Africa and the southern United States.

Externalization factors such as authoritarianism are associated with prejudice in both the South African and the southern samples at levels roughly comparable with other areas. Data from the South African students hint, however, that susceptibility to conform may be an unusually important psychological component of prejudice in regions where the cultural norms positively sanction intolerance. In addition, there is no indication in either of these samples that there is any more externalizing personality potential for prejudice in these areas

than in more tolerant parts of the globe.

The extensive racial prejudice of the South African and southern groups seems directly linked with the antiblack dictates of the two cultures. Sociocultural factors which reflect the mores consistently relate to prejudice—place of birth, political party preference, upward mobility, and ethnic-group membership in the South African data and sex, church attendance, social mobility, political party identification, armed service, and education in the southern data. The pattern is clear: conformity to South African or southern mores is associated with racial intolerance, while deviance from these mores is associated with racial tolerance.

Taken together with other published work, these limited results suggest a broad, cross-national hypothesis:

In areas with historically imbedded traditions of racial intolerance, externalizing personality factors underlying prejudice remain important, but sociocultural factors are unusually crucial and account for the heightened racial hostility.

Should future, more extensive, research support such a hypothesis, its implications for prejudice theory would be considerable. Regions or peoples with heightened prejudice against a particular outgroup would not necessarily be thought of as harboring more authoritarianism; the special conflict may reflect the operation of particular historical, cultural, and social factors. Such a prospect may be encouraging to many action programs—efforts which typically are more successful at changing a person's relation to his culture than they are at changing basic personality structure. Desegregation is a case in point. The success of the movement in the South does not depend—this hypothesis would contend

—on changing the deeply ingrained orientations of prejudice-prone personalities; rather, it rests on the effectiveness with which racial integration now going on in the South can restructure the mores to which so many culturally intolerant southerners conform.

A second implication of the hypothesis is that personality factors such as authoritarianism and susceptibility to conform cannot be overlooked in understanding bigotry even in parts of the world like the Union of South Africa and the southern United States. Most psychological approaches to prejudice, it has been noted, are concerned chiefly with the externalization function of attitudes. Perhaps, as the object-appraisal and social-adjustment functions of attitudes are studied in more detail, the direct personality concomitants of cultural pressures will be isolated and better understood.

NOTES

1. This article is a revision of a paper delivered in September, 1957, at the New York meetings of the American Psychological Association. The author wishes to express his deep appreciation to Professor Gordon W. Allport for his advice and encouragement and to Dr. Herbert Kelman, this issue's special editor, for his theoretical and editorial suggestions.

2. This investigation was conducted during 1956 when the author was an honorary research associate of the University of Natal's Institute for Social Research. The study would not have been possible without the aid of the institute's co-operative staff, particularly Professor Arnold Lloyd (now of the University of Witwatersrand), Dr. Hamish Dickie-Clark, Miss Len Kuyper, Dr. Jack Mann, and Professor Max Marwick (now of the University of Witwatersrand).

3. Comparisons between this one-third sample and the total student body of the University of Natal reveal that, in terms of sex, age, and field of concentration, the sample's distributions are quite similar to the student body at large.

4. All thirteen of the F-scale items are from the original California study on authoritarianism (1, pp. 255–57); the C scale is a new scale composed of both new items and adaptations from the conformity measures of Hoffman (15) and MacCrone (22); and fourteen of the A-scale items are new, while four are adaptations from the E scale (1, items 8, 31, and 34 on p. 105 and item 29 on p. 117).

5. Comparisons across diverse groups with varying forms of the F scale are difficult and tenuous at best. American college samples generally average slightly below the neutral point on F-scale statements, while the present South African sample averages slightly above the neutral point. This small difference can probably be accounted for by (a) the use of a disproportionate number of high-agreement items in the thirteen-item F scale employed with the South African sample and (b) the inclusion in the South African group of fields of concentration not usually included in tested American college groups (e.g., agriculture) whose members tend to score high on the F scale (due probably to social class factors).

6. Again, comparisons are difficult. Correlations between long-form F scales and ethnocentrism scales (measuring prejudice against a variety of out-groups) have

sometimes reached the sixties and even occasionally the seventies in American college samples (1, 2, 5). But correlations of the magnitude found in this study have been consistently reported when—as in this study—a short form F scale and a prejudice scale against a single out-group are related.

7. Authoritarianism can be controlled out in two ways. First, separate chi-square analyses of father's employment and anti-African attitudes were made for low and high F-scale halves. Second, the A- and F-scale scores were employed in an analysis of covariance that partialed out F scores. Both analyses indicate that father's employment is a significant correlate of anti-African attitudes even after authoritarianism is controlled out of the relationship.

8. Authoritarianism was controlled out by both of the analyses described in the previous footnote. With their F-scale differences corrected for, Afrikaners in the sample are still significantly more hostile to the African than the English students. The cultural determination of this ethnic-group difference is made apparent when we survey the attitudes of the English students toward the Indians of South Africa. In sharp contrast to their African attitudes, the English members of the sample are considerably more anti-Indian—one-fifth of them "wish someone would kill all of them."

9. This is true because the prejudiced personality is predisposed to disliking all socially recognized out-groups—Negroes, Jews, Catholics, etc.—and not just one. Being functionally necessary, prejudice generalizes to out-groups of all varieties (1, 2, 13).

10. There is considerable overlap in items used in the two investigations. Again, all ten of the F items are taken from the work of Adorno *et al.* (1); seven were used in South Africa (Table 2, items *a, b, c, f, h, i,* and *k*); and the others are items 1, 13, and 21 of p. 255 in *The Authoritarian Personality* (1). The A-S items are all from the California investigations, too (1, items 3, 4, 13, 15, 22, and 24 on pp. 68–69 and items 4 and 15 on p. 70). Save for the word substitutions of "white" for "European" and "Negro" for "native," all twelve N-scale items were used in the South African A scale (Table 8, items *b, c, d, e, f, j, k, m, n, o, q,* and *r*). That virtually the same prejudice and authoritarian statements can be successfully used in the Union of South Africa and in the northern and southern United States suggests that racial prejudice and its personality concomitants take extremely similar forms in many parts of the Western world.

11. This was not necessary in the South African data because the college sample is relatively homogeneous in terms of age and education. In heterogeneous, randomly drawn adult samples, however, age and education must be controlled, since both authoritarianism and prejudice are positively related to age and negatively related to education (2, 5, 16, 23).

12. The church attendance, social mobility, political party identification, and armed service findings reported here were all established with matched-pair analyses. This design made it possible to control the age, education, and sex variables out of these relationships. The detailed results are published elsewhere (29).

13. It might be thought that Republican party membership in the South constitutes deviance, too. Actually, the "solid South" is not that politically solid; three of the four southern communities polled have favored some Republican candidates in recent elections.

14. Presumably this increased authoritarianism of veterans is related to their service experience in authoritarian environments, though Christie (5) failed to note an increase in F scores of army recruits after six weeks of infantry basic training.

REFERENCES

1. Adorno, T. W., Frenkel-Brunswik, Else, Levinson, D. J., and Sanford, R. N. *The Authoritarian Personality*. New York: Harper & Bros., 1950.

2. Allport, G. W. *The Nature of Prejudice*. Cambridge, Mass.: Addison-Wesley Press, 1954.

3. Bettelheim, B., and Janowitz, M. *Dynamics of Prejudice*. New York: Harper & Bros., 1950.

4. Cash, W. *The Mind of the South*. New York: Knopf, 1941.

5. Christie, R. "Authoritarianism Re-examined." In R. Christie and M. Jahoda (eds.), *Studies in the Scope and Method of " The Authoritarian Personality,"* pp. 123–96. Glencoe, Ill.: Free Press, 1954.

6. Davis, A., Gardner, B., and Gardner, Mary. *Deep South*. Chicago: University of Chicago Press, 1941.

7. Deutsch, M., and Collins, M. *Interracial Housing*. Minneapolis: University of Minnesota Press, 1951.

8. Dollard, J. *Caste and Class in a Southern Town*. New Haven, Conn.: Yale University Press, 1937.

9. Dollard, J., Doob, L., Miller, N., Mowrer, O., and Sears, R. *Frustration and Aggression*. New Haven, Conn.: Yale University Press, 1939.

10. Greenblum, J., and Pearlin, L. "Vertical Mobility and Prejudice: A Sociopsychological Analysis." In R. Bendix and S. Lipset (eds.), *Class, Status, and Power*, pp. 480–91. Glencoe, Ill.: Free Press, 1953.

11. Harding, J., and Hogrefe, R. "Attitudes of White Department Store Employees toward Negro Co-workers," *Journal of Social Issues*, VIII, No. 1 (1952), 18–28.

12. Harris, D. B., Gough, H. G., and Martin, W. E. "Children's Ethnic Attitudes. II. Relationship to Parental Beliefs concerning Child Training," *Child Development*, XXI (1950), 169–81.

13. Hartley, E. L. *Problems in Prejudice*. New York: Kings Crown Press, 1946.

14. Hellmann, Ellen (ed.). *Handbook on Race Relations in South Africa*. Cape Town, South Africa: Oxford University Press, 1949.

15. Hoffman, M. L. "Some Psychodynamic Factors in Compulsive Conformity," *Journal of Abnormal and Social Psychology*, XLVIII (1953), 383–93.

16. Hyman, H. H., and Sheatsley, P. B. "Attitudes toward Desegregation," *Scientific American*, CXCV (1956), 35–39.

17. Jones, E. "City Limits." In D. Shoemaker (ed.), *With All Deliberate Speed*, pp. 71–87 New York: Harper & Bros., 1957.

18. Kutner, B., Wilkins, Carol, and Yarrow, Penny. "Verbal Attitudes and Overt Behavior Involving Racial Prejudice," *Journal of Abnormal and Social Psychology*, XLVII (1952), 649–52.

19. La Piere, R. T. "Attitudes versus Actions," *Social Forces*, XIII (1934), 230–37.

20. McLean, Helen V. "Psychodynamic Factors in Racial Relations," *Annals of the American Academy of Political and Social Science*, CCXLIV (1946), 159–66.

21. MacCrone, I. D. *Race Attitudes in South Africa*. London: Oxford University Press, 1937.

22. ———. "Ethnocentric Ideology and Ethnocentrism," *Proceedings of the South African Psychological Association*, IV (1953), 21–24.

23. MacKinnon, W. J., and Centers, R. "Authoritarianism and Urban Stratification," *American Journal of Sociology*, XLI (1956), 610–20.

24. Malherbe, E. G. *Race Attitudes and Education*. Johannesburg, South Africa: Institute of Race Relations, 1946.

25. Milton, O. "Presidential Choice and Performance on a Scale of Authoritarianism," *American Psychologist*, VII (1952), 597–98.

26. Minard, R. D. "Race Relations in the Pocahontas Coal Field," *Journal of Social Issues*, VIII, No. 1 (1952), 29–44.

27. Myrdal, G. *An American Dilemma*. New York: Harper & Bros., 1944.

28. Pettigrew, T. F. "Desegregation and Its Chances for Success: Northern and Southern Views," *Social Forces*, XXXV (1957), 339–44.

29. ———. "Regional Differences in Anti-Negro Prejudice" (manuscript presently submitted for publication).

30. Prothro, E. T. "Ethnocentrism and Anti-Negro Attitudes in the Deep South," *Journal of Abnormal and Social Psychology*, XLVII (1952), 105–8.

31. Roper, E. "United States Anti-Semites," *Fortune*, XXXIII (1946), 257–60.

32. ———. "United States Anti-Semites," *Fortune*, XXXVI (1947), 5–10.

33. Rose, A. M. "Intergroup Relations vs. Prejudice: Pertinent Theory for the Study of Social Change," *Social Problems*, IV (1956), 173–76.

34. Saenger, G., and Gilbert, Emily. "Customer Reactions to the Integration of Negro Sales Personnel," *International Journal of Opinion and Attitude Research*, IV (1950), 57–76.

35. Samelson, Babette. "The Patterning of Attitudes and Beliefs Regarding the American Negro: An Analysis of Public Opinion." Unpublished doctoral dissertation, Radcliffe College, 1945.

36. Sims, V. M., and Patrick, J. R. "Attitude towards the Negro of Northern and Southern College Students," *Journal of Social Psychology*, VII (1936), 192–204.

37. Smith, C. U., and Prothro, J. W. "Ethnic Differences in Authoritarian Personality," *Social Forces*, XXXV (1957), 334–38.

38. Smith, M. B., Bruner, J. S., and White, R. W. *Opinions and Personality*. New York: John Wiley & Sons, 1956.

39. Stouffer, S. A., Suchman, E. A., DeVinney, L. C., Star, Shirley A., and Williams, R. M., Jr. *The American Soldier: Adjustment during Army Life*. ("Studies in Social Psychology in World War II," Vol. I.) Princeton: Princeton University Press, 1949.

40. Wilner, D. M., Walkley, R. P., and Cook, S. W. "Residential Proximity and Intergroup Relations in Public Housing Projects," *Journal of Social Issues*, VIII, No. 1 (1952), 45–69.

THE EFFECT OF PUBLIC POLICY IN HOUSING PROJECTS UPON INTERRACIAL ATTITUDES

- ## Morton Deutsch and Mary Evans Collins

... The strength of the social and psychological barriers to democratic race relations as well as the pervasiveness of discrimination and prejudice suggests that a reduction in prejudices will require strong influences.

The social scientist is rarely in the position where he, himself, has the opportunity to create these influences. He has neither the political power nor the financial resources to produce of his own accord a major social experiment. Nevertheless, social "experiments" are going on all the time; or, perhaps more accurately, major attempts at producing social and psychological changes of one sort or another are a commonplace.

With the aid of scientific controls, the social scientist may occasionally be able to convert an attempt at social change into a social experiment. This is the purpose of our study. *We wish to investigate the effects upon prejudice of what is perhaps one of the most important "social experiments" in the area of race relations—the establishment of publicly supported non-segregated interracial housing projects.* Unfortunately, as in most "social experiments," social scientists did not participate in the design of the "experiment." The prob-

lem we face, then, is to convert *ex post facto*, a "social change" into a scientific "social experiment."

o   o   o

The Research Problem

To orient ourselves to the various factors which might influence race relations in public housing projects and to determine the social urgencies and vital issues, we interviewed officials with experience in interracial housing throughout the country. From our survey of expert opinion and from other social-science knowledge, it was apparent that one of the most crucial influences affecting race relations in housing communities is the *occupancy pattern*. To determine the impact of different occupancy patterns, we decided to do a comparative study of race relations in two types of housing projects: the *integrated interracial* project (families are assigned to apartments without consideration of race) and the *segregated biracial* project (Negro and white families live in the same project but are assigned to different buildings or to different parts of the project).

We obtained the cooperation of two large housing authorities[1] in neighboring cities, Newark and New York, which differ in policy with respect to the type of occupancy pattern in interracial public housing projects. In Newark, the projects, which house both Negro and white families, have a segregated occupancy

Above selection reprinted from: *Readings in Social Psychology*, by E. Maccoby, T. Newcomb, and E. Hartley, "The Effect of Public Policy in Housing Upon Interracial Attitudes," an adaptation from *Interracial Housing* by Morton Deutsch and Mary Evans Collins. Copyright 1951 by the University of Minnesota. Deletions have been made by the editor in the interest of brevity.

pattern; in New York the pattern is integrated. In each city two projects were selected for study. Realizing that the ratio of Negro to white families might be an important influence on race relations, we selected projects in the two cities that had approximately the same ratios. In one project in each of the two cities, there are about 70 Negro families to 30 white families; in the other project in Newark the ratio is 50–50, while the second project in New York has 60 white to every 40 Negro families.

Of course, other factors in addition to the ratio of Negro to white families may influence race relations. Fortunately the projects we were comparing are similar in many relevant respects: they all are low-income projects containing families who had to meet similar eligibility requirements in order to move in; they were all built at about the same time, just before World War II, the neighborhoods surrounding the various projects are much alike—all of them are predominantly Negro neighborhoods, and one of the projects in each city is located in a neighborhood that is considerably deteriorated and characterized by much delinquency; the staffs in each of the four projects include both Negro and white personnel; the project managers have all had considerable experience in interracial public housing projects; etc. The projects differ somewhat, as one would expect, e.g., one New York project is larger and the other smaller than the corresponding projects with similar racial ratios in Newark. Also, it should be indicated that population differences exist that act to enhance some of the results reported below. However, statistical analysis reveals that these population differences are by no means sufficient to "explain away" the differences we

attribute to the effects of occupancy pattern.

The data for this study were collected primarily through systematic interviewing of white housewives. The home is, after all, largely the domain of the woman. She spends more time in it than anyone else; she is, by and large, the initiator of activities and contacts that develop directly out of the home. Whether or not she "wears the pants in the family," she is the key person in activities centered about the place of residence.

The funds at our disposal made it unfeasible to interview both Negro and white housewives in equal proportion. We decided to interview more white housewives as a result of our conviction that prejudiced interracial attitudes are more socially crucial among whites than among Negroes, since the practices of segregation and discrimination are enforced by the white and not by the Negro segment of the population.

We interviewed approximately 100 white and 25 Negro housewives in each of the four projects. In addition, a total of 24 Negro and white adolescent boys and girls were interviewed in one project in each of the two cities. The interviewees were selected by a random procedure.

The Interview

The interview was long and intensive; on the average, it lasted about one and a quarter hours. Some interviews ran over two hours. In the course of the interview, data were obtained about five major areas:

1. *The Attitudes of the Housewife toward Living in the Project:* What she liked most and least about the project; her feelings about public housing, the neighborhood,

the apartment, etc.; the anticipations she had before moving into the project; her future plans; and her feeling toward people in the project.

2. *Attitudes toward Negroes:*[2] A series of questions attempted to uncover the attitudes of the housewife toward Negroes, her feelings about them, her "knowledge" and beliefs about them, and her feelings about living in an interracial project.

3. *The Amount and Intimacy of Contact with Other Women in the Project:* Questions were asked about neighborly contacts (such as visiting, shopping together, minding children, going to movies together), friendships, how one gets to know people, etc. Information was obtained about the types of contacts with Negro women.

4. *The Social Supports for Attitudes:* The housewife was asked, for example, to tell how her relatives, friends, people in the project, management staff, etc., would react to her being friendly with Negro people.

5. *The Characteristics of the Housewife:* A miscellaneous assortment of questions was asked about the housewife: her age, number of children, her activities, her education, her religion, her interests, etc., to obtain information about the comparability of the populations in the projects we were studying.

The interview, for the most part, encouraged the respondent to answer freely in her own words rather than restricting her to "yes" or "no" answers. Interviewing was done in the respondent's home.

Research Results

In an *ex post facto* experiment such as we are here reporting, there is always

need to be cautious in making causal inferences. One must inevitably face the critical question, "Which came first?" That is, did the attitudinal differences between the housewives in the integrated interracial and the segregated bi-racial projects exist prior to their residence in public housing and perhaps *cause* them to move into the one or the other type project? Or did the differences in attitudes *result* from their living in the different types of projects? In the book from which this article is adapted and condensed considerable indirect evidence is brought to bear upon these questions. This evidence for which we do not have space here, leads us to believe that the differences primarily reflect the effects of the different occupancy patterns. The evidence is of several sorts: (1) an examination of the socio-psychological situation of prospective tenants; (2) an examination of refusal rates and voluntary move-outs; (3) an examination of the housewives' prior interracial experiences; (4) the reports of the housewives about their prior attitudes; (5) comparison of housewives who did or did not know about the nature of the occupancy pattern before they made their applications; (6) a comparison of housewives in the different projects who were equated for education, religion, and political beliefs. All these types of evidence give credence to the interpretation that the occupancy pattern had causal efficacy.

Getting to Know Each Other

As our knowledge about the development of prejudice has increased, it has become more and more evident that prejudice rarely originates in personal experiences with the members of a minority group. We know that many people who are extremely prejudiced against Negroes or Jews have never known a Negro or a Jew.

Further, we know that the nature of prejudice is such that it results in a reduction of intimate, equal-status contacts with the objects of prejudice. Prejudices combine with social custom to prevent the bigot from having the types of experiences, with Negro people, for example, which would destroy his prejudices. Hence, the main source of information about Negroes comes to be the "experiences," beliefs, and feelings of other prejudiced members of his own group. As a consequence, members of the prejudiced group, through contact with each other, tend mutually to confirm and support one another's prejudices. A vicious circle or a "socially shared autism"[3] is established whereby, without personal experience with members of a minority group, contact with the prevailing attitude toward them provides the "experience" to support a prejudice.

Perhaps the first problem that faces the person who wishes to change the attitudes of a prejudiced individual is that of breaking through this vicious circle so as to bring to bear upon the bigoted the experiences necessary to a change in attitudes. Something must be done to "prevent" the prejudiced person from selectively avoiding the experiences which might disrupt his prejudices. One method of accomplishing this objective would be to "compel" him to get to know Negro people in equal-status contacts of a sufficiently intimate and extended nature to resist perceptual or memorial distortion. This latter qualification must be inserted because we know that attitudes tend to select and distort experiences so as to maintain themselves. However, persistent, intense experiences

that are repeated are likely to survive attitudinal distortion, if only because of the individual's need to accept the reality of his own senses and experiences.[4]

One of the basic hypotheses of the study is that *the greater physical and functional proximity of Negro and white families in the integrated interracial projects will result in more frequent and more intimate contacts between Negroes and whites in these projects as contrasted with the segregated bi-racial projects.* Let us consult the data.

In the interview, we asked the housewife to indicate whether she thought that a person who moved into the project would "be likely to get to know any colored people in the project." The differences in responses of the housewives in the two types of projects are striking. More than 95 percent of the women in each of the two integrated projects assert that a person will get to know some Negro people in the project; the few dissenters voice the opinion that "it depends upon you." In contrast, only a minority (30 percent in one and 21 percent in the other) of the housewives in the segregated bi-racial projects feel that there is any chance of getting to know Negro people; the majority are quite convinced that no such likelihood exists.

Clearly, then, the opportunity to get to know Negro people is considerably greater in the integrated than in the segregated project. Table 1 helps to explain why there is such a striking difference in this respect between the two types of projects. The most frequently mentioned places of contact with Negro people for white residents in the integrated projects are the buildings in which they live, laundry facilities located in or near their buildings, or outside on benches. (People in the projects, for the most part, during the warm season customarily sit on benches located near their buildings.) It seems evident that the major source of Negro–white contact—contacts that arise from living in the same building—is not available to residents of a segregated bi-racial project.

Several of our questions in the interview of the housewives had the purpose of finding how intimate the contacts were with Negro women in the two types of projects. Only 3 percent of the housewives in each of the two segregated projects report "knowing any Negro people in the project pretty well—well enough to call them by their first names;" in contrast 77 percent of the housewives in one and 49 percent in the other integrated project report having at least this degree of intimacy. The tenants were also asked to tell us the five people in the project they know best. Table 2 indicates the percentage of persons "known best" who are Negro. None of the women in the segregated projects include Negro people among those they know best in the project. In contrast, 27 percent of the women

in Koaltown and 62 percent in Sacktown indicate that at least one of the women they know best is Negro.

Similar differences obtain in "neighborly" activities, such as *visiting back and forth; helping one another out*, for example, with shopping or taking care of the children or when somebody is sick; *informal club activities*, such as "card" clubs, sewing or ironing clubs; and going out together, such as going to the movies, shopping together, or going "downtown" together. Only a very small percentage (1 percent and 4 percent) of white housewives in the segregated projects engage in any such activities with Negro women; in the integrated projects many of the white women (39 percent and 72 percent in the two projects, respectively) engage in such activities with their Negro neighbors.

To sum up, the data we have presented so far have demonstrated that the likelihood of white tenants getting to know Negro people and of having intimate social relationships with them is

Table 1

Percentages of Housewives Indicating Their Most Likely Contacts with Negro People

MEETING PLACE	Integrated interracial projects		Segregated bi-racial projects	
	Koaltown*	Sacktown*	Bakerville*	Frankville*
As neighbors in the building	60	53	0	0
Through laundry facilities located in or near building	13	17	0	0
Outside on benches	46	64	7	21
In office, etc.	2	1	7	17
At tenant meetings	2	17	28	28
Shopping in stores, in the streets around project	12	13	81	60
Through the children's schools	1	3	14	0
Total cases†	102	86	43	42

* The project names are pseudonyms.

† Only the people who responded "yes" or "uncertain" to the question of getting to know Negro people are included. The percentage figures add up to more than 100 because many people named more than one place.

Table 2

Percentage of Persons Known Best Who Are Negro

PERCENTAGE OF NEGROES AMONG PEOPLE "KNOWN BEST"	Integrated interracial projects		Segregated bi-racial projects	
	Koaltown	*Sacktown*	*Bakerville*	*Frankville*
0	73	38	100	100
20–39	19	18	0	0
40–59	6	23	0	0
60 or over	2	21	0	0
Total cases	96	84	99	98

considerably less in the segregated than in the integrated projects. Our interviews with Negro housewives and with children of both races give the same results. Further, when we compare people in the two types of projects of the same religion or of similar educational backgrounds, or with similar political attitudes (or people who are similar in all three respects—religion, education, and political attitudes) it is still strikingly clear that the occupancy pattern markedly affects interracial contact. . . . The integrated project is, thus, considerably more successful in stimulating unprejudiced behavior toward Negroes among the white people in the project. Many more white people in the integrated than in the segregated projects violate, in actual behavior, the social prejudices and social customs which have the consequence of preventing intimate, equal-status contacts between Negroes and whites. In effect, living in the integrated projects produces a *behavioral* change with respect to race relations for many of the white people.

Social Standards for Behavior with People of the Other Race

A housing project may be seen as composed of many informal groups organized around various types of goals. These groups are intricately connected through the overlapping memberships of individuals within each group. Within this complex network it is likely that group standards or social norms will develop with regard to issues which are collectively important to the interconnected groups. In a society where prejudice is commonplace and where interracial association is a possibility, race relations will be such an issue. It is our hypothesis that *the social norms in the integrated projects will be more favorable to friendly interracial relations than will the corresponding social norms in the segregated projects.*

There are several reasons for advancing the foregoing hypothesis. First of all, it has long been recognized that people tend to behave as they are expected to behave. The expectations of others in a social situation, particularly if these others are important to the individual, help to define what is the appropriate behavior. There is little doubt that a public housing authority looms importantly in the life of residents in public housing projects, since it controls their only means of obtaining decent housing at a low rental. Thus, to the people who live in the projects, the action of a housing authority in establishing a policy of integration or of segregation is not likely to be without significance. Further, the policy of integration or segregation is an "official" decision implicitly carrying public sanction, and as such it may set up standards for what one "should" or "should not" do. The policy of segregation may be seen as implying the notion that Negroes and whites should be kept apart; the policy of integration, that race should *not* be a criterion for distinguishing among tenants.

In addition to the direct psychological impact of official policy decision in shaping social norms, the policy decision has indirect effects upon social norms through the physical environment that it creates for race relations. In the previous section, we have seen how interracial contact is promoted or hindered by the physical nature of the occupancy pattern. The differences in interracial behavior resulting from the different occupancy patterns are likely to have consequences for the social norms which emerge in the projects. Thus, a housewife in the integrated projects is more likely to have friendly relations with Negroes, as well as to see other housewives as having similar relations. These differences combined with the inclination to moralize one's own behavior (to rationalize the status quo) and with the tendency to conform to and to accept as "right" the behavior of one's peers would work in the direction of producing more favorable social norms in the integrated projects. Another factor working in the same direction would be the comparatively greater number of cooperative relationships between Negroes and whites in the integrated projects.

Several questions were designed to determine whether and to what extent the decision with respect to occupancy pattern by a public authority and the fact of occupancy pattern do establish a standard for interracial conduct. Such a standard, we felt, would be reflected in the housewife's description of how "the other people in the project would react if she were friendly with Negro people" and in her answer to questions about whether it would influence her reputation in the project if she had much to do with the colored people.

The evidence strongly indicates that the housewife in the integrated project expects more approval than disapproval from others in the project if she is friendly with the Negro people. She thinks it is better rather than not better for her "to have much to do with the colored people." In contrast, the housewife in the segregated project expects to be socially ostracized by the other white women if she is friendly with the Negro people, and asserts that it is better not to have much to do with them. Thus, one woman in a segregated project said: "They'd think you're crazy if you had a colored woman visit you in your home. They'd stare at you and there'd be a lot of talk." Another said, "I used to be good friends with a colored woman who worked with me at the factory before I moved here. She lives in the other side of the project but I never have her over to my side of the project—it just isn't done. Occasionally, I go over and visit her."

Perhaps the most striking evidence as to the effects of occupancy pattern in creating guides for behavior comes from interviews with the children. The children in Lakerville (a segregated project) go to unsegregated elementary schools, where Negro and white children mix freely. As a consequence of meeting in the schools, they all have at least speaking acquaintances with members of the other race. Many of them play games together and belong to the same clubs. Yet in no single instance among the children interviewed in Bakerville do they engage in such activities with children of the other race in the project. The children in Bakerville implicitly understand that different standards with respect to interracial association exist in the school and in the housing project. In contrast, the children in Sacktown (an integrated project) play together at the project as well as in the school, visiting in each other's homes freely.

Some examples will illustrate the effects of social norms on children in Bakerville (a segregated bi-racial project):

One twelve-year-old white girl stated that she had made friends with a Negro girl at camp and she thought the girl was very nice. The girl lived in the project, but they never saw each other.

A Negro girl who feels that she is friendly with a number of white children stated, " I play with them at school and go to the movies with them. In the project, I have nothing to do with them."

Thus, it is clear that the occupancy pattern brings along with it a frame of reference which helps to establish expectations and values with respect to race relations within the project. Since this frame of reference is *shared* by other housewives with whom one is interacting, it can be said that a consequence of moving into one or another project is that the housewife becomes exposed to one rather than another social norm with respect to being friendly with the Negro people in the project. It is apparent that the social norm that one is exposed to as a result of moving into an integrated project is more likely to favor friendly interracial association than the norm of the segregated project; the latter is more likely to favor avoidance (with the more or less inevitable connotation in American society that interracial association brings trouble or that it is socially degrading).

The fact that the tenants in the various projects are exposed to "shared frames of reference," as Newcomb[5] calls them, rather than merely their isolated individual experiences, is a matter of some significance. Lewin and Grabbe have pointed out that "only by anchoring his own conduct in something as large, substantial, and superindividual as the culture of the group can the individual stabilize his new beliefs sufficiently to keep them immune from day-by-day fluctuations of moods and influences to which he, as an individual, is subject."[6] This is why attempts to change significant social attitudes must be directed not only at the individual but also at the social institutions and social norms which determine the individual's values and which help to induce the goals for which he strives.

The Effects upon Interracial Attitudes

So far, the results have indicated that the integrated occupancy pattern creates more opportunities for close contact with members from the other race, an atmosphere more favorable to friendly interracial associations, and friendlier interracial relations.

Let us now make the assumption that the tenants who moved into the two types of projects had, like most people of similar education and circumstance, rather prejudiced attitudes toward Negroes. If this were the case, one would expect many of the tenants in the integrated projects through their experiences and relationships with Negro neighbors, to shift their attitudes in a more favorable direction; few of the tenants in the segregated projects could be expected to change. That is to say, we hypothesize that *the differences between the two types of projects with respect to interracial contacts and social norms which have already been indicated would result in attitudinal differences between the residents in the two types of projects.* These attitudinal differences would be most directly reflected in attitudes toward the Negro people in the project; they might be generalized somewhat to include Negro people in general, and perhaps might even extend to other minority groups.

In our data we have many different indicators of attitudes toward the Negro people in the project; some of the measures of interracial association and interracial contact may be so considered. All give the same results: the attitudes of the housewives in the integrated projects are considerably less prejudiced than those of the women in the segregated bi-racial projects. Almost three times as many women in the segregated projects (36 percent and 31 percent as compared with 13 percent and 10 percent) in describing the Negro people spontaneously use words like "aggressive," "dangerous," "trouble-makers." There are approximately *two* housewives who want to be friendly *to every one* who wishes to avoid contact with Negroes in the integrated projects; in the segregated developments there is approximately only *one* who wishes to be friendly to *every ten* who wish to avoid relationships.

We also obtained many different indicators about attitudes toward *Negro people in general:* reactions to social-distance questions, acceptance of stereotypes about Negroes, interviewer ratings, reports of the housewives about their own attitudinal change, etc. Again, all provide the same result. The attitudes of the housewives in the integrated projects are

considerably more favorable than those of the women in the segregated developments. We can infer that the *changes* in attitudes toward Negroes in general among the women in the integrated projects have been considerable. In other words, many of the women in this type of development have not only come to respect and like the Negro people with whom they have associated, but they have also changed their notions about Negroes in general. Their experiences in the project with Negro people have become partially *generalized*, so that they now have more favorable attitudes toward Negroes as a group.

Perhaps the most striking data come from the reports of the housewives themselves about their own attitude changes toward Negroes in general.[7] We asked the housewives a series of questions which included: "Can you remember what you thought colored people were like before you moved into the project?" "How much have your ideas about colored people changed since you have lived in the project?" (If some change occurred) "In what ways have they changed?" And, "What do you think made you change your ideas?"

Results which cannot be presented in full here indicate that the *net gain* (percent of housewives reporting favorable changes minus percent reporting unfavorable changes) for the two integrated projects among housewives who indicated that they were initially highly prejudiced is 71 percent and 78 percent; for the housewives reporting moderate prejudice initially, it is 46 percent and 61 percent; for housewives reporting favorable initial attitudes it is 13 percent and 28 percent. In the two segregated projects, the corresponding net gains are much smaller: for those reporting much initial prejudice it is 26 percent and 19 percent; for those indicating moderate initial prejudice, it is 18 percent and 2 percent; for those reporting that they were originally unprejudiced, there is a net gain of 15 percent in one and a *net loss* of 18 percent in the other segregated project.

The interview material provides dramatic illustration of the nature of the attitudinal changes that occurred among many of the housewives in the integrated projects. Thus one woman, when asked to tell how she felt about living in the project, said: "I started to cry when my husband told me we were coming to live here. I cried for three weeks. . . . I didn't want to come and live here where there are so many colored people. I didn't want to bring my children up with colored children, but we had to come; there was no place else to go. . . . Well, all that's changed. I've really come to like it. I see they're just as human as we are. They have nice apartments; they keep their children clean, and they're very friendly. I've come to like them a great deal. I'm no longer scared of them. . . . I'd just as soon live near a colored person as a white; it makes no difference to me."

Another woman put it quaintly: "I thought I was moving into the heart of Africa. . . . I had always heard things about how they were . . . they were dirty, drink a lot . . . were like savages. Living with them my ideas have changed altogether. They're just people . . . they're not any different."

Another one said: "I was prejudiced when I moved in here but not any more. . . . I find there is no such thing as 'my kind.' . . . I was under the impression that every colored man that looked at you wanted to rape you or was going to

pull out a razor. . . . I don't feel that way any more. . . . I know the people. I have been in their homes . . . been to church with them. . . . I know they're not dirty. My doctor is colored . . . my dentist is colored. He's a surgeon and he's wonderful."

In contrast with the above, the following remarks express typical findings in the segregated projects: "I don't have anything to do with the colored people . . . they don't bother me . . . I don't mingle with them. I guess I don't like them because they're colored . . . the Bible says 'God created them equal' so I guess they're equal, but I don't like them. I don't like living so close to them. I think they ought to be in separate projects. Let them live their lives and let us live ours. . . . My ideas haven't changed any since I've lived here. . . . They're colored and I'm white. They don't like us and we don't like them."

Conclusions

Our results provide considerable evidence to discredit a notion that has characterized much of social-science thinking in the field of race relations: the notion originating with William S. Sumner that "stateways cannot change folkways." The implication of our study is that official policy, executed without equivocation, can result in large changes in behavior and attitudes despite initial resistance to that policy. Thus, it is clear from our data that, although most of the white housewives in the integrated projects we studied did not, upon moving into the projects, like the idea of living in the same buildings with Negro families (and certainly the community as a whole did not favor it), a considerable change has taken place in their beliefs and feelings as well as in their behavior. *It is evident that from the point of view of reducing prejudice and of creating harmonious democratic intergroup relations, the net gain resulting from the integrated projects is considerable; from the same point of view, the gain created by the segregated biracial projects is slight.*

Further, our results are consistent with the growing body of evidence about the effects of equal-status contacts, under certain conditions, upon prejudiced attitudes. Studies by Allport and Kramer,[8] by Brophy,[9] by the Information and Education Division of the U. S. War Department,[10] by Mackenzie,[11] among others, all support the notion that prejudices are likely to be diminished when prejudiced persons are brought into situations which compel contacts between them and the objects of prejudice, provided:

(*a*) that the behavior of the objects of prejudice is such as not to conform with the beliefs of the prejudiced. That is, the Negroes with whom the prejudiced person has contact are not "lazy," "ignorant," "delinquent," etc.

(*b*) that the intimacy and amount of contact with objects of prejudice not conforming to the stereotypes of the prejudiced are such as to result in experiences which are sufficiently compelling to resist marked perceptual and memorial distortion.

(*c*) that the contact takes place under conditions which make the nonconforming behavior seem relevant to the basis on which the objects of prejudice are grouped together. Thus, if a Negro attendant is seen to be clean and honest, there may be little effect on stereotypes if the perception of cleanliness and honesty is corrected primarily with the requirements of the situation, with the classification of the individual as an attendant rather than as a Negro or Negro attendant.[12]

(*d*) that the prejudiced person has values or is exposed to social influences (e.g., democratic values or the social influences emanating from a policy of an official, public body) which would strongly conflict with the unabashed retention of unrationalized prejudices.

In addition, if the contact situation is such that it encourages the development of new sentiments to replace prejudiced sentiments either as a result of the experience of cooperative activity with the objects of prejudice or as a result of the internalization of the social norms of an unprejudiced group, the reduction of prejudiced sentiments will be much facilitated.

NOTES

1. We wish to express gratitude to both the Newark and New York Housing Authorities for their constructive cooperation throughout the study. Without their objectivity and their concern with the broadening of knowledge this study would not have been possible.

2. Essentially the same questions were asked of the Negro housewives but, of course, we asked them about white people.

3. Gardner Murphy has originated the term "socially shared autism" to refer to phenomena such as these in which members of a social group develop considerable confidence in their belief about something with which they no longer have contact, as a consequence of their mutual reinforcement of each other's beliefs. See his *Personality: A Biosocial Approach to Origin and Structure* (Harper & Bros. 1947).

4. It is important to emphasize the strength of the motivation to accept as real one's perception and experiences. If they were not customarily accepted, the individual would be in a continuous state of insecurity and indecision.

5. T. M. Newcomb, *Social Psychology* (New York: Dryden Press, 1950).

6. K. Lewin and P. Grabbe, "Conduct, Knowledge, and the Acceptance of New Values," *Journal of Social Issues*, I (1945), 53–64.

7. To be sure, such reports must always be evaluated with caution because of distorting effects in recall. We have examined the data to see if differential distortion between the two types of project has occurred and could find no such indications.

8. G. W. Allport and B. M. Kramer, "Some Roots of Prejudice," *Journal of Psychology*, XXII (1946), 9–39.

9. I. N. Brophy, "The Luxury of Anti-Negro Prejudice," *Public Opinion Quarterly*, IX (1946), 456–466.

10. Information and Education Division, U.S. War Department, "Opinions about Negro Infantry Platoons in White Companies of Seven Divisions," pp. 502–506 in this book.

11. B. K. Mackenzie, "The Importance of Contact in Determining Attitudes toward Negroes," *Journal of Abnormal and Social Psychology*, XLIII (1948), 417–441.

12. Just as there is likely to be little effect upon prejudiced beliefs if "good" behavior upon the part of the objects of prejudice is seen to result from the requirements of the situation rather than from the person or from the person's membership in a minority group, so too, one can expect a reduction in prejudice if "bad" behavior upon their part comes to be seen as emanating from their circumstances rather than from their personality or minority-group membership. This is why changes in theories of behavior (from a genetic to an environmental emphasis) may have a subtle influence even upon prejudice.

[EXCERPTS FROM] THE MORAL BASIS OF A BACKWARD SOCIETY

- Edward C. Banfield

[The excerpt which follows is from Banfield, Edward, *The Moral Basis of a Backward Society*, a study of Montegrano, a small community of farmers and laborers in southern Italy. Montegrano is characterized by severe poverty and by lack of political organization. In the selection which follows, Professor Banfield asks himself the question, "What accounts for the political incapacity of the village?" To this question six answers are given.]

1. Most people in Montegrano are desperately poor. Many have nothing to eat but bread, and not enough of that. Even the well-to-do are poor by American standards. Such a town cannot support a newspaper or the kinds of activity which a newspaper would report. The peasant must go to his fields at dawn and he must work there until it is dark. The blacksmith must be at his forge when the peasant passes on his way to his fields. There is no time for political life in a society so poor.

2. The peasant is as ignorant as his donkey and the artisan is hardly less so. One-third of the men and two-thirds of the women of Montegrano cannot read or write. Some peasants have never been beyond the next village, four miles away. People so ignorant can have no notion of

Above selection reprinted with permission of The Macmillan Company from *The Moral Basis of a Backward Society* by Edward C. Banfield, The Free Press, a Corporation, 1958. Deletions and condensations have been made by the editor in the interest of brevity.

what it is possible to accomplish politically and they cannot make meaningful choices among parties and candidates. Indeed, such things do not enter into their world at all. The peasants, Carlo Levi wrote, "were not Fascists, just as they would never have been Conservatives or Socialists, or anything else. Such matters had nothing to do with them; they belonged to another world and they saw no sense in them. What had the peasants to do with Power, Government and the State? The State, whatever form it might take, meant 'the fellows in Rome.'"[1]

3. Political behavior reflects class interests and antagonisms. The upper class gives the village no leadership because it lives by exploiting the peasant and can do so only by keeping him in poverty and ignorance.[2] The lower class hates the upper and seeks for revenge upon it. Collaboration between the classes is impossible, although nothing can be done without it.

4. Workers who have a plot of land, however small, want to maintain the *status quo*. On the other hand, those who are landless and must depend upon a large employer see that security is to be had by collective action, the only effective vehicle of which is the Communist Party. Thus Montegrano peasants, most of whom have a bit of land, are conservative or politically indifferent, whereas those of nearby Basso, who are mostly laborers on large estates, are Communists. Differences in political

behavior are to be accounted for by the circumstances of land tenure.

5. Centuries of oppression have left the peasant with a pathological distrust of the state and all authority. "To the peasants," Carlo Levi writes, "the State is more distant than heaven and far more of a scourge, because it is always against them."[3]

6. The southern Italian is a despairing fatalist. He believes that the situation is hopeless and that the only sensible course is to accept patiently and resignedly the catastrophes that are in store.[4]

These theories have obvious implications for action. If the political incapacity of the southern town is due to poverty, then increasing incomes will increase political capacity. If it is due to ignorance, then increasing the level of education will increase political capacity. If it is due to a pathological distrust of the state, then a sufficiently long experience with a welfare state will overcome that distrust. Similarly, the solution may be, as Levi advises, the suppression of the upper class and the substitution for it of something better; large-scale undertakings (like *La Cassa per il Mezzogiorno*, a government corporation for resource development in the south) to convince the southerner that all is not hopeless, or perhaps some combination of these.

There is an element of truth in each of the theories, but none of them is fully consistent with the facts that have to be taken into account, and one could not on the basis of any of them—or of all of them together—predict how the people of Montegrano would behave in a concrete situation.

The peasant's poverty is appalling to be sure, but it does not prevent him from contributing a few days of labor now and then to some community undertaking like repairing the orphanage. In fact, he uses his poverty as an excuse for not doing what he would not do anyway: he does not go to mass on Sunday, he explains sadly, because he must be off to his field at dawn. But his field is a tiny patch of wheat on which, except for three weeks a year, he can do almost nothing. There is hardly a man in Montegrano who could not contribute a third of his time to some community project without a loss of income.

Nor is the peasant's ignorance sufficient to account for his political incompetence. Of forty-two peasants who were asked what the Communists *claim* to stand for, only one was without an opinion. Most of the opinions were reasonable. Twenty-six persons said that the Communists claim to stand for equality, and the replies of most of the others—e.g., "peace, liberty, and work," "work for all," "opposition to the church," and "taking from the rich" —also showed comprehension. Some were very thoughtful. Here, for example, is Prato's:

> They say they are going to divide the property and give us all a piece. But what are they going to divide in Montegrano? The only land that could be divided is the Baron's. But he has it all in tenant-operated farms now. They are quite large and perhaps they could be divided. But you have to remember that as matters stand each of those farms supports ten families when you consider the year-round and the day-laborers who work for the tenants. Who is to say it would be better if that land were divided? Who is to say that the land would be better cultivated or that more people could live on it?

Most of the peasants warmly approve the ideal of social equality. They are not so simple-minded, however, as to suppose that Communist claims can be taken at face value. Fourteen of those who were asked what the Communists claim to stand for went on to say that their claims had to be distinguished from their real intentions. The Communists, these peasants said, use the equality argument to get themselves into power.

The Communists would like us all to be equal and so they would install equalization in Italy. In reality, however, it is certain that they don't like us and are probably looking after their own interests and wanting the command.

Certainly the erratic swings of the electorate to and from Communism cannot be explained on the grounds that the peasant has no idea of what is at stake. He has a sufficient idea—as much or more, perhaps, as the working class voter in the United States—and the artisan has an even better idea. "Italy," one of them remarked, "is too poor a country to afford the luxury of Communism."

The history of the American frontier provides numerous examples of people whose poverty and ignorance were as great or greater than that of the Montegranesi, but whose capacity for self-government and mutual aid was nevertheless extraordinarily great. St. George, Utah for example, . . . was a century ago a desert of sand and rock inhabited only by a handful of miserable Indians subsisting on vermin. The resource base of southern Italy, poor as it is, is far better than that which the Mormons found on the site of St. George. In St. George, incidentally, as in many frontier towns, there was a weekly newspaper at a time when the local economy was based on handicrafts and self-sufficing agriculture and most of the population spelled out its letters painfully one by one.

If the Montegrano peasant had a mystical or sentimental attachment to the land or if he "belonged to another world" which he could not see beyond or which he would not leave, he should be compared to the American Indian rather than to the frontiersman. But with few exceptions, he loathes the land, is acutely aware of the larger society about him, and wants desperately to be fully a part of it.

Class antagonism does not explain Montegrano's political behavior either. If it did, one might expect to find the peasants uniting in action *against* the upper class. But there is no such action, nor is there likely to be. Class and status relations do, however, influence the situation profoundly in ways that are diffuse, indirect, and hard to identify. Like poverty and ignorance, they are general conditions which, so to speak, form the causal background.

In Montegrano peasants do not have a pathological distrust of the state. Such distrust as they have is better described as "normal" and "healthy." When they were asked, "What kind of people are in authority today?", they usually said, in effect, "All kinds." Here are some unexceptional replies:

Do you mean people in the Chamber of Deputies? Most of them are Christian Democrats. The Christian Democrats are the better people—they are thoughtful . . . really trying to help. With the others, so long as they are getting theirs they don't care.

You mean the military, like the generals, and the pope and his cardinals? Some are good and some are bad.

The chief of the government is Pella. Pella is a good type—intelligent. If he were not intelligent, they would not let him be head of the government. Always it is those who are very intelligent.

Sometimes the peasant thinks of the state as a source of help. Eighteen were asked what they would do if someone owed them $3 or $4 and would not pay. All but five said that they would take the debtor to the Marshal of the *carabinieri*. The others would not go to law, not, however, from pathological distrust of the state, but because they would not want to make enemies.

When they were asked what they would do if someone in the neighborhood hid a person who was sick with a contagious disease, twelve said they would inform the doctor (who is the town health officer). Eight others would do nothing, not, however, from distrust of the state, but because they would not want to "humiliate" the family or act in a way that would be thought unfriendly.[5]

Fourteen peasants (some of them women) were asked, "What would you do if you saw a policeman give a bad beating to someone who had done nothing wrong?" The replies were as follows:

Try to convince him of his error.	(Four)
Report him to the Marshal.	(Three)
Nothing, because before the law one must be quiet.	(Three)
Let him taste some blows.	(Four)

Fear of the authorities is not a specifically peasant attitude; many peasants are not fearful and some who are not peasants are extremely so. The Communist director of schools, among the best educated men in Montegrano, when asked what he would do if he saw a policeman beating an innocent man, said he would not interfere unless the victim were a friend or relative. The police, he pointed out, might make reprisals against one who interfered.

Many peasants regard the government as a friend: they say it is the only source from which they have ever received help.

The theory that the southern Italian is prevented by melancholy fatalism from taking effective action does not, of course, explain the choices he makes when he *does* act. Nor is it consistent with the fact that when individualistic action is called for he is not incapacitated by despair or fatalism. . . .

These theories, it should also be noted, do not explain—and may even be inconsistent with—the tendency of voters to shift erratically between right and left from election to election. In the town of Addo, for example, there was a shift from Christian Democratic to Communist and back again to Christian Democratic, although of course there had been no change in per capita wealth, in literacy, or in the distribution of land ownership.

o   o   o

A very simple hypothesis will make intelligible all of the behavior about which questions have been raised and will enable an observer to predict how the Montegranesi will act in concrete circumstances. The hypothesis is that the Montegranesi act as if they were following this rule:

Maximize the material, short-run advantage of the nuclear family; assume that all others will do likewise.

One whose behavior is consistent with this rule will be called an "amoral familist." The term is awkward and somewhat imprecise (one who follows the rule is without morality only in relation to persons outside the family— in relation to family members, he applies standards of right and wrong; one who has no family is of course an "amoral individualist"), but no other term seems better.

In this chapter, some logical implications of the rule are set forth. . . .

1. *In a society of amoral familists, no one will further the interest of the group or community except as it is to his private advantage to do so.* In other words, the hope of material gain in the short-run will be the only motive for concern with public affairs.

This principle is of course consistent with the entire absence of civic improvement associations, organized charities, and leading citizens who take initiative in public service.

    o   o   o

2. *In a society of amoral familists only officials will concern themselves with public affairs, for only they are paid to do so. For a private citizen to take a serious interest in a public problem will be regarded as abnormal and even improper.*

    o   o   o

Farmuso, the director of the school district and formerly the Communist mayor of a town in another province, is earnest, energetic, and intelligent. He listed several things which might be done to improve the situation in Montegrano, but when he was asked if he could bring influence to bear to get any of them done, he said that he could not. "I am interested only in the schools," he explained. "If I wanted to exert influence, with whom would I talk? In Vernande there are six teachers in two rooms, but

no money for improvements. I have talked to the mayor and others, but I can't get anything even there."

The feeling that unofficial action is an intrusion upon the sphere of the state accounts in some measure both for Mayor Spomo's haughty officiousness and for the failure of private persons to interest themselves in making stop-gap arrangements for a school and a hospital. In nearby Basso a reclamation project will increase vegetable production and make possible the establishment of a canning factory. The large landowners of Basso will not join together to build a factory, however, even though it might be a good investment. It is the right and the duty of the state to build it.

3. *In a society of amoral familists there will be few checks on officials, for checking on officials will be the business of other officials only.*

    o   o   o

4. *In a society of amoral familists, organization (i.e., deliberately concerted action) will be very difficult to achieve and maintain. The inducements which lead people to contribute their activity to organizations are to an important degree unselfish (e.g., identification with the purpose of the organization) and they are often non-material (e.g., the intrinsic interest of the activity as a " game "). Moreover, it is a condition of successful organization that members have some trust in each other and some loyalty to the organization. In an organization with high morale it is taken for granted that they will make small sacrifices, and perhaps even large ones, for the sake of the organization.*

The only formal organizations which exist in Montegrano—the church and the state—are of course provided from the outside; if they were not, they could not exist. Inability to create and maintain organization is clearly of the greatest importance in retarding economic development in the region.[6]

Despite the moral and other resources it can draw upon from the outside, the church in Montegrano suffers from the general inability to maintain organization. There are two parishes, each with its priest. Rivalry between the priests is so keen that neither can do anything out of the ordinary without having obstacles placed in his way by the other, and cooperation between them is wholly out of the question. (On one occasion they nearly came to blows in the public square; on another the saint of one parish was refused admittance to the church of the other when the *festa*-day procession stopped there on its route.) When some young men tried to organize a chapter of Catholic Action, a lay association to carry Catholic principles into secular life, they encountered so much sabotage from the feuding priests, neither of whom was willing to tolerate an activity for which the other might receive some credit, that the project was soon abandoned.

The Montegranesi might be expected not to make good soldiers. However brave he may be, the amoral familist does not win battles. Soldiers fight from loyalty to an organization, especially the primary groups of "buddies," not from self-interest narrowly conceived.

Lack of attachment even to kindred has impeded emigration and indirectly economic development. In the half century prior to 1922, there was heavy emigration from Montegrano to the United States and later to Argentina. In general, however, ties between the emigrants and those who remained at home were not strong enough to support "chains" of emigration. Hundreds of Montegranesi live in the hope that a

brother or uncle in America will send a "call," but such calls rarely come. People are perplexed when their relatives in America do not answer their letters. The reason is, probably, that the letters from Montegrano always ask for something, and the emigrant, whose advantage now lies elsewhere, loses patience with them. The relative absence of emigration, as well as of gifts from persons who have emigrated, is a significant impediment to economic development. Some Italian towns, whose ethos is different, have benefited enormously from continuing close ties with emigrants who have prospered in the New World.[7]

5. *In a society of amoral familists, officeholders, feeling no identification with the purposes of the organization, will not work harder than is necessary to keep their places or (if such is within the realm of possibility) to earn promotion. Similarly, professional people and educated people generally will lack a sense of mission or calling. Indeed, official position and special training will be regarded by their possessors as weapons to be used against others for private advantage.*

In southern Italy, the indifference of the bureaucracy is notorious. "A zealous official is as rare as a white fly," a man who had retired after 49 years in the public service remarked.

○   ○   ○

7. *The amoral familist who is an officeholder will take bribes when he can get away with it. But whether he takes bribes or not, it will be assumed by the society of amoral familists that he does.*[8]

○   ○   ○

8. *In a society of amoral familists the weak will favor a regime which will maintain order with a strong hand.*

Until it involved them in war, Fascism appealed to many peasants—at least so they now say—because by enforcing the laws rigorously, it protected them.

o   o   o

9. *In a society of amoral familists, the claim of any person or institution to be inspired by zeal for public rather than private advantage will be regarded as fraud.*

o   o   o

11. *In a society of amoral familists there will be no leaders and no followers. No one will take the initiative in outlining a course of action and persuading others to embark upon it (except as it may be to his private advantage to do so) and, if one did offer leadership, the group would refuse it out of distrust.*

Apparently there has never been in Montegrano a peasant leader to other peasants. Objectively, there is a basis for such leadership to develop: the workers on road gangs, for example, share grievances and one would expect them to develop feelings of solidarity.

Suspicion of the would-be leader probably reduces the effectiveness of the doctor, the midwife, and the agricultural agent as teachers. When a peasant was asked whether she could get birth control information from the midwife, she replied, "Of course not. It is not to her interest that I limit the size of my family."

o   o   o

12. *The amoral familist will use his ballot to secure the greatest material gain in the short run. Although he may have decided views as to his long-run interest, his class interest, or the public interest, these will not effect his vote if the family's short-run, material advantage is in any way involved.*

Prato, for example, is a monarchist as a matter of principle: he was born and brought up one and he believes that monarchy is best because Italy is too poor to afford frequent elections. These principles do not affect his vote, however. "Before elections," he explains, "all the parties send people around who say, 'Vote for our party.' We always say 'Yes,' but when we go to vote, we vote for the party we think has given us the most." The Christian Democratic party has given Prato a few days work on the roads each year. Therefore he votes for it. If it ceased to give him work and if there were no advantage to be had from voting for another party, he would be a monarchist again. If Mayor Spomo has influence with the Minister of Agriculture, he should be kept despite his haughtiness and his stealing. But if Councilmen Viva and Lasso can get a larger project than the mayor can get, or if they can get one quicker, then down with him.

13. *The amoral familist will value gains accruing to the community only insofar as he and his are likely to share them. In fact, he will vote against measures which will help the community without helping him because, even though his position is unchanged in absolute terms, he considers himself worse off if his neighbors' position changes for the better. Thus it may happen that measures which are of decided general benefit will provoke a protest vote from those who feel that they have not shared in them or have not shared in them sufficiently.*

In 1954, the Christian Democratic party showed the voters of Basso that vast sums had been spent on local public works. Nevertheless the vote went to the Communists. There are other reasons which help to account for the vote (the Christian Democratic candidate was a merchant who would not give credit and was cordially disliked and distrusted), but it seems likely that the very effectiveness of the Christian Democratic propaganda may have helped to cause its defeat. Seeing what vast sums had been expended, the voters asked themselves: Who got it all? Why didn't they give me my fair share?

No amoral familist ever gets what he regards as his fair share.

14. *In a society of amoral familists the voter will place little confidence in the promises of the parties. He will be apt to use his ballot to pay for favors already received (assuming, of course, that more are in prospect) rather than for favors which are merely promised.*

o   o   o

15. *In a society of amoral familists it will be assumed that whatever group is in power is self-serving and corrupt. Hardly will an election be over before the voters will conclude that the new officials are enriching themselves at their expense and that they have no intention of keeping the promises they have made. Consequently, the self-serving voter will use his ballot to pay the incumbents not for benefits but for injuries, i.e., he will use it to administer punishment.*

In subsequent chapters of his book Professor Banfield proceeds to show the interrelationship between amoral familism, economic poverty, and lack of political organization. He argues that where poverty may once have been a root cause of amoral familism, the continued practice of such an amoral ethos in everyday life prevents economic development and acts as a formidable barrier to economic cooperation and progress as well as to political participation and leadership. Thus ethos affects politics and economics, and the latter two in turn reinforce the ethos. His prognosis for the future of such a village is gloomy unless the villagers can change their ethos, the likelihood of such change depending in turn on improvements in the standard of living and general education.

The author concludes, "Finally, it must be said that there is little likelihood that any such measures will be tried. Even if it were certain—which it is not, of course—that they would work, they probably would not be tried. Nations do not remake themselves in fundamental ways by deliberate intention any more than do villages" (ed.).]

NOTES

1. Carlo Levi, *Christ Stopped at Eboli*, Penguin Edition, p. 52.

2. The real enemies of the peasant, according to Carlo Levi, "those who cut them off from any hope of freedom and a decent existence, are to be found among the middle-class village tyrants. This class is physically and morally degenerate and no longer able to fill its original function. It lives off petty thievery and the bastardized tradition of feudal rights. Only with the suppression of this class and the substitution of something better can the difficulties of the South find a solution." *Op. cit.*, p. 176.

   It should be remembered that Levi's observations were made during an exile which began in 1935 and that his book, which was widely read by the upper class in Montegrano and other southern towns, no doubt produced an effect. At any rate, it was curious in 1955 to find upper class people quoting him with approval, although with reference not so much to their own town as to others and to the Fascist period.

3. Levi, *op. cit.*, p. 52.

4. *Ibid.*, p. 129.

5. In answer to the question, "What would you do if you knew that someone was contemplating suicide?" most people said they would advise or plead with the person; a few said they would tell his family, and still fewer would call the police or the doctor. No one mentioned the priest.

6. Max Weber remarked in *The Protestant Ethic and the Rise of Capitalism* (Allen and Unwin edition, London, 1930, p. 57) that "the universal reign of absolute unscrupulousness in the pursuit of selfish interests by the making of money has been a specific characteristic of precisely those countries whose bourgeois-capitalistic development, measured according to Occidental standards, has remained backward. As every employer knows, the lack of *coscienziosità* of the laborers of such countries, for instance Italy as compared with Germany, has been, and to a certain extent still is, one of the principal obstacles to their capitalistic development."

7. McDonald writes in a personal letter: "Since 1927 Italians who are not officially assisted may be nominated and paid for by relatives or friends resident here in Australia. Solidarity of some kind is needed for chains of such emigration to have continued 30 years. Montegrano folk apparently would not help each other. In Reggio Calabria, community solidarity is lacking yet there is nuclear family solidarity plus relatively strong identification with and participation in cliques of certain relatives selected from the kindred kinship system plus certain friends (especially *compari* and *commare*). I have found that these nuclear family-clique members are the Calabrians who form the links in the migration chains. Since cliques of relatives and friends overlap in their system, these chains are snowballing despite the lack of community solidarity. In fact, comparing the rate of growth of Calabrian settlements of the above clique-nuclear family solidarity type with Calabrian settlements of the Montegrano solidarity nuclear family type, I have found that the former grew very much faster than the latter."

THE INTERNALIZATION OF POLITICAL VALUES IN STATELESS SOCIETIES

- Robert A. LeVine

The purpose of this paper is to suggest the following proposition: To understand and predict the contemporary political behavior of African peoples who were stateless prior to Western contact, one must take account of the traditional political values involved in their local authority systems, particularly since such values continue to be internalized by new generations after their society has come under the administration of a modern nation-state. Most anthropological students of stateless societies have concentrated their attention on the total-society level, analyzing the structure of inter-group relations in the absence of a central authority. In my opinion, a concept such as "segmentary society," which is at the total-society level of analysis, is an inadequate tool for the investigation of political variation and adaptation in African societies. To illustrate this point, I shall compare political behavior in two East African societies having segmentary lineage systems: the Gusii of Kenya, among whom I did field work,[1] and the Nuer of the Sudan, on whom four excellent monographs have been published by two independent field workers.[2]

The Nuer and Gusii are similar in many aspects of indigenous socio-political organization. First of all, the two societies resemble each other in size and scale. The Nuer population is about 350,000, that of the Gusii, 260,000.

Above selection reprinted from: *Human Organization*, 19 (1960), 51–58.

Among the Nuer, there are fifteen so-called tribes, within which compensation for homicide could be collected; the Gusii have seven such units based on the same principle. Both societies lacked superordinate political structures and were, in that sense, "stateless." There were no permanent positions of leadership with substantial decision-making power, and no formal councils. The major social groups within the tribes of both societies were patrilineal descent groups, each of which was associated with a territory and was a segment of a higher-level lineage which contained several such segments. Lineage structure is similar in many details for Nuer and Gusii: a lineage is named after its ancestor; its segments derive from the polygynous composition of the ancestor's family and are named after his several wives or their sons; the growth of lineage from polygynous families and their progressive segmentation are regular features of the system. Although Gusii lineages are more highly localized than Nuer ones, in both societies lineage segments and the territorial units associated with them engaged in armed aggression against segments of the same level. Two segments of equal level within the tribe would combine to fight a different tribe, but would conduct blood feuds against each other at times. This multiple-loyalty situation, plus the effect of mutual military deterrence, resulted in the maintenance of a certain degree of order which Evans-Pritchard has called "the balanced opposition of segments." Thus, in comparing Nuer and Gusii, it is possible to hold constant major structural variables in the pre-contact political systems.

There are also many similarities in the conditions which the Gusii and Nuer faced in coming under colonial admin-istration. For both peoples, serious administration began in a punitive ex-pedition brought on by an attempt to assassinate the District Commissioner (the Nuer succeeded in killing a D.C., while the Gusii only wounded the first one sent to rule them). British-led forces conducted the punitive expedition in both cases, and the aims of the early administrators were identical: to estab-lish law and order on the pattern of British colonies elsewhere. This meant the abolition of feuding and warfare, and the establishment of chieftainship and native courts for the peaceful settlement of disputes. A major difference in the ex-posure of the two societies to British administration is chronological. The Gusii came under colonial rule in 1907, while the Nuer were not conquered until 1928. This twenty-year lag must be borne in mind as the analysis proceeds, so that the extent to which it contributes to the sharpness of the contrast may be assessed. With this qualification, it may be said that a comparison of political changes in Nuer and Gusii societies has the advantage of using groups which are matched on pre-existing political struc-ture (in gross aspect) and on the nature of the political institutions introduced.

Contemporary Political Behavior

The contemporary political behavior of the Nuer and Gusii will be compared on two points: the adjustment of indi-viduals to leadership roles in the intro-duced judicial system and the tendency of the traditional blood feud to persist or die out under British administration. Howell, writing in 1954 of the Nuer courts, states:

. . . there is still everywhere a reluctance to give anything in the nature of a judgement. In many disputes, where the rights of one or another of the disputants are abundantly clear, a rapid and clear-cut decision might be expected. This is rarely forthcoming. . . .[3]

He goes on to say with respect to sentencing:

. . . although Nuer chiefs and court members may be aware of the value of punishment, they are still reluctant to inflict it, especially as they are often subjected to recriminations by their fellows when the case is over. A fixed penalty (which they desire) absolves them from this and throws the responsibility on the Government.[4]

It is clear from these statements that Nuer judges do not relish their positions of authority over their fellow men, whose disapproval they fear. They attempt to avoid using the authority of their office by making indecisive verdicts and by demanding that the government set fixed penalties for offenses. By contrast, the government in Gusiiland has never had any trouble finding men willing to deliver judgment on their fellows. If anything, Gusii chiefs and judges have, from the early days of admin-istration, tended to err on the side of arbitrariness and severity. Some of them may be charged with favoritism and accepting bribes but not with vacil-lation. Gusii Tribunal Court presidents complain of the puny sentences they are empowered to inflict. Location chiefs, who act as constables and informal courts of first instance, go far beyond their formal powers, incarcerating young men for insolence to their fathers, threatening legal sanctions against husbands who neglect their wives, punishing their personal enemies with legal means at their disposal. Gusii judicial leaders do not fear the adverse opinions of their fellow men because they know that their judicial authority is respected and even feared by the entire group. Chiefs and Tribunal Court presidents are the most powerful individuals in Gusiiland; immoderate criticism of them to their faces is considered impolite as well as simply unwise.

The second point of comparison concerns the persistence of the blood feud in the face of an established court system for the peaceful settlement of disputes. Howell states of the contemporary Nuer:

Spear-fights between rival factions are not uncommon, and the blood-feud is still a reality among the Nuer despite severe deterrents applied by the Administration. Casualties are sometimes heavy, and most Nuer bear the marks of some armed affray . . . it would be a mistake to believe that the Nuer do not frequently use in earnest the spears and clubs which they keep always at their sides.[5]

Howell also mentions occasional "extensive hostilities" when "the intervention of State police armed with rifles is sometimes necessary."[6] He relates an incident in which he, as District Commissioner, intervened prematurely in a developing feud and

. . . was publicly and most soundly rebuked by the elder statesmen of the area, and was told that such matters should be left to the chiefs themselves.

The Nuer chiefs, though, are sometimes "unwilling or afraid to intervene and restrian their fellows."

The Gusii situation is strikingly different. Despite the persistence of ill feelings between lineage segments, the blood feud was replaced by litigation in the early days of British administration. Nowadays the only occasion on which overgroup aggression occurs is at the funeral of a childless married woman whose death is attributed to the witchcraft of her co-wives. People from her natal clan attempt to destroy her belongings so they will not be inherited by her "murderers," and they may even attack her husband for his complicity in the affairs leading to her death. Significantly, however, women are usually the aggressors on such occasions, which are more likely to result in a court case than an all-out brawl. Fights are normally personal and show little tendency to involve groups of individuals. The Gusii, long reputed to be among the most litigious of Africans in Kenya, utilize assault charges in court as an alternative to physical aggression.[7] Soon after one individual insults or threatens another, they are both on their way to chief or court to lodge assault charges. Two-thirds of the vast number of assault cases are dismissed, most of them on the grounds that there is no evidence that assault has taken place. The Gusii are so eager to involve a higher authority in their quarrels that victims of alleged assaults would relate their stories to me and show me their injuries if I happened to meet them on their way to the chief.

To summarize this point: Nuer judicial leaders are more uneasy about making decisions and inflicting punishments on their fellow men than are their Gusii counterparts. Nuer men continue to practice the blood feud after twenty years of colonial rule, while the Gusii have a strong tendency to resolve their conflicts in court. The hypothesis that these differences are due to the twenty-year head start which Gusii political acculturation had, can be rejected on the grounds that the present tendencies of rulers and ruled in Gusiiland manifested themselves in the early years of British administration.

Political Values

Can these differences in the political behavior of the Nuer and Gusii be related to more general differences in their political values? It is instructive in this connection to examine their values (as expressed in behavior) concerning authority and aggression. Both Evans-Pritchard and Howell use the words "democratic," "egalitarian," and "independent" in characterizing Nuer behavior. Evans-Pritchard also mentions the Nuer possession of "a deep sense of their common equality,"[8] and states, "There is no master and no servant in their society, but only equals. . . ." Both investigators give detailed accounts of the Nuer avoidance of using the imperative mode of speech, and the anger with which a Nuer reacts to an order which is not couched in terms of polite request. Nuer men refused to help a sick Evans-Pritchard carry his equipment when he was leaving the field because his way of asking them to do it was not euphemistic enough.[9] They refuse to be ordered about by other Nuer or by Europeans, and they also exhibit little deference to persons in political roles. Referring to the Nuer leopard-skin chiefs, Evans-Pritchard states:

. . . The chiefs I have seen were treated in everyday life like other men and there is no means of telling that a man is a chief by observing people's behavior to him.[10]

Howell says of the contemporary situation:

. . . though the Nuer have a proper respect for the authority of their District Commissioner, no one could argue that this in any way curbs their blunt methods of expressing approval of his decisions, or more often, disapproval. . . . He is addressed by his "bull-name," greeted as an intimate by men and women of all ages, praised, but often severely criticized, by the chiefs.[11]

In characterizing the Gusii attitude toward authority, one finds it necessary to use terms such as "authoritarian" which connote dominance and submission. Command relationships are a part of everyday life and are morally valued by the Gusii. A higher-status person has the right to order about persons of lower status, and this right is not limited to a functionally specific relationship. The contemporary location chief, for example, is surrounded by lackeys ready to do his bidding, and these lackeys have considerable command power over the populace in matters unrelated to the governing of the location. The chief, or someone in his immediate family, can stop anywhere in his location and order a man he does not know to do a personal favor for him, and it will be done. Schoolteachers, by virtue of their prestige; traders, by virtue of their wealth; elders, by virtue of their age; and subheadmen, by virtue of their political position, all have the privilege of telling other people what to do, and they use this privilege to pass onerous tasks on to persons of lower status. Orders are given in imperative terms and often in harsh tones, yet this is considered normal and proper conduct. Europeans are accorded considerable command power, whether or not they are government officials. Deferential behavior to persons of higher status is also pronounced among the Gusii and this was the case in the past as well as today. Traditionally, local community decision-making was dominated by the elders and the wealthiest individuals of the area; the local lineage was an age-hierarchy in terms of deference and dominance. Old men enjoy relating tales of the awe in which people held Bogonko, a nineteenth-century hero and leader of the Getutu tribe. It is said that when he walked out of his home area people fled from their houses until reassured that he would do them no harm. Songs in praise of his wealth, power, and accomplishments were composed. When he attended his grandson's wedding, woven mats were laid down so that he should not have to walk on cow dung. A soft voice and downward glance constitute traditionally proper demeanor for someone talking to an elder, chief, or other figure of importance. It is significant that some of the major political leaders of contemporary Gusiiland started out as servants to the major figures of their day, and that uneducated men with political aspirations often want to be cook or chauffeur to a chief. Gusii leaders are deferential to the District Commissioner and do not often contradict him.

The Gusii, then, appear to have authoritarian values while the Nuer are extremely egalitarian. This difference in values is manifest if one examines community or family relationships in the two societies. Nuer village life is characterized by economic mutuality, and an ethic of sharing surplus goods so intense that it is impossible for a man to keep such goods as tobacco if his supply exceeds that of his neighbors; they simply take it from him.[12] Among the Gusii, who live in scattered homesteads rather than villages, each homestead tends to be an independent economic unit; communal sharing is not considered desirable and the privacy of property is guarded. Although Gusii men, like Nuer, eat at each other's places, they have a greater tendency to congregate at the homestead of a wealthy man, who can afford to feed them well and who dominates them economically and politically to some extent. Both Nuer and Gusii are formally patriarchal in family organization. The available evidence indicates that the Gusii *paterfamilias* is much more powerful vis-à-vis his wives and sons than his Nuer counterpart. Among the Nuer, men do not beat their wives; sons can go off to live with their maternal uncles; and the eldest sons can curse their parents. Among the Gusii, wives are frequently beaten; sons can find no refuge at their mother's brothers'; and only parents may curse their children. Thus, the contrast between egalitarian and authoritarian values can be found in spheres of Nuer and Gusii life.

Values concerning aggression are also of interest here. The Nuer have been described as "truculent"[13] and easily roused to violence."[14]

A Nuer will at once fight if he considers that he has been insulted, and they are very sensitive and easily take offense. When a man feels that he has suffered an injury . . . he at once challenges the man who has wronged him to a duel and the challenge must be accepted.[15]

No such code of honor obtains among the Gusii, who consider it preferable to avert aggression whenever possible. Gusii men tend to be quiet and restrained in interaction and, although enemies try to avoid meeting one another, when they are forced into contact they will be civil and even friendly, although they have been backbiting or sorcerizing one another covertly. This is summed up in the proverb, "Two people may be seen together but their hearts do not know one another." Another proverb epitomizes Gusii avoidance behavior toward persons of a quarrelsome disposition: "A biting snake is pushed away with a stick." Serious crimes of violence are committed almost exclusively by intoxicated individuals. Thus the Gusii preference to avoid interpersonal aggression, and to resolve it in the courts when it comes to a head, contrasts sharply with the Nuer tendency to settle quarrels by fighting.

Using the classification of political systems proposed by Fortes and Evans-Pritchard[16] or the revision of it proposed by Southall,[17] the Nuer and Gusii both fall into the same class, that of stateless segmentary societies. Yet, as has been shown above, they are poles apart in terms of political values which are significantly involved in their contemporary political situation.[18] If authority values were the criteria of classification, the Nuer would probably fall with societies like the Masai, whose political organization is based on age groups,[19] or with the Fox Indians, whose opposition to the concentration of power and authority was expressed in their political, religious, and kinship organization and their resistance to European domination.[20] The Gusii, in terms of authority values, might be classed with African kingdoms or with smaller-scale and less stratified chiefdoms in which inequalities in the allocation of authority were cherished rather than reviled. The corporate lineage is sometimes thought of as an inherently egalitarian institution, but, as the Gusii case indicates, it is also flexible enough to be able to develop in a non-egalitarian direction with an emphasis on generational status differences and a recognition of seniority based on wealth.

Certain aspects of Nuer and Gusii sociopolitical organization which would be considered peripheral under the Fortes-Evans-Pritchard scheme indicate the divergent tendencies of the two societies. The Nuer have an age-set organization which, while it is not an important factor in their political life, nonetheless exhibits some degree of group organization based on relationships of equality. The Gusii have no organized group of peers. In the nineteenth century, Getutu, largest of the seven Gusii tribes, developed a hereditary chieftainship which resulted in some centralization of judicial power in that tribe. The chieftainship later bifurcated along lines of lineage segmentation but the leadership tradition remained strong in Getutu and is so today. This development, although limited to one part of Gusii society, was a movement in a distinctly authoritarian direction, especially when compared to temporary leadership movements among the Nuer. It is probable that, if the Gusii had lived in an area which contained a centralized chiefdom, they would have, as the Uganda-Congo tribes described by Southall did, voluntarily accepted its domination for the authoritarian order it offered. This is speculation and cannot be verified. But one thing seems certain from the above, and that is that classifying political systems on the basis of their predominant political values, particularly concerning authority, yields insights into them which cannot be obtained by a scheme based purely on the broad outlines of political structure. The authority structure of cohesive groups within stateless segmentary societies has been neglected by investigators in favor of the structure of lineages and their relation to territorial units.[21] It is time that this situation be remedied by closer attention to problems in the allocation and exercise of authority.

Childhood Experience

The contrasting values of the Nuer and Gusii described above indicate differing means of making decisions and different paths of action concerning the settlement of disputes, in short, basic differences in the political systems of the two groups. In stateless societies with segmentary lineages, decisions are made mostly at the level of the local community and local lineage group, where permanent solidary bonds exist. The extended family as minimal lineage is a unit in the local political system, and its authority structure tends to resemble that of larger units. This resemblance has been made explicit for the Nuer and Gusii. Since the extended family functions both as a political unit and as an institution for the care and training of the young, the individual's induction into the political system actually begins in early childhood. His socialization into the authority structure of the family leaves him with values and role expectations which are adaptive in sociopolitical units above the family level. Because of this connection between the early family environment of the child and the political system, it is reasonable to expect differences in the early learning experiences of typical individuals in Gusii and Nuer societies. Psychological theory and research suggest two aspects of childhood experience as particularly relevant to the learning of values concerning authority and aggression: parent-child relations and aggression training. It should be possible to develop some theoretical expectations about these aspects for the Nuer and Gusii, and to check the available evidence for confirmation or disconfirmation.

1. Parent-Child Relations

Several investigators in the fields of social and developmental psychology, among them Frenkel-Brunswik,[22] Riesman, and Whiting, have proposed the general hypothesis (based on psychoanalytic theory) that the individual's attitudes toward authority are a function of his early relationships with his parents. The factors often held responsible for the development of such attitudes are: a) the authority structure of the family, i.e., the extent to which family authority is concentrated, in hierarchical fashion, or equally distributed among its members. In a family in which authority is concentrated, the child is held to develop authoritarian or rigid absolute values, and where it is equally shared, he internalizes egalitarian, group-oriented, and cooperative values. b) The closeness and warmth of the relationship between the child and the parent with most authority in the household. In particular, Frenkel-Brunswik found that American men scoring high on the F (authoritarianism-ethnocentrism) scale characterized their fathers as "distant," "stern," and "with bad temper," while those scoring low said their fathers had been "warm" and "demonstrative."[23] This finding appears to have had a major influence on thinking in this field of study. c) The degree to which the discipline administered is severe, with physical punishment most important. It is held that the child who has been beaten by a powerful parent will grow up submissive to arbitrary authority and to cherish a nonegalitarian ideal. The comparison of the Nuer and Gusii on these characteristics will be limited to (b) and (c), since (a) has been described above.

The father-son relationship is the appropriate category for studying childhood antecedents of authority values among Nuer and Gusii since both groups are strongly patrilineal, with men occupying all positions of authority in the kinship and political systems. Furthermore, residence at marriage tends to be patrilocal in both societies, so that many men live in close proximity to their fathers until the latter die. For the father, the father-son relationship is one between lineagemates and is, therefore, likely to reflect the authority values which characterize his relations with other members of his lineage. For the son, the relationship represents his induction into the authority system of the minimal lineage, of which he is likely to remain a member as an adult, and it probably serves also as a prototype for other intralineage authority relationships. Concerning the Nuer, Evans-Pritchard states:

... the father also takes an interest in his infant children, and one often sees a man nursing his child while the mother is engaged in the tasks of the home. Nuer fathers are proud of their children and give much time to them, petting and spoiling them, giving them titbits, playing with them and teaching them to talk: and the children are often in the byres with the man. I have never seen a man beat his child or lose his temper with him, however aggravating he may be. When a father speaks crossly to his child, as he does if, let us say, the child goes to the edge of a river or among the cattle, where he may be injured, it is evident that the child is not afraid of his loud words and obeys from affection rather than fear.[22]

Among the Gusii, fathers rarely take care of infants, as most mothers have daughters or sisters aged five to eleven who are charged with the responsibility of caretaking in her absence. If there is no such child caretaker (*omoreri*), the mother's co-wife or mother-in-law helps her out in this regard, but the father's role in infant care is minimal. Nor do fathers spend much time with their children, play with them, or act otherwise nurturant. On the contrary, the Gusii father tends to be aloof and severe, being called in by the mother primarily when the child needs to be disciplined. Fathers threaten their sons with punishment, and administer harsh beatings with wooden switches, explicitly intending to make the sons fearful and therefore obedient. The mother and older siblings help to exaggerate the punitive image of the father by warning the child of the dire paternal punishments which await him if he does wrong. At the end of his son's initiation ceremony the father ritually promises not to beat him any more, as an acknowledgement of his maturity. Most Gusii men recall a thrashing by the father for neglect of cattle-herding as one of their outstanding childhood experiences.

The patterns of father-son relations in Nuer and Gusii childhood experiences conform to the expectations generated by psychological hypotheses. The Nuer, who as adults have egalitarian values, grow up with warm, demonstrative fathers who do not beat them physically. The Gusii, who exhibit authoritarian behavior as adults, have experienced, as children, fathers who are remote, frightening, and severely punitive. This indicates the possibility that the difference in values concerning authority between Nuer and Gusii is related to the concomitant difference in early father-son relations.

2. Aggression Training

Psychologists have done considerable research on childhood antecedents of aggressive behavior. One of the most recent and comprehensive research studies on the topic is that of Sears, Maccoby, and Levin on the child-rearing patterns of 379 American mothers. They found a positive relationship between the mother's permissive attitude toward the aggressive behavior of her child and the degree of his aggressiveness. The more permissive the mother, the more aggressive the child.[25] Although no direct relationship between the aggressive behavior of an individual as a child and his aggression as an adult has been established, it is possible to use the above finding as an hypothetical basis for predicting that the Nuer, who are more aggressive and who set a high value on physical aggression, will be found to permit more aggressive behavior in their children than the Gusii, who tend to disvalue aggression and seek to avoid it. Evans-Pritchard states of the Nuer:

. . . From their earliest years children are encouraged by their elders to settle all disputes

by fighting, and they grow up to regard skill in fighting the most necessary accomplishment and courage the highest virtue.[26]

. . . A child soon learns that to maintain his equality with his peers, he must stand up for himself against any encroachment on his person or property. This means that he must always be prepared to fight, and his willingness and ability to do so are the only protection of his integrity as a free and independent person against the avarice and bullying of his kinsmen.[27]

With the Gusii, on the other hand, parents do not encourage their children to fight but rather to report grievances to the parents. Adult disapproval of fighting is so strong that most children learn at an early age not to fight in the presence of parents or other adult relatives. When they are by themselves, herding cattle, however, boys do engage in physical aggression against one another. If a boy is hurt badly or beaten by a boy he does not know well, he will run to a parent, usually the mother, who will question him about it and then angrily cross-examine the other children involved. Mothers describing this procedure said that they "make a case," using the expression for conducting a trial. If the mother concludes that her own child was at fault, she will warn him and tell him he got what he deserved. If she concludes that the fault lay with someone else's child, she will loudly complain to the parents of the aggressor and demand that he be punished and controlled in the future. I have seen this happen and believe it is the normal procedure. When injury to a child is serious or permanent, an actual assault and damages litigation is initiated with the local elders. Older boys are warned against fighting on the grounds that they will involve their parents in lawsuits. Thus, as predicted on grounds of a psychological hypothesis, Nuer parents are permissive toward the aggression of their children and, in fact, actively encourage it, while Gusii parents do not tolerate fighting but promote reliance on adult intervention for the settlement of disputes.

This finding suggests that there may be a relationship between the difference in values concerning aggression on the part of Nuer and Gusii adults, and the concomitant difference in aggression-training of children in the two societies.

Discussion

Since Nuer and Gusii are both segmentary lineage societies, a theory which uses total-societal structures (acephalous segmentary lineages, central state organization, etc.) as the sole means of differentiating one political system from another would be hard put to explain why their contemporary patterns of political behavior under British rule are divergent. I have attempted to explain the divergence in terms of differing values, institutionalized in their political systems and internalized by individuals as they grow up in the family.

The Nuer, whose present-day judicial leaders shrink from passing judgment on and penalizing their fellow men, are seen as having an egalitarian ethic manifested in many aspects of their life, including community and family relations. In their early years, Nuer boys are treated in a nurturant and non-punitive way by their fathers, a pattern which personality theorists have hypothesized as antecedent to the learning of egalitarian values. The persistent feuding of the Nuer is part of a wider value-orientation favoring personal aggressiveness in which

honor is easily offended and violence begun on trifling provocation. On the childhood level, Nuer individuals grow up in a mileu of adults who permit and encourage their fighting, and it is suggested here that this promotes the development of aggressive behavior patterns.

The Gusii, whose present-day judicial leaders are only too willing to pass judgment on and to punish members of their own group, are characterized by authoritarian values exhibited in many facets of interpersonal behavior on the local and family levels. Gusii fathers are emotionally distant from and physically punitive toward their young sons, which may be a necessary prerequisite for the internalization of authoritarian values. The tendency of Gusii men to disvalue aggression, attempt to avoid it, and to resolve aggressive conflict in court whenever possible is paralleled by the tendency of parents to express disapproval of childish aggression and to encourage children to report fighting to their elders. This child-training experience probably serves to inhibit overt aggressiveness in the individual and to strengthen litigiousness as an alternative behavior pattern.

By virtue of their greater willingness to submit to hierarchical authority and their greater inhibitions concerning the expression of aggression, the Gusii were able to make a more rapid and "satisfactory" adaptation to a colonial administration which required these very characteristics of them than were the Nuer, whose values concerning authority and aggression were contradictory to the demands of the British government. If and when the Nuer accept the idea of decision-making and peaceful conflict resolution at the level of the total society, they are likely to develop leadership patterns which are less autocratic than those of the contemporary Gusii, but their intergroup antagonisms and preference for local autonomy may block the acceptance of large-scale political integration.

It is not suggested here that child-training variables are independent determinants of political behavior but rather that they are shaped and selected by the functional requirements of local authority systems, just as any social group trains its members to conform to the rules which help maintain it. Thus child training may be *cause* with respect to the behavior of individuals, but is *effect* with respect to the traditional values which aid in the maintenance of social structures. If a pattern of child training is operating effectively, it is producing individuals whose personal values conform to the social values of the groups in which they participate as adults. Furthermore, the analysis presented here does not suggest that value-influenced child rearing practices are the only, or even the most important determinants of political behavior. Since the Gusii and Nuer are matched on two important sets of independent variables, i.e., the traditional structure of group affiliations and the nature of the colonizing power, it has been possible to detect in clearest form the influence of other variables such as child training. My claim is that these latter variables account for some of the crosscultural variance in political behavior, but not for all of it. While the validity of the analysis presented here is by no means established, it has, at the very least, the advantage of differentiating between two societies whose outward forms of political organization are similar. Furthermore, the aspects of child-

hood experience in which differences were found were not selected on an impressionistic basis but were investigated because of the indications from psychological theory and research that they are antecedents to personal behavior concerning authority and aggression. The differences in childhood experience conform to the expectations generated by psychological research. Finally, the theoretical approach used here is consistent with the hypothesis of Bruner based on research among American Indians:

> That which was traditionally learned and internalized in infancy and early childhood tends to be most resistant to change in contact situations.[28]

This hypothesis lends plausibility to the persistence, under British administration, of those traditional Nuer and Gusii political values which are internalized in the early years of life.

It has not been the purpose of this article to launch an attack on the study of political structure as such, but to add to it a new dimension which, hopefully, will increase its explanatory power by bringing it simultaneously closer to the realities of contemporary politics and to the findings of behavioral sciences other than social anthropology. In line with this aim, it is possible to draw two conclusions from the above study which bear on the comparative analysis of political behavior.

Conclusions

1) An invariant correspondence between sociopolitical organization at the total-society level and values concerning

authority should not be assumed to hold cross-culturally. In the particular case of stateless societies, it is fallacious to assume synonymity between the balanced opposition of equal segments and egalitarian political values, or to assume that corporate lineages are inherently egalitarian. The notion that sociopolitical organization at the total-society level varies concomitantly with authority values should be treated as an hypothesis to be tested empirically. For this purpose, the unit of comparison should be a relatively universal decision-making unit such as the local community. The degree of concentration of authority[29] within local units could be rated for a large number of societies which would also be classified according to their total-society organizations (see Figure 1). If the hypothesis is valid, then most societies would fall in the cells on the upper-right and lower-left of the chart, i.e., stateless societies would prove to have a low concentration of authority within their local units and states would prove to have a high concentration of authority in comparable units. It would also be possible to compare the authority structures of stateless societies having different types of total-society organization, as well as the local authority systems of states of different kinds of central organization. If there were no significant correlations between total society organization and local authority structure, then the influence of other variables on local authority structure would assume high priority for future research.

2) All societies have authority structures and values concerning the allocation of authority. In stateless societies, the proper unit for the analysis of such phenomena is not the total society, where we are likely to mistake lack of a central political hierachy for egalitarianism, but the maximal decision-making unit (or some cohesive subgrouping within it). Most often this unit corresponds to the village, but it may be a cluster of villages, a hamlet or neighborhood, or even a domestic group such as the polygynous extended family. The local decision-making unit provides adult individuals with a model for behavior toward incipient authority structures in the wider society, and it is simultaneously the

Figure 1

DEGREE OF CONCEN-TRATION OF AUTHORITY WITHIN LOCAL UNITS	TOTAL SOCIETY ORGANIZATION					
	Stateless Societies			States		
	Multikin Villages and Bands	Segmentary Lineages	Age and Associational Groups	Segmentary States	Federative States	Centralized States
Very High						
High						
Low						
Very Low						

model from which the child learns values concerning authority. This dual function is likely to continue even after national administration has drastically altered the nature of total-societal political organization by bringing it under state control. For this reason, the analysis of authority and other political values at the local level is most likely to yield valid predictions about contemporary political behavior in newly introduced governmental institutions.

NOTES

1. In 1955–1957 on a Ford Foundation Fellowship and with the assistance of the author's wife, Barbara B. LeVine.
2. Evans-Pritchard, 1940, 1953, 1956 and Howell.
3. Howell, pp. 230–231.
4. *Ibid.*, p. 236.
5. *Ibid.*, p. 39.
6. *Ibid.*, p. 66.
7. Phillips, writing in 1944, states, ". . . Comments on the intensely litigious disposition of the Kisii are to be found in official reports for at least thirty years past. . . ." He goes on to cite 1942 court records to show how much more litigation was brought by the Gusii (Kisii) than by their Nilotic neighbors, the Luo, p. 31.
8. Evans-Pritchard, 1940, p. 134.
9. *Ibid.*, p. 182.
10. *Ibid.*, p. 176.
11. Howell, p. 3.
12. Evans-Pritchard, 1940, pp. 183–184.
13. *Ibid.*, p. 134.
14. *Ibid.*, p. 181.
15. *Ibid.*, p. 151.
16. *Ibid.*, pp. 5–6.
17. Southall, pp. 241–263.
18. There is the question of why the political values of the Nuer and Gusii are so different. One possible hypothesis is an ecological one: the environment of the Nuer in the swampy upper Nile region necessitates local community cohesion and mutuality while tending to isolate one community from another. The Kenya highlands, where the Gusii live, provides an abundant agricultural base, with much less need for local cooperation and allows more contact between relatively distant parts of the society. This is consistent with the facts that the Nuer have more than twice as many tribal units as the Gusii, although their population is far from twice as large, and that, for the Gusii, the whole society is the maximal lineage, descended from Mogusii, while, for the Nuer, maximal lineages are

components of the total society. Thus, Nuer social organization and values seem adapted to an environment which forces the cohesion of small groups but prevents that of large ones, while Gusii social organization and values seem less constrained by the physical environment.

19. Fosbrooke.

20. Miller.

21. The most recent example of this is the volume entitled, *Tribes Without Rulers: Studies in African Segmentary Systems*, Middleton and Tait, 1958, in which six political systems are described with a minimal treatment of problems of internal authority. Leach represents an approach taking greater account of authority values.

22. Frenkel-Brunswik, 1955 and in Adorno, *et al.*, pp. 337–389.

23. Adorno, *et al.*, pp. 359–360.

24. Evans-Pritchard, 1953, p. 137.

25. Sears, Maccoby, and Levin, p. 259.

26. Evans-Pritchard, 1940, p. 157.

27. *Ibid.*, p. 184.

28. Bruner, p. 194.

29. In actual research this would have to be broken down into a number of specific variables, but elaboration of the concept is beyond the scope of this paper.

BIBLIOGRAPHY

ADORNO, T. W. *et al.*, *The Authoritarian Personality*, Harper & Bros., New York, 1950.

BRUNER, EDWARD M., "Cultural Transmission and Cultural Change," *Southwestern Journal of Anthropology*, XII (1956), 191–199.

EVANS-PRITCHARD, EDWARD EVANS, *The Nuer*, Oxford University Press, London, 1940; *Kinship and Marriage Among the Nuer*, Oxford University Press, London, 1953; *Nuer Religion*, Oxford University Press, London, 1956.

FORTES, MEYER AND E. E. EVANS-PRITCHARD (ed.), *African Political Systems*, Oxford University Press, London, 1940.

FOSBROOKE, H. A., "An Administrative Survey of the Masai Social System," *Tanganyika Notes and Records*, No. 26, 1948, pp. 1–50.

FRENKEL-BRUNSWIK, ELSE, "Differential Patterns of Social Outlook and Personality in Family and Children," in Margaret Mead and Martha Wolfenstein (eds.), *Childhood in Contemporary Cultures*, University of Chicago Press, 1955.

HOWELL, P. P. *A Manual of Nuer Law*, Oxford University Press, London, 1954.

LEACH, E. R., *Political Systems of Highland Burma*, G. Bell and Sons, London, 1954.

MIDDLETON, JOHN AND DAVID TAIT (eds.), *Tribes Without Rulers: Studies in African Segmentary Systems*, Routledge, Kegan Paul, London, 1958.

MILLER, WALTER B., "Two Concepts of Authority," *American Anthropologist*, LVII (1955), 271–289.

PHILLIPS, ARTHUR, *Report on Native Tribunals*, Government Printing Office, Colony and Protectorate of Kenya, Nairobi, 1944.

RIESMAN, DAVID, *The Lonely Crowd*, Yale University Press, New Haven, Conn., 1950.

SEARS, ROBERT R., ELEANOR MACCOBY, AND HARRY LEVIN, *Patterns of Child Rearing*, Row, Peterson, Evanston, Ill., 1957.

SOUTHALL, AIDAN W., *Alur Society: A Study in Processes and Types of Domination*, Heffer and Sons, Cambridge, England, 1956.

WHITING, JOHN W. M. *et al.*, *Field Manual for the Cross-Cultural Study of Child Rearing*, Social Science Research Council (mimeographed); "Inculcation of the Mechanisms of Social Control" in *Field Guide for a Study of Socialization in Five Societies* by Whiting, Irvin Child, W. W. Lambert *et al.*, Laboratory of Human Development, Harvard University (mimeographed).

THE MAKING OF A BLACK MUSLIM

• John R. Howard

The Lost-Found Nation of Islam in the Wilderness of North America, commonly known as the Black Muslim movement, claims a small but fanatically devoted membership among the Negroes of our major cities. The way of the "Messenger" is rigorous for those who follow it. The man or woman who becomes a Muslim accepts not only an ideology but an all-encompassing code that amounts to a way of life.

A good Muslim does a full day's work on an empty stomach. When he finally has his one meal of the day in the evening it can include no pork, nor can he have drink before or a cigarette after; strict dietary rules are standard procedure, and liquor and smoking are forbidden under any circumstances. His recreation is likely to consist of reading the Koran or participating in a demanding round of temple-centered activities, running public meetings or aggressively proselytizing on the streets by selling the Muslim newspaper, *Muhammad Speaks*.

Despite allegations of Muslim violence (advance publicity from the slaying of Malcolm X supports the erroneous notion that Muslims preach violence), the member's life is basically ascetic. Why then in a non-ascetic, hedonistically-oriented society do people become Muslims? What is the life of a Muslim like? These are questions I asked in research among West Coast

Above selection reprinted from: *Trans-Action*, 4 (December 1966), 15–21. Deletions have been made by the editor in the interest of brevity.

members. Specifically, I wanted to know:

What perspective on life makes membership in such an organization attractive?
Under what conditions does the potential recruit develop those perspectives?
How does he happen to come to the door of the temple for his first meeting?
The Black Muslims are a deviant organization even within the Negro community; the parents or friends of many members strongly objected to their joining. So how does the recruit handle pressures that might erode his allegiance to the organization and its beliefs?

Presenting my questions as an effort to "learn the truth" about the organization, I was able to conduct depth interviews with 19 West Coast recruits, following them through the process of their commitment to the Nation of Islam.

Two main points of appeal emerged—black nationalism and an emphasis on self-help. Some recruits were attracted primarily by the first, and some by the second. The 14 interviewees who joined the organization for its aggressive black nationalism will be called "Muslim militants." The remaining five, who were attracted more by its emphasis on hard work and rigid personal morality, may be aptly termed "Protestant Ethic Muslims."

Muslim Militants: Beating the Devil

Of the 14 Muslim militants, some came from the South, some from border states, and some from the North. All lived in California at the time of the interviews; some migrated to the state as adults, others were brought out by their families as children. They varied in age from 24 to 46, and in education from a few years of grade school to four years of college. Regardless of these substantial differences in background, there were certain broad similarities among them.

At some point, each one had experiences that led away from the institutionally-bound ties and commitments that lend stability to most people's lives. Nine had been engaged in semi-legal or criminal activities. Two had been in the military, not as a career but as a way of postponing the decision of what to do for a living. None had a stable marital history. All of them were acutely aware of being outsiders by the standards of the larger society—and all had come to focus on race bias as the factor which denied them more conventional alternatives.

Leroy X came to California in his late teens, just before World War II:

I grew up in Kansas City, Missouri, and Missouri was a segregated state. Negroes in Kansas City were always restricted to the menial jobs. I came out here in 1940 and tried to get a job as a waiter. I was a trained waiter, but they weren't hiring any Negroes as waiters in any of the downtown hotels or restaurants. The best I could do was busboy, and they fired me from that when they found out I wasn't Filipino.

Leroy X was drafted, and after a short but stormy career was given a discharge as being psychologically unfit.

I tried to get a job, but I couldn't so I started stealing. There was nothing else to do—I couldn't live on air. The peckerwoods didn't

seem to give a damn whether I lived or died. They wouldn't hire me and didn't seem to worry how I was going to stay alive. I started stealing.

I could get you anything you wanted—a car, drugs, women, jewelry. Crime is a business like any other. I started off stealing myself. I wound up filling orders and getting rid of stuff. I did that for fifteen years. In between I did a little time. I did time for things I never thought of doing and went free for things I really did.

In my business you had no friends, only associates, and not very close ones at that.... I had plenty of money. I could get anything I wanted without working for it. It wasn't enough, though.

Bernard X grew up in New York City:

As a kid . . . you always have dreams—fantasies—of yourself doing something later—being a big name singer or something that makes you outstanding. But you never draw the connection between where you are and how you're going to get there. I had to—I can't say exactly when, 13, 14, 15, 16. I saw I was nowhere and had no way of getting anywhere.

Race feeling is always with you. You always know about The Man but I don't think it is real, really real, until you have to deal with it in terms of what you are going to do with your own life. That's when you feel it. If you just disliked him before—you begin to hate him when you see him blocking you in your life. I think then a sense of inevitability hits you and you see you're not going to make it out—up—away—anywhere—and you see The Man's part in the whole thing, that's when you begin to think thoughts about him.

Frederick 2X became involved fairly early in a criminal subculture. His father obtained a "poor man's divorce" by deserting the family. His mother had children by other men. Only a tenuous sense of belonging to a family existed. He was picked up by the police for various offenses several times before reaching his teens. The police patrolling his neighborhood eventually restricted him to a two-block area. There was, of course, no legal basis for this, but he was manhandled if seen outside that area by any policeman who knew him. He graduated in his late teens from "pot" to "shooting shit" and eventually spent time in Lexington.

William 2X, formerly a shoeshine boy, related the development of his perspective this way:

You know how they always talk about us running after white women. There have always been a lot of [white] servicemen in this town—half of them would get around to asking me to get a woman for them. Some of them right out, some of them backing into it, laughing and joking and letting me know how much they were my friend, building up to asking me where they could find some woman. After a while I began to get them for them. I ran women—both black and white. . . . What I hated was they wanted me to do something for them [find women] and hated me for doing it. They figure "any nigger must know where to find it. . . ."

Things Begin to Add Up

Amos X grew up in an all-Negro town in Oklahoma and attended a Negro college. Because of this, he had almost no contact with whites during his formative years.

One of my aunts lived in Tulsa. I went to see her once when I was in college. I walked up to the front door of the house where she worked. She really got excited and told me if I came to see her anymore to come around to the back. But that didn't mean much to me at the time. It is only in looking back on it that all these things begin to add up.

After graduating from college, Amos joined the Marines. Then he began to "see how they [the whites] really felt" about him; by the end of his tour, he had concluded that "the white man is the greatest liar, the greatest cheat, the greatest hypocrite on earth." Alienated and disillusioned, he turned to professional gambling. Then, in an attempt at a more conventional way of life, he married and took a job teaching school.

I taught English. Now I'm no expert in the slave masters' language, but I knew the way those kids talked after being in school eight and nine years was ridiculous. They said things like "mens" for "men." I drilled them and pretty soon some of them at least in class began to sound like they had been inside a school. Now the principal taught a senior class in English and his kids talked as bad as mine. When I began to straighten out his kids also he felt I was criticizing him. . . . That little black man was afraid of the [white] superintendent and all those teachers were afraid. They had a little more than other socalled Negroes and didn't give a damn about those black children they were teaching. Those were the wages of honesty. It's one thing to want to do an honest job and another thing to be able to. . . .

With the collapse of his career as a public school teacher and the break-up of his marriage, Amos went to California, where he was introduced to the Muslim movement.

I first heard about them [the Muslims] in 1961. There was a debate here between a Muslim and a Christian minister. The Muslim said all the things about Christianity which I had been thinking but which I had never heard anyone say before. He tore the minister up.

Finding an organization that aggressively rejected the white man and the white man's religion, Amos found his own point of view crystallized. He joined without hesitation.

Norman Maghid first heard of the Muslims while he was in prison.

I ran into one of the Brothers selling the paper about two weeks after I got out and asked him about the meetings. Whether a guy could just go and walk in. He told me about the meetings so I made it around on a Wednesday evening. I wasn't even bugged when they searched me. When they asked me about taking out my letter [joining the organization] I took one out. They seemed to know what they were talking about. I never believed in nonviolence and love my enemies, especially when my enemies don't love me.

Muhammad Soule Kabah, born into a family of debt-ridden Texas sharecroppers, was recruited into the Nation of Islam after moving to California.

I read a series of articles in the Los Angeles *Herald Dispatch*, an exchange between Minister Henry and a Christian minister. It confirmed what my grandfather had told me about my African heritage, that I had nothing to be ashamed of, that there were six thousand books on mathematics in the Library of the University of Timbucktoo while Europeans were still wearing skins. Also my father had taught me never to kow-tow to whites. My own father had fallen away. My parents didn't want me to join the Nation. They said they taught hate. That's funny isn't it? The white man can blow up a church and kill four children and the black man worries that an organization which tells you not to just take it is teaching hate.

Protestant Ethic Muslims: Up by Black Bootstraps

The Protestant Ethic Muslims all came from backgrounds with a strong tradi-

tion of Negro self-help. In two cases the recruit's parents had been followers of Marcus Garvey; another recruit explicitly endorsed the beliefs of Booker T. Washington; and the remaining two, coming from upwardly mobile families, were firm in the belief that Negroes could achieve higher status if they were willing to work for it.

When asked what had appealed to him about the Muslims, Norman X replied:

They thought that black people should do something for themselves. I was running this small place [a photography shop] and trying to get by. I've stuck with this place even when it was paying me barely enough to eat. Things always improve and I don't have to go to the white man for anything.

Ernestine X stressed similar reasons for joining the Muslims.

You learned to stand up straight and do something for yourself. You learn to be a lady at all times—to keep your house clean —to teach your children good manners. There is not a girl in the M-G-T who does not know how to cook and sew. The children are very respectful; they speak only when they are spoken to. There is no such thing as letting your children talk back to you the way some people believe. The one thing they feel is the Negroes' downfall is men and sex for the women, and women and sex for the men, and they frown on sex completely unless you are married.

Despite their middle-class attitudes in many areas, Protestant Ethic Muslims denounced moderate, traditional civil rights organizations such as the NAACP, just as vigorously as the militant Muslims did. Norman X said that he had once belonged to the NAACP but had dropped out.

They spent most of their time planning the annual brotherhood dinner. Besides it was mostly whites—whites and the colored doctors and lawyers who wanted to be white. As far as most Negroes were concerned they might as well not have existed.

Lindsey X, who had owned and run his own upholstery shop for more than 30 years, viewed the conventional black bourgeoisie with equal resentment.

I never belonged to the NAACP. What they wanted never seemed real to me. I think Negroes should create jobs for themselves rather than going begging for them. That's why I never supported CORE.

In this respect Norman and Lindsey were in full accord with the more militant Amos X, who asserted:

They [the NAACP and CORE] help just one class of people. . . . Let something happen to a doctor and they are right there; but if something happens to Old Mose on the corner, you can't find them.

The interviews made it clear that most of the Protestant Ethic Muslims had joined the Nation because, at some point, they began to feel the need of organizational support for their personal systems of value. For Norman and Lindsey, it was an attempt to stop what they considered their own backsliding after coming to California. Both mentioned drinking to excess and indulging in what they regarded as a profligate way of life. Guilt feelings apparently led them to seek Muslim support in returning to more enterprising habits.

Commitment to Deviance

The Nation of Islam is a deviant organization. As such it is subject to public scorn and ridicule. Thus it faces the problem of consolidating the recruit's allegiance in an environment where substantial pressures operate to erode this allegiance. How does it deal with this problem?

The structural characteristics of the Nation tend to insulate the member from the hostility of the larger society and thus contribute to the organization's survival. To begin with, the ritual of joining the organization itself stresses commitment without questions.

At the end of the general address at a temple meeting, the minister asks those nonmembers present who are "interested in learning more about Islam" to step to the back of the temple. There they are given three blank sheets of ordinary stationary and a form letter addressed to Elijah Muhammad in Chicago:

Dear Savior Allah, Our Deliverer:
I have attended the Teachings of Islam, two or three times, as taught by one of your ministers. I believe in it. I bear witness that there is no God but Thee. And, that Muhammad is Thy Servant and Apostle. I desire to reclaim my Own. Please give me my Original name. My slave name is as follows:

The applicant is instructed to copy this letter verbatim on each of the three sheets of paper, giving his own name and address unabbreviated at the bottom. If he fails to copy the letter perfectly, he must repeat the whole task. No explanation is given for any of these requirements.

Formal acceptance of his letter makes the new member a Muslim, but in name only. Real commitment to the Nation of Islam comes gradually—for example, the personal commitment expressed when a chain smoker gives up cigarettes in accordance with the Muslim rules even though he knows that he could smoke unobserved. "It's not that easy to do these things," Stanley X said of the various forms of abstinence practiced by Muslims. "It takes will and discipline and time, . . . but you're a much better person after you do." Calvin X told of periodic backsliding in the beginning. but added, "Once I got into the thing deep, then I stuck with it."

This commitment and the new regimen that goes with it have been credited with effecting dramatic personality changes in many members, freeing alcoholics from the bottle and drug addicts from the needle. It can be argued, however, that the organization does not change the member's fundamental orientation. To put it somewhat differently, given needs and impulses can be expressed in a variety of ways; thus, a man may give vent to his sadism by beating up strangers in an alley or by joining the police force and beating them up in the back room of the station.

"Getting into the thing deep" for a Muslim usually comes in three stages:

Participation in organizational activities— selling the Muslim newspaper, dining at the Muslim restaurant, attending and helping run Muslim meetings.
Isolation from non-Muslim social contacts— drifting away from former friends and associates because of divergent attitudes or simply because of the time consumed in Muslim activities.
Assimilation of the ideology—marking full commitment, when a Muslim has so absorbed the organization's doctrines that he automatically uses them to guide his own behavior and to interpret what happens in the world around him.

The fact that the organization can provide a full social life furthers isolation from non-Muslims. Participation is not wholly a matter of drudgery, of tramping the streets to sell the paper and studying the ideology. The organization presents programs of entertainment for its members and the public. For example, in two West Coast cities a Negro theatrical troupe called the Touring Artists put on two plays, "Jubilee Day" and "Don't You Want to Be Free." Although there was a high element of humor in both plays, the basic themes— white brutality and hypocrisy and the necessity of developing Negro self-respect and courage—were consonant with the organization's perspective. Thus the organization makes it possible for a member to satisfy his need for diversion without going outside to do so. At the same time, it continually reaches him with its message through the didactic element in such entertainment.

Carl X's experiences were typical of the recruit's growing commitment to the Nation. When asked what his friends had thought when he first joined, he replied: "They thought I was crazy. They said, 'Man, how can you believe all that stuff?'" He then commented that he no longer saw much of them, and added:

When you start going to the temple four or five times a week and selling the newspaper you do not have time for people who are not doing these things. We drifted—the friends I had—we drifted apart. . . . All the friends I have now are in the Nation. Another Brother and I get together regularly and read the Koran and other books, then ask each other questions on them like, "What is Allah's greatest weapon? The truth. What is the devil's greatest weapon? The truth. The devil keeps it hidden from men. Allah reveals it to man." We read and talk about the things we read and try to sharpen our thinking. I couldn't do that with my old friends.

The Problem of Defection

Commitment to the Nation can diminish as well as grow. Four of the members I interviewed later defected. Why?

These four cases can be explained in terms of a weak point in the structure of the Nation. The organization has no effective mechanisms for handling grievances among the rank and file. Its logic accounts for this. Muslim doctrine assumes that there is a single, ultimate system of truth. Elijah Muhammad and, by delegation, his ministers are in possession of this truth. Thus only Elijah Muhammad himself can say whether a minister is doing an adequate job. The result is the implicit view that there is nothing to be adjudicated between the hierarchy and its rank and file.

Grievances arise, however. The four defectors were, for various reasons, all dissatisfied with Minister Gerard X. Since there were no formal mechanisms within the organization for expressing their dissatisfaction, the only solution was to withdraw.

For most members, however, the pattern is one of steadily growing involvement. And once the ideology is fully absorbed, there is virtually no such thing as dispute or counterevidence. If a civil rights bill is not passed, this proves the viciousness of whites in refusing to recognize Negro rights. If the same bill *is* passed, it merely proves the duplicity of whites in trying to hide their viciousness.

The ideology also provides a coherent theory of causation, provided one is willing to accept its basic assumptions. Norman X interpreted his victory over his wife in a court case as a sign of Allah's favor. Morris X used it to account for the day-to-day fortunes of his associates.

Minister X had some trouble. He was sick for a long time. He almost died. I think Allah was punishing him. He didn't run the temple right. Now the Brothers make mistakes. Everyone does—but Minister X used to abuse them at the meetings. It was more a personal thing. He had a little power and it went to his head. Allah struck him down and I think he learned a little humility.

When a man reasons in this fashion, he has become a fully committed member of the Nation of Islam. His life revolves around temple-centered activities, his friends are all fellow Muslims, and he sees his own world—usually the world of an urban slum dweller—through the framework of a very powerful myth. He is still doing penance for the sins of Yakub, but the millennium is at hand. He has only to prepare.

The Nation of Islam does not in any real sense convert members. Rather it attracts Negroes who have already, through their own experiences in white America, developed a perspective congruent with that of the Muslim movement. The recruit comes to the door of the temple with the essence of his ideas already formed. The Black Muslims only give this disaffection a voice.

FURTHER READING SUGGESTED BY THE AUTHOR

Outsiders: Studies in the Sociology of Deviance, by Howard S. Becker. London: Free Press of Glencoe, 1963. Provides a theoretical framework for analyzing behavior such as joining the Nation of Islam.

Black Nationalism: a Search for an Identity in America, by E. Essien-Udom. Chicago: University of Chicago Press, 1962. Valuable mainly in that it was done by an African.

The Black Muslims in America, by C. Eric Lincoln. Boston: Beacon Press, 1961. A standard work on the Nation of Islam.

The Social Psychology of Social Movements, by Hans Toch. Indianapolis: Bobbs-Merrill, 1965. An excellent treatment of a wide variety of political and non-political social movements.

POLITICS

- Charlotte Leon Mayerson

Many of these conversations* took place between the time President John Kennedy was assassinated and the 1964 Presidential race between President Lyndon Johnson and Senator Barry Goldwater. Juan is always very aware of the political scene. He spends a lot of time talking about politics and trying to work out for himself a political philosophy appropriate to his own situation. He listens to speeches, is always "looking for a fight" about the latest political development, and frequently asks for information about political figures with whom he is unfamiliar.

Peter is not interested in politics or in government in any theoretical sense. He has participated in some of his family's political activities on the local district level and he is interested in politicians or officials with whom he can personally identify. He was extremely disturbed by President Kennedy's assassination and he is still very moved when he refers to it.

* The selection above consists of tape recorded interviews with two seventeen-year-old boys living in the same New York City neighborhood. They are both high-school seniors and both belong to the same Catholic parish. They do not know each other. Juan is Puerto Rican and poor; Peter is white and middle-class (ed.).

- Juan Gonzales

Whenever I hear a political speech or something like the Governor is not quitting, he's going to go on running, or things like that, I don't understand what it is all about. But pretty soon I start thinking.

You know I felt bad when Kennedy was assassinated because that's wrong, to kill anybody. But I figured out that all the people that have a lot of money are the ones that are in politics. You see in the news all the time that another Rockefeller goes into politics or a Kennedy. Those are the only people that can get anywhere and I can't see it. It's supposed to be that the people, they govern themselves. But it seems as if the rich guy controls all the others. They move and we follow. We pay taxes and they get rich and that is all wrong.

Abraham Lincoln's supposed to be very poor, and poverty-stricken, and finally he worked himself up to be the President of the United States. Anybody that's poor *now* couldn't get in. Like, they showed a picture of Johnson on his ranch or someplace. He didn't go there by car. He didn't go there by bus. He didn't go there by train. He went there by helicopter. Now how many people do you think can afford a helicopter? Who could afford a limousine? That just tells me that the rich man is running the government.

And even the Puerto Ricans who managed to get elected to something, they never can get to the point where they can say to anybody, "Do this, do that." They can only get to the point where their own ignorant people, the Negroes and the Puerto Ricans, can say, "Well, we have somebody up there now. We can really tell the big shots what we want." But they are really like nowhere. It is just the same as if they were still out on the street saying, "I want my rights."

Now I don't believe in the Nazi Government or anything like that, but I believe that once the poorer people get to a stage where they can just *take* their rights, *that's* when the people will run their government.

Like that class stuff? It's really color that's class now. If the Negroes weren't Negroes, if they were all white, if there were all whites in the world, the upper class couldn't have any way to keep so much power.

Now, we have people going around saying, "Oh, look at that colored guy. I don't want to see him with a white woman." Things like that. This is where you get your problems, your riots.

And nothing helps so far. Even Malcolm X, he starts a campaign, but then he doesn't go all the way through. He leaves the Negroes hanging on a string, just dangling. He says he's going to do something, but all of a sudden he changes his mind and goes to something else.

But anyway, Malcolm has a problem. He organized the Negroes, but then they wouldn't go behind him. They wouldn't help him, so Malcolm himself was left there hanging. He thought he was leading a group and all of a sudden he found there was nobody there. Everybody was home, criticizing, or getting criticized.

Like when you have those sit-down strikes. All right, so you get a little, maybe even a lot, of newspaper stories out of it. But what is it doing for them? Nothing. They are only being arrested and they are being put in jail and their money's being taken away from them. They are being *destroyed*. What chance can a Negro or a Puerto Rican have if he goes to school? He can't get where the power really is. Like he can't go into the Treasury Department or into the Defense Department or be a general. He can't go like to be working as a Secretary of State.

Well, I figured out that the Negroes, since they *are* segregated, if they would form a group all by themselves, but with the Puerto Ricans, then they could try to get money, power. They could form into a great empire. You see, then no one could tell them, "Do this, do that." They'd be on their own.

The way it is now, what's the use of having a Negro who's a genius? They won't give him a chance to work. What's the use of having guys, Negro guys, that can solve diseases? If he does solve them, then someone else takes the credit. It's no use for the Negro unless he gets organized. I'm not saying that they'd be better off living someplace off by themselves. I'm saying that they should stand up for their rights, get something done for themselves. Live in *this* society, but, I mean, why plead to the whites when the whites close their ears to them? Why don't they plead with the others who are down? Why doesn't the Negro say to the Puerto Ricans, "Why don't you help us? Why don't you join us and get something done about the things that we both want? Why don't you help us get more money? Why don't you help us get more power? Why don't you help us get credits and distinctions so you know who's who?"

But, you know, that's tough. Like, I've never met any Puerto Rican kid who thinks on his own the way I do. Like I'm alone.

That's because the Puerto Ricans and the Negroes hold everything back. Because they fear if they say something it's just that they'll be hurt and be hurt bad. They're afraid. They know what's what. No one wants to listen.

O.K., say a lot of people start to say, "Well, here are these boys, fifteen- sixteen-year-old boys, if they can go on strike for their rights, why shouldn't we help them?"

Well, maybe some people do say that, but most of them are not going to listen, they're just going to lay back and die. These strikes or these boycotts don't have any effect. The people with power, they hear, and maybe some of them are losing money, but they are not really getting hurt that bad. If a Puerto Rican who has a job went on strike, didn't make money, he'd die. He couldn't support himself or his family and sooner or later he'd just perish. They'd be nothing left for him. A person of the upper brackets, he can go on a one-man strike. Just do what he wants. He would lose out in the little business profit, or maybe close down one business, but he'd still have another chain there.

Then, another thing, people with a lot of money have everything they want. They've got money, power, but that's not enough for them. They want to be able to know that their grandchildren will see their name written down in a book someplace, as Governor, as President. They want something to be remembered by, but that doesn't mean that they are qualified to be a leader. You can have a

Puerto Rican over here and really he's not making over $2,000 a year, but he can have the experience enough to go over there and run the government.

But what happens now? A guy who's got the money starts campaigning and gets a big job. He doesn't have to know a thing about it. Then, on the other side, you have someone like me. I can know everything about politics, but I can't go and start a campaign. I don't have the power. I could say something to my people, to Negroes, but until I get some power I just have to keep my mouth shut.

You know, I never had a lot of money, I don't know how I would react with power. But I don't think I would look down on my own. Let's put it this way: if I am a middle-class person who has enough power to make me want to go mad, I think I would do right and bring in more Puerto Ricans here and try to get them higher. I wouldn't leave the Puerto Ricans flat. I would try to bring them up. But people don't do that.

Puerto Rican politicians are more crooked than even the cops because you see they are up there, maybe one Negro, one Puerto Rican, among all those whites. They don't know what's going on, they feel dumb. They feel dumb and they are treated dumb even though they are all politicians together. The whites, they give that one poor slob all the lousy things to do. He takes orders and he obeys them. Whatever the white politicians want, the Negro or the Puerto Rican goes through with it. I don't think until another generation will you find a Puerto Rican politician that can think on his own, to go out there and do his job, as if for his own people. Now he'll do what the others want him to.

The only one who's got power is

Adam.* You can see that they listen to Adam Clayton. He came to our school once and he gave a long speech and every kid there applauded. We believe in what he says because he has power, maybe not as much as the other people up in Congress, but enough to try to help.

Not like Malcolm X.† He has no power. He can't even get the people behind him. And instead of trying to think his way out of a problem, he uses the gun, and the fists, and riots. That's how all of this riot problem came up. There is nothing in Harlem now. All the wars, breaking up the stores. Now that's stupid. I mean, what do they get out of it? Usually the people that have the stores are the whites. I guess they figure that they will hurt the whites by breaking up their little companies, but it just gets the Negroes into trouble.

You know, kids are more restless than old people. The old people can afford to wait, they are used to it. But the younger group, they say, "Well, we've got to do it now, because when I grow up I want to be able to walk down the street free. I don't want to walk, like down the street, a slave."

And the shooting of that kid before the riots got them mad. First of all, a policeman is supposed to give a person a warning shot. If he is going to shoot, he shoots at the legs and he won't kill the person. Now I know it didn't happen like the cops say. I can't see a little boy, fifteen years old, grab a knife and try to attack an officer. Now that's not easy to believe. I'd be scared to attack an officer with a knife, when I know the cop had a gun. I

don't believe that cop was telling the truth.

But, really, that shooting didn't have anything to do with the riots. It just set off the fuse. Harlem was tensed up because they got their civil rights bill, but they were still going backwards. They were still being treated like privileged savages and so they finally said, "Well, let's *be* savages. I mean, they treat us like savages, we might as well become savages."

And where does it get them? Have you heard from Adam Clayton lately? Nothing. How can he help when they are in these riots. Can he say that his people are nervous? He can't say nothing. He can't help them just because they are rioting. If they keep it up, they are just going to get themselves in a lot of trouble. You notice you didn't see many Puerto Ricans out that night because the Negroes can't sometimes tell a Puerto Rican from a regular white person in the middle of the night, when it's dark, unless the Puerto Rican talks up. But the Puerto Rican can get out of hand just as well as the Negroes. Now, the Negroes are just out, and the whites are stopping them, but suppose, all of a sudden, suppose the Puerto Ricans went out of hand, too. They would be too much to handle and if the Puerto Ricans and the Negroes ever join up, they'll be like a revolution.

The trouble is that nobody is looking ahead, everybody's looking out for now. And I just watch, and I just see how everything's going and I am making plans to move out of this little city, because I know there's going to be a lot of more trouble. There's just the beginning now. Everybody thinks the worst has ended, but the worst hasn't even shown up yet.

* Adam Clayton Powell, Congressman from New York. Mr. Powell is a Negro.

† Malcolm X, Negro nationalist leader, was assassinated in February, 1965, several months after this conversation.

• Peter Quinn

I have never enjoyed politics much. I've watched the news almost every night for years and I've listened to the commentators asking politicians questions about current events. I have never yet experienced a straight answer from any of them, and I just don't like that.

The only time I ever had much to do with the whole subject was when my uncle ran for district leader. That was fun. I got my friends and my cousins and we put up signs and stuff like that. I didn't pay too much attention to the political part of it and though I was disappointed that he didn't get in, I have to say that the part I liked best about the campaign was climbing lampposts to get the signs up.

The only election I ever paid much attention to was when Kennedy was running, but I don't consider that politics. I said to myself then, "If Kennedy isn't going to be elected, I want to die." I really went for him because he was Irish, because he was Catholic, because he was so very good in politics, I thought. Everybody I knew or spoke to liked him and didn't like Nixon. Then, when he got in, I was very proud to see him there, and he was doing a great job. He put a lot of new things in and tried for many things that Eisenhower would never even think of. My father took me to see him once when he was coming into New York and that was the greatest thrill of my life.

Then—well—I guess I'll never forget the day he died. It was the last period in school and we were doing our geometry homework and then Brother Joseph, the principal of the school came over the P.A. System and said, "Attention, stop everything and listen. Very important." And

then a radio came on and through the microphone a voice said, "We have confirmed that the President died." He was dead and everybody was stunned. I was terrified. I was really afraid. I said that the world was going to come to an end and I kept thinking about it and thinking about it and I was really more afraid than I have ever been in my life or than I ever will be.

The thing that got me was how he could be killed by such a small man. How such a small creature could really ruin us, could really shock the whole nation, how easily this could be done. I felt that way for a long time, but then when I saw what kind of person Johnson was I got over it.

That day everybody thought it was a joke, they were too shocked to believe it. The school was very quiet. Usually there's a lot of hustle and bustle after the day is over with everybody throwing books around and going crazy, but that day nobody said anything.

Then, when I watched the funeral, I was terribly depressed, and yet I was very proud of how all that honor was given to the President, to someone who came out of the same background as I did. Everybody really loved him. So many heads of state and leaders of other countries came, and it really struck me when the caisson came out of the White House through those gates and all the heads of state walked together in a crowd as if they were no one compared to Kennedy. Just for this man. Then they all attended Mass and it was really beautiful. I was proud of the Presidency and how it was and, then, remembering him, I felt terrible.

As a matter of fact the only time I ever paid any attention to political speeches was during that campaign. Now, I don't pay much attention because politicians always get around the questions and never really say much. But that Kennedy-Nixon debate, that was the greatest! Nixon was falling all over himself and I loved it.

In this last campaign that we had for President, I was for Johnson, but my family was not. We didn't talk much about it, but I was worried about some of the things that Goldwater said he would do. They were really wild. I never discuss it much with my brother because he generally approves of Goldwater and I know that if I got into a big discussion with him I don't know enough. If I had a fight with him, a mental fight, I would be only half armed.

I don't think much of Johnson either, but about war he seems to be more sensible. He's more or less following Kennedy's lead, though on a smaller scale. Kennedy showed, in the Cuban blockade, that he wasn't taking any nonsense from anybody, though he wasn't recklessly dropping bombs.

Johnson is a hard man to like. I don't like his Southern way of speaking and that really bothers me. As for Humphrey, I can't stand him. He acts like a fool talking too much and not being dignified. He just doesn't seem to know how to behave.

The thing that really surprised me in the last election was that Robert Kennedy beat Senator Keating. I thought he was great and a very good politician, but that he wasn't going to win. I thought that Senator Keating had Senator Javits* on his side and the Jewish population would vote for Keating. I don't know why, but I

* Senators from New York, 1964. Jacob Javits is Jewish; Kenneth Keating, who was defeated by Robert Kennedy, is not.

expected all the Jews in New York to vote for him. Of course, all the Irish and all the Catholics always knew who they were going to vote for, not only because the Kennedys are Irish Catholics, but because they knew that Bobby was a very good organizer and someone who would carry on his brother's program.

I suppose it's only natural to be glad to see one of your own group in a high office. Not everybody has that chance. For example, I think there would be very small chance for a Puerto Rican person to reach a really important position in government. I suppose you can achieve something, if you're good enough, through contributions, but it takes an awful lot of money to go through politics and someone who just starts out with nothing would have to work awfully hard. Usually, politicians have some resources of their own. Just look at other politicians as an example. Goldwater is worth 2 million, Johnson is worth 17 million, and the Kennedy family is worth something like 300 million. To get where they are takes a lot more than any Puerto Rican or Negro has right now.

Although everybody in this country has a chance to run for office, probably a Negro or Puerto Rican now wouldn't be accepted. He has the right, but I don't think he can be elected. I suppose if the major party had very good faith in a Negro they might let him come in, but they'd have to have a very good idea that he'd win and that wouldn't happen very often. Another problem is it would be harder to find a Negro that was educated or qualified enough. I'm not saying that they are dumb people; they just haven't had the opportunities because we haven't given it to them. Maybe, sometime, there will be a time when they are ready. Fifty years from now.

But I don't spend too much time thinking or talking about politics. I guess there are some things that politicians could do, like cleaning up the slums and living conditions. Or something that bothers me personally, is that there ought to be more privileges for the teen-age boy in New York. For example, there are places to play now, but they're not nearly large enough, so that if a team wants to play hard ball without getting into some organized league, there are very few fields that are big enough. It would be nice if someone were to take care of that kind of thing, but I don't think that I've ever even talked about it to anybody.

I have one friend, though, who really can talk. We're always telling him that he is going to be a lawyer when he grows up. Once we got into a quarrel on the street with some man who just came up to us and began talking about Goldwater and saying that Goldwater would ruin the government. We were just sort of ignoring him, but when our talking friend came over he jumped right into that guy. He pointed a finger right in the guy's face and said, "You're a Commie." It seems that there was a picture of a man in the paper recently who was a Communist, and it looked just like this man. Maybe it even was. And my friend demolished that fellow and he went away without having much more to say. John's really a great talker, about any subject.

But it's not something we argue about or get all excited about. Even in my own family my father, brother, and sister are for Goldwater; my mother is for Johnson. Nobody ever quarrels about it, though, no worries.

THE MALEVOLENT LEADER: POLITICAL SOCIALIZATION IN AN AMERICAN SUB-CULTURE*

- Dean Jaros, Herbert Hirsch, and Frederic J. Fleron, Jr.

Introduction

Perhaps the most dramatic finding of recent research on the political socialization of children is that youngsters appear to be overwhelmingly favorably disposed toward political objects which cross their vision. Officers and institutions of government are regarded as benevolent, worthy, competent, serving and powerful.[1] The implications of such findings are striking indeed. Childhood political dispositions may represent the roots of later patriotism; we may be observing the building of basic regime-level supportive values at a very young age.[2]

These findings are by no means new; in fact, they might be classified as part of the conventional wisdom of the discipline. Moreover, they are extremely well documented. And, the study of childhood political socialization has advanced to consider far more than basic regime-level norms. Despite all this, however, there are still many empirical questions to be asked about such norms. Perhaps the recent assertion that the political scientist's model of socialization is "static and homogeneous,"[3] is particularly apropos here. Consider two closely related characteristics of the appropriate literature: 1) the "positive

Above article reprinted from: *The American Political Science Review*, LXII, 2 (June 1968), 564–575.

* The data on which this paper is based were collected under Contract #693 between the University of Kentucky Research Foundation and the Office of Economic Opportunity.

image" which children have about politics and political figures has been synthesized from data gathered largely in the United States and to some extent in urban, industrialized communities within the United States;[4] and 2) empirical explanation of the favorable disposition which children manifest has not progressed very far. Though there may be hypotheses about how children get this way, there has been little systematic testing of the relationships between variables.

There is some danger that the major findings may be essentially "culture bound." There are few data on the political values of children in other countries or even in rural, racial, or ethnic, sub-cultures within the United States. Moreover, what evidence there is hints at important cross-cultural variations in political learning;[5] less positive images may characterize other cultures. "Political socialization is the process by which the child learns about the political culture in which he lives."[6] The content of what is socialized may well differ from culture to culture or from sub-culture to sub-culture.

The failure to explain children's positive orientations toward politics may be a function of the cultural problem. If the great majority of children in one culture manifest a glowing image, variance in disposition is not prominent, and empirical explanation in terms of accounting for variance may not suggest itself as a crucial task; also it may be quite difficult.

In order to explain children's political images, one has to have a distribution of affect; there have to be some relatively negative images to come by. Research into children's political views in other cultures or sub-cultures may provide us with such negative images. But even if it does not generate the necessary data to conduct explanatory analysis, it would lessen the culture bound nature of findings in political socialization.[7]

This paper attempts to realize these desiderata through a study of childhood socialization in the Appalachian region of eastern Kentucky. Appalachia may be classified as a sub-culture within the United States for at least two reasons. The poverty and isolation of the region impose characteristics that differentiate it from most other areas in the country. Secondly and relatedly, many cultural norms of Appalachia differ radically from those considered to be standard middle-class imperatives.[8]

Two Explanations of Children's Political Authority Orientations

There are several relatively untested hypotheses about the sources of the positive notions children are observed to hold toward the political. Many of them prominently involve the family as a socializing agent. Because of the intriguing nature of family related variables in Appalachia, the region provides an excellent context in which to investigate these assertions.

Among these explanations is the view that the family directly transmits positive values about government and politics to the child while shielding him from stimuli which have negative connotations, such as stories of political corruption, expedient bargaining, etc.[9] In short, the family directly indoctrinates the child as to the benevolent nature of political authority, to view the political world in essentially the same terms as characterize the parents' generally supportive outlook on the political regime.[10] In Appalachia, in contrast to most of the rest of the United States, there is a great deal of overt, anti-government sentiment in the adult population. Rejection of and hostility toward political authority, especially federal authority, has long characterized the region.[11] It is very difficult to believe that here parents could transmit positive images of regime symbols to their children. In fact, ". . . the civic instruction which goes on incidental to normal activities in the family,"[12] suggested as a likely cause of children's favorable affect, would in Appalachia be a source of political cynicism. Singularly negative values may be communicated.

Secondly, we might take the thesis that the family is an important socializing agent because the child's experiences with his immediate authority figures (parents) are somehow projected to include more remote agencies, including the political. The father, perceived as providing and benevolent, supposedly becomes the prototypical authority figure.[13] For the child, the regime becomes "the family writ large,"[14] especially sacred as its image benefits from the emotional kind of bond that exists between parent and child. In Appalachia, there is a high degree of family disruption. The father may well not live at home. Far from providing a glowing prototype of authority, he may be a pitifully inadequate figure, unemployed or absent, not providing for his family, deserving of (and receiving) scorn.[15] If the Appalachian child generalizes the father figure or the family authority structure to the political, he is not very likely to be generalizing a positive configuration. Far less favorable political dispositions would result from this cause.[16]

Method

Data were gathered from a nearly complete enumeration (N = 2,432) of rural public school children in grades 5–12 in Knox County, Kentucky during March, 1967. Paper and pencil questionnaires were administered in classrooms in connection with an evaluation of a Community Action Program of the Office of Economic Opportunity. This paper is based on the responses of a random sample of 305 of these subjects.[17]

Affect toward political authority was measured in two ways: through reports of images of the President,[18] and through "political cynicism" scale scores.[19] Images of the President were used because this figure apparently occupies a key position in the development of both cognitions of and affect toward the regime.[20] The Presidency provides an introduction; notions first held toward this role are probably subsequently generalized to other political institutions and to the entity of government itself.[21] The specific instrumentation is that developed by Hess and Easton.[22]

By contrast, political cynicism, "Rather than referring to specific political issues and actors . . . is a basic orientation toward political actors and activity. It presumably pervades all encounters with political objects."[23] In short, political cynicism relates to a basic, general evaluative posture toward politics. Though perhaps a developmental descendant of images of the

President, this variable represents far less specifically focussed regime-level affect. The specific instrumentation is the political cynicism scale developed by Jennings and Niemi.[24]

In addition to desiring variables important in the introduction of children to politics and ones which seem to encapsulate a more generalized and developed kind of regime-level affect, we chose these measures because of the fact that they have generated reliable data. We wished to take advantage of direct replicative possibilities.

Unfortunately, no direct information about the political values of the parents of our sample is presently available.[25] Though the aggregate view of political institutions and personalities held by Appalachian adults is reportedly less positive than those of other Americans, the only personal level data available are child-reported. Our indicators of parental affect toward political authority consist of two family-related items from Easton and Dennis' scale of political efficacy.[26] Two problems attend to use of these items as indicators of parental values. First, the index in question was designed to measure a variable in children, not adults. However, the items "inquire about the relationship between government and the child's family . . ." The index is not regarded as a direct reflector of children's efficacy *per se*. In fact, it shows how a child has come to "view expected relationships between adult members of the system and the authorities" as well as it taps a "nascent attitude" of the child himself.[27] Youngsters tend to evaluate political objects in child-related terms.[28] Clearly this index does not measure that kind of dynamic. The items can be interpreted as a report on family (adult) orientations to political authorities. Indeed, such a report, involving the perception of children, may be a more significant independent variable than the actual values of the parents. A person's values, of course, can have no direct impact on the behavior of another individual. Any effect must be mediated through the influencee's cognitive and evaluative processes.

Secondly, given this, can items which tap efficacy be said to reveal anything about "positive" or supportive regime-level attitudes among adults? Though it is easy to imagine people highly enthusiastic about their political authority without their possessing "citizen competence,"[29] it is probable that in democratic societies sense of efficacy is in fact related to general affect toward political authority. Inefficacious feelings are related to alienation and what has been called "political negativism."[30] These are the very antithesis of supportive dispositions. Moreover, recent scholarship has specifically considered efficacy to be a crucial variable in regime-level supports.[31]

The nature of the family authority structure is measured by 1) "father image" items analogous to Hess and Easton's "Presidential image" items[32] and 2) noting whether the father in fact lives at home.[33]

The Appalachian Child's Affect Toward the Political

Our subjects' evaluations of political authority have a very prominent feature: they are dramatically less positive than those rendered by children in previously reported research.

Table 1 describes the affective responses of the Appalachian children to the President and directly compares them to Hess and Easton's findings on Chicago-area children. Though our sample includes children from fifth through twelfth grades and Hess and Easton's from second through eighth, it is possible to make comparisons using only the fifth through eighth grade portions of both. It is clear that for all five President-evaluation items, the distribution of responses of the Knox County youngsters is significantly less favorable than that of the Hess and Easton sample. In fact, when compared against "most men," the President does not do particularly well. On aggregate, he is not a paramount figure; and there are a fair number of youngsters (about a fourth) that express overtly unfavorable reactions to him.

Hess and Easton, it will be recalled, note that age greatly affects the nature of their sample's responses. Generally, they showed that the very favorable view that the very young have of the President's personal qualities (Items 2, 3, and 5) declines with increasing age, while high regard for his performance capabilities is maintained or even increased as the child grows older.[34] The diminution of "personal" portions of the image is not interpreted as a disillusionment with authority, but as increasing realism. The maintenance of the role-filling portions is regarded as most relevant to future adult behavior, translating into respect for political institutions.[35] In short, the changes of children's images of the President with age present a very fortunate configuration considered from the standpoint of loyalty and support for the regime. The Knox County data, bleak to begin with, show few such encouraging tendencies when controls are imposed for age. Even extending the analysis to the older portions of the

Table 1

Fifth–Eighth Grade Children's Evaluations of the President

	Response	*Knox County data**	*Chicago area data***	*Smirnov two-sample test*
1. View of how hard the President works compared with most men.	harder	35%	77%	
	as hard	24	21	
	less hard	41	3	$D=.42, p<.001$
	Total	100% (N = 128)	101% (N = 214)	
2. View of the honesty of the President compared with most men.	more honest	23%	57%	
	as honest	50	42	
	less honest	27	1	$D=.34, p<.001$
	Total	100% (N = 133)	100% (N = 214)	
3. View of the President's liking for people as compared with most men.	likes most everybody	50%	61%	
	likes as many as most	28	37	$D=.20, p<.01$
	doesn't like as many	22	2	
	Total	100% (N = 125)	100% (N = 214)	
4. View of the President's knowledge compared with most men.	knows more	45%	82%	
	knows about the same	33	16	$D=.37, p<.001$
	knows less	22	2	
	Total	100% (N = 124)	100% (N = 212)	
5. View of the President as a person.	best in world	6%	11%	
	a good person	68	82	
	not a good person	26	8	$D=.19, p<.01$
	Total	100% (N = 139)	101% (N = 211)	

* The Knox County subjects were provided with a "don't know" option apparently not available to their Chicago-area counterparts. This was done to avoid forcing the subjects, who are relatively undeveloped intellectually, to choose among possibly meaningless options. As expected, choice of the don't know alternative was very frequent. For each of the five items above, approximately 30% responded that they did not know. In the interest of comparability, the data do not include these responses. Reported non-responses (about 1%) to items 4 and 5 are likewise excluded from the Chicago-area data.

** These data are compiled from those reported in Hess and Easton *op. cit.*, pp. 636-637.

sample does little to effect change. To be sure, the personal portions of the image appear slightly less positive than those of younger children. Only 31% of the high-school seniors think the President likes almost everybody while 31% think he likes fewer people than most men; no twelfth graders think the President is the best person in the world while 31% think he is not a good person. But overall, the picture is static. *Tau* correlations between age and positive responses to the personal image items range between .02 and .04 and are not significant.

In those portions of the image supposedly more crucial to adult regime-level behavior, there is no increase in favorable response to the President. However, a decline in the proportion of overtly unfavorable reactions does produce a significant relationship between age and positiveness on the item dealing with how hard the President works ($\tau c = .14, p < .05$) and a perceptible though not significant relationship between age and positiveness on the item dealing with the President's knowledge ($\tau c = .09, p > .05$). At best, these are modest trends. There is relatively little ground on the basis of which to say, "The President is increasingly seen as a person whose abilities are appropriate to the demands of his office . . ."[36]

Furthermore, the very high incidence of "don't knows" does not decline significantly with age (see note to Table 1). Such a high rate was to be expected of a deprived, unsophisticated population. But the fact that it remains high even among high-school seniors (mean nonresponse rate 27%) provides further evidence that politically speaking nothing is happening to these Appalachian youth as they mature. They certainly do not appear to be developing into adults devoted to symbols of extant political authority.

Finally, the stark contrast of these data to those on other American children is heightened when the consideration of social class is introduced. It has often been observed that lower class children have a greater propensity to idealize political figures.[37] This may well be due to the fact that such children are less

politicized than their middle-class counterparts. Being less developed and less knowledgeable, they have developed fewer critical faculties and continue to exhibit the "immature" response of excessive deference. It is impossible to determine whether the same class phenomenon operates within Appalachia for the sample as a whole is overwhelmingly lower class.[38] But because of their lower class position relative to the rest of the country, Knox County youngsters generally should be highly idealizing. The data of course reveal the diametric opposite. It is clear that Appalachia constitutes a distinct subculture, one in which there are operative variables sufficiently powerful to prevent the occurrence of what is by now expected as a matter of course.

Table 2 describes the more generalized affect manifested in political cynicism. The scores of the Knox County youngsters are compared to those of the Survey Research Center's nation-wide sample of high school seniors.[39]

The greater cynicism of the subculture sample is evident. Since The Survey Research Center deals only with high school students, perhaps comparisons should be made only with the high school portion (grades 10–12) of the Knox County sample. Though this portion is significantly more cynical, the small number of subjects in it perhaps recommends use of the entire sample. One might think that the introduction of younger respondents would depress cynicism scores (age and cynicism are reportedly positively related in children),[40] but this does not happen to any great degree. In any event, even the entire 5–12 grade Knox County sample is significantly more cynical than the SRC twelfth graders. The implication of

Table 2

Political Cynicism Scores

		Knox County data (whole sample)	Knox County data (high school only)	SRC national sample	Smirnov two sample test
most cynical	6	8%	26%	5%	Knox County data (whole sample) and SRC national sample, D = .16, $p<.001$
	5	11	22	3	
	4	19	11	13	
	3	19	20	37	
	2	23	15	25	Knox County data (High school only) and SRC national sample, D = .40, $p<.001$
least cynical	1	21	6	17	
Total		101%	100%	100%	

this, of course, is that in Appalachia, unlike the rest of the United States, there is relatively little change in cynicism with maturation. That this is the case is revealed by the non-significant $\tau c = -.02$ between school grade and political cynicism score. Early in life these children appear to become relatively cynical and they stay that way.

Thus, though at this point it remains unexplained, there is no doubt that Appalachian children manifest far less favorable political affect than do their counterparts elsewhere in the United States. Regardless of the index in question, the responses of our sample stand in sharp contrast to other research. Just as supportive dispositions in citizens have been asserted to have early roots, so may the Appalachians' often noted rejection of political authority germinate during tender years. Moreover, also in some contrast to other research, the affective orientation of these subjects does not change greatly with increasing age. These negative images are relatively static. This nonvariant affect suggests the operation of a pervasive socialization agent early in the lives of these children.[41]

This in turn suggests the desirability of examining the causal efficacy of variables related to an early agent frequently assumed to be an important socializer: the family. It is to this task that we now turn.

The Family as Transmitter of Specific Political Values

What kinds of general explanatory propositions about the socialization process are consistent with these data? If parents typically transmit the substantive content of their values about government to their children, then the very negative political affect observed among Appalachian youngsters should be related to similar assessments on the part of their mothers and fathers.[42] Evidence on this can be gained by examining the nature of the relationship between our family political orientation items and childrens' political affect (Table 3).

Since responses to family political orientation items were recorded in terms of degree of agreement (from disagree very much to agree very much), they constitute ordinal variables as do the presidential image and cynicism measures. The evidence on the amount of impact they have on these child political affect variables, however, is mixed. Some fairly substantial *taus* are complemented by others approaching zero. But it is interesting to note where the significant relationships occur. Primarily, they involve Presidential competence items and the cynicism scale. These may be the most important dependent variables. Several scholars have observed that childhood evaluations of the personal qualities of the President, which here do not relate to family political orientation, are "less functionally relevant" to future adult behavior than are assessments of role-filling capabilities. As stated above, those observers express no alarm at the decline with age of evaluations of Presidential benevolence. Similarly, the fact that parental values do not seem to influence them may not be great evidence about the inefficacy of

familial values in conditioning important childhood orientations.

If political cynicism represents a more developed kind of evaluation, it is significant that it appears to depend upon these parental variables. Regarded as an important encapsulator of youthful political affect, this contrast may be a crucial indicator whose antecedents should be known.

Family political values, then, appear to have some effect on children's political affect. Especially given the fact that the affective variables in question appear to be among the most significant kind, the direct transmission hypothesis takes on some credibility. This suggests the desirability of more detailed investigations of the content of intrafamilial political communication.

The Family as Prototypical Authority Structure

A totally different kind of dynamic is implied in the notion of relations with

Table 3

Relationship Between Family Political Orientation and Child's Political Affect

Family political orientation item	Child's political affect measure	τc	Significance
"I don't think people in the government care much what people like my family think"*	view of President's works	.23	p <.001
	view of the honesty of the President	.06	p >.05
	view of the President's liking for people	.18	p <.001
	view of the President's knowledge	.01	p >.05
	view of the President as a person	.05	p >.05
	political cynicism scale	−.20	p <.001
	view of how the President works	.10	p >.05
"My family doesn't have any say about what the government does."*	view of the honesty of the President	.06	p >.05
	view of the President's liking for people	.07	p >.05
	view of the President's knowledge	.13	p <.01
	view of the President as a person	.06	p >.05
	political cynicism scale	−.13	p <.01

* Disagreement scored as positive value.

Table 4

Relationship Between Family Authority Characteristics and Child's Political Affect

Family Authority Characteristics	Child's political affect	τc	Significance
View of father's liking for people	view of President's liking for people	.05	p >.05
	political cynicism	−.07	p >.05
View of father's knowledge	view of President's knowledge	.02	p >.05
	political cynicism	.02	p >.05
View of father as a person	view of President as a person	.05	p >.05
	political cynicism	−.03	p >.05
Father living with family*	view of how hard President works	−.08	p <.05
	view of President's honesty	−.09	p <.05
	view of President's liking for people	−.12	p <.05
	view of President's knowledge	−.23	p <.001
	view of President as a person	.00	p >.05
	political cynicism	.05	p >.05

* This is a dichotomous variable—either the father lives at home or he does not. However, since father's living at home constitutes a less disrupted family authority structure, we continue to apply ordinal statistics.

the family as a model for political affect. It is not, however, incompatible with the notion that the family transmits specific value content to the young. It is entirely possible that both processes operate simultaneously. Moreover, since the relationships are relatively small, our data on value transmission fairly demand that additional explanatory tacks be taken. Table 4 demonstrates the effects of father-image and of integrity of the family on Appalachian children's political orientations. Again, evidence is somewhat mixed. Three father-image items[43] are placed against their Presidential-image parallels and against cynicism. There is almost a complete lack of relationship. Not only does the "great overlap of the images of father and President"[44] fail to appear among these children, but the more generalized political affect measured by cynicism does not depend on how they see their

fathers. In short, there is no evidence at all to support the hypothesis that evaluations of family authority figures are directly projected to remote, political ones.

If the father-image hypothesis thus suffers, another dynamic by which the family might serve as a model for regime affect fares even worse. The presence or absence of the father might be thought to have political consequences for children. A fatherless home is disrupted and generally thought to have negative implications. Children might project their negative evaluations of such homes onto the political authority.[45] If this were the case, children from fatherless homes should have less positive views. Table 4 reveals exactly the opposite. There are generally low to moderate, but significant, negative relationships between having a father at home and evaluating the President in a favorable light.

Fatherless children are more positive toward the political. How can this remarkable result be interpreted? One could argue that there is a cathartic process at work; that there is some sort of psychic necessity (possible anxiety-related) to regard authority as benign. Perhaps unfortunate home life heightens this need which is then manifested in positive evaluations of the political.[45] This does not seem likely, for as we have just seen, specific negative evaluations of their fathers are not related to children's positive political orientations.

Rather than resulting in negative authority orientations, father-absence could interfere with the transfer of specific political value content from family to child. A major agent in the transfer process may be absent. Though mixed, there is some evidence in previous research of "male political dominance" in the family. Fathers may be particularly important communicators of political values.[47] Children from fatherless homes become more dependent upon their mothers. But mothers are not typically strong political cue-givers. Hence, the typical adult political values of Appalachia will not be so effectively transmitted in the fatherless home. These adult values supposedly involve relatively unfavorable assessments of political authority. The fatherless child

Table 5

Relationship Between Family Political Orientation and Child's Political Affect, with Father-Presence Controlled

Family political orientation item	Child's political affect measure	Father-present childrenτ	Father-absent childrenτ	Significance of difference
I don't think people in the government care much what people like my family think*	view of how hard the President works	.25	.12	p <.001
	view of honesty of the President	.12	−.10	p <.001
	view of President's liking for people	.23	.04	p <.001
	view of President's knowledge	.00	.06	p < .01**
	view of President as a person	.10	−.11	p <.001
	political cynicism scale	−.18	−.26	p < .01**
My family doesn't have any say about what the government does*	view of how hard the President works	.17	−.15	p <.001
	view of honesty of the President	.10	−.06	p <.001
	view of President's liking for people	.17	−.23	p <.001
	view of President's knowledge	.17	.03	p <.001
	view of President as a person	−.06	.08	p <.001**
	political cynicism	−.13	−.16	p < .05**

* Disagreement scored as positive value.
** Relationship not in predicted direction.

escapes close contacts with these values and emerges more positively disposed toward political authority. When this agent is absent, perhaps the media, or other agents bearing more favorable cues, assume a more prominent role in the socialization process.

This interpretation, which of course returns us to the transmission-of-specific-values hypothesis, is strongly supported by additional analysis of the data. First, it is clear that there is no unknown process operating to produce more positive adult political values in father-less families. Fatherless and two-parent families are identical in this regard (*tau's* between father at home and family political value items are —.03 and .00). Though the starting point is the same, it is also clear that the transmission process is greatly attenuated in fatherless homes. This can be seen by imposing a control for father-presence on the relationship between family political orientation and child's political affect (Table 5). The data for father-present children are very similar to the collapsed data shown in Table 3, except that the relationship between family value and child affect is generally somewhat stronger. But for father-absent children, the relationship generally declines and in several cases is actually reversed. Not only can the fatherless family not promulgate its political values, but it seems to leave its children very vulnerable to the socialization of other agents, agents with rather different (more positive) values. To be sure, child political cynicism, which is related to family political values, does not appear to be governed by these considerations. Other family-related roots may affect this variable—perhaps those which relate to generalized cynicism.

Conclusion

Children in the relatively poor, rural Appalachian region of the United States are dramatically less favorably inclined toward political objects than are their counterparts in other portions of the nation. Moreover, the image which these children have does not appear to develop with age in the fashion observed for others; there is no indication that a process conducive to the development of political support is operative in Appalachia. Here, children's views appear to be relatively static. These findings have two implications. First, they point to the possibility that the often-emphasized highly positive character of children's views of politics may be a culturally bound phenomenon. One should exercise much caution in accepting such views as a universal norm. Secondly, the occurrence of such divergent findings underscores the desirability of *explaining* children's political orientations.

Since, at the sub-cultural level, these atypical findings are paralleled by 1) atypical adult (parent) political values, and 2) atypical family structure, two broad hypotheses involving the effect of family-related variables on children's political affect were tested. Examination of the hypothesis that parents directly transmit the content of their political values to their children produced some confirming evidence. Reported parental values showed moderate relationship to certain aspects of children's political affect. This was especially true of the competence items in Presidential images (supposedly the most important for subsequent behavior) and of political cynicism, a more generalized kind of system affect.

The thesis which posits the family as

prototypical authority structure fares less well, however. There is no support at all for the notion that affect toward the father is extended to remote, political authority. Relationships between specific aspects of children's father images and parallel components of Presidential images are not significant. Nor is there evidence that disrupted family structure, measured by father-absence, contributes to negative political evaluations. In fact, father-absence is associated with more favorable political valuations in Appalachian children! This remarkable result is interpreted as supporting the first hypothesis regarding the direct transfer of value-content from family to child. Where the father is absent, an agent communicating the predominantly negative adult political values to youngsters is lost. This notion seems the more plausible when it is observed that there is a marked relationship between family political values and child political affect among father-present families, but no such relationship—if anything a slight negative gradient—among father-absent families.

Thus, of the two broad hypotheses posited at the outset, our data support the notion of direct value transfer, while leading us to doubt that the family is an effective authority prototype. Though these findings are offered as significant in and of themselves—they certainly suggest the importance of closer examination of parent-child political communication processes in the understanding of regime-level values—there are other implications. The explanatory relationships presented here are of relatively modest magnitudes. The small amount of variance in children's political affect which is explained here by the family suggests that we should search for other agents of socialization, or for other dynamics which may operate within the family. A preliminary view of other of the Knox County data suggests that there may be conditions under which other, less personal agents assume a great role. Fortunately, the move toward cross-cultural and explanatory analysis of childhood socialization will proceed and these and other related questions will be joined.[48]

NOTES

1. Robert D. Hess and David Easton, "The Child's Changing Image of the President," *Public Opinion Quarterly*, XIV (Winter, 1960), 632–642; Fred I. Greenstein, *Children and Politics* (New Haven: Yale University Press, 1965), pp. 27–54; Robert D. Hess and Judith V. Tourney, "The Development of Basic Attitudes Toward Government and Citizenship During the Elementary School Years: Part I," (Cooperative Research Project No. 1078; University of Chicago, 1965), pp. 102–105; Dean Jaros, "Children's Orientations Toward the President: Some Additional Theoretical Considerations and Data," *Journal of Politics*, XXIX (May, 1967), 368–387.

2. David Easton and Robert D. Hess, "The Child's Political World," *Midwest Journal of Political Science*, VI (August, 1962), 243, Greenstein, *op. cit.*, p. 53.

3. Roberta S. Sigel, "Political Socialization: Some Reactions on Current Approaches and Conceptualizations," (Paper presented at the 1966 Annual Meeting of the American Political Science Association, New York, Sept. 6–10, 1966), p. 14.

4. The Chicago area, New Haven, and Detroit provided the research environments for some of the studies cited in Note 1.

5. Robert D. Hess, "The Socialization of Attitudes Toward Political Authority: Some Cross-National Comparisons," *International Social Science Journal*, XIV (No. 4, 1963), 542–559.

6. Gabriel A. Almond and G. Bingham Powell, Jr., *Comparative Politics: A Developmental Approach* (Boston: Little, Brown, and Co., 1959), p. 23.

7. Michael Argyle and Peter Delin, "Non-Universal Laws of Socialization," *Human Relations*, XVIII (February, 1965), 77–86.

8. Several analyses contributory to this assertion are: Virgil C. Jones, *The Hatfields and the McCoys* (Chapel Hill: University of North Carolina Press, 1948); Jack E. Weller, *Yesterday's People* (Lexington: University of Kentucky Press, 1965); Harry M. Caudill, *Night Comes to the Cumberlands* (Boston: Little, Brown and Co., 1963).

9. Greenstein, *op. cit.*, pp. 45–46; Easton and Hess, *Midwest Journal of Political Science*, VI, 229–235.

10. Herbert Hyman, *Political Socialization* (Glencoe, Ill.: Free Press, 1959), Chapter 4; Leonard W. Doob, *Patriotism and Nationalism* (New Haven: Yale University Press, 1964), pp. 119–126.

11. Weller, pp. 33–56, 163; also Thomas R. Ford (ed.), *The Southern Appalachian Region: A Survey* (Lexington: University of Kentucky Press, 1960), pp. 12–15. These may characterize the entire American South. Indeed, some basic socialization data from the South could be most interestingly compared with that gathered elsewhere. But apart from South-wide considerations, there are historical reasons why one would expect such values to be especially strong in Appalachia.

12. Greenstein, *op. cit.*, p. 44.

13. Harold D. Lasswell, *Power and Personality* (New York: Viking Press, 1962), pp. 156–159; Sebastian Degrazia, *The Political Community* (Chicago: University of Chicago Press, 1948), pp. 11–21; James C. Davies, "The Family's Role in Political Socialization," *Annals*, CCCLXI (September, 1965), 10–19.

14. Easton and Hess, *Midwest Journal of Political Science*, VI, 242–243.

15. The effects of widespread unemployment in the coal industry and other economic malaise are well known. Because they are unable to provide, men reportedly invent physical disabilities or contrive "abandonments" of their dependents in order to qualify their familes for public assistance. Such men become ciphers. Weller, pp. 76–78; Ford, pp. 245–256. In addition to anecdotal accounts of such situations, there are some hard data which are consistent with these assertions. The great proportion of Appalachian men who are not in the labor force (23% in Knox County, site of the present study, as opposed to 11% in the U.S. as a whole) plus a high unemployment rate (11% in Knox County) suggests a large number of non-providing fathers (Source: U.S. Census of Population,

1960). A high incidence of incomplete families can also be confirmed. Fully 22% of the Appalachian children sampled for the present study reported father-absence, while only 12% of the Survey Research Center's national sample of high-school seniors are from fatherless homes. The authors wish to thank Richard Niemi for the last datum.

16. At this point, it should be noted that these two general hypotheses do not ex-haust the list of suggested socialization processes. In fact, some observers stress the efficacy of altogether different agencies, for example the public school: Hess and Tourney, *op. cit.*, pp. 193–200. But even with this emphasis, such observers believe that some political values are implanted in youth by their parents, namely, those which, "insure the stability of basic institutions." (p. 191). This is a reference towhat we have called "regime level" values, which are the sole topic of this paper. At least for socialization to this kind of political affect, testing of family-related hypotheses is of undoubted importance. See M. Kent Jennings and Richard Niemi, "Family Structure and the Trans-mission of Political Values" (Paper presented at the 1966 annual meeting of the American Political Science Association, New York, Sept. 6–10, 1966).

17. A few schools, not accessible by road, did not participate in the study. The cost of including them would have been very high and the returns realized very small. These schools had a total enrollment of less than fifty and a somewhat smaller number than this in grades five through eight. The questionnaire was administered by regular classroom teachers who had been instructed in its use. Every attempt was made, however, to convince the subjects that despite the context, they were not being tested. Teachers were asked explicitly to communi-cate this notion. This mode of administration probably produced fewer invalid responses than exposing the subjects to a non-indigenous investigator who would have aroused suspicion.

Knox County was chosen as the site for this study because it to some extent typifies Appalachia. That is, it is isolated, rural, and poor. No air or rail pas-senger transportation is available and only one U.S. highway crosses the county. The county has an annual per capita income of $501 as compared with $2223 for the U.S. as a whole. It is 84% rural while the nation is 70% urban. (Source: U.S. Census of Population, 1960).

18. For commentary on images of the President, see Fred I. Greenstein, "More on Children's Images of the President," *Public Opinion Quarterly*, XXV (Winter, 1961), 648–654.

19. For remarks on political cynicism, see Robert E. Agger, Marshall N. Goldstein, and Stanley A. Pearl, "Political Cynicism: Measurements and Meaning," *Journal of Politics*, XXIII (August, 1961), 477–506.

20. Fred I. Greenstein, "The Benevolent Leader: Children's Images of Political Authority," *American Political Science Review*, LIV (December, 1960), 936; Easton and Hess, *Midwest Journal of Political Science*, VI, 241.

21. Greenstein, *Children and Politics*, Chapter 4, p. 54.

22. Hess and Easton, *Public Opinion Quarterly*, XIV, 639.

23. Jennings and Niemi, *op. cit.*, p. 13.

24. *Ibid.*, footnote #30.

25. The evaluation of the Community Action Program in Knox County involved the solicitation of data from a sample of adults. These data can be arranged with those on youngsters to form parent-child pairs. These data are being exploited by Herbert Hirsch in his forthcoming doctoral dissertation.

26. David Easton and Jack Dennis, "The Child's Acquisition of Regime Norms: Political Efficacy," *American Political Science Review*, LXI (March, 1967), 25–38.

27. *Ibid.*, p. 32.

28. Greenstein, *American Political Science Review*, LIV, 938–939.

29. Gabriel A. Almond and Sidney Verba, *The Civic Culture* (Princeton: Princeton University Press, 1963), Chapter 6.

30. John E. Horton and Wayne Thompson, "Powerlessness and Political Negativism," *American Journal of Sociology*, LXVII (March, 1962), 435–493.

31. Easton and Dennis, *op. cit.*

32. Hess and Easton, *Public Opinion Quarterly*, XIV, 635–642.

33. On father-absence see: David B. Lynn and William L. Sawrey, "The Effects of Father-Absence on Norwegian Boys and Girls," *Journal of Abnormal and Social Psychology*, LIX (September, 1959), 258–262; George R. Bach, "Father-Fantasies and Father-Typing in Father-Separated Children," *Child Development*, XVII (March, 1946), 63–80.

34. Hess and Easton, Public Opinion Quarterly, XIV, 635–642.

35. *Ibid.*

36. *Ibid.*, p. 639.

37. See for example, Greenstein, *Children and Politics*, Chapter 5.

38. No reliable information on social class could be secured from the children themselves. Information on occupation or estimated family income simply was not given by these youngsters. Assigning class on the basis of the neighborhood in which individuals live, as Greenstein did, requires that virtually every subject be placed in the lowest social stratum. These rural residents are universally poor. Only 9% of the county's families have incomes over $6,000, and these are almost entirely to be found in the "urban" county seat, which was not sampled. (Source: U.S. Census of Population 1960).

39. Jennings and Niemi, *op. cit.*, p. 15.

40. Greenstein, *Children and Politics*, pp. 39–40.

41. This non-variance, a preliminary look at our data suggests, may be due to the homogeneity and isolation of the area. Family, peer groups, schools and other possible agents of socialization indigenous to the region probably manifest substantially the same configuration of values. Thus if families transmit an initial set of political notions to children, subsequent exposure to school, peers, etc., is likely to reinforce rather than effect any change in values. The remote location of the county probably insulates it from electronic or printed media and other external stimuli. Any value implications at variance with indigenous norms which such sources might transmit are thus prevented from having a widespread effect on maturing children.

42. In the absence of additional data, it is difficult empirically to show that the parents of this sample have negative dispositions toward political authority. However, responses to the family political value items, when the distribution is dichotomized, reveal about equal number of agreements (negative dispositions) and disagreements (positive dispositions). Following each item is the percentage of respondents expressing agreement:

"I don't think people in the government care much about what people like my family think," 58%;

"My family doesn't have any say about what the government does," 43%.

The authors are fully aware of the precarious nature of the family value measures. Their proxy nature makes them somewhat suspect. The data they generate are displayed, however, because they are "suggestive" and because they indicate the kind of research which, in the author's opinions, should be performed more often. In subsequent publications based on the Appalachian data, direct information on parental values and children's perceptions thereof will be available (See note 25).

43. The father image items are analogous to the Presidential image items used by Hess and Easton. Though there are five Presidential image items, only three father image analogues are used because of objection to asking respondents to evaluate their fathers' honesty or diligence at work.

44. Hess and Easton, *Public Opinion Quarterly*, XIV, p. 640.

45. Davies, *op. cit.*, pp. 13–15.

46. Judith V. Tourney, "The Child's Idealization of Authority" (Unpublished M.A. Thesis, University of Chicago, 1962).

47. Greenstein, *Children and Politics*, p. 119; Kenneth P. Langton, "The Political Socialization Process: The Case of Secondary School Students in Jamaica," (Unpublished Ph.D. dissertation, University of Oregon, 1965), p. 119. On the other hand, male-dominance in the political learning of the young fails to appear in some research: Hyman, *Political Socialization*, pp. 83–89; Eleanor E. Maccoby, Richard E. Matthews, and Anton S. Morton, "Youth and Political Change," *Public Opinion Quarterly*, XVIII (Spring, 1954), 23–39.

48. Forthcoming doctoral dissertation by Herbert Hirsch explores other socialization agents at greater length.

THE ACTIVISTS IN THE DETROIT RIOT: A STUDY OF THEIR FAMILIES AND THEIR ATTITUDES TOWARD MILITANCY*

- Robert A. Mendelsohn and Elliot D. Luby[1]

Civil disorder in major American cities has aroused enormous anxiety among its citizenry who show unmistakable signs of becoming polarized along a black-white axis. Riot, rebellion, or insurrection, whatever label may be applied, Los Angeles, Newark, and Detroit strongly suggest that long-established patterns of black behavior toward white communities are changing from passivity and conformity to violence. That such violence is purposeless and is viewed positively by only a small segment of Negro society are myths which have been amply dispelled by the Watts' Study of Tomlinson and Sears.[5] Mass violence in Los Angeles was received with substantial, though ambivalent, support as an effective form of social protest by a surprisingly large number of Negroes, who attributed its causes to mistreatment, economic deprivation, police brutality, and accumulated hostility and resentment. That such support in Watts had ominous portent for other cities has now been verified by events of the two succeeding summers.

Above selection has been written especially for this volume.

*This paper is from the Lafayette Clinic and Wayne State University Departments of Psychology and Psychiatry and was supported by a grant from the National Institute of Mental Health. The authors wish to express their appreciation to Miss Jacqueline Giering and Mrs. Sue Smock for their invaluable contributions and to Dr. Nathan E. Cohen, coordinator of the Los Angeles Riot Study for granting permission to adapt their arrestee form as our situation demanded.

The fact that support is fairly general in the Negro community does not, of course, mean that most people are willing to take to the streets. Like people everywhere they avoid direct involvement and cheer from the sidelines, not wishing to place themselves in jeopardy. Who then are the "troops" who perform the acts that many perceive to be a protest against an indifferent and hostile white society? What are the characteristics of those who convey the message that increasing numbers of blacks are despairing of the possibility of progress through peaceful means?

The closest we can come to an understanding of the action group at the present point in our analyses is a study of those persons who were arrested during the riot (henceforth called "arrestees"). They are, of course, not the only group involved nor need they have committed actual criminal offenses. Many undoubtedly happened to be in the wrong place at the wrong time, for example, curfew violators or bystanders. Conversely, many who were involved in criminal offenses were not arrested. They thus cannot be considered to be synonomous with the classification "rioters" if one means by that the complete group of persons who engaged in looting, burning, or sniping. Nonetheless, in a certain sense, they were "in action" against white authority and obviously were on the streets during the civil disturbance. There is accordingly some justification for considering them an approximation of a major segment of the action troops of the riot.

Our approach to the arrestee population was in many respects similar to our approach to the other groups we are studying. We were less interested in the immediate precipitants of the riot than in the long-term social, economic, political, and psychological forces that were more fundamental to its etiology. We have thus studied a variety of factors that were considered to be influencing forces. Thus, our instrument,* a carefully drawn and exhaustive questionnaire, covered such areas as basic demographic variables; awareness of and attitudes toward Negro leaders and institutions; feeling about community forces such as store owners, police, and so on; responses to arrest and method of arrest and imprisonment; involvement in federal programs; attitudes toward, and explanations of, the riot; beliefs about the future of race relations in Detroit; and, finally, past and present family structure data.

In this paper we shall focus our attention upon only a certain portion of the data from arrestees—the family structure, past and present, and some data on attitudes toward militancy in the young. Because data on family structure are charged with controversy and arouse powerful emotions, we wish to make several points entirely clear. First, we do not feel that experiences within the family of those arrested provide anything approaching a complete explanation of either the behavior of arrestees or the

mass violence that erupted in Detroit. Second, insofar as is possible, we are not taking a value stand about this data. Thus, we are neither arguing that some lower-class Negro families are "sick" because they have a particular structure; nor, are we, on the other hand, arguing that they are valuable because they produce a kind of person who expresses grievances openly—grievances that might not be expressed at all by those living in stable family structure. Stated simply, then, our purpose is only to describe the family patterns of the action group and integrate such a description with knowledge already in existence about family structure.

Our arrestee sample was drawn from a complete listing of 6,500 persons, seventeen years and older, who were apprehended during the riot. From the list, every fourteenth name was drawn. A large minority of the sample could not be located; but statistical comparisons on a number of key variables* of the obtained sample with the full population of arrestees led us to believe that the obtained sample is representative. The comparisons are described elsewhere.[1]

Results

Despite warnings that talking to Negroes jailed during the riot would be an exercise in futility and would serve only to further inflame them, we were impressed by the cooperativeness and candor of the respondents. The refusal rate was strikingly low. It was obvious that many welcomed the opportunity to unburden themselves and to describe their riot experiences. 87.7 percent of our sample was male and 12.3 percent was female.

---

* The interviewers were those with previous survey interview experience, schoolteachers from central city schools, and individuals sent by local civil rights organizations. The race of the interviewer was matched to the race of the respondent. Respondents were seen in their homes.

* For example, race and offense charge are two such comparisons.

90.3 percent of the sample was Negro and 9.7 percent was white. They clustered predominantly in the seventeen to twenty-eight age group. The most frequent alleged offense was breaking and entering or entering without breaking—essentially "looting."

Inasmuch as comparative data from the community sample are not yet available, it is not possible on many variables to evaluate whether the characteristics of arrestees differ from those of the community from which they come. We recognize, therefore, that a full understanding must await the completion of these comparisons. We will make those comparisons that are possible utilizing data available from census sources. The arrestees discussed here are both Negro and white, male and female, but the sample is overwhelmingly male and Negro.

Turning first to family life, present and past, we find that only 35.5 percent are married and living with spouses as compared to 60.4 percent of the non-white males in the city of Detroit over fourteen years of age in 1960.[6] Since our group is over seventeen and the marriage rate increases with age, it is obvious that our sample is strikingly less often married than the general population of non-white males in Detroit. Past family life contains features that appear to be those described by the previous reports of Gunnar Myrdal, Charles Silberman, Daniel Moynihan, and Lee Rainwater, and William Yancey.[2,3,4] Only 49.2 percent of the sample of arrestees lived with their natural fathers continuously for the first seventeen years of their lives, because the fathers left the home somewhere between birth and the age of seventeen. Even more striking is the fact that 20.6 percent never lived with their natural fathers at all. Since children from broken families would be expected to stay with their mothers, it is surprising to find that only 75.7 percent of arrestees lived with their mothers continuously for the first seventeen years of their life, and 3.7 percent did not live with their mothers at any time during childhood. Perhaps even more significant, only 50.2 percent of the arrestees, when asked which adult male they felt closest to as a child, selected their father. A full 12.6 percent felt close to no man.

[The paragraph which follows is from: "A Preliminary Report on Two Populations Involved in Detroit's Civil Disturbance", by the authors and Gerald Wehmer (ed.).]

Psychiatric evaluations were done to determine how many suffered from emotional disorders as a result of traumatic riot experiences after which the data in the areas previously described were obtained. These latter data are now being coded and analyzed, but the results are not yet available. Impressions were carried away, however, that do not require statistical summarization. Many uninvolved people grievously suffered as a result of being trapped in crossfire between snipers and police or being burned out of their homes. The older Negro male and the Negro woman and her children were the most seriously victimized. We saw elderly people with heart failure or in early diabetic coma precipitated by both intense excitement and inability to obtain proper medication. A surprisingly small percentage of the dislocated were psychiatrically disabled by severe anxiety or depression. In general, they were quietly resigned and bland, as though this were another in a series of lifelong catastrophes that had to be accepted and over which they had no control. In the elderly men and in the women of this somewhat passive group, a curious return to earlier more ingratiating and servile ways of relating to whites was noted. They appeared to share a collective guilt and sense of shame about looting and burning, despite their non-participation. The older Negro male expressed his perplexity, his inability to understand the massive destruction and the utter disrespect for law and order, which he attributed to parents who were unwilling to discipline their children.

To answer the question of militancy in the young, we have chosen to utilize the data concerning the relative popularity of different leaders and groups. It is our assumption that their popularity indicates what people's sentiments are as to the form social action should take even though we recognize, of course, that part of a leader's appeal may be a function of his "public personality" irrespective of the type of social action he stands for. We also assume that leaders and groups can in fact be typed as to the kind of social action they represent. Accordingly, we have analyzed the popularity of three individuals and groups that we assumed stand for three different viewpoints. Martin Luther King and the NAACP we see as representing "progress through reform;" Stokely Carmichael and SNCC are interpreted as representing "revolutionary militancy;" and Elijah Muhammad and the Black Muslims are viewed as representing "separation." The question that provided the data is "How good a job do you think _____ is doing? Is he doing well, fairly well, doing nothing, or doing harm?"

The results, reported in detail elsewhere,[1] indicate that for all ages, Martin Luther King is far and away the most popular leader and the NAACP the most popular organization. Among middle-aged and older persons, Carmichael, Muhammad, SNCC, and Black Muslims are distinctly unpopular; but among the younger (under age twenty-five) group, these Negro leaders and organizations have substantial popularity. This is especially true of Carmichael, who received a favorable rating from 65 percent of the young respondents who knew him. It is notable, however, that even among the young King is still the more popular leader being favorably viewed by 84 percent of the respondents. It would appear that in the younger group, then, there is a considerable amount of pull from the different ways of reacting to the problem of prejudice and discrimination. These data are in accord with impressions obtained from a sample of persons dislocated, inconvenienced, or burned out in the riot and who were interviewed during its latter stages by our staff. We found there too a fairly clear-cut generation gap. The man beyond forty utterly disavowed civil disorder and did not feel that it could serve any useful purpose.* The young black male, on the other hand, seemed less concerned about retaliation and often found justification for some of the acts that occurred in the riot in the long history of white exploitation of his race. This did not mean that all acts were approved of—quite the contrary. But there was less overall shock at the riot events

* We do not believe that the responses of the over-forty individuals from this group represent the opinion of all members of that age group. The dislocated persons in this sample tend to come from the lowest socioeconomic groups and tend to be a somewhat passive group. We expect that data from the arrestees and community sample will show this age group to have a substantial amount of ambivalence about the riot.

and more attempts to justify them. Impatience was seen and there was an unwillingness to merely hope that our democratic system would eventually provide him with a status in our society comparable to his white counterpart.

Discussion

That group of "activists" in the Detroit riot represented by "arrestees" come from families in which a parental coalition was all too frequently not maintained during developmental years. In about half these families, the father ceased to live in the home before the child's seventeenth year; and the same is true of a surprisingly high percentage of the mothers. In addition, a remarkably small number of arrestees were married, which is another indication of deviance from the dominant pattern of Western society.

Can these characteristics contribute to an understanding of the activist role taken by this group? We believe that they can, although until we have completed the data analyses from all relevant samples, we are inclined to view the following discussion as representing hypotheses rather than conclusions.

As we noted earlier, most people, no matter how deep their grievances are reluctant to take action that will endanger their personal safety or social positions or disrupt important personal relationships. This is even more true for those with deep personal and legal commitments. Men who do not have marital ties then are most likely to be on the streets during a civil disturbance, inasmuch as they have no family to protect and no loved ones to exert pressure for noninvolvement. The absence of marital ties in the arrestee group probably stems in part from ex-

periences during early years that are discussed below. The point being made here, however, is not dependent on any explanation for their single state.

The second reason why family structure data help explain who was active and who was not stems from a consideration of the socializing and cultural experiences of the under-class Negro, during crucial developmental years, which seem to particularly characterize the history of our arrestees. It is well known that poverty has a corrosive and disorganizing impact upon families, interfering with solidarity and the assumption of essential parental roles. This is particularly true in families in which the father (or adequate father surrogate) is absent or is present but a poor emulative model. Whether, to what degree, and in what manner these difficulties manifest themselves depend on many circumstances such as the general cultural environment in which the child matures. It is clear, however, that the situation of the child in the ghetto all too often conspires to maximize developmental difficulties, particularly when the father is absent. We will discuss some of these consequences as they apply to the fatherless family.

First, the father's absence often places an intolerable burden on the mother. She must, without support from a husband, be both the breadwinner and the guide and tutor of her children. Harrassed and overwhelmed by what is often a daily battle for survival, she can offer her children only insufficient emotional and cognitive stimulation. Children enter the school system disadvantaged in every way. Middle-class families prepare their children for school, for there is both time and money. Because the Negro mother does not have the time or sometimes even the strength, the early learning of the disadvantaged child is often grossly neglected, resulting in deficits in the use of and understanding of formal language and abstract thinking.[4] When he enters the school system, he finds an inflexible bureaucracy, itself organized around certain assumptions as to the kind of readiness and ability to learn of the under-class child. The ensuing clash between the child and the system produces a repeated cycle of failure, humiliation, apathy, defeat, and a growing reactive defiance and aggression. The inadequacy of inner city schools contribute to the cycle together with the resignation and low achievement expectancies of some teachers. Education has always been the vehicle for upward mobility in America; and if the lower-class Negro child cannot compete in our educational system, he certainly cannot compete as an adult for jobs and economic security. The combination of high defiance and aggression, economic insecurity, and job uncertainty make him an excellent recruit for the ranks of the activists.

Secondly, the child growing up in a stressed, under-class family (which may be the case even if the father is present) suffers from an absence of or a disruption in reciprocal relationships that create enduring affectional attachments. Strife within the home is common, and there is often open contempt on the part of the mother toward males in general for their failure to meet marital obligations. The Negro boy suffers far more than the girl when repeatedly confronted with devalued and ineffectual paternal images. Ordinarily it is the father who represents the family in the external world, determines its prestige, and interprets the outside world to it. This role often cannot be

performed, however, by many lower-class Negro fathers who have neither status nor a validated family role, a heritage of slavery, and a consequence of current discriminatory practice.* Not surprisingly, the child often turns to models available within a community that is itself either alienated, disorganized, or at best organized in a way markedly different from that of the dominant society.

In summary, it is our tentative conclusion that the nature of family life, past and present, did play a role in determining who were the activists. The absence of a current family life removed one possible barrier from taking to the streets. The nature of family life during the developmental years encouraged the emergence of significant hostility, frustration, and despair, and, with the family (and the school's) failure to provide an education leading toward upward mobility, helped contribute to the behavior that led to arrest.

Turning next to the attitudes toward militancy in the arrestee, we find the generation gap, which is characteristic of all groups. The fact, however, that reform still seems to be the predominant sentiment is encouraging, particularly since the arrestees are the activists and have been shown in the past to be more militant than the general community.[5]

* As is well known, slavery destroyed the family structure of the Negro by forcibly separating man and woman and refusing to recognize marital bonds. The substantial amount of unemployment or degrading employment permitted Negro males following emancipation deprived many males of a chance to enact a valid marital role. Furthermore, these conditions encouraged the development of a family structure organized around women, who often were the sole valued adults in the family, thereby completing the emasculation of the male and often his departure from the family setting.

It is possible, however, that the popularity of the militant leaders in the young is a reflection of a growing trend toward revolutionary militancy, a trend that will achieve a permanent status. If this is so, we face a serious crisis, for not only are the families we have been describing proliferating, but the frustrated and angry persons they produce are increasingly the targets of mobilization by Black Nationalists. With the rise of young Negroes possessed of an ideology, toleration of slow progress will decrease and with it the fear that has prevented revolutionary action in the past.

NOTES

1. Elliot Luby, Robert Mendelsohn, and Gerald Wehmer, "A Preliminary Report on Two Populations Involved in Detroit's Civil Disturbance" (unpublished manuscript, 1967).

2. Gunnar Myrdal, *An American Dilemma*, rev. ed. (New York: Harper & Row, 1962).

3. Lee Rainwater and William Yancey, *The Moynihan Report and the Politics of Controversy* (Cambridge, Mass.: M.I.T. Press, 1967).

4. Charles Silberman, *Crisis in Black and White* (New York: Random House, 1964).

5. T. T. Tomlinson and David Sears, "Los Angeles Riot Study, Negro Attitudes Toward the Riot" (unpublished manuscript, 1967).

6. Final Report PHC (1)-40, U.S. Censuses of Population and Housing, 1960, Detroit, Mich., Standard Metropolitan Statistical Area (Washington, D.C.: U.S. Bureau of the Census).

Change, Conflict, and Socialization

9

INTRODUCTION

This last set of selections pinpoints what must have become clear through most of the readings in this volume, namely, that the course of political socialization is neither unchanging nor completely smooth. The conceptual model of political socialization envisages a rather uninterrupted transmission belt by which political norms and values are passed on intact from one generation to the other. The model has little room for the impact of change and/or conflict upon the course of socialization.* It proceeds rather as though there were no conflict (or only minimal conflict) between generations

or between the larger political environment and specific socializing agents, such as family, ethnic group, and so forth. It also assumes but minimal external change, so that the content of socialization remains relatively unchanged over time. In real life such a state of continuity and serenity does not exist or prevails only in the most static and simplistic types of political society, where there is no change, not much intergroup variation, and where there are no sharp boundaries between family, society, and state. Whether or not such societies actually do exist today is certainly debatable. Most societies, as we know them, change over time; and with change conflict is a fact of life. To be sure, the rate of change and the degree of differentiation as well as the depth of conflict may vary and may be rather minimal in some systems but comprehensive

---

* Since the book went to press a few studies have appeared which no longer operate from such a simplistic model but take cognizance of the dynamic nature of the process. The most explicit statement so far is the just published work by David Easton and Jack Dennis, *Children In the Political System* (New York: McGraw-Hill, 1969).

in others. But when we talk about political socialization these days, we must count on change. Of course, not all political change affects socialization. Changing from a mayor to a city-manager form of government, extension of the suffrage to eighteen-year-olds, and so on, does not necessarily conflict with previously learned attitudes and behaviors and hence requires no resocialization. But far-reaching change must by definition engender conflict because it implies that people are required to unlearn attitudes, values, and response patterns to which they have become attached— what once was considered true or moral, say deference to highborn persons, suddenly becomes false and immoral. To put it another way,

In relation to ideological and value systems ... the thesis seems inherent in recent work by a number of students that if, under conditions of change, the basic cultural rationale retains its validity, even extensive behavioral changes can take place without threat to group or individual integrity and morale. ... But if these basic elements are threatened or undermined, the group or individual concerned is likely to lapse into states of disorganization, insecurity, anxiety, self-depreciation, and low morale, though usually accompanied by attempts to establish a new rationale.... Several theorists have suggested that, so long as the basic value systems stand reasonably firm, selective change can proceed with minimum strain and stress. At the other extreme, some groups and individuals have undergone, or are in the process of undergoing, the experience of having their value systems in jeopardy or shattered, catastrophically or through a prolonged series of crisis episodes.[1]

Political change can arrive from a variety of directions and with a variety of speeds. There can be sudden change in the political system as the result of revolution, war, newly won national independence, or other sudden and radical structural changes. (See Alex Inkeles and Kenneth Prewitt below). There can be a more gradual but nonetheless profound change as a consequence of technological or social changes; transitions from agricultural to industrial societies being a case in point. There can be changes in the balance of power in a society wherein a previously docile and exploited subgroup ceases to remain submissive and begins to make far-reaching demands of the ingroup, as in the case of the Negro civil rights movement in the United States.

There is, however, yet another form of change, change initiated by the individual himself, as, for example, in the case of emigration to a foreign country, or within one's own country—as in the case of moving from farm to city or from lower social class to middle class. Such voluntary change presumably would entail a readiness on the part of the individual to become resocialized. The selections below roughly illustrate some of these types of change and demonstrate that the severity of the conflict which accompanies change varies with the conditions under which such change takes place. The greater the attachment of individuals to the old ways (perhaps because of benefits received), the more traditional (that is, change resistant) the society, the sharper the discontinuity between old and new, the more perilous, presumably, will be the path of resocialization.

Change in the Structure of the Regime

The selection by Inkeles below shows how the Russian Revolution brought on changes in political adaptation within the generation that had grown up in tsarist days. The article demonstrates not only the effect of change but the fact that rational human beings who have a fair amount of control over their own emotions can deliberately pursue goals and norms different from those to which they have been socialized if they consider this change to be to their advantage. Thus, many families who had grown up in tsarist Russia self-consciously helped their children develop new and different attitudes toward family, religion, and politics—attitudes with which the parents were not necessarily in accord but whose adoption they hoped would help their children's advancement under communism and would keep them from political harm. Kent Geiger[2] in another study of the Russian family shows some case histories in which families in a totalitarian society often voluntarily abdicated responsibility for the moral and ideological training of their offspring in order not to cause conflict between their children and the political system. Studies on German youths under the Nazis[3] clearly document how through youth organizations, school, and other agents the state deliberately tried to lure the children away from their families and how some families learned voluntarily to adapt to these changes and not to compete with the state for the loyalty of their children.

Perhaps few families can accept change and adapt to it quite as deliberately as the above illustrations would imply. Many families and subgroups find change discomforting and actually painful. The discomfort often finds expression in social disorganization (family breakup, crime) and in political turmoil, as old and new ways clash. For example,

Robert Jay Lifton[4] thinks that postwar Japan experienced turmoil in part because of the absence of fathers from many families and in part because of conflict between traditional ways of conducting politics and modern pseudo democratic ways, the latter foisted upon the family by the occupying forces. These dislocations, Lifton argues, contributed much to the unrest, radicalism, and lawlessness witnessed among Japanese students of the 1950s and 1960s.

The article by Prewitt and Okello-Oculi vividly illustrates the difficulties that schools have in trying to socialize young people to national consciousness and loyalty in a nation which to many young people is nothing but a name. Other studies from developing nations yield rather similar results and also show that not all groups in a society are equally ready at a given time to adapt to changes in the external environment. Rural elements are often the most resistant. The better educated and the more politically ambitious are the groups most likely to adopt new ways of feeling and behaving politically, provided of course they can see a future with good prospects for them in the adoption of these new ways. Thus, the military in newly developing countries very often is the most emphatic in urging the adoption of new technological and political ways, not because they are themselves necessarily so much more progressive but because they see in these ways the best chance for national development and with it for an insured future for themselves.

Change in Power Distribution

So far we have looked only at change in the structure of the political regime. Another type of change involves power distribution changes within the system—changes that need not necessarily affect the external structure of the regime. An example of this would be changes in the balance-of-power maintained among various political groups. A study of India after the caste system had been legally abolished shows the real agony, deviance, and outright hostility with which the main Indian society tried to avoid the full impact of the changed political status of the untouchables.[5] Interestingly enough, even the untouchables themselves—or at least part of them—resisted the changes and tried to evade accommodation to them either from fear or as a result of previous socialization. The book is an agonizing portrayal of the real reluctance with which political change is accepted in a very tradition-bound society.

History is full of other examples of subgroups that try to effect change in the political environment when they judge it to be unfavorable to them. How does the larger society react to these demands? Probably the more stratified the society and the greater and more time-honored the distinctions in the powers and privileges allocated to different groups, the more unlikely it is that resocialization will take place without much conflict or violence. After all, societies from time immemorial have known of inequalities, injustices, and preferential treatment of some groups and exploitations of others. The main goal of socialization has always been to get people to accept the distinctions as just. So long as the setup remains relatively stable from generation to generation, it is feasible to assume that various groups learn to accommodate more or less grudgingly to this state of affairs. When some previously disadvantaged groups suddenly refuse to make the customary accommodations, objection is apt to develop in all of society or at least among its more advantaged members.

Deviancy and Change

When great changes occur in society as a result of new technology, new national borders, new population groups absorbed, new ideologies afloat, or a host of other reasons, then it is likely that certain previously deprived groups or newly assimilated groups might not accept their position of inferiority and might resort to legal or extralegal means to rectify the situation. Under such conditions of rapid change the customary socializing agencies often find themselves relatively ineffective. If socializing agencies cannot succeed in resocializing the malcontents to their status, or all of society to the new distribtuion of power, they will court open group conflict or subgroup deviancy. They will see the advent of subgroups with values so deviant that far from preparing the child for performance within the mainstream of society, the subgroup will actually teach him antisocial behaviors. Mendelsohn and Luby, by focusing on the generational difference in the Detroit Negro families show clearly that recourse to violence rather than to more legitimate political means of improving the position of the Negro is far more prevalent among young Negroes than among middle-aged or older ones and is most characteristic of those subgroups that by family structure, income, or other indications seem more deviant than the average working or middle-class Negro family. White backlash, growth in the radical right, and similar phenomena must be perceived as yet another form of deviancy, triggered by large-scale sociopolitical change. They represent the reactions of people who could not or would not become resocialized to the change.[6] Ira Rohter's study of the radical right seems to imply that many joined such groups in the hope that this movement could offer a bulwark against the political change they felt engulfing them. They were keenly aware that the United States was changing politically and socially, and they deeply resented the change because they were incapable of reaping its benefits. To us they may seem deviants from the mainstream of society but to them it is we who have deviated.

Self-Initiated Change

So far no mention has been made of the political change that may affect a person when he deliberately moves to a new country because he thinks its political system may be more in harmony with his own ideas. Harold Isaacs wrote two books about people who thought they could find more congenial fatherlands elsewhere. One deals with the American Negro[7] who went back to an African country in the hope of finding there the link to his past and the respect denied him at home; the other book dealt with American Jews[8] who went to Israel for somewhat the same reasons. In each case the author observed that the transition was far from smooth; in fact it was usually painful and was more often than not unsuccessful. Why should this be so? There are of course a variety of reasons, but a very important one (although the author does not label it so) seems to have been that the force of previous socialization had caused the new arrival to have internalized certain norms, values, and expectancies that left him unable to re-

socialize in another country whose norms were very dissimilar. The selection by Oscar Handlin below attests to the tribulations, failures, and agonies experienced by immigrants to this country in their attempt to come to terms with an environment that made unaccustomed social and political demands of them (such as voting) and that required them to develop completely new yardsticks by which to measure officials, organizations, and ideas. Even within the same country a move from rural to urban life brings with it first social and then, eventually, political changes. Unfortunately we do not have much information about the ways in which people react politically to such a change in their way of life. The few studies here and there would seem to indicate that those who arrive in the city determined to stay quickly adopt city ways of participating, joining, voting, and so forth, whereas those less committed reject the new norms and either become alienated or drift back to the country. One observation the editor has often heard from welfare workers in larger urban areas is that Southern mountain people are not at all averse to accepting welfare benefits once they move to the city, yet these same people often rejected such payments most vehemently and considered them an insult to their pride and self-reliance while still living in the mountains. There is no hard data known to the editor to support this observation; but if it should be true, the question really is, What is it in the urban environment that can so change a traditional political outlook or were the in-migrants ready to become resocialized?

Comments like these imply first of all that adaptation to change is never totally without conflict and that it always violates at least some norms learned previously. It also implies that people vary in their adaptiveness to change and that this adaptiveness may in part be motivational and in part a function of the position and capacity of the group or individual who has to do the adapting. Thus a first generation immigrant with lower skill levels, less literacy, less sophistication, and more thoroughly imbued with the old ways is much less able to adapt than his children who have attained a higher skill level and who have been, so-to-speak, socialized in two worlds, the American world and the old world of their parents.

Finally, change will probably be accepted most readily when it can build on at least some norms or behavior patterns established earlier in childhood. In other words, adaptation to change is probably difficult, if not impossible, when it requires so drastic a departure from the past that the person almost has to learn to look, think, feel, and act in a completely new way. This may be the case of the immigrant just alluded to. When, however, as in the case of Red China, resocialization can build on certain mechanisms used by people over many generations, then political change can probably proceed with somewhat less strain. Lucien Pye, for example, explains the recent outbursts of rage and hatred observed among warring Chinese factions as being deeply rooted in their national culture. The target for hatred may have varied with time, but the mechanism of hate-ventilation apparently is time-honored and considered socially desirable.

No other political culture places as much stress upon the emotion of hate as does the Chinese. Both in extolling hate as a positive virtue and in seeking to tap hostile feelings, the Chinese Communists have carried to new extremes a trend which was well established in modern Chinese politics.[9]

Just as individuals and groups vary in their ability to incorporate change, so do political regimes and political cultures. Some nations pride themselves in their adherence to tradition and view all suggestions of change with fear and suspicion. Other countries look upon change as a sign of progress and manage to make some truly radical transitions—as did the United States in its transition from rural elitist to urban democratic society —without much radical dislocation, much less revolution. Since change is inevitable, those countries are possibly the most stable who have the capacity to adapt to it without too much internal dissension, whereas those who cannot do so are either doomed to frequent turmoil or to underdevelopment or both.

Unfortunately socialization theory has not yet specified clearly the types of changes that individuals and groups can accept most easily or what the nature of the political outcome is under those circumstances where prior political socialization conflicts significantly with existing political and social changes. Since change is a fact of life and since today more countries than not experience such change, it would seem that one of the first orders of business would be that in the future we explore this topic more fully and more thoughtfully. In summary we could perhaps say that the selections in this chapter merely accentuate what we have seen previously, namely that each generation is socialized by the previous generation. But each new generation must also become somewhat resocialized by the new environment with which it has to cope; and for each generation the environment is always somewhat different from that in which the previous generation grew up. In times of drastic change political socialization is put to a severe test and the greater the discontinuity, probably the more difficult the task. It may even be possible to say that where the discontinuity is too sharp, stability for the regime can only ensue under at least one of the two following conditions: (1) the regime is so strong and totalitarian that it can force submission from the older generation while it is in pursuit of the mind and heart of the generation not yet of age or (2) the material and other values that the new regime can bestow upon its members is so great as to outweigh the pain of the political conflict and that eventual peace and stability can be bought via the great material comfort the new regime has to offer.

NOTES

1. Felix M. Keesing, *Culture Change* (Stanford, Calif.: Stanford University Press, 1953), pp. 80, 85.

2. Kent Geiger, "Changing Political Attitudes in Totalitarian Society," *World Politics*, 8 (1955–1956), 187–205.

3. Robert A. Brady, *The Spirit and Structure of German Fascism* (New York: Fertig and Howard, 1937).

4. Robert Jay Lifton, "Youth and History: Individual Change in Postwar Japan," *Daedalus* 91 (Winter 1962), 172–197.

5. Harold R. Isaacs, *India's Ex-Untouchables* (New York: John Day, 1965).

6. For a theoretical discussion, see Talcott Parsons, *The Social System* (New York: Free Press, 1951). For specific data on ethnic prejudice and mobility, see also Bruno Bettelheim and Morris Janowitz, *Dynamics and Prejudice* (New York: Harper & Row, 1950). For data on the radical right, see Daniel Bell (ed.), *The Radical Right* (New York: Anchor, 1965).

7. Harold R. Isaacs, *Emergent Americans: A Report on Crossroads Africa* (New York: John Day, 1961).

8. Harold R. Isaacs, *American Jews in Israel* (New York: John Day, 1967).

9. Lucian W. Pye, "The Dynamics of Hostility and Hate in Chinese Political Culture," mimeographed manuscript (Cambridge, Mass.: Center for International Studies, M.I.T.), p. 1.

SOCIAL CHANGE AND SOCIAL CHARACTER: THE ROLE OF PARENTAL MEDIATION[1]

- Alex Inkeles

In his general essay on national character Gorer (3) provides a clear and succinct formulation of one of the major premises underlying most of the related literature. Gorer indicated that we can deal with the simple but imposing fact that "societies continue, though their personnel changes" only because we can assume that "the present generation of adults will be replaced in due course by the present generation of children *who, as adults, will have habits very similar to their parents.*"[2] Implicit in this general pattern, of course, is the further assumption "that the childhood learning of the contemporary adults was at least very similar to the learning which contemporary children are undergoing."

Gorer recognizes, and indeed states explicitly, that this model is probably not applicable to "societies which are in the process of drastic change." As Margaret Mead (8) points out, however, so few individuals may now hope to grow up under conditions of sociocultural stability that we may regard this situation as almost unusual, and its products as in a sense "deviants." Gorer's model, therefore, requires elaboration, extension, and adjustment to enable it to deal adequately with national character as it develops and emerges under conditions of social change. The question is essentially this: Insofar as rapid social change interrupts the simple recapitulation of child training practices and produces new modal

Above selection reprinted from: *Journal of Social Issues*, XI, 2(1955), 12–23.

personality patterns, by what means are such changes mediated or effected?

The literature on national character contains several important and interesting efforts to answer this question. Margaret Mead (8), for example, has explored the significance for personality development of growing up in a culture that is no longer homogeneous and posits the development under those circumstances of what she calls a "tentative" personality syndrome. Riesman (10), developing in full detail a point also made by Mead (7), has discussed the significance for social character of growing up under the strong influence of peer group pressures and standards. Erikson (2) has stated the implications for personality development that arise from the absence of adequate and valued role models with which to identify, and from the associated lack of roles through which the individual can find socially sanctioned and culturally meaningful outlets for the discharge of his emotions.

Despite the diversity of these studies they seem to have one element in common in their approach to the role of the parent as "child rearer" under conditions of social change. Implicitly, if not explicitly, the parent is conceived as having available a relatively fixed repertory of child training procedures provided by his culture and learned by him in the period of his own childhood. Two main alternatives as to his utilization of those techniques are then generally considered. On the one hand, the parent is seen as acting as the passive agent of his culture, raising his children according to the procedures he had learned earlier in his own childhood, even though these techniques may have lost their appropriateness. It is assumed in that case, that as his children grow up the gulf between parent and child will rapidly grow great, and relations will become strained as the child meets and learns the conflicting behavior patterns and underlying values of his "own" new culture. On the other hand, the parent may know enough not to try to apply the training procedures under which he was raised, and in that case he either surrenders to other cultural surrogates such as peer group, teachers, mass media, etc., or borrows, and of course generally ineptly applies, some prefabricated set of rules. In the lower classes the borrowing might be from the local baby clinic, and in the upper classes from books and lectures on child rearing. In short the parents will manifest what Mead (8) terms "disturbed and inconsistent images of their children's future."

Without doubt these descriptions are faithful to the facts in many situations. Nevertheless, they seem to have made inadequate allowance for the positive adjustive capacity of human beings and for the process of continuous interaction that goes on between them and their sociocultural environment. Very often the global impact of Western contacts on a non-literate people may be almost totally disorienting, but parents need not be either unimaginative and passive agents of their culture, raising their children by rote, nor so disorganized and disoriented as is suggested by Mead's discussion. Although parents are adults, they may nevertheless still *learn*, and learn what they feel to be major

"lessons," from their experiences under conditions of social change. This learning, furthermore, may influence the parents to seek purposefully to bring their children up in a way different from that in which they were raised, and in a manner intended better to suit the children for life in the changed social situation. This has been clearly recognized by Aberle and Naegele (1), who in a passage not easily duplicated elsewhere in the literature affirm that:

All in all child rearing is future oriented to an important extent. The picture of the desired end product is importantly influenced by the parents' experiences in the adult world, as well as by their childhood experiences. When adult experience changes under the impact of major social change, there is reason to believe that there will ultimately, although not necessarily immediately, be shifts in the socialization pattern as well.

Of course, if either the parental experience of change or the response to it were purely idiosyncratic, then even where such experiences were widely distributed their effect on the character of the next generation would be essentially randomized. But it is in the nature of social structure, particularly in modern industrial society, that large groups of the population will be exposed to and perceive on-going change in similar fashion. Furthermore, it follows both from the existence of modal personality patterns and the shared cultural heritage of those in the subgroups of any population that they are very likely to react to this experience in systematically patterned ways. One very probable reaction to the experience of social change is to adjust the training of children to better prepare them for life in the future as the parent now anticipates that life in the light of his own experience. There is reason to assume, therefore, that the influence of large-scale social change occurring at any one time may be reflected in the character of the *next* generation because of mediation by parents living under and experiencing the change.

To test these assumptions one would ideally want a research design permitting the exploration of two distinct although intimately related questions. The first involves the hypothesis that parents who have experienced extreme social change seek to raise their children differently from the way in which they were brought up, purposefully adapting their child rearing practices to train children better suited to meet life in the changed world as the parent now sees it. To test this hypothesis we would need detailed information about the child rearing practices utilized by two consecutive generations of parents in the same culture, the first of which lived and raised its children in a period of relative stability, whereas the second lived and brought up its children under conditions of fairly extreme social change. A different requirement is posed by the question of how effective the parents in the second generation are in developing new traits or combinations of traits in their children. The extension of the ideal research design in this direction would require that we secure data on the modal personality patterns prevalent in the third generation. We would anticipate that as a result of their different socialization experience those in the third generation would manifest modal personality patterns different in important respects from those of their parents in the second generation.

Clearly such a design is extremely difficult to execute. Fortunately, however, we can approximate the ideal, although admittedly very imperfectly, through the utilization of some of the materials collected by the Harvard Project on the Soviet Social System. In that research program detailed life history interviews were conducted with about 330 former Soviet citizens, yielding a well-balanced sample in regard to such factors as age, sex, and occupation. The interview extensively explored the life of the respondent in both his family of orientation and procreation. Particular attention was paid to the values in regard to character development and occupational goals that dominated in child rearing as practiced by the respondent's parents and by the respondent himself in the role of parent. Through an exploration of these data we may hope to see some of the effects of social change in the Soviet Union as the parents who "lived" the change adjusted their child rearing practices in response to their own adult experiences, and thus acted as intermediaries in transmitting the effects of their current change to a future generation.

We may begin by testing the first assumption, namely that a generation experiencing extreme social change in adulthood will adapt the methods whereby it raises its children, and that as a result its children will be reared differently than it had been and yet more in keeping with the changed social realities. For our first generation, which we shall call the "Tsarist" generation, we need a group that raised its children during a period of relative social stability. The most recent period of that sort in Russia unfortunately falls as far back as the time immediately preceding the First World War, roughly from 1890 to 1915. Since we are interested in child rearing practices, and particularly of people who raised their children to adulthood (taken here as age 15) in those years, then eligible respondents would have been at least 33 by 1915 and at least 68 by the time of our interview in 1950. Indeed, most of those who could qualify as parents in our first generation were probably dead by 1950, and in any event only three of those living appear in our sample. We can learn about the child rearing practices utilized by that generation, therefore, only by relying on what their children report to have been true of the parents. The children of the Tsarist generation do, of course, appear in our sample. In this group we include all respondents over 45 in 1950,[3] and we call it the "Revolutionary" generation because its members, born in 1905 or before, were young adults at the time of the Revolution and lived as mature individuals through the subsequent Civil War and the later periods of momentous social change represented by the forced collectivization and industrialization programs. It was this second generation that was raising its children to adulthood during the main period of Soviet development.

It will be recognized, therefore, that, although dealing with the child rearing practices of two different generations of parents, we draw our information from but a single set of respondents, namely those in our sample over 45 years of age in 1950. In telling us how their parents brought them up they provide us with data about the child rearing practices of the Tsarist generation, whereas in describing the training of their own children, they provide our materials on the child rearing practices of the Revolutionary generation. Although limits of space do not permit presentation of the evidence, we have data that indicate

that this procedure of ascertaining the child rearing values of an earlier generation by accepting the description given by those who had been the children of the group being studied, is methodologically less suspect than might appear to be the case. The description by the youngest generation in our sample of the manner in which it was reared agrees so closely with the report of how the training was done as related by the middle generation, which actually reared the children, as to yield correlations of .89 and .95 on the two available comparisons.

Relative to the child rearing materials we have a detailed summary code of the dominant values governing child rearing, both as to character and occupational goals, characteristic for each generation acting as parents. In no case, however, is the rating of the parent based on his observed behavior, but only on the values deduced by us to have been operative on the basis of the interview. Furthermore, as already noted, the respondents from the prerevolutionary Tsarist generation could not speak for themselves and we had to rely on the retrospective report of their children.

In the following analysis a larger number of code categories has been grouped into a set of six major dimensions that were prominent value orientations in the child rearing efforts of those in our sample. The value of "tradition" was coded mainly for emphasis on religious upbringing, but it included as well references to maintenance of strong family ties and traditions; "adjustment" reflects emphasis on "getting along," staying out of trouble, keeping an eye on your security and safety, etc; "achievement" was coded when parents stressed attainment, industriousness, mobility, material rewards, and similar goals; "personalistic" was checked when the parent was concerned with such personal qualities as honesty, sincerity, justice, and mercy; "intellectuality," where the emphasis was on learning and knowledge as ends in themselves; and "political" when the focus was on attitudes, values, and beliefs dealing with government and particularly with *the* government of the land.

When we consider the profound differences, during their years of child rearing, in the life experience of the Revolutionary generation as contrasted with that of its parents in the Tsarist generation, what differences may we expect in their values with regard to child rearing? The revolutionary upheaval of 1917 and the subsequent programs of forced social change struck a great blow at the traditional structure of Russian society and profoundly altered it.[4] Massive programs of expansion were undertaken in industrialization, in urbanization, in formal organization and administration. The pattern of rural life, in which the bulk of the population was involved, was drastically revised through the forced collectivization of agriculture. Centralized political control and political terror were ruthlessly imposed. Opportunities for mobility increased greatly. Under these circumstances we might well expect the traditional values to suffer the greatest loss of emphasis, with a consequent shift to stress on either simple successful adjustment or the more secularized morality represented by the personalistic values and the pursuit of knowledge as an end in itself. In addition, our knowledge of the growing opportunities for advancement, associated with the generally expanded development of the formal occupational structure, leads us to

anticipate that greatly increased weight would be given to achievement. Finally the central role played by the state in Soviet affairs, the existence of the political terror, and the additional fact that our repondents were disaffected from the political system, lead us to anticipate heightened concern with political considerations in child rearing.

In Table 1 we have indicated the distribution of emphasis among the dimensions in our set of dominant value orientations. The relative stability of the gross rank order is testimony to the fact that both generations of parents represented a common cultural tradition which they carried forward through time. Nevertheless, it is clear that there have been very substantial shifts in the relative weight of several value orientations, and they go largely in the expected direction.[5] Perhaps the most striking finding is the sharp decrease in emphasis on the traditional values, accounted for overwhelmingly by the decreased emphasis on religious training and belief. Under the impact of industrialization and urbanization, perhaps abetted by the antireligious and "proscientific" propaganda conducted by the regime, parents in the Revolutionary generation clearly shifted toward an emphasis on more secular values.[6] This shift is reflected in the increased emphasis on learning (intellectuality) and positive personal qualities *as ends in themselves* rather than as *means* to the attainment of the good life lived, as it were, "in the sight of God." Thus secular morality replaced traditional and religiously based morality.

Perhaps most directly and explicitly related to the intervening experience of the parents under conditions of social change is the increased attention paid to

Table 1

Child Rearing Values of Parents in Russian Pre-Revolutionary and Post-Revolutionary Times

AREAS	Distribution* of Emphasis in	
	Tsarist Period	*Post-Revolutionary Period***
Tradition	75%	44%
Achievement	60	52
"Personalistic"	32	44
Adjustment	16	21
Intellectuality	12	22
Politics	12	20
Number of Respondents	77	78

* These percents total more than 100, since respondents were scored for as many themes as cited, but percentaging is on the basis of total respondents.

** The percentages in this column have been adjusted to equalize for the effect created by the larger number of responses given by our informants in describing their own activity as parents, as against the manner in which they had been raised by the Tsarist generation.

political considerations in the education of one's children. The greater emphasis on political problems arises from the fact that the Soviet regime has progressively "politicized" more and more areas of human activity that in most Western societies fall outside the political realm. A person at all alert to his situation and surroundings could therefore hardly fail to realize that if he wished to prepare his child adequately for life under Soviet conditions he must train him to an awareness concerning the political realities of the system, even though such training had not been important in his own childhood. This interpretation is borne out by the statements made by our interviewers.

Finally, it is necessary to comment on the major instance in which the data fail to confirm expectation, namely in regard to emphasis on achievement values. This failure is, of course, only relative, since achievement was the most emphasized value in the rearing of children by those in the Revolutionary generation. Nevertheless, in absolute weight it declined in

importance even though it had been expected to increase. It might be that since our respondents were refugees from the system, and since many of them looked upon too active pursuit of a career as suggesting involvement with the regime, they did not admit fully the importance they actually attributed to inculcating achievement strivings in their children. On the other hand, it may be that the expectation was unrealistic quite apart from specific Soviet conditions. There is some evidence that values such as security, adjustment and personal attractiveness are becoming ever more important foci in child rearing in the United States (10) and that stress on achievement as an *end in itself*, although still prevalent, has become somewhat old fashioned. This pattern may be associated with the combination of mass industry, education and communication, and the consumer culture of which the Soviet Union is but one example.

All told, however, the data certainly seem strongly to support the assumption that the experience of extreme social change that the Revolutionary generation underwent did have a marked effect on that generation's approach to the rearing of its children. As compared with the way their parents raised them, they can hardly be assumed to have merely "recapitulated" the earlier pattern of child rearing. On the contrary, having experienced marked social change, they adjusted their child rearing practices, the better to prepare their children for the life they expected those children to lead.

To test the effectiveness of the changed general child rearing orientations of the Revolutionary generation, we would need data on the personality patterns prevalent among their children in the third generation, which we unfortunately do not have.[7] Nevertheless, we can make a very approximate approach to our second question concerning the effectiveness of the changed child rearing emphases if we shift our attention to the realm of occupational choices. In that area we have data not only on the values stressed by parents, but we also have information on the values which the individual held in regard to himself. In treating value orientations relative to the occupational world we are, of course, dealing not with personality patterns in a psychodynamic sense, but rather with something more closely akin to "social character" as it has been defined by Riesman (10) and Inkeles (4).

The influence of their experience with social change on the child training practices adopted by the Revolutionary generation is perhaps even more strikingly evident in the area of occupational choices. In addition to asking about the specific occupations for which parents wished to prepare their children, we asked the reasons for the selection. The reasons cited provide us with a guide to the values that were dominant in the home atmosphere created by the parent for the child. Considering the nature of the social change experienced by the Revolutionary generation and described above, we might again well expect that as part of the general weakening of the traditional way of life there would have been a decline in the importance of family tradition, as against self-expression or free choice, as values emphasized in orienting the child toward the occupational world. In addition it is reasonable to assume that economic and material rewards would have come to be much more stressed among the goals set before the child, as would the necesssity of finding work that permitted an appropriate accommodation to the highly politicized occupational structure in Soviet society.

As a comparison of the first and second columns of Table 2 indicates three of these four expectations are rather strongly supported by the responses of our interviewees. We see, to begin, a sharp decline in the importance of family tradition as a criterion in shaping the child's occupational orientation, along with a marked increase in the role played by self-expression or free job choice. In addition, we may note the much greater emphasis on guiding the child toward a job that is politically desirable, which for our respondents generally meant one safe from danger of political arrest and not too directly involved in the regime's political objectives. Finally, it should be observed that here again the data fail to support our expectation that the material and psychic rewards on the job—roughly equivalent to earlier discussed achievement value—would be more emphasized

Table 2

Changing Values Concerning the Occupational Realm

| VALUE AREAS | DISTRIBUTION OF EMPHASIS AMONG VALUES STRESSED | | |
| | In Child Rearing by: | | In Hypothetical Choice by |
	"Tsarist" Generation	*"Revolutionary" Generation*	*"Soviet" Generation*
Rewards	41%	25%	14%
Tradition	35	14	11
Self-expression	21	38	62
Politics	3	23	13
Number of Responses (equal to 100%)	58	63	931

by the Revolutionary generation than by the Tsarist generation. Indeed, the relative weight of such rewards as values to be emphasized in orienting children toward the occupational world declined markedly from the one generation to the next.

Now to return to our original research design, do we have any evidence that the different child rearing patterns utilized by the middle generation as a response to their experience of social change actually were effective? Or did the parents in that second generation, despite their apparent intention, act in fact as passive agents of the culture and, *nolens volens*, raise their children in their own image and much as the first generation would have done the job? For a proper answer to this question we should have access to the children of the Revolutionary generation, and to data on their job choices coded by the same categories used to describe the child training values of their parents. Unfortunately we can only approximate each requirement. Respondents on both our written questionnaire and oral interview remained anonymous, and we therefore have no way of identifying the actual children of

the Revolutionary generation. But we can secure a reasonable equivalent of that third group which we call the "Soviet" generation, by taking all respondents under 35 in 1950. Most of them were raised and reached adulthood in the same period in which the Revolutionary generation was acting in the parental role and could well have been their children. As for the values that governed their job choices, we are obliged to draw on our written questionnaire, which presented the respondents with a choice of precoded categories not strictly comparable with those used in assessing child training values.[8] For example the check list included the omnibus category "I feel suited to it," which we have equated here with "self-expression," but which obviously could have meant many more things to the respondents.

Quite apart from such methodological difficulties, it would be naive to expect a near-perfect correlation between the values that the parents in the Revolutionary generation stressed while they reared the Soviet generation and the ones which that generation emphasized in its own job choices.

Such training always produces only an approximation of the parents' desire. More important, those in the Soviet generation have had their values shaped by many influences other than those exerted by their parents. Nevertheless, our expectation is that on the whole the pattern of value orientations of the Soviet generation will be quite close to those that were stressed in child training by their parents in the Revolutionary generation as contrasted with those inculcated in an earlier era by the Tsarist generation. The relative degree of fit between the two sets of orientations may be taken as a rough measure of how successful the Revolutionary generation was in training the Soviet generation to orient in new directions.

The appropriate comparison may be obtained by examining the third column of Table 2—which contains the distribution of emphasis in the operative values guiding the job choices of the younger generation—in relation to the first and second columns. The over-all comparison strongly suggests that those in the Revolutionary generation were highly successful in their purposive effort to shape the values their children would carry into adulthood. This is most evident in the marked emphasis that the Soviet generation places on self-expression rather than family tradition as a criterion for its job choices, much in keeping with the lesser emphasis that its parents had put on tradition in orienting their children's thoughts about the world of jobs and work. Even if we make allowance for the strong pull of the actual code category, "I feel suited for it," this interpretation would clearly not be materially affected.

It will be noticed, further, that in raising children those in the Tsarist generation gave extremely slight attention to political considerations, whereas those in the Revolutionary generation stressed it very heavily, indeed more heavily than tradition. In their own job choices, those in the Soviet generation again show the apparent influence of their parents' concern for this dimension, although in their own value scheme it does not loom quite so large as it did in their parents' efforts at socialization. Finally, we may note that material and psychic rewards such as income and prestige had roughly similar relative weight, as compared to politics and tradition, in the child rearing practices of the Revolutionary generation and in the actual job choices of the Soviet generation.

It seems reasonable to conclude again, therefore, that the Revolutionary generation did not merely act passively as the agent of the old culture, recapitulating in its own parental activities the socialization practices that had earlier been used by *its* parents. On the contrary, it may be said that the middle generation responding to its experience of social change under the Soviet regime, in large measure turned away from the pattern of child rearing under which it had been raised earlier and in its approach to the new Soviet generation stressed goals and values of a different sort. It appears, furthermore, that this training of the youth in new value orientations was relatively successful.

Because the numbers are small and the sample unusual, the material presented here is perhaps little more than suggestive of the results that might be yielded by research specifically designed to increase our knowledge in this area. Indeed, a stronger case could have been made with the material at hand had not rigorous limits of space precluded the presentation of quotations from our interviews that show graphically the way in which conditions of social change experienced by the parents influenced their approach to raising their children. Nevertheless, the material presented should serve to alert us to the role that the parent plays, through both purposive and unconscious adjustments in his child rearing practices, in mediating the influence of social change to his children and consequently in better adapting them for the changed social conditions they may meet as adults. Furthermore, although the demonstration presented above dealt only with the more surface level of attitudes and value orientations, there is reason to believe that similar processes operate with regard to the development of personality at deeper levels.

NOTES

1. This paper was read by Alice Rossi and David Gleicher, to whom thanks are due for several valuable suggestions. The data reported on were collected as part of the Harvard Russian Research Center's Project on the Soviet Social System, under contract AF No. 33(038)-12909 with the Officer Education Research Laboratory at Maxwell Field, Alabama.

2. Italics mine. For a detailed statement of the position that national character should be defined in terms of modal adult personality patterns rather than in cultural or structural terms see Inkeles and Levinson (6).

3. The median age in the group was 52, and only six respondents were over 65. Such an age class admittedly does not represent a truly distinctive generation. In part this results because the limited number of cases we have forces us to use a gross dichomotization of those over 45 and under 35 in 1950. But even larger numbers and finer age gradations would not eliminate overlapping, because at any one time some children are being raised who are the *last* to be raised by a given generation of parents whereas others of the same age are the *first* to be raised by the next generation. Since we have no reliable absolute measure of generation, the respondent's own age is used as the basis for classifying the respondent's generation and that of his parent. We are not unaware of the complications thereby raised, but feel the procedure adequate for present purposes.

4. See Moore (9) and Inkeles (5) for discussion of this process, and for evaluation of its significance as a program of planned social change.

5. There is some evidence that the strength of the shift varies by class on certain dimensions. Limits of space preclude the exploration of such difference. It must suffice to say that on the whole class differences represent only special case of the general points being made here.

6. Alice Rossi (11) has prepared an outstanding analysis, as yet unpublished on the declining importance of religious belief in a succession of Soviet Russia generations.

7. The Harvard Project on the Soviet Social System did collect data on personality patterns among former Soviet citizens. However the small size of the clinical

sample, and the nature of the personality variables investigated, largely rule out the possibility of an adequate test.

8. The respondent was asked what job he would have chosen while in the U.S.S.R. if he had had a completely free choice, and was then asked to check off the reason for his choice.

REFERENCES

1. Aberle, D. F., and Naegele, K. D. Middle-class fathers' occupational role and attitudes toward children. *American Journal of Orthopsychiatry*, 1952, *22*, 366–378.

2. Erikson, E. H. *Childhood and society*. New York: Norton, 1950.

3. Gorer, G. The concept of national character. In J. L. Crammer (Ed.), *Science news*. Harmondsworth Middlesex: Penguin Books, 1950. No. 18. Pp. 105–122.

4. Inkeles, A. Some sociological observations on culture and personality studies. In C. Kluckhohn, H. A. Murray, and D. M. Schneider (Eds.), *Personality in nature, society, and culture*. (2nd. ed.) New York: Knopf, 1953. Pp. 577–592.

5. Inkeles, A. Social change in Soviet Russia. In M. Berger, T. Abel, and C. H. Page (Eds.), *Freedom and control in modern society*. New York: Van Nostrand, 1954. Pp. 243–264.

6. Inkeles, A., and Levinson, D. J. National character: The study of modal personality and sociocultural systems. In G. Lindzey (Ed.), *Handbook of social psychology*. Cambridge: Addison-Wesley, 1954. Pp. 977–1020.

7. Mead, Margaret. Social change and cultural surrogates. *Journal of Educational Psychology*, 1940, *14*, 92–110.

8. Mead, Margaret. The implications of culture change for personality development. *American Journal of Orthopsychiatry*, 1947, *17*, 633–646.

9. Moore, B. *Soviet politics: The dilemma of power*. Cambridge: Harvard University Press, 1950.

10. Riesman, D. *The lonely crowd*. New Haven: Yale University Press, 1950.

11. Rossi, Alice S. *Generational differences in the Soviet Union*. Russian Research Center, Harvard University, 1954. (mimeographed).

POLITICAL SOCIALIZATION AND POLITICAL EDUCATION IN THE NEW NATIONS*

- Kenneth Prewitt assisted by Joseph Okello-Oculi

Introduction

Policy maker and research scholar alike have become sensitive to the critical attitudinal component of the development process in the newer nations of the world. The assumption guiding policy maker and researcher is a simple but crucial one. Innovations in any program, be it political, social, or economic, will meet with greater or lesser success depending on whether the target population is psychologically receptive to innovation in general and specific programs in particular.[1] For example, a self-help, cooperative agricultural scheme will only be as good as the willingness of peasant farmers to show local initiative and to combine their efforts. The examples are many, but the principle remains the same. Nation-building and modernization are not only a matter of programs. In critical ways they are a matter of citizen attitudes.

Above selection has been written especially for this volume.

* This paper is part of a larger study concerned with political socialization in East Africa. This study, "Citizenship and Education in East Africa," is being carried out under the general direction of Kenneth Prewitt, George Von der Muhll, and David Koff. Initial support for the project has been provided by the Rockefeller Foundation through a grant administered by the Political Science Research Program, East African Institute of Social Research. Additional help has been provided by the Center for the Comparative Study of Political Development and by the Social Science Division, both of the University of Chicago.

Awareness of the attitudinal aspect of economic development and nation-building has focused attention on political socialization, the social mechanisms and processes that provide a population with its political manners and values. New nation leaders and new nation scholars have begun inquiry into the way in which agencies in society might influence the political values internalized by the citizens. In particular, interest turns to those agencies that condition the political beliefs of the young—the generation on whose shoulders will fall the major burden of translating the promises of independence into the realities of a new social order. It is not surprising therefore that increasing attention is being paid to the educational systems of the new nations. It has been assumed, perhaps too readily, that independence from colonial control would lead directly to nationalization of schools, politicization of the curricula, and mobilization of the teachers to the tasks of creating "junior citizens."

It is not difficult to see why such conclusions are tempting. Many nationalist movements that swept into power at the time of independence embodied within them a program for a national political culture. The observer of those events might assume that the new political and administrative elites would search for a vehicle through which to disseminate their plans and that the school system would be a likely candidate. The educational system monopolizes the time and the instruction of youth during the impressionable years of late childhood and early adolescence. Unlike other agencies of political socialization, such as the family or peer group, the schoolroom is relatively susceptible to centralized control. In theory, it is possible for political authorities to design and implement a fairly uniform program of political education for the majority of youth in society. Finally, the school is already labeled as an instrument of modernization and national development.

In addition to the apparent availability of the school system for programmed political education, there is a second reason why commentators might conclude that teacher-directed political socialization is widespread in the newer nations. There are dramatic models for such programs. Among the newer nations, Indonesia and Guinea are well-known examples. Among older nations, schoolroom indoctrination has been a prominent feature of such centrally directed polities as Stalinist Russia, Imperial Japan, Nasser's Egypt, and Communist China.

However, in spite of the availability of the school system and identifiable models of programmed political education, such practices do not seem as widespread in the newer nations as was first suspected. In this brief essay we take a look at a new nation, Uganda, which has *not* harnessed its educational system to the tasks of instilling political values in the country's youth. Our intent is to counter the assumption that the school system can be used effectively for programmed political education. We will also argue on theoretical grounds that even when such programs do exist they can expect only limited success at best.

Why Uganda?

Uganda suggests itself as a useful case for examining the question of schools and political education for two sets of reasons:

1. The leadership of Uganda self-consciously articulates sentiments that link education to a new and better political future. Prime Minister Milton Obote sprinkles his speeches with such phrases as "the schools will mold the young people and ensure that they grow to become the driving force in the nation for progress." Education is to "develop the personality of the nation" and to "promote democracy." These are not the isolated sentiments of one leader. They are reflective of the currents of thought to be found whenever political and educational personnel discuss the country's future. Living in Uganda, reading the daily press, listening to and watching the national leaders, one is impressed by an almost embarrassing self-consciousness about the "need to modernize," to "create a new nation," and to use the schools as a major vehicle in such tasks. As expressed in the influential 1963 Report of the Uganda Education Commission, a major aim of education is "To promote in the pupils a knowledge of their civic rights and responsibilities, and a love of their country which are basic for creating a sense of national solidarity."[2]

More to the point perhaps, is the fact that such sentiments have been supported with hard-cash policies. The central government expends nearly a third of its total revenue in the educational sector; district and local-level authorities often invest even higher proportions. In educational spending, as indicated by the percent of the budget so invested, Uganda is in the upper decile of all nations of the world. In addition, postindependence Uganda has nationalized its schools; control has been shifted from the mission to the civil authorities. This policy is defended on grounds of making the classroom more reflective of Uganda's national values. A more subtle but no less important policy has been the practice of placing some of the most articulate and qualified Ugandans in positions of educational policy-making. Especially at the national and district level, an impressive array of talent has been marshalled to manage the educational enterprise. There is no better testimony to the seriousness with which the political leadership treats the schools than to see how scarce economic and human resources are being disproportionately invested in the education sector.

2. There is a second factor that makes Uganda compelling as a test case for the "programmed political education and nation-building" arguments. The range of problems facing Uganda are precisely those that require a frontal attack on the attitudinal predispositions of the population. Uganda, a nation only five years old fits the popular description of an African country arbitrarily created out of diverse elements. More than a dozen vernacular languages are spoken. The country is roughly divided, politically as well as geographically, between the Bantu of the South and the Nilotes and Nilo-Hamitics of the North. Many of the tribes that make up the nation were bitter enemies both before and during colonial rule. The objective conditions for a "crisis of identity" are abundant.

Uganda is equally a textbook case for hypotheses about the "crisis of legitimacy." No nationalist movement, no charismatic leader, no independence ideology is available to those who face the tedious task of building legitimacy for the postindependence regime. The young nation cannot depend on the legitimacy-building mechanism of transferring legitimacy from the nationalist party or independence leader to the newly installed governing bodies.[3] The problem is exacerbated by certain traditional authorities and customs that are well entrenched. Four traditional kingdoms, each virtually controlled by a priest-king prior to British arrival, survive today in a legal sense (recognized in the constitution through a sliding-scale federalism)[4] and, more important, in the minds and values of the people. In the absence of a unifying ideology or a charismatic leader and in the presence of semiomnipotent traditional rulers, the new leaders can well do with help from whatever agencies are available as they attempt to build legitimacy for the new political order. Problems of political integration have been considered solvable, at least in part, through the effective application of a large-scale "nationalization" operation. National leaders in Uganda and social science observers agree that unless the young of the new nation come to share a new set of values it will not be easy for the country to take its first steps toward effective nationhood.

The Thesis

It is the thesis of this essay that Uganda has not, indeed cannot, depend very much on programmed political education to help resolve the critical needs of nation-building. Our essay is in the tradition of those case studies that examine a proposition under conditions most likely to disaffirm it.

Two general lines of argument will be presented to make our case. In the first instance we argue that political-administrative educational realities in Uganda do not lend themselves to intensive efforts at explicit citizenship training. In the second instance we suggest that even if they did, political socialization theory as currently developed casts considerable doubt on the success of such explicit efforts.

Before presenting these arguments a qualifying note is in order. We are not contending that the Uganda school system is failing to make a tremendous impression on the youth of the country. Nor are we arguing that the impression made in the schools is irrelevant to the tasks of nation-building—to creating a sense of national identity, to legitimating the regime, to cementing a political community, and so forth. Quite the opposite. As a later publication will attempt to show,[5] we feel that the educational system is making a major contribution in socializing the youth into a Uganda national community. However, the school's impact is occurring for reasons *other than* programmed political education. It is the latter topic that is of concern here.

Observations About Conditions in Uganda

The Content of Programmed Political Education

It is a truism to suggest that the first condition to be met in any focused program of political education is for the country to have a doctrine or ideology to which the student can be introduced. The doctrine should be fairly specific. A diffuse, amorphous message does not lend itself to highly structured teaching programs. Furthermore, the doctrine should be sufficiently stable that the time it takes to communicate it through teachers and textbook writers does not overlap with radical shifts in the ideology.

Uganda has yet to articulate a coherent nationalist ideology. Neither the economic, the social, the political, nor even the historical doctrines have been more than sketched in rough outline form. And the sketches themselves are subject to change. Unlike many of the new African nations, Uganda does not have the advantage of at least one major unifying ingredient on which to build an ideology. There is no easily grasped political doctrine such as "one party democracy" nor an easily understood economic doctrine such as "African Socialism." There is no national victory over an obstinate colonial enemy as in the case of the white settlers in Kenya and the French in Guinea. There is not even a common history or shared political folk heroes to evoke national pride. With the leaders of the nation trying to find and agree on a set of common national values, it is difficult to see what could be taught as a program of political education in the schools.

Very little in Uganda's political past or her current situation lends itself to codification as a "national ideology." The one call that can be issued by the leadership is to urge the population to wage war against ignorance, disease, and poverty. Though such innocuous slogans may become part of the *lingua franca*, they are no substitute for a coherent and emotionally compelling ideology. Uganda is still groping for an anchor in the way of either an economic or a political doctrine. Programmed political socialization cannot encode into the values of school children a nonexistent doctrine.

Without a past to celebrate or a present to eulogize, the directors of any (hypothesized) political education program would find lesson plans and materials in short supply. No wonder that the leaders find themselves in disagreement even on such basic questions as "traditionalism" versus "modernization" in the history curriculum. Shortly after independence one outspoken member of Parliament argued that if Uganda were to maintain her individuality as a nation then "The Minister of Education should encourage our children to learn more about African songs ... and African musical instruments." Debating the merits of various educational policies, this M.P. went on to bemoan the students' "abysmal ignorance when asked questions about African history, about African kings and the like." In a subsequent speech on educational goals, the Prime Minister differed on the merits of celebrating the past. Obote urged his listeners to "move away from the tentacles of tradition." Otherwise, he argued, "you are imprisoning yourselves."

That this basic ambivalence among the country's leadership is reflected in the schoolroom is indicated by the perceptive director of Uganda's National Institute of Education. "Teachers in Africa are tip-toeing rather precariously between these two conflicting culture worlds (the traditional tribal life and the Western ideals), not knowing which set of values to emphasize."[6] This educational leader is suggesting to us a larger truth as well. National leaders, disagreement, diffuseness, or transitoriness about the appropriate ideology will be reflected as lack of coherence in the classroom.

Administering Political Education Programs

But even if the elite shared more values with each other and even if the nationalism of Uganda were such as to embody a political culture program, it might still be argued that the administrative infrastructure is such that the program could not be effectively and quickly diffused. The national doctrine —to be diffused—must get from the capital to the upcountry schoolroom, and once in the schoolroom, it must be impressed on the minds of the youth. The first step in this flow concerns the administrative structures; the second concerns teachers and teaching materials.

Uganda, as many of the newer nations, lacks the administrative expertise and channels for effectively transmitting directives from the political capital to the field. Administrative breakdowns—what has been called lack of structural integrations—characterize all polities. Ubiquitous though such difficulties might be in political life, they appear in their most exaggerated form in the new nation. The reasons for this have been well documented. In common with most recently decolonized African countries, Uganda has lost considerable civil service expertise through the departure of large numbers of expatriates. Though programs of Africanization and rapid upgrading can fill the posts, the experience acquired over many years is not easily replaced.

The difficulty of finding trained personnel is compounded by a critically inadequate communication and transportation system. We were told by a civics teacher in a primary school some distance from the capital that the time lag between placing a book order and receiving the books was frequently longer than the school year. The District Educational Offices are understaffed and the clerk and secretarial help grossly undertrained. Given their overwhelming problems of opening, maintaining, equipping, and staffing schools, it is no surprise that relatively little of the district and regional personnel's effort goes into establishing political education programs.

These are only three of many factors contributing to administrative difficulties. Another factor is the instability of many of the agencies and the tasks assigned to them. For example, the responsibility for inspecting the schools and setting the teaching standards shifted from a University Institute of Education to an Inspectorate in the Ministry of Education to the District Education Office within the period of a few years. A country that has just had its fourth birthday, as Uganda has, is understandably still groping for the administrative structures which are most suitable to the tasks at hand.

Yet another factor concerns the rigidity of any set of structures that have become institutionalized over time. Educationists, many of whom predate the new leadership by a considerable number of years, have evolved their own ways of doing things and their own set of values. It is a mistake to think that school systems are without wills of their own, that they are easily manipulable when a new political and administrative elite comes to power. Rupert Emerson has noted:

The available evidence is scanty, but it is improbable that the educational authorities have thus far made any significant direct effort to use the schools as agencies for "nationalizing" the pupils. The missionary and colonial origins of the schools, which precluded nationalist indoctrination, have continued into the period of independence.[7]

Parents' associations, local foundation boards, headmasters, teachers, and other educational policy-makers at the district and local level have views of their own. It is not self-evident that any clash between the values of those local groups and those of central leadership is necessarily resolved in favor of the latter.

A second barrier to effective diffusion of national doctrines concerns the lack of resources for transmitting a coherent set of values through the school system. The resource gap manifests itself both in teaching materials and teachers. Material that could form the backbone in African history of Uganda is not yet available. In fact, it should be noted that when one speaks of Africanizing the syllabus, it is generally Europeans who are organizing the syllabi, writing the textbooks, and preparing the teaching materials. The civics and history material available at present is told either through the eyes of the colonialists or with the colonial era as the major referent. Whether or not this is a serious "neocolonial" problem cannot be answered here. We can surmise that it is likely to reduce the production of a truly African syllabus, however well intentioned the expatriate staff.

We should also keep in mind that political education programs must compete for scarce resources with a curriculum largely established in colonial times and still dominated by the British examination system. As presently constructed, the exam system offers few rewards for those who study African history or current events in Uganda. English and arithmetic are the subjects that must be mastered for success in the primary leaving examination. The secondary Cambridge Certificate examination demands world history and geography in addition. It is a commentary on Uganda, one consistent with the thesis argued here, that if a school actually devoted itself to intensive political education and nationalization programs, it would without doubt severely handicap its students in the exams. We were told by a regional inspector that civics and local history were second only to physical education as the poorest taught subjects in Uganda. Our own examination of the materials available, school periods alloted, and teachers assigned to such topics confirms this judgment.

Lack of resources is further compounded by school staffing practices. The secondary schools are almost entirely staffed by expatriates. In 1960, 83 percent of the teaching staff in the senior secondary schools was non-African. In 1964, two years after independence, this figure had actually increased to 86 percent. John Kakonge, Uganda's outspoken Director of Planning, has noted some consequences of expatriate-staffing. He pointed out that "it is impossible to develop an African outlook and attitude to life in the country's youth if the schools are manned by people with an English or American outlook. . . . There is such a thing as African personality. . . . It is often very difficult for a young eager child to understand why a white man should still be able to order him around and even beat him."[8] Kakonge is an astute enough

politician to recognize that European "Teachers for East Africa" and American "Peace Corps Volunteers" are not suitable channels for transmitting values and attitudes particular to the Ugandan setting.

Primary schoolteachers, though overwhelmingly African, have certain disadvantages as well. The 1963 Education Report mentions the difficult task teachers have in fitting the youth to Uganda's needs: "Themselves educated in the past, they have to teach children in the present for life in a future which is unknown."[9] Primary schoolteachers, many of whom do not speak English and most of whom have only limited educations themselves, will not necessarily be effective agents of modernization. Against nearly overwhelming odds the primary teachers are making a tremendous dent in the ignorance characterizing large portions of the population. Educational authorities are pleased when reading, writing, and arithmetic can be taught. They can hardly place an additional burden on the teachers by instructing them to expend energy in political education. Even were the authorities predisposed in this direction the primary schoolteachers do not have sufficient training, knowledge, or even disposition for the task. Educated by preindependence mission teachers, today's primary teachers are often more reflective of colonial values and teaching practices than postindependence themes. A certain "conservatism" has been built into the school system in this regard.

We have here reviewed some conditions in Uganda that mitigate against effective programs of focused political socialization in the classroom. We argue that necessary, though not sufficient, conditions for programmed political education are a nationalistic doctrine and a means of transmitting it. Uganda does not meet these preliminary conditions. Neither doctrine, administrative structures, teaching materials, nor teachers have been adequately marshalled to the tasks of citizenship training or political indoctrination.

Before leaving this section, we might add one footnote for those readers whose images of African education are too much shaped by their experiences in the Western world. A major factor accounting for the ineffectiveness of schools in the newer nations for the tasks of programmed political education concerns the relatively small proportions of students who actually continue schooling long enough for such programs to take hold. In Uganda the proportion of children of primary school age in classes is about 50 percent. At the secondary level, where the concentration on citizenship training is heaviest, the proportion drops to less than 2.5 percent. In addition, the number of children in school is distributed very unevenly throughout the country. In other words, as the carriers of citizenship ideology, the school directly reaches less than half of the target population and distributes the message around the country in very uneven patterns.

The problem of instilling citizenship values extends beyond the student population. By definition, appropriate *nationalistic* orientations should come to be the property of all the youth, not just the few who make their way into and through the schools. But universal education is many years away. Thus, even if the administrative and resource difficulties outlined in this section were to be overcome, it is still years in the future before the majority of Uganda youth could be directly exposed to such programmed political education.

Observations About Political Socialization Theory

In this section we shift focus from the conditions particular to Uganda and the new nations to some general notions from political socialization theory.[10] Our goal remains the same however. We shall probe the premise that programmed political education is a useful vehicle for instilling into the youth of new nations those values considered appropriate for nation-building.

We acknowledge that the strategy of this section is somewhat premature, for political socialization "theory" is still in the developmental stage. Nearly any finding leads to a quantum rather than incremental jump in our understanding. A small empirical study of seemingly marginal import can upset what had previously been considered a major prop in the theory. Further, data on which theories about the process of political socialization have been built are often attitude surveys that tell us more about what children believe than about the mechanisms through which these beliefs came to be internalized. Finally, socialization theory tends to be culture-bound. The sample of research sites is heavily biased toward the more established nations where the young are introduced to an ongoing, coherent political culture and drawn into a stable well defined political community. Such a bias limits the applicability of the theory to the newer nations.

To draw on "theory" to refute a particular hypothesis presumes that the theory has successfully escaped falsification from attack enough times that for operational purposes we consider it confirmed. Such an assertion can hardly be made about political socialization theory. These caveats in mind, it is still useful to note three areas in which the theory would bid us to be cautious in assessing the value of attempts at programmed political instruction. That is, even if the inherent difficulties of articulating and diffusing a political culture were not characteristic of new nations, we would have theoretical reasons for being dubious about the success of programmed political education.

Congruent versus Incongruent Political Socialization

A more or less confirmed proposition in political socialization theory is that the greater the number of socialization agencies operating in the same direction, the more effective will any one of them be. If the parents, teacher, school curriculum, scout leader, symbol system, peer group are all urging the child to "obey the law," the correlation will be high between the message of any one agent and the child's attitude. On the other hand, if various agencies are pulling in different directions, the less successful will any one of them be. Cumulative or congruent socialization describes the first situation; noncumulative or incongruent describe the second.

As pointed out earlier, one reason social observers and political leaders regard the school system as a valuable agent for programmed political socialization is that the classroom, of all the major socialization agencies, is the most susceptible to public control. Family and peer groups, the two other critical agents of early political instruction, are generally "free" with respect to the political messages they diffuse. Efforts of certain totalitarian regimes notwithstanding, the family and play group have never been brought under the control of political authorities. They are difficult to program.

This observation has particular relevance for an understanding of cumulative political socialization. In some countries, the United States for example, it is of little importance that the various influencers of the young cannot be programmed. The family, church, friendship groups, media, leisure activities, and associational life reinforce and complement each other in providing new members of society, especially the young, with appropriate political values. If the classroom and the teacher induce patriotism, expect obedience, and instill suitable attitudes, they are successful not because of their program but because they are congruent with the remainder of society's socialization mechanisms.

The question of whether political socialization is cumulative or not is a relative one. No society's agencies are perfectly conguent with respect to the citizenship images portrayed. In any society the political socialization agents can diffuse conflicting messages. However, the problem of incongruent political socialization is particularly acute in the new nations. Like all societies, most of the important political socialization agents are beyond effective control by the political leadership. In addition, and here the new nations are less like established nations, critical socialization agents, such as the family, are almost necessarily in conflict with the modernization and nationalization attempts of programmed political education. The more rapidly a country is trying to change, the more likely will the various socialization agents be out of phase with one another. Uganda can depend very little, if at all, on the social and cultural milieu to be uniformly supportive of any programmed political education.

Reasons for this have been well reviewed in the "new nation" literature.[11] One theme concerns the incongruence between the "modern, progressive, Western, national" values of the school system and the "traditional, conservative, parochial" values of such important political socialization agents as tribal elders, parents, religious leadership, and even some teachers. The second theme, usually discussed under the heading of continuities and discontinuities in political socialization, is the varient on socialization incongruence which stresses how things learned at one age are inappropriate for the demands of citizenship associated with a later age. Since both of these themes are so well developed in general socialization theory we need do little other than recognize that congruence among various political socialization agencies in new nations is more the exception than the normal case.

Highly self-conscious instructional efforts, such as programmed political education, must struggle against numerous other currents. There is nothing in political socialization literature to suggest that programmed instruction will fare well in such a struggle. Indeed, the theory tends to predict the opposite: the more self-conscious the instruction, the less likely is it to succeed. The very obviousness of the program works to its disadvantage. Boredom, cynicism, and even antagonism are common responses of youth to explicit ideological indoctrination.[12]

Indirect versus Direct Political Socialization

A second package of political socialization propositions relevant to our argument concerns the tension between indirect modes of learning. Indirect political socialization refers to the internalization of values not themselves political but which subsequently influence the acquisition of analogous values that are political. The classic example is how the child learns what to think about authority. Through his interactions with parents, teachers, and other "nonpolitical" authorities, the young child comes to expect certain things of persons in authority positions. He acquires a general disposition toward authority. Subsequently this general disposition is attached to political authorities. His socialization with respect to attitudes toward political authority has been indirect; it is a two-step process involving the initial acquisition and the later transference. Direct political socialization refers to learning situations where the content of what is transmitted is specifically political. The attitude is attached to a political object from the beginning.

Although socialization theory is far from clear about the relationship between these two modes of political learning, the literature, in a hypothesis reminiscent of the cumulative proposition already noted, does suggest that direct political socialization can be seriously undermined by contradictory indirect socialization.

Almost by definition, programmed political education stresses the direct mode of learning. Specific political orientations are to be attached to identified political objects. The curriculum materials, the patriotic ritual life and the teacher explicitly point out that this rather than that political value is the suitable one. But coterminous with his instruction in these "appropriate values," the student is involved in continuous learning experiences with latent political consequences. If the values he acquires in nonpolitical but politically relevant experience contradict the specific values channeled through an explicit program of political socialization, we expect the impact of the latter to be consequently weakened. Three examples, all drawn from the East African situation, help clarify the mechanisms at work.[13]

Our first illustration comes from Uganda's neighbor, Tanzania. Tanzanian political leaders frequently make references to "African socialism" and urge the classroom to become a vehicle for instilling values appropriate for moving the classroom toward such an economic system. The attitude set considered proper for African socialism is one in which individualistic values are suppressed in favor of cooperative predispositions. Teachers and textbooks are expected to stress the need for cooperative endeavors. However, the culture of the classroom stresses the contradictory values of competition and individual achievement. At the primary level the struggle to obtain one of the few openings in secondary school can be intense. This highly competitive situation repeats itself at every stage of the educational ladder. The political orientations indirectly acquired from the "culture of competition" are not consistent with the message of the political education program. The cooperative, sharing ideology of African socialism is difficult to internalize when competition

for scarce resources is the dominant experience of every schoolchild.

Another value repeatedly stressed by East African leaders, and at times even to be found in the civics teaching materials, states that a sense of national identity should transcend parochial, tribal, or racial loyalties. However, in boarding school after boarding school, students of different tribes (or races in the case of Asian versus African) group together in the dorms, share a common dining table, and speak in their vernacular. The day to day living conditions have latent political consequences that overwhelm any textbook lesson in national integration. This pattern is not limited to East Africa, of course.

A final illustration, drawn again from our observations of East Africa, focuses on the contradiction between school lessons in egalitarian democracy and school practices constructed around the British prefect system. Headmasters throughout the ex-British colonies continue to run their schools according to the elitist, hierarchial patterns borrowed from the famous British public schools. The prefect system, indirectly if not directly, teaches the students that recruitment into positions of student leadership is a function of satisfying the authorities rather than a student constituency. The prefect system further emphasizes that that which the powers give they can also take away. There is no appeal beyond the absolute power of the staff. Such experiences with authority are not reflective of the egalitarian-democratic values presumable being taught in programs of civic education.[14]

These brief examples do not prove that direct political socialization is always the loser when undermined by indirect learning. Being only illustrations, they simply indicate how direct and indirect lessons can be in contradiction. They further suggest some very concrete ways in which this contradiction expresses itself in the new nation classroom. Although political socialization theory cannot with confidence assert that indirect learning is necessarily more compelling than direct learning, it can suggest that a program of political education is weakened to the extent that other political socialization experiences, direct or indirect, are pulling in different directions.

The Development Sequence of Political Socialization

The efforts at political education are also weakened because they reach the pupil so late. Of relevance here is a thesis with respect to the development sequence that appears to characterize much political learning. We must limit ourselves to a very brief overview. The argument can be capsuled as follows: the individual acquires a "political self" as a result of his movement through the political socialization process. The core of an individual's political self is made up of basic political attachments, identifications, and loyalties. These basic orientations are characterized by high affect. Also as part of his core orientations, the individual acquires a set of basic interpretative categories through which political events, personalities, and programs are interpreted. The citizen trusts or does not trust his fellow man. He feels efficacious or powerless in the face of a political event. He either thinks in terms of "class politics" or does not. Racial classifications may or may not be salient. Along with his basic identifications, these interpretative ori-

entations serve the individual as political eyeglasses. They filter, screen, distort, magnify, illuminate, or block, depending on the political object.

At a somewhat less basic intermediate level the individual political self has various forms of specific knowledge about and feelings toward political structures and processes. These orientations involve at least minimal knowledge about the form and operation of political life in his country. Finally, the political self is characterized by transitory responses and reactions to particular political policies, programs, and personalities.

This schematic description of the political self is useful for understanding political socialization. As more and more socialization data become available, it increasingly appears that these three different types of orientations are sequentially related to a political maturation process. The more basic attachments and the interpretive orientations are acquired quite early in life. Subsequently, in later years the information and knowledge necessary for participation in political life is added. It is much later, normally during the adult years, that an individual acquires specific views about political programs and policies.

A critical assumption in the argument as briefly presented is that the basic or core values acquired early serve as the foundation upon which the political self is constructed. Subsequently acquired political values are shaped by basic identifications and predispositions. Politically speaking, the adolescent or adult is not an entirely free agent. What he comes to believe about politics is conditioned—though not determined—by his basic values. We cannot here go into the many facets of this quite complex assumption, and surely it merits qualification from many angles. It is presented only to shed additional light on the difficulties under which programmed political education must operate.

In most new nations the earliest point at which a program of political education can be introduced into the school curriculum is during the late primary school years, that is, when students are about fourteen or fifteen. Neither the materials nor the teachers are available for specific political instruction at levels much below this. Further, students in their early primary years lack both the conditioning and the literacy skills necessary for absorbing much in the way of citizenship training materials. Explicit efforts at political indoctrination in the classroom necessarily have as their target students who are well past the stage when such a teaching program might be successful.

To cast our argument in the specific Meadian language alluded to above, much of a person's social self, and by extension his political self, is well established by early adolescence or, for that matter, by late childhood. Basic interpretative categories, attachments and loyalties, identifications, and social identities are relatively fixed. To the degree that a political education program builds upon these core values it will be successful. To the degree that it runs counter to such core values, programmed political education will fare ill. Readers of this volume need no reminding that a nationalistic and modernistic political education program will not be congruent with the parochial and traditional values likely to be at the core of the nascent political self of "new nation youth."

A Caveat

It has not been possible to develop ideas from political socialization theory in any detail. They are added to our discussion of programmed political education as a corrective to a tendency in social analysis. Observers of social behavior occasionally slip into the error of inferring the attitudes and beliefs of a group from the doctrines to which that group is exposed. This is to think that we know what values all Catholics hold if we only read the Papal Encyclicals or that we can deduce the beliefs of all communists from the writings of Marx. This error, what we might call the "fallacy of misplaced inference," is particularly acute when the observer is unable to get attitudinal data. Lack of such attitudinal data, especially from schoolchildren, is the fate of many commentators on the new nations. One purpose of this part of our essay has been to correct any tendency to infer the values of African schoolchildren from content analysis of political education programs. Such analysis might instruct us about the goals of the political directorate. It cannot inform us of the degree to which the message has been internalized by the target audience.

Conclusions

Plato devoted much attention in *The Republic* to the role of education and childhood training for instilling appropriate political values in the citizen. In his utopia citizens would believe suitable things about the political order and their place in it if only they received the proper education. Plato suggested a second notion of importance when he raised the question of how the distribution of individual political beliefs might affect the stability of political structures. In his language, the cyclical degeneration of politics is traceable to defects in political education.

New nation leaders tend to share with Plato a faith that difficulties of development or threats to political order can be overcome with the "right" program of political education. Though we agree with the general thesis that the making of the citizen is an essential ingredient in nation-building, we are doubtful about the feasability of a political education program as the most effective first thrust instrument for this task.

Using Uganda as the illustrative case, we have wished first to show the tremendous difficulties under which new nation leaders are operating. Problems of agreeing upon and articulating a national doctrine, difficulties in administering programs, and lack of properly oriented teachers and suitable teaching materials are the more obvious, but not the only, barriers to diffusing a nationalist ideology through the classroom. However

attractive programmed political education might appear on paper, the political and administrative realities caution us not to expect significant results.

Further, even if a program could be mounted, our knowledge about the political socialization process suggests that we take a skeptical view with respect to its likely impact. The schoolroom is but one of the many sources of political values for the youth of a nation. Its success as political instructor depends in large measure on the configuration of political socialization agencies and messages. It is our argument that the political socialization configuration in new nations works against the success of programmed political education. Those who would effect an attitudinal revolution to accompany the political and economic modernization programs must work on many more fronts than the school system. Political socialization theory indicates to us that significant alteration in a nation's political culture is unlikely to follow the introduction of a politicized curriculum into the schoolroom.

NOTES

1. The literature pertinent to this topic is large and growing rapidly. Our own efforts have been guided by Gabriel Almond and Sidney Verba, *The Civic Culture* (Princeton: Princeton University Press, 1963), and the collection of essays in Lucian Pye and Sidney Verba (eds.), *Political Culture and Political Development* (Princeton: Princeton University Press, 1965). A study that examines some of the notions connected with political culture analysis in the context of Uganda can be found in Kenneth Prewitt, "Political Values of Opinion Leaders in Uganda," *Information of the Social Sciences* (June 1969).

2. *Education in Uganda: The Report of the Uganda Education Commission* (Entebbe, Uganda: Government Printer, 1963) p. 22.

3. David Easton has written persuasively on how to increase legitimacy by transferring it from one political institution to another. See his *A Systems Analysis of Political Life* (New York: Wiley, 1965), especially chap. 19. For a study that attempts to examine this mechanism in the context of East Africa, see Kenneth

Prewitt and Goren Hyden, "Voters Look at the Election," in Lionel Cliffe (ed.), *The Tanzanian Election of 1965* (Nairobi: East African Publishing House, 1967).

4. The present state of federalism in Uganda is unclear. Events of 1966 have made the legal status of Buganda particularly difficult to determine. The Kabaka, the traditional ruler of Buganda, was forced from his position as President of Uganda and has fled to England. Irrespective of the legal status of federalism, the sense of identification with one's Bantu kingdom appears to remain strong among the Bantu-speaking tribes of Southern Uganda.

5. Preliminary papers from this study can be found in Kenneth Prewitt (ed.), *Education and Political Values* (Nairobi: East African Publishing House, 1969).

6. Senteza Kajubi, "Crisis and Values in East African Education," paper of the National Institute of Education (Makerere University College, 1963), p. 12.

7. Rupert Emerson, "Nation-Building in Africa," in Karl W. Deutsch and William J. Foltz (eds.), *Nation-Building* (New York: Atherton, 1963), p. 112. Coleman makes a similar point. He suggests that in those countries where there "continues to be a marked dependence for teaching staff upon the former metropolitan country, overt ideological indoctrination in the schools would obviously be difficult if not impossible. Moreover, in many instances, indigenous members of the teaching staff tend to be either to the left or to the right of the government of the day; they are, therefore, unreliable agents for political indoctrination in the ideological line of the regime." See Coleman, *op. cit.*, p. 48.

8. From a speech reported in *The People*, August 21, 1965.

9. *Education in Uganda, op. cit.*, p. 12.

10. Much of the argument presented in this section is drawn from Richard E. Dawson and Kenneth Prewitt, *Political Socialization* (Boston: Little, Brown, 1969).

11. In particular see Robert LeVine, "Political Socialization and Culture Change," in Clifford Geertz (ed.), *Old Societies and New States* (New York: Free Press, 1963), pp. 280–303.

12. For a particularly instructive treatment of how programmed political education can generate disaffection see Jeremy R. Azrael, "Soviet Union," in James Coleman (ed.), *Education and Political Development* (Princeton, N.J.: Princeton University Press, 1965), pp. 233–271. Azrael writes, for example, that some students in the Soviet Union are politically apathetic from "sheer overwhelming boredom aroused by the regime, whether in the classroom, the Komsomol, or the mass media." p. 256.

13. Our thinking about this question has been aided greatly by conversations with George Von der Muhll. In an unpublished working paper, "Education and Citizenship in Tanzania: Some Preliminary Notes," 1966, Von der Muhll outlines the examples upon which this section draws.

14. Certain evidence from the United States suggests that the extracurricular life is a more potent political learning experience than formal instruction. Roy A. Price, reviewing this literature in his "Citizenship Studies in Syracuse," *Phi Delta Kappan*, 33, 180 (December 1951), concludes that "Classroom instruction fails to achieve the goals of citizenship and appears to be less effective than the extracurricular program of the school." p. 181.

DEMOCRACY AND POWER

- Oscar Handlin

o   o   o

To many pursuits of the New World the immigrant was strange upon arrival; to politics he was strangest of all. His European experience had included no participation in government; every question related to these matters would be new to him.

In the Old World (except perhaps in France), the State had been completely external to the peasant's consciousness. In the business of ruling he did not act, was only acted upon. Nowhere but in France (not even in England until 1884) did he possess the privilege of taking part in the selection of administrators or in the determination of policy. Nowhere therefore did he seriously expect that the State might further his welfare or safeguard his rights.

Indeed, he knew well—and this experience did teach—that the government was the tool of those who governed; and those who governed—the gentry, nobility, or the Crown—acted from interests that were remote from, or hostile to, his own. Where parliaments existed they were the arenas in which middle-class city people debated with his own masters; he had not yet the notion that this might be the means of redressing his own grievances.

Quite the contrary! The peasant never learned to understand how power could emanate from that impersonal abstraction, the State. That Boards or Benches could do anything he refused to believe. Behind the bureaucrat's desk, beneath the judge's robe, he could see only a man. But these men played always the official with him, refused to respond as human beings; and that he could not comprehend. He preferred therefore, in need, to turn to the local nobility, who might be cajoled or appealed to, and who could be held to the personal standards of behavior that befitted their stations. Or, sometimes, he thought of the religious figure of the sanctified King as his distant protector who, if only he were told, would surely intercede for his devoted subjects. In Ireland and Poland, where the overlords were alien, the peasants had not even the consolation of that daydreaming.

Realistically, the villagers knew the State only in its role of harsh, unfriendly exploiter. Its taxes were worse than the landlords' dues; the latter at least were visibly expended in the manor house, the former went off to some remote incomprehensible purpose. The government exacted forced labor to build and mend roads the husbandman could have done without. Most oppressively of all, in many places, it conscripted the young men to serve in the remote world. At the most crucial point of their lives, when they were ready to marry and to create families, the army took them away, interfered with the whole order of inheritance and upset the stability of the village.

Above selection from: *The uprooted: The Epic Story of the Great Migrations that Made the American People*, by Oscar Handlin (Boston: Atlantic-Little, Brown and Co., 1951), pp. 201–218, excerpts.

The State assumed its most horrifying guise when the perverse foolishness of its officers dragged it into war. The peasants dreaded the bloody disasters which no pen could describe, no mind embrace. Men were so fearful at the very thought of it that they wept; they knew that all would perish when it came. It was not glory the trumpets blew for them, but doom, in ravaged fields and flaming homes and men on horseback trampling over the supplicating bodies.

This was power; and it was not theirs. In the face of it nothing could be done. The tillers of the soil resented it as they resented everything that despoiled the fruits of their labor. But there was no escape. As with the weather or with any other unpredictable superior force, passive resignation was the only tolerable reaction. After all, it was the docile calf that thrived and lived to suck much milk. The gendarme encountered no resistance, only sullen, silent suspicion, or a grudging appeasement by gifts to keep trouble away.

The same grievances shaped the attitudes of the dissenting people. They were fully as remote from the State as the peasant and in addition suffered from discriminatory legislation if not from outright persecution.

And what was government that any immigrant should acquire a more favorable impression of it in the course of his journey? Government was a succession of malevolent obstacles in the way of getting to America. It foreshortened the earth, putting up high walls in the way of the free movement of people. In its name men found themselves betagged with strange papers, herded about like cattle. Its visible symbol was the outstretched, uniformed palm. Such, on arrival, was the newcomers' conception of power.

Perhaps they thought the New World would be different. If so, the first contacts disabused them of the idea. The immigration officials of the Land of Liberty were not unlike those anywhere else. Subsequent experiences also confirmed the old assumptions.

In pillared halls the laws are made, the briefs are read, the judgments rendered, in proper form, engrossed, signed, sealed. Of the majesty of the law, however, the immigrant has another view. Down by the corner the policeman twirls the symbol of his authority. Within the beat, he is government. But the limits of his power are well recognized. Shyly he averts his eyes as he passes this house or that. He cannot see where cards are dealt, where liquor flows beyond its hours, where ladies peep through curtained windows. With the shopkeeper, on the other hand, he is severe, and the incautious peddler often knows his wrath. Fortunately it is not hard to turn away that wrath; a soft answer and a generous purse deflate his zeal.

The wise laborers stay out of the way, make themselves unobtrusive. They expect to help, and count themselves lucky if only they can remain unnoticed. They know the dangers of entanglement with the law.

o o o

Having settled and survived the five years, the newcomer was expected to become a citizen. Docile, he did what was expected of him. One day he took an oath, received a certificate, was naturalized.

You might say, *Well, what was one paper more? In his lifetime, many had been given him.* This one, carefully hidden in the bottom of the trunk, was unique. It made the foreigner an American, equal in rights with every other man. With this document, he was told, came a prompt accession to power. Now he was no longer a mere subject, but a person of consequence, one who shared in the selection of his rulers. How? By casting the vote. Why? Because, he was told, the United States was a democracy.

Now this was a conception the immigrants found it difficult to comprehend. The underlying assumption that in political relationships there was a fundamental equality among men did not square with their own deep-rooted ideas of status, with their own acceptance of differences of rank. Everyone knew that respect was due to the elders in a community, that a farm hand was not on a level with a farmer, an ignorant cottier with a husbandman of substance. Each individual had a place within which he ought to stay. To push oneself forward, to set oneself high, was a grievous sin. Otherwise there would be no order in the world. Search the memory of their experience as they would, these people could find nothing in their life in the Old World or the New that would confirm the democratic hypothesis that they themselves could participate meaningfully in the exercise of power.

Naturalization did not therefore immediately make voters. That would come only when their own American needs led the new citizens to the ballot box.

o   o   o

[In the passages that follow Handlin describes how the political boss and his machine assisted the new immigrant in his dealings with the bureaucracy and the law. The bribes and corruption that often accompanied such services were not resented by the newcomer because

"all this was entirely as it had been in the Old Country." (p. 205). No wonder he distrusted the political movements that tried to do away with bossism and corruption. Reformers, progressives, much less socialists or anarchists found no converts among the immigrants of peasant origin (ed.).]

It was not surprising that the boss should see in the stirring of reform interests a threat to his own position. But it was significant that the mass of immigrants should regard the efforts of the various progressives with marked disfavor. In part this disapproval was based on the peasant's inherited distrust of radicalism; but it was strengthened by a lack of understanding among the radicals that deprived them of all influence among the newcomers.

In the case of the Italians and other central Europeans, the revolutions of the mid-nineteenth century had added fear of the pillaging reds to the traditional suspicion of revolutionaries. All these old misgivings crossed the ocean to the New World. Conservative enough at home, the peasants had become more conservative still in the course of migration. They dreaded political change because that might loosen the whole social order, disrupt the family, pull God from His throne; the radicals themselves talked that way and confirmed the worst such suspicions. Naturally the influence of the churches on both sides of the Atlantic was thrown in the balance on the side of stability and confirmed the unwillingness of the immigrants to be involved in any insurgent movements.

At only one point, and that very early, had there been the basis of a rapprochement of the newcomers with radicalism. In the 1840's and 1850's the émigré nationalist leaders were strongly tinged in their thinking by liberalism. But they had difficulty even then in controlling their following; and the outcome of the revolutions in Europe, together with the hostility of the clergy, forced them either to surrender their heterodox ideas or to sink themselves into obscurity.

As to the native reformers, those were always an outlandish breed to the immigrants. The insistence upon framing platforms which included such curious planks as women's rights, temperance, and Sabbatarianism cast upon them all the suspicion of eccentricity. Their religious tolerance and nonsectarianism seemed to reflect a lack of interest in religion; and already before the Civil War the battle lines were drawn over such issues as the public school system.

o   o   o

THE GENESIS OF POLITICAL RADICALISM: THE CASE OF THE RADICAL RIGHT

- Ira S. Rohter

"*Washington has been taken over*! By which we mean that Communist influences are now in full working control of our Federal Government. . . . And we believe that the Communists and their dupes, allies, and agents, throughout this vast apparatus of government, now actually determine almost all policies, actions, and decisions."[1]

These pronouncements by Robert Welch, founder and head of the John Birch Society, succinctly state the guiding premise of today's radical rightists:* in their eyes America is almost completely in the hands of a massive communist conspiracy. The symptoms of this "communization" of America are many: increasing crime and civil strife, the decline of home life and religion, poor education, and a vast catalogue of socialistic governmental programs, particularly "federally imposed" civil rights activities, the war on poverty, the progressive income tax, foreign aid and United States participation in the "one-world" oriented United Nations, mental health, urban renewal, and medicare.[2]

How can we account for the fact that a sizable number of American citizens[3] believe our political leaders are traitors,

that the United States is in the tight grip of a diabolical clique that "controls 80%" of our lives, and are unalterably opposed to so many aspects of our contemporary social order?

One frequently voiced interpretation argues essentially that radical rightism represents inadequate socialization into proper citizen roles, that right-wing extremism is a phenomenon led and populated mainly by embittered misfits and nuts swept up in paranoid delusions. Such psychopathic explanations must be rejected since they are not supported by any substantive evidence.[4] A more tenable interpretation sees rightism as a form of deviant political behavior engendered by a conflict between the strongly socialized central values, beliefs, and personality needs of some individuals, and certain modern trends in the larger society.[5]

In the analysis that follows, we will first examine in depth two factors found to be crucial to the genesis of rightist behavior, these being (1) a strong adherence to traditional values in concert with a deeply felt alienation from current prevailing moral standards; (2) a distinctive personality structure characterized by a close-minded cognitive style and the tendency to cathect frustrations by directing hostility against scapegoat enemies. These behavioral dispositions represent the "products" of earlier socialization. We shall then explore their roots, focusing particular attention on

Above selection has been written especially for this volume.

* In this paper the term "rightist," uncapitalized, refers to adherents to this movement in general. Other commonly used terms are "right-wing extremists," "superpatriots," "ultra-rightists," and "rightwingers."

(a) the role of parental child-rearing practices and their relationship to the rightists' later personality system and (b) the role of religious fundamentalism as a cultural milieu that strongly influences both value orientations and personality.

The Products of Socialization

Beliefs

The interpretation that rightists give to certain events and situations in their environment may be conceptualized as their belief system related to these phenomena. Beliefs provide structure, organization, and meaning for the individual as he attempts to relate to his world.[6] Talcott Parsons usefully distinguishes between three types of beliefs: (1) *cognitive* beliefs, which consist of concepts and conceptualizations through which the world is viewed (knowledge); (2) *affective* beliefs, which are basically emotional feelings and reactions; and (3) *evaluative* beliefs, which involve the assessment of alternatives in terms of value preferences.[7] Cognitive, affective, and evaluative beliefs inextricably combine to form attitudes, ideologies, opinions, views, and orientations toward social objects.[8]

A further refinement to the study of a *political* belief is to classify it on the basis of its major object of focus. Easton and Hess, for example, suggest three distinct levels of orientation—toward the regime (the political system as a whole), toward the government (the day to day running of government), and the political community (the social order in general and fellow citizens).[9] Or, beliefs may be cataloged into citizen roles (partisan attachment, ideology, motivation to participate), about role incumbents (President Johnson), or system outputs (medicare).[10]

Most of the right's political views are charged with negative *affect*: nearly all its programs and goals consist of repealing something or removing someone from an office or position. The often-voiced proposals to "get the U.S. out of the U.N.," "to impeach Supreme Court Justice Earl Warren," to repeal the income tax, social security, and medicare, to sell the Tennessee Valley Authority, and to stop foreign aid are characteristic of its almost completely negative orientation to policies and political leaders at the governmental level. At the political community level the right is vehemently opposed to a great many aspects of contemporary life that it feels are undesirable: "forced" racial integration, mental health programs, urban renewal, progressive education, labor unions, and liberal churches are only a few. Because the right is so dissatisfied with most governmental policies, public officials, and political representatives, it views the system as practically rotted to the core. Frequent accusations charging the country with "going socialist," the President and the Supreme Court having usurped power and destroyed the founding fathers' checks and balances system and the Constitution having been substantially overturned are again only a few indicators of the right's fundamentally hostile orientation toward the current political system.

The right's *cognitive* beliefs (how its adherents see their personal and social environments) are distinctively colored by its intense hostility toward and rejection of many facets of modern society. Rightists explain this by attributing everything they dislike to Communist agents: America is in the grip of sinister men bent on destroying all they hold sacred.

In order to understand the rightists' current political beliefs we must examine the attitudinal predispositions that they bring to the situation. These antecedents represent the products of their earlier socialization and may be classified into two major analytic categories: values and personality traits.

Values

Values are affectively charged *standards* that people employ substantially to organize and define their environment. They play a major role in shaping behavior; according to Talcott Parsons and Edward Shils, writing in *Toward A General Theory of Action*, values are the single "most crucial cultural elements in the organization of systems of action."[11] Values always consist of emotional and cognitive components, and operate as norms, standards, criteria, or rules that guide the selection of alternatives in a choice-making situation.[12] Although the normative influence of values is evident, their intimate relationship with cognitions is often overlooked. How an individual acts in a particular situation is shaped by his perceptions, which, when carefully scrutinized, are revealed as stimuli selected, organized, and imputed meaning by conceptions of what is available and desirable, that is, values.

The *evaluative* mode is the predominant element in the right's political orientation; the rightists' value commitments supply the emotive energy and subsume all cognitive beliefs to their service.

This finding is one of the best-supported hypotheses that emerged in my empirical study of actual radical rightists. In 1965, 169 rightists* and 167 Non-Rightists (who served as a control-comparison group) living in the Pacific Northwest were administered a 35-page instrument by professional interviewers. Radical rightists are defined as people who believe that an overwhelming conspiracy of communists has secretly taken over and controls the government, the schools and universities, the churches, the mass media, ad infinitum. A sample of such people was constructed from the following sources: lists of John Birch Society and Liberty Amendment Committee members published in newspaper articles, a content analysis of "letters to the editors" in several newspapers, and finally, from a list of members of a local rightist organization.

The sample of Non-Rightists was selected in a similar fashion, their names also came from the content analysis of other "letters to the editor" and from referenda petitions. These people showed themselves to be concerned with the same issues, but did *not* link them to communism.

Applying our attitudinal definition to both samples, individuals were ranked on two empirical dimensions: their extent of belief in, and activities directed against, internal communist subversion. This recognizes that some followers are more committed than others to the ideology and practices of radical rightism and allows us to work with distinctions of degree rather than a simple dichotomy of rightist, nonrightist. In all, twenty-five separate items were used to

* "Rightists," with a capital "R," are those individuals in the sample classified as radical rightists on a 25-item empirical index. Rightists believe significantly in the communist conspiracy and take part in anticommunist activities.

Table 1

Belief in Traditional Values Scale* Versus Radical Rightism Index

Degree of Radical Rightism	Traditional Beliefs				
	(high) I	II	III	*(low)* IV	*(N)*
(low) I	12%	11%	33%	44%	(75)
II	17	26	29	27	(92)
III	30	28	28	13	(92)
(high) IV	30	36	27	7	(77)

Kruskal-Wallis H-Test = 41.5 P < .001

Gamma = .38

* The other items in this scale are: "Too many people today are spending their money for unnecessary things, instead of saving or investing it for the future," "A man can't be respected unless he's worked hard for some important goal," and "Obedience and respect for authority are the most important virtues children should learn." The internal consistency of this scale is quite high, with the Kuder-Richardson Coefficient being .87.

classify the respondents' degree of rightism. Low scores (quartiles I and II) on the Rightism Index may be thought of as Non-Rightists, high scorers (quartiles III and IV) are the Rightists.[13]

We discovered that the *evaluative* components of the Rightists' beliefs were heavily colored by a strong commitment to traditional values that emphasize religious morality, individualism, and the affirmation of hard work, saving, investing, and limited personal gratification, in sum, the old Protestant ethic.[14] Rightists overwhelmingly subscribe to such statements as "What this country needs most is a return to the simple virtues of individual initiative and self-reliance," "Thrift and industriousness are the most important traits a man should develop," and "What youth needs most is strict discipline, rugged determination, and the will to work and fight for family and country." (See Table 1). Their religious beliefs are greatly influenced by fundamentalism as well: "The Bible is God's word, and all that it says is true," "In the next life people will be punished by

God."[15] 42 percent of the Rightists* (compared to 17 percent of the Non-Rightists), in fact, attend churches of fundamentalist denominations.[16]

Radical rightism attracts traditional value-holders to its ranks because it affirms their older principles and styles of life and simultaneously mounts a bitter attack against their erosion. Rightism provides a standard ("anticommunism") behind which those who oppose many aspects of an increasingly complex, cosmopolitan society can rally. Although "communism" is the symbolic enemy, rightism is really a protest movement directing much of its wrath against the fact that America has moved away from ascetic Protestant values. Considerable evidence from the interviews shows that Rightists are individuals extremely disturbed by what they see around them as the disestablishment of their own strongly held values and their replacement by newer, different ones. Throughout their interviews they protested that

* Rightists are those individuals in quartiles 3 and 4 of the Radical Rightism Index.

"morality and standards are going bad," and argued that "we need a moral and spiritual revival among our leaders." Statements that drew immediate and emphatic agreement included "[We now have] a general breakdown of moral standards in our country," "What this country needs most is a return to love of country and old-fashioned patriotism," and "If we would return to the religious, moral, and family values of the past, we could solve most of today's social problems." (The association (gamma) between the Rightism Index and a moral breakdown scale is .66).

That Rightists equate communism with attacks on their own strongly held traditional values is indicated by their responses to questions which asked them "What kinds of things do communists believe in?" and "What kind of people are they?" Rightists disproportionately described "communists" as antireligous and anti-Christian, as immoral and dedicated to the destruction of traditional values, as coming from "liberal" or "modern" churches.

Personality

Personality is the second major determinant that plays a significant part in the genesis of radical rightist beliefs. Following Gordon Allport, we can consider personality traits to be relatively stable neuropsychic structures within individuals, which produce consistent and generalized responses to a variety of situations.[17] The relationship between personality and political behavior is becoming increasingly clarified,[18] and, as the study of political socialization becomes more encased in broad theory, personality variables are drawing increasing attention from political scientists.[19]

One of the distinctive personality traits that characterize the typical Rightist is close-mindedness, a particular mode of cognitive style. One of rightism's primary attractions is that it offers its adherents a way of understanding their immediate environment in terms consistent with their psychological need for simplistic explanations. Confronted with social and cultural changes that they cannot readily grasp, the right's conspiratorial interpretation for everything massively simplifies and provides meaning for what was previously an unintelligible but very frightening world. Politics, world events, civil turmoil, all become reduced to one overriding cause: the communists.

Considerable psychological research shows that persons who readily accept oversimplified views do so because they have a general psychological need for uncomplicated, firm, stereotyped views of people and events; there is no place in their beliefs for ambiguity or ambivalence.[20] Such people also reject, in a dogmatic fashion, individuals who disagree with—or merely fail to share— their beliefs, and they hold their opinions so rigidly that compromise is impossible. Lack of self-guidance makes them unusually dependent upon external authority-figures and "experts" for guidance and information. This mode of cognizing is amply manifested in rightist ideology, in its literature and its organizations.

For the typical rightist, the conspiracy theory of history unravels what was previously baffling. Rightist literature also reflects the close-minded style in its presentation of issues, no matter how complex, as always involving only *two* sides (American or anti-American, moral or immoral, good or evil). Among rightists, compromise is a betrayal that

Table 2

Intolerance of Ambiguity Scale* Versus Radical Rightism Index

Degree of Radical Rightism	Intolerance of Ambiguity				
	(high) I	II	III	(low) IV	(N)
(low) I	15%	13%	28%	44%	(75)
II	8	28	37	27	(92)
III	25	38	22	15	(92)
(high) IV	49	23	21	6	(77)

Kruskal-Wallis H-Test = 57.5 P < .001

Gamma = .46

* The other items in this scale are: "Of all the different philosophies which exist in this world, there is probably only one which is correct," "People can be divided into two distinct classes: the weak and the strong," and "You can classify almost all people as either honest or crooked." The Kuder-Richardson Coefficient of Internal Consistency is .79.

cannot be tolerated; differing points of view and political systems cannot co-exist: one must triumph and the other be completely destroyed. Most rightist organizations are leader-centered and authoritarian in structure; the initiative always flows from the top downward (the Birch Society's monthly bulletin contains an "agenda" of programs that members dutifully carry out) and elected officials or leaders are unheard of.

When measured, our Rightists' views on matters concerning communism and Russia are extremely dogmatic; to them "Communism is a total evil." "As philosophies of government, modern liberalism, socialism, and communism are all essentially the same," and it is *not* true that "the Soviet Union is 'mellowing' and the way is opening for peaceful cooperation between the Russians and the United States."* The Rightists' re-

* The association (gamma) between the five-item "dogmatic views on Communism and Russia scale (Kuder-Richardson Coefficient = .82) and the Rightism Index is .69. The other two items are "The current fight between the Russians and the Communist Chinese shows there are some great differences between them (reversed in scoring)," and "The United States and Communist Russia have nothing in common."

sponses on psychometric scales[21] show them clearly to be *more* intolerant of ambiguity ("There is usually only one right way to do anything"), opposed to compromising their beliefs ("The compromising of principles leads to nothing but destruction"), generally close-minded ("In the long run, the best way to live is to pick friends and associates whose tastes and beliefs are the same as one's own"), and more opinionated than Non-Rightists. (Table 2 is typical of the relationship between rightism and the cognitive style measures.)

The strident negativism and combativeness displayed in rightist writings and speeches points to a second important psychological function of radical rightism. The acceptance of the conspiracy theory not only greatly simplifies the believers' system of reasoning and conception of social causation but provides concrete targets against whom anger can be discharged. The tendency to express personal discontents in the form of hostility directed against scapegoated enemies is characteristic of the personality trait "extrapunitiveness."[22] When confronted by frustrating situations, individuals who employ this mechanism typically react (1) by manifesting anger; (2) by making judgments that condemn other people or the outer world as the source of their personal difficulty; and (3) by directing aggression outward, against their environment.

The two main features of the extrapunitive personality style—the display of considerable *aggressive needs* directed against supposedly blameworthy objects, and their selective *perceptions* which justify these hostile attacks[23]—are disproportionately exhibited by Rightists. Rightism allows its adherents, under the guise of Americanism and anticommunism, to express their resentments belligerently against those who have the respect and influence they do not—the social, political, and intellectual leaders of their communities and nation.*

The image Rightists hold of communists reflects selectively organized cognitions and the projective attribution of personal hatreds. Communists become grossly exaggerated repositories of vileness; in rightist literature communists are often portrayed as "gangsters," "barbarous animals," "foul creatures," "sex perverts," and "megalomaniacal murderers," thus serving as convenient symbols against which hostility can be vented with a clear conscience. When asked in the interviews to describe "the typical American communist" and the "kinds of things they believe in," our Rightists associate with, or attribute to, their enemies traits that are the absolute antithesis of things they value most. Inordinately concerned with religion and moral principles, our Rightists see communists as the Antichrist, as immoral and dedicated to the destruction of moral standards, as coming from "liberal" or "modern" churches. Often threatened occupationally by better-educated persons, unsurprisingly Rightists more often describe communists as well educated.

In the interviews the Rightists' aggressiveness showed up in their attitudes toward safe scapegoat adversaries. They favored *severely* punishing people whom they consider to be communists (a category, you will recall, which *to them* encompasses a sizable proportion of Americans). That Rightists are generally aggressive is demonstrated by their hostile reactions to nonpolitical deviants: they believe homosexuals "should be severely punished," those who commit sex crimes "deserve more than mere imprisonment, such criminals ought to be publicly whipped or worse," and "There is hardly anything lower than a person who does not feel a great love, gratitude, and respect for his parents."*

---

* Data reported on elsewhere (see Rohter, *Radical Rightists: An Empirical Study*, or forthcoming article "Rightists in the Far West," in R. A. Schoenberger (ed.), *Analyses of the American Right* (Holt, Rinehart and Winston, 1969)), lend considerable support to the contention that Rightists are persons experiencing certain kinds of status and value conflicts, which their participation in rightism allows them to express while at the same time allowing them to enhance their personal feelings of social status, importance, and self-worth.

* These three items, taken from the F-Scale, constitute a well-defined scale (Kuder-Richardson Coefficient = .89). Although the items specifically measure hostility toward deviants, several empirical studies have shown that expressing hostility toward persons who violate conventional norms of behavior represent displaced feelings of general hostility and aggressiveness. (For a detailed justification of this assertion, see my *Radical Rightists*, pp. 226–228.) The degree of association (gamma) between this general aggressiveness measure and the Rightism Index is .31 (P < .001).

The Authoritarian Syndrome

A factor analysis of a number of the scalar-measured variables employed in my study found these personality traits clustered together statistically—intolerance of ambiguity, close-mindedness, anticompromise, hostility, traditional values, and lack of trust of other people.* These variables correspond to the classic authoritarian personality syndrome first systematically studied by Adorno and his associates.[25] The "authoritarian" type of individual tends to have these characteristic personality traits:

a. *Conventionalism*—rigid adherence to conventional values, institutions, and ways of doing things.

b. *Authoritarian submissiveness*—uncritical submissiveness to and dependency upon authority figures.

c. *Aggressiveness*—tendency to look for, punish, and reject those who violate conventional values. Blame for own difficulties is directed toward others, outer events, circumstances.

d. *Power-oriented*—personal relations characteristically regarded in terms of power and status.

e. *Categorical thinking*—prominent cognitive style follows two-sided logic, displays considerable rigidity, close-mindedness, need for certainty.

---

* Factor analysis is a statistical technique for reducing a large number of variables into the fewest underlying dimensions. The factor analysis tells us that the same individuals who score highly on the intolerance of ambiguity measure also score highly on the close-mindedness, anticompromise, hostility, and lack of trust of other people scales. The same negative relationship holds true for low scores. Applying the law of parsimony, the "something" that is assumed to account for this commonality of responses over a variety of items is called a factor. In our case, we identify the "factor" as a personality syndrome since the variables that cluster together correspond to the well established authoritarian pattern.[24]

f. *Threat-oriented*—lives in fear of punishment, retaliation, broadly suspicious of other people's behavior and motives.

This seems like a fair description of rightists in general. We have already examined the data which show that Rightists are conventional in their value orientations, are categorical and simplistic thinkers, and are prone to aggressiveness. They are also greatly concerned with power and feel quite threatened. They feel personally powerless ("More and more I feel helpless in the face of what is happening in the world today," "It is only wishful thinking to believe that one can really influence what happens in society at large");* they see the government wielding too much power over them, believe that many groups in our society have too much power and influence (and they too little), and are convinced that public officials and their elected political representatives do not represent or listen to them. (See Table 3.) And finally, we can note that the original Adorno, et al., study (and a great many others), also finds "authoritarians" distinctively anti-Negro, antisemitic, and generally ethnocentric. Forster and Epstein, using data collected by the Anti-Defamation League, have documented the blatant antisemitism of many major rightist leaders and the prevalence of such views in the literature circulated by many rightist groups. Others have pointed out significant racist undercurrents as well.[26]

These then are the major parameters of the Rightists' personality traits and values, the elements that so importantly

---

* A three-item "sense of personal powerlessness" scale (the third item being "Life is primarily a matter of struggle for survival") discriminates between Rightists and Non-Rightists at $P < .05$.

figure in their political orientations. If these are the "products" of their socialization experiences, what can we say about the processes that created them?

A Developmental History of Radical Rightists

Several distinctive lines of theory have arisen to explain the process of socialization. From Freud and his successors we have learned the importance of early life experiences for subsequent personality structure. Psychoanalytical theory, one of the major forces in the study of personality and child-development, focuses considerable attention on early child-parent relationships.[27] Behavioral analysis, grounded in experimental methods and empirically based theories, provides a second major focus of study. Learning takes place according to definite psychological principles; what we call socialization represents histories of past conditioning, that is, the schedules of when, how, for what, and by whom the child was rewarded and punished.[28] Cultural and social variables constitute a

third major socialization influence, for *what* an individual learns, the normative and cognitive standards that he internalizes as his own, are transmitted to him by his culture, mediated through his particular position in his society's social system.[29] Basic value and behavioral standards are significantly shaped by "role relationships," through which "the individual learns the behavior appropriate to his position in a group through interaction with others who hold normative beliefs about what his role should be and who reward and punish him for correct or incorrect actions."[30] Although this is not the place to examine or evaluate these alternative approaches, they alert us (1) to the influence of child-parent relationships within the family setting on later *personality* (particularly by the shaping of behavior through rewarding certain responses and punishing others) and (2) to the fact that *values* and behavioral expectations are significantly related to culture and position within the society. For rightists, childhood person-to-person interaction within the family was marked

Table 3

Political Alienation Scale* Versus Radical Rightism Index

Degree of Radical Rightism	Degree of Alienation				(N)
	(high) I	II	III	(low) IV	
(low) I	9%	21%	33%	36%	(75)
II	13	21	40	26	(92)
III	20	32	30	18	(92)
(high) IV	40	31	21	8	(77)

Kruskal-Wallis H-Test = 41.02 P < .001
Gamma = .38

* Political alienation scale: (1) People like me should have more of a say about how things are run in this country; (2) Public officials really care how people like me want things to be done; (3) I wish public officials would listen more to people like me; and (4) If it were possible, I'd throw most public officials out on their ears. Kuder-Richardson Coefficient of Internal Consistency = .84.

by hierarchical relationships, strong pressures to meet parental expectations, and strictly enforced obedience to moral and personal standards. Secondly, their families adhered to a life-style culturally identified with fundamentalism, which supplied both traditional value and belief orientations and the normative atmosphere that justifies harsh control-centered patterns of child-rearing. This family life-style bears great resemblance to the one to which the so-called "authoritarian personality" (as observed by Adorno, et al.) was accustomed in its childhood and youth.

The Authoritarian Family

It is axiomatic that the earliest, and usually the most significant, socialization takes place within the family. What is learned during this time evolves from series of interactions with other persons who control rewards and punishments. The small child's dependency on others for food, warmth, and protection operates as the primary fulcrum for applying the leverage of training.[31] The influence of the parents is so great because of their frequency of contact with and degree of control over the child. Their expectations and ability to control sanctions, furthermore, continue over a long period of time. Orville G. Brim offers this useful conception of personality as the resultant of interaction with significant others:[32] "Analytically, personality is a set of learned self-other relationships or systems, themselves constituted of thousands and thousands of remembered expectations, appraisals of one's own performance by self and others, the resultant perceived conformity or deviance (or success or failure) of the action,

and the consequent rewards or disapprovals given by society."[33] Recent statistical studies have demonstrated that relationships between children and their parents can be ordered along two global dimensions. One dimension taps the degree of *control* exerted over the child's behavior, which ranges from strict demands and restrictions to virtual autonomy. The *affective* quality of the relationship, which varies from intense love and affection to rejections and hostility, comprises the second basic factor.[34] An interaction pattern that falls into the control and emotional coldness quadrant (see Figure 1), often called the "authoritarian" pattern, is particularly relevant for our study since its behavioral consequences and the behavior manifested by radical rightists are strikingly similar.

In the authoritarian child-rearing pattern the parents place strict demands and restrictions on the child's behavior, insist on compliance, and maintain their authority through harsh discipline or the withdrawal of the little affection that characterizes the emotional aspect of the relationship. The child is thus forced to be highly submissive to parental expectations governing many areas of everyday life: sex play, table manners, toilet training, neatness, orderliness, noise, aggression toward siblings, peers, and parents, and so forth.[35]

Coercive training, while leading to surface submission, results in considerable underlying resentment on the part of the child. If the child is unable to express hostility naturally (either because of punishment or threats, or more subtly, by the fear of having the little affection he receives withdrawn), he learns to postpone or denounce direct instinctual gratification. If this pattern recurs often enough, the child's adaptation results in a rigid personality structure.

The propensity to direct aggressive impulses against those social objects not able to punish him is typical of this kind of individual.[36]

According to learning theory, the displacement of aggression can be explained as the consequence of counteracting forces of excitation and inhibition. In the home the child is spurred to aggressiveness by his parents; but at the same time they punish any expression of his aggression against them, thus forcing the child to inhibit the response. The aggression becomes generalized; but because the inhibition is more specified, it is directed toward other, noninhibited figures. Role theory also makes a contribution to this discussion, since research shows that physically punitive parents set examples of aggressive behavior for the child, who models himself after them.[37] These findings are consistent with research on prejudice, which finds that prejudiced parents produce prejudiced children: the parents in this instance give the child

direct cues on whom to dump their resentments.[38] That a rigid personality structure is the consequence of a stern autocratic rearing is one of the best documented propositions in the literature of child development.[39] On the basis of a survey of research in this area, Wesley Becker concludes that

... power-asserting techniques in controlling the child are more likely to correlate with externalized reactions to transgressions (fear of punishment, projected hostility), and with non-cooperative, aggressive behaviors.[40]

The child's dependency on parents who strictly enforce many demands furthermore forces him to attend constantly to their expectations. This sensitizes him to authority figures who control sanctions over him, to conceptualize the social order as arranged hierarchically (leaders-followers), and to repress thinking about feelings that might, if expressed, lead to displeasure and perhaps punishment (anti-intraception).[41] Thus do we end up with individuals who psychologically require uncomplicated,

Figure 1   Two Dimensions That Depict Basic Parental Behavior Toward Children*

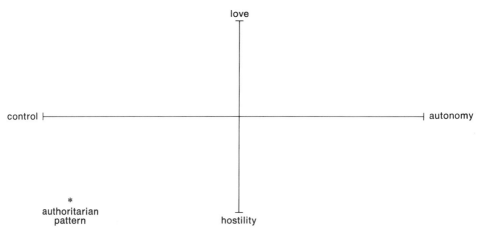

*The basic dimensions for Figure 1 come from E. S. Schaefer's factor analysis reported in his "A Circumplex Model for Maternal Behavior," *Journal of Abnormal and Social Psychology*, 59 (1959), 226—235; the "authoritarian pattern" label in the lower left quadrant has been added by the author.

firm, stereotypical views of people and events; there is no place in their beliefs for ambivalence of ambiguity.[42] The authors of one study, working with ten-year-olds, found our familiar punitively oriented pattern of child-rearing among those who were unable to break out of a rigid style of response to situations calling for cognitive reorganization:

Parents of field-dependent children on the whole had punished them more severely, using both aggressive modes of punishment and the withdrawal of love. They had forbade them to show assertive or overly independent behavior, and in general imposed their own standards upon the children.[43]

The Rightists' Upbringing

All the direct evidence we have on the Rightists' upbringing, although fragmentary, points to the same conclusion: they were sternly raised, and taught to achieve "character" and to follow clear-cut normative standards. The Rightists interviewed in my study agreed overwhelmingly with these authoritarian child-rearing propositions: "What youth needs most is strict discipline, rugged determination, and the will to fight for family and country," "Obedience and respect for authority are the most important virtues children should learn," "We should increase the teaching of respect for authority in schools," and "There is hardly anything lower than a person who does not feel a great love, gratitude, and respect for his parents."*

* We assume here a continuity of child-rearing practices, with the Rightists repeating with their children the pattern they experienced as children. Although there is a general societal trend toward permissiveness,[44] making many parents more flexible than their parents, we find little reason to assume the opposite, that permissively raised children in turn raise their children punitively.

Data collected by Lawrence Schiff in his clinically oriented study of college-age rightists reveal the same picture; he characterized their family backgrounds as generating "enormous pressure to measure up to parental demands and expectations."[45] In describing one student's youth he talks of the "low impulse gratification of his father's tutelage," of others he mentions "parental values writ large through exhortation and example." Other phrases in Schiff's report mention "adherence to strict moral standards," "hard work and frugality," "orthodox religiosity and stern moralism," and "achievement, excellence, character."

Similar backgrounds emerge when one examines the biographies of noted rightist leaders.[46] Taylor Caldwell, well-known author and frequent contributor to Birch Society publications, for example, reflecting approvingly on her own strict upbringing, comments "Americans have been smothering their children with the syrup of 'tender, loving care' instead of driving character into their backs like a ramrod."[47]

The Fundamentalist Subculture

Substantial linkages exist between the radical right and antimodern fundamentalist religious organizations.[48] Many of the more prominent rightist groups combine fundamentalism and rightism; Billy James Hargis' "Christian Crusade," Carl McIntire's "Twentieth Century Reformation Hour," Fred Schwartz's "Christian Anti-Communist Crusade," and Edgar Bundy's "Church League of America" are all headed by ministers or former preachers. The John Birch Society is named after an evangelical Baptist who combined zealous missionary preaching with his military career before he was killed in China. What in fundamentalism makes its adherents so ripe for radical rightism? Two general answers are proposed: one, that its distinctive values produce an ideological proclivity to the acceptance of rightist political views and, second, that the cultural milieu of fundamentalism produces and reinforces authoritarian personality traits.

The influence of religion on politics is well documented and seems related to two major factors.[49] Religion *indirectly* affects political behavior in that it is related to *social factors* (such as ethnic or economic status), which in turn have political consequences. Our focus in this paper, however, is on the second of these influences, namely the *theological and value* elements of religion. Such beliefs play either a direct role in politics (the condemnation of the Communist party by the Catholic hierarchy in Italian elections or the enactment of "blue law" by local governments) or create dispositions that support certain secular political ideologies. Religious fundamentalism is connected to radical rightism in both ways.

The major value-orientations of the fundamentalist subculture[50] have been described as follows:

The Ascetic Protestant idea of the calling emphasized methodical and consistent striving toward the accomplishment of long-range goals. It stressed output of effort from the individual toward the physical and social environment and markedly de-emphasized the input of gratifications from the environment to the individual. In short, the idea of the calling constrained the believer to adopt an instrumental, manipulative posture, to produce and achieve, and to curtail his interest in immediate consumption. At the same time it strengthened his determination to be self-reliant and to reap only rewards of his own making.[51]

Fundamentalists find many of America's current values and practices clashing with these standards and expectations. Fundamentalist groups—Pentecostal, conservative orthodox groupings having split off from mainline denominations—comprise what J. M. Yinger calls "contracultures." The "normative system of the group contains, as a primary element, a theme of conflict with the values of the total society."[52] These same dissatisfactions resound throughout the right's condemnation of modern society.[53] Rightist literature bristles with indictments against the social gospel, "liberal theology," and forcefully demands a return to strict fundamentalist doctrines in the churches. Current social welfare practices grate hard on those dedicated to the principles of the Protestant ethic.

Fundamentalists are drawn to rightism not only because they share its disgust at modern moral practices but for religious reasons as well. Communism, when considered in theological terms, is viewed as the Devil's own work.

The world is a battlefield and there are two contestants. One is God, who leads the legions of good. The other is Satan . . . Satan, who is the father of Communism, works in very deceptive ways. To prepare the way for Communism in other parts of the world, Satan has devised a remarkable scheme. He is spreading modernism and disbelief across our land. He is using Christian clergymen to deny the fundamentals of the Christian faith—the virgin birth of Christ, his physical resurrection, the inerrancy of the Word of God. When faith is thus polluted, it can be destroyed.[54]

Note also the reduction into dichotomist alternatives, characteristic of both rightist and fundamentalist thinking: two contestants—the good and the bad; Satan vs. Christianity; victory or destruction. This simplistic style of thinking is learned early and is difficult to overturn. Thus is Billy James Hargis able to mobilize his followers with statements that "there is a master conspiracy loose in the world today headed by Satan himself," then attack groups like the National Council of Churches, or the ADA, as part of this "Satanic conspiracy."[55]

Research into the development of "moral character" and "moral ideology" consistently shows that basic normative standards are pretty well internalized during early childhood.[56] Moral standards are the products of the child's interaction not only with his parents but with other influences, particularly peer groups and media.[57] Nevertheless the impact of the family situation is primary in most instances, for empirical research shows that the child's earliest morality is oriented to obedience and punishment, and that only later does it become anchored in more subjective internal values. Piaget has also observed that the cognitive limitations of the young child (three to eight) make him confuse moral rules with physical laws and view them as fixed external, sacred objects. Sears, Maccoby, and Levine offer this proposition:

So far as we can tell, there is a learning of internal control that goes on mainly in the years before puberty, perhaps chiefly in the first six to ten years, determining the extent to which conscience will operate throughout all the rest of life.[58]

Our Rightists' adherence to traditional moral values can thus be attributed to their fundamentalist upbringing. It could be argued that Rightists, although now fundamentalists in terms of church attendance and beliefs, were raised in mainline religions and converted in later life. Although we have no systematic evidence to test this possibility, the existing biographical data support the first assumption. Furthermore, given the continuity of value orientations and personality patterns once established in childhood, it seems likely that any converts were raised with the same values which fundamentalists share, thus making them ripe for formal conversion when the proper situation arose later in their lives. Lawrence Schiff found this kind of value-inculcation process in the backgrounds of the young rightists he studied. Their parents had exhorted them to follow strict moral guidelines in their daily activities, to work hard and be frugal, to keep an orthodox religious faith, and to value and achieve success.[59]

The fundamentalist subculture also has a very significant impact on the personalities of those raised within it. In an extensive review of the literature on the "fundamentalist personality," E. Mansell Pattison (a psychiatrist) finds these traits typically manifested by fundamentalists:

. . . deep feelings of dependency and passivity, crippling self-doubt, pervasive reactive hostility, restrictive social relationships, aggressiveness and covert hostility, frequent use of paranoid mechanisms.[60]

He concludes:

. . . in sum, the present data consistently described the fundamentalist personality as one who has basic passive-dependent attitudes . . . , deep feelings of guilt, inadequacy, inferiority, and self-reflection. . . . There is a lack of social adaptability with a tendency toward aloof schizoid types of social relations, with a defensive, hostile, ethnocentricism . . ., with constriction of cognitive and perceptual functions reflected not only in dogmatic attitudes, but [in other areas as well].

From our brief discussion of the authoritarian personality syndrome, these traits should be familiar to us. The roots of these personality attributes lie, of course, in early infancy, and the key to the child-rearing practices of the fundamentalist is found in the doctrine of original sin. According to this view, man is inherently accursed with evil impulses. Child-rearing thus becomes a matter of bringing the infant's "sinful desires" under conscious control. Pattison gives a succinct summary of the profound psychological implications of this normative notion:

The effects of the orientation toward *man as evil* may be briefly reviewed. Because the infant is seen as bad, his behavior is interpreted as hostile. The mother may then treat the child in hostile fashion, as well as presenting a hostile image for identity formation. The interpretation of all aggressiveness

as hostility and the rejection of all overt expressions of aggression, much less hostility, inhibit ego maturation. Further, the culture does not provide mechanisms for the development or utilization of sublimating or mediating mechanisms in the ego. The use of the obsessive-compulsive or intellectualizing defenses against basic hostile impulses is undercut by the culture. Ego identity revolves around identification with God, which leads to an ambiguous uncertain identity of guilt omnipotence. Sexual identity is confused and immature. Relationships with others are based on the perception of self as inferior which is defended against by an attitude of superiority and hostile omnipotence.[61]

Fundamentalisms' emphasis on the inhibition of natural emotions, enforced by strict discipline, prevents the development of mature ego mechanisms for controlling and expressing anger and hostility. This leads to a series of obsessive-compulsive defenses. With morality a hostile demand to be adhered to, rather than a positive affirmation, there is a compulsive need to control and dominate other people to maintain their "self-control."[62] Fundamentalists and others strongly committed to orthodox religious beliefs tend to be extremely

Figure 2   Suggested Causal Relationships Between Specific Variables and Religious Fundamentalism Index (Product Moment Correlation Coefficients)

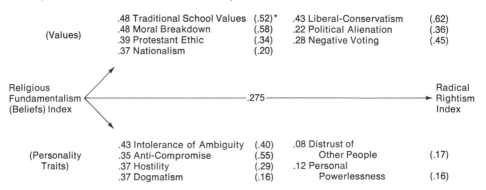

(Values)	.48 Traditional School Values	(.52)*	.43 Liberal-Conservatism	(.62)
	.48 Moral Breakdown	(.58)	.22 Political Alienation	(.36)
	.39 Protestant Ethic	(.34)	.28 Negative Voting	(.45)
	.37 Nationalism	(.20)		

Religious Fundamentalism (Beliefs) Index ⟵ .275 ⟶ Radical Rightism Index

(Personality Traits)	.43 Intolerance of Ambiguity	(.40)	.08 Distrust of Other People	(.17)
	.35 Anti-Compromise	(.55)		
	.37 Hostility	(.29)	.12 Personal Powerlessness	(.16)
	.37 Dogmatism	(.16)		

*Figures in parenthesis next to each variable represent correlation between that variable and Radical Rightism Index.

Figure 3   Causal Model of Significant Factors Related to Genesis of Radical Rightism (correlation coefficients)

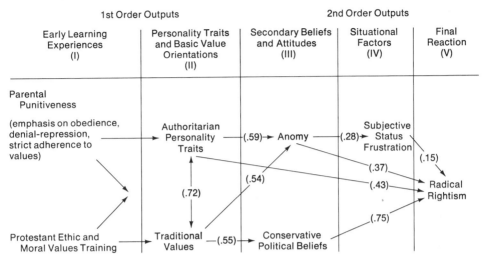

severe in the moral judgments of others.[63] Again we have the displacement mechanism at work: with normal expressions of hostility proscribed, fundamentalists direct their aggressions against "sinners" and other transgressors of the moral order, thereby "defending the faith." Cognitive defenses also characterize fundamentalists. Ambiguity is not tolerated in interpreting the Bible (it is *absolutely* true), it is always God versus the Devil, the world is divided into the forces of good and the forces of evil, the danger is always from within, from a corruption of insidious doctrines.[64]

Fundamentalism, as a subculture oriented toward sacred values and the observance of God's will, tends to circumscribe its adherents' involvement in the larger culture, which is viewed as contaminated and inescapably evil. This social isolation makes them strangers in the larger society, distrustful of its inhabitants, and prevents them from developing a tolerance of dissimilar in-

dividuals. Fundamentalists are thus highly susceptible to distorted perceptions of the society:

The adult who is especially vulnerable to paranoid developments is one in whom this process of socialization has been seriously defective. His deficient social learning and poorly learned social skills leave him unable to understand adequately the motivations, attitudes, and intentions of others.[65]

When forced to live within the society, feelings of insecurity, social isolation, and an absence of a sense of belonging often result.[66] Mental illness, depression, psychosomatic symptoms, and maladjusted behavior are also associated with religious dissonance.[67]

The parallels between rightist and fundamentalist value and belief orientations, as well as personality configurations, indicate the importance of cultural fundamentalism as a socializing environment with distinctive political effects. Figure 2 shows the significant association between religious fundamentalism (as measured by *beliefs*, which we can consider an approximate if somewhat crude indicator of early socialization) and our familiar cluster of value and personality measures. As expected, the direct influence of these experiences decreases as we move away from variables linked mainly to *early* socialization; political beliefs and reactions to current situations (personal powerlessness, for example) form much later. (The correlations behind each variable, in brackets, represent the product moment correlation between the variable and the Radical Rightism Index.)

Conclusions

The developmental sequence that leads to radical rightism is summarized in Figure 3.

Early learning experiences that stress obedience to parental demands and strict adherence to traditional values produce distinctive values and personality traits which, in turn, significantly shape later-formed beliefs and attitudes.

A causal model analysis[68] of the factors in stages II and III supports the conclusion that conservative political beliefs and anomy are the resultants of the traditional value orientation and authoritarian personality syndrome, respectively. The intercorrelations between factors are also given.[69]

It should be reiterated that socialization produces only *predisposition* to action. Whether such action is taken, and its form, depends on other, situational variables, which we have not considered here. Later socialization influences should also be mentioned although necessarily only in passing, since we lack the space to go into any detail. The socialization of rightists after they enter an organization deserves further attention, for example. Group activities, intragroup support and reinforcement, and selective reading and information exposure are all activities that have definite behavioral consequences. Impressionistic evidence suggests that these factors are cumulative and reinforcing of the orientations analyzed here, however.

NOTES

1. This excerpt is taken from a pamphlet titled "The Time Has Come," written by Robert Welch, printed and distributed by the John Birch Society, Belmont, Mass. (copyrighted 1964). Similar statements can be found in the published literature of all rightist organizations.

2. See John A. Stormer's *None Dare Call It Treason* (Florissant, Mo.: Liberty Bell Press, 1964), and Robert E. Ellsworth and Sarah M. Harris, *The American Right Wing* (Washington D.C.: Public Affairs Press, 1962).

3. Today's Right is well organized. For instance, the John Birch Society has about 80,000 dues-paying members, over 200 employees in its 5 regional offices, and 75 professional full-time field coordinators supervising 4,000 local chapters, and 350 American Opinion Bookstores spread throughout the United States (Benjamin Epstein and Arnold Forster, *The Radical Right: Report on the John Birch Society and Its Allies* [New York: Random House, 1967]). Prominent

national organizations like the Christian Anti-Communist Crusade, We The People!, the Twentieth Century Reformation Hour, the Christian Crusade, and the Church League of America make up with literally hundreds of local groups a political movement with 300,000 active members in total. The movement spends more than 20 million dollars a year propagating its particular conspiratorial views (*ibid.*). Formal membership is only a partial indicator of the magnitude of rightist influence. National opinion surveys consistently show Birch Society sympathizers number between 4 and 6 million (Gallup Polls, reported in *Chicago Sun Times*, March 6, 1962; *Milwaukee Journal*, December 19, 1965, and an Opinion Research Corporation Poll reported in the *New York Times*, July 31, 1964). And this influence is increasing. Through more than 5,000 weekly radio and TV broadcasts, periodicals with circulations exceeding half a million a month, and stepped-up recruiting efforts the Right fills its coffers and attracts more and more adherents (Epstein and Forster, *op. cit.*).

4. Richard Schmuck and Mark Chesler, "On Super-Patriotism: A Definition and Analysis," *Journal of Social Issues*, 19 (1963), 31–50; Lawrence F. Schiff, "The Conservative Movement on American College Campuses" (unpublished doctoral dissertation, Harvard University, 1964) (An abridged version of part of the dissertation is "The Obedient Rebels: A Study of College Conversion to Conservatism," *Journal of Social Issues*, 20 [1964], 74–95.); Ira S. Rohter, "Radical Rightists: An Empirical Study" (unpublished doctoral dissertation, Michigan State University, 1967) (See "The Righteous Radicals," Trans-Action, IV (May 1967), 27–35.).

5. Talcott Parsons, *The Social System* (New York: Free Press, 1951), chap. 7; Albert K. Cohen, "The Study of Social Disorganization and Deviant Behavior," in Robert K. Merton, Leonard Broom, and Leonard S. Cottrell, Jr. (eds.), *Sociology Today* (New York: Basic Books, 1959), 461–484. For the data that support this contention see Schmuck and Chesler, *op. cit.*; Rohter, *op. cit.*; Murray Havens, "The Radical Right in the Southwest: Community Response to Shifting Socio-Economic Patterns" (paper delivered at 1964 meetings, American Political Science Association); J. Allen Broyles, *The John Birch Society* (Boston: Beacon Press, 1964); Daniel Bell (ed.), *The Radical Right* (New York: Doubleday, 1963); Richard Hofstadter, *The Paranoid Style in American Politics and Other Essays* (New York: Knopf, 1965); Joseph R. Gusfield, *Symbolic Crusade: Status Politics and the Temperance Movement* (Urbana: University of Illinois Press, 1963).

6. See Daniel Katz, "The Functional Approach to the Study of Attitudes," *Public Opinion Quarterly*, 29 (1960), 163–204; M. Brewster Smith, Jerome Brunner, and Robert White, *Opinions and Personality* (New York: Wiley, 1955); David Kretch, Richard S. Crutchfield, and Egerton L. Ballachey, *Individual in Society* (New York: McGraw-Hill, 1962), chap. 2; Hadley Cantril, *Psychology of Mass Movements* (New York: Wiley, 1941).

7. Parsons, *op. cit.*, chap. 8. See Gabriel A. Almond and G. Bingham Powell, Jr., *Comparative Politics* (Boston: Little, Brown, 1966), chap. 3, and Gabriel Almond and Sidney Verba, *The Civic Culture* (Princeton, N.J.: Princeton University Press, 1963) for political applications of this scheme.

8. Parsons, *op. cit.*, chap. 8. Milton Rokeach, *The Open and Closed Mind* (New York: Basic Books, 1960); Milton J. Rosenberg, "Cognitive Structure and Attitudinal

Affect," *Journal of Abnormal and Social Psychology*, 53 (1956), 367–372; Katz, *op. cit.*; Nora Jenkins, "Affective Processes in Perception," *Pyschological Bulletin*, 54 (1957), 100–127. For a political manifestation of this phenomenon see Angus Campbell, *et al.*, *The American Voter* (New York: Wiley, 1960), chap. 2.

9. David Easton and Robert D. Hess, "The Child's Political World," *Midwest Journal of Political Science*, 6 (1962), 229–246.

10. See William C. Mitchell, *The American Polity* (New York: Free Press, 1962), chaps. 5 and 6.

11. Talcott Parsons and Edward Shils (eds.), *Toward A General Theory of Action* (Cambridge: Harvard University Press, 1951).

12. See Parsons and Shils, *op. cit.*, and Robin M. Williams, Jr., *American Society: A Sociological Interpretation*, 2nd ed., revised (New York: Knopf, 1963), chap. 11.

13. See Rohter, *Radical Rightists: An Empirical Study, op. cit.*, for a detailed discussion of the procedures employed. In essence a form of item analysis was used to arrive at unidimensional scales. The resulting scales displayed excellent internal consistency.

14. Max Weber, *The Protestant Ethic and the Spirit of Capitalism*, Talcott Parsons (trans.) (New York: Scribner, 1958).

15. The Index of Religious Fundamentalist Beliefs was drawn from Gerhard Lenski's *The Religious Factor* (New York: Doubleday, 1961). The degree of association (gamma) between the rightism and religious fundamentalism indices is .31 (p < .001).

16. See Benton Johnson, "Ascetic Protestantism and Political Preference in the Deep South," *American Journal of Sociology*, 69 (1964) for listing of fundamentalist denominations.

17. Gordon Allport, *Pattern and Growth in Personality* (New York: Holt, Rinehart and Winston, 1961).

18. Significant major reviews of this literature can be found in Robert Lane, *Political Life: Why People Get Involved in Politics* (New York: Free Press, 1959); Robert Lane, *Political Ideology* (New York: Free Press, 1962); James Davies, *Human Nature in Politics* (New York: Wiley, 1964); Herbert C. Kelman (ed.), *International Behavior: A Social-Psychological Analysis* (New York: Holt, Rinehart and Winston, 1965).

19. Herbert H. Hyman, *Political Socialization* (New York: Free Press, 1959); Lewis A. Froman, Jr., "Personality and Political Socialization," *Journal of Politics*, 23 (1961), 341–353; Richard E. Dawson, "Political Socialization," in James A. Robinson (ed.), *Political Science Annual: Volume I* (Indianapolis: Bobbs-Merrill, 1966), 1–84; Fred I. Greenstein, "Political Socialization," in *International Encyclopedia of the Social Sciences* (New York: Crowell-Collier, 1965).

20. Milton Rokeach's *The Open and Closed Mind* provides one of the best discussions of this form of cognitive style, as well as reporting original research in this area. Other major sources include Theodore W. Adorno, *et al.*, *The Authoritarian Personality* (New York: Harper & Row, 1950); Else Frenkel-Brunswick, "Intolerance of Ambiguity as an Emotional and Personality Variable," *Journal of Personality*, 18 (1949), 108–143; Jerome S. Bruner, Jacqueline J. Goodnow, and George A. Austin, *A Study of Thinking* (New York: Wiley, 1956).

21. These unidimensional scales were constructed from items taken from Rokeach's "Dogmatism Scale" (*The Open and Closed Mind*) and the "F Scale" developed by the authors of *The Authoritarian Personality*.

22. Saul Rosenzweig, "The Experimental Measurement of Types of Reactions to Frustration," in Henry Murray (ed.), *Exploration in Personality* (New York: Science Editions, 1962), 585–599.

23. See Theodore M. Newcomb, Ralph H. Turner, and Philip E. Converse, *Social Psychology: The Study of Human Interaction* (New York: Holt, Rinehart and Winston, 1965), 157–163; Victor H. Vroom, "Projection, Negation, and the Self-Concept," *Human Relations*, 12 (1959), 335–344, for experimental evidence. Also Gustav Ichheiser, "Projection and the Mote-Beam Mechanism," *Journal of Abnormal and Social Psychology*, 42 (1947), 131–133; Gordon Allport, *The Nature of Prejudice* (New York: Doubleday, 1954), 367; Henry H. Murray, "The Effect of Fear upon Estimates of the Maliciousness of Other Personalities," *Journal of Social Psychology*, 4 (1933), 310–329.

24. See Calvin S. Hall and Gardner Lindzey's *Theories of Personality* (New York: Wiley, 1957), chap. 10, for a nontechnical discussion of the factor analysis technique's application to the study of personality. Citations of the basic statistical literature are also given. A superb explanation of the technique, using data more familiar to the political scientist, is found in Lee F. Anderson, Meredith W. Watts, Jr., and Allen R. Wilcox, *Legislative Role Call Analysis* (Evanston, Ill.: Northwestern University Press, 1966), chap. 7.

25. Adorno, *et al.*, *op. cit.*, 482–484, and especially chap. 20. For methodological and theoretical critiques of the study see Richard Christie and Marie Jahoda (eds.), *Studies in the Scope and Method of the "Authoritarian Personality"* (New York: Free Press, 1965); Rokeach, *op. cit.*; Roger W. Brown, *Social Psychology* (New York: Press, 1965); Robert F. Peck, "Family Patterns Correlated with Adolescent Personality," *Journal of Abnormal and Social Psychology*, 57 (1958), 347–350.

26. Arnold Forster and Benjamin R. Epstein, *Danger on the Right* (New York: Random House, 1964); Ralph L. Roy, *Apostles of Discord* (Boston: Beacon Press, 1953); Arnold Forster and Benjamin Epstein, *Report on the John Birch Society: 1966* (New York: Random House, 1966). T. Allen Comp and Julian F. Foster in a well-documented article in the March 1966 issue of *Reason: A Review of Politics* (Vol. 2, No. 3) that the Birch Society has strong racist undercurrents. The Anti-Defamation League reports that the society has grown substantially in Georgia and Alabama and that membership is increasing in Louisiana and Mississippi as White Citizen Councils decline in strength. (*Facts*, 17, 1 [February 1966], 353.)

27. See Irving L. Child, "Socialization," in Gardner Lindzey (ed.), *Handbook of Social Psychology* (Cambridge, Mass.: Addison-Wesley, 1954), 655–692. For a systematic discussion and critique of psychoanalytical theories of child development see Arthur L. Baldwin's *Theories of Child Development* (New York: Wiley, 1967).

28. Ernest R. Hilgard, *Theory of Learning*, 2nd ed. (New York: Appleton-Century-Croft, 1965); Ernest R. Hilgard and Donald G. Marquis, *Conditioning and Learning*, revised by Gregory A. Kimble, 2nd ed. (New York: Appleton-Century-Croft, 1961). An excellent introduction to learning theory is Sarnoff A.

Mednick's *Learning* (Englewood Cliffs, N.J.: Prentice-Hall, 1965), a paperback in Prentice-Hall's Foundations of Modern Psychology Series. For a learning theory approach to development see Sidney W. Bijou and Donald M. Baer, *Child Development I: A Systematic and Empirical Theory* (New York: Appleton-Century-Croft, 1961).

29. Parsons and Shils, *op. cit.*; Newcomb, Turner, and Converse, *op. cit.*; Parsons, *op. cit.*

30. Orville G. Brim, Jr., "Socialization Through the Life Cycle," in *Socialization After Childhood: Two Essays*, by Orville G. Brim, Jr., and Stanton Wheeler (New York: Wiley, 1966), 1–50.

31. See Bettye M. Caldwell's "The Effects of Infant Care," in Martin L. Hoffman and Lois W. Hoffman (eds.), *Review of Child Development Research* (New York: Russell Sage Foundation, 1964) for a systematic review of child-rearing practices and later personality, emphasizing empirical studies. An interesting and extremely comprehensive survey on family patterns and illness is contained in William W. Meissner's "Family Dynamics and Psychosomatic Processes," *Family Processes*, 5 (1966), 142–161. See also his "Thinking about the Family— Psychiatric Aspects," *Family Processes*, 5 (1966), 1–40.

32. Sidney W. Bijou and Donald M. Baer view "child development" not in terms of age but as a continuous sequence of interactions—"Therefore, a developmental analysis is not a relationship of behavior to age, but a relationship of behavior to events which, requiring time in order to occur, will necessarily have some correlation with age." ("Some Methodological Contributions from a Functional Analysis of Child Development," in Lewis P. Lipsitt and Charles C. Spiker (eds.), *Advances in Child Development*, Vol. I [New York: Academic Press, 1963], 197–232, quote on 198.) In Vol. II (published in 1965), see Harold W. Stevenson's chapter on "Social Reinforcement of Children's Behavior," 98–126, for a similar approach.

33. Brim, *op. cit.*, p. 12.

34. See Earl S. Schaefer, "A Circumplex Model for Maternal Behavior," *Journal of Abnormal and Social Psychology*, 59 (1959), 226–235; also Wesley C. Becker, "Consequences of Different Kinds of Parental Discipline," in Hoffman and Hoffman, *Review of Child Development Research*, *op. cit.*, 9–88.

35. Jane Loevinger and Blanche Sweet, "Construction of a Test of Mothers' Attitudes," in John C. Glidewell (ed.), *Parental Attitudes and Child Behavior* (Springfield, Ill.: Charles C. Thomas, 1961), 110–123; Becker, *op. cit.*

36. Adorno, *et al.*, *op. cit.*; Maurice L. Farber, "The Anal Character and Political Aggression," *Journal of Abnormal and Social Psychology*, 51 (1955), 486–489; Theodore M. Newcomb ("Autistic Hostility and Social Reality," *Human Relations*, I [1947], 69–86) makes this comment: "Persistently hostile attitudes will develop when interpersonal relations remain autistic, its privacy maintained by some sort of communication barrier." See also Ross Stagner, "Studies of Aggressive Social Attitudes: I. Measurement and Interrelation of Selected Attitudes," *Journal of Social Psychology*, 20 (1944), 109–120; Else Frenkel-Brunswick, "A Study of Prejudice in Children," *Human Relations*, 1 (1948), 295–306. See A. Irving Hallowell, "Aggression in Saulteaux Society," reprinted in Clyde Kluckhohn and Henry Murray (eds.), *Personality in Nature, Society, and*

Culture, 2nd ed., revised (New York: Knopf, 1961), for an example of cultural determinants that channel manifestations of aggression into socially acceptable forms. Many of the studies in this book show the effects of culture on socialization.

37. Albert Bandura, Donald Ross, and Sherman Ross, "Transmission of Aggression Through Imitation of Aggressive Models," *Journal of Abnormal and Social Psychology*, 63 (1961), 575–582; William McCord, Joan McCord, and Alan Howard, "Familiar Correlations of Aggression in Nondelinquent Male Children," *Journal of Abnormal and Social Psychology*, 62 (1961), 79–93; Albert Bandura and Richard H. Walters, *Adolescent Aggression* (New York: Ronald Press, 1959); Robert R. Sears, Lucy C. Rau, and Richard Alpert, *Identification and Child Rearing* (Stanford, Calif.: Stanford University Press, 1965); Leonard Berkowitz, *Aggression* (New York: McGraw-Hill, 1962); O. Ivar Lovaas ("Interaction Between Verbal and Non-Verbal Behavior," *Child Development*, 32 [1961], 329–336) showed that positive reinforcement is an important variable in increasing the rate of emission of aggressive responses; John W. M. Whiting, "Resource Mediation and Learning," in Ira Iscoe and Harold W. Stevenson (eds.), *Personality Development in Children* (Austin: University of Texas Press, 1960), 112–126, offers this postulate to account for learning by identification: "The more a child envies the status of another with respect to the control of a given resource, the more he will covertly practice that role."

38. Adorno, *et al.*, *op. cit.*; Frenkel-Brunswick, "Study in Prejudice," *op. cit.*; major reviews include Nathan W. Ackerman and Marie Jahoda, *Anti-Semitism and Emotional Disorder* (New York: Harper & Row, 1950); Allport, *Nature of Prejudice*, *op. cit.*; Bruno Bettleheim and Morris Janowitz, *Dynamics of Prejudice* (New York: Harper & Row, 1950).

39. Robert R. Sears, *et al.*, "Some Childrearing Antecedents of Aggression and Dependency in Young Children," *Genetic, Psychological Monographs*, 47 (1953), 135–234; Robert R. Sears, "Relation of Early Socialization Experiences to Aggression in Middle Childhood," *Journal of Abnormal and Social Psychology*, 63 (1961), 466–492; McCord, McCord, and Howard, *op. cit.*; Peck, *op. cit.*; Bandura and Walters, *op. cit.*; Leonard D. Eron, Leopold O. Walder, Romolo Toigo, and Monroe M. Lefkowitz, "Social Class, Parental Punishment for Aggression, and Child Aggression," *Child Development*, 34 (1963), 849–867; Elleanor Hollenberg and Margaret Sperry, "Some Antecedents of Aggression and Effects of Frustration in Doll Play," *Personality*, 1 (1951), 32–43; Jerome Kagen and Howard A. Moss, *Birth to Maturity: The Fels Study of Psychological Development* (New York: Wiley, 1962): Amy R. Holway, "Early Self-Regulations of Infants and Later Behavior in Play Interviews," American Journal of Orthopsychiatry, 19 (1949), 612–623; Goodwin Watson, "Some Personality Differences in Children Related to Strict or Permissive Parental Discipline," *Journal Psychology*, 44 (1957), 227–249; Eleanor E. Maccoby, "The Taking of Adult Roles in Middle Childhood," *Journal of Abnormal and Social Psychology*, 63 (1961), 493–503; Robert R. Sears, "The Relation of Early Socialization Experiences to Aggression in Middle Childhood," *Journal of Abnormal and Social Psychology*, 63 (1961), 466–492; Wesley C. Becker, Donald R. Peterson, Zella Luria, Donald J. Shoemaker, and Leo A. Hellmer, "Relations of Factors Derived from Parent-Interview Ratings to Behavior Problems of Five-year-olds," *Child*

Development, 33 (1962), 509–535; Leonard D. Eron, Thomas J. Banta, Leopold O. Walder, and Jerome H. Laulicht, "Comparison of Data Obtained from Mothers and Fathers on Childrearing Practices and their Relation to Child Aggression," *Child Development*, 32 (1961), 457–572.

40. Becker, *op. cit.*

41. Adorno, *et al.*, *op. cit.*; Frenkel-Brunswick, "Intolerance of Ambiguity," *op. cit.*

42. Frenkel-Brunswick, "Intolerance of Ambiguity," *op. cit.*; Rokeach, *op. cit.*; Theodore Milton, "Authoritarianism, Intolerance of Ambiguity and Rigidity, Under Ego and Risk—Involved Conditions," *Journal of Abnormal and Social Psychology*, 55 (1957), 29–33; Jack Block and Jeanne Block, "An Investigation of the Relationship Between Intolerance of Ambiguity and Ethnocentrism," *Journal of Personality*, 19 (1951), 303–311; Charles D. Smock, "The Relationship Between 'Intolerance of Ambiguity,' Generalization and Spread of Perceptual Closure," *Child Development*, 28 (1957), 27–36.

43. John Shaffer, Sarnoff A. Mednick, and Judith Seder, "Some Developmental Factors Related to Field-Independence in Children," *American Psychologist*, 12 (1957), 399. Herman A. Witkin, *et al.*, *Personality Through Perception* (New York: Harper & Row, 1954) found "field-dependent" individuals manifest these personality traits: dependency on environmental supports, conformists, not initiators, submit readily to authority, not introspective, low self-esteem and self-acceptance. See also George S. Klein, "Personal World Through Perception," in Robert R. Blake and Glenn V. Ramsey (eds.), *Perception: An Approach to Personality* (New York: Ronald, 1950); Harold M. Schroder, Michael J. Driver, Siegfried Streufert, *Human Information Processing: Individuals and Groups Functioning in Complex Social Situations* (New York: Holt, Rinehart and Winston, 1967).

44. See Urie Bronfenbrenner's "Socialization and Social Class Through Time and Space," in Eleanor E. Maccoby, *et al.* (eds.), *Readings in Social Psychology*, 3rd ed. (New York: Holt, Rinehart and Winston, 1958), 400–425, for a systematic analysis of trends. Also Melvin L. Kohn, "Social Class and Parental Values," *American Journal of Sociology*, 54 (1959), 337–351.

45. Schiff, "Conservative Movement on American College Campuses," *op. cit.*, 38.

46. See Harry Overstreet and Bonaro Overstreet, *The Strange Tactics of Extremism* (New York: Norton, 1964), for detailed biographies of some noted rightists.

47. Taylor Caldwell, "Taylor Caldwell on Growing Up Tough," *American Opinion*, 10, 7 (September 1967), 103–112, quote on 103.

48. See particularly Roy's *Apostle of Discontent*, *op. cit.*, for a detailed discussion of fundamentalist groups. For a discussion of rightist-fundamentalist organizations see Forster and Epstein, *Danger on the Right*, *op. cit.*; David Danzig, "The Radical Right and the Rise of the Fundamentalist Minority," *Commentary* (April 1962); and "Special Supplement on the Far Right," *The Reformed Journal* (January 1965). Alan Rosenbaum in "Religious Orthodoxy and Political Attitudes," paper presented at Midwest Conference of Political Scientists (April 1967), found "orthodox" individuals generally "estranged from American Society," "patriotic," "internationally belligerent," "authoritarian," and "conforming."

49. Campbell, *et al.*, *op. cit.*; Seymour M. Lipset, *Political Man* (New York: Double-day, 1959) 257–261; Lenski, *op. cit.*; Paul Lazarsfeld, Bernard Berelson, Hazel Gaudet, *The People's Choice*, 2nd ed. (New York: Columbia University Press, 1948); Seymour M. Lipset, "Religion and Politics," in Robert Lee and Martin M. Marty (eds.), *Region and Social Conflict* (New York: Oxford University Press, 1964).

50. See Florence R. Kluckhohn and Fred L. Strodtbeck, *Variations in Value-Orientations* (Evanston, Ill.: Row, Peterson, 1961).

51. Benton Johnson, "Ascetic Protestantism and Political Preference," *Public Opinion Quarterly*, 26 (1962), 35–46, quote on 37. For a systematic discussion of religious belief-systems see Parsons, *The Social System*, *op. cit.*, chap. 8.

52. J. Milton Yinger, "Contracultures and Subcultures," *American Sociological Review*, 25 (1960), 625–635, quote on 629. For a discussion of sects and other similar "contracultures" see Willard C. Sperry, *Religion in America* (New York: Macmillan, 1946); Martin M. Marty, "Sects and Cults," *The Annals of the American Academy of Political and Social Science*, 332 (November 1960), 125–135; Bryan R. Wilson, "An Analysis of Sect Development," *American Sociological Review*, 24 (1959), 3–15.

53. See Hofstadter, *The Paranoid Style in American Politics and Other Essays*, *op. cit.*, chap. 2.

54. Ralph L. Roy, "Conflict from the Left and Right," in Lee and Marty, *op. cit.*, 68.

55. Forster and Epstein, *The Radical Right*, op. cit., 17.

56. Three major works stand out in this area: Jean Piaget, *The Moral Judgments of the Children* (New York: Macmillan, 1955); Parsons and Bales, *General Theory of Action*, *op. cit.*, and a recent review of the literature, Lawrence Kohlberg, "Development of Moral Character and Moral Ideology," in Hoffman and Hoffman, *op. cit.*, 383–431.

57. For a discussion of moral values imparted by role-taking in the family, see Talcott Parsons, *Family, Socialization, and Process* (New York: Free Press, 1955); in larger social institutions, Parsons and Bales, *General Theory of Action*, *op. cit.* For peer influences see Piaget, *op. cit.*; John D. Campbell, "Peer Relations in Childhood," in Hoffman and Hoffman, *op. cit.*; Urie Bronfenbrenner, "Soviet Methods of Character Education," *American Psychologist*, 17 (1962), 550–564; James S. Coleman, *Adolescent Society* (New York: Free Press, 1961); Robert F. Peck and Robert J. Havenghurst, *The Psychology of Character Development* (New York: Wiley, 1960); Robert J. Havenghurst and Hilda Taba, *Adolescent Character and Personality* (New York: Wiley, 1949); Muzafer Sherif and Carolyn W. Sherif, *Reference Groups: Exploration into Conformity and Deviation of Adolescents* (New York: Harper & Row, 1964); for mass media, Eleanor E. Maccoby, "Effects of the Mass Media," in Hoffman and Hoffman, *op. cit.*, 323–348.

58. Sears, Maccoby, and Levine, *op. cit.*, 367–368. Additional studies that support this proposition are cited in Kohlberg, *op. cit.*, 392–394; see also George G. Thompson, "Age Trends in Social Values During the Adolescent Years," *American Psychologist*, 4 (1949), 245–251; Roy G. Bose, "Religious Concepts of

Children," *Religious Education*, 24 (1929), 831–837; Ernest Harns, "The Development of Religious Experience in Children," *American Journal of Sociology*, 50 (1944), 112–122.

59. Schiff, "Conservative Movement on American College Campuses," *op. cit.*, 38.

60. E. Mansell Pattison, "The Effects of a Religious Culture's Values on Personality Psychodynamics," paper read to the American Association for the Advancement of Science (Berkeley, Calif.: December 1965).

61. *Ibid.*, 24–25.

62. Pattison, *op. cit.*; see also Monica B. Holmes, "A Cross-Cultural Study of the Relationship between Values and Modal Conscience," *The Psychoanalytical Study of Society*, I (1960), 98–184.

63. Eric Klinger, Anita Albaum, and Mavis Hetherington, "Factors Influencing the Severity of Moral Judgments," *Journal of Social Psychology*, 63 (1964), 319–326; Derek Wright and Edwin Cox, "A Study of the Relationship Between Moral Judgment and Religious Beliefs in a Sample of English Adolescents," *Journal of Social Psychology*, 72 (1967), 135–144. Fundamentalist ministers, for example, consistently favor punitive retaliatory techniques for handling children's social problems; William E. Alberts, "Personality and Attitudes toward Juvenile Delinquency: A Study of Protestant Ministers," *Journal of Social Psychology*, 60 (1963), 71–83.

64. Lawrency Hong, "Religious Styles, Dogmatism, and Orientation to Change," *Sociological Analysis*, 27 (1966), 239–242; Martin L. Hoffman, *Progress Report: Techniques and Processes in Moral Development* (Detroit: Merrill-Palmer Institute, 1961, mimeographed), cited in Kohlberg, *op. cit.*, 421–422.

65. Norman A. Cameron, "The Paranoid Pseudo-Community Revisited," *American Journal of Sociology*, 65 (1959), 53–58.

66. Morris Rosenberg, "The Dissonant Religious Context and Emotional Disturbance," *American Journal of Sociology*, 58 (1962), 1–10.

67. *Ibid.*, James J. Keene, "Religious Behavior and Neuroticism, Spontaneity and Worldmindedness," *Sociometry*, 30 (1967), 137–157; Clifford M. Christensen, "The Occurrence of Mental Illness in Ministry: Family Origins," *Journal of Pastoral Care*, 14 (1960), 13–20.

68. The construction of "causal models" is a technique for validating *empirically* the causal relationship between variables, an extremely necessary step in theory building. For three recent applications of this technique to political data see Thad L. Beyle, "Contested Elections and Voter Turnout in a Local Community," *American Political Science Review*, 59 (1965), 111–117; Charles F. Cnuddle and Donald J. McCrone, "The Linkage between Constituency Attitudes and Congressional Voting Behavior: A Causal Model," *American Political Science Review*, 60 (1966), 66–72; and Arthur S. Goldberg, "Discerning A Causal Pattern Among Data on Voting Behavior," *American Political Science Review*, 60 (1966), 913–922. Although there is a vast technical literature on this method, Herbert M. Blalock's *Causal Inference in Nonexperimental Research* (Chapel Hill: University of North Carolina Press, 1964) is a readable introduction to the subject.

69. From the factor analysis of 18 scale measures, four dummy variables were constructed, using factor loadings as weights. An individual's "anomy" score, for example, was computed by multiplying his political alienation scale score by .689 (the loading of this scale on the anomy factor), adding to this his sense of personal powerlessness score multiplied by .635 (the factor loading), etc. In this way an overall score on this and the other three dimensions was calculated for each respondant. The correlations are product-moment (Pearson's) r's. Regression and partial-correlation analysis show that conservative political beliefs are almost totally determined by traditional value orientations and that anomy is largely the product of the authoritarian personality factor, at least for this sample.